Creative Human Resource Planning and Applications
A Strategic Approach

Elmer H. Burack PH.D., S.P.H.R.

Professor of Management
University of Illinois at Chicago

Prentice Hall
Englewood Cliffs, New Jersey 07632

Library of Congress Cataloging-in-Publication Data

BURACK, ELMER H.
Creative human resource planning and applications.

Bibliography: p.
Includes index.
1. Manpower planning. 2. Personnel management.
3. Strategic planning. I. Title.
HF5549.5.M3B874 1988   658.3'01   87-35696
ISBN 0-13-189648-2

Cover design: *Lundgren Graphics*
Manufacturing buyer: *Lorraine Fumoso*

© 1988 by Prentice-Hall, Inc.
A Division of Simon & Schuster
Englewood Cliffs, New Jersey 07632

The publisher offers discounts on this book when ordered
in bulk quantities. For more information, write:

Special Sales/College Marketing
College Technical and Reference Division
Prentice-Hall, Inc.
Englewood Cliffs, New Jersey 07632

Printed in the United States of America

10 9 8 7 6 5 4 3 2 1

ISBN 0-13-189648-2

PRENTICE-HALL INTERNATIONAL (UK) LIMITED, *London*
PRENTICE-HALL OF AUSTRALIA PTY. LIMITED, *Sydney*
PRENTICE-HALL CANADA INC., *Toronto*
PRENTICE-HALL HISPANOAMERICANA, S.A., *Mexico*
PRENTICE-HALL OF INDIA PRIVATE LIMITED, *New Delhi*
PRENTICE-HALL OF JAPAN, INC., *Tokyo*
SIMON & SCHUSTER ASIA PTE. LTD., *Singapore*
EDITORA PRENTICE-HALL DO BRASIL, LTDA., *Rio de Janeiro*

Dedication

To my family and friends—who have helped me to see some of the creative possibilities ever present in our lives—for ourselves and in the places and organizations where so much of our lives are spent.

Contents

2 Organization and Job Planning for the Productive Organization: A
        Strategic View   **30**

3 Corporate Culture Viewed Strategically   **95**

4 Managers: Defining Functions and Performances for Success   **125**

5 Strategic Succession Planning and Management Development:
Concepts and Applications   **163**

Contents

8 Management Development Methods: Individual Learning and Effectiveness   **287**

9 Managerial Career Development: Strategic Approaches   **337**

11 Viewing Information and Computers Strategically   **413**

12 Implementation Strategies   **439**

Preface

This book is written primarily for practicing managers and human resource people who must grapple with numerous and practical human resource issues. Organizations are changing rapidly in terms of their structures, systems, work processes, and activities. Competitive strength due to economic size and the barriers to industry entry enjoyed by various companies in the past are disappearing. Creative people are constantly coming up with innovative ways to make and market products or to provide new(er) services. Markets have opened up and competitive threats are worldwide in character.

In part, the new competitive environment includes smaller businesses that have broken market entry barriers through new and flexible technologies and creative partnership arrangements. Third World products and know-how no longer can be ignored or considered third rate as they compete head on with the products of our highly industrialized society.* These turbulent conditions place even greater stress on proactive planning rather than reactive responses. Organizational leadership, supported by a highly competent and dedicated managerial group and employee force, are crucial to enterprise continuity, let alone renewal and growth.

These dynamic conditions require a comprehensive approach to the managerial work force. Strategic approaches to management succession and development are required to achieve a practical, effective, and integrated system and human resource effort. The objective, however, is not just one of planning strategically but also one of managing strategically.

---

*Frederick W. Gluck, "Strategic Management: An Overview," in James R. Gardner, Robert Rachlin, and H. W. Allen Sweeny, eds., *Handbook of Strategic Planning* (New York: John Wiley, 1986).

Strategic thinking is a responsibility of managers at all levels. It is not an "ivory tower" exercise. Consequently, planning activities must be integrated among all authority levels and functions. The objective of integrated and proactive planning is to make sure that the organization increasingly creates its own future—one in which the organization best utilizes its resources, capabilities, and market opportunities.

Today's strategic thinking and approaches are best described as a Gestalt of various planning activities. These include sales forecasting, financial analysis, technological forecasts, organization structure planning, succession analysis, and managerial development. The companies that have been successful in assembling this complex puzzle are those that recognized planning requires going much beyond questions of "what to do." Successful planning today requires thoughtful integration of the "what to do" with line management's expertise in "how to do it." Minimally, the planner's role change requires close work with line management. New ways must be identified for building the organization's capabilities. Planners, line managers, and human resource officials must be joined together in this task.

Strategic Planning for Managerial Succession and Development

"Strategic thinking about human resource planning and development," this book's general focus, involves a complex set of concepts, issues, systems, and practical ideas. Simplistic notions won't fit the circumstances. Approaches must be flexible enough to adapt to widely different organizational and work circumstances, uncertainties attendant to these processes, and individual differences.

A basic problem often encountered in strategic discussions is: Who are managers and what do they do to be successful? Management development and succession systems and methods are shaped greatly by the situational context. Contextual factors such as organization culture and aspects of structure and systems planning need to all receive attention.

The successful outcome of strategic human resource planning actions ultimately comes down to performance management. Topics that need to be addressed from the viewpoint of the individual include motivation-behavioral matters, stress, and wellness. Career development also needs to receive attention since it represents the joint resolution of organizational and individual needs, both of which are tied to performance. Performance also reflects the nature of work itself, and thus I have included discussions on ways to plan for and approach the design of managerial work.

Realistic strategic thinking and approaches must confront the need to identify feasible alternatives. Getting these underway calls for creative thinking and dealing with unfamiliar subject matter, consequently, the inclusion of case studies, numerous application sections, and the writer's sharing of varied and diverse corporate experiences.

The above notwithstanding, the appetite of planners and strategists is great for considering what's new or promising for future planning agendas and discussions. Thus the inclusion of a concluding chapter on an *emerging agenda* for "strategic management development."

A Note on Terminology

The title for this book could easily create quite different expectations among readers as to coverage. Aside from the differing experience or background of readers, there is a confusion of terms due to the rapid advancements in the numerous fields of study related to this subject matter.

In simpler times, perhaps 20 years ago, the major terminology problem related to systematic people planning approaches was described by the term "manpower planning." Governmental planners and Labor Department analysts used this term for years. It involved general labor trends and particular occupational categories such as scientists, engineers, and teachers. The main concerns were technological displacement of personnel, obsolescence and retraining, set against a backdrop of regional and national labor markets.

"Manpower planning" was also carried out in the private sector. Initially, the substantive base was largely the heritage of excellent application work in England. Manpower planning, as it developed along company lines, dealt with having the "right numbers at the right place at the right time and with the right skills."

Two parallel developments subsequently led to the semantic jungle with which we are currently confronted: advancements in business planning spawned longer-range approaches, and these were complemented eventually by "strategic approaches" in the late 1960s. Some confusion arose because many assumed that if you were doing long-range business planning you were also doing "strategic planning." In the 1970s and 1980s, this picture was further obscured by a proliferation of planning innovations identified under various terms such as "strategic business units," "portfolio planning," "PIMS" (profit impact of market strategies, re: General Electric), "industry structure models" (re: Michael E. Porter of Harvard), and "value-based planning" (e.g., increasing market value of stock and paying dividends).

The other development contributing to the confusion was related to the advancement of people planning methods in the 1980s. First, the "manpower planning" designation gave way to "human resource planning," and more holistic approaches required the incorporation of "career management." A comprehensive approach to planning for human resources was needed. The advancements in corporate experiences and the attendant body of knowledge led to the development of overarching approaches (and terms). *Human resource planning and development* and *human resource management* became popular.

Work in the career field also expanded, and analyses concerned particularly with this were captured under the title of *career development*, comprising both corporate career management and individual career planning.

Added fuel for the terminology confusion was provided as human resource people started to link with business planners and strategists. "Strategic human resource planning," "strategic planning for human resources," "strategic human resource management," "human resource planning strategies," and "strategic career development" were terms used with increasing frequency. Thus the concern with terminology is a significant one; participants in "strategic" discussions affecting human resources need to approach these with care. In subsequent discussions, we have tried to minimize the use of terms likely to contribute further to this confusion. In general, functional descriptions have been emphasized that stress what is to be done or accomplished. Where economy of word usage dictates descriptive terms, these are defined intially, and consistency in subsequent usage was sought.

Book Focus Restated

Perhaps it is worth recapping briefly the focus of the book's discussions. Managers are the primary individuals considered as they become a part of succession planning and development. General familiarity is assumed with the foundations of human resource planning and personnel management reflecting either experience or as covered by basic texts in these fields. This book underscores the need for comprehensive strategic approaches that emphasize coordinated efforts between human resource and personnel staff groups, business officials, planners and strategists, and line managers. Because of the vastness of the subject area, particular stress is placed on corporate culture, management systems, and contextual and individual matters as they affect succession and management development. Implicit within this approach is the view that these HR approaches are shaped by, and affect, business planning and the identification of feasible enterprise directions in the future. Planning for human resources is linked directly to management of human resources.

Acknowledgments

I am grateful to many individuals and organizations for sharing their information and experiences. A list of contributors is provided in this acknowledgments section. Also, others such as Diane Wilson, at Roosevelt University, stimulated my thinking regarding many career and human resource issues.

Additionally, a group of dedicated reviewers read various versions of early manuscript drafts. Their useful ideas and frankness were of considerable help in stimulating my thinking and motivation to "try it again."

I am quite grateful for the highly detailed comments, suggestions, and positive support of Alan A. Yelsey (Honeywell, Inc.) and Richard Zalman (Electro-OPTICS). Robert Edwards (Drake Beam Morin, Inc.) also provided a number of useful suggestions on an early draft.

A note of appreciation is due also for the viewpoints and comments of Laurie Borne (Ontario-Hydro), which provided useful insights for me as to balance of subject matter and usefulness to various groups that were helpful in the subsequent revisions.

I would like particularly to acknowledge, with appreciation, practitioners such as Brett Avner, of Nationwide Insurance Company, whose zest for improving the usefulness of human resource planning applications stimulated the efforts of myself and others to meet these needs.

Finally, a note of grateful appreciation goes to those people and institutions that provide the ambience and cordiality desperately needed by writers (and others) seeking to express useful ideas simply. It is with much thanks that I am pleased to acknowledge Monique and Guy Barusseau, and Michael Stillwell of Maison Barusseau in Highland Park, Illinois, for their patience and warm hospitality.

Despite the type of support and helpful comments noted, the responsibility for the final project lies with the author.

Albrecht, Maryann H., Ph.D.
Associate Professor of Management
University of Illinois at Chicago

Avner, Brett, Ph.D.
Director, Management Development
and Planning
Nationwide Insurance Co.

Borne, Laurie
Director, Human Resources Planning
Ontario-Hydro

Browne, Philip J., Ph.D.
Director, Human Resource Planning
and Development
Rexnord, Inc.

Buckner, Marilyn
Manager of Continuity Planning
The Coca-Cola Company

Campbell, Sam
Manager of Management Development
Honeywell, Inc.

Corrigan, Jay M.
Director, Personnel Development &
Research
Bristol-Myers Company

Delbecq, André, Ph.D.
Dean, School of Business
University of Santa Clara

Desatnick, Robert L.
President
Robert Desatnick & Associates

Doerflein, Steve, Ph.D.
Director, Human Resources Research
Holiday Inns of America

Dotlich, David, Ph.D.
Director of Corporate Human Resource Development
Honeywell, Inc.

Douglas, Parrie
General Manager, Internal Development
Procter & Gamble

Dyer, Sherry G.
Manager, Human Resource Planning
Boise-Cascade Co.

Edwards, Robert
Vice President
Drake Beam Morin, Inc.

Elsen, Paul
Manager of Human Resource Development
Honeywell, Inc.

Gill, Sandra L.
Principal
Organizational Development Associates

Gridley, John, Ph.D.
Human Resources Manager
EBASCO Services, Inc.

Gustafson, Robert
Manager of Manpower Planning
Honeywell, Inc.

Hauser, William L.
Director, Career Development
Pfizer, Inc.

Hemphill, Karen
Manager, Honeywell Training Center
Honeywell, Inc.

Jacobson, Marilyn, Ph.D.
Associate
Hay Career Consultants

Johnson, Harold H.
Manager, Human Resource Planning
Defense Systems Division
Honeywell, Inc.

Kroeger, Tom
Director of Personnel, Stores
Division Sherwin Williams

Lantz, Kathy, A.P.S.
Employment Manager
Systems and Data Processing
Nationwide Insurance Co.

Leigh, David
Manager, Corporate Managerial Planning & Development
Robbins & Myers

Lightle, Juliana, Ed.D.
Personnel Specialist
Nationwide Insurance Co.

Lundberg, Craig, Ph.D.
Professor of Management
Cornell University

Manzini, Andrew O.
Vice President, Human Resources
EBASCO Services, Inc.

Margolis, Jan
Corporate Director, Personnel Development
Bristol-Myers Company

Mayer, Robert
Management Development Training
Manager
Nationwide Insurance Co.

McConnell, David
Manager, Development
Procter & Gamble

Melone, David L.
International Manager, Italy
Procter & Gamble

Page, Ronald C., Ph.D.
Manager, Job Analysis Services
Control Data Business Advisors, Inc.

Patinka, Paul, Ph.D.
Manager, Human Resource Planning
Motorola, Inc.

Richter, Carl
Manager, Human Resources
Honeywell, Inc.

Schrenk, Larry P., Ph.D.
Manager of Manpower Planning
Honeywell, Inc.

Sonnino, Daniel
Project Manager, International Group
Foster-Wheeler

Tiffany, Nancy A.
University of San Francisco

Tornow, Walter, Ph.D.
Vice President
Control Data Business Advisors, Inc.

Wyatt, Larry L.
Manager, Systems & Planning
Aluminum Company of America

Yelsey, Alan A.
Manager, Corporate Human Resource Planning
Honeywell, Inc.

Zalman, Richard, Ph.D.
Vice President, Administration
Electro-OPTICS, Inc.

1

Business and Strategic Planning and Its Integration with Human Resource Planning

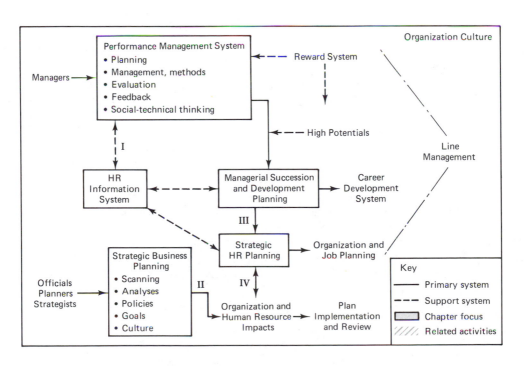

The Right Issues, the Right Questions

This book is concerned with the strategic aspects of management development and closely allied activities such as succession planning. Corporate officials, managers, and specialists need to understand and exploit fully newer and more effective means of developing managers and officers, since the fulfillment of longer-range business plans and strategies is vitally dependent on them. Before this can be accomplished, effective linkages must be established with long-range and strategic business planning activities and the operational or performance-related activities of the organization.

Strategic analyses related to human resources (HR) should result in the identification of realistic alternatives and effective approaches for managerial succession and development in the future which are thoughtfully integrated with strategic business thinking and directions.

Since strategic business analyses frequently impact organization and work structures, structure and working planning are early candidates for strategic analysis of human resources (HR). In a large insurance company, for example, the strategic decision to enter a new line of business resulted in the creation of an organization structure and positional responsibilities quite different from those in the traditional insurance form. The decision of a manufacturer to phase out its fabricating facilities and to emphasize products built around purchased components led to a major internal reorganization with a mix of positions and work processes far different from those used in the past.

As longer-range and strategic HR processes mature, planning and strategic analyses turn toward equally potent but more subtle factors affecting succession and development. Of major importance among these is organization culture and individual behavioral matters affecting performance, including career development and motivation. In all cases, it is of utmost importance that strategic discussions taking place in a particular company be shaped to the specifics of that organization. The essence of strategic thinking flows from the core of a given organization's situational features and its future possibilities and limitations.

This book provides a framework for longer-range planning and strategic thinking affecting human resources, with particular emphasis on succession and management development. The unique features and aspects of a given organization such as its markets, clientele, location, size, and philosophy of management are the contingencies defining the specifics of planning and strategic designs.

2

Why a Longer-Range and Strategic Perspective for Management Development?

The strategic perspective in management development is meant to focus top management thinking on the most critical features of its preparation of officials and managers to lead and run the business. It follows that these discussions and analyses must bridge from the present to "where" the organization wants to be in the future. The challenge to HR planners and strategists is to devise the human resource means of achieving business planning objectives and goals, including the alteration of these in the light of HR possibilities and limitations. Due to the fact that most of the factors and circumstances involved in these analyses are constantly changing, strategic processes must be renewed regularly. Strategies and plans previously defined must be reviewed for continuing relevance. For convenience and economy of word usage, subsequent references to "strategic approaches (HR)" will also include longer-range planning.

Why Strategic Approaches for Succession and Management Development?

Early and basic questions raised by company officials are, "Why the 'sudden' interest in strategic planning affecting human resources?" "Is this just another way to expand HR staffing?" "What's in it for us?" These are tough questions to answer, but officials need to have clear answers to these before proceeding. Exhibit 1-1 summarizes some of the main reasons for these approaches.

The exhibit presents compelling reasons for undertaking strategic approaches to succession and management development. Strategic approaches are highly useful in directing an organization's attention to significant issues affecting corporate survival, stability, growth, and renewal (point 1). Exhibit 1-1 serves to emphasize the importance assigned to strategic approaches as these meet, in a timely way, basic staffing needs with appropriately prepared people (point 2). From a strategic viewpoint, this approach is even more critical as the heart of the organization's future leadership is involved. These considerations alone would be compelling ones for undertaking these approaches.

Strategic thinking also acknowledges the fact that widely different ideas exist in organizations as to what comprises the experience, knowledge, and abilities (skills) for managerial success in the past, present, *and* future. The fact that widely different ideas or values exist and are frequently used by managers in selection, development, and promotion processes *destabilizes* the solidarity of managerial groups and leadership (points 3 and 4). For example, in a large, divisionalized service organization, operating under a decentralized managerial mode, division heads differed greatly in the values that guided their identification of high potentials and promotion discussions. In a period of rapid growth opportunity, newly

EXHIBIT 1-1

An Agenda of Factors for Undertaking Longer-Range Planning and
Strategic Approaches for Succession and Management Development

1. Directing the organization's attention to major human resource issues affecting enterprise survival, growth, and renewal.

2. Assuring the availability of *adequate numbers* of talented people to assume *leadership and managerial roles.* This is indispensable to corporate solvency and renewal to meet future business requirements.

3. Establishing guidelines and a degree of uniformity in development. Also included in the developmental process is succession to key corporate positions to *avoid widely disparate experience, knowledge, and abilities* (*skills*) being used that may prove dysfunctional or at cross purposes with corporate needs.

4. Coordinating the actions of senior managers. This recognizes that frequently quite *different sets of performance criteria and planning bases* are used where operations are decentralized. Also, this is especially important where actions or decisions taking place in one area have consequence or affect the range off choice(s) in another area.

5. Establishing *priorities* among the *major and concurrent problems and issues* characteristically facing the firm. Lack of priorities dilutes resources or may make those used ineffectual. Also, failure to define priorities leads to drifting or ill-defined directions and purposes which can affect the attraction of capable people. It can also result in the "turn-off" of major accounts or clients, failure to rally company personnel, or failure to gain needed commitment to corporate purposes and directions.

6. Determining environmental uncertainties due to a variety of forces and change necessitates the establishment of *priorities.* There is a need for concentration on the *scarce or limited resources* of the organization to deal with these. Strategic processes provide a structure for this thinking and attendant analyses.

7. Shedding light on the *underlying factors, resources,* and *circumstances* contributing to *successful actions* in the past as well as the "why" of poor performance or failure. The "why" of organizational successes (and failures) in the past is often incompletely understood as a variety of circumstances enter into the consideration. Strategic thinking helps to "unearth" these, forming a valuable base of experiences from which the organization can draw.

assigned managers in key positions were often at odds with each other on basic corporate policy matters. Additionally, executive management, in seeking out appropriately oriented and developed people for senior succession positions, found suitable candidates seriously lacking, "We can't afford to take a chance on 'Shirley', her sense of important factors in marketing strategies is out of focus with 'our' approaches."

Since the available analysis and decision time of senior people and others is severely limited (point 5), strategic approaches help to establish priorities. These priorities help to avoid drifting, conflicts in actions, and failure to meet targeted objectives.

Due to the increasing environmental uncertainty and complexity faced by most firms, the encouragement of these discussions and resolution of these issues is a compelling one. Merger, downsizing, reorganization, international competition, and economic fluctuations are factors contributing to this picture. Strategic actions move beyond the statement of issues and actively seek out superior means of successful accomplishment. Also, underlying causal factors are actively searched out (point 7) to avoid recurrence of problems or to establish a superior base of future performance.

Strategic approaches *cannot* be used in a mechanistic or slavish way. In fact, establishing a climate for recognition and discussion of key issues is a central part of the process. The importance of effective strategic approaches to corporate welfare is so great that from the start, it is important to have a healthy regard for things that go wrong.

Things That Go Wrong

National surveys by major affiliates of the Human Resource Planning Society, studies by its research committee, and analyses undertaken by various researchers have confirmed the high priority assigned to strategic HR matters. Establishing means of better *integrating* human resource planning with business planning and strategic processes is among the key issues. But devoting attention to this point assumes that things are working well on both the business and human resource planning sides of the organization and that the major need is integration. This assumption often turns out to be a poor one.

The recent and often drastic changes in the organization, staffing, and processes of business planning and strategic units have vividly demonstrated that many corporate strategic approaches are *not* working well. Various studies including a large-scale study of business planning units (Midwest Academy of Management, May 1985; Burack, 1985) and a cover story in *Business Week* (1985, esp. pp. 62–70) have reported on major difficulties in this area. The study reported in *Business Week* considered strategic decisions made by leading corporate units in the period from 1979 through 1984. The study was meant to be illustrative of problems and issues and not a general study of the strategic "batting average of success." The results nevertheless were quite sobering. The "strike-outs" of major corporates such as Adolph Coors, Campbell Soup, Exxon, General Motors, Oak Industries, Shaklee, Toro, and Wang Laboratories was impressive. According to the study, the "misses" included poor estimates of demand for new products, straying too far from core business competencies, underestimating the impact of international competition on main product lines, and the failure to interpret the need to introduce newer product innovations. If human resource planning strategies had been better integrated with the business strategies, staffing up for new product introductions and strategic decisions *not* to proceed for lack of talent or distance from core capabilities would have proved profitable. However, it would be premature to conclude that strategic thinking is an expensive exercise in futility. The same *Business Week* study also reported notable strategic successes for such corporations as Abbott Laboratories, American Motors, Borg-Warner, Dayton Hudson, Ralston Purina, and Southern California Edison (SCE). SCE's strategic decision to develop a balance in connection with power sources contributed handsomely to its profitability and financial soundness. Its correct readings of nuclear power complexities, demand, and alternate power sources for exploitation were all a part of its successful decision.

The statistics of the hits and strike-outs provide no insights as to why failures occurred or whether some of these could have been avoided. Similarly, some of the successses may have simply "lucked out." The *Business Week* article attempted to provide some explanations for the failures and how particular companies organized their strategic approaches. Some companies lost sight of their planning and strategic analysis purposes, and this process became an end in itself. Others lost the commitment of their line management because they were insufficiently involved. Some of the results were also fortuitous and involved occurrences that couldn't have been anticipated. More on these matters in a moment.

It is clear that organizational strategists need to stay focused on the right questions and issues. There simply is no point in worrying about how to (better) integrate the human resource system with the strategic business system if the latter or the former is in jeopardy or not working right. The adequacy of the organization and staffing of the human resource function is also an important point and not to be ignored. It is developed in detail in other books, including one of the author's earlier books (Burack and Mathys, 1980, 1987 rev.) and other books too (e.g., Fombrun, Tichy, and Devanna, 1984). Much can be learned from failures as well as successes. Since subsequent chapters assume the validity and need for strategic approaches, it is important that basic issues related to success and failure using these approaches be explored at this time.

Business Strategic Planning: Bases for Failure and Success

Strategic business thinking ultimately affects organizational survival, growth, and renewal. Two mainstreams of analysis are involved. The first is one of trying to understand the organization's positioning in "today's" economic and competitive world. This involves many marketing, economic, competitive, technological, and organizational considerations. The second stage of analysis deals with identifying potentially attractive alternatives for future operation(s) and assessing their value and likelihood of achievement. In general business planning, the analyses cover such significant areas as changes in markets, competition, and technology as well as financial matters. Corresponding to these business strategies, human resource analysts probe succession planning and management development issues. Included with these HR approaches is an attempt to understand and rationalize managerial roles, development structures and processes, and sources of strengthening managerial knowledge and skills. Also included is assessing the relative effectiveness of various approaches being used and the fit of these with longer-range business developments. Strategic management thinking related to HR is future oriented.

Thus, it is charged with identifying the structures, systems, processes, and activities for succession and development likely to fit best with the goals and organization of the future.

Failure of Strategic Business Approaches

General sources of uncertainty accompanying planning processes are well known, especially those related to the environment. Unexpected changes in weather patterns, international crises, and unanticipated innovations are common. They form part of the standard repertoire of events that have (always) complicated future-oriented analyses.

Strategic planning, introduced for the first time in the 1960s, offered a systematic approach for analyzing an organization's competitive and economic environment. It also involved identifying prospects for future corporate activities and bases for charting a long-term action program. Thus, the advent of strategic approaches in the 1960s, pioneered by the Boston Consulting Group, and with the added impetus of leading companies such as General Electric and General Motors, promised a significant step beyond long(er)-range planning. A rapidly swelling number of major corporations either introduced or expanded their planning groups to foster the new strategic thrust. The growth in strategic applications was catalyzed by their usage in prestigious corporations and the expansion of major professional planning societies. Also, expansion of MBA programs featuring strategic approaches, and popularization through publications and workshops, were other contributing factors.

Although interest in strategic processes grew rapidly, lacking was a solid foundation of application information regarding conditions or situations, assumptions, processes used, and results. The fact that the results of strategic designs took years to unfold and that much company detail was confidential, effectively shielded assessing the validity of these approaches. Contributing further to the difficulties were the complex internal organizational processes and relationships about which characteristically little was known. In short, the bases for either success or failure and the circumstances contributing to these had not been established. The "sudden" reporting of failures in strategic approaches in the mid-1980s came as a shock to many. Quite likely, the disclosure of poor strategic results turned off many corporate CEOs (chief executive officers) and executives entertaining the use of these approaches. In some cases this may have been premature.

The purpose of these introductory remarks, the foregoing situation notwithstanding, has been to set a realistic foundation for critically examining and using strategic approaches. Now, why the failures?

Specific Factors in the Failure of Strategic Approaches

Three types of factors accounted for most of the failures of corporate strategies, aside from fortuitous circumstances. These three classes of factors were:

1. *Distortion of the strategic concept or philosophy.* Some organizations concentrated on only portions of strategic approaches without adequate attention to internally related procedures. There was a tendency to dismiss the importance of initially establishing a foundation for change or to midjudge internal management needs or competencies as in the acquisition of dissimilar businesses. Another example here was the overemphasis on formula market share studies with insufficient emphasis on requisite tactics to accomplish these.

2. *Breakdown of interpersonal processes and relationships and changes in the staff role.* The sudden favoring of planning and strategic approaches resulted in staff groups gaining much power and authority in organizations. Planning processes became elaborate rapidly and were overseen by senior planners—seemingly plans became an end in themselves. These conditions fostered traditional line-staff rivalries. Plans became staff's, "not ours (line's)." Also, in the press to get on with things, many strategies blossomed without adequate involvement or commitment of key line management people—who nevertheless had to assume responsibility for implementation and results.

3. *Violation of basic assumptions or distortions in strategic procedures or the thoroughness with which these were carried out.* In some instances of failures, strategic procedures became overly quantitative and formulas (e.g., for market share) were used in a slavish, mechanistic fashion. Another characteristic set of circumstances involved the change of marketing or environmental conditions from those of relative stability to rather turbulent ones. Formula approaches that worked relatively well under stable conditions fell apart under shifting circumstances—environmental scans either weren't carried out or if done, were carried out in cursory fashion.

The applications section of this chapter provides a corporate case study of the evolution of strategic approaches.

The three classes of factors contributing to failure of strategic designs involve some 11 different points, which are summarized in Exhibit 1-2. Overly quantitative techniques (point 1) hastened the breakdown of interpersonal processes and relationships. Staff (planners) increasingly took charge of strategic approaches as these grew in complexity and were converted to computerized analysis. Understanding the dynamics of competition was endangered by an overreliance on numbers (point 4). The loss of credibility by planning and strategic groups (point 7) was not an unexpected outcome since line managers realized that computational power was overcoming logic (point 10) or failing to take realistic account of technology, human resources, and competitive tactics. Line was also being charged with the responsibility to carry out plans in which they had not (fully) participated so that line-staff hostility grew (point 9).

The "refinement" of strategic procedures swept away in-depth analyses or distorted strategic approaches. Needed tactics to make strategies work assumed relatively lower priorities (point 2) in favor of paperwork which frustrated managers who might otherwise be willing process participants (point 8).

EXHIBIT 1-2
Major Factors in the Failure of Strategic Business Planning Approaches

1. Use of overly quantitative techniques in a mechanical or formula approach.

2. Overemphasis on market share studies and portfolio analysis, with insufficient emphasis on the requisite tactics to accomplish these strategies, including the conversion of unprofitable to profitable operations.

3. Degeneration of strategic processes into essentially business acquisitions, but which fail to deal adequately with the fact of highly dissimilar businesses and requisite managerial know how.

4. Failure to take adequate account of competition because of highly formulated approaches.

5. Changing conditions which negated underlying market assumptions and thus the suitability of formulated approaches. The assumption of market stability initially lent itself to some formulated approaches—and then emerged the growing uncertainty of changing conditions for which the subject approaches were inappropriate.

6. Overstaffing of planning/strategic groups creating very costly overhead structures.

7. Loss of credibility by planning and strategic groups because of business "blueprints" that appeared to be overly precise relative to the time spans, uncertainties, or events involved.

8. Overemphasis on paperwork and reports for strategic planning documentation that became an end in themselves. Operating management felt that these grew increasingly remote from customers and competition.

9. The resurgence of major line management–staff hostilities as planners assumed an often dominant role in planning and strategic activities—furthered by new language and techniques that alienated line people.

10. Planning and strategic staffs who played key roles and relied primarily on data analysis, with deemphasis on "common sense," experience, or intuitive thinking.

11. Deterioration of the strategic process, particularly among divisions of conglomerates, into an "art form" of written reports and oral presentations best characterized as "pony shows," without appropriate candor for open, effective communications.

In some firms strategic business analyses were seen as essentially processes for systematically studying acquisition candidates (point 3). Even in this rather narrow view of strategic purposes, core business strengths and the compatibility of organizational cultures and executives received too little attention.

A final point concerns the deterioration of strategic processes into an artifact of "desirable corporate actions," virtually an art form (point 11). The proliferation of paperwork, written reports, and top management presentations became part of annualized procedures. Time for dialogue or interaction to talk things out was inadequate. For those who participated in these affairs, they were often described as "pony shows." Needed candor and open, effective communications were either lost or never emerged.

There is another, more general criticism that can be leveled at these failed strategic plans, and this goes to the heart of the organizations themselves. Planning and strategic design deals with extended time horizons—a long-term orientation toward economic, technological, social, and marketing circumstances. Yet many of the firms experiencing failures were trying to connect long-term orientations to structures, systems, and processes, with situations heavily committed to short-term approaches and results.

The rapid growth in planning groups and overemphasis on math models or formula approaches were part of a "knee-jerk" organizational reaction to the promise of strategic thinking. Few bases existed for establishing an enduring internal network of working relationships and sensible allocations of role responsibilities in the strategic processes. Staff was thrust into the role of proponent and doer (of plans)—too often, line management, the "real doers," were pushed aside! The record of corporate strategic undertakings shows that many of the business planning strategies were relatively successful in terms of securing economic objectives though the same record shows that internal coordination and human resource processes did poorly. The failure to integrate strategic business planning successfully with human resource planning activities is a "linkage problem."

Successful Strategic Business and Human Resource Planning Approaches

Sufficient information now exists to outline general organizational guides for improving business and human resource approaches to strategic processes.

Long-term Thinking and a Supportive Climate/Culture.   At a most basic level is the need to establish an organization climate (culture) that is synchronous with long(er)-term planning and programming or plan execution. In many organizations, "culture" simply "happens" with no conscious attempt on the part of top management to define its basic features, let alone use it as a positive force for change or in support of policies and plans.

A culture which supports deliberate and critical approaches to new(er) undertakings may well lose some degree of short-run flexibility. However, the trade-off favors more stable performance patterns for long(er)-term results. With this orientation, needed planning capabilities are carefully groomed. Responsibilities are assigned mindful of those who will be responsible for results and the expertise needed for accomplishing the strategic design. Line management is central to these planning processes. Rotational assignments of line managers into staff positions and the use of "staff" to provide training are means of developing planning capabilities. Staff may also be called on to provide coordination or technical know-how to get things underway, to help solve problems, and to keep things running smoothly.

The Why and What before the How.   Strategic thinking involves many interrelated environmental and organizational factors, only a portion of which are reducible to numbers. The convenience and appeal of "formula approaches" must be bridled by the reality of circumstances. Realistically, situations are mixtures of widely different types of factors, only portions of which permit numerical approaches. But even beyond this is the recognition that *both* cognitive and affective thinking will be called on to render judgments and make decisions. Unfortunately, achieving this type of managerial wisdom is frequently the consequence of "learning the hard way"—experiencing much of what goes wrong and profiting from these lessons.

These considerations have to do largely with the "why" and "what" of strategic thinking and organizational processes. There are important "how" questions as well, aside from the technical specifics of particular models or approaches. Yet the "how" questions frequently are the first point brought up in strategic discussions. The viewpoint expressed here is that the "why and what" should receive much initial attention—these establish the basic orientation and focus of strategic discussions.

A Comprehensive Arrangement of Structure, Systems, and Processes.   Strategic thinking requires a comprehensive arrangement of structures, systems, and processes that link the various organization levels engaged in the planning and the personnel contributing to those processes. Opportunity and threat, feasible future directions, alternatives, and priorities are among the strategic factors that must be confronted or decided upon in this approach. To the extent that planning responsibilities have been carefully parceled out, strategic approaches isolate the top five or six issues facing the organization that affect survival, growth, containment, or renewal. All firms have a cookbook list of "major" problems or issues. But resource limitations dictate that the time and concentration of organizational leadership be confined to only a small number, say, five or six, which are really crucial—and manageable.

Staying Abreast of New Developments, Change.   The actions flowing out of strategic decisions take many years to work out. Thus results have to be monitored regularly and means and criteria devised to detect deviations from initial assumptions and occurrences likely to have adverse outcomes. While it is true that strategies result in tangible activities, few are for all time. Businesses are acquired, new plants are built, and new product lines are introduced. But the only aspects of these that is a given is the fact of a *past* decision. It often is not necessary to live with a decision if it is a bad one. But it is important to be able to determine if it is a bad one and that the organization capability exists to do "something" about it!

Initial assumptions regarding future marketing conditions, no matter how soundly conceived, may be violated because of fortuitous circumstances. Losses or sunk costs will (likely) have to be accepted. It is critical to monitor events so that it can be determined if the initial and basic assumptions have changed and, thereby, the need for refocusing strategic approaches. In short, strategic approaches are not "once and for all" decisions. They are subject to change and new(er) strategic interpretations and considerations. *Even though* the strategy may have paid off in the initial years of operations, what happens subsequently is relevant! Thus, regular environmental scans and audits and the interpretation of these relative to ongoing strategic processes and action programs for implementation are a must.

Realistic Time Frame for Change.   Instead of insisting that the organization go "on line" at a particular time, for example, it may be prudent to provide more time. Our experience suggests at least two or three years and often five years is needed before the smoothing out of procedures and relationships—and the absorption of needed changes. This much time is required often for the massive reorientation required in the successful undertaking of many strategic approaches.

Processes as a Means to an End.   Strategic thinking is literally just that—a way of thinking about current and future circumstances. Procedures or paperwork are meant to support, not complicate, this activity. Documentation needs to be adequate but not so voluminous that it becomes an end in itself. Strategic purposes must not be obscured by paperwork or reports! Also, line management must not be stripped of its central role. Although referenced in many points in the preceding discussion, this latter prescription is well worth repeating.

Many line managers are action oriented and not attuned to the contemplative, reflective, and deliberate approaches characteristic of strategic planning. The tendency is to let the "experts," the planners, take over various key planning and strategic steps. This is a tendency that needs to be resisted or rejected outright. Interaction patterns affecting line and staff must be established that include the various planning phases and the initial states of plan implementation.

The actions and deliberations of planning must be joined in a thoughtful way to the launching of these plans. This involves a dynamic, interactive, continuing process and good working relationships. Thus, in the strategic and longer-range planning phases, planning officials will need to organize planning processes and provide inputs reflective of their expertise. At the same time, planning officials need to create the formats (one-on-one discussions, committees, small-group meeting, weekend conferences) where line management can confront planning issues, provide inputs reflective of their resource knowledge and experience, and temper proposed strategic actions. The extent of line management's involvement in these planning phases will be reflected in the quality of the plans, their degree of plan commitment, and the results.

As plans and strategies start to move toward implementation, the relative contributions of participants change. Line management assumes a major role in implementation, yet planners and strategists need to stay in close touch with developments. Line management will likely need technical counsel and support. Planners need to know how well assumptions are working and how events are playing out.

Since subsequent discussions increasingly involve the human resource aspects of strategic approaches, a schema that outlines book topics in relationship to business planning and strategic approaches is next described.

Strategic Approaches—An Integrative Model

Because the subject matter of this book is relatively complex, I have provided a diagram (model) that includes the main discussion topics and general relationships among these and closely allied factors. The sketch is for general orientation purposes; details are omitted because they are numerous and would greatly complicate the picture. Highlights of the model are discussed at this point since it is intended that it serve as both a clarifying and integrative device. A replica of the diagram also heads up each chapter with shading indicating the main chapter subject matter.

As an aside, it has been my experience that a carefully developed model (sketch) can prove highly useful in executive/managerial orientation sessions. However, it usually is helpful to "ease" the viewing group into this type of subject matter because "diagram shock" is always a possibility. These visual representations provide a practical means for orientation and generating discussion. They can also readily project the overall scope of a complex subject and show general relationships. However, it is only fair to say that these types of diagrams run the risk of implying a rigidity of approaches or oversimplification of underlying processes. They may fail to communicate the dynamics of relationships or change. However, if carefully organized, the advantages can substantially outweigh the disadvantages.

Overview

There are four main activities shown in Exhibit 1-3. Each is specialized as to purpose. Together, they form parts of a comprehensive whole coupling business planning and strategic analyses (activity II) to performance (activity I). The other two activities are managerial succession and development planning (activity III) and strategic HR planning (activity IV). These four elements are either directly involved in or related to all discussions in this book.

The performance management system is heavily oriented to people, what they do, how they do it, how well they do it, and the means by which these may be established, maintained, or improved. It includes managerial work assignments, performance appraisals, and supportive activities, including accurate, timely information and rewards. An important offshoot of this activity is the identification of those possessing high potential, those exhibiting good performance, and those likely capable of fast upward movement.

The performance management system represents an ultimate "bottom line" in all organizations. If plans and strategies cannot be transformed into practical and efficient work activities, the best laid plans will fail. The effective functioning of the performance system relative to the strategic planning system can't be ignored. The danger is that the role of performance tends to be underplayed in the complex planning picture because it is distant in orientation and direct impacts. The former is tangible; the latter requires much conceptual, global, or visionary thinking. Performance management lends itself to varying degrees of measurement, some very specific. Progress in measuring managerial performance has been slow, but the area

EXHIBIT 1-3
Strategic Approaches to Managerial Succession and Development:
Overview

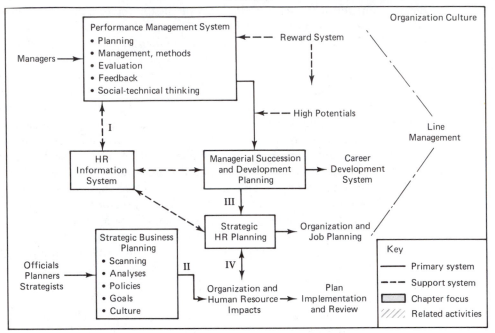

has received much attention lately. As for the strategic planning system, the record is virtually a blank when it comes to *measuring* how effective these have been. "After all, there are so many factors involved." This situation is starting to be corrected, but as noted elsewhere in this chapter, much remains to be done.

Another aspect of performance management is the recognition that people, jobs, and working systems must be approached collectively since performance is a joint product of people and technology. In performance matters, position holders can't be ignored any more than work and work desgin. This is the basis for a "sociotechnical" approach to improving performance and the individual's response to the work situation.

Activity II is a conceptualization of the long-range and strategic planning system. A complex series of determinations build on (1) scanning of the business's environment for opportunities and threats, (2) scans of the internal environment for general resource capabilities and limitations, and (3) confirmation or change of longer-range organizational objectives and examination of organizational culture as to its relevance to organizational purposes and actions. Attention also is directed toward how culture can be approached so that it is more strategically relevant and supportive of plans and programs. This system (II) gives rise eventually to connections with related activities which help to shape strategic thinking and actions on the lower rungs of the planning hierarchy (e.g., tactical planning). The "organizational distance" in orientation and approaches is great between the performance management (I) and strategic system (II) but one that must be bridged effectively.

From the viewpoint of human resources as well as various operational planning and management functions, coupling and mediating activities are needed. Two of those given much attention in this book are "managerial succession and development planning" (activity III) and "strategic HR planning" (activity IV).

Business strategies shape the direction and thrust of the work of the HR planning strategists. Human resource inputs to the strategic business planning process (activity IV) need to provide environmental scanning information (external and internal) which effectively highlights and interprets trends, capabilities, and limitations affecting business strategies in HR terms. Severe shortages of systems or technical personnel or a relative decrease in the availability of young people are examples of environmental trends often included in this type of analysis. Organization and job planning also emerges as an extension of strategic analyses since choices need to be made as to the structure best suited to future business requirements. General Motors' choice of styling centers to coordinate automotive designs across divisions, the establishment of financial service groups at Sears and General Electric, the creation of internal entrepreneurial efforts ("intrepreneurships") as self-standing businesses, and the merging in of various Van Camp organizational units and personnel into the Quaker Company—all are examples of major corporate strategies involving organization structure with great human resource consequences. Internal reorganization, hiring of new personnel, retraining of existing people, and outplacement of people no longer needed or affordable were some of the consequences of the referenced strategic actions. Needless to say, major policy questions (e.g. outplacement matters) were also involved.

Managerial succession and development planning (activity III) represents two major aspects of human resource planning, often acknowledged as the basic ones in this area. Strategic HR thinking is bent toward the future organizational leadership, who they will be, and how they will be developed.

A first level of analysis deals with competent and immediately available personnel for promotion, and then those likely to be ready. An important related question is how will limitations in access to people and available information affect strategic HR choices and thereby strategic business decisions?

Another plateau of decisions rests on the firming up of general HR directions. This is followed by the need to design systems, jobs, and mobility paths likely to "deliver" the needed people. This design step must meet the assumptions and expectations of the performance management activities. Planning approaches which have progressed to this point of discussion also need to start to consider how the individuals and (technical) systems can be joined effectively. A "sociotechnical" approach is a term used to capture this type of comprehensive thinking and approach.

As successively lower rungs of planning analysis are reached, thinking must be initiated as to how individuals will be motivated to make major commitments of their personal and professional lives to the organization, let alone to perform well. The "career development" activity jointly meets the needs of the organization and the person. The career development system includes bases for people to explore career opportunities. It involves support of managerial succession and development planning (activity III), identification of effective career ladders for managerial mobility, and defining the career development role of supervisory or senior people.

Reserved for last in this discussion of Exhibit 1-3 is the role of line management. Its role is a major one in all the previously mentioned systems and processes. On the one hand, valid strategic planning depends on the thoughtful contributions of line managers who know their responsibility areas and operations well. Line management is also central to meeting performance expectations, especially where they have been an integral part of setting achievable goals or a part of planned change. Line management also directly interfaces with the individual (manager) whose future in the organization often depends on the supervising manager's coaching abilities, communication skills, and inspirational talents.

The success of strategic business and human resource planning approaches often turns on the skill with which business and human resource planning activities are integrated. This topic is viewed as among the most urgent by many officials and managers. It receives specific attention in the next section because of its importance.

Issues in Linking Business and Human Resource Planning

In contrast to previous discussions, the emphasis here is on the strategic aspects of human resources planning and linking these to strategic business planning. Some characteristic strategic business matters with important human resource issues are suggested by the following:

- Facility closing and the redeployment or outplacement of employees.
- Succession planning for officer and senior managerial positions to address the need for business continuity, expansion, or consolidation.
- Management development strategies due to the expansion of international operations.
- Merger, acquisition, or reduction in the scope of business activities and the needed redesign of organization and job structures.
- Introduction of major new technologies involving information, robotics, or work automation.
- Enterprise productivity and new(er) "quality of work life" experiments and designs.
- New services or product line introductions requiring knowledge, skills, abilities, or experience in (very) short supply.

These key human resource–related issues are quite common, and thus it is natural that interest has grown in comprehensive planning and strategic systems which effectively use human resource contributions. They are seen as increasingly instrumental to the successful fulfillment of long-range and strategic plans.

Many corporations are trying to make human resource planning part of their long-range and strategic business plans, but much remains to be done (Burack, 1985, 1986). If human resource components are to be effectively merged into a long-range/strategic business planning system, the important organizational and change questions must be faced. As stated by a senior human resource officer, "The problems are not technical or logistical—they are often emotional and political and, thus, much harder to fully identify, let alone solve." For example, what new organization structures or arrangements and policies will be needed? Also, in the process of change, "organizational cultures" and subcultures, as in Personnel, are often involved. Thus, "What new roles will be required of senior people?" "Who are the newer participants in decision processes and politics, or for making particular decisions, and what new power or/and political issues emerge from these?" These types of questions formed a central part of a study which we conducted, some key results of which are highlighted in the following discussion.

Some Study Results

The referenced study covered over 60 corporations in the United States and Canada, including those engaged in worldwide activities (Burack, 1985, 1986). This "convenience sample" involved 12 different industrial classifications, including manufacturing, banking, insurance, consumer products, services, and high technology. Ninety percent had comprehensive planning approaches. One fact immediately apparent from study results was that many organizations assumed that long-range business planning (LRBP) and strategic business planning (SBP) were one and the same, or virtually indistinguishable. A point of fact: an evolutionary process had been taking place with a shift in corporate orientation from long-range business planning to long-range *and* strategic business planning.

Although long-range business planning had pretty much matured in these corporations and had become an integral part of company life, strategic business planning was still in the *formative stages* in many! And to the extent that these emerging strategic processes called for new(er) planning or strategic "partners" (planners, officials, and managers), important adjustments and rebalancing of responsibilities were needed and taking place, albeit slowly and at times with much conflict.

The shift to a more strategically oriented business approach was much more than a change in procedures. For example, the clarification or refocusing of "organizational culture" was a characteristic concern. This involved possible attempts to change the philosophy of management, assumptions underlying major decisions, or shifts in the seat(s) of corporate power.

The study results indicated that the integration of human resource planning with long-range/strategic business planning was (and will be) a slow process. The degree of recognition and thoughtful utilization of human resource planning components has varied widely. The introduction of human resource planning as an integral part of the business planning process was a radical change relative to the more traditional (often) secondary role of Personnel in the past. Past Personnel activities were often reactive rather than proactive. A common example of the reactive approach in the past was communications to Personnel of a "list of positions" to be filled reflecting short-term line management needs. Rarely did the Personnel Department have enough esteem to be factored into longer-range planning and strategic analyses. Recruitment planning wasn't possible because Personnel often lacked information on future business plans! Unfortunately, the initiators of the personnel requisitions often had not taken the longer-range business requirements into account.

"Linkage problems" often underlying the problems described above masked several, quite different issues:

1. Strategic business planning processes, its state of development, the designation of roles to be played by key participants, and how well these are carried out.
2. Connecting effectively the systems, structure, processes, and people comprising strategic business and human resource planning.
3. Development and integration of human resource activities, including planning, career development, and Personnel activities.

Involvement of Human Resource Activities.   In this selection of firms, most of which were involved in longer-range planning, over half *involved* HR people in strategic processes but less than one-quarter assigned it an interactive role. In short, at this stage of development, HR was not an active planning partner. Yet most study firms expected this situation to change rather rapidly, with Human Resources playing a much more important role in high-level planning activities. The redeployment of the Human Resource function was already underway in many.

Focus of Human Resource Functions as a Part of Strategic Approaches.   In organizations where Human Resources was involved in some way with the strategic business plan, the main emphasis was on top- and middle-level management. Succession planning, management development to help meet longer-range plans, and the progress of high potentials were common activities. About one-half of these companies also involved first-line management and technical employees. Other perspectives on this topic may be found in the applications section for this chapter.

HR's Future Role.   Corporate representatives felt that their companies benefited most from HR planning in the area of management succession, but only somewhat so in the area of human resource utilization, cost savings, employee job satisfaction, and development. However, it was expected that the latter areas would receive much greater attention in the future.

If the expected benefits from HRP (planning) are obtained, it is likely that the partnership of HRP and LRBP will continue to mature. But the inability to clarify or demonstrate the specific contributions of the HR function relative to the other individuals and functions who are a part of LRBP, remains a block to its more complete integration in business planning and strategic processes. The *intuitive sense* of officials that business plans will benefit from some type of HR component needs to be replaced with more well-defined specifics. Better criteria and assessment techniques are needed to judge the contribution of HR planning to the success of the LRBP. Also, more definitive areas of HR responsibility are needed in the planning process as well as the specification of measurable objectives.

HR officials in some cases expressed a lack of familiarity with some of the planning specifics of HR, especially in larger firms. This lack of familiarity with planning aspects stems commonly from several causes. First, responsibilities were often delegated to specialists, and thus senior people got out of touch with what was happening. Also, technically complex procedures inhibited communications. Other problems included a high degree of division of responsibilities and specialization involving planning units, with Personnel Management (simply) being uninformed.

The lack of comprehensive knowledge by key company people concerning corporate system functions and available HR forecasting techniques also represented a major block to the emergence of a more complete strategic business planning process. Approaches to strengthening strategic system approaches based on the corporate experiences described here are summarized in Exhibit 1-4 (Burack, 1985).

The points outlined in Exhibit 1-4 for improving strategic system functions and approaches cover essentially the three areas of problems outlined earlier. Points 1 and 2 deal with the understanding and competencies of HR personnel who became a part of strategic planning processes. A central problem (complaint) voiced consistently by top executives has been the lack of understanding (by HR people) of (their company's) major business functions, how these dovetail, and the foundation of assumptions, knowledge, and skills involved in longer-range business planning and strategies. Points 3, 6, and 7 deal with the soundness of planning and strategic approaches as these are affected by the reality of time parameters, effectiveness of communications and working relationships, and reality of approaches. A comprehensive planning and strategic program is often most difficult at its inception— when attempting to gain acceptance and get things underway. Thus points 4, 5, 6, 8, 9, and 10 describe specifics of gaining organizational acceptance, promoting change, and building a valid base of information and methods. Finally, point 11 emphasizes the critical importance of monitoring processes and activities and assuring the needed flexibility for adapting to changed circumstances or making procedural improvements.

Information to Support HR Approaches. In the study companies, much emphasis was (still) placed on internal data versus external sources of information. It is important to note that the areas of information deficiencies were significant ones. These included economic trends and various sources of competition including inter-

EXHIBIT 1-4
Strengthening Strategic Systems Development

1. Reflect an understanding of the basic character and work of the business and the financial, marketing, engineering, and operational functions attendant to these companies.

2. Underscore the need for self-preparation or development in the light of an expanded and more demanding role for Human Resources.

3. Focus on undertakings fully capable of completion within realistic time frames and progress reporting to key officials and senior managers.

4. Establish a solid program of activities likely to be successful to gain organization acceptance. Establish benchmarks for measuring progress and objectives attainment.

5. Gain top management's commitment and support at an early point and use this as the basic building block in a program for planned change.

6. Establish good working relationships with other staff support groups whose input will be critical to human resource and strategic planning (e.g., wage and salary administration regarding job analyses for existing and new staffing and the managerial reward system, and with data processing systems or information groups).

7. Establish/plan approaches that will withstand the basic managerial tests of understandability, common sense, involvement (theirs), and usefulness.

8. Work toward approaches that will facilitate critical examination of the common denominator for top management analyses and discussions—crisp, specific language and quantification where possible.

9. Assure good communications and working relationships among corporate and divisional Personnel groups who will be expected to explain and support programs during installation and functioning.

10. Build carefully and thoroughly, the information base and systems that will be expected to support planning and strategic approaches.

11. Stay close to emerging developments and be prepared to refocus approaches as circumstances dictate.

Source: Elmer M. Burack, "Linking Corporate Business and Human Resource Planning," *Human Resource Planning*, Vol. 8, no. 3 (1985): 133–145.

national. Environmental scanning capabilities and the skills to interpret trends and business impacts were often lacking, although this is a singularly difficult task.

Another potentially valuable but deficient information source area was the lack of models that were user oriented and available to (line) managers. Environmental scanning for outside (external) trends was just starting to emerge, though some years will be required to develop this capability. Environmental scanning methods and know-how and user-oriented "personal computer" systems are inexorably involved with LRBP/SBP in current approaches. This is a highly undeveloped area that will have to receive much more attention in the future. Aspects of this situation as related to personal computers are discussed in Chapter 9.

Conflicting Outlooks: Business Versus Human Resource Planners. The lack of mutual understanding as to the various planning techniques, their capabilities and limitations characterized many internal relationships among planners, especially business planners relative to HR's role and inputs. Thus it would follow that lack of confidence, even mistrust, could arise under these conditions. Yet in the interest of improving overall strategic and planning approaches, the need for strengthening these relationships holds whether due to being uninformed, unsure, or unaccepting.

Summary

Massive changes are underway in many different corporate settings affecting strategic and long-range business planning. Major priorities have been assigned to developing comprehensive longer-range systems that include planning and strategic analysis (and thinking!) and program execution. The fact that these efforts have been launched under dynamic and often rapidly changing circumstances mandates that a flexible and highly adaptable approach be used.

Line managers are central to the successful launching and maturing of these systems. This is truly a challenge in change involving the business and strategic planning activities as such, human resource planning in the strategic framework, and the Human Resource/Personnel function. Line managers and HR people must be artfully woven into this tapestry. All must be thoughtfully linked through excellent communications, understandings of mutual purposes, and organization and systems. Contrary to some popular thinking, models' and/or methods' sophistication will not make a successful strategic undertaking.

This chapter has provided a number of problems and prescriptions based on actual experiences to improve the likelihood of success in these undertakings. Successful strategic undertakings possess the potential for significant advancements in corporate fulfillment of longer-range plans, the fuller utilization of managerial resources, and greater opportunities for individual fulfillment. Human Resources will have a central role to play in these events, but its role change is contingent upon (among other factors) demonstrated expertise in the broader domain of strategic planning and analyses. Its acceptance and role change also is connected to major internal organizational changes that involve definition or refocusing of corporate culture and realignment of decision-making responsibilities and power.

In past years, corporate planning and more recently strategic planning, were responsibilities frequently assigned to a group of specialists within "planning." In the past, this unit was heavily oriented to finance or marketing or other basic organization functions. At best, Human Resources was factored in after the basic long-range plans were developed. For various reasons discussed here, top Personnel/Human Resource officials were often absent from these processes during the basic conceptual, discussion, or scenario stages.

A central consideration that has retarded integration of human resource planning with strategic business planning has been an inherent lack of widespread long-range thinking *and* actions. The "rites" of long-range and strategic planning are performed often in many companies, but these may be in reality "pony shows." For the most part, corporate values have been geared toward the "short-term" way of thinking. The "quick fix" is often demanded within an organization and at virtually every level.

One of the major themes emerging from the study results described in this chapter is that companies need to examine critically the planning functions, processes, and relationships attendant to both the business and human resource activities. Their collective effort in strategic undertakings must also be reviewed.

Themes for improving roles and performance in both the business and human resource planning system, described in detail in this chapter, include the following:

- Assure a central role for line management in information inputs, planning, and program execution, and preserve staff unit roles as support groups, facilitators, and problem solvers. Avoid staff units gaining "ownership" of plan/strategies. Be wary of approaches that by their nature "force" staff to assume dominant roles.
- Assure that line management gains identification and commitment to plans and strategies. Encourage line management to assume an active, even leading role in information processing and exploring alternatives.
- Establish or solidify a key contributing role for Human Resources in business planning and strategic processes. Assure that HR approaches this role understanding the enterprise's activities and with the full support of top management and the people and functions involved in planning and strategic processes.
- Produce planning and strategic documents that avoid being lengthy or overly complex—seek out ones that will be seen as understandable, sensible, and helpful. Seek to develop thinking and dialogue on major planning and strategic matters.
- Decrease dependence on formula approaches that fail to deal with the realities of competition or that lose sight of the dynamics of the marketplace.
- Establish and maintain close and continuing communications between staff and line management groups as strategies are launched.
- Establish benchmarks and monitoring capabilities—maintain flexibility to adapt to needed changes.

Chapter Development—What Follows

Chapter 2 deals with organization and job planning. It is a broadly oriented topic which, along with corporate culture in Chapter 3, deals with contextual factors in strategic thinking regarding HR.

Beginning with Chapter 4, the focus of discussions shifts toward "managers."

The development emphasizes who they are and the systems and methods for planning succession and development, including information management (with "personal computer" emphasis).

Several chapters, starting with Chapter 9, deal with career development and important individual problems attendant to this, including stress, aging, and tapping creativity as in (internal corporate) entrepreneurial approaches.

Concluding chapters take up, respectively, implementation strategies (Chapter 12) and an emerging planning agenda for HR strategists (Chapter 13).

REFERENCES

Burack, Elmer H. "Corporate Business and Human Resource Planning Practices: Strategic Issues and Concerns." *Organizational Dynamics* Vol. 15, no. 1 (Summer 1986): 65–87.

Burack, Elmer H. "Linking Corporate Business and Human Resource Planning." *Human Resource Planning*, Vol. 8, no. 3 (1985): 133–145.

Burack, Elmer H. and Nicholas J. Mathys. *Human Resource Planning: A Pragmatic Approach to Manpower Planning and Development*. Lake Forest, IL: Brace–Park Press, 1980, 1987 rev.

Business Week. "Special Feature Issue," September 17, 1985.

Fombrun, Charles, Noel Tichy, and Mary Anne Devanna. *Strategic Human Resource Management*. New York: John Wiley, 1984.

Midwest Academy of Management. "Indiana University Workshop on Corporate Strategic Approaches" (May 1984).

APPLICATIONS SECTION

Strategic Business Planning and Human Resource Strategies— A Life Cycle Case

Larsen & Goldsmith (L&G) was founded in 1938 for the manufacture of industrial controllers. Military contracts during World War II and the postwar industrial growth led to a manyfold expansion of L&G's product line and sales. By 1970 almost 3,000 people were employed. Organization structure was drawn along traditional functional lines emphasizing marketing, production, and engineering.

Along with company size, the product line had changed a great deal and included controllers (still an important area), small electric motors, and allied equipment. The products, though mainly industrial, also included a small but growing number of consumer offerings. Although the business had expanded greatly, the considerable experience and expertise of the supervisory and managerial group met most customer demands. Budgetary planning, in force for many years, provided a workable basis for developing and meeting cost objectives, including those related to managerial staffing and work force employment.

However, the company subsequently found itself in a tough competitive period with competition increasing and cost of materials escalating rapidly. General corporate problems worsened as demand for their basic products plateaued, piling up inventory and further tying up scarce funds.

L&G had to adopt a more powerful and longer-range planning approach. Longer-range planning horizons and forecasting were introduced. The planning capability was achieved through the hiring of an MBA (the first) whose specialization was business and financial planning. He was assigned to the comptroller. Subsequently, sales forecasts were developed as a joint product of the sales vice president and the comptroller's office. Sales forecasts and multiyear budgets provided a sounder basis for managerial planning and execution. Capital funds, working capital, staffing, and inventory were brought into better alignment and better internal control was achieved.

Human resource staffing was demand driven. Succession was largely a one-at-a-time consideration since most of the executives were (still) relatively young and replacement came up infrequently. Management development focused on job-related needs and was almost entirely experience based. Though the sales picture had been changing, the improvements in planning and internal controls adequately met general business needs.

In the 1970s the pace of change accelerated as the competitive picture became more international and new technological innovations led to rapid product obsolescence. L&G's business and staffing planning approaches and bases for internal controls were inadequate. Its financial position darkened and then became precarious.

A change of corporate leadership was mandated, and Tom Fitzgerald, a successful young officer from an industrial products company, was hired as CEO. Fitzgerald brought with him two people with whom he had worked closely. They eventually become the vice presidents of marketing and finance.

The new CEO assessed the desperate situation and set to work on several different fronts simultaneously. "New product development" was reorganized and strongly supported with a rejuvenated marketing group and strong financial management. Also a new position of human resource development (HRD) manager was created and filled by promoting one of the divisional Personnel managers. One of the main tasks of the new HRD manager was to develop an integrated human resource planning system which brought together sales forecasts and coordinated internal staffing planning and development of supervisors and managers.

Fitzgerald believed strongly in the power of a dedicated managerial group, focused on common objectives and rallying around a central managerial theme. The motto created for these purpose was inscribed on wall plaques and placed in all managerial offices. It was "Think and Act Strategically." To back up his view of the company and its circumstances further, a number of additional internal changes were instituted. The concept of strategic business units (SBUs) was introduced. The SBU concept, developed jointly by General Electric and McKinsey & Co., Inc. in the late 1960s, was that the marketplace activities of a company had to be understood and then segmented strategically for the best allocation of key resources and to assure a competitive advantage. In the past, the SBU system was designed to answer these key planning related questions: What business are we in? Who is our competition? What's our position relative to that competition?

The growing complexity of L&G's business served to make it a prime candidate for the innovative SBU approach. In essence, six freestanding businesses were created. Each unit had a unique business segment with its competition clearly defined. Each SBU, headed by a general manager, carried out its own integrated planning activities and "controlled" sales personnel, product development directions, and inventory levels. A corporate planning unit integrated the plans of the individual SBUs, which were then reviewed by an executive committee. After general approval, the comprehensive plan was sent to the HRD manager for staffing analyses. Comments as to recruiting or development problems and issues were noted and then the plan was returned to the individual SBU. Before SBU plans were finalized, the SBU general managers were expected to interact with the HRD Manager to reconcile any difficult matters.

Although the SBU reorganization served to improve financial matters, it was not without its problems. The introduction of SBUs within L&G led to a basic and almost complete change from the internal planning and management processes of the past. Formerly, the organizational culture and values strongly supported the functional structure. Powerful vice presidents headed these up. Under the SBU concept, much of the power of the functional vice presidents of manufacturing, engineering, and sales was reduced. SBU business heads made decisions or had a major "say" in resource discussions previously reserved for the vice presidents.

Practical organizational problems also emerged from several other sources. Crucial resources such as L&G's product development groups and salespeople representing multiproduct lines had to be shared among the SBUs. Also, production runs to stock often-encountered problems, since common manufacturing and packaging facilities processed the products of various SBUs.

Another difficulty that emerged was the role of department managers under the SBU concept. In past years the functional vice presidents carried out general planning activities, but the real planning (and execution) took place at the departmental level, and department managers pretty well ran their own show. Under the SBU concept, several developments completely changed this picture. The SBU general managers developed their own planning staffs, and department managers then provided planning information as solicited from these staff groups. Also, since many SBUs drew on common resources, corporate planning was expanded and assumed an increasing monitoring, coordinating, and integrating role.

Department managers and the older functional vice presidents became further estranged as more "powerful" planning and analytical models were introduced within the SBUs and at the corporate level. Computer applications, probabilistic models, and much new terminology were representative developments in this difficult situation.

After several years, other "messy" organizational problems emerged at the corporate level. Tensions arose from the shared resources approach. Several SBUs were authorized to establish their own product development capability. Autonomy and accountability, given high top management priority under the SBU approach, led to the dilution of the expertise possessed by the former (consolidated) product development group. The interactive collegial nature of development engineer relationships was reduced. Also, Fitzgerald and his direct reports had to grapple with the number of SBUs to create. "Six" seemed like a manageable number, but it was difficult to arrive at a focused strategic mission fitting together all the businesses within the SBU.

Complications for Fitzgerald and the executive committee also came from other directions. This was especially the case as the planners sought to improve the SBU approach by including "portfolio planning." Portfolio planning provided a model for evaluating the individual corporate businesses formed under the SBU umbrella. Each SBU was evaluated on a table (matrix) that purported to measure the strength of the SBU relative to its competitors and the growth prospects of its markets. Strategic missions and strategies resulted from these analyses, and top management reviewed these results for mission accomplishment and financial acceptability.

In portfolio approaches, industry attractiveness and business strength were interpreted in terms of a specialized terminology. The terminology, described as "more jargon" by its critics, included terms such as "harvest" (divest) and "grow" (invest). The systematic format of portfolio approaches lent itself readily to the inclusion of various factors interpreted in numerical terms (e.g., price trends, market growth, and concentration). Computer programming and the use of multiple regression models as in PIMS (profit impact of market strategies, from the Strategic Planning Institute) appeared to be a "logical next step."

The portfolio approach, its quantification and computerization, was readily handled by the planning groups at the corporate and SBU levels. The models and approaches were an excellent fit with their educational background. The moves also had the full support of the executive committee since these were a clear demonstration of "thinking strategically." The staff planners by 1982 had become quite powerful and exerted much influence on L&G's strategic planning and decisions.

Some of the staff planners' impact on strategic directions was also shared by HRD. HRD, now staffed by three people, was called on increasingly to provide inputs to strategic discussions and to do the systems planning and monitoring needed for a comprehensive human resource system.

The foregoing notwithstanding, the focus, language, and methods of the planners, executive group, and SBU heads became largely foreign to middle-level (department) management. Increasingly, line managers had the main task of implementing plans devised elsewhere in the organization. Not surprisingly, "glitches" occurred more and more as the model/theory (and indicated directions) failed to match marketing and operational realities. The improvement in the general financial picture and increased sales which reflected L&G performance for some five years seemed to be peaking out.

"Thinking strategically" had indeed led to widespread corporate improvements, but it had also created its own problems. A 1985 management consultant's report indicated that "the sophisticated planning approaches undertaken in recent years had lost contact with corporate realities, namely, its capabilities and limitations. The failure to gain line management's involvement resulted in strategic approaches absent of line management commitment."

A New Conception of Planning and Management for the Future

The consultant's analyses acknowledged the rapidly changing character of L&G's business needs and the proactive, positive steps taken by top management. Especially noted was management's willingness to alter, even radically change, its thinking in seeking to exploit new opportunities, meet competitive threats, and adjust internal processes and systems to these requirements. What was proposed for the future was *not* an abandonment of its relatively advanced managerial approaches; rather, what was called for was a systematic reassessment of altered economic and competitive conditions and environmental trends, and the fitting of internal organization and approaches to these for a better match. In part, the proposed internal remedy involved a newer conception of future planning and management. Features of the newer approaches included the following:

1. The complex circumstances with which the firm was confronted called for a high level of understanding of external and internal factors and creative approaches in dealing with these.
2. Plans and strategies could benefit significantly from greater involvement of line management and the latter's commitment was crucial to accomplishable programs.
3. Creative processes and improved communications called for carefully organized dialogues among officials, planners, and managers. These "staged" interactions should benefit from strategic analyses of both external and internal factors. But, if anything, these approaches should err on the side of models, analyses, and data which maximized participant understanding, communications, and involvement, although the inherent uncertainties and complexities of the factors would limit in a practical sense, how far simplification efforts could be taken.
4. Human Resources Development should be an active participant in all planning discussions and should assume an important contributory role in identifying HR issues, problems, and strategies connected with business plans and approaches. HRD's role would reflect its expertise and professionalism in HR matters but in all cases should benefit from line management experience and know-how.

5. Strategic human resources approaches would have to come to grips with a group of interrelated matters. Some would require immediate attention relative to strategic business planning analyses while others would affect the longer-term human resource management picture. The former included organization and structure planning and replacement (succession) planning involving key and critical positions. Management development would also be of immediate concern to the extent it influenced the nature and feasibility of recruitment plans and involved incumbent managers.

For the longer term, strategic thinking related to human resources would have to be expanded. It would be necessary to take fuller account of factors affecting the cultivation and performance of the organization's leaders and managers. Matters likely to require attention would include

- The organization's culture affecting values related to planning, promotions, and decisions.
- Managerial performance factors, including work design and more deep-seated matters related to individual career development, motivation, behavior, and healthfulness, especially dealing with stress.
- Systems and processes by which succession and development took place.

The Larsen and Goldsmith Case in Perspective

The L&G case provides a condensed picture of organizational problems and issues spanning many years, attendant to the birth and growth of strategic approaches and practices. Serendipity played a role, at times a major one, in uncovering the malfunctions of existing arrangements and leading to improved means for the organization's executives to deal with their environment.

In a comparatively short time, L&G progressed through several significantly different stages of planning approaches and strategic thinking. At one point a radical change in organization leadership and structuring was signaled to move forward into a newer and fast-changing competitive world quite distinct from the past.

The growing complexity of L&G's circumstances called for more powerful means of planning, identifying, and "testing" out business alternatives prior to resource commitments. Also needed were more adaptive and flexible means of dealing with complexity and fast-changing conditions. The use of strategic business units and more comprehensive models was a partial answer to the needs.

Another part of the confrontation with complexity came from human resource's newer role as planner and strategist. It had become apparent that successful business strategies turned more and more on the organization's ability to identify and develop its human resources. Of particular importance were its key and critical personnel forming the cadre of tomorrow's leadership, management, and technical competency.

Overdependence on planning and strategic methods and failure to note fully changing circumstances, created (again) internal problems and issues of growing proportions. It was to the credit of L&G's leadership that it was willing to seek help in solving the difficult organizational problems they had encountered. Top managers were aware that a candid view of the firm's circumstances was likely to call for major changes in their own actions. They nevertheless accepted the challenge and viewed the consultant's report as a positive means of launching needed future changes.

2

Organization and Job Planning
for the Productive Organization
A Strategic View

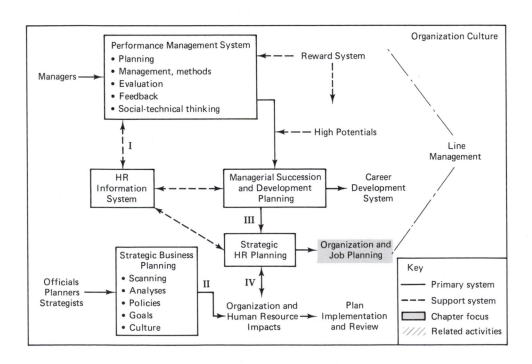

The design of managerial work, which involves the job itself as well as work context, is an important topic in strategic management development. This chapter deals primarily with the strategic aspects of work and job design, including reward systems. Chapter 3 deals more with the work context, particularly organization culture.

Some notes on approaching organization and work design from a strategic perspective lead off the chapter discussions. Next, there is a brief presentation of the background underlying the topics introduced in this chapter. The main chapter discussions that follow are divided into two parts. Part I presents some of the newer bases for organization and job planning, including reward systems. Part II gets into some of the detail of position analyses commonly associated with managerial position design.

Approaching Organization and Work Design Strategically

Two general levels of analysis are considered, both of which are of interest to strategic planning analyses. But they came about in quite different ways. One set of circumstances, broad in nature, emerges as a "follow-up" of business and strategic planning. Here, organization structure and job/work planning take their direction from strategic planning processes and analyses that establish the study parameters. In this approach, which is macro oriented, *general* strategic planning considerations are prominent. Organization structures may be created, modified, or eliminated in consequence of planned changes in the complexion, processes, products, or services of the future enterprise. Models and approaches that deal with overall features of structures, systems, or relationships prove helpful.

The second approach is more specific and micro in nature; it serves to define the character of managerial needs, positions, and design requirements. It is derived from specific human resource strategies correlated with business strategies. "Improving managerial productivity" in connection with a particular business plan is a common focus, often involving redesigning or redefining positions. One aspect of the productivity picture might include "strategies to strengthen the performance management system" (a topic developed in a subsequent chapter). Analyses might come to grips with updating individual knowledge, or abilities, or using behavioral approaches in job design to improve related satisfaction. Another example of micro approaches relates to the establishment of new business components where it is desired to know the new(er) position characteristics for various managerial jobs relative to existing ones.

The organization and work-design approaches described here are often well suited for specific types of strategic applications or planning needs. A characteristic group of these are summarized in Exhibit 2-1. Analysis of organization culture, also included in this exhibit, is discussed in detail in Chapter 3.

Exhibit 2-1 provides several different classifications that reflect the diverse applications for which these approaches are used. The seven categories of organization and job design approaches referenced in this chapter differ in such fundamental areas (column 2) as to whether they are mostly conceptual or systematic (procedural) or some combination of these. For example, most discussions involving organization culture are quite general ("conceptual") and deal with overall characteristics or properties. However, when specific aspects of culture are considered, like the values used in making decisions, "systematic" study approaches are carried out. In job-analytic approaches, most of these are quite detailed (systematic), and newer approaches emphasize competencies and end-job performances. It is possible to deal with job-analytic approaches conceptually, but management development applications usually involve specific dimensions and procedures.

The third column in Exhibit 2-1 is a descriptive classification reflecting the intended end application or types of information desired.

The fourth column highlights approaches which are primarily oriented to performance, careers, or job-related satisfaction. In reality, there is extensive overlap so that, for example, even though a "career-stage model" is intended for bettering individual career planning, improved job satisfaction and performance may be added "bonuses" from this approach.

The last column in Exhibit 2-1 is intended to convey the utility of the various approaches for assessing the impact of change. The usefulness of some are confined to the job (micro focus), while others, such as "culture," fit well with the impact of overall organizational changes.

Another consideration is recognizing that various approaches may prove useful at an early point in organization and work-design planning stages, while others are more valuable in operational planning. Environmental analysis (no. 1) provides a general guide to needed features of organization structure and desirable properties of communications, working relationships, and decision-making systems. Sociotechnical approaches, for example, are useful in planning for the introduction of a new (major) work system. If major changes are anticipated in the nature of the business or organization, the first three approaches would likely be helpful.

Where management development requirements must be examined closely in terms of individual needs, much detail is provided through approaches 6 and 7 in Exhibit 2-1. In general, the newer job-analytic approaches for job design (6 and 7) usually provide job details, including convenient categories for analyzing the impact of change. However, these provide little information for viewing events in the broader context of organizational change. Conversely, the first four approaches provide a good picture of the broader organizational impacts affecting work units or groups, but lack the type of detail identified with approaches 6 and 7.

EXHIBIT 2-1

Organization and Job Design Approaches in Relation to Strategic Management Development Needs

Organization/job design approaches	Nature of Strategic Management Development Needs or Approach			
	Conceptual vs. systematic schema	Work flow as systems or relationships vs. individual job design	Career planning vs. performance/satisfaction design	Utility for assessing the impact of change
1. Environmental	Conceptual	Systems, work flow	—	Useful, general changes
2. Sociotechnical	Conceptual	Work flow, relationships	Performance/satisfaction designs	Highly useful, broad
3. Organization culture	Mostly conceptual	Job orientation, relationships	Performance (general)	Useful, general changes
4. Organization development	Conceptual and systematic	Relationships	Performance/satisfaction design	Useful and broad
5. Career stage model	Conceptual	Systems	Career planning	Useful at individual level
6. Job/career matrix (e.g., Honeywell)	Conceptual and systematic	Systems, relationships	Career planning	Useful generally
7. Job-analytic responsibilities and end behaviors (e.g., Control Data)	Systematic	Individual job design	Performance design	Limited to job
8. Job (re)design behavioral (Hackman and Oldham or Herzberg)	Systematic (and some conceptual)	Individual job design	Performance/satisfaction design	Limited to job

PART I: ENVIRONMENTAL ANALYSES
AND SOCIOTECHNICAL APPROACHES

Environmental Assessments and General Managerial Orientation

General environmental descriptors are used as a basis for structure and position planning. For example, comparatively *stable* external environments relative to economic, technological, and competitive changes are contrasted with dynamic or volatile environments. The latter involve fast, often unpredictable, forms of change. The benefit of this environmental approach is that it is very broad and helps to establish at an early point in planning and strategic analysis the link between it and general structure and decision-making features. General relationships are summarized in the following table.

ENVIRONMENT AND STRUCTURE

Environmental Characteristics	Structural Position and Communication Features
Stable	Mechanistic form or variations emphasizing centralized decision making; reliance on procedures, coordination, and control; detailed planning; communications through channels; slow adaptation to change.
Volatile	Organic relationships, decentralization of decision making; high level of personnel interaction; reliance often placed on participative approaches; stress on adaptive style and sound risk taking.

Two examples illustrate this first step in environmental assessments. An electric power utility serviced an industrial-residential market which had stabilized many years ago. Demand increases were related primarily to industrial expansion reflecting mostly small manufacturers and service-type companies. This demand pattern was relatively stable and permitted a long planning horizon. A conventional, hierarchical structure with vertically oriented planning, communications, and decision making proved adequate for its needs. Another electric power utility had quite a different environmental picture—a volatile one. Business and residential demand patterns were changing a great deal due to the decline of several major industries and the outward movement of family units to other area of the country. Additional "volatility" was lent by an early commitment to atomic energy for power and the many unknowns which had moved into the picture, affecting its financial situation, cost structure, and even community relations. Reorganization of its traditional type of bureaucratic structure into one with fewer authority levels, emphasis on communication, and deemphasis on formalistic approaches was providing

EXHIBIT 2-2

Relation of Environment or Philosophy of Management to Structure
and Management Processes

Environmental Characteristic	Philosophy of Management	
	"Traditional"	"Human resource development"
Stable	"Reactive" • Centralizes decision making. • Channels communications. • Reacts to needs as they arise. • Relies on short(er)-term planning. • Views positions in terms of main responsibilities and considers them fixed. • Emphasizes functional or administrative management, geared largely to job experiences.	"Proactive" • Undertakes long(er)-range planning. • Is highly systematic, often relying on models. • Attempts to integrate strategic business planning with human resource planning and development. • Utilizes systematic change management—well detailed. • Systematically draws out and develops individual competencies. • Positions viewed as a design variable—subject to enrichment or redevelopment and upgrading as part of a sociotechnical system.
Volatile	"Conservative" • Is slow to change. • Follows change leaders. • Relies on systematic, deliberate actions. • Minimizes risk taking. • Requires some personnel involvement. • Views positions in context of detailed responsibilities and largely fixed. • Encourages individual development largely through assignment to progressively more complex or alternate assignments.	"Satisfying" • Is adaptive. • Is decentralized. • Is participative. • Uses organic communications style. • Views communications as a strategy. • Avoids intricate or detailed planning. • Engages in periodic monitoring. • Has flexibility to redirect efforts. • Stresses tolerance and conflict resolution. • Emphasizes management of change. • Views positions as a design variable but with a conscious attempt to avoid too much detail. • Undertakes enrichment of individual jobs or group approaches.

needed internal flexibility for a very difficult period in its history. The types of general organization planning approaches illustrated in the preceding table are often fleshed out to provide added detail (Exhibit 2-2).

The four classifications used in Exhibit 2-2 are for convenience in referencing. The purpose of the exhibit is to juxtapose environmental features with various organizational philosophies of organization and managerial roles and performance. The exhibit also contrasts traditional approaches to organization planning (the first column) with organizations that have more of an HRD approach.

The general profiles suggest that top management's philosophy, or cultural features, can establish the "tone" for valued managerial activities. However, profiles differ from organization to organization. Why? Strong cultures that are highly supportive of developmental approaches provide design options usually *not* encountered in more traditional enterprises. In the latter, relatively low priorities are assigned to managerial (human) development (Exhibit 2-2). Conversely, those organizations emphasizing personnel development seek to integrate strategic and business planning with management development planning. This is done to establish positional performance requirements and the boundaries within which design actions for individual improvement can be initiated. Where environments are stable, approaches tend to be more systematic and detailed in *matching* requirements and capabilities. There is a willingness to make job modifications based on available talent. Stable conditions permit reasonable latitude in personnel selection or job (re)design decisions while recognizing the complex complementarity of human skills and abilities. Volatile environments favor an integrative orientation too, but with much greater flexibility for adaptation to changing conditions.

Mitigating Factors.   From a prescriptive viewpoint, internal environmental characteristics have an important bearing on the form that structure and positions (*ought to*) assume. There are, however, mitigating circumstances: one would be strong top management philosophies or organization cultures which affect managerial performance behavior patterns. Another consideration would be the fact that many companies oriented to human resource development have introduced structural and positional modifications or particular development approaches as a deliberate strategy to strengthen or change managerial roles.

> For example, a financial services business enjoyed steady growth for a number of years. Although many changes were affecting the industry generally, its market segment involving the financing of particular equipment was quite stable. Its founder had left the business years ago. It was then sold and eventually became a publicly held corporation with offices in several major cities. Its top management group, possessing much industry experience and excellent educational credentials, gradually introduced longer-range planning approaches. These planning approaches, subsequently augmented by strategic analysis, provided good tracking of changes in (its) equipment field and competition. The appearance of new financial service opportunities led to the

creation of internal teams which were charged with becoming highly knowledgeable in certain equipment applications and service areas. Corporate growth was paced to take full advantage of market opportunities and internal competencies. Well-trained people, always viewed as "our real assets," were carefully nurtured by talented supervisors. "Trainees" were exposed to numerous and challenging situations to assist their development—while their progress was monitored, and feedback and support given by designated service people.

Sociotechnical Systems Design in the Strategic Perspective

The concept of "sociotechnical systems" is a relatively mature concept but one that has received relatively little attention in the past. It is now used in design and development approaches which cover a wide spectrum of work situations in *both* manufacturing and service-type industries.

This approach lends itself well to thinking in strategic planning terms. The sociotechnical model involves systemic ideas, planning, and analyses for adaptation to change and has at its heart the managerial role and its relationship to other major organization functions. The origins for this approach, as well as its features and how they can be used in strategic approaches, are addressed in this section.

Past progress in this area was slow because of the lack of concrete corporate experiences, let alone an appropriate framework of theory and perspectives. The advancement of strategic thinking for management development rests (importantly) on being able to translate planning and strategic changes to managerial work. Better than 20 years of work in this area has resulted in some notable progress. It is now possible for Human Resource officials, business and organization planners, and senior managers to draw on a growing body of information in a selective, critical manner—and with considerable potential benefits for their organization. For many years, it was thought that organizational performance depended mainly on structural considerations involving responsibility and authority, spans of reporting relationships, number of authority levels, and the distribution of decision responsibilities. Change, whether internally initiated or in response to external forces, simply occurred and the organization coped with it as best as it could.

The realization grew, however, that forces of change could be better planned for and managed. This accomplishment required more comprehensive approaches to organization, work, and job design. Organizations had grown too complex to be approached through singular means or methods. Structural considerations continued to be important, but newer approaches were needed as well. Long-term planning helped to enlarge the scope of factors included, but it proved to be no panacea. This was particularly true where planning was coupled essentially to short-term (reaction type) managerial actions or remained unconnected to the identification of new(er) managerial needs associated with change. No focused or sustained effort could be mounted in personnel development under these conditions. Not only did organizations fail to achieve the full potential of their managerial groups, but their managerial ranks lacked the required durability and flexibility to cope with tougher competition. Organizations were also coming up increasingly short in developing adequate numbers of talented people for growth and succession purposes.

The recognition grew that work systems and people were closely joined together with various aspects of the work context and organization structure. Also, shorter-term actions had to be better coordinated with longer-term plans. Major changes, when these occurred, moved through all these interconnected factors. This recognition led to a whole new line of analysis for approaching organizational performance. Jobs, work units, and people were seen as common denominators of performance, and planned change (e.g., new process lines or corporate expansion) was increasingly analyzed to establish its impact on these. This understanding led to more comprehensive organization and work designs in which change was first analyzed, and then a balanced "bottom-up" and "top-down" (macro and micro) approach was taken. Sociotechnical thinking, a new term for this more comprehensive view, included change forces, organization goals and plans, individuals, jobs, structure, and work systems. This viewpoint became prominent in general organization and work planning. Although the subject approach initially involved manufacturing industries as a dominant focus, applications soon blossomed in hospitals, insurance companies, banks, fast-food organizations, and all types of service industries.

Progress in the application of sociotechnical approaches helped to increase needed attention in the improvement of the processes by which people worked together on interpersonal and intergroup relations. A partial answer was found in organization development (OD), which served to strengthen group processes and performances and to link groups and units together better. Managers had a relatively powerful weapon at their disposal to facilitate change and improve performance, but they had to master its intricacies. Because of the importance of OD in support of design approaches, a case illustration is provided in the applications section of this chapter.

Supervisory and managerial personnel, involved in all the change situations described here, were not always clear as to their role. In job-enrichment designs, for example, it was not always recognized that supervisors could provide positive support to subordinates and thereby improve the person's sense of "enrichment." Where autonomous work groups were created as part of a work-group–enrichment effort, it was important to recognize that the activities of supervisory and managerial roles changed greatly. Their new roles emphasized increased planning, building cooperative work relationships with other groups, and improving intragroup relationships.

Sociotechnical analyses were used to examine the general effects of change on managerial and work systems. This was a big step in development approaches (previously referenced), which helped to smooth the path for change through improved group performance and work relationships!

An enterprise which today is deeply involved in sociotechnical analyses and in organization development procedures illustrates some of the compelling circumstances for these approaches.

The organization, a medium-sized communications company, experienced rapid growth as much commercial business developed in its marketing area. When demand for its services and products started to level off, it was evident that while a lot of change was taking place, only a portion of it could be accounted for by product/market maturity. Corporate officials and planners, however, had not perceived the cumulative impact of numerous and diverse environmental changes involving new technology, competition and marketing/business demographics. Technological developments affected internal administration, and planning and control procedures, as well as the uniqueness and utility of their products and services. Several new competitors, including a foreign company, entered its marketing picture and cut deeply into existing customer groups as well as potential areas of new business. Its functional organization and traditional communications and work relationships (oriented to hierarchy and lacking time management) were ineffective. Product superiority, enjoyed in the past and a main basis for maintaining and gaining customers, no longer worked. Management needed access to good and timely information to make informed production, sales, and engineering decisions. Part of the requirement was attainable through improved internal communications which included working relationships, computer information files, and communications hardware (e.g., a "two-way talk-back TV" system). Thus it was realized that internal management was faced with a new game involving a complex combination of environmental circumstances and internal organization, technology, and processes. The situation facing field sales managers was similarly problem ridden and required comprehensive solution approaches.

Sociotechnical Systems—Particulars

Sociotechnical thinking is inherently an "open systems" approach, and, as already noted, change management is deeply imbedded within the concept. As an *open* systems model, it is acknowledged that organizations are highly vulnerable to change whether the source is external or internal. The enterprise's adaptation to change, how rapidly it adapts, and whether it does so successfully, become some of the relevant questions. These give rise to even more basic questions such as, "What are the factors affecting the ability of the organization's units or key personnel to adapt successfully to change?" Related analyses involve determinations as to whether change is an inherent part of particular departments and how this affects the orientation of managerial development for future staffing. In regard to the latter point, some units such as marketing, or research and development, are formally "delegated" change responsibilities, but their change roles are quite different. These differences reflect responsibilities for the detection of change and its interpretation, and the proposal of newer strategic approaches which may "involve change." Also related to this point is, "How can change effectiveness of a particular unit be increased?" "How well do they 'engineer,' handle, or process change so that it can be 'used' in a strategic or positive manner elsewhere in the organization?" Correspondingly, "How do other organizational units handle unexpected or unplanned change?" Thus, various organizational functions or units assume roles different from their normal mission when confronting change. What are the strategic implications for management development that the responses to these questions present?

A second characteristic of the sociotechnical approach is its systemic makeup (Exhibit 2-3A). Organizations are viewed as being composed of a systems hierarchy including the primary work processing activities and those (subsystems) that support this primary work mission. The organizational mission or character of the enterprise defines the primary work activities. This means that in many organizations, performance of the major work system is constrained by the degree of effectiveness with which support systems function.

For ease of discussion and to facilitate planning analyses, especially those including succession and management development, it is convenient to think of five interactive components (Exhibit 2-3A):

A. *Goals, policy, and the mission subsystem*—consisting of the strategy planning and policy determining officials and functions which establish organizational goals and mission(s). The senior people who in part make up this area "define" or preserve the organization's culture.

B. *Work-technology subsystem*—involving work procedures, and work technology. This subsystem is often defined in terms of the primary work activity.

C. *Structure*—containing the formal organization's body of rules, regulations, and position responsibilities, including those related to planning, coordination, and control.

D. *Human resources*—relating to the personnel resources of the organization. For purposes of specific analyses, these may be defined in terms of those assigned to the primary work system or support groups, for example. This covers individual work assignments and those organized as groups.

E. *The management subsystem*—including supervisory and managerial personnel in either a line or staff capacity.

All these components are housed within, affect, and are impacted by the organization's culture. The interrelatedness of these components is expressed in the small panels of Exhibit 2-3B; the dynamic qualities are expressed by the "arrows."

EXHIBIT 2-3A
Work System Design: A Sociotechnical Perspective

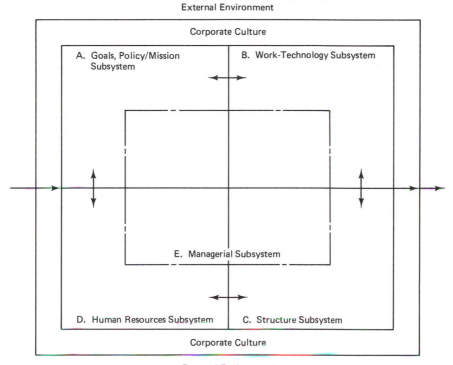

External Environment

Corporate Culture

A. Goals, Policy/Mission Subsystem

B. Work-Technology Subsystem

E. Managerial Subsystem

D. Human Resources Subsystem

C. Structure Subsystem

Corporate Culture

External Environment

This sketch, for example, can be used to interpret an externally based change and its reverberation through the subsystems (shown previously in Exhibit 2-3A) of the organization. Consider (A) another breakthrough in microchip technology as it might affect a microcomputer manufacturer. Change that starts out in or impacts in one area eventually affects all the sociotechnical components because of the force and potency of this major change. Organizational goals and mission change as the possibility of a whole new generation of computers is factored into long-range and strategic planning. Gearing up to produce and market new products involves the operational subsystem (B) plus the various departments related to developing, producing, and marketing this new product.

Both the technical and organizational changes affect personnel staffing, training, and required knowledge, skills, and abilities (D). Needless to say, all of the above, A-B-C-D, dramatically redefine the "life space" of managers—or in short what they have to do to be successful. From the standpoint of strategic planning, the changes outlined here would be a challenging assignment in planning and strategizing for change. Other types of changes vary in their impact on particular components depending on the specifics involved.

EXHIBIT 2-3B
Change Dynamics and the Sociotechnical System

I. External Change

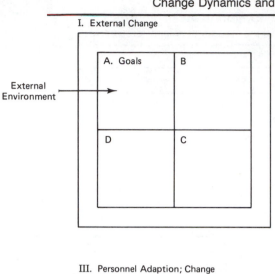

II. Work-Structure Adaptive Change

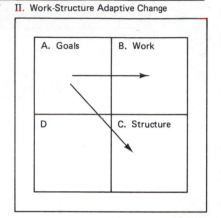

III. Personnel Adaption; Change

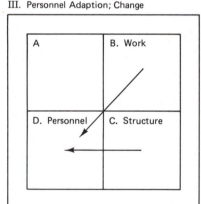

IV. Manegerial Dynamics of Change

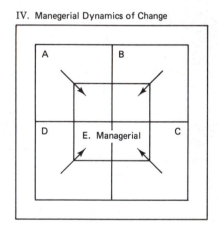

V.

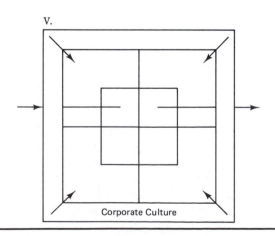

Corporate Culture.   Often overlooked, is the need to reexamine corporate culture (discussed at length in the next chapter) and to establish its role as a part of strategic analysis. More often than not, culture tends to be "fixed" so that strategies are built upon it. If it appears that some cultural changes must be considered, these must be approached cautiously because of both the difficulty and complexity involved. Typical points considered include the reward systems, mobility paths to key positions, decision criteria, and valued work performances. Because of their deeply rooted nature, changes in "culture" are difficult to undertake and frequently require years to implement. Chapter 3 is devoted exclusively to this topic.

Internal Organization for Sociotechnical Analyses

Because of its potential, general schema have been developed for organizing internal managerial efforts to support sociotechnical approaches. An important group for this purpose is a "sociotechnical design committee." The organization of a sociotechnical design committee and some of its major functions are presented in Exhibit 2-4.

   This committee typically involves varied membership because of the diversity of applications and the necessary expertise required to deal with them (Exhibit 2-4, items 1 and 7). The composition and activities of this type of "committee" are provided in some detail because of their importance and the role they play in strategic activities. These groups represent a concrete way to carry out strategic actions and to stay in touch with strategy planning groups. Programming, procedures, and design projects are meant to be carried out under "committee guidance"; it serves as the organizationwide catalyzing and coordinating force for these efforts. These groups also provide assistance in dealing with important issues and problems which arise. Characteristic problems and issues encountered include

- Dealing with the politics of change as, for example, people who may gain or lose power in consequence of change
- Planning for and anticipating staffing changes
- Identifying units that are to incur staffing reductions
- Qualifying incumbents to assume roles in new or modified units or systems
- Determining managerial behaviors for changes in organization success
- Anticipating the consequences of needed changes in organization culture and how to effectuate these
- Disposing of existing systems
- Instituting purposeful innovative work-design approaches to deal with serious employee turnover or/and job satisfaction matters
- Recommending job and work designs
- Modifying strategic plans (12) where these may pose major problems in organizational adaptation

A comprehensive case application ("Dorothy's") based on sociotechnical approaches is presented in the applications section of this chapter.

EXHIBIT 2-4

Approach to Establishing a Sociotechnical Design Committee and Its
Major Activities

1. Establishment of a sociotechnical design committee appointed by a senior officer or CEO. Staffing involves all major functions plus the person who has professional competency in staffing planning, and committee functions (usually someone from Human Resources).

2. Organization change and role analyses.

   Trace the impacts of major technological, procedural, or policy changes within and between main subsystems. Once identified, these factors help to determine main activities, relationships, and points of (major) modification. They also help to establish key managerial, staff, and employee roles.

3. Organization work analysis and design. This focuses on managerial positions and jointly considers senior positions, first-level supervisory positions, and middle-level managerial and support positions.

   a. Establish primary work flow(s)/technology and the identification of main activities and relationships.

      Examine relationships and functions to determine which are required or fixed plus factors which may serve as *design variables,* useful in enrichment approaches.

   b. Examine points where formal structure, responsibilities, and end behaviors for success match work demands, or where these fall short of meeting work requirements. Also, examine these to establish where change is most likely and its thrust.

   c. Identify existing nonformal or informal patterns of relationships or activities which are required for performance purposes. Then determinations are made of which of these might be formalized or serve as additional design options for individual career paths or work improvement. To the extent that nonformal or informal relational and activity patterns remain, it is necessary to determine which may require some form of organizational support.

4. Organization role analysis and design of employee jobs relative to the work/technological, structural, and managerial subsystems or components.

5. Examination of the work context and broader features of the organizational culture for needed modifications and changes. This phase of the work has a specific offshoot in what is described commonly as "designing the social support system."

6. Design of educational and development activities or recommendations for these where units exist for these purposes. Also, may recommend recruitment and selection activities to determine whether personnel are to be drawn from internal or external resources. Since sociotechnical analyses often seek to improve group processes as well as individual situations, organization development activities may include interpersonal effectiveness, managers facilitating group processes, or stress management and conflict resolution. They may also include cross-functional moves to develop a broad(er) perspective, and technical training commensurate with new technologies.

EXHIBIT 2-4 (Continued)

---

7. Design implementation. Design committees which are broadly based in skills and represent different organizational approaches can facilitate the implementation of sociotechnical designs. Too, they can prove supportive to resident managements whose units may be involved directly in these changes. Significant changes in position descriptions and requisite role performance are commonly involved in sociotechnical changes. These place significant demands on individual change and adaptation. These also require close monitoring of outcomes and/or responses to change.

8. Design evaluation. Understandably, multiple and diverse criteria are used to assess the success of sociotechnical designs. Effectiveness and efficiency measures are involved, including growth needs of the person, absenteeism and turnover, quality levels, cost performance, sales, group problem solving, and creativity or new idea generation. Committee recommendations may include new managerial or general performance criteria.

Summary

In general, sociotechnical improvements were combined with a growing maturity regarding the role of and planning for human resources. If these approaches are "merged," a consolidated picture emerges which is useful to strategic thinking and approaches (Exhibits 2-3A and B.) The degree of change from past orientations becomes quite evident. Organization and work planning in the HR perspective has a solid base in HRP, behavioral, and sociotechnical systems concepts. It merges in the organization's culture, performance considerations, and career thinking (Exhibit 2-5).

Exhibits 2-3A and B stress, for example, the shift in "general orientation" from the short(er)-term, impersonal structural, or methods-oriented approach. The one replacing it has a longer planning horizon, including personal and impersonal elements, and viewing the organization's culture strategically as well. Achieving the economic purposes of the organization means that "individuals" have to be factored explicitly into the picture in terms of their careers and the development experiences attendant to these. "Jobs" can no longer be viewed in isolation but rather as a part of a complex arena of structure, systems, activities, and processes, and these within the context of the organization's culture. Not surprisingly, communications assumed new and strategic importance as a key vehicle to help weld the many of these elements together.

Thus organization–job planning is now approached in a more comprehensive way involving time horizon, individual, job, organization structure and processes and culture, and performance. Working relationships and communications are strengthened through organization development processes. Contemporary management development and succession planning approaches and performance planning and management clearly have moved into a potentially rich but complex terrain.

EXHIBIT 2-5

Changes in the Bases for Strategic Approaches to Management
Development

	Traditional Model	Human Resource—Organization Culture Model
General orientation	• Short(er) term • Focus on system elements • Economic performance, returns • Dependence on structural or methods approaches	• Long-term planning, activities, and behaviors • Systemic, comprehensive • Joint view of development as taking place outside the organization as well as internally • Activities affected by external and internal developments
Individual	• Used to achieve economic purposes of organization • Assumes competent people will "rise" through their own initiative • Skill development largely oriented to job experience	• Person in charge of his or her own career . . . but with thoughtful support of organization • Adult learning mode—self-directed, need oriented • Skill development reflects both informal and formal experience and educational processes • Feedback and self-assessment stressed and supported • Works often in group for mat—skills in interpersonal relationships important.
Job	• Job responsibilities play central role • Performance-oriented primarily to individual job or high dependence on technology • Job enrichment seen often as manipulation to improve performance	• Behavioral view of the job as being able to meet substantially both organizational and individual needs • Multidimensional perspective incorporating responsibilities and behavior for success. • Work design includes individual, work, and group relationships • Job design, staffing, and development seen as major variables in creating the productive organization

EXHIBIT 2-5 (Continued)

Organization	• Hierarchical orientation • Limited feedback, primarily oriented to work task • Communications closely parallel organization structure	• Substantial attempt to gain convergence of organization and individual concerns • Visualizing internal environment as possessing the potential for becoming a strong "organization culture" • Organization development approaches to improve relationship and performance within and between groups and units—systems orientation • Seeking to develop a strong culture, the features of which are reasonably uniform and compatible with individual life and career needs • General management policy and actions supportive of the "new era" organization
Performance	• Heavy emphasis on efficiency criteria involving various aspects of quantity, quality, on-time performance, cost containment, etc. • Short-run budgetary orientation—limited view of management objectives	• Merger of short- and longer-term planning and action approaches • Joint consideration of performance dimensions in terms of efficiency and effectiveness • Recognition of broader relationships and impact of organization on community and environment • Reflects joint effects of people and work system technology

PART II: MANAGERIAL WORK DESIGN AND CAREER DEVELOPMENT

Introduction

Renewed emphasis on the planning for managerial change as well as managerial roles in promoting change was in part a derivative of sociotechnical analyses described in Part I. However, the desire to advance these analyses ran into a surprising stumbling block. It turned out that there was a considerable lack of knowledge regarding managerial behavior and the factors defining successful performance. This was a startling revelation in light of the years of writing about managers.

Efforts were intensified in the study of managerial behavior and performance. These analyses led to the identification of "critical incidents" that defined the specific actions (behaviors) on the job, the sum of which equaled successful job performance. Also, end-job behaviors were organized into related groups, with general applicability to many different jobs, regardless of title. They formed a part of a more general structure of managerial characteristics or behavioral dimensions. In any given company, a relatively small number of these "groups" (clusters or dimensions), perhaps 15 to 25, described the general requirements of a significant number of all managerial jobs. Thus, the study of managerial work for purposes of performance improvement and management development planning was refocused to include both position responsibilities *and* end-job behaviors. The accuracy with which jobs could be defined, and a given needs analysis conducted, improved considerably. Career planning, performance appraisal, and assessments of potential and planning for change all benefited.

Contemporary approaches to the design of managerial work are based on broad needs analyses involving organization, work, and the individual. A growing body of research (e.g., Hackman and Oldham, 1980; Davis and Rayler, 1978; Tornow and Gartland, 1980; Nadler and Lawler, 1982; Rhodes and Walker, 1984) indicates that organizational structures, processes, and the work itself form a necessary part of strategic planning considerations. Work context, individual career orientation and progress, and job specifics potentially affect job-related satisfaction and the motivation to perform. For example,

- Decision to expand, contract, or modify business or work units which affect staffing, job structures, work relationships and responsibilities and thus required knowledge, skills, and abilities (KSAs). At the same time, established career ladders or mobility paths in the organization may be greatly modified or completely disrupted.
- Decisions that result in major changes in primary work technologies (e.g., production or computer information based) which alter requisite job responsibilities, staffing, and required KSAs.

The kinds of staffing and job changes described here might result, for example, in a strategic specification for an entrepreneurial, high-competition unit:

> Measured risk taking, rapid adaptation to change, high level of personnel interaction, team skills.

Also, attempts are made frequently to crystalize or strengthen corporate cultures or those existing in particular units (i.e., subcultures). These actions help to achieve greater unity of purposes among managerial groups.

The results of work and human resource planning analyses may suggest necessary modifications in strategic business planning approaches. Recognizing that needed organization changes may be unlikely in the strategic time frame may dictate reexamining the strategic plan. Also, if good communications are established between business and human resource planning units, alternate and useful planning scenarios can be generated. If strategic business plans are viewed largely as "givens," however, then organization and work planners need to understand what organization and work design options exist in seeking to implement business plans or strategies.

The material in Part II is divided into two discussions as follows:

A. Career stages and individual development
B. Work context and content

A. CAREER STAGES AND INDIVIDUAL DEVELOPMENT

"Job-Career Matrix" (Honeywell, Inc.)

This approach is based on long-term career development, spanning four phases of individual skill and competency building. The career development model serves as an overlay for a conventional salary structure (some five major grades); thus both career *and* salary progress can be viewed simultaneously. In total, some 20 or more combinations of these variables (number of levels and career stages) comprise this design. Honeywell undertook years of research and the careful cataloging of its own and other organizational experiences. The result is an impressive approach to career and salary planning backed up by solid information concerning the design of individual jobs, job families, and work structures.

In their approach, individual job design was viewed as part of an interrelated whole involving learning, career development, individual career planning, HR development, and salary matters. Honeywell lends considerable reality to the picture by integrating its salary structure with the career structure. Various career paths are traced over time with numerous options combining career and skill development with position and salary progress.

Their "job-career matrix" also provides for dual-career options, that is, technical or more general management-administrative careers with appropriate cross-over points. The "matrix" identifies critical developmental experiences to qualify for promotion or mobility between stages and further integrates the corporation's formal educational program to facilitate achieving career and work objectives! This type of model ("matrix") can be used for the total organization, a major business unit, or a division.

Learning Strategies

The general orientation of the four phases of skill building paralleling career development are (1) *initial assignment* emphasizing work orientation and gaining familiarity with work basics; (2) *learning*/building basic job skills; (3) *maturity*, focused on efficient performance; and (4) *"mastery"* or expertness at a consultive level. Emphasis is placed on the types of knowledge, competencies, and insights to be developed during each skill/career stage. These then comprise learning objectives with job designs and assignments arranged accordingly.

Development Strategies.   Three developmental approaches form the basis for their learning approaches. They are (1) formal classroom education and training; (2) coaching by the supervising manager, staff members, or colleagues; and (3) strengthening relational (interpersonal) abilities. Each career/skill phase was approached from a design standpoint so that the derived benefits from any of the learning strategies (schooling, coaching, relational) was the best possible. For example, in the first phase, "initial assignment," getting acquainted with the requirements of a particular job and starting to understand how the organization works, were probably of equal importance. Work-design approaches for this period might involve a variety of assignments which brought the person into contact with many different units, personalities, problems, and issues. It would also facilitate the person getting into the "meat" of the job in an informed way and as rapidly as possible.

At the *"mastery"* or expertness stage, job design and assignment approaches had quite different objectives because functional performance capabilities were assumed. Developing expertness in an assigned area requires excellent coaching, often formal educational experiences, and personal reflection by the jobholders as to how expertness will be best achieved and what complex set of behaviors these comprise. Managers have to take account of the organization's culture and the role it plays in defining "expertness," let alone how they achieve it as a technical, political, or administrative matter. Strategic business plans and expected changes often lead to the need to redesign job roles. These may favor expanded product development knowledge, enlarged customer contacts, more familiarity with computer usage, or approaches to new account development. "Expertness" is typically built with a pattern of increasingly challenging applications expanding the scope and/or depth of the person's know-how. In technical career tracks, the "design" emphasis is directed toward expertise at a consultive level. The "state of the art" of applied or basic sciences heavily flavor the specifics of the approaches.

More details on the Honeywell approach are provided in the applications section of the chapter on management development systems. A relatively brief case application example of the Honeywell-type approach will follow (Hoskins Systems). Variations of the Honeywell learning strategy have been introduced into a wide variety of organizations. Although these differ in specifics due to organization size, products, or internal culture, the genre is still evident.

Hoskins Systems started out in the highly specialized area of electronically oriented process controls. At an early point, it adapted computers to these applications and enjoyed considerable growth. The decline of many "smokestack" industries, its mainstay business area, was anticipated by Hoskins. It searched for alternate markets where its competencies and computer know-how could be used. Repositioning its business led to the development of two different enterprises: one specializing in a line of computer-based controllers and the other technical services, including consulting. Its president expected numerous internal personnel problems from the vast changes; thus he recommended and the executive group endorsed the hiring of a Human Resource Manager. Most "personnel" work in the past was handled by department managers and their staffs. The new HR manager, Joan McBride, had much general experience and good interpersonal skills, plus formal training in the HR field. She was thus able eventually to gain the acceptance of senior managerial and technical people alike.

For better than a year her time was taken up with a large number of transitional problems involving retraining, compensation matters, recruiting, and separations. As the situation became more stable, she started to bring together the bases for a longer-term human resource development program. It was a response to top management's wishes for consolidating its gains from the reorganized business, which rested on personnel competency and creativity. More particularly, assuring adequate numbers of highly talented people, avoiding obsolescence, and creating an appropriate reward system were their goals in this area.

The Action Research Program Underpinning Long-Term Managerial Development

Joan undertook an action research study in connection with the Hoskins Learning and Growth Program (HLGP). Central to information development was a series of interviews she conducted with almost 40 people representing both sides of their newer business. It included all major functional areas, technical specialties, and managerial areas such as senior executive positions and the president. Of particular interest was information such as how individual careers developed, skills or competencies associated with these benchmarks of career progress, and changes likely to result from future technical, competitive, and economic changes. Joan also reviewed personnel files to verify times and dates and visited four other companies which had formalized career systems, the general circumstances of which were not unlike Hoskins. Key study findings included the following.

1. The specifics of career advancement differed widely among people but certain regularities appeared among many of these.
2. Major career moves and progress, if these took place, covered a period of 15 to 20 years and reflected three or four major development phases.
   a. Early career development was taken up with initial assignments, getting to learn the job requirements, trying to understand how the organization works, and starting to develop basic technical and general (e.g., communications) skills.
   b. Those advancing their careers evidenced good progress in building and strengthening job-related skills. Aside from better than average salary advancement, their progress was marked by some number of supervisory or coordinating roles or assignment to more difficult technical projects.
   c. Continued career progress was marked by assignment to managerial positions, project management of technical activities, or success in technically oriented or development work in which they demonstrated much independent effort.
   d. Achieving a relatively senior position in the organization signaled considerable maturity on the individuals' part and their value to the organization, although there was much variation in their levels due to general management or technical assignments. General management positions reflected much scope and breadth of responsibility. Positionholders planned, made decisions, and dealt with people inside and outside the organization (in terms of power and politics). Maturity of judgment was a necessary part of success in these positions. Technical positions involved either the management of important technical groups or managing units affecting main areas of the company's profits, costs or welfare, or original development work, studies, or systems designs. The former leaned somewhat more heavily on administrative abilities in connection with technical competencies at a consultive level. The latter was more purely focused on the technical aspects, and the person involved was considered an in-house expert (with subject matter "mastery"), frequently called in for technical consultation.
3. The potential for individual career advancement was usually in evidence before a promotion and was often indicated months or even years prior to the change. The competencies to bridge from one career phase to another were often different from those judged in performance appraisals. At any point in his or her career, the person was forced to balance the demands of the existing job with demonstrations of competencies seen as valuable in more advanced positions. At early career stages, the factors demonstrative of potential were mostly unknown to the person. As careers progressed, individuals became more knowledgeable of factors affecting their career progress; this was particularly true among more senior personnel. Competencies evidencing future potential could vary greatly, even be at odds, with those needed most in current assignments. For example, risk taking and creativity was vital in some work, yet the person had to give evidence that they could exercise risk taking in a responsible way reflective of more complex corporate circumstances typical of higher-level positions.

4. Supervising managers played the central role in individual development. Excellent coaching, counseling, work assignments, and constructive feedback were almost always in the "background" of the individual's success. Beyond the impact of the supervising manager, formalized instruction, including both short-term instruction for specialized topics (two days or less, workshops and seminars) and regular classes (30 or more contact hours), were critical incidents in individual career progress.

5. Information on aspects of the reward system provided some important data from the viewpoint of individuals.

   a. Steady progress in career advancement usually was paralleled by better than average growth in compensation. In fact, at a relatively early career point, the salary spread between "acceptable" and superior performances increased rapidly. The salary maturity curve for high performance (salary versus years of service) evidenced fairly characteristic form. It could potentially provide another benchmark of individual competency and progress.

   b. Many managers and technical personnel, though welcoming salary increases and promotions, were vitally concerned with nonmonetary aspects of the reward system. The intrinsic rewards of their assigned work, independence, awareness of progress (feedback), variety, and recognition for achievements were frequently repeated themes that salary alone would not meet.

Hoskins' Learning and Growth Program

The designation "Hoskins Learning and Growth Program" was the direct outgrowth of the almost year-long action research study program. The learning plan, conceived of as a strategic design to help fulfill longer-range corporate objectives, reiterated the company's strong orientation to, and dependence on, its talented people. It also acknowledged that the interest of its people, even those similarly trained, might be such that they would desire quite different career paths.

Hoskins endorsed the idea that varied career paths meeting the joint needs of the individual and company, were acceptable, even desirable. A "dual-career ladder" model was established which consisted of general managerial and technical work. It stipulated that people should be able to achieve comparable rewards for similar progress in taking on greater responsibilities and demonstrated performances. An HR policy statement, including the above, also set out two of its key learning strategies, namely, that learning progress could be accomplished in various ways depending on the person, their background, abilities, and situations and that supervisory coaching, and formal and informal instruction, were important at all career levels to assure continuing technical or managerial relevance. Learning by doing, building know-how through experience, and even gaining subject matter mastery, reflected career progress and transitions.

For individual progress to take place, thoughtful coaching by the supervising manager and interaction with knowledgeable people elsewhere in the organization, often gained through rotating assignments, would be important and increasingly used sources of learning. However, since required individual competencies would vary considerably with individual level and scope of responsibility, it would be helpful to identify particular career phases or stages signaling progress.

Stages of progress required two important determinations: (1) the general set of competencies for high performance *within* any particular phase and the specific competencies related to an assigned position and (2) the general and particular competencies giving evidence of individual potential for work at more advanced levels. Since most managers measured career progress in part through salary progress, general stages of competency development and the compensations structure were combined.

Their five-level salary structure was combined with four stages of competency development. They created 20 building blocks (the five salary levels × four stages) of individual, professional, and career progress. Similar approaches were taken in both of their businesses.

Each "block" contained information on "normal" career development in terms of salaries, salary progress, and competencies. Each block provided for four competency levels involving indoctrination, developing know-how, job competency, and senior skills—whether pursuing technical or more general managerial career tracks.

In general, the four career stages and increases in compensation were marked by some newly created positional titles. Lower-level positions involving stages of "indoctrination" or "know-how" building had titles such as Engineer I or II. Exceptional progress might witness an Engineer III title, with the person progressing to the "job competency" stage (third phase). In technical tracks, individual career progress could be evidenced by growing technical administrative/management responsibilities (e.g., Technical Administrator I or II or Project Manager I or II); these were most likely in the second and third phases. Additional career maturity and salary progress, as in career phases III and IV, were marked by additional new titles such as Unit Manager, Manager, Service Manager, and General Manager; Senior Engineer I and II and Scientist and Senior Scientist; or Technical Manager I, II, or III. As an aside, no connection was intended between career stage numbers and position titles (I, II, or III).

Redirection of careers was also facilitated in the new program. Once having achieved "performance competency," career directions were reviewed in considerable depth. Individuals could study future company staffing opportunities relative to their current career situation and had the benefit of counsel (optional) from an outside professional psychologist. During earlier career phases, career directions were reviewed frequently in the light of individual competency gains, potential, and longer-term corporate needs.

Career Stages, Developmental Tasks, and Learning Requirements

A conscious attempt is made to align career stages, skill development, and progress through salary grades, as part of the Honeywell approach. Upon reflection, it is clear that these general connections are present in many organizations—although they may not be systematically "blueprinted." In sales, for instance, people typically don't start out as managers; rather, the authority structure often represents a "natural" progression of responsibilities. Over time, for the person to progress, he or she must increasingly "tap" and display more difficult and comprehensive sets of knowledge, skills, and abilities. What is sometimes not realized is that each assignment can represent some aspect of an individual's career development and thus be another rationale for the "career-stage" approach.

Organization and work design in this perspective recognizes that positional assignments and job content should be motivating factors and give people a sense of career fulfillment. Organization requirements and personal needs are blended. Yet certain positions, by virtue of their responsibilities and required job behaviors for success, may be ill suited to the needs of a particular manager. Strategic approaches may dictate that, when possible, the position be redesigned, responsibilities altered, or alternative assignments be considered as an immediate approach to ensure the potential long(er)-term gain.

In the chapter on *career development* (Chapter 9), the subject of career stages per se is discussed in some detail. The thinking of many people who have worked in this field also coincides with the Honeywell career stages to the extent that four stages are considered (Schein, 1978; Hall, 1976; Burack, 1984; Dalton and Thompson, 1986). This approach emphasizes individual career development and includes the following terms and concepts:

1. *Entry*—job activities are varied, which serves to qualify individual interests, test out knowledge, skills, and abilities and develop competencies. The Honeywell counterparts are "initial assignment," "learning," and to some extent "maturity."

2. *Establishment/advancement*—job activities and assignments are sought which challenge the person and stretch knowledge, skills, and abilities. Competence is often developed in some area of specialization, and good opportunities (should) exist to build individual creativity. Also, people are faced with competition and conflict and need to come to grips with these. The need exists to rotate the person into new areas which afford a continuing challenge and expansion of individual knowledge, skills, and abilities. The Honeywell counterparts are "maturity" and "mastery." If a person should be assigned to a new area, then "initial assignment" and "learning" phases may be the relevant ones.

3. *Mid career*—job designs need to emphasize updating of knowledge, skills, and abilities where state of the art changes are frequent relative to the manager's early formal education. Individuals also need to enlarge their competencies for coaching/developing younger or more junior members of their units. Work and organizational designs should help people to develop a broader view of the organization and its relationships to their role. Cross-functional assignments and new areas of specialization are common means by which an enlarged perspective is achieved. Any of the Honeywell phases may apply here depending on organizational and individual needs.

4. *Late career*—emphasis here is often on consultation and guidance and facilitating preliminary planning for other careers beyond those in the organization. Organization and work design needs to incorporate flexibility in necessary work activities. It needs to facilitate significant role change for the person while undertaking such necessary tasks as identifying their successor. The relevant Honeywell phases here would most likely be "maturity" or "mastery." Career-stage models embody the idea of "developmental tasks," which is an essential concept and relevant to management development planning.

Developmental Tasks.   Work assignments serve dual purposes: the first and obvious need is to get a particular job done successfully. However, assignments also help in the identification and cultivation of people displaying promise (potential) for more responsible positions. At the "entry stages," for example, a young graduate has to master job details and often do things involving close supervision—though these may move counter to personal expectancies or the desire to prove one's self. Yet at the same time, especially after preliminary orientation assignments, opportunities need to be provided to demonstrate potential for more responsible or demanding work. As a consequence, particular assignments or classes of positions may be designated as "developmental." They are especially good for bringing out specific competencies and permit observation of these (potential) capabilities for senior managers to make more realistic judgments of potential or promotion readiness.

In summary, the career-stage approach emphasizes individual development which is geared to performance and individual careers.

B. WORK CONTEXT AND CONTENT

An individual's satisfaction with the "work context" is a basic starting point for coming to grips with behavioral issues and performance. For the moment, the highly relevant questions of the person's *capabilities* to perform well, or even his or her desire/need for personal *growth through work,* are set aside.

Also relevant but not considered here is the manager's *perception* of his or her environment. What people "see" or think to be true is very important in performance questions. (See Chapter 7, Managerial Performance: Strategic Aspects.)

Work context may affect the inclination of people to respond to enriched or challenging jobs (Hackman and Oldham, 1980, esp. pp. 86–87). They may include for example, relationships with supervisors or co-workers, or the formality of the work climate. If much of a manager's energies are absorbed in coping daily with poorly trained co-workers or people who resist change or people who are uncooperative, chances are that little energy or desire will remain to take advantage of "stimulating" job features or assignments. Consequently, the potentially positive impacts of a redesigned (enriched) job are moderated by contextual factors.

Chapter 3 is devoted to organization culture because of its central importance in strategic matters and the growing conviction of its bearing on overall organizational performance. Culture is an essential part of work context. Many job-(re)design approaches glibly slip over it. It deals with the "climate," "tone," or "feel" of the organization. Not to be ignored, too, are the behaviors valued by the organization, including decision criteria, the organization's valuing of human resources, or even its orientation to the external community (social responsibility). It affects the person's sense of mobility opportunities, job security, and co-worker relationships.

Equally potent as a contextual issue and part of strategic analyses are reward systems, including salary.

Reward Systems, Performance, and Strategy

A carefully designed organizational reward system can contribute significantly to organizational effectiveness and performance. Achieving the full potential of this contribution requires that reward systems be thoughtfully included in strategic plans and processes. Since the term "reward systems" will be used frequently, it is worthwhile to pause and consider what's included. Aside from benefits, a familiar factor to all is compensation (salary). This includes bonuses and deferred arrangements as well.

The "reward system" concept desirably provides for a good degree of flexibility, permitting adjustment to individual needs and situations within policy and financial constraints. This concept also includes nonmonetary aspects of work, the purpose of which is to motivate particular behaviors and performance. Corporate recognition, car arrangements, office layout, and work design are some of the many options exercised in behavioral approaches.

Money's role as a universal medium of exchange for goods and services assigns to salary, as the average person's main source of money, a prominent place in the life of any person. Also, it is widely known that salary level stands as a visible "marker" of an individual's business or social achievement. In particular organizations, internal salary comparisons underlie equity issues of great importance to many. In our experience, even where salaries are *not* outrageously low or deficient in some obvious way, equity matters are of central concern to managers and professional people. Monetary needs and wants, and fairness issues, are constantly intermingled in salary discussions to a point that "real" salary matters are difficult to define or simply get lost. This particular topic is so rich that whole books are devoted to discussions of these points.

In short, "reward systems" alert strategists to both monetary and nonmonetary planning alternatives.

Reward systems enter the strategic picture in two different ways (Lawler, 1986). The first way is to note the current situation, that is, the existing human resource management practices, behaviors, climate, and structure. Also included are the organization's financial capabilities and constraints. New operational systems or lines of business, the shrinkage of organization structures (and the number of positions), or marketing repositioning will require quite different managerial performances and thus modifications or considerable changes in the reward system.

The second way in which reward systems enter the strategic picture is as a part of organization/human resource planning. Determining the kinds of human resources, behaviors, culture, and management practices indicated by strategic plans calls for designing a reward system which attracts desired personnel, motivates desired performance, and becomes a significant part of culture supporting these results (Lawler, 1986:10.3).

Design Factors and Reward System Objectives

Strategic thinking needs to take into account the ways in which reward systems affect both individual behaviors and cost structures and therefore organizational efficiency and effectiveness:

1. Costs are quite tangibly associated with reward systems since they may represent 50 or 75 percent of operating costs. Strategic determinations include the establishment of cost "ceilings" and determinations of their variability relative to competition or the company's ability to pay. For example, in good times, managerial incentive bonuses may be a significant percentage of base pay, say, 15 to 30 percent. But how much will be available if times are tough and yet managers put forth equal or even greater effort? Strategic thinking must be a factor in both eventualities as well as the policies and approaches for handling them when they arise.

2. Reward systems also play a major role in an organization's culture (see Chapter 3). One basic feature displayed in this regard is the extent to which the reward system is largely hierarchical and based on promotion, or whether a significant attempt is made to include the recognition of individual competence or the enactment of valued actions. Another dimension of the reward system is the relative division and amount of rewards in career systems, including both technical and more general managerial career ladders. Reward systems send quite visible signals to organization members through the culture.

3. A third strategic aspect of reward systems relates to their impact on attracting and retaining people. The reward system is often a major factor in who is attracted to the organization and who stays. Management trainees and seasoned managers are both affected in their "decision to join." Competency (or merit) -based rewards may attract superior performers since better performers want more tangible recognition (higher rewards) than those provided to average or poor performers. More generally, the match between what (better) performers value and what the organization offers is instrumental in attracting and retaining top-notch people.

4. The motivation to act or perform in a particular way is greatly affected by

reward system features. A key point developed at some length elsewhere in this chapter indicates that managers (people) behave in ways they they believe will lead to valued rewards (outcomes). For rewards to motivate desired performances, they must be seen by the person as *valued*, *"connected,"* and *achievable*. In brief, the reward must have value for the person, be seen as "connected" to performance, and be achievable. "Valuation" lies entirely within the person and thus requires acute perception on the part of officials as to this state of needs. The second idea involves both the person and organization. The individual needs to have a valid picture of the reward system, and the organization must communicate its relationships and have the integrity to stand by it. For the person to see the reward as achievable, he or she needs to have the appropriate competencies (the role of development!), and the organization needs to have supported the individual's development through needs analyses and involvement of supervising personnel.

5. Self-development and individual competency can be viewed as human resource–related strategic design options. Does the organization want to motivate a significant improvement in the scope and level of individual competencies? Involved here are issues of performance improvement and broadening the talent pool of promotable people. The matter of self-development also figures prominently in career development systems which serve as a conduit to valued individual accomplishments and help to meet organizational staffing requirements.

Reward Systems and Performance

Probably the most important strategic decision to be made in designing a reward system is to determine whether or not it will be based on performance (Lawler, 1986: 10.6). Allied with this determination is deciding the scope and detail which will be communicated to organization members. The major alternatives to a performance-based system are to tie pay structures to the particular positions, which are mostly hierarchical, or to relate it to seniority. Although many organizations claim that they have performance-based reward systems, many do not, and others wish they used alternative approaches! This seeming contradiction with the general thrust of discussions here and elsewhere in the book requires explanation.

Let's deal, first, with the simplest issue. Some companies claim that they have performance-based systems, but in fact, this is untrue. Although they may desire this type of system, their actual approach is a traditional one based on position in the pay structure, or it is related to length of service.

Developing a performance-based system that is reliable, consistent, and acceptable to most organization members is probably the major deterrent to this accomplishment. Many external conditions affect performance, yet managers may have little or no control over these. Identifying relevant performance criteria is a significant task. It becomes even tougher when it is recognized that these multiple measures will vary with the position being considered, and they must be accepted by both the organization and the individual. Also, they must be maintained in a timely way. The specification of performance criteria subsumes the ability of officials and managers to specify desired performances, no small task in itself! The corollary of this determination is then establishing whether in fact the valued performances have been demonstrated.

Numerous reward options can be used as a part of a strategic game plan. Reward parameters include time interval, amount, deferrability, individual versus group basis, and degree of individual choice. Some organizations deal with many of the problems in a pragmatic way, rewarding short-term performance because it is more quantifiable and easily dealt with. Unfortunately, this approach may submerge strategic considerations and encourage a managerial preoccupation with short-term returns.

This subject is clearly a major topic, and because of its length will not be pursued here.

On balance, the cumulative thrust of research indicates that the reward-performance model is sound and accomplishable from an individual behavioral viewpoint. Yet numerous practical problems exist when organizations attempt to apply this model under the myriad real-life uncertainties and organizational pressures and circumstances. Practical means exist, however, for dealing with these matters if circumstances permit, and it has been determined that this is the system to pursue.

No clear-cut answers exist as to whether a reward system should be open or secretive. An open system encourages people to raise questions and challenge particular reward decisions under unique circumstances not completely or generally known. Secretive systems encourage the grapevine and often lead to distortions as to what factually is happening. They may also undercut the ability of an organization to meet basic motivational conditions related to effort, competency, value to the person, and rewards. No hard guides exist as to what reward system strategy best fits particular circumstances. Lawler (1986:10.6) offers some general guides in this regard, and these may prove useful to planners and strategists.

- Competency-based systems appear to fit well with organizations wanting stable, relatively permanent, work forces which are oriented to individual development, learning, and growth. An organized career development effort may serve as a highly important supportive system for this approach. Firms where there are many knowledgeable workers or which are high-tech, for example, seem well suited to these strategic approaches.
- Reward structures related to position or derivatives of seniority seem to work where organizational circumstances are complex or changing rapidly to a point that measurement and administrative problems are too great. Also, if circumstances dictate a long-term staffing reduction, these simpler, more stable structures would seem desirable.

It is evident that contextual factors play an important role in how jobholders respond to redesigned positions.

Analysis of job content, the next topic, frequently takes work context as a given or acceptable to the person. Clearly, job content is an important, perhaps major, consideration for human resource planning strategists.

Job-Analytic Approaches—The "Job-Person Matrix" (Control Data)

Job analysis plays a major role in management development planning and performance and career management. Job-analytic approaches provide a specific model to guide job (re)design since they deal with job particulars and work dimensions. At one time it was thought that statements of position responsibilities containing position title, reporting relationships, main duties, lists of key responsibilities, and sometimes important working (communications) relationships, supported by position specifications, could meet these needs. "Job specifications" entered the picture because they outlined the education, experience, skills, and often personality features of "qualified" candidates. Too often, the inherent uncertainties in these approaches were never questioned. Although traditional job design approaches were focused on performance, increasingly they fell short of this important but limited objective.

The limitations of these approaches regarding "equal (employment) opportunity" also became well known. One of the demands imposed on equal employment opportunity was that more work-related approaches should be used. General descriptive statements of work responsibilities or educational specifications usually were inadequate. More powerful means were needed for job design, with a greater likelihood of achieving the multiple objectives of development, salary administration, career planning, and performance management.

The years of job-related research carried out at Control Data and directed by Dr. Walter Tornow (e.g., Tornow and Gartland, 1980) are representative of these superior and more powerful approaches. Another is the job-analytic approach which established a solid competency basis for the performance management and career planning system at Holiday Inns, Inc., which was established by Dr. Steven Doerflein (1985) and his associates.

In the Control Data approach, action research resulted in the establishment of general sets of "position description factors" and corresponding "performance behavior dimensions" applicable to most (managerial) positions. Additionally, each position was backed up with a detailed itemization of activities and behaviors needed for success in a particular assignment. Consequently, this job analysis approach provided an excellent basis for job and organization design. Individual positions could be adequately described and families of jobs were more readily identified. Also, relationships between positions were better understood so that systematic career development programs could be designed. Other positive results included more uniform bases for performance appraisal and assessment of potential, and more equitable bases for administering salary systems.

The following represents a brief summary of this approach—more details are provided in Burack and Mathys (1987). Though some aspects of this approach changed as Control Data (and others) gained more experience with its use, the essence of the model is still highly applicable to a variety of organizational situations.

The job-analytic research at Control Data resulted in the identification of 13 position description factors and 17 performance behavior dimensions. The former profiled key elements of positions and the latter what jobholders had to do ("behaviors") to be successful on the job. Each of the general behavior dimensions was supported with much detail relative to a given job. These sets of factors permitted job-to-job comparisons; a uniform group of factors by which a given job could be described, a useful basis for development, and an excellent way to describe job changes for planning purposes. Examples of position description and performance behavioral dimensions follow (Tornow and Gartland, 1980).

Position Description Factors

1. *Strategy planning*—a high score on this factor in a management position indicated a significant emphasis on long-range thinking and planning. The concerns of the incumbent are broad and are oriented toward the future of the company. They may include determining areas of long-range business potential or objectives of the organization, identifying the business activities in which the company should engage, and the evaluation of new ideas.

2. *Internal business coordination*—a high score on this factor in a management position indicates that the incumbent exercises business controls, that is, reviews and controls the allocation of manpower and other resources. Activities and concerns are in the areas of assignments of supervisory responsibility, expense control, cost reduction, setting performance goals, preparation and review of budgets, protection of the company's monies and properties, and employee relations practices.

Performance Behavior Dimensions

1. *Innovation*—developing and applying innovative procedures to accomplish assignments; developing new ideas and unique solutions to planning and problem solving, anticipating and coping effectively with change in circumstances which impact the functional area.

2. *Crisis action*—recognizing critical problems and acting promptly and decisively to alleviate them; taking charge quickly in crisis situations; behaving deliberately and rationally under stress; deciding promptly on an alternative course of action when necessitated by unforeseen emergencies.

3. *Communication*—providing complete, concise, accurate, and prompt information to superiors; disseminating full information to subordinates about company policies and objectives; sharing information with other units as necessary; reporting truthfully on job activities and progress toward objectives.

These sets of factors facilitated important and growing applications in the human resource planning–strategic area as well as in personnel management practices. Another advantage of this job analysis approach was gained from the fact that any given job could be examined in terms of those behavioral (performance) factors seen as most important in meeting critical position (responsibility) requirements (Exhibit 2-5). The "job-person" matrix summarized in Exhibit 2-6 shows one format for making these job-design analyses. The "matrix" also permitted recording how strategic actions or planned positional changes were likely to affect requisite performance behavior dimensions *and* position description factors!

End-Job Behaviors and Managerial Style Including Male-Female Considerations

The determination of end-job behaviors required for successful performance specify performance-specific activities but give little attention to the effects of individual style differences. That is, managers with a particular set of job responsibilities have associated with these a set of critical incidents related to "innovation," "crisis action," and "communication," as in the Control Data example cited. However, individual style differences, including those related to sex, enter into this picture. For example, females may emphasize some factors more than others as a matter of personal style—and with equal effectiveness.

In this book, little attention has been given to male-female considerations simply because the weight of evidence indicates no practical performance differences exist under a variety of work conditions. However, where sex considerations do enter into strategic considerations (as, for example, in EEO planning), these have been addressed specifically.

Practical differences, however, do exist between men and women which affect their management style. The derivation of end-job behavior profiles and even the emphasis on various critical incidents used in many organizations were often based on male models. The considerable period in which women have occupied managerial roles has helped to clarify important alternate approaches to successful performance (Loden, 1986). For instance, characteristic masculine leadership models make much of the individual's competitive style while maintaining high control in strategic and analytical matters. An unemotional demeanor is usually prized, and the objective is to win. Many successful women emphasize the quality of relationships with their colleagues and subordinates. This may mean less emphasis on control, being more empathetic, using collaboration, being cooperative—while maintaining high performance standards.

Bottom-line results form an absolute basis for determining the success with which individual or stylistic differences enter into the picture. Performance appraisal sessions between the manager and his or her superior represent a common and practical format within which style differences can be discussed and reconciled. For strategic planners and officials, they need to be alert to the preconceived notions that frequently exist in (their) organizations as to a "one best style" for performance

EXHIBIT 2-6

The Job Person Matrix in Position Planning and Design (After Control Data)

Position Factors		1. Know-How	2. Plan and Allocate	3. Document	4. Effort/Persistence	5. Innovate	6. Crisis Action	7. Responsibility/Accomplishment	8. Integrity	9. Commitment	10. Communicate	11. Coordinate	12. Represent	13. Consideration	14. Train	15. Delegate	16. Motivate	17. Coach
1	Strategy Planning																	
2	Organizational Coordination																	
3	Internal Business Coordination		G				G				G			G		G	G	
4	Products and Services Responsibility		G					G						G		G		
5	Public Relations								G		G		G					
6	Internal Consulting																	
7	Autonomy								G	G								

Performance (Behavior) Dimensions

Position Factors										
8 Financial Approval Commitment										
9 Staff Service	G	G								
10 Supervision							G		G	G	G
11 Complexity				G				G		
12 Financial Management			G					G		
13 Human Resource Management										

Source: Based on Walter W. Tornow and Timothy Gartland, internal corporate documents, Control Data. For added details, see E. H. Burack and N. J. Mathys, *Human Resources Planning*, (1987).

success. Valid policy and planning considerations require explicit consideration of alternate performance models and the infusion of this recognition into the many systems underlying planning processes and operations management.

Behavioral Approaches to Job Design

Two approaches to job design are discussed in this section: "work redesign," developed by J. Richard Hackman and Greg R. Oldham (1980), and "job enrichment," based on the pioneering work of Frederick J. Herzberg (1968). The discussions here are developed in a work-design format. Behavioral motivation issues more generally linked to planning for performance (management) are covered in the next chapter.

The work of Hackman and Oldham is probably among the more widely used approaches today to job design, and consequently it is emphasized in this section. This systematic approach to work analysis, gathering of job data, and continuing research to improve the model and its application, helped to establish its well-deserved reputation. Although changes are likely to take place in the methods or instrumentation with which users will want to be acquainted, it stands as an excellent point of departure for redesign of jobs. Data gathering regarding work is critically important in this approach; thus, an example of their job analysis instrument is included in the applications section of this chapter. In the past, Herzberg's "job-enrichment" approach was widely used. However, many organizational researchers have examined it critically and identified major limitations due to its underlying research methods. Yet its imprint is clear in many contemporary approaches including the work of Hackman and Oldham.

Common to design approaches based on behavioral concepts is the desire to improve various job characteristics leading to superior performance and a sense of individual well-being. In brief, if a person desires change in his or her job situation, and features of the job can be redesigned, then the work redesign should be such as to bring about a more positive human experience; thus, job-related satisfaction improves.

Initially, individual suggestions are actively sought in considering a job-design approach; individuals usually know their own needs best. Participation of the person in the work redesign customarily comes out of the day-to-day interactions of the person with their supervisor, formally scheduled preimplementation interviews, regularly scheduled performance appraisal sessions, and action research analyses. Numerous observational and attitude instruments exist for action research purposes, the description of which goes much beyond space limitations in this book. However, in the applications section of this chapter, there is a short version of the Job Diagnostic Survey (JDS) developed by Hackman and Oldham (which is not copyrighted). The fact that much data have been compiled using the JDS means that a given organizational application may be able to draw on a rich base of comparative data through contacts with the researchers. The short form of the JDS included in this chapter is an *attitude survey* form with all the advantages and limitations that these provide.

In the Hackman-Oldham "work-redesign approach," the focus is on achieving high(er) levels of interal work motivation, work efficiency, and effectiveness; an improved sense of job-related satisfaction; and the experiencing of personal growth. These results were seen as a possible result of the person achieving more personal potential. From almost anybody's viewpoint, these are enviable outcomes, though their accomplishment is not easily brought about.

Hackman and Oldham's "Work-Redesign" Approach—Model Specifics

This work-design model is a logical point of departure for work planning or design analyses. It incorporates many of the "job-enrichment" ideas, but in a more rigorous analytical framework. The essence of this job-design approach is contained in four points:

1. Understand what it is that we are trying to help the person experience or feel ("critical psychological states") and establish a means of assessing these and the hoped-for end results.
2. Identify selected aspects of the person and the work situation which are known to affect how well the person responds to a work-redesign approach. These are called *moderators* and include job competencies (skills, experience, and training), desire to grow or achieve, and the person's outlook regarding the general work environment or organization (e.g., satisfaction with pay and supervision). These factors, both individually and collectively, if acceptable or met reasonably well, are likely to promote a strong and positive response to work (re)design. If the person is not satisfied with, say, pay or supervision, this situation will limit (some of) the positive effects of job redesign. The more adverse these circumstances, the less likely that work redesign will be effective.
3. Examine the motivational potential of the job. Jobs are subject to widely different opportunities for redesign and thus influencing the jobholder. Hackman and Oldham developed a formulated approach for making this calculation, which is included in the application section of this chapter. This analysis is undertaken from the viewpoint of the job holder.
4. Identify "core job (motivating) factors" that contribute to motivational potential. These have been identified in previous research and include task variety, identity, and significance; autonomy; and feedback to judge how one is doing or where they stand. This analysis combines "job-design engineering" and the psychological aspects of these.

Some of these points require greater explanation, and this is provided in the following discussion.

Moderators. The redesign of work, even if artful in a behavioral sense, may accomplish nothing if certain general preconditions are not satisfied. There were three preconditions which were identified in the Hackman and Oldham (re)design approach described first (point 2). Although all are important, their relative importance will vary with the person, their priorities, and the situation. The three factors are known more specifically as "knowledge and skill needed for satisfactory performance," "satisfaction with work context," and "growth-need strength."

Knowledge and skill (or job-related competency) of the person involved is a universal requirement in job-(re)design approaches and handled more directly than other preconditions. From a strategic viewpoint, it is necessary to establish whether the management development "candidate" has at least the minimal requirements of knowledge and skills for successful performance in the targeted position. The fact that months or years, in some cases, may be required to strengthen or develop these skills, as in the Honeywell approach, makes it important that the results of a job design not be judged prematurely—adequate time must pass. Thus, individual needs analysis must be part of the initial management development and job-design strategy. Baselines of knowledge and skill criteria need to be established for subsequent comparisons. The fact that room exists for the person to expand his or her knowledge and skills beyond these baselines may also prove to be motivating for the candidate in that it builds self-confidence in the person's ability to grow.

Context satisfaction is much broader in concept. It involves the strength and "positiveness" of the person's feelings regarding such factors as salary, work conditions, nature of supervision, career mobility and opportunities, co-workers, job security, and benefits structure. Many of these were related to organization culture. Obviously, appraisal of each of these points differs widely among individuals and situations. However, unless (any of) these represent particularly severe or difficult problems for the person, it is likely that the "growth-need" strength of the "candidate" manager, discussed in the next paragraph, would be equal to or even more critical in achieving a positive human experience.

Individual growth-need strength reflects the value that the person places on being assigned greater responsibility or their need for personal achievement opportunities or accomplishment. Involved too is their desire for recognition and/or the opportunity to advance. The growth-need strength of an individual can play an important role in management development planning since it often ties into assessments of potential and promotability decisions. Put another way, strength of growth needs influences both the attractiveness of a position assignment for the person (the question of how the work redesign or assignment is perceived by the managerial candidate) and also describes a characteristic often sought-after in managerial promotion (or high-potential) candidates!

Core Job Characteristics, Impact on the Person, and End Results.   If the "moderator" conditions just outlined are met in a reasonable way, then work designs that are high on "core" work-design features become the "blueprint" for the job design. In the work carried out by Hackman and Oldham, three core design features were identified.

The first, *work meaningfulness,* contained three interrelated elements: skill variety, opportunity to identify with the task, and task significance. Practically speaking, work assignments which are challenging, include, for example, reasonable complexity, a variety of significantly different situations, or a changing pattern of contacts.

Autonomy involved "reasonable" independence of the jobholder in task performance. It was another characteristic of a successful work design assuming the "moderator" conditions were met. Autonomy meant that the person had some control over time-place-methods resources thus permitting their experiencing responsibility for work outcomes. Autonomy in managerial positions might also mean responsibilities (and authority) which had been allocated (decentralized) to the person facilitating (more) independence in handling difficult problems (e.g., customer complaints), or making commitments for actions based on the results for which they will be judged.

Feedback, the communication of progress or performance-related information, is critical for the person to judge the results of their work. Baselines to evaluate change are also very much a part of this picture. For managerial positions, this is an especially demanding requirement. At times, it is difficult to meet because of the interdependent nature of much managerial work and the length of time required for events to unfold. There is an obvious need for agreed-on and measurable baselines or performance criteria. The strategic considerations set out in Chapter 1 argue in general for the lengthening of the time horizons considered critical for judging the "actual" performance outcomes of managerial decisions or actions. This doesn't mean that an activity be played out to failure just to see what happened—that would be naive. Yet a number of strategic plans or programs have been launched, seemingly without suitable evaluation and control mechanisms.

> In a large multiple-unit hospital system, an ambitious effort was launched to strengthen substantially the identification and development of managerial personnel. An extensive series of top-level planning sessions led to the identification of substantially modified organizational goals and objectives. Strategic planning sessions led to a much better understanding of the type of complex organization it had become and viable alternatives to accomplish its future competitive positioning. Considerable modifications in organization structure were indicated in consequence of new or modified hospital missions and business ventures. Managerial work was studied intensively, and an extensive management development program was launched. Yet almost two years passed *after* program initiation before it was realized that no data baseline had been specifically identified to document the course of change.

Knowledge of actual accomplishments is important for managerial motivation, and to the organization as well.

Baselines to Evaluate Change.   The need to have knowledge of "actual" results may pose informational challenges of a type not ordinarily encountered yet really necessary for an informed, strategic approach. Many internal control systems or programs which (are supposed to) provide critical information in a timely way, such as budgets or MBO (management by objective), in reality are inadequate. Often these are purely numbers oriented or geared to shorter-term results. Lack of thoughtful procedures may also lead to the burying of individual results in consolidated figures. In turn, the managerial person (candidate) will need to understand the possibilities and limitations of (available data in) a given situation so that they build realistic expectations regarding the timing, form, and substance of work results. Thus the system capability must exist for judging performance outcomes, only a portion of which fall into the conventional category of "objective" results. The "efficiency" outcomes, which are more numbers related (Chapter 7, on performance management), include production efficiency (output, quality), number of customers served, profits or degree of cost containment. However, from the viewpoint of an organization's general goals and the people instrumental to these, important descriptive information is also needed. Desired "effectiveness" outcomes would include level of internal work motivation; degree of career progress; experiencing of growth, particularly job-related satisfaction; and a general sense of (work-related) well-being. The effectiveness factors require thoughtful consideration to identify useful benchmarks for comparison. Managerial survey techniques dealing with perceptions of organization culture and work-related satisfaction are examples of these.

Some possible limitations of the "work-redesign" approach described in this section include the fact that the requirements of new positions may involve factors not previously experienced by the individual. Also they may represent a pattern of activities over time, the sum total of which may be overly demanding or even frustrating. Measurement problems for data gathering include changing individual or situational needs. Needless to say, since strategic actions involve future time frames, deterministic approaches are limited by uncertainty. Initial estimates or judgments of managerial role needs will change as circumstances unfold.

Herzberg's Job-Enrichment (JE) Approaches

Only a few brief highlights will be presented here since key background factors have already been covered in the discussion of Hackman and Oldham's work. The fact that the "job-enrichment" model was used extensively within AT&T member units for many years (Ford, 1973, 1979) provides an important rationale for considering this approach. More on this in a moment.

The "job-enrichment" approach is based on the recognition of two sets of factors. Most of the type of "work context" factors identified by Hackman and Oldham are classified as *hygiene* or "dissatisfiers" by Herzberg (1968). These factors include company policy and administrative work conditions, supervisory relationships with the jobholder, salary, co-worker relationships, and a sense of job security. To the extent that "hygiene" factors are not major problem sources, the major JE design thrust is on intrinsic work factors or *motivators*. The latter include work itself, facilitating achievement and recognition for the person by providing meaningful responsibility (with commensurate authority), establishing good advancement opportunities, and the person experiencing personal growth.

Experiences at AT&T and those of researchers such as Hackman and Oldham emphasize that certain conditions must be met if a job-redesign effort is to be successful. Thus, these work-redesign specifics provide necessary, but not sufficient conditions for performance improvement. For example, both this and the Hackman/Oldham work-design approach stress the importance of a cordial, supportive environment for job enrichment. Strategic approaches to management development assume that supervising managers are apprised fully of the work redesign purposes. Also, it is important that their support and cooperation be actively enlisted to help improve performance outcomes!

Summary

Business and strategic planning has increasingly involved substantial and complex organization and work-design issues because these are inexorably connected. Thus it has become necessary to develop newer perspectives on managerial work and its connection to general planning and strategic human resource thinking. The sociotechnical model is part of a whole new era of organizational thinking and approaches which have been applied to these situations. Because of the difficulty in analyzing change and complex systems, and due to the many different areas of information which must be drawn upon, "sociotechnical" advisory groups are frequently formed. They deal with these matters on an organizationwide basis and provide planning, counseling, and help to support implementation. They facilitate strategic planning processes. A "sociotechnical design committee" can prove highly useful for planning and strategizing as planners seek to understand better and capitalize on the impacts of change. Additionally, the committee can serve as the major internal vehicle or catalyst for organizing or guiding a complex group of activities and processes. They help to assure needed adaptation to change covering structure, systems, processes, job functions, and work itself.

Organization and Work Planning as a Contingency Strategy

A basic starting point is initiation of strategic human resource planning processes needed to establish positional staffing requirements. These are relative to the current and proposed organizational design. Needs analyses then take account of organizational and job requirements and those of the individual. If a new organizational design is being proposed, or a new work system is to be installed, or the job structure is to be extensively changed, then the impact of these changes needs to be traced out. Of particular interest will be their impact on managerial positions. Sociotechnical analyses are helpful in this regard.

Organization and work planning approaches also need to deal with the added alternatives provided by the reward system which consists of numerous monetary and nonmonetary factors. Initially, analyses must take into account the financial capabilities and limitations of the enterprise to establish the current situation. Next, the impact of strategic plans on managerial roles and performances are noted, and thereby requisite changes in the reward system. The approaches described in this chapter advocated five design approaches which take into account costs, culture, attraction, and retention of people, performance motivation, individual competency, and the motivation for self-development. A basic decision to make in connection with the reward system is determining whether rewards will be based on performance, and if so, how these will be determined. Enlightened techniques for studying managerial work can be instrumental in these determinations.

At a micro level, detailed job analyses which consider responsibilities and performance behaviors for success will prove useful for anticipating the impact of changes. At a macro level, the overall impact of change on the primary organizational structures and systems is more readily detected.

Job-(re)design planning, as it relates to managerial positions, is clearly a complex process because of the numerous factors involved. Thus, a contingency approach is required with the choice of particular models or analyses or combinations of these reflecting the specific situation. Sociotechnical approaches provide a general framework for analysis. Specific factors discussed in this chapter included contingency options such as organization culture, use of career-stage approaches, and job redesign. Organization culture, especially if it is a strong one, is a potent factor in organization and job planning. It affects the pragmatics of the reward system to the general tone or orientation toward human resources. It also establishes the reality of work requirements and the clarity with which individuals view these. The Dorothy's case in the application section (B) provides an integrated demonstration of these concepts.

Individual maturity, career progress, and growth in competencies (knowledge, skills, and abilities) form a much-needed and additional perspective in design approaches. The opportunity for individual progress and the programming of individual development can be related to individual maturation, salary, progress, and psychological needs. Also, visualizing changing situational needs, as these affect individual career progress, provides an opportunity to fuse organizational opportunities and needs with those of the person. This viewpoint also provides a logical basis to tie in alternate development strategies as to how learning is to be provided for the person.

Specific work/job-design activities center on core task features with important behavioral implications for the person. Those listed were identified with the work of Hackman and Oldham and Herzberg. The applications section of this chapter includes a shortened version of the JDS (Job Description Survey) developed by Hackman and Oldham. The information gained from this data gathering approach has been found useful in establishing individual needs and the possible responsiveness of individuals to these designs.

Strategic human resource thinking needs to take account of the person's desire and readiness for change. Part of this question includes the person's desire for personal growth, given the acceptability (i.e., his or her satisfaction) of supervisory relationships and contextual conditions surrounding the job. If the design is carried out well and the person's "inner feelings" have been stimulated, the level of motivated effort should be significant. Persons, correspondingly, should be able to exercise more personal discretion and exploit knowledge they possess. Performance results for both the organization and person should be positive. Another point in this behavioral view is to recognize that the person builds their understanding and interpretation of the situation based on their perceptions. If these are faulty, the best intended design will fail. Their supervisor plays a key role in this regard. The person's supervisor must be fully understanding of the rationale for job (re)design and be prepared to support it actively. Thus strategic thinking must encompasss enlisting the helpful cooperation of senior people.

The implementation of strategic actions is a matter of consequence in planning. At times much effort and time may have to be considered with regards to strengthening cooperative and working relationships both within and between groups or units. The group context is a fact of managerial work. Thus the applications section for this chapter includes a summary presentation on organization development approaches which can materially facilitate the transition from planning to programs.

In Part B of the applications section for this chapter, a comprehensive application example is provided. It includes strategic planning issues, sociotechnical analysis, and work-design approaches. The subject company is Dorothy's, a rapidly growing, fast-food chain.

REFERENCES

Birchall, David. *Job Design*. London, England: Gower Press, Ltd., 1975.

Buchanan, David A. *The Development of Job Design Theories and Technique*. New York: Praeger, 1979.

Burack, Elmer H. "The Sphinx' Riddle." *Training and Development Journal*, Vol. 38, no. 4 (April 1984): 52–61.

Burack, Elmer H. and Nicholas J. Mathys. *Human Resource Planning*, 2nd. ed. rev. Lake Forest, IL: Brace-Park, 1987.

Burack, Elmer H. and Nicholas J. Mathys. *Introduction to Management: A Career Perspective*. New York: John Wiley, 1987.

Burack, Elmer H. and Robert D. Smith. *Personnel Management: A Human Resource Systems Approach*. New York: John Wiley, 1982.

Davis, Louis E. and F. Raylor. *Job Design*, 2nd ed. Pacific Palisades, CA: Goodyear, 1978.

Dalton, Gene W. and Paul H. Thompson. *Novations: Strategies for Career Management*. Glenview, IL: Scott, Foresman, 1986.

Dalton, Gene W., Paul H. Thompson, and R. L. Price. "The Four Stages of Professional

Careers: A New Look at Performance by Professionals." *Organizational Dynamics,* Vol. 6 (1978): 19–42.

Doerflein, Steven. "Directions, for Career Planning." *Personnel Administrator,* Vol. 30, no. 10 (October 1985): 93–107.

Ford, Robert N. *Why Jobs Die and What to Do About It.* New York: AMACOM, 1979.

Ford, Robert. "Job Enrichment Lessons from AT&T." *Harvard Business Review,* Vol. 51 (January–February 1973): 96–106.

Hackman, J. Richard and Gregg R. Oldham. *Work Redesign.* Reading, MA: Addison-Wesley, 1980.

Hall, Douglas T. *Careers in Organizations.* Reading, MA: Addison-Wesley, 1976.

Herzberg, Frederick. "One More Time: How Do You Motivate Your Employees." *Harvard Business Review,* Vol. 46 (January–February 1968): 53–62.

Huse, Edgar F. and Thomas G. Cummings. *Organization Development and Change,* 3rd ed. St. Paul, MN: West, 1985.

Kirkman, Frank. "Who Cares About Job Design? Some Reflections on Its Present and Future." *International Journal of Operations and Production Management* (UK), Vol. 2 (1981): 3–13.

Lawler, Edward E. III. "Reward System and Strategies." In James R. Gardner, Robert Rachlin, and H. W. Allen Sweeney, eds., *Handbook of Strategic Planning.* New York: John Wiley, 1986, Chap. 10.

Lippitt, Gordon. *Organization Renewal: A Holistic Approach to Organization Development,* 2nd ed. Englewood Cliffs, NJ: Prentice-Hall, 1982.

Loden, Marilyn. *Feminine Leadership; or How to Succeed in Business Without Being One of the Boys.* New York: Times Books, 1986.

McCormick, Ernest J. *Job Analysis: Methods and Applications.* New York: AMACOM, 1979.

Morse, John T. "A Contingency Look at Job Design." *California Management Review,* Vol. 16 (Fall 1973): 67–75.

Nadler, David and Edward Lawler III. "Quality of Work Life: Perspectives and Directions." Working paper, Center for Effective Organizations, University of Southern California, Los Angeles, 1982.

O'Conner, Edward J. "Individual Differences and Job Design Reconsidered: Where Do We Go from Here?" *Academy of Management Review,* Vol. 5 (April 1980): 249–254.

O'Toole, James. *Making America Work, Productivity and Responsibility.* New York: Continuum, 1981.

Pasmore, W. and John J. Sherwood. *Socio Technical Systems: A Source Book.* La Jolla, CA: University Associates, 1978.

Pierce, Jon L. "Job Design in Perspective," *Personnel Administrator,* Vol. 25 (December 1980): 67–74.

Pinder, Craig. *Work Motivation: Theory, Issues, and Applications.* Glenview, IL: Scott, Foresman, 1984.

Rhodes, David W. and James W. Walker, "Management Succession and Development Planning." *Human Resource Planning,* Vol. 7, no. 4 (1984): 157–174.

Ross, Joel E. *Productivity, People, and Profits.* Reston, VA: Prentice-Hall, 1981.

Schein, Edgar H. *Career Dynamics*. Reading, MA: Addison-Wesley, 1978.

Shaw, James B. "An Information-Processing Approach to the Study of Job Design," *Academy of Management Review*, Vol. 5 (January 1980): 41–48.

Schoderbeck, Peter P. and William E. Reif. *Job Enlargement: Key to Improved Performance*. Ann Arbor: University of Michigan Press, 1969.

Slocum, John W., Jr., and Henry P. Sims, Jr. "A Typology for Integrating Technology, Organization and Job Design." *Human Relations*, Vol. 33 (March 1980): 193–212.

Tornow, Walter W. and Timothy C. Gartland. "An Integrated Research and Development Program for Enhancing Managerial Effectiveness." In Edwin L. Miller, Elmer H. Burack, and Maryann Albrecht, eds., *Management of Human Resources*. Englewood Cliffs, NJ: Prentice-Hall, 1980.

Umstot, Dennis D., Terence R. Mitchell, and Cecil H. Bell, Jr. "Goal Setting and Job Enrichment: An Integrated Approach to Job Design." *Academy of Management Journal*, Vol. 21 (October 1978): 867–879.

Woodman, Richard W. and John J. Sherwood. "A Comprehensive Look at Job Design." *Harvard Business Review*, Vol. 56 (July–August, 1977): 384–390.

APPLICATIONS SECTION

Part A. The Organization Development Orientation in Human Resource Approaches

Background

It is with much justification that practitioners view organization development (OD) as one of the more useful behavioral/change products imported into the world of work. Its broad focus and growing track record of practical contributions to improving organizational processes and relationships establish it as a potentially important source of work-design ideas. Of particular interest in this approach is the simultaneous view of work context, job content, and (relational) processes. This approach contributes to programming effective working relationships and performance. In other words, modern OD approaches recognize the complex interplay of various situational factors on job-related satisfaction, motivated behavior, and performance, although much of the emphasis is still on the group. Exhibit 2-7, based on a tabulation of factors identified by Gordon Lippett (1982) and others, comprises a "wholistic" approach to successful OD designs. Included are four sets of factors: organization (context), supervision, person (or people as in a group), and work relationships.

Organization   The organization is required to support individual activities and to create a climate that is motivationally satisfying and challenging. Quite naturally, the organization must assume general responsibilities for the design of the overall job structure and climate and to manage, proactively, work-related processes. Organization culture, budgets, policies, and leadership in the management of change form part of the essential role of "organization."

EXHIBIT 2-7
Organization Development Approaches to Organization and Work
Design for Managers

Person(s)	Work
Grow through roles/relationships and facilitating career programs	Increase accountability, responsibility, and authority or independence to act
• Increase independence. • Clarify roles. • Strengthen intergroup communications, relations. • Pursue learning opportunities. • Expand individualism, identification with work. • Relate work to career goals. • Require meaningful support of superior. • Build sense of strength affecting knowledge, skills, and abilities.	• Reduce task controls and emphasize results. • Establish more accountability. • Clarify work goals or objectives. • Exercise reasonable choice in work approaches. • Involve person(s) in decision making. • Expand achievement, recognition and personal growth opportunities. • Provide feedback, emphasizing self-analysis and thus self-control.
Organization	**Supervising Managers**
Establishes climate, support, and management of processes	Serve in a facilitative or supportive role
• Establish a supportive culture, build a climate of trust. • Establish requisite internal policies, budgets • Create an open system—support communications and relations. • Provide orientation to people combined with performance realities. • Take the lead in managing change. • Enhance two-way communications. • Strengthen the climate for creativity, innovation. • Expand meaningfulness of individual work tasks. • Reward quality and quantity of performance. • Combine approaches: use of organization, management, and individual development.	• Enlarge role of planning and general management. • Expand coaching roles for individual development. • Provide feedback on an accurate, timely basis (relational roles). • Develop group and interpersonal skills. • Enlarge work group responsibilities. • Expand supportive activities as opposed to directive activities. • Enlarge role of planning and general management. • Expand change management skills; adaptation and coping with change. • Build trust with subordinates, work group members. • Expand counseling/mentoring role for bettering individual career planning. • Facilitate individual desires for growth, recognition, independence of action, and achievement.

Source: Based in part on the work of Gordon Lippitt (1982) and others.

Supervising managers The key question here is to consider how to expand the facilitative or supportive role. The specifics of Exhibit 2-7 have been modified somewhat relative to the customary OD model for greater emphasis on general managerial rather than task group roles. The potential impact of the supervising manager's role on individual development is substantial. It may include helping to expand individual capabilities, counseling regarding individual career plans, work assignments to build new areas of expertise, and facilitating personal growth opportunities.

Work This factor emphasizes expanding individual job responsibility with commensurate opportunity for the person to act in a reasonably independent and accountable way. Supervising managers have to "let loose" and assist in expanding the capabilities of managerial "trainees." At the same time, the "work" factor stands as a reminder of the need for work documentation in terms of job descriptions and the identification of the expected job behaviors for success. Work assignments should include clear work goals or objectives and reasonable options in work approaches to bring out individual capabilities. Feedback needs to increasingly emphasize self-assessment as a practical basis to reduce the direct involvement of a supervising manager and expand the individual's sense of independence and self-determination.

Person(s) Individual managerial roles need to provide substantial opportunities for growth through work roles and role relationships. A number of the entries in Exhibit 2-7 echo points made under the "work," "supervising manager," or "organization" captions. An additional point is to emphasize the need for policymakers, strategic planners, and the supervising manager to facilitate or to provide efficient and valid learning opportunities. For example, people can be assigned to a position from which they may *eventually* synthesize a useful group of experiences and personal learnings. The trouble is that this informal approach may take far longer than necessary. Careful coaching and feedback on the part of a supervising manager and job assignments which are richer in the needed experiences, usually turn out to be a much more efficient approach.

Part B: Dorothy's—A Comprehensive Application Example*

Background

The fast-food business in the United States is often seen as being purely "American" in origin but almost universal in satisfying, admirably, valued "needs and wants" of people. Although only dating back to the 1950s, themes of quality food,

---

Names and selected figures have been altered to preserve the anonymity of corporate participants. Any relation to actual people or events is purely coincidental.

fast service, and an often-pleasant social setting helped to provide a cordial welcome to "fast foods" around the world. At the same time, the quick growth of this
field attracted a large number of tough competitors who sought to establish significant and recognizable differences in product quality, service, ambience, and price.
The dominance of well-established chains (company owned and franchised) such as
McDonald's and Burger King were challenged by newer "upstarts" such as
Wendy's and Fuddrucker's. Some idea of the rate of growth can be gained from the
fact that Wendy's, established in 1969, had over 3,000 company-owned and -fran-
chised units by 1984, despite this tough competition.

Dorothy's, a Northeastern regional chain, opened almost 1,500 stores in a
10-year period. Its founder, when interviewed, indicated that "current" planning
called for the store chain to grow almost 30 percent in the next 5 years. Yet he
emphasized strongly that Dorothy's would continue to maintain its high standards
of quality and service—and at least equal or improve the profitability of stores in
past years.

Chains such as Dorothy's had to resort to a number of marketing, product,
and operational strategies to maintain their share in primary markets. When firms
sought to increase market penetration, all the strategic factors had to be exercised.
Understandably, corporate resources, including finance, franchising, site development, product development, marketing, and store operations, were pushed to the
maximum.

At Dorothy's, to get the sales "numbers" up, hours were extended and a
number of new products were introduced. As sales went up, absenteeism or turnover increased among store managers, store crews, and even area managers. Although wages and salaries rose to some degree in consideration of customer load,
store hours, and general work demands, attitude surveys indicated that work demands exceeded "rewards."

Two years previously, the company prepared its first five-year business and
strategic plan. Among other strategic activities, it confirmed the president's ambitious plan for store growth and profitability, while maintaining its reputation for
product quality and service. However, the subsequent and alarming rise in personnel turnover, especially among managers, and the increasing difficulty of recruiting
managerial trainees in already over strained labor markets, prompted a
(re)assessment of human resource planning and management approaches by its Corporate Personnel Department.

Key Developments

Personnel Analyses and Reorganization.   An employee survey was taken
which covered almost one-third of all employees from crew members to middle-
level managers. Also, some exit interviews and contacts with former employees
were made. Although there were some differences in results between the various
groups surveyed, these were primarily a matter of emphasis, and most were similar. They emphasized inequitable compensation relative to hours; frequent and

unexpected changes; and poor employee, supervisory, and managerial training. Managers and supervisors were sorely in need of training to handle employee training and the identification and development of supervisory and managerial potential.

Other findings indicated work overload, understaffing of stores and administrative units, lack of staff support, and poor communications. Many of the managers and supervisors felt that there were too many surprises regarding new products and services—nobody seemed to know about them in advance.

When survey results were reviewed with Dorothy's executive committee, it was clear to all members that immediate action had to be taken to achieve their strategic program and targeted objectives. A decision was made to reassign almost the entire corporate Personnel Group to the Operations organization. Store operations were responsible for company-owned domestic and international stores plus the engineering and layout of these. The Personnel Group was to become involved in such areas as organization development, management development, employee training, and compensation and benefits.

Over the next one and one-half years, all of the store profit and cost "numbers" moved in the right direction as Operations benefited from what was essentially a task force type approach by the newly assigned Personnel unit. However, subsequently, the operating figures from various major marketing areas showed a bottoming out or what the controller described as "diminishing returns."

Reappraisal of Issues by the Vice President, Human Resources. The vice president for human resources (the group was renamed) had to change his style and role considerably. He was faced with a far greater number of short-range planning and administrative problems characteristic of Operations. However, he didn't allow himself to be drawn in so deeply into daily issues that overall problems were lost to sight. It was apparent that something more than just a nominal reorganization would be required. The pressure from the executive committee to take quick action was great. He "invited" in several consultants; one was to be chosen to act in an advisory capacity. He was to help Dorothy's Human Resource Unit put together a longer-term solution for the types of problems identified in the survey. Also, the timing of the situational appraisal coincided with an update of the (first) corporate strategic plan requested by the chief financial officer and the president in preparation for the annual stockholders meeting.

Human Resource Planning and Strategic Analysis. (Refer to the "Self-audit Questionnaire in the applications section of Chapter 8.) The external consultant set to work immediately with the Human Resource Staff. The general "game plan" was to assess internal (expertise) capabilities of Human Resources, establish "where" the organization stood as a personnel–human resource system, and to learn how various corporate executives viewed the company's current problems and solution priorities relative to the first corporate strategic plan. After gathering this information, Human Resources was to crystallize three to five major human resource issues. The issues selected were those likely to result from current strategic business plans; their task was to examine the possible need to develop alternate planning scenarios. These analyses were also to include an examination of the managerial function including store operations and staffing generally. The possibilities of work redesign were also included in the "charge." Essential steps and highlights from these analyses follow.

1. Human resource department assessments. These analyses confirmed the existence of a highly competent professional group, strong in personnel skills, but one which had not worked together frequently as a team in the past. This teamwork was especially critical in regards to complex interrelated matters as involved with strategic planning. These analyses also confirmed that none of the Human Resource members had experience with human resource planning approaches nor possessed some of the technical skills (e.g., human resource forecasting) supporting these. It was also apparent that recruiters and trainers who worked with the operation's area, district and regional managers, and officials lacked both the understandings and technical skills required for the more complex store operations and the field organization that had emerged.

2. Personnel/human resource system assessment. The analysis of the personnel/human resource system based on conventional personnel standards revealed one that was largely traditional in nature. (See the sample system audit form in Chapter 8.)

The existing system lacked important personnel and job information including data on competencies, career interests, and formal training. No data were available on job structures, and only standard (cursory!) job descriptions were available. Also, in the area of performance management, much individual information was available on the meeting of store profit, cost, quality, and service targets, but there was very little beyond this for development of store management. For higher levels of supervisory and administrative management, only general performance data was available, based largely on overall ratings. Most available information on potential was informal and was sometimes included as part of a "commentary." "High potentials" were tentatively identified by their supervisors. A recommendation for a "high-potential" classification was sent up to a regional manager who had to review and approve it. If accepted, the person received a special salary increment as part of their annual review.

Personnel analyses reflected a consolidation of the referenced forms submitted to the Human Resource staff and Personnel supervisors assigned to the regional operations groups. A number of critical comments were made regarding these forms. Among other things they indicated that the "high-potential" designation had became largely meaningless—it was used as a way to supplement store manager salaries.

It was felt that there was a need to achieve some type of consensus on the state of the personnel/human resource system as many different views were held as to how complete or advanced it was. Major changes could involve considerable financial expenditures. The Human Resource Vice President and his staff plus several senior managers and officers in operations and marketing were asked to make note of their perceptions as to the *state of the art* of the overall system. For these purposes, a form showing stages of Human Resource systems development was used (see discussion in Chapter 4). Consensus was attained through general discussions and reviews of individual appraisals. These results revealed a highly uneven picture of human resource systems development. Performance management at the store level was comprehensive and fairly complete from a technical viewpoint. They were based on standards, procedures, and objective measures of performance. Personnel data to support this part of Personnel Administration and performance management were in good shape. On the other hand, most elements of a human resource planning and development capability were nonexistent. That is, management development, succession planning analysis, human resource forecasts, and career development information were generally not available. Also, no systematic information had been gathered on the possible bases for redesigning work or managerial positions. The consensus on the *state of the art* of the human resource system advancement helped to establish a more selective basis for judging what had to be done. It also facilitated estimating costs and times to achieve a particular level of capability for strategic planning. Put another way, the act of drawing up strategic planning scenarios would be meaningless unless the correlated needs for human resource systems and organization could also be developed. This approach for information gathering also helped to alert key managers and executives as to current organization capabilities and to establish greater support for strengthening the human resource effort. It helped to bring key people together on the bases of common understanding as to organizational capabilities and limitations.

3. *Managerial and executive outlooks and priorities.* The interviews with managers and executives involved a representative group from Operations, Administration, Marketing, Finance and Business Planning, and Franchising. The "hidden agenda" in regard to these interviews was to make key people more aware of a group of strategic-level competing demands. These competing demands in subsequent discussions became known as components of a "dynamic balance" that included the following important factors:

a. Expanding store operations—an average of some 10 percent per year.
b. Increasing store sales and store and corporate profits through greater market penetration and expansion of store products and hours, while holding the line on costs and quality. This also included enlarging the relative number of company-owned stores through new openings and taking over some of the franchisees.
c. Undertaking corporate continuity (succession) planning for long(er)-term growth and renewal.
d. Reassessing the organization structure for improved planning and performance.

EXHIBIT 2-8
The Dynamic Balance: Central Strategic Business and Human
Resource Planning Issues

Forces for Stability	Destabilizing Forces
Business/Strategic Issues	
Corporate continuity planning for stability and renewal.	Rapid expansion of store operations.
	Increased store sales (total and by unit)—while holding the "line" on costs and quality.
	Expanding the base of company owned stores (conflict with franchisees and a major change).
Human Resource Approaches	
Enlargement of the base of capable middle-level managers for succession.	Introduction and development of a new "breed" of managers (conflict with traditional people).
Improvement of managerial inventories for mobility, retention.	Labor shortages in traditional regional skill pool.
Expansion of the base of "real," high-potential people.	
Reduction of store managerial and crew turnover.	
Expansion of base for internal recruiting.	

Corporate executives assigned high priority to a group of human resource–related planning issues: enlarge the base of capable middle-level managers for succession, improve managerial incentives for internal career mobility and retention, identify and develop a "real" cadre of high-potential people, reduce store management and crew turnover, introduce and develop a new "breed" of Dorothy's managers, develop managers geared to a more complex and challenging environment, and expand the base of capable employees to permit more internal rather than external managerial recruitment. The dynamic balance that was exposed through the managerial interviewing indicated a group of challenging strategic business issues which would have to be resolved *before any* specific human resource plans (as itemized) could be drawn up. Consequently, the dynamic balance between stabilizing and destabilizing forces was as indicated in Exhibit 2-8. This analysis led to some highly interesting discussions among top-level managers when it was revealed that almost all the top-priority strategic business plans were likely to be (highly) destabilizing for Dorothy's with the exception of continuity planning. In contrast, most human resource plans, with the exception of developing a new type of store manager, could help to achieve stability. In short, "how was a dynamic balance to be achieved between these important but largely opposed actions?" The "answer(s)" to the questions formed part of a complex series of strategic business and human resource planning analyses, a portion of which was carried out with sociotechnical approaches—highlights are recorded next.

   4. Sociotechnical systems analyses. [Refer to Exhibit 2-9]. The format and model for this approach was described earlier in this chapter. Defining the changing managerial role resulting from modified organization and business circumstances helped to establish a link with business strategic planning. This proved helpful in reconciling the major but "opposed" forces in the dynamic balance.

   Dorothy's first strategic plan made it clear that the president's vision for the future had been captured in the strategic market penetration and store expansion objectives. To facilitate achieving this objective, Property Development's efforts were expanded, and Finance was alerted to the need to take over a growing number of franchised stores. This move was necessary because of the inability to construct enough new stores and because of the generally good profitability of many of these.

   5. Strategic human resource planning and sociotechnical analyses including forecasting. The analyses of the company's Human Resource Group indicated adverse major demographic trends and impacts on its labor market sources, including the growing difficulties for recruitment in their key age categories. Nevertheless, the results failed to dampen their zest for expansion. Given the "go-go spirit" of the organization's leaders and managers, this was perhaps understandable. But this analysis was only part of a more complex series of analyses that had to be made to round out an understanding of some of the explosive features of the "dynamic balance" referenced previously. In Exhibit 2-9, the scope of the "explosive changes" are suggested by the operations (A) and human resource (B) summaries. The company's strategic plan imposed a demand for change management and coping, virtually impossible to satisfy in the targeted time interval. The planned expansion was likely to ripple ("ripped" might be more appropriate) through the organization, from top to bottom and from East to Midwest to West and from Canada to Florida. For example, one promotion of a senior manager to take over a newly formed district required two to three internal promotions, each involving significant training and development time. The alternative to internal recruitment, going to the outside, led to a lot of bitter feelings among employees because it frustrated individual career ambitions and plans. Outside recruitment also required orienting a new person to the organization's culture, even if she or he possessed the needed skills. Successful integration into their culture was no small accomplishment, especially at the managerial level.

   Strategic planning analyses helped to identify some of the chief features of the new managerial roles—very different from those that existed but a few short years

EXHIBIT 2-9
Sociotechnical Analyses

A. Business and Strategic Planning—Impact on Organization and Work Technology
   1. Corporate Strategic Objectives for Growth and Profitability
   2. Sales Penetration
      • Enter new markets.
      • Develop new products.
   3. Strategic Approach
      • Build new stores in current markets.
      • Convert some franchised stores.
      • Limit new franchises.
      • Introduce new products.
   4. Operations, Administration, and Store Managers
      • Increase numbers.
      • Expand responsibilities.
      • Increase coordination and control.
   5. Store Work Technology
      • Develop new equipment.
      • Greatly change methods.
   6. Store organization
      • Study crew staffing ratios.
      • Analyze store manager responsibilities.
B. Impact of Changes in Organization and Work Technology on Human Resources
   7. Human Resource Impacts
      • Recruiting, selection.
      • Develop/train manager, crews.
      • Review work conditions.
      • Change of managerial roles.
      • Change of individual roles.
      • Review benefits and salary structure.
   8. Changes in Managerial Function and Roles in Stores
      • Emphasize planning and management versus doing skills.
      • Increase coordination and controls for cost and inventory control.
      • Emphasize training.
      • Emphasize expanding knowledge, skills, and abilities to enlarge base of promotables.
      • Work more closely with recruiters.
      • Do store staffing planning.
C. Administration
      • Increase regional, district, and area coordination and control.
      • Improve recruitment planning.
      • Expand managerial development.
      • Identify high-potential personnel.
      • Start human resource forecasting.
      • Devise new operational, cost, and revenue controls.
      • Emphasize new store location, development.
      • Expand internationally.

ago. The employee surveys made it clear that the failure to adequately change the reward structure commensurate with newer managerial responsibilities would have adverse results. It was likely that managerial morale, productivity, and turnover would be negatively affected—the other organizational and human resource shortcomings notwithstanding.

6. *Sociotechnical analysis, job design, and strategic planning issues.* The sociotechnical analyses provided a blueprint for identifying the redefined managerial roles of store and administrative groups. These roles and job redesign, however, were incapable of implementation without the backup of a new job analyses. These involved reexamination of the organization's reward structure including both monetary and nonmonetary features. Necessary modification in the reward structure involved reinforcing the importance of the managerial role in developing people. This analysis also included assessment of the part played by organizational culture, including, potentially, the need to refocus it.

The corporate culture (refer to Chapter 3) required intensive review and analysis. Many of the values that had accounted for the "go-go spirit" of the organization and its fast growth in the past were likely to have a distinctly negative affect in the future. This was likely to be the case unless some of the problems were dealt with in an adequate and timely fashion. Other managerial matters that required solution involved gut-feel decisions, hands-on involvement of managers in store operations, and a strongly held idea that managers with good potential were mostly good work performers. These types of values were in conflict, partially or wholly, with the type of managers Dorothy's was attempting to develop to achieve its future. Officer discussions on "desired" and contemporary operative (actual) values and those values likely to be needed in the future set the stage for a major, internal organization change. The direct and visible participation of the founder and president and the other executive officers plus open meetings (presentations, questions and answers) helped to initiate the change program.

7. *Strategic business and human resource planning and development and the "dynamic balance."* Corporate officials and senior managers at last came to grips with what easily was the most difficult part of the challenge facing top management—the need to moderate the destructive effects of unplanned internal change by reassessing corporate, planning, and strategic objectives. In the past, the short-run disruptive effects were great and likely to be greater in the future unless immediate steps were taken. On the one hand, growth *had* to be sustained—but at a pace that permitted reasonable personnel, organization, and procedural changes to be digested. Short-run profit objectives became a variable ("could be reduced") rather than a given—in an effort to secure a more stable high-profit organization in the future. Growth plans were cut back to achieve shorter-term stability and longer-term profitable growth potential.

Part C: Job Diagnostic Survey: Short Form*

The purpose of this form is to establish how jobs can be better designed by obtaining individual reactions to different kinds of jobs. There are no right or wrong answers—what is wanted is the person's perception of their job and his or her reactions to it. Answers are kept confidential and each item should be answered in an honest and frank manner.

Contents of the Job Diagnostic Survey (JDS)

The JDS provides information regarding the jobholder's assessment of his or her current work situation and preferences should the work be reorganized. The JDS also captures more general individual information so that it is possible to assess generally their degree of satisfaction with the work environment or context of work, job-related satisfaction with specific factors, and growth-needs strength. In brief, a basis is provided for gathering the data identified by Hackman and Oldham as basic to work-design approaches. Thus, it is possible to judge the person's degree of satisfaction with features of the work context, work itself, and personal preferences. Data are also generated as to how important (strong) individual growth needs are, at least to the extent these can be met or improved upon through work "redesign."

A. Ratings of Job and Context Features

Section One	An objective, general description of the person's current job (7 questions).
Section Two	An objective and specific description of the person's current job (14 statements).
Section Three	The individual's feelings regarding the job (7 agree/disagree statements).
Section Four	The person's degree of satisfaction/dissatisfaction with various aspects of the job (14 satisfaction/ dissatisfaction statements).
Section Five	Individual preferences for various job and context features (11 features).

---

*This questionnaire was developed as a part of a study at Yale University conducted by J. Richard Hackman and Greg R. Oldham and appears in *Work Redesign* (Reading, MA: Addison-Wesley, 1980). The JDS was funded by Manpower Administration, U.S. Department of Labor, to Yale University (No. 21-09-79-14) in 1974. Since the completion of this early work, numerous organization researchers and analysts have used the JDS and the models developed by Hackman and Oldham. Interested parties are advised to see the book *Work Redesign* by the researchers, and the journal literature for various recent studies, and to contact them for information sharing. This material is not copyrighted.

Section One

This part of the questionnaire asks you to describe your job as objectively as you can.

Please do not use this part of the questionnaire to show how much you like or dislike your job. Questions about that will come later. Instead, try to make your descriptions as accurate and as objective as you possibly can.

A sample question follows:

To what extent does your job require you to work with mechanical equipment?

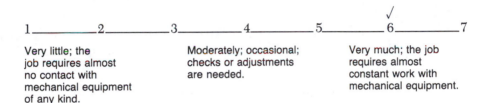

You are to *mark the number* that is the most accurate description of your job. If, for example, your job requires you to work with mechanical equipment a good deal of the time—but also requires some paperwork—you might mark the number six, as was done in the example above.

1. To what extent does your job require you to work closely with other people, either clients or people in related jobs, in your own organization?

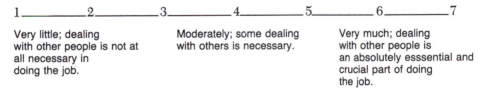

2. How much autonomy is there in your job? That is, to what extent does your job permit you to decide on your own how to go about doing the work?

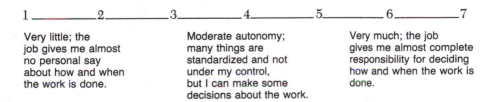

3. To what extent does your job involve doing a whole and identifiable piece of work? That is, is the job a complete piece of work that has an obvious beginning and end? Or is it only a small part of the overall piece of work, which is finished by other people or by automatic machines?

1_____2_____3_____4_____5_____6_____7

| My job is only a tiny part of the overall piece of work; the results of my activities cannot be seen in the final product or service. | My job is a; moderate-sized chunk of the overall piece of work; my own contribution can be seen in the final outcome. | My job involves doing the whole piece of work, from start to finish; the results of my activities are easily seen in the final product or service. |

4. How much variety is there in your job? That is, to what extent does the job require you to do many different things at work, using a variety of your skills and talents?

1_____2_____3_____4_____5_____6_____7

| Very little; the job requires me to do the same routine things over and over again. | Moderate variety. | Very much; the job requires me to do many different things, using a number of different skills and talents. |

5. In general, how significant or important is your job? That is, are the results of your work likely to affect significantly the lives or well-being of other people?

1_____2_____3_____4_____5_____6_____7

| Not very significant; the outcomes of my work are not likely to have important effects on other people. | Moderately significant. | Highly significant; the outcomes of my work can affect other people in very important ways. |

6. To what extent do managers or co-workers let you know how well you are doing on your job?

1_____2_____3_____4_____5_____6_____7

| Very little; people almost never let me know how well I am doing. | Moderately; sometimes people may give me feedback; other times they may not. | Very much; managers or co-workers provide me with almost constant feedback about how well I am doing. |

7. To what extent does doing the job itself provide you with information about your work performance? That is, does the actual work itself provide clues about how well you are doing—aside from any feedback co-workers or supervisors may provide?

1_____2_____3_____4_____5_____6_____7

| Very little; the job itself is set up so I could work forever without finding out how well I am doing. | Moderately; sometimes doing the job provides feedback to me; sometimes it does not. | Very much; the job is set up so that I get almost constant feedback as I work about how well I am doing. |

Section Two

Listed below are a number of statements that could be used to describe a job. You are to indicate whether each statement is an accurate or an inaccurate description of your job. Once again, please try to be as objective as you can in deciding how accurately each statement describes your job—regardless of whether you like or dislike your job.

Write a number in the blank beside each statement, based on the following scale: *How accurate is the statement in describing your job?* 1, very inaccurate; 2, mostly inaccurate; 3, slightly inaccurate; 4, uncertain; 5, slightly accurate; 6, mostly accurate; 7, very accurate.

_____ 1. The job requires me to use a number of complex or high-level skills.

_____ 2. The job requires a lot of cooperative work with other people.

_____ 3. The job is arranged so that I do not have the chance to do an entire piece of work from beginning to end.

_____ 4. Just doing the work required by the job provides many chances for me to figure out how well I am doing.

_____ 5. The job is quite simple and repetitive.

_____ 6. The job can be done adequately by a person working alone—without talking to or checking with other people.

_____ 7. The supervisors and co-workers on this job almost never give me any feedback about how well I am doing my work.

_____ 8. This job is one where a lot of other people can be affected by how well the work gets done.

_____ 9. The job denies me any chance to use my personal initiative or judgment in carrying out the work.

_____ 10. Supervisors often let me know how well they think I am performing the job.

_____ 11. The job provides me the chance to finish completely the pieces of work I begin.

_____ 12. The job itself provides very few clues about whether or not I am performing well.

_____ 13. The job gives me considerable opportunity for independence and freedom in how I do the work.

_____ 14. The job itself is not very significant or important in the broader scheme of things.

Section Three

Now please indicate how you personally feel about your job. Each of the following statements is something a person might say about his or her job. You are to indicate your own personal feelings about your job by marking how much you agree with each of the statements.

Write a number in the blank for each statement, based on this scale: *How much do you agree with the statement?* 1, disagree strongly; 2, disagree; 3, disagree slightly; 4, neutral; 5, agree slightly; 6, agree; 7, agree strongly.

_____ 1. My opinion of myself goes up when I do this job well.
_____ 2. Generally speaking, I am very satisfied with this job.
_____ 3. I feel a great sense of personal satisfaction when I do this job well.
_____ 4. I frequently think of quitting this job.
_____ 5. I feel bad and unhappy when I discover that I have performed poorly on this job.
_____ 6. I am generally satisfied with the kind of work I do in this job.
_____ 7. My own feelings generally are not affected much one way or the other by how well I do on this job.

Section Four

Now please indicate how satisfied you are with each aspect of your job listed below. Once again, write the appropriate number in the blank beside each statement, based on this scale: *How satisfied are you with this aspect of your job?* 1, extremely dissatisfied; 2, dissatisfied; 3, slightly dissatisfied; 4, neutral; 5, slightly satisfied; 6, satisfied; 7, extremely satisfied.

_____ 1. The amount of job security I have.
_____ 2. The amount of pay and fringe benefits I receive.
_____ 3. The amount of personal growth and development I get in doing my job.
_____ 4. The people I talk to and work with on my job.
_____ 5. The degree of respect and fair treatment I receive from my boss.
_____ 6. The feeling of worthwhile accomplishment I get from doing my job.
_____ 7. The chance to get to know other people while on the job.
_____ 8. The amount of support and guidance I receive from my supervisor.
_____ 9. The degree to which I am fairly paid for what I contribute to this organization.
_____ 10. The amount of independent thought and action I can exercise in my job.
_____ 11. How secure things look for me in the future of this organization.
_____ 12. The chance to help other people while at work.
_____ 13. The amount of challenge in my job.
_____ 14. The overall quality of the supervision I receive in my work.

Section Five

Listed below are a number of characteristics that could be present on any job. People differ about how much they would like to have each one present in their own jobs. We are interested in learning how much you personally would like to have each one present in your job.

Using the scale below, please indicate the degree to which you would like to have each characteristic present in your job. *Note:* The numbers on this scale are different from those used in previous scales.

4_____5_____6_____7_____8_____9_____10

| Would like having this only a moderate amount (or less). | Would like having this very much. | Would like having this extremely much. |

____ 1. High respect and fair treatment from my supervisor.
____ 2. Stimulating and challenging work.
____ 3. Chances to exercise independent thought and action in my job.
____ 4. Great job security.
____ 5. Very friendly coworkers.
____ 6. Opportunities to learn new things from my work.
____ 7. High salary and good fringe benefits.
____ 8. Opportunities to be creative and imaginative in my work.
____ 9. Quick promotions.
____ 10. Opportunities for personal growth and development in my job.
____ 11. A sense of worthwhile accomplishment in my work.

B. Scoring

I. Job Dimensions
  A. Skill Variety
  B. Task Identity
  C. Task Significance
  D. Autonomy
  E. Feedback from the Job Itself
  F. Feedback from Agents
  G. Dealing with Others
II. Affective Response to the Job
  A. General Satisfaction
  B. Internal Work Satisfaction
  C. Specific Satisfactions (pay, security, social, supervision, growth opportunity)
III. Individual Growth-Needs Strength
IV. Motivating Potential Score

Scoring Key for the Short Form of the Job Diagnostic Survey

Each variable measured by the JDS short form is listed below, along with (1) a one- or two-sentence description of the variable and (2) a list of the questionnaire items that are averaged to yield a summary score for the variables.

I. Job Dimensions: Objective Characteristics of the Job Itself

   A. *Skill variety*   The degree to which a job requires a variety of different activities in carrying out the work, which involve the use of a number of different skills and talents of the employee. Average the following items (note the items where reversed scoring is used, that is, subtract the number entered by the respondent from eight (8):

> Section One   #4
> Section Two   #1
>   #5 (use reversed scoring)

   B. *Task identity*   The degree to which the job requires the completion of a whole and identifiable piece of work, that is, doing a job from beginning to end with a visible outcome. Average the following items (note reversed scoring):

> Section One   #3
> Section Two   #11
>   #3 (use reversed scoring)

   C. *Task significance*   The degree to which the job has a substantial impact on the lives or work of other people—whether in the immediate organization or in the external environment. Average the following items (note reversed scoring);

> Section One   #5
> Section Two   #8
>   #14 (use reversed scoring)

   D. *Autonomy*   The degree to which the job provides substantial freedom, independence, and discretion to the employee in scheduling his or her work and in determining the procedures to be used in carrying it out. Average the following items (reversed scoring):

> Section One   #2
> Section Two   #13
>   #9 (use reversed scoring)

E. *Feedback from the job itself* The degree to which carrying out the work activities required by the job results in the employee obtaining information about the effectiveness of his or her performance. Average the following items (reversed scoring):

> Section One   #7
> Section Two   #4
>   #12 (use reversed scoring)

F. *Feedback from agents* The degree to which the employee receives information about his or her performance effectiveness from supervisors or from co-workers. (This construct is *not* a job characteristic per se and is included only to provide information supplementary to construct E above.) Average the following items (reversed scoring):

> Section One   #6
> Section Two   #10
>   #7 (use reversed scoring)

G. *Dealing with others* The degree to which the job requires the employee to work closely with other people (whether other organization members or organizational clients). Average the following items (reversed scoring):

> Section One   #1
> Section Two   #2
>   #6 (use reversed scoring)

II. Affective Response to the Job

The affective reactions or feelings an employee gets from working on his or her job.

A. *General satisfaction* An overall measure of the degree to which the employee is satisfied and happy in his or her work. Average items 2, 4*, and 6 from Section Three (*reversed scoring).

B. *Internal work motivation* The degree to which the employee is self-motivated to perform effectively on the job. Average items 1, 3, 5, and 7* from Section Three (*reversed scoring).

C. *Specific satisfactions* These short scales tap several specific aspects of the employee's job satisfaction.

1. Pay satisfaction: Average items 2 and 9 of Section Four.
2. Security satisfaction: Average items 1 and 11 of Section Four.
3. Social satisfaction: Average items 4, 7, and 12 of Section Four.
4. Supervisory satisfaction: Average items 5, 8, and 14 of Section Four.
5. Growth satisfaction: Average items 3, 6, 10, and 13 of Section Four.

III. Individual Growth-Need Strength

This scale taps the degree to which an employee has a strong desire to obtain growth satisfactions from his or her work. Average the following six items from Section Five. Before averaging, subtract 3 from each item score; this will result in a summary scale ranging from 1 to 7. The items are 2, 3, 6, 8, 10 and 11.

IV. Motivating Potential Score

A score reflecting the potential of a job for eliciting positive internal work motivation on the part of employees (especially those with high desire for growth need satisfaction) is given below:

$$\begin{matrix}\text{Motivating} \\ \text{Potential} \\ \text{Score (MPS)}\end{matrix} = \frac{\begin{matrix}\text{Skill} \\ \text{Variety}\end{matrix} + \begin{matrix}\text{Task} \\ \text{Identity}\end{matrix} + \begin{matrix}\text{Task} \\ \text{Significance}\end{matrix}}{3} \times [\text{Autonomy}] \times \begin{bmatrix}\text{Feedback} \\ \text{from the} \\ \text{Job}\end{bmatrix}$$

3

Corporate Culture
Viewed Strategically

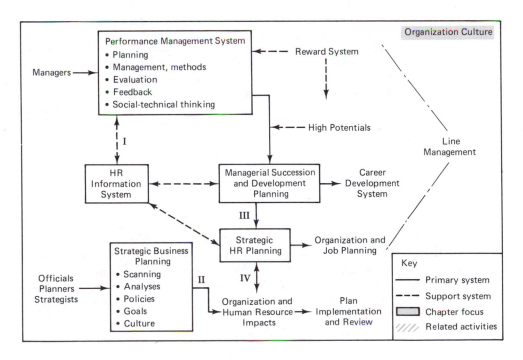

The rapid popularization of "corporate culture" in business literature led many officials and policymakers to believe that at long last a universal remedy or cure was at hand. It is extraordinary indeed that for years human resource (HR) officials had tried to get the attention and active involvement of policymakers in human resource matters and now HR officials are being called into the president's or CEO's office and told "let's get into corporate culture." Thomas Peters's and Robert Waterman's revelation that successful companies had strong corporate cultures in part explains this "turning of the tables." Senior officials found it easy to identify with company incidents that legitimized corporate heroes, picnics, friendly poker games, locker-room stories, and once-a-year (dull) speeches. Actions seen as irrational by outside standards are all right for the company because "that's the way we do it here!"

Of course, many ignore the fact that a strong culture may at times prove to be undesirable for the company as is brought out in the following experiences.

Milkin and Brown (M&B) was a highly reputable general management consulting organization. Although perceived by other consultants and even its clients as rather conservative, the reputation it enjoyed was a good one. The founding partners were still actively involved in the business, though almost 30 additional partners had been taken into the business and offices opened elsewhere in the United States, Canada, and Australia. M&B's culture manifested itself in numerous ways. The partners dressed conservatively. In their new consultant's indoctrination program, lasting three days, they stressed "careful and thoughtful analysis of client problems and leaning on the quality and weight of information gathered. Avoid speculation! Wherever possible, firm up your information and be sure *before* you make client recommendations." The indoctrination program included many client situations built around case studies with the different partners discussing how these were diagnosed and written up for client presentations. M&B also stressed a group project approach with balanced representation from various functional fields of management (e.g., marketing, finance). Consensing was important. If a consultant survived to her or his third year with the firm, that individual was deeply steeped in M&B's ways of consulting and client management.

As a final note regarding the M&B firm; its internal management formula worked for many years, but its leadership had much difficulty in refocusing to the needs of newer types of clients, some of whom were used to faster-moving and changing business and competitive environments. These clients felt that M&B's approaches were too conservative, took too long to reach solutions, and frequently lacked contingency programs for changed circumstances. However, this company's negative experience with corporate culture is far distant from the highly positive ones at NPC, Inc. (New Product Concepts).

Mary Murphy was among the very few women completing an MBA in the early 1960s. She had always worked during her school years and had a rich and varied series of part-time experiences in waitressing, credit collections, setting up point-of-sales displays, and market research. After completing her graduate work, she spent a few years working for a large consumer products firm since this seemed to fit well with her "double major" in marketing and management. However, she was restless to advance her career and felt that too many obstacles to mobility existed in the company, "they were just discovering women in their work force, let alone in management."

Through some friends of her father, she was able to secure financing for starting a new business. Her concept was that many household and personal consumer products had pretty well run their course. The way was clear for a fast-moving, flexible type of organization that could develop and distribute "new concept" products. Thus the company name, New Product Concepts (NPC) was created to signal a break with tradition and the "arrival" of new(er) products which fit in with the life-styles of younger men and women. NPC's personal care products became almost instant hits because of their high and rigid quality standards, excellence in (convenience) packaging, and aggressive sales and advertising approaches.

From the beginning of her company, Mary had determined that she would have to seek out people who were both creative and adaptable to what surely would be a fast-moving period of activities and changes. As for the organization, she was sensitive to the need to support conscientiously internal structures, processes, and programs that would back up NPC's marketing philosophy and concepts.

NPC's first five years were very difficult for Mary. There were many times when she had to pause to ask whether it was worth it. The organization at first was moving counter to mainstream directions in almost all respects. Private label manufacturers, chain store buyers, and even owners of specialty shops strongly resisted the product line and marketing tactics of NPC. Yet despite the difficulties, progress was made, and out of these organizational and marketing conditions a closely knit group of key people emerged. They had shared both troubles and triumphs and even periods when payroll was "delayed" (until some large bills were paid).

In subsequent years the company grew rapidly. Although the employee group increased several times over, and a network of franchised "House Hostesses" was added to the picture, NPC infused a tremendous sense of enthusiasm, loyalty, and company identification. The original core group of key people formed a solid base for subsequent organizational growth. Strong company identification emerged from a variety of activities and relationships. Company insistence on minimizing paperwork and harnessing (computer) technology to serve company members (rather than vice versa!), plus frequent direct contacts, helped to assure people staying abreast of current and newer developments. "Real" recognition awards for achievements, company parties, "valued" prizes for accomplishments including time off, were a few of the ways that company solidarity grew. At NPC's twentieth birthday party, Mary Murphy enthusiastically anticipated a continuation of the excitement and profitable growth that characterized its preceding years.

To an important extent, the development of corporate culture reflects the intermingling of various social science concepts, and the views of experienced organizational researchers and seasoned organization members. For example, the social anthropologist thinks of culture as an integrated pattern of human behavior that includes values, customs, rituals, and artifacts. Norms of behavior are deeply rooted and take years, decades, or even centuries to unfold in society. Culture, in the general sense, depends on people's capacity for learning and transmitting knowledge to succeeding generations.

Being accepted into a culture is (or "should be") its own reward, for it brings the privileges of membership: acceptance, identification, recognition, and social and psychological support. However, the reward of "just being accepted" as a member of a given organization, especially a business-oriented one, is not as compelling for most people as the awarding of organizational power, status, and income. And yet there are parallels between the general societal model and the organizational model.

These common ideas form the basis for an organizational model of culture which can serve important strategic purposes:

- An integrated pattern of human behavior in which membership per se is valued.
- Membership in the culture as a form of reward for the person because it provides a sense of belonging or identification and protection against adverse (external) incidents or forces.
- Valued association of participants built on a foundation of shared values, customs, rituals, and artifacts.
- Solidification of values which govern important behavior over an extended time period.
- Individual (and organizational) learning as a basis for bringing people into the culture and for survival—adaptation to needed change.
- Suitable communications media for knowledge transmission to future generations (new culture/organization members).
- Appropriate reinforcement by values, rituals, artifacts, and leadership actions with which members can identify.
- Member behavior that is consonant with a desire to preserve membership in the (organization or) culture.

This chapter deals with corporate culture in the context of strategic human resource thinking: what it is, how it relates to the strategic management development of human resources, and how it can be used. It also provides some case studies illustrating practical and positive ways of dealing with or using corporate culture. Organization culture, as a part of a modern comprehensive approach to strategic organizational planning for performance, is presented in an application section.

Organizational Adaptations of the Culture Idea

An understanding of culture in general makes possible the more critical consideration of organization culture. It is recognized that values gradually emerge in organizations which define success, the actions needed to achieve it, and the heroes who
personify the values and expected behavior. Key values are reinforced by rites and
rituals and transmitted through communications, work, and informal relationships.
Terrence Deal and Allan Kennedy in their book on *Corporate Cultures* (1982) talk
about the insights and understandings of policymakers, officials, and organization
members which are prerequisite to establishing a viable organization's culture.
These understandings build on insights as to how the external business environment interacts with successful corporate actions/behaviors.

Edgar H. Schein (of M.I.T.), based on his years of study and familiarity with
organizations, proposed that organization cultures pattern the basic assumptions
developed by the group (or organization) in learning to cope with its environment.
Coping actions initially require conscious adaptation to environmental developments, both opportunities and/or threats. These are then integrated with internal
structures, systems, processes, and behaviors that work well and that help to assure
continuity and organizational renewal. Structure, systems, processes, and behaviors
are validated by valued results, and they come to serve as ways to perceive problems, issues, plans, policies, and strategies in future actions. Many of these are then
internalized, and subsequently organization members may respond to specific situations in particular ways without even realizing the "why" of their response.

Some of the central ideas of corporate culture are diagrammed in Exhibit 3-1.
The points made in the diagram reflect the following time sequence of events,
factors, and relationships:

1. Business environment, comprising various economic, social, and political
   forces, is a basic source of factors and changes (eventually) leading to the
   definition of culture.
2. Opportunities and threats to corporate leaders presented by the environment.
3. Organization's founders/leaders—they provided the assumptions or "theories"
   as to how things work, and bases for behavior, relationships, and performance.
4. Philosophy and strategies developed by founder(s) to exploit or deal with the
   situation they perceived.
5. Formal processes and behaviors which incorporated a growing body of values
   and behavioral guides which served as the gradual fleshing out of the organization's philosophy, values, and desired behaviors ("culture").
6. Adoptive processes and behaviors developed over time reflecting preferred
   leadership role, attributes, and approaches. These increasingly come to serve
   as models of valued/desired behavior. Understandably, these also cover an
   ever-widening scope of organizational actions, including planning, decision
   making at all levels, and many functional activities.

EXHIBIT 3-1
Emergence of Corporate Culture

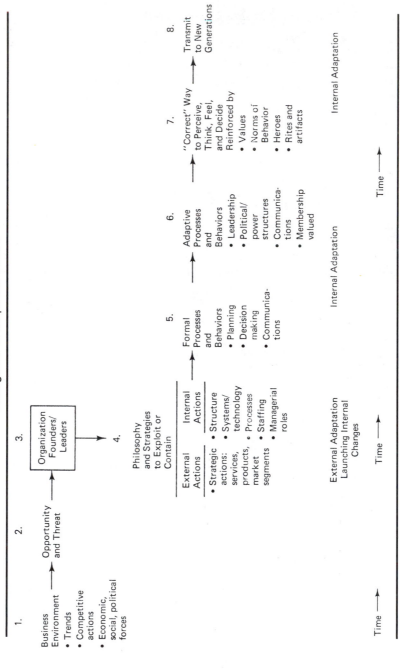

1.

Business
Environment
• Trends
• Competitive
  actions
• Economic,
  social, political
  forces

2.

Opportunity
and Threat

3.

Organization
Founders/
Leaders

4.

Philosophy
and Strategies
to Exploit or
Contain

External Actions	Internal Actions
• Strategic actions: services, products, market segments	• Structure • Systems/ technology • Processes • Staffing • Managerial roles

External Adaptation
Launching Internal
Changes

Time ⟶

5.

Formal
Processes
and
Behaviors
• Planning
• Decision
  making
• Communica-
  tions

6.

Adaptive
Processes
and
Behaviors
• Leadership
• Political/
  power
  structures
• Communica-
  tions
• Membership
  valued

Internal Adaptation

Time ⟶

7.

"Correct" Way
to Perceive,
Think, Feel,
and Decide
Reinforced by
• Values
• Norms of
  Behavior
• Heroes
• Rites and
  artifacts

8.

Transmit
to New
Generations

Internal Adaptation

Time ⟶

7. "Correct" ways to perceive, think, and feel about organizational matters, reinforced by rites/rituals and people who became the organization's heroes.
8. Transmission to new generations of the organization's culture and/or values. Modification is only allowed after extended validation experiences. This assures slow change and adaptation, increasing the chances for organizational survival, continuity, and renewal.

The elements in Exhibit 3-1 provide some of the basics of organization culture formation. The ways organization culture can be applied to human resources and strategic management development are discussed in the following sections.

Organization Culture and Its Human Resource and Strategic Dimensions

To the extent that an "organization's culture" has been defined, it can serve as a (remarkable) framework within which to view human resource and strategic planning events.

1. *Employee recruitment and initial expectations.* The ability of managerial recruits to blend into the organization often revolves around "cultural" issues like dress, mannerisms, working hours, equality of treatment, reward structures, and the organization's commitment to training/development. When people face the employment decision, virtually anybody is willing to "waive" some personal preferences, or even perceived mismatches, to join an organization. However, there is a critical set of behaviors which will be required if the person is to be accepted and promoted.
2. *Assessment of political and promotion decisions.* The informal agenda used for the appraisal and assessment of performance includes how well a person demonstrates understanding of the core values and accepted behaviors of an organization. These are aside from technical and/or managerial skills factors, which are the most common part of performance approaches.
3. *Management development programming.* An essential part of coaching by senior people is seeking to cultivate subordinate abilities and "organizational finesse." The latter is concerned with such things as "the way things work" and "who to talk to to get things done." Thus, cultural considerations become woven into the fabric of functional responsibilities and actions. Senior managers also serve as behavior models for various decision-making situations.
4. *Career paths and valued experiences.* Certain types of work experiences are more important than others for promoting upward mobility. Many paths may provide upward movement, but most often a characteristic pattern of functional experiences and time in grade identify the "comer" or the high-potential person. Time and experience provide a *surer* path to senior, or valued, positions for the person cognizant of the culture.

5. *Managerial (executive) decision making.* The preferred mode for executive decision making is often reflected in the handling of uncertainty; the amount, quality, and timeliness of information used; and specific types of alternatives considered. This is especially apparent in planning- or policy-related decisions where qualitative or objective information must be balanced.

"Organization Culture": Do You Have One?

An organization's culture is fun to discuss at company events and perhaps even to reminisce about at stockholder meetings. However, the general subject of *organization culture* has little to do with the strategic aspects of management development. If organization culture is to serve as a useful guide and reference framework for viewing management development in a human resource planning and strategic framework, it must be

- Modeled by the organization leader(s) and chief powerholders.
- Consistently identifiable by key organization leaders and senior managers.
- Working well over an extended time interval.
- Perceived as the correct or preferred way that organization members view, feel, and think about problems and situations.
- Regularly reinforced through leadership behaviors, ceremonies, and artifacts so as to sustain the essence of the critical behaviors over time.
- Adaptable to needed changes to assure organizational survival, growth, and renewal.

To some degree all organizations have a culture of sorts, but the fact that this culture lacks predictability of behaviors, cohesion, or continuity over time substantially reduces its utility for management development. Moreover, it often is unclear whether a particular cultural configuration best lends itself to high performance levels! That is, as brought out earlier, even if the culture is a strong one, it may have adverse organization or individual consequences.

A format for making assessments of organizational culture is provided in the application section of this chapter (Exhibit 3-7). A variety of forms have been used in attempting to gather information on an organization's culture (climate), some of which are referenced in the company examples which follow. These short case examples (as opposed to forms) have been included here rather than in the applications section because the definition and application of organizational culture is still in a fluid state and thus part of the main picture. Because of its formative state, organization culture applications must be approached in a thoughtful and critical way.

It will be apparent in reviewing Exhibit 3-7 (applications section, this chapter) that precise definitions and numerical evaluation have been avoided. For a complex issue like organization culture, a qualitative assessment may provide the greatest understanding of what exists in a company. We have found the greatest benefits from a format of this type in which senior executives and managers initially assess these points independently of each other. Group discussion of individual views of cultural factors create spirited exchanges, often requiring several sessions. In any case, organization cultures differ, and each organization must decide for itself the extent to which these factors exist and their strength (Section A of Exhibit 3-7), how pervasive these are (Section B), and the extent to which they integrate work, social, and behavioral processes.

The Normative Side of "Organization Culture" Assessments.   The type of rating form in Exhibit 3-7 has limited utility unless the assessors also consider "what should ideally exist." One side of the picture is that a strong culture can project considerable corporate identification, spirit, and individual willingness to go the extra distance. It can reduce wheel spinning, increase people's confidence (certainly) in the rightness of actions, and substantially improve recruiting effectiveness and efficiency. It is often an informal but key basis for acceptance to the inner power circle. But a strong culture may also repel newer values of behavior, dress, or other important social changes already important in society generally.

How long a company should preserve its culture and when it should try to modify or shift cultural anchor points is a tough issue for review by corporate leadership. If an increasing number of high-potential people are being lost or are turning down what otherwise appears to be attractive offers, maybe it is high time that a corporation look inward. If indicators such as profit or loss, turnover, absenteeism, poor cooperation, or pervasive bad-mouthing of the company exists, deep-seated internal problems may call for a critical examination of the corporation's culture. An example of corporate culture at work follows.

Formalizing Corporate Culture Indoctrination

Corporate culture sometimes just happens, but in some companies such as Hewlett-Packard (H-P), organization culture has been a conscious design. They have made it a tangible and recognizable part of employee relationships, decision style, and specific events with which people identify. H-P is a good example of a corporation which took specific steps to concretize its sense of a corporate culture. It is one which features *shared beliefs, values,* and *assumptions* as to how to do things, ranging from personal relationships to decision making. Its culture also contained many informal guidelines or rules which channeled behaviors much of the time.

The "H-P Way" of doing things probably best summarizes the various and diverse behaviors that the founders, Dave Packard and Bill Hewlett helped to infuse in their business. Their sense of faith in people, an intangible feeling of how to approach particular situations and people staying in touch with things by "wandering around," involved both formal and informal processes—the H-P way of doing things. Well-known stories and their telling, as for example, about the partners' founding of the company, trade-offs of (short-run) corporate profit to achieve higher quality, and layoff avoidance even in the face of declining business, were characteristic of their culture. These stories were anchored in the minds of H-P members. The key historical events, behavior models, and ways of approaching situations were passed onto a new generation of employees. Communications of these stories was reinforced through internal house organs, meetings, presentations at special events, speeches, daily conversations, and new employee orientation. But the limitations of person-to-person recitals became apparent as the organization became increasingly complex. Thus, the increasing reliance on formalizing approaches. The conduct of formal training sessions in H-P methods and values and executive seminars provided solid and more assured means of defining the "H-P way" (of conducting business). Even this effort, however, was improved through the creation of a modular course describing work at H-P. As many as 16 contact hours could be "taken" in this program and substantial numbers of its total employee group were exposed. Included in the course were involvement of senior managers and personnel, question and answer sessions, telling of the history and corporate accomplishments, and hands-on exercises. Modules also included descriptions of personnel policies and practices and bases for evaluating performance.

Some examples of experiences with organization cultural analysis follow. They illustrate the complexity of the issues. Some of the approaches taken to better understand and deal with particular decisions are given.

Case 1: A Survey Study of Organization "Culture"

The following discussion involves a company in existence for over 20 years that found the need to assess certain management problems which had arisen. A survey study was undertaken in an attempt to evaluate how major organizational changes had affected "culture" and its potential impact on managerial behavior.

Background.   Thompson Insurance* was a successful full-line insurance company with over 7,000 employees. Over the years, a highly qualified nucleus of key salespeople provided the basis for product line development and continuous growth. Prudent financial management and a succession of strong and gifted officers had provided the necessary guidance for profitable performance. In the 1970s, however, it became apparent that the organizational solidarity for which the company had become known was developing some serious flaws.

The hard-driving salesmanship and executive leadership characteristic of the period from 1950 to the mid-1970s was not adequate for the numbers and types of issues found in the 1980s. Myriad problems started to surface at *all* organizational levels, including turnover among high performers, individual dissatisfaction with career progress, varying standards of performance, and a seeming inability to mount a thoughtful and well-coordinated management development program.

In previous years, line management served as the core of company operations

---

*Disguised to preserve the identity of the company.

and assumed key responsibility for individual development as it was needed. Corporate-level personnel handled mostly routine maintenance functions such as salary administration and overseeing headquarters' staff. The growing number of personnel-related problems prompted top management to reorganize the Personnel Department with the intention of strengthening it. The corporate level hiring of a manager of human resource development (HRD) was an unprecedented move for the organization, it being the first time that an outsider was brought into the corporate-level Personnel Department. Also, the "human resource" designation was intended as a signal to the organization that new and important changes were forthcoming. However, four years were required to attend to basic personnel matters before a corporatewide program of human resources development was initiated.

The growing attention given to organization culture studies suggested an approach to the HRD manager for diagnosing problems that might prove useful for future planning strategies. The Thompson culture study acknowledged the people orientation of the company. A portion of it was devoted to morale. The second, and major, part of the study was concerned with management styles and the credibility of managerial behaviors and decision actions. Thus, Thompson's culture study sought to define pragmatic issues with which key managers could identify.

There was no question that the transmittors of the organization's culture were the tenured senior management group. They had a major employment and financial stake in the company. The entire group, some 400, were surveyed on a voluntary basis; over 90 percent participated.

The manager of HRD, knowing how key company people were likely to react to the company survey figures, took care to collect information on other companies which could be used by the senior people for comparative purposes. People at Thompson, and elsewhere for that matter, placed a lot of credibility in figures showing how they compared to others (their industry generally and similar companies in other industries). In fact, the availability of comparative figures influenced their decisions to go forward with (or to drop) some topics. The agreed-upon format for the study generated data (1) specific to Thompson and (2) comparisons with other insurance companies and other types of companies as well.

Study Results.   The main areas of managerial study were organized around morale, planning, and managerial performance.

Morale

- Overall assessment
- People orientation
- Provision of a sense of security

Planning and Performance

- Existence of a performance ethic
- Perception of desire for change

- Clarity of corporate goals and the means to achieve them
- Assignment of responsibilities for goal accomplishment
- Formulation and implementation of decisions
- Relation of daily decisions to long(er)-term goals or objectives
- Effectiveness with which decisions were implemented
- Commitment and support of major decisions by unit heads or managers

Discussion of the Thompson Study Results.　　The following comments parallel the presentation of the study results in Exhibit 3-2. Note, this exhibit includes two different types of figures: percentiles, indicating the percentage of companies with lower results (columns 1 and 2), and percentages (column 3), indicating the percentage of Thompson managers "very strongly" or "strongly" agreeing.

> *Morale.* Thompson's managerial group clearly liked to work at the company and displayed a strength of conviction much beyond other enterprises including other insurance companies. Thompson's orientation to its people was undoubtedly a key factor in the managers' strong overall morale assessment. Thompson was also seen as providing a great deal of security compared to enterprises in general (85th percentile) and compared to other insurance companies (65th percentile).

> *Planning and Performance.* Concerning the tasks, relationships, procedures, and standards associated with a contemporary, profit-oriented culture, Thompson managers saw their organization as deficient in these areas. According to their key managers, the company did *not* project a strong performance ethic. Three-fourths of other companies were seen as stronger in this factor. Although the key company people were aware of the low performance ethic, the motivation or sense of urgency for change was lacking. The requisite skills for building clear organizational goals, precise profit objectives, and the means for achieving these were lacking. The company was at the midpoint or the lower one-third of both comparison groups on these factors.

Meeting the emergent competitive demands while maintaining profit levels of past operations indicated the need for a *comprehensive* organizational effort. Planning had to be supported by thoughtful strategic analyses and sound follow-up programming. Unfortunately, the deficiencies perceived by managers in goal and strategy setting, and the general tone, carried over into programming areas. Relatively poor organization or lack of accountability, lack of coordination of major decisions with planning activities and day-to-day decisions, and poor efforts at implementation (including timing) were major issues highlighted by the management group. Perhaps the single most important factor underlying all the planning and performance comments was the belief by fully half the managers that there was little or no commitment to decisions, even after they had been made! It was understandable that change without notification of those affected would undermine confidence considerably. It is interesting to note that to some degree the managers were describing themselves as well as policymakers and higher-level personnel.

Some Inferences of Study Results.　　Thompson's approach to studying its culture made it clear to top executives that there were many different ideas as to what it was. Managers were pragmatic and performance oriented. Of all possible

EXHIBIT 3-2

Thompson's Culture as Seen by Its Senior Management:
Survey Results

Items	Company vs. general industry results (% of companies lower) (1)	Company vs. other insurance companies* (% of companies lower) (2)	Company only† (% agreeing) (3)
Morale			
Overall assessment	80%	75%	60%
Orientation to people	70	65	
Provision of a sense of security	85	65	
Planning and Performance			
Existence of a performance ethic	20	25	
Perception of desire for change	30	50	
Clarity of corporate goals	35	40	
Clarity of means to achieve goals	50	55	
Clear assignment of responsibilities for goal accomplishment	—	—	45
Formulation and implemention decisions	30	50	
Relation of daily decisions to long(er)-term goals or objectives	—	—	40
Effectiveness with which decisions are implemented	30	65	
Commitment and support of major decisions by units	—	—	50

*Numbers are based on percentiles and show percentage (%) of companies that scored lower. Thus a percentile score of 80 shows that 80 percent of the group scored lower than Thompson and/or Thompson scored higher than 80 percent of the group.
†Percentage with very strong or strong agreement.

culture-related factors, those with a "bottom-line" orientation held the biggest attraction. Yet the very cultural features that contributed to its successes in the past, including pragmatism and independence in actions, were proving increasingly dysfunctional in a world of changes and competitive challenges. The spirit of managerial independence and the idea of the company as a "good place to work" had not been adjusted in a timely way. The internal climate and the "Thompson way of doing things" needed overhauling—a difficult task with major consequences.

Study Instruments. The instrumentation used in the Thompson study was useful to them to the extent that it provided comparative data and a perspective on vital managerial functions. Many points concerned the senior management group, and they struck home. However, the diagnosis of the underlying problems and issues was complex. The study helped to identify problems which in turn led to more in-depth analyses. Instrumentation useful in more comprehensive approaches included those developed by Harry Levinson (1972), or Van de Ven and Ferry (1980), or Lawler et al. (1980).

Another example of an instrument used to gather valuable internal data regarding managerial orientations, and the organization type of management perceived to exist, is facilitated by the tools shown in Exhibit 3-7 of the applications section. This particular form is based in part on the climate analysis of Litwin and Stringer (1968) and the managerial assessment style of Margerison (1979). We have used these types of tools with individual organization members and executive officers to help in establishing "where we are" and "where we want to go" from the viewpoint of cultural values or managerial styles. These descriptors can also be grouped to suggest the overall sense of organization structure and the degree of individual flexibility, participation, and communications processes these imply (Exhibit 3-8 in the applications section). Wallach (1983) and Margerison provide a good discussion of the managerial styles as suggested by these analyses.

Case 2: "A Change of Focus"*

Of the organizations currently undergoing "large-scale change and cultural adaptation," the most outstanding example occurred in the early 1980s, namely, the court-ordered dissolution of AT&T and the subsequent formation of various regionally based enterprises and a successor AT&T corporate unit. Certain organization descriptions in this narrative have been changed to preserve the anonymity of the particular regional company member involved.

Background. In less than 18 months, the total employment of one of the regional companies was reduced by almost 40 percent. One-half of the displaced employees were transferred to AT&T operations, and the remaining either took early retirement or were laid off over an extended time period. In a matter of months, the organization structure for this regionally based business was formalized. Even more dramatic than the structural changes was the new mission of the regional corporations "conferred" on them by the dissolution orders. The basic mission shifted from one of telephone utility monopoly to one of competition in the

---

*The views and interpretations expressed in this case are those of the writer and don't necessarily reflect the company's official position or statement on these matters.

communications and information processing field, and many other competitors moved rapidly into the markets of the old "Bell System." The services, staff capabilities, decision-making and planning capabilities, and activities of the regional corporations were separated from the former parent. Each of the new regionally based corporations included varying numbers of the previously existing Bell Company members. Redefinition of regional corporate missions plus competitive, economic, and technological changes had a major impact on regional structures, systems, processes, and needed behaviors. The focus and direction of the internal changes in the regional units, however, had to be worked out in detail and appropriate strategies developed for the future.

Correspondingly, each of the member companies of a regionally based enterprise had to understand the type of culture that existed in the past and the type that would be preferred in the future. The new(er) cultural form had to be well suited to the member company's changed mission and role as a part of a regional corporate group. As a note of explanation, even under the old AT&T form, Bell companies were organized along individual or multistate lines. However, they assumed their own distinct personalities which reflected that company's leaders, the influence of the area's general social culture, and various historical circumstances, the common communications mission of all of AT&T member units notwithstanding. Thus, the organization of the former AT&T corporation was hardly monolithic. There were many strong cultural features associated with particular units—which had never been formalized for human resource planning purposes.

Various cultural features were quite pronounced in the subject company. They were functional to the extent that they defined the qualifications for "high-potential," modes of expected dress and work behavior, decision patterns, valued performance appraisal factors, and valued patterns of promotion criteria. These culturally based norms and behaviors had developed over a period of many decades, so that virtually every entry of a culture audit (as described earlier in this chapter) could be filled out in specific terms. The company was generally conservative, deliberate, and slow paced with planned changes, and it promoted entirely from within. In contrast, to be able to compete, it was challenged to bring about an internal environment (Exhibit 3-3, step 3) that could be characterized as fast moving, aggressive, encouraging of individual mobility, and more prepared to take risks. Also, high-talent and/or senior personnel needed to be externally recruited— a move virtually without precedent in the past.

Also of interest in these writings is step 2 (Exhibit 3-3) in which Human Resources assumed a greatly expanded role in the corporation. This new role had major implications for strategic processes and managerial development. Also, the orientation of results defining successful performance changed; managers were to be judged increasingly in terms of efficiency (old standard) and effectiveness (e.g., with people), along with both short-term and longer-term (step 4) results. The newer attributes of successful managers, including leadership qualities and performance, illustrates just how greatly the organization mission and redefinition of culture had changed things.

EXHIBIT 3-3

Case 2: Changing Corporate Culture in a Communications Company: A Planning Model for Analysis

Intentional Changes			Performance			
			Efficiency Measures*		Effectiveness Measures*	
			Short Term	Long Term	Short Term	Long Term
• Organization Culture	Policymakers/ Planners	• Redefinition of Valued Behavior and Bases to Judge Successful Performance				
• Structure, Systems, Processes, and Needed Behaviors	→ Human Resource Functions	• Redefinition of What Comprised Valued Leadership and Managerial Qualities—and thus Management Development Approaches	→			
1.	2.	3.	4.			

*General economic measures such as quantity, quality, cost containment, and number of people per limit of time.
*General goal attainment measures with particular emphasis on individuals or groups served or involved (e.g., employees, customers, suppliers, community groups).

Development of New Performance Criteria.　　A feature of Exhibit 3-3, which receives too little attention, is "performance." (This is discussed in added detail in Chapters 2 and 7.) Increasing numbers of companies have come to view performance as having two distinctly different thrusts: *efficiency*—concerned with financial profit, cost, quantity, and quality matters—and *effectiveness*—measures that pertain to securing organization goals and key corporate constituencies (e.g., customer, stockholder, and employee) but that emphasize behavior or satisfaction of their valued needs. A format for summarizing these performance measures is presented in Exhibit 3-4. In sum, these performance criteria represented a radical departure from past patterns of official concern in the communications company. For example, in the past, general "efficiency" criteria centered on financial measures. These justified investment expenditures and rates subject to approval by regulatory bodies. These efficiency measures were also the basis for making its common and preferred stock an attractive investment for trusts and the public at large. Cost justification was, of course, a part of this with "passthrough" of cost increases to the customer. Stockholders were attracted by consistent and secure earning patterns and returns on investment that were also incorporated in the rate base. Efficiency measures were elaborately developed to cover virtually every aspect of cost expenditure or investment. In the effectiveness area, stockholders were

EXHIBIT 3-4

Case 2: Changing Corporate Culture in a Communications Company:
A Planning Format for Short- and Longer-term Results

	New(er) Performance Measures			
	Efficiency		Effectiveness	
Groups Involved	Short Run	Long Run	Short Run	Long Run
• Customers	————	————	————	————
• Organization members				
. Executive	————	————	————	————
. Senior management	————	————	————	————
. Middle management	————	————	————	————
. Supervision	————	————	————	————
. Employee group	————	————	————	————
• Stockholders	————	————	————	————
• Suppliers	————	————	————	————
• Community	————	————	————	————
• Regulatory bodies	————	————	————	————

EXHIBIT 3-5

Case 2: Shifting Mission and Culture and Redefinition of Valued
Managerial Features in the Marketing Function-Selected Ones*

	Old Mission and Culture	New Mission and Culture
Mission	• Being an efficient phone utility within and in response to public regulation.	• Being an efficient and competitive unit in the communications industry plus undertaking other related services providing good long-term possibilities for profits and financial returns.
Planning	• Finance driven with major emphasis on secured rate of return.	• Short and long term, market driven. Returns to investors, increasingly subject to competition.
Organizing	• Classic AT&T mode with some variations reflecting territorial or sectional difference reflecting the number, types of concentration of business and consumer accounts.	• New and innovative-type units with orientations to various customer groups; product considerations, new communications technologies, and interfacing of these with communications operations.
Customer Orientation	• General public relations. • "A complete phone related service" within the constraints of approved, pass-along costs and stockholder returns. • Response on need basis—so long as requests could be meshed with existing structures and systems. • General and institutional.	• Competitive. • Cost consciousness. • Flexible pricing. • Willingness to bid for and take on new communications and information services. • New product/service introductions to meet competitive offerings.
Decision Making	• Prescribed formats. • Narrow band or latitude of activity. • Market research component and information of nominal importance. • Often a formulated approach with company prescribed elements and carefully proscribed boundaries—often	• Entrepreneurial actions encouraged where decision maker must be more aggressive to confront competition. • Market research information and its effective use critical. • Fast-changing conditions required flexible formats for controlling personnel and

EXHIBIT 3-5 (Continued)

	Old Mission and Culture	New Mission and Culture
	entailed highly detailed analyses. • Viewed frequently as "bureaucratic." • Group mode–formal head makes decision.	also for the type of information sought out. • Organic group with spirited discussion sought.
Communications	• Culture dictated, largely along authority lines. • Informal processes reinforced formal authority structure. • Heavy, downward acting.	• Less formal and flexible lines desired. • Growing emphasis on cultivating informal modes and new modes to introduce "valuable" information. • Upward flow consciously encouraged.
Controls	• Formal and cost oriented. • Formal reporting relationships seen as central vehicle and institutionalized. • Nominal customer contacts.	• Multiple formats actively developed with customer contacts seen as indispensable. • Wide use of personnel computers to track changing events and to provide needed guidance for subordinates and information seen as vital to customer development or preservation.

*The views and interpretations expressed in the summary are those of the writer and don't necessarily reflect the company's official position or statement in these matters.

"romanced" with corporate financial information; community awareness was built on a warm and cordial picture of "Ma Bell," and employees attested to the stability and security of employment.

The shift in mission and corporate culture changed all this. The new performance criteria built on the competitive model required a distinctly different orientation affecting all the strategic constituencies making up the effectiveness component (e.g., employees, stockholders, suppliers, and community groups). The types of new behavior patterns illustrated by the exhibit for marketing management (Exhibit 3-5) are representative of these many changes.

The strategic side of management development had the purpose of translating the new mission and culture into specific management behavior patterns. New behavior models were constructed on a foundation of key managerial features which served as a comparative basis for individual needs analysis. These types of features were discussed briefly in Chapter 2 and are discussed in detail in Chapter 4.

Shifting Mission and Culture: Impact on Marketing.   The company's changed culture is illustrated by the changed mission of marketing. In past years, the organization's culture encouraged the soft sell: warm, friendly, technically competent, available when needed, responsive to inquiry, not pushy, and with pricing considerations secondary. Management trainees, as a matter of course, cycled through "customer relations" or marketing units to gain an understanding of customer outlook and needs. Little specific experience or formal education background was needed for this type of assignment. In the past, some areas of marketing required a special background or training in customized communications installations. Technical support as needed was provided by experienced operations personnel or electronics/communications engineers. Also, customized communications frequently involved competitive bidding, but this was a very small part of the total business. This all changed as the new mission (and culture) started to emerge (Exhibit 3-5).

The marketing unit was reorganized and new people were hired who revised mission statements and policies which were distributed to unit members. Although the new marketing strategies were carefully articulated, these were imposed on a company culture deeply rooted in the minds of older corporate members. Successive waves of general managers and marketing managers waded through orientation and strategy sessions, but the knowledge of what needed to be done was confronted by myriad built-in approaches and responses established over decades through the heritage of the (Bell) family. Changes, as a result, were slow in coming.

The difficulty they had instituting new culturally based ideas is yet another example of the powerful hold that culture has and the challenges inherent in bringing about cultural change.

Case 3: Individual Career Actions in a Cultural Context

Organizational career management heavily stresses individual "needs analyses" that take into account three areas of requirements. These are the *organization* (human resource planning, staffing, and strategic requirements), the *job* (responsibilities, competencies, and end behaviors for success), and the *individual* (skills, knowledge abilities, and career aspirations for the future). But, in the context of organization culture, what the organization expects of the individual goes beyond required skills or abilities. An individual's success is also affected by his or her personality, motivation, style, and demeanor. The following case note stresses the (often unnoticed) role that individual characteristics play in career success within an organization.

History.   Tom Duncan was product manager—field sales for a consumer products company. He was interviewed initially at his university several months before graduation. The fact that Tom received the "Goldwater" medal as outstanding junior in marketing/advertising and was consequently on the dean's list made him a much sought-out student for recruiting. He was subsequently hired by the company and placed in its "fast-track–sales trainee" program. This results-oriented program emphasized challenging the individual. Tom's strong analytical and communications skills and his aggressive style won him a promotion and choice of assignments. Tom selected field sales in the company's Consumer Products Division.

For the next few years, Tom received very good ratings on his performance appraisals with "excellent" ratings in "knowledge and skill" categories. Yet at the same time two of his supervisors also noted that he had "a tendency to be abrasive" or "works hard himself, but pushes others around him too much and without much tact."

Subsequently, Tom's career went into a holding pattern and five years after he was hired, he left the firm. In his exit interview he noted that the "company provides a good setting for learning but really doesn't want to have people around who rock the boat, even if it pays off."

Discussion.   What happened to Tom is not unusual. The development of individual careers within a particular organization may potentially pass through several culture orientation–acceptance stages, and there is nothing automatic about the process and individual survival, let alone success. Many may never make it, though they remain in the organization. Others leave because "they never understood me or what *I* wanted to do."

Success, as *viewed by the organization*, is a complex combination of performance and cultural fit. At the point of individual entry into the organization, much energy is used just becoming familiar with the organization, and performance is stressed. But, as time passes, promotion starts to turn on the demonstration of (or potential for) broader, more sophisticated managerial or technical skills. These skills include a growing understanding of how the organization works. Tom passed the first stage of evaluation when he received his initial promotion because of his clear demonstration of valued (performance) skills. But his personality and lack of understanding concerning the organization's culture froze his career. He could not pass into a more advanced stage, where an understanding of the company's culture was necessary, and he quit. Two of Tom's supervisors described him as pushy or abrasive. Certainly, his poor rapport with these individuals and perhaps other key figures affected his career adversely.

Growing acceptance by (a) key and powerful figure(s) may be necessary, but the specifics are contingent on situational factors reflecting "inner-circle (cultural) qualities." It is unlikely that many managers will develop beyond the first or second career stage (as in the Honeywell model, Chapter 2) without the encouragement of key figures. These mentors, or sponsors, are often critical to a person's career, assuming a reasonable competency level, if they are to reach stage 2 or 3. From a strategic standpoint, it is important that there be a convergence of thinking, beliefs, or assumptions regarding the corporation's current culture and its desired profile for the future. Defining the form of an organization's culture, and reaching consensus among key officials (and leaders) as to its appropriateness, or about needed change, requires lengthy consideration by top-level people.

Subcultures and Cultural Change

Although a "dominant" culture may exist in an organization, many variations of it may also exist in organizational units. At times, these may be in conflict with the values and ingrained behaviors of the "dominant culture."

Multiple Cultures within a Given Organization.   In conglomerates, divisionalized structures, and geographically dispersed units, internal cultures may vary significantly between units. A little reflection on the historical emergence of particular units is enough to suggest why some important cultural differences may exist internally. Differences (subcultures) may also help to explain why conflicts exist between valued unit behaviors and those described by the organization culture of the corporation as a whole.

For example, a large corporation undertook expansion through acquisition in the mid-1960s. Its policy was one of retaining the leadership of the acquired organizations and permitting them much autonomy. Most of the acquisitions were derivations of vertical or horizontal diversification, that is, directly related to its original core business (heavy equipment, precision machinery, and high quality). The cultures of the acquired units stayed intact, and even though the parent company imposed financial and planning constraints, it was largely business as usual. In one large division, "Rainbow Precision Products," an acquired company, conflict became increasingly evident between the divisional and corporate management groups. The corporation wanted to establish a uniform quality image throughout the company; Rainbow's management felt that the needed statistical techniques were not applicable to Rainbow. Rainbow had prided itself on direct and informal means of operational controls and did not want to add to its overhead, even though it was to take over manufacture of several lines from other divisions and would need high(er) quality standards than it normally exercised.

In management development, high-potential people from the Rainbow group who rotated to other divisions often posed difficult problems due to their work orientations and approaches.

This case note emphasizes the importance of cultural measurements and the necessity for sensitivity to possible differences and what these may imply for policy or executive action. When these measurements are carefully drawn, it becomes possible to consider normative-type questions. Namely,

- "Do you want these differences to exist, and if so, how are they to be successfully integrated?"

• "If a dominant set of cultural values and behaviors is to be established, how will existing differences be overcome and how will the culture change program be implemented?"

As a partial response to these questions, it should be said that changing a culture can be as difficult as establishing it initially. Our greatest successes with change, and these have been modest ones, have been with the use of organization development strategies.

Changing Divisional or Organizational Missions. Recession, foreign competition, and/or the drastic cutbacks in some industries have forced some companies to alter radically corporate missions for survival. The U.S. steel, electronics, and textile industries are but a few examples of areas where major corporate changes have taken place for survival. Whether operating at a reduced scale or being forced to move into different product or service areas, corporate missions have had to be altered. Cultural analyses have provided a tangible basis upon which to examine the adjoining alterations in values, career paths, valued knowledge and skills, and bases for promotion. The events at Ford Motor Co. are a case in point (Halberstam, 1986). Diagnostic models of the type described in this chapter represent means of profiling the existing culture and launching critical examination of these relative to new or modified strategic missions.

Use of Mentors or Sponsors. The formal identification and development of (senior) people to assume mentoring or couseling roles often proves a decisive factor in the enculturation of individuals.

Summary and Implications

This chapter has discussed some of the emerging concepts in thinking through organizational cultures strategically, and some characteristic experiences with using these approaches. The notion of a corporate culture caught on quickly, but the efforts to convert it into a viable concept, as a part of longer-range and strategic planning, has required much effort and the process continues.

Benchmarks of progress in strategizing with corporate culture have been accomplished through the painstaking work of people like Schein (M.I.T.) and a growing number of researchers. Increasingly comprehensive frameworks, the growing body of corporate experience, and improved study instruments have all aided this work.

At this stage of development, enough information and experience exists to assert that organizational culture can be usefully related to general planning and strategic approaches. Essential to applications development has been the definition of corporate culture in meaningful terms within the diverse community of organizations. Both general and operational definitions were set forth in this chapter, the latter dealing with specific characteristics associated with corporate culture. A significant advancement in these concepts beyond older related ones, such as climate or values, is that corporate cultures represent a more comprehensive approach in the explanation of both formal and informal behaviors with connections to key means by which the enterprise achieves performance and impacts its employees and clientele. Progress in the refinement or development of instrumentation to study organizational culture as an action research undertaking, has been steady and a boon to application. Several application examples and some short cases were provided to further illustrate viable uses of these concepts to stimulate top-level thinking and strategizing.

Corporate culture characteristics can provide valuable means of initiating thought about the orientation, underlying assumptions, and behavioral processes affecting key measures. For example, how does an organization create a *strong* corporate culture and is it necessarily an achievement likely to contribute to valued goals? Instances were presented in this chapter where strong corporate cultures led to successful organizational performances (e.g., Hewlett-Packard) as well as situations in which it represented a major block to needed changes (e.g., the phone company example). Thus, a strong culture per se is not necessarily advantageous. The circumstances must be examined in depth. This point may well be counterintuitive relative to "commonsense" thinking.

Another point regarding corporate culture is the fact that it often contains subcultures within it. Subcultures may strongly reinforce the dominant culture, be at cross-purposes with it, or be stronger and/or more viable than cultures existing elsewhere in the organization. When strategic thinking enters into the realm of change, various interesting possibilities can be considered. For example, "how long will it take to bring about a particular type of culture and what are the necessary organizational strategies and changes for its accomplishment?" "How long will it take to introduce organizational change which accomplishes a *cultural* form, and all that that implies, as opposed to accomplishing only the outward signs of change?" Accomplishing a viable corporate culture is decidedly in the realm of *long-range* human resource planning and best thought of in terms of *years* to meet particular behavioral objectives.

What are some of the more effective means of achieving a particular cultural form or changing one? How can management development and succession planning become key instruments in strategies relevant to change? How can this work be further supported through organization development processes? Aside from practical plans and procedures, effective change often turns on well-prepared and key people who know what has to be done, how to do it, and further, who also serve as models of actionable changes. The fact that organizational change related to culture typically stretches out over extended time periods means that officials need to approach this area with realistic expectations. It also means that careful definition of culture change criteria and benchmarks will be indispensable to the needed monitoring of progress.

REFERENCES

Business Week. "Can John Young Redesign Hewlett-Packard,?" December 6, 1982, pp. 72–78.

Deal, Terrence and Allan Kennedy. *Corporate Cultures*. Reading, MA: Addison-Wesley, 1982.

Lawler, Edward III, David Nadler, and Cortland Camman. *Organizational Assessment*. New York: John Wiley, 1980.

Lee, Chris. "Raiders of the Corporate Culture" *Training*, February 1984: 26–33.

Levinson, Harry. *Organizational Diagnosis*. Cambridge, MA: Harvard University Press, 1972.

Litwin, G. H. and R. H. Stringer. *Motivation and Organization Climate*. Cambridge: MA: Harvard University Press, 1968.

Margerison, C. *How to Assess Your Management Style*. New York: AMACOM, 1979: 112–123.

Peters, Thomas and Robert Waterman. *In Search of Excellence*. New York: Harper & Row, 1982.

Schein, Edgar. "What It Is and How to Change It," circa 1984, Report N00014-80-C-0905, NR170-911. Arlington, VA: Office of Naval Research, Organization Effectiveness Group (Code 452).

Tunstall, W. Brooke. "Cultural Transition at AT&T." *Sloan Management Review*, Vol. 25, no. 1 (Fall 1983): 1–12.

Van de Ven, Andrew and Diane L. Ferry. *Measuring and Assessing Organizations*. New York: John Wiley, 1980.

Wallach, Ellen J. "Individuals and Organizations: The Cultural Match." *Training and Development Journal*, Vol. 37, no. 2 (February 1983): 29–36.

Wessowetz, Richard G. von and Michael Beu, "Human Resources at Hewlett-Packard," Case No. 482-125. Cambridge, MA: Harvard Business School Case Service, 1982.

APPLICATIONS SECTION

The two exhibits that follow have been used in different types of organizations and with many individuals, including staff and line supervisors and officers. Results, similarities, and differences can often serve as a highly stimulating basis for group discussions on "what we are" and "what we should strive to become in the future."

EXHIBIT 3-6
Assessing Corporate Culture

Ratings

	?? Don't Know 1	Not a Factor 2	Low—Done Infrequently, Little Recognition 3	Some Importance— in Regularity or Recognition 4	Important— Ingrained, Value or Behavior Guide 5

A. Common Elements

1. *Corporate philosophy, policy*
   Organization's tone or climate
   "Who" we are and "what" we are trying to do and what
   we stand for
   Clarity of corporate mission or objectives

2. *Valued performance features and behaviors*
   Competitiveness, assertiveness, aggressiveness
   Demonstrated company loyalty, acts of organization
   commitment
   "Macho," stoic, "hanging-in"
   Productivity, performance ratings, workaholism
   Control of resources, information
   Valued departmental assignments

3. *Decision making*
   Centralization vs. decentralization
   Factors considered
   Degree of support documentation
   Scope of participation

4. *Organization's reward system*
   Management by objectives, accomplishments
   Performance appraisal ratings
   Assessments of potential
   Wage/salary increases, bonuses
   Internal recognition (communications, ceremonials)

120

5. *Sponsorship*
   "Adoption" by power figure
   Expert guidance
   Having a home department

6. *Mentoring*
   Guidance/counseling by key person

7. *Career ladders*
   Knowledge of valued routes
   Qualifications to "enter" valued career routes
   How to navigate valued routes

8. *Social networking*
   Acquaintance with key, power, or in-group figure(s)
   Part of recognized "old boy" or "old girl" network
   Support of "favored" charities
   Participation in selected sports/recreation activities

9. *Dress, mannerisms, personal features, education*
   Type of dress
   Posturing that is recognized/valued
   Knowing when to take a position or to "back off"
     (be flexible)
   Age, physical size
   Education: type of degree, school

10. *Political system*
    Knowledge of the key "actors" and their areas
      of influence
    Who has the power and the bases for it
    How is power asserted, that is, influence on decisions
      (e.g., succession, recruiting, selection)

(Continues)

121

EXHIBIT 3-6 (Continued)

	Ratings				
	?? Don't Know	Not a Factor	Low—Done Infrequently, Little Recognition	Some Importance— in Regularity or Recognition	Important— Ingrained, Value or Behavior Guide
	1	2	3	4	5

B. Comprehensiveness and Social Integration

1. Extent to which the "common elements (A)" are identifiable by corporate leadership

2. Extent to which *formal* corporate communications feature regularly, "cultural" elements

3. Extent to which *informal* corporate and organizational communications include culture elements

4. Consistency with which values and desired aspects of behavior have been transmitted to incoming and successive generations of managers and corporate leaders

5. Extent to which "culture" elements are seen as working (adequately) well

6. Consistency with which elements of supervisory and managerial decision/behavioral patterns reflect "culture" (elements)—thereby, serving as models of behavior

122

EXHIBIT 3-7
Profiling the Behavioral Dimensions of Organization Culture

Scale Key			
(0)	(1)	(2)	(3)
Not at all descriptive of my organization	Describes my organization a little	A fairly good description of my organization	Quite descriptive of my organization

Descriptors	Scale Values			
1. Conservative	0	1	2	3
2. Trusting	0	1	2	3
3. Hard driving	0	1	2	3
4. Well established	0	1	2	3
5. Results oriented	0	1	2	3
6. Innovative, leader	0	1	2	3
7. Innovative, follower	0	1	2	3
8. Creative	0	1	2	3
9. Risk taking	0	1	2	3
10. Procedural	0	1	2	3
11. Hierarchical, channels	0	1	2	3
12. Supportive (individual) action	0	1	2	3
13. Structured	0	1	2	3
14. Enterprising aggressive	0	1	2	3
15. Informal	0	1	2	3
16. High pressure for results	0	1	2	3
17. Balance—short/long-term results	0	1	2	3
18. Challenging	0	1	2	3
19. Sociable	0	1	2	3
20. Independent action (individual)	0	1	2	3
21. Power oriented	0	1	2	3
22. Secure, safe	0	1	2	3
23. Equity oriented	0	1	2	3
24. Reward-performance oriented	0	1	2	3
25. Entrepreneurial orientation	0	1	2	3
26. Collaborative decision making	0	1	2	3
27. Open and trusting	0	1	2	3
28. Relationships oriented	0	1	2	3
29. Encouraging	0	1	2	3

Source: Based in part on G. H. Litwin and R. A. Stringer, *Motivation and Organization Climate* (Cambridge, MA: Harvard University Press, 1968); C. Margerison, *How to Assess Your Managerial Style* (New York: AMACOM, 1979), pp. 112–123; Ellen J. Wallach, "Individuals and Organizations: The Cultural Match," *Training and Development Journal,* Vol. 37, no. 2 February 1983: pp. 29–36.

EXHIBIT 3-8
Managerial Style Interpretation of the Cultural Profile*

Bureaucratic Orientation
1. Conservative
4. Well established
7. Innovative follower
10. Procedural
11. Hierarchical, channels
13. Structured
21. Power oriented
22. Secure, safe
    ($N_1 = 8$)

Supportive (People) Orientation
2. Trusting
12. Supportive (individual) action
15. Informal
18. Challenging
19. Sociable
24. Reward-performance oriented
28. Relationships oriented
29. Encouraging
    ($N_2 = 8$)

Innovative, System 4, "Z" Orientation
3. Hard driving, aggressive
5. Results oriented
6. Innovative leader
8. Creative
9. Risk taking
14. Enterprising, aggressive

16. High pressure (manageable)
17. Balance: short/long-term results
20. Independent action oriented
23. Equity orientation
24. Entrepreneurial orientation
26. Collaborative decision making
27. Open and trusting
    ($N_3 = 13$)

*For a good practical discussion of these relationships as they apply to the corporate setting, see C. Margerison, *How to Assess Your Managerial Style* (New York: AMACOM, 1979), pp. 112–123.

4

Managers
Defining Functions and Performances for Success

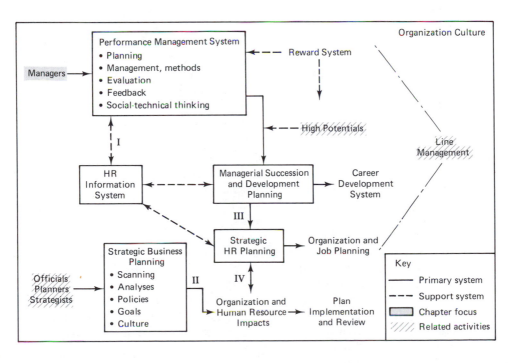

Synopsis

The question of "Who is a manager?" or for that matter, "What is a manager?" has been debated for many years, often, I think, fruitlessly. No idea will meet universal agreement because many diverse needs must be served. Executives universally would agree that managerial roles and performances are pivotal for organizational survival, continuity, and renewal. Instinctual feelings, beliefs, and general experiences validate this idea. But how much is really known in your organization about why some "managers" are better than other "managers"?

Human resource planning and strategic approaches of late have helped to bring some degree of convergence in this area. Experienced officials, planners, and specialists have recognized the important connection between a knowledge of managerial role behaviors for successful performance and the achievement of strategic plans and programs. Quite naturally, then, individual factors likely to lead to successful performance have received much attention. Several significant studies of successful managerial performance (behavior) have achieved workable agreement on general factors closely identified with these accomplishments. These results serve as an important body of information in this chapter. Through critical and thoughtful use, this information can prove greatly beneficial to management development strategies.

To sharpen the issues to be discussed in this chapter, the following questions are posed:

- Do sets of job-related factors exist that provide a useful way to think about managerial behaviors and performance?
- To the extent that these factor sets exist, what are some of the organizational circumstances that emphasize particular elements in success?
- What are some useful ways to describe managerial behavior or performance to facilitate development and staffing planning?
- Are managers leaders and leaders managers?

Your position may be that "On balance, the *managerial* designation is rather arbitrary—and anyhow, what difference does it make?" Contrary to this position, the experiences in many different organizations indicate that the "who" and "what" kinds of questions are basic to soundly conceived human resource planning and development strategies. The "how" question is reserved for several subsequent chapters (5, 6, 12) and the applications section at the end of other chapters.

Background—Breaking Down the Traditional View of What a Manager Is

In some of the companies, we have studied the term "manager" had little meaning unless it was coupled with a functional term such as "product," "marketing," engineering," or "production." Although at first this may seem to be a commonsense attempt to establish identification with an area of responsibilities, it frequently assumed much more that went unspoken. One company's situation helps to illustrate this point.

In a large electronics manufacturing firm, the term "management development" was *not* recognized or used. The inevitable response from a person in the organization was, "What kind of a manager are you talking about, electronics, marketing, product development, or what?" Not surprisingly, perhaps, promotional paths or career ladders were almost entirely within major product or systems groups. Cross-transfers between groups were generally discouraged and not considered in a management development context. Does this mean that there was no general management preparation or executive program? No, there were in fact many general management and executive programs that ran for many years in this company. But these were consistently seen as a means of enriching jobs viewed as essentially technical or generally functional in nature.

Marketing managers had to deal with customer accounts, products, complaint handling, bidding, and the like. A *production* manager in a given unit had to know how to schedule production runs, think through the fit of new technologies, or consider where to go to resolve a complex production problem.

Job entry, managerial seasoning, and promotion of sales or marketing personnel took place primarily in the sales unit or marketing organization. The production or manufacturing person followed a similar pattern. If a person performed well in his or her functional specialty, he or she frequently became a part of the pool of "qualified" candidates for higher-level technical or administrative positions—*within* the functional area or technical specialty. It was at this point in the individual's career that he or she was encouraged to take a smattering of courses or personally broadening workshops in "management." Senior employees qualified for an "executive program." This program consisted of several alternative activities: (1) an off-site, two-week workshop at their conference center, (2) a six-week part-time program at one of several local universities, or (3) a part-time two-year certificate or master's degree programs depending on the participant's qualifications.

In reality, the conference center "executive program" was as much an assessment center as an individual developmental activity. Aside from attendance at various seminars and workshops, attendees were administered a number of psychological instruments and also were interviewed extensively. Many of these participants resented the treatment they received and felt that the "center" program was misrepresented to them. Those who attended the academic (part-time) programs were a part of more conventional, formal educational development. Regardless of the program in which individuals participated, however, the learnings were seen as

complementary administrative, technical, or functional skills—the potential for career mobility to other corporate areas was not especially great. Also, there was no
coordination of programs or candidates between groups or sectors, nor was any link
made to human resource planning except at the most general level of staffing
analyses.

In this corporation and many others with which we have dealt, the common
knowledge and skill base for managers, to the extent one existed, was found in the
Fayol tradition. That is, to some degree all managers planned, controlled, coordinated, directed, and administered. Job descriptions were traditional in format (and
often outdated) and organized around the types of functional terms just enumerated. There were no well-defined standards for judging successful job performance.
It was assumed that the general outline of responsibilities and specification of
educational level, type(s) of experience, and occasionally personality features was
adequate for assignment, training, and promotion purposes.

In short, company supervisors and managers were viewed, appraised, and
assessed for potential primarily on the basis of past and current work. Management
development activities were nonsystemic and fragmented; there was no overall
organization or thrust. There was little effort to coordinate these within groups,
divisions, or sectors, let alone at the corporate level. "Managers" were not seen as a
general class or even as a central core of individual skills—at least in so far as the
actual workings of the systems.

The most recent developments at this company related to succession planning
for senior managerial positions. Management inventories indicated that many excellent people had been developed in the diverse technical and functional fields of the
corporation—but there was a severe shortage of qualified candidates for a newly
structured "pool" of general management talent.

Newer Developments in Concepts of Managers

One of the more important breakthroughs in the traditional views of "managers"
was questioning the (logic and) results "promised" by the "rational managerial
model." This model placed professional or management practice largely in a problem-solving mode. The individual focused on problem definition and identification
of alternatives (means) to achieve well-defined ends. Models were used extensively,
and bases were also provided for making choices. Its prescription of specific steps
for a particular end objective (problem solution) were understandably appealing.
Some successes and the well-defined structure of this approach led to wide-scale
adoption in much managerial and professional practice. As noted in Chapter 1,
these approaches spilled over into strategic planning, and they were quickly absorbed. Formulated strategic approaches diffused rapidly throughout major corporate units—much to the dismay of policy officials, subsequently. The use of the
"rational managerial models" had also been reinforced by formal educational programs that emphasized rational models and methods. As noted in the instance of
strategic planning, these approaches also ran into problems, including environmen-

tal changes that "wouldn't behave" in rational ways. The highly erratic, often poor, results in the longer term brought many of these programs to a halt or led to a major restructuring of these managerial activities.

In managerial situations, it became increasingly common to have highly complex, uncertain conditions. Managers were forced to think well and respond appropriately, often as events unfolded. These managerial actions required changing the rational model into an art form which was more adaptive and action oriented. Some have termed this "reflection in action." Managers needed to act intelligently when confronted with unstable, unique, and/or uncertain situations. Each had to draw from a broad repertoire of knowledge and experience, which was then tailored to the situation they faced. This dynamic managerial process called for more inductive and reflective thinking. It was action oriented but guided by information gathering and focusing which reflected the individual's intelligent use of past experience, knowledge, and developed skills. It involved predigesting all manner of "what ifs" and thinking through in advance various scenarios and the potential influence or consequences of these. It was reinforced by creative processes that committed the immediately unsolvable to temporary mental "storage"—for subsequent retrieval, in redefined form, use, and problem resolution or creative innovations. This creative view portrayed managerial thought and approaches in a new form. The new picture was one in which experience, technical and general abilities, and formal educational preparation were combined and shaped to one's functional assignment(s). This combination of skills, experience, and education was then focused on a range of specific situations. These situations spanned the range from those permitting "rational approaches" to many where adaptation and change were much more characteristic and called for "reflection in action." However, all these situations had in common the need to update and clearly specify job responsibilities, and to identify, where possible, generic and specific behaviors characteristic of managerial actions for successful performance.

This newer perspective on managerial action also suggested an alternate definitional approach to *managerial potential:* the ability to span a range of situations from those requiring pure rationality to those complex approaches calling for highly adaptive behavior. Since comparatively few people were likely to possess this versatility, strategic management development approaches also provided some alternatives, for example,

1. Identifying the general environmental and business features peculiar to specific business sectors and better matching situation and person or
2. Developing *dual*-career ladder models in which the provision of technical and administrative career tracks capitalized on quite different combinations of individual interests, skills, and versatility.

The newer managerial view and strategic perspective described in this section was only feasible in the organizational settings where managerial roles were defined, where traditional assumptions were questioned, organizations were viewed in a comprehensive way, and where organizations were prepared to change to improve managerial actions.

Popular Concepts, Myths, and the Search for Useful Models

A typical response to the question of "What is a manager?" is that "Managers are those who supervise others." However, many staff positions, for example, require little direct supervision of subordinates. Most wage and salary administrators have set aside the broader issues that are part of these questions, approaching some of them in a very practical way. The pragmatic assumption is that "when one reaches salary/grade level 'X,' one has become a manager." Some companies attempt to distinguish exempt from nonexmpt as a basis to designate managers. Indeed, this approach separates managerial, professional, and staff people from the other workers. But this dichotomy fails to tell us what a manager is, let alone what a manager does.

The Classical View—"Nothing Could Be Farther from the Truth"

An often-cited study of the manager's role was done by Henry Mintzberg (1974). Although some view his evidence as flimsy and restricted to executive roles, there are some useful points to be considered. Mintzberg noted that since French indus-trialist Henri Fayol first defined the managerial role in 1916, most businesses seem to think about managers as those who do planning, coordinating, controlling, and organizing. Mintzberg felt that this classical view was no longer relevant—if it ever was! His own studies, including some company analyses, indicated that many myths had grown up around the managerial role. Mintzberg stated that managers were often perceived to be careful and thoughtful planners. His research dispelled this impression. Instead of managers quietly contemplating abstract business issues, a consistent finding in his studies was the "unrelenting" pace of managerial activities. These activities were more like mixed-up movie frames—brief, varied, and seem-ingly unrelated across time. True, his analyses were primarily concerned with executives, but it does give one cause for questioning widely held assumptions.

   More recently, John P. Kotter conducted a still broader and more intensive analysis of a group of successful general managers representing many different American industries. (Kotter's work can be viewed in a broader career framework in Sonnenfeld and Kotter, 1982.) Although the notion of the unrelenting pace of managers was further validated in Kotter's work, he shed light on the nature of managerial planning that was underplayed in Mintzberg's analyses. Because of their rapid job pace and their relatively complex positions, managers plan in ways that are quite subtle. Managers were found to develop agendas made of "loosely con-nected, time-related goals and plans that address their long-, medium-, and short-term responsibilities." This meant that "agenda" construction required considerable time and that issues may not be shared with others because of their incompleteness or sensitive nature. Also, ideas and approaches needed to ferment creatively over appreciable time periods as circumstances changed and information became available. *The most efficient managers* were best at constructing and modifying these "agendas."

Another commonly held belief is that efficient managers have few routine job duties to perform. Many studies, however, indicate that managers and executives have a significant group of recurring and relatively routine activities. Some of these are indispensible to maintain external and internal relationships; attendance at community meetings or ceremonial recognition gifts would be examples of routines "designed" to achieve important end purposes. Some of these rituals and routines are passed on to subordinates in condensed form.

Dependence on Information

Managerial role performances also reflect the reality of an increasingly complex environment in which managers are dependent on the contributions of subordinates, alternate viewpoints, or the technical expertise of others, especially staff specialists. As a consequence, managerial work styles for information gathering must reflect these dependent and often critical relationships. Centralized information gathering or even decision making often isn't feasible. Decision requirements imposed upon individual managers move beyond information technology, available time, and areas of individual competency. The commonsense conclusion is that one person simply can't be astride all the critical information needed for a broad sweep of decision matters.

Managers attempt to make the best use of their available time for information gathering—this often comes out as a considerable dependency on verbal media, namely, telephones, meetings, and increasingly telecommunications. Body language *connected* to voice through telecommunications is beneficial to interpreting verbal communications and simultaneously increases the possibilities to influence others. Important information is often derived informally. Such "soft" information helps to validate ideas, assists in formulating new(er) areas to investigate, and very importantly, also helps to anticipate "tomorrow's facts."

There are serious drawbacks unfortunately to a managers' heavy reliance upon verbal media. This information is usually *not* documented, and it is greatly limited with regard to its use by others—albeit many managers want it that way. The microcomputer revolution, however, may dramatically alter this picture. The opportunity to personalize computer outputting processes and modes to individual work styles has expanded individual capabilities and, potentially, the range of individual influence. Highly flexible information compiling options, with the capability to "download" information from more comprehensive and powerful corporate systems, is providing managerial opportunities for planning analyses and decision styles without precedent. These points are developed much more fully in the chapter on strategic uses of microcomputers in managerial development (Chapter 11).

Organizational size and the physical aspects of these are among the organizational "facts of life" that greatly affect communications patterns for managerial actions. Multiunit organizations, and assuredly internationals, would be handicapped (paralyzed?) by undue reliance on verbal communications. In general, the greater the physical decentralization, the more crucial the role of communications and information technology. Also, the greater the dependence on policy and procedures, the greater the importance of strengthening corporate culture (Chapter 3) as an implicit guide to decisionable actions. Even in the multinationals, however, verbal communications and enculturalization opportunities are exploited by senior managers through periodic field trips, face-to-face meetings, and bringing "home" key managers for debriefing or rebriefing. In one large multinational, for instance, foreign-born managers spend months in U.S. facilities until it is felt that they fully understand the "company's way" of managing its businesses and its human resources. Of necessity, verbal communications persist, but they are supported extensively by information technology. Communications formats increasingly are consciously formatted to organization needs and individual work styles, circumstances, customary ways of doing things, and available technology.

Management as a Profession

Another commonly held belief is that management has become a profession and a science. For some, this is a highly controversial point and one that increasing numbers of internal consultants, educators, and researchers have addressed. Mintzberg's answer was simple. He believed that what he observed in his research was not science, since what managers had to learn for success in their position was not specified. At one time this assertion was largely true. But the managerial studies carried out in the last two decades at companies such as AT&T, Control Data, General Electric, Honeywell, Inc., and Xerox, and societies such as ASTD* and ASPA† changed all this. They addressed, specifically, the definition of who is a manager and what they do. The indicated business organizations framed the answers in terms of the managerial skills *and* position performances (behaviors) defined as successful in (their) organizations. They also specified the training and development needed to achieve successful performance. The behavioral models or managerial prototypes were often drawn from successful managers in their firms or through cooperative field studies. Thereby results of selection and management development were more predictable and the potential for success increased. Managers in these and other firms could draw upon a structured base of knowledge, concepts, experiences, information, and methods. The managerial art was advanced significantly. It took on increasingly professional characteristics reflecting a defined body of knowledge, recognized concepts and methods, dedicated publications, and

---

*American Society for Training and Development.
†American Society for Personnel Administrators.

a formal educational structure. Studies by professional societies and a growing number of academic studies have contributed to this progress.

The professionalization of managerial activities and performances for success represented an artful blending of work experiences and advancements in the knowledge of work and its connection to performance. Yet there is a respectful recognition of individual learning differences. These factors can be separated for discussion purposes, and they comprise the main focus of this section. While the chemistry that catalyzes their blending can be fully appreciated but not completely described, we do have much information to go on in the growth of the manager. Its strategic aspects are discussed in this and subsequent chapters.

Selected Studies Usefully Defining Managerial Roles and Performance

The information that forms the basis for a systematic and useful view of managerial roles comes from a handful of research studies. The reader should not be misled by the modest number because they all involve extensive work, numerous organizations, and analyses by informed and dedicated people over a period of many years. Unfortunately, since these studies used many different study techniques, a point-by-point comparison is not possible. What is important for practitioners and researchers is that all these studies provide useful information and guidelines, and also show some general agreement about what makes a capable and professionally successful manager. Taken together, these studies already are the basis for management development programs in many organizations. There are four main studies described in this section. Bray et al. (1974) spent eight years at American Telephone & Telegraph studying some 300 new managerial recruits. Their report provides one of the most comprehensive analyses available on the development of the successful manager. Also, subsequent studies were conducted. Whetten and Cameron (1984) developed an inventory of critical managerial skills based on their study of company and continuing education programs. In a sense, these two studies anchor almost two decades of work in the management development field. Two other useful studies that helped to define successful management were undertaken by Walter W. Tornow and his associates Timothy Gartland and Patrick Pinto of Control Data (1980) and Melaney Baehr (1980). The orientation and approach of these four major studies are presented in summary form in Exhibit 4-1. More detail appears in the application section of this chapter.

The AT&T Management Progress Study: A Newer Perspective on Who Are Managers

In 1956, Bray and his associates at AT&T began their eight-year "management progress study," which was described in their classic book, *Formative Years in Business* (1974). Assuming that companies need to most of all use the abilities and

EXHIBIT 4-1

Orientation and Approach of Four Major Studies of Managerial Characteristics and Performances

	Study Teams*			
	Bray et al.	Whetten and Cameron	Tornow et al.†	Baehr
Orientation	Psychological attributes.	Behavioral: general management skills	Behavioral: job-related skills for general job responsibilities.	Behavioral: time spent on specific activities.
Methods	Longitudinal interviews; observer assessments of characteristics; executive opinion.	Literature reviews; analyses of management activities.	Informational interviews with managers and executives; developed "job-person matrix."	Quantified judgments of specific task dimensions in the "work-employee inventory" (WEI).
Number of dimensions	7	9	17†	12

General emphasis	Administrative and interpersonal and general skills; stress-effective leadership and adaptability; unique emphasis on intellectual abilities and work motivation.‡ Stress factor seen in "stability of performance."	Administrative and interpersonal skills, with approaches for greater self-awareness, skill building including "managing personal stress."	Includes five administrative dimensions and six for interpersonal/communications, "Know-how" a behavioral analogue to Bray et al.'s "intellectual" ability." Stress that management is "persistence" and "integrity." Unique means of gaining organizational commitment.	Three administrative dimensions, two employee relations. Unique mention of relations with outer community. Mentions "self-development" as wellas "employee development." Stress management is "coping with" emergencies.

*Full citations are provided in the References for this chapter.

†Tornow et al. also developed 13 job description dimensions which emphasized the kinds of job-related skills different managers needed for successful performance. This reflected Control Data's organizational arrangements. CD's "manager" is a generic class with common responsibility dimensions regardless of specific assignments. More traditionally organized companies focus more on specific assignments (i.e., marketing, production, and so on), each with distinct knowledge, skills, or competencies and general abilities.

‡Perhaps too "psychological" to be behaviorally analyzed in other studies.

motivation of people they already employ, the team tried to track the development of individuals through their professionally formative years—before they assumed managerial responsibilities.

At the beginning and end of the study, some 300 participants spent three days in an "appraisal center," in which researchers used simulated work activities and psychological instruments to try to define aspects of personality, intellectual abilities, and knowledge of current events. Annual open-ended interviews were also conducted, to record the significant events in the participants' work lives that were thought to have influenced them. As time went on, the cohort groups were expanded; more recently, study groups were further expanded to include women and minorities. Participants who left AT&T continued to be followed by the study group.

The AT&T Management Progress Study described here was referred to by Campbell et al. (1970) as the largest and most comprehensive study of managerial career development ever undertaken. Because the data were gathered in an unobtrusive way, and since there was a reassessment of subjects periodically and on a continuing basis over many years, the study contained a wealth of data.

Bray and his colleagues drew on the psychological and management literature, as well as on the opinions of senior executives, to examine personal qualities that might be related to job advancement. Selected features of the study are summarized in Exhibit 4-1 and added details of the study are provided in Exhibit 4-2 and the application section (Exhibit 4-7). Seven groups of characteristics (see Exhibit 4-1) proved to be closely associated with managerial success. Three of the dimensions related to knowledge, skills, or particular abilities; the other 4 were more general personality or motivational features of the person. Individual characteristics furnishing the basis for these dimensions are in Exhibit 4-7 of the applications section. Exhibit 4-2 lists 11 groups of essential characteristics for managerial success based on the seven management dimensions identified in the AT&T study (Exhibit 4-1).

The formative years study provided impressive results. The results indicated that the multiple criteria used for assessment ratings were effective predictors of future managerial achievement. Put another way, overall ratings based on multiple criteria predicted success better than any single measure alone.

Findings from the Bray study indicated that

- 51 percent of those predicted to do so, reached middle management as opposed to 14 percent of those *not* predicted who (also) reached middle management.
- Of the 55 men achieving middle management, 78 percent were correctly predicted.
- Of the 73 men who did not advance beyond first level, 95 percent were correctly predicted.
- Of those promoted who were assessed as "unacceptable," most tended to be below-average performers.

EXHIBIT 4-2

Summary of Characteristics for the Managerial Role*

Bray et al.'s "Groups of Essential Characteristics to Managerial Success"	Whetten and Cameron's "Management Skill Topics"	Tornow et al.'s "Management Performance Dimensions"	Baehr's "Job Dimensions"
Administrative Skills			
1. Organize and plan efficiently	1. Creative problem solving	1. Plan and allocate	1. Setting objectives
2. Make decisions quickly—and wisely	2. Improving group decision making	2. Innovate	2. Improving procedures
	3. Effective delegation and joint decision making	3. Document	3. Developing technical ideas
		4. Responsibility/accomplishment	4. Decision making
		5. Delegate	5. Promoting safety
			6. Supervisory practices
Interpersonal Skills			
3. Strong/favorable personal impact	4. Gaining power and influence	6. Train	7. Developing employee potential
4. Effective leadership of others for task accomplishment	5. Improving employee performance by motivating others	7. Coach	8. Developing teamwork
5. Oral communications	6. Establishing supportive communications	8. Cordinate	9. Handling outside contacts
6. Behavioral adaptability to attain goals	7. Managing conflict	9. Motivate	10. Community-organization relations
	8. Self-awareness	10. Consideration	11. Self-development
		11. Communicate	
		12. Represent	
General Abilities, Motivation, Behaviors			
7. Intellectual ability	9. Managing personal stress	13. Know-how	12. Coping with emergencies
8. Stability of performance		14. Effort, persistence	
9. Work motivation		15. Crisis action	
10. Career motivation		16. Integrity	
11. Dependence on others		17. Organizational commitment	

*Complete citations are provided in the References for this chapter.

Emerging Definitions from Research

The 11 groups of "essential management characteristics" based on the Bray et al. study (Exhibit 4-2) deserve considerable attention from business officials and development specialists. Thought provoking in themselves, their conclusions were supported in several contemporary studies that identified similar clusters of characteristics for effective management. Because of different study techniques and data, the total number (and labels) of the clusters varies somewhat, but the overall similarities are striking.

Bray and his associates decried what they regarded as an unwise emphasis in research on analytical techniques and theory while the actual skills relevant to (the) job performance were neglected. "Up to now, students have been taught more *about* management," but not actually how to manage. Bray and his associates examined the psychological aspects of management and factors contributing to managerial success. Subsequent researchers aimed to find still more specific information by examining the particular behaviors managers performed to be rated as "successful" by their senior managements. As Whetten and Cameron (1984) concluded in studying this area, understanding how and why a particular managerial act is undertaken is important. However, "skill delivery" involves more than knowledge alone.

Whetten and Cameron

To discover essential managerial actions, Whetten and Cameron reviewed previous managerial studies of what managers (actually) do; examples of these types of analysis would include studies by J. Livington, John Miner, Richard E. Boyatzis, and John Flanders. They also observed and interviewed over 400 managers in diverse positions and organizations. From these two study phases they developed a group of nine personal and interpersonal skills (Exhibit 4-3) that were consistently shown to be important for effective management in many organizations and for a great number of managerial positions. Essential as these skills were, they were not necessarily products of innate individual talent. All could be taught to some degree and some (perhaps much) improvement could be exhibited in most.

Whetten and Cameron noted that the basis for individual learning, and the one on which all the others rested, was self-awareness. Understanding one's values, cognitive style, factors contributing to stress, and interpersonal orientation made it possible for the manager to adapt other critical skills to his or her own needs and working style.

This was a very powerful idea; it opened the door to strategic management development approaches that centered importantly on strengthening self-awareness as an initial thrust. For example, self-awareness as to learning style can assist an individual in identifying self-learning approaches best suited to particular situations. Another area involving self-awareness concerned stress management. A person lacking in self-awareness regarding his or her vulnerability to stress might approach

EXHIBIT 4-3
Critical Management Skills

1. Developing self-awareness
   Determining cognitive style, values, and interpersonal orientation
   Becoming aware of personal strengths and weaknesses
   Understanding the impact of your interpersonal style on others

2. Managing personal stress
   Developing effective time management techniques
   Identifying major life and work stressors
   Developing effective coping mechanisms

3. Solving problems creatively
   Developing competence in rational problem solving
   Dealing with conceptual blocks
   Creating flexibility in thinking

4. Establishing supportive communication
   Becoming adept at active listening
   Developing empathetic response to others
   Using appropriate response formats

5. Gaining power and influence
   Establishing a strong power base
   Converting power into influence
   Avoiding power abuses

6. Improving employee performance through motivation
   Distinguishing ability versus motivational problems
   Providing highly valued incentives
   Making rewards contingent on performance
   Timing rewards for maximum impact

7. Delegating and decision making
   Developing competence in task assignments
   Fostering successful task completion in others
   Determining when to involve others in making decisions

8. Managing conflict
   Balancing assertiveness and sensitivity
   Handling personal criticism
   Registering complaints effectively
   Mediating conflicts between subordinates

9. Conducting effective group meetings
   Making adequate preparations
   Effectively managing both task and process aspects
   Making effective presentations

Source: Based on David A. Whetten and Kim S. Cameron, *Developing Management Skills* (Glenview, IL.: Scott, Foresman, 1984).

difficult situations and lose control of initiative or get into conflicts without knowing why. The Whetten and Cameron work emphasized the individual's self-identification and strengthening of this set of nine skills found widely applicable to many managerial situations—for successful behavior or performances.

Tornow and the Work at Control Data Corporation

Dr. Walter Tornow and his colleagues at Control Data Corporation undertook an approach that considered *both* position responsibilities and endjob behaviors for successful performance (Tornow and Gartland, 1977). The continuing program of study at Control Data Corporation resulted in further improvements in their earlier work, and this too is described here. Their earlier studies involved extensive research, which included consultation with some 600 managers and executives in Control Data. This first major study stage led to the identification of 13 "position description factors" which effectively included almost all the diverse managerial positions represented by their initial group of study participants. Each of the 13 factors emphasized job-related skills to carry out position responsibilities in a successful way. Examples of the titles for these "position description factors" included "human resource management," "financial management," "supervision," and "public relations." From this list, it was possible to create a general descriptive profile of different managerial work assignments. In turn, each job description factor was then detailed as it applied to a specific position (See the applications section in this chapter, Exhibit 4-8, Part A).

Similarly, an exhaustive list of 17 "managerial performance dimensions" was also developed. Here the emphasis was on work-related behaviors for successful performance of the work assignments. These are summarized in Exhibit 4-2 and detailed in Exhibit 4-8, Part B. Thus this work led to the identification of two sets of factors, the combination of which constituted a powerful means of proscribing a particular management position. A substantial base was provided for new person orientation, management development, assessment of potential, and position planning, including the impact of change.

To develop a comprehensive set of general terms which described managerial responsibilities and a characteristic set of essential behaviors was a useful innovation in itself. It represented one of the first large-scale applications of job-analytic research which demonstrated the utility of capturing both job descriptive and behavioral information to define a position adequately. In addition, positions were detailed in much depth; this provided the needed information to carry out a variety of planning and programming activities.

Tornow et al. integrated the 13 "position description factors" and the 17 "management performance dimensions" into a "job-person matrix." In this matrix, essential performance dimensions were matched to the various positions factors by a consensus of experts. This matrix helped to answer the question of which behaviors appeared to be most closely related to specific position description factors. For example, the position description factor "human resource management" was found to draw upon four different performance dimensions: "plan and allocate," "crisis action," "control," and "motivate." Details of the matrix are provided later, in Exhibit 4-9. These job descriptive and performance dimensions provided a general set of criteria and guides for selecting individuals for a "talent pool" for future development and advancement. Also, the matrix provided an objective guide to the particular behaviors which would be most critical to success in meeting the requirements of a particular position description responsibility. Further, the matrix served as a general model to study differences among positions or job families, thus facilitating both planning and development. They also facilitated succession planning by providing a systematic basis for needs analysis in establishing competencies for promotion or/and succession.

In more recent work, Tornow and his associates at Control Data, including Ronald Page, have extended these results into comprehensive analyses of managerial competency. These are discussed in Chapter 8, Management Development Methods.

The "management performance dimensions," developed by Tornow and his associates at Control Data stress interpersonal skills. All the studies described in this section emphasized this dimension. In the Tornow et al. study, the related skills included training, coaching, coordinating, motivating, communicating, representing, and expressing considerate behavior. Some 40 percent (7 of the 17) of the sets of factors identified by the Tornow et al. study support expertise in interpersonal relationships.

Tornow's work is consistent with the other studies in a second way, and that is the importance of administrative management skills or behaviors. What is labeled "plan and allocate," "innovate," "document," and "delegate" are similar to Bray et al.'s "making decisions quickly and wisely" and the "creative problem solving" and "effective delegation" noted by Whetten and Cameron.

Control Data Update.   The continuing advancements in Control Data's job analysis work, and as described in this section, are too voluminous to describe adequately here ("SYNCHRONY," 1985). A representative development in their more recent work is incorporated in the company's "personal (micro) computer" systems work and identified as "SYNCHRONY." In this systems work, a *general* set of managerial competencies were identified which were widely applicable to many different organizations. In brief, 7 general areas of competency were identified, which in turn incorporated 39 different types of behaviors and abilities. The structure of this system is highlighted in Exhibit 4-4.

Some representative areas of behaviors and abilities are as follows:

- *Organizational Culture:* Understanding the company's history, structure, operations, decision-making channels, and planning systems. (Organizational knowledge)
- *Measurement and Evaluation:* Understanding the methods for assessing the effectiveness of strategies, processes, programs, and policies. (Managerial knowledge)
- *Organizational Perspective:* Ability to see the "big picture" of how the organ-

EXHIBIT 4-4
Control Data's "SYNCHRONY" System-competency Dimensions

Organizational Knowledge
1. Business strategy
2. Organization culture
3. Products and services
4. Policies and procedures
5. Business trends

Managerial Knowledge
1. Professional/technical
2. Human resource management
3. Financial Management
4. Marketing and sales management
5. Computer literacy

Decision-Making Skills
1. Information management
2. Problem solving
3. Organizational perspective
4. Participative management
5. Creativity
6. Entrepreneurship

Administrative Skills
1. Budgeting
2. Financial analysis
3. Planning
4. Administration
5. Work scheduling/time management

Leadership Skills
1. Delegating
2. Motivating
3. Coaching and training
4. Coordinating
5. Team building
6. Meeting management

Communication Skills
1. Active listening
2. Feedback
3. Presenting
4. Writing
5. Conflict resolution
6. Negotiating

Personal Effectiveness Skills
1. Networking
2. Human relations
3. Persuasiveness
4. Perseverance
5. Career planning

Source: Based on "SYNCHRONY: A Job Person Assessment, Profiling and Matching System," Technical Bulletin, Control Data Business Advisors, Inc., 1985.

ization operates and how one's position affects and is affected by other parts of the organization. (Decision-making skills)

- *Motivating:* Ability to identify employee preferences for job-related rewards, to administer rewards fairly, and to create group enthusiasm and cooperation. (Leadership skills)
- *Conflict Resolution:* Ability to channel people's differing needs, interests, ideas, and feelings into constructive communication and problem solving. (Communication skills)
- *Networking:* Ability to increase one's organizational effectiveness by using formal and informal communication channels, ability to bridge the gap between the technical and business areas of the organization. (Personal effectiveness skills)

These competency dimensions provided a rich source of functional skills from which specific behaviors could be identified for particular jobs.

Baehr's "Components" of Managerial Work

The fourth (and final) approach serving as a foundation for these discussions is that of Melaney Baehr. Baehr, affiliated with the University of Chicago, carried out an extensive series of studies in all kinds of businesses and organizations. She developed various quantitative procedures such as the "Work Elements Inventory" (WEI) to describe the "component" tasks of officials, middle-level managers, and supervisors. These studies yielded 12 job dimensions which were applicable across a broad cross section of different positions and different organizations. Results from these studies emphasized the "specific underlying work behaviors" needed to execute these tasks successfully rather than personal features or task responsibilities. The fact that the instrument was originally developed from a wide range of occupational groups helped to assure that a diversity of skills was represented in her subsequent studies. According to Baehr,

> The basic theory in the construction of the WEI was that there was considerable overlap among the functions performed in even dissimilar, higher level positions. (Baehr, 1980, p. 226)

EXHIBIT 4-5

Job Dimensions from the "Work Elements Inventory"

1. Setting objectives
2. Improving procedures
3. Promoting safety
4. Developing technical ideas
5. Decision making
6. Developing teamwork
7. Coping with emergencies
8. Developing employee potential
9. Supervisory practices
10. Self-development
11. Community-organization relations
12. Handling outside contacts

Source: Based on Melaney E. Baehr, "Job Analysis Objectives, Approaches and Applications," in Edwin L. Miller, Elmer H. Burack, and Maryann Albrecht, eds., *Management of Human Resources* (Englewood Cliffs, NJ: Prentice-Hall, 1980).

The WEI results provided a picture of the relative importance of the 12 functions performed on particular managerial jobs (see Exhibit 4-5).

Professional-Technical Versus General Management Positions. Baehr's studies provided another insight into managerial position that proved useful to many management studies. In her 1967 study, participants were selected to represent two managerial types: professional managers who manage other (technical) professionals and general or line managers. Subsequent studies have often referred to this type of "split" as the basis for a dual-career ladder structure. For both the technical and general managerial hierarchies, different levels were recognized as a basis to distinguish key behavior elements. Among the managers of (technical) professionals, the "higher-level" managers were those who managed other professionals; the lower-level managers were those who managed technicians or skilled laborers. Among the general or line managers, the higher-level people were executives who managed senior managers or organizational members at the vice-presidential level or above. The next managerial level (in the general line) were those in positions in middle management who directed managers, supervisors, or staff up to (but not including) the vice-presidential level.

The comparison of WEI profiles on 12 job dimensions for the professional/technical and the general managers revealed important areas of similarities *and* dissimilarities across position *type* and hierarchical *level*. The profiles of higher- and lower-level managers of professionals resembled each other in most respects. However, the former spent significantly more time on "decision making" and "setting objectives"—factors commonly associated with senior managerial positions where planning and establishing objectives were emphasized.

On the whole, the two levels of general managers were more dissimilar than the two levels of professional/technical people. The greatest dissimilarity was that lower-level general managers gave little or no job emphasis to "developing employee potential" and placed more emphasis on "supervisory practices." Lower-level general managers also gave higher ratings to "self-development," likely reflecting a strong upward career orientation need. As an aside, this lack of emphasis on potential development poses an important challenge to senior line people and HR officials.

Higher-level managers, both professional and general, showed similar job behavior profiles. The general managers reflected the more traditional managerial dimensions. Greater differences appeared between the two types of lower-level managers.

The importance of Baehr's work was both in theoretical and methodological areas. First, it demonstrated, clearly and objectively, how managerial responsibilities and the specific behaviors needed to accomplish them vary according to the type of manager one is, and from what authority level one operates. From the point of view of organizational structure (let alone individual personality), one manager is just not the same as any other! Second, the WEI is another promising means by which to quantify aspects of behavior and thus analyze more precisely the emphases of particular work assignments.

As can be seen in Exhibit 4-5, Baehr's 12 work element dimensions in managerial positions overlap considerably with the three previous approaches. Her factors were generally most similar to the behaviors described by Bray et al.'s (1974) administrative and interpersonal skills. The innovative or creative aspect of administrative skills are represented in her work by the "improving procedures" and "developing technical ideas" factors. "Setting objectives" is a traditional administrative skill which is discussed in some way by the other analysts except Whetten and Cameron. However, Whetten and Cameron's otherwise unique focus on "getting in touch with self" is included in Baehr's "self-development" factor. Although all four approaches mention an ability to handle stress effectively, its importance is made explicit in Baehr's "coping with emergencies" factor.

Like Tornow's et al.'s "train" and "coach" dimensions, Baehr found "developing employee potential" a significant part of managerial behaviors, particularly for those in high-level positions. The collaborative focus in work relations is also seen in her "developing teamwork" dimension.

Baehr's "developing outside contacts" and community-organization relations" factor relate to Tornow's "represent" and emphasized that a growing component of managerial work was related to external linkages and communications affecting community groups, customers, suppliers, and even stockholders. Baehr also has a factor "promoting safety" that directly reflects (undoubtedly) the safety and hygiene legislation (e.g., OSHA) which has influenced managerial practices since the late 1960s.

The ASTD Competency Study

In contrast to other referenced studies in this section which dealt with managers generally, this study dealt with HRD managers. This has the obvious benefit of providing important and specific details on this key group, but at the same time, comparison opportunities with "managers" (unspecified) are reduced.

This is a notable study because it was among the first large-scale studies which attempted to "define excellence in the training and development (T&D) field . . . useful as a standard of professional performance and development." Although the results are sometimes taken as advisory because of the study methods, it provides much helpful information if used in a thoughtful way. There are other special purposes served for this chapter in highlighting the ASTD study. Study background and approaches have been described in much detail, and therefore key study products can be identified which correlate with other studies referred to in this chapter or which together provide a model for individual company efforts.

Study Highlights

Because of the scope of the ASTD study, only a few summary highlights can be provided here. The study led to nine products of which several are briefly described here. The reader is referred to an excellent overview article written by McLaglan and Bedrick (1983).

Human Resource Wheel.   This defines nine application areas or specialties in human resource practices. These are categories of convenience for referencing and description purposes. These include T&D per se, organization development, organization design, HRP, selection and staffing, personnel research, and three support activities (compensation/benefits, employee assistance, and union/labor relations). These areas share a "bottom-line" focus of productivity, individual satisfaction, personnel development, change readiness, and quality of work life; yet each approaches these quite differently. Unique methods and technology characterize each area. In reality, individuals often take on multiple roles which cross several of these.

Training and Development Roles.   People enact various roles across the nine application areas previously referenced. Roles played by specialists are often narrowly defined and might involve instruction, counseling, *or* task analysis. Generalists often take on multiple roles; these might include those already named plus "strategist," "marketer" (selling T&D or HR viewpoints and approaches to general management), *and* "manager" (organization, staffing, control, etc.). All told, 15 roles were identified which provided a flexible basis for thinking about particular jobs since these varied greatly from situation to situation and company to company.

These roles represent an important step toward defining *what people do* to be successful on the job. This is the type of approach discussed elsewhere in this chapter and described as "dimensions of managerial work," or end-job behaviors. In the ASTD study, roles comprised small clusters or groups of work-related activities. For example, the role of *instructor* involved "presenting" information and "directing structured learning experiences so that individuals learn."

Outputs.   The subject study focused on the outputs (end results or behaviors) which people in the field had to produce for their work to be judged as "excellent." This step provided the specific type of information described elsewhere in the chapter as "end-job behaviors." One hundred and two were identified. Examples included the need of an instructional writer to produce computer software and the strategic role "identifying" forces/trends impacting training and development."

The specification of outputs (end-job results or behaviors) for any (managerial) position provides the basis for establishing particulars needed to deal with competency questions. That is, what knowledge, skills/abilities, and experiences must an individual have to meet positional (output) requirements? This is an essential and all-important determination in needs analyses for managerial development. The answers are essential to determining the most appropriate and efficient methods for managerial or career development and thereby providing a concrete basis to determine required time, institutional support, and those who might best serve for coaching purposes.

Competencies. In training and development work, needed competencies quite naturally flow from the roles enacted by field professionals, managers, and the personnel in general, who are related to these activities. Examples of 31 widely used competencies identified in this study included (McLagan and Bedrick, 1983)

- *Adult learning understanding*—"knowing how adults acquire and use knowledge, skills, and attitudes, understanding individual differences in learning."
- *Career development knowledge*—"understanding the personal and organizational issues and practices relevant to individual careers."
- *Feedback skill*—"communicating opinions, observations, and conclusions, and (assuring) that they are understood."
- *Research skills*—"selecting, developing, and using methodologies, statistical, and data collection techniques for a formal inquiry."

After competencies have been identified, particulars would have to be adjusted to individual situations. For example, research skills for a large professionally oriented work force may call for the use of quite sophisticated methods and statistical models. Additionally, these might have to be supported for interpretive purposes by the type of preparation ordinarily associated with industrial/organizational psychologists or quite advanced Personnel management people. A small "low-tech" organization with infrequent employee problems might require only general research competencies, that is, general experience and academic preparation plus an acquaintance with research methods.

Managers and Performance

The subject study provides an opportunity to draw together several of the items introduced in these initial chapters. Related to Chapter 2 (performance), the identification of job outputs (behavior) is a critical first step in establishing performance benchmarks (standards) for which jobholders will be held accountable. This is an essential step in performance management. It also signals the supervising manager as to what is expected of him or her in carrying out his or her development role.

Performance management also dictates that the needed competencies for average or superior performance be identified; therefore, relevant and efficient management development methods must be prescribed. One needs good background in the relevant options and their use (Chapter 7), and how these become part of a more comprehensive system for accomplishing other corporate purposes (Chapter 5, 6, and 8) as, for example, succession or developing high potentials.

The ASTD study description also provided a general schema for developing work outputs (end-job behaviors) and various related accomplishments. Thus, the definition of who a manager is or what she or he does is an essential understanding, but only one of several that together provide a basis for more informed approaches in strategic thinking and planning affecting human resources.

Business Imperatives, Change, and Managerial Behavior

The behavior and attributes fundamental to effective management are influenced by the demands of particular work assignments. Managerial positions are embedded in business organizations, which, in turn, exist within the context of an increasingly complex political, social, and economic environment. Within these interrelated developments, the organization must respond wisely to an external environment that seems at different times to be threatening, encouraging, or constraining. Classic work by Larry E. Greiner (1967) has shown how managerial tasks change in response to the evolving and changing character of the organization and its environment. As organizations develop strategies for dealing with change, managerial roles will change too. Thus a full description of a managerial position must include some mention of its organizational context. For instance, continuing business growth, as Burack and Mathys (1987) have shown, often creates new situational demands leading to new(er) managerial tasks and thereby the need for changed or radically new managerial behavioral patterns.

Managerial responsibilities are affected by organizational change. Perhaps partly because the postwar "baby boom" generation is growing up and growing older, research in recent years has paid increasing attention to psychological development beyond childhood and throughout one's life span. Work such as that of Bray et al. (1974) has helped to bring about a general interest in study of the workplace as part of this lifelong change process. "Career development" as a field of study (see Sonnenfeld and Kotter, 1982) is one of the results. Because of the scope and importance of these occurrences to strategic planning processes for managerial development, they are discussed as part of the chapter on career development (Chapter 9).

Managerial Behaviors and Environmental Change

Burack and Mathys (1987) analyzed the managerial characteristics demanded by three types of business environments: high, low, and no growth. Oriented toward human resource planning, these conclusions helped to show how individuals were groomed for particular kinds of managerial positions based on the environmental conditions with which they were (to be) faced. While various critical task behaviors must be considered in positional analyses, strategic planning for businesses is now giving special consideration to the different management prototypes for dealing with widely different external environments (Exhibit 4-6).

In comparing managers in high-growth business environments with those in low- and no-growth situations, sharp differences can be observed. Among other factors, they involve needed intellectual and interpersonal styles. High-growth business managers characteristically take more original and autonomous action. Strategic planning, or drawing up long-range planning agendas, appears to be an important part of their work. Their coordination, communications, and decision-making activities are far less routine. Delegation of some tasks may be required

EXHIBIT 4-6
Managerial Characteristics: High-growth, Low-growth, and No-growth
Business

	No Growth	Low Growth	High Growth
Focus	Internal cost containment	Internal-external cost benefit; management of technology	Coping, experiment; external opportunistic; resource management
Risk	Avoidance cost, cost-benefit assessments	Reduction, minimize	Acceptance, risk assessment
Decision making	Routine, historical basis; structured	Traditional values; many opinions; group oriented	Information oriented; departs from patterns
Structure	Important	Good tolerance	Use in flexible way
Clarity, ambiguity	Clarity	Preference for clarity	Tolerance for ambiguity
Change	Avoided unless "to plan"	Generally resisted	Inherent, may initiate
Skills	Technical, experience	Technical, structural	General management
Planning focus	Short range	Tactical	Strategic
Performance expectation	Often accept "adequacy"	Standards oriented	High
Rewards	Often little	Some recognition	Performance oriented
Autonomy	Gets little	Accepts moderate level; sets limits	Desires high level
Innovations	Little/none	Out of channels, some	Horizontal necessary, persistent need
Coordination	Routine, resource usage	Some personal flexibility	Use of special support, flexible, internal
Coaching, training	Standardized, delegated	Need some personal ability	Key to growth; developing new people
Communications	Routine	Some variety	Vertical, diagonal
Delegation	Little	Some	External resources; must be able to delegate

SOURCE: Based on work of Hershel Kranitz and David Coulam. Reproduced with permission from Elmer H. Burack and Nicholas J. Mathys, *Human Resource Planning: A Pragmatic Approach to Manpower Staffing and Development,* 2nd ed. (Lake Forest, IL: Brace-Park Press, 1980: rev. 1987).

involving resources outside their own sphere of competency or responsibility, yet the skills of the staff must be developed if the unit as a whole is to live up to the high expectations that have been placed on it. The manager's job is likely to be demanding under these conditions but high performance typically yields high rewards. In light of these challenges, it is understandable that to be a successful manager in a high-growth environment, the manager's tolerance for uncertainty in his or her actions must be high relative to the risks taken.

Executive Attitudes Regarding Management Skills

Managers and senior executives are a part of a major redirection in organizational thinking. In the past, managerial thinking was anchored heavily in a short-term reaction mode. The reorientation is toward modes in which longer-range planning and strategic activities are increasingly involved. Although each managerial position requires a unique set of actions for success, chapter discussions suggest the existence of a general structure of managerial behavior dimensions which vary in emphasis with authority level and general responsibility assignments (e.g., administrative verses technical). Management development techniques serve as a conduit to build individual knowledge and competencies. The content of management development individual needs analyses takes into account current competencies, position responsibilities, and those end behavioral actions crucial to success. Senior line managers who assume general administrative responsibilities have a growing need to demonstrate competencies that take into account both the individual and organization.

In this respect, a study of 370 executives with senior line and administrative responsibilities provided a sense of their competency needs and their view of the utility of various management techniques used in the daily conduct of their work. The usefulness of these techniques was generally as follows (Broedling et al., 1979):

Most useful	Next most useful	Least useful
Building teamwork	Conflict resolution	Varying leadership style
Assigning/staffing	Technical education*	Administering rewards
(matching person and job)	Job (re)design	and punishment
Appraising performance	Training unit member	Distributing authority
	Interpersonal	Management by objectives
	relationships	Operational research
		techniques

*Executives were top civilian executives in the U.S. Navy.

When these management techniques were regrouped as either individually or organization centered, the *average* usefulness ratings were essentially the same. Many of these executives felt that they were frequently thrust into problem solving or reactive management approaches with insufficient time or environmental support for longer-term planning approaches. *Heavy* reliance was placed on their own staff members plus their own personal experience and knowledge. Not surprisingly, in an action research–oriented mode of management, use was also made of literature sources and members of other staffs to develop general information. Many executive actions were interpersonally oriented, regardless of whether their assignment was technical (e.g., research and development) or general administration.

In this study, some differences in managerial approaches were ascribed to differences in authority level, similar to Baehr's findings. "Executives" differed significantly from midlevel managers on the greater importance they assigned to building teamwork, staffing assignments (matching person and job), and conflict resolution.

Summary and Implications

The question of "who" is a manager is clearly an arbitrary matter, with companies evoking various criteria based on corporate history, philosophy, or decision rules from their compensation unit. A precise definition is unimportant. For the purpose of this book, it is someone with the title supervisor, manager, officer, or professional staff (managers) at comparable corporation levels. However, the question of "what" is a manager in terms of function clearly poses some complex issues long in need of clarification. Notable research and the experience of many leading companies have made it clear that job descriptions, even if responsibilities are up to date and in detail, usually won't suffice for planning and development purposes. Rather, it is the combination of job-descriptive factors *and* performance/behavioral dimensions for success which more fully proscribe the managerial function and role. What is important to systematic strategic planning is that major areas of convergence in these behavioral dimensions have started to emerge. These cut across authority level, organization type, and functional responsibility. The study results presented in this chapter suggest that a highly promising and significant body of information has started to emerge. They can substantially improve strategic planning approaches to management development.

The work of Bray et al. (1974), Tornow and his associates (1977), and Baehr (1980) indicate that some important variations in skills and traits exist according to particular work assignments or specific organization needs. Nonetheless, these studies and the Whetten and Cameron analyses reveal a general and significant cross section of managerial behavioral dimensions likely to be found in many different organizations. Their results provide a basis for defining what comprises managerial actions and bases for critically analyzing performance. Managerial ability to plan and organize work load so that organization objectives can be reached includes documenting procedures and solving problems creatively. Being forceful and "stable," and a good communicator, can motivate and help to support subordinates and encourage their career development. Managers also frequently carry out relational responsibilities with people or groups outside of their own organization—in the community and beyond. For many organizations, these activities also provide a basis for defining managerial mobility and potential.

This mixture of organizational and interpersonal responsibilities and behaviors characteristically impose much stress on the manager. Stress is characteristic of all organizational activities and often beneficial—but stress has to be managed! In studies we have conducted with specialists and managers in all kinds of industries, being able to deal *successfully* with stress is a central issue. In fact, stress coping is critical to the business as well as individual well-being and career progress. The area of stress management is of such widespread concern that it is one of the major themes in a subsequent chapter (Chapter 10).

Effective managers need both administrative and interpersonal skills; these are valued because they help the manager reach his or her goals. Communicative skills are a critical element of managerial leadership; aside from carrying out job-related activities, managerial communications and actions can serve as a basis to spark a desire for effectiveness among subordinates.

The study undertaken by ASTD illustrates the type of rich detail which can be developed when position responsibility and behavioral orientation focus in on a specific field—namely, "defining excellence in the training and development (T&D) field. Although some of the specifics of the results are perhaps debatable because of study techniques, nonetheless, approaches discussed at length in this chapter are well illustrated as they apply to the T&D field. The nine application areas making up the "human resource wheel," role definitions of positionholders, and identification of behaviors needed for solid performance provide a model for conducting analyses which may prove useful to many.

What Is a Manager . . . in Perspective

In this chapter we have dealt with the difficult question of "What is a manager?" We went from explorations of the folklore about managerial role to comprehensive field studies of the managerial role and function. Individual companies, such as AT&T, Honeywell, and Control Data, have contributed much to the nomenclature of who, and what, is a manager. They have confronted successfully questions such as, "What do managers do?" and "What do successful managers do?" Others such as Whetten and Cameron (1984) and Baehr (1980) have synthesized research and theory. All this information presents a view of what a manager is today.

In the most general sense, managers are individuals responsible for organizational units or subunits. Individual responsibility and activities are influenced by the particulars of an organization's culture. However, one constant feature of the role is the often unrelenting pace at which managers encounter both demands for decisions and new information important to meeting their organizational objectives.

To cope with these challenges, most managers undertake a number of different and important activities which may be difficult to see in a tangible way, at least at the outset. They develop personal agendas or informal plans to guide their goal attainments. They also develop networks of supporters to help implement their plans.

To develop agendas and networks, managers spend time and energy in interactions aimed at gathering information from peers, subordinates, superiors, and sources from outside the organization itself. Managers are involved in many activities, from public director of organizational ceremonies to modest actions which motivate subordinates. They are involved with conducting meetings, handling conflicts, giving presentations to superiors, delegating work, and handling their own level of stress. Decision making, a potentially universal aspect of the managerial role, often dictates their agenda-development and networking process. MIS (management information systems) systems may provide valuable support in some situations.

Generally speaking, successful managers are those who can plan and realistically update their (mental) agendas for meeting their portion of the organization's goals. To do so they must have the interpersonal skills to be able to collect relevant information and the savvy to draw upon the "hard" (e.g., management information systems) sources of information whenever necessary. Successful managers also (can) help to satisfy the needs of others. An awareness of individual career development needs and patterns can facilitate this. In short, successful managers are perceptive and forceful and can organize well.

It is possible to make some general statements about what a manager is, what a manager does, and what a manager needs to do to be successful. However, the handling of the managerial role differs across time and circumstance. Within a single manager's own professional life, challenging experiences and maturation will enhance some performance skills over time, provided that managers are not overtaxing their developed abilities or cognitive potential for abstraction. At higher managerial positions in the organizational structure, more abstractional activities will be involved. Long-range planning activities will increasingly influence most higher-level positions. Important as abstractional ability is, interpersonal and administrative skills particularly need to be emphasized and to be improved over time. Successful managers are carefully placed and challenged in their work.

Two other factors will affect the handling of the managerial role: the degree or rate of business growth and the nature (mission) of the manager's unit. Rapidly growing organizations require managers capable of more autonomy, innovation, and tolerance for uncertainty. Such qualities are far less important in environments which are not rapidly growing. The kind of work the manager's unit does will also draw on particular skills.

While the classic management activities of planning, organizing, coordinating, and controlling are still fundamental, the expanding managerial role will probably call for newer descriptive terms in the future. Just as the human resource movement is making succession planning and "talent pools" for managers more prevalent, managers will in turn make development of the careers of their subordinates a more significant part of their role. For example, the four classic activities noted here have already been joined by a fifth, "employee development."

The dynamic aspects, both of business environments and the individuals within them, are critical to our understanding of effective management. Attributes necessary for effectiveness will, to a considerable extent, be contingent upon the organization's responses to the external environment. These responses create an organizational environment within which the necessary managerial actions are determined. The nature of the external environment and stages of business growth are valuable ways to start to understand the bases for planning managerial needs and thereby cultivate effective managerial performance characteristics. On the psychological side, the attributes that managers bring to their work will depend on their basic knowledge, skills, abilities, and temperament and the extent to which these have been nurtured over time. The experiences and opportunities managers are "given" appear to have a major impact on the extent to which they can develop their capabilities and handle the demands of higher-level jobs. All managers can, and do, possess some fundamental and innate talents. Careful job placement will allow the organization to use these effectively within the organization. For those managers whose career aims and career realities match, career development can be less hectic. Overall, as managers develop their abilities, they can meet the changing needs of subordinates on whom they rely to help meet organizational goals.

REFERENCES

Baehr, Melaney. "Job Analysis: Objectives, Approaches and Applications." In Edwin L. Miller, Elmer H. Burack and Maryann Albrecht, eds., *Management of Human Resources*. Englewood Cliffs, NJ: Prentice Hall, 1980.

Boyatzts, Richard E. *The Competent Manager*. New York: John Wiley, 1982.

Bray, Douglas W., Richard J. Campbell, and Donald L. Grant. *Formative Years in Business: A Long-Term AT&T Study of Managerial Lives*. New York: John Wiley, 1974.

Broedling, Laurie A., Arthur Newman, and Alan W. Lau. "Executive Attitudes Toward Management Techniques." *Academy of Management Proceedings*, Naval Personnel Research and Development Center, Atlanta, GA, 1979.

Burack, Elmer H. and Nicholas J. Mathys. *Career Management in Organizations: A Practical Human Resource Planning Approach*, Lake Forest, IL: Brace Park Press, 1980.

Byham, William C. "Dimensions of Managerial Competence." Monograph VI. Pittsburgh, PA: Development Dimensions International, 1982.

Greiner, Larry E. "Patterns of Organizational Change." *California Management Review*, (May–June 1967).

McLagan, Patricia A. and David Bedrick. "Models for Excellence: The Results of the A.S.T.D. Training and Development Competency Study." *Financial and Development Journal*, Vol. 37, no. 6 (June 1983): 10–20.

Mintzberg, Henry. *The Nature of Managerial Work*. New York: Harper & Row, 1973.

SYNCHRONY: A Job-Person Assessment, Profiling, and Matching System," Technical Bulletin. Control Data Business Advisors, Inc., 1985.

Sonnenfeld, Jeffrey and John P. Kotter. *The Maturation of Career Theory,* Vol. 35, *Human Relations* (1982):19–46.

Tornow, Walter W. and Timothy C. Gartland. "An Integrated R&D Program for Enhancing Managerial Effectiveness at Control Data," Personnel Research Report#100-77 (February 1977).

Whetten, David and Kim S. Cameron. *Developing Management Skills.* Glenview, IL: Scott, Foresman., 1984.

APPLICATIONS SECTION

The exhibits that follow provide some added details on research studies and instruments referenced in the main body of the chapter material. Exhibit 4-7 lists 25 personal qualities appraised in the now famous "management progress study" carried out at AT&T by Bray and his associates (1974). Exhibits 4-8 and 4-9 provide position descriptions and performance information as well as a sample of analyses from the work at Control Data, undertaken by Tornow and his associates. This approach to describing and analyzing managerial work is one of the pioneering efforts in applying this advanced thinking to work-job structures.

EXHIBIT 4-7
25 Personal Qualities Appraised in the "Management Progress Study"
at American Telephone & Telegraph Co.*

Personal Qualities Description	Correlation to Advancement Level†
1. "Oral Communications Skill" Ability to give oral presentations on subjects with which the manager is well versed.	
"Written Communication Skill" Ability to construct informative formal statements on subjects with which the manager is well versed.	.33
2. "Human Relations Skill" Ability to lead a group to task accomplishment without engendering hostility.	.32
3. "Need Advancement" How important is it for this manager to be promoted well before his peers are promoted.	.31
4. "Resistance to Stress" Ability to sustain effective performance even while encountering stress.	.31
5. "Tolerance of Uncertainty" Ability to sustain effective performance in situations which are ambiguous or lack structure.	.30
6. "Energy" Ability to consistently sustain work activity at a high level.	.28
7. "Organizing and Planning" Ability to plan in advance and order work activities information and materials for effective performance.	.28
8. "Creativity" Can solve management problems with unique and innovative solutions.	.25
9. "Range of Interests" Extent interests are pursued which encompass a broad spectrum of different activities (e.g., art, science, and sports).	.23
10. "Behavioral Flexibility" Ease with which the manager can adapt or change his behavior to attain a goal.	.21
11. "Inner Work Standards" Extent to which the manager is determined to achieve own criteria for performance even when this exceeds those of his superiors and peers.	.21
12. "Need Security" Extent to which the manager is motivated by the need for job security.	−.20
13. "Scholastic Aptitude" Mental ability of a general nature.	.19

EXHIBIT 4-7 (Continued)

14. "Ability to Delay Gratification"
    Extent to which the manager can sustain work activity with-
    out rewards to achieve the rewards of long-term goals.   −.19

15. "Decision Making"
    Ease with which decisions can be made and the quality of
    decisions made.   .18

16. "Goal Flexibility"
    Ability to change the content of goals in life to correspond
    with realistic opportunities.   −.18

17. "Primacy of Work"
    Extent to which work provides satisfactions which are more
    important than those attained in other areas of activity.   .18

18. "Need Approval of Peers"
    Extent to which the manager relies upon the emotional sanc-
    tion of co-workers and subordinates.   −.17

19. "Perception of Threshold Social Cues"
    Ability to detect subtle nonverbal clues from others in inter-
    personal situations.   .17

20. "Personal Impact"
    Favorability and strength of the manaager's early impression
    on others.   .15

21. "Need Approval of Superiors"
    Extent to which the manager relies upon the emotional sanc-
    tion of figures of authority.   −.14

22. "Social Objectivity"
    Extent to which the manager is unbiased by prejudices
    against race, ethnic, sex, or other groups.   .13

23. "Realism of Expectations"
    Extent to which career goals reflect realistic opportunities for
    this manager.   .08

24. "Self-Objectivity"
    Extent to which the manager's perceptions of his own mo-
    tives, stengths, and weaknesses are realistic.   .04

25. "Bell System Value Orientation"
    Extent to which the manager is likely to adopt or has
    adopted the work values of the Bell System   −.02

*In rank order of relative correlation.

†Correlational relationship to advancement level based on reassessment (eight years after start).

Ties exist in the rank ordering of personal qualities in terms of their correlational relationships with level of advancement. The ordering of these tied qualities (e.g., "Behavioral Flexibility" and "Inner Work Standards") is random.

$\rho = .18$ or more is significant with a probability level of .05.

$\rho = .23$ or more is significant with a probability level of .01.

Based on Douglas W. Bray, Richard J. Campbell, and Donald L. Grant, *Formative Years in Business: A Long-Term AT&T Study of Managerial Lives* (New York: John Wiley, 1974).

EXHIBIT 4-8

Walter Tornow et al. and the Research at Control Data Corporation

A. Position Description Factors

I. STRATEGY PLANNING

A high score on this factor in management position indicates long-range thinking and planning. The concerns of the incumbent are broad and are oriented toward the future of the company. They may include such areas as long-range business potential, objectives of the organization, solvency of the company, business activities in which the company should engage, and the evaluation of new ideas.

II. ORGANIZATIONAL COORDINATION

A high score on this factor of a management position indicates that the incumbent coordinates the efforts of others over whom he or she exercises no direct control, handles conflicts or disagreements when necessary, and works in an environment where he or she must cut across existing organizational boundaries.

III. INTERNAL BUSINESS COORDINATION

A high score on this factor in a management position indicates that the incumbent exercises business controls; that is, reviews and controls the allocation of manpower and other resources. Activities and concerns are in the areas of assignment of supervisory responsibility, expense control, cost reduction, setting performance goals, preparation and review of budgets, protection of the company's monies and properties, and employee relations practices.

IV. PRODUCTS AND SERVICES RESPONSIBILITY

A high score on this factor of a management position indicates activities and concerns of the incumbent in technical areas related to products, services, and their marketability. Specifically included are the planning, scheduling, and monitoring of products and services delivery along with keeping track of their quality and costs. The incumbent is concerned with promises of delivery that are difficult to meet, anticipates new or changed demands for the products and services, and closely maintains the progress of specific projects.

V. PUBLIC RELATIONS

A high score on this factor in a management position indicates a general responsibility for the reputation of the company's products and services. The incumbent is concerned with promoting the company's products and services, the goodwill of the company in the community, and general public relations. The position involves firsthand contact with the customer, frequent contact and negotiation with representatives from other organizations, and understanding the needs of customers.

VI. INTERNAL CONSULTING

A high score on this factor in a management position indicates that the incumbent is asked to apply technical expertise to special problems, issues, questions, or policies. The incumbent should have an understanding of advanced principles, theories, and concepts in more than one required field. He or she is often asked to apply highly advanced techniques and methods to address issues and questions which very few other people in the company can do.

EXHIBIT 4-8 (Continued)

VII. AUTONOMY

A high score on this factor in a management position indicates that the incumbent has a considerable amount of discretion in the handling of the job, engages in activities which are not closely supervised or controlled, and makes decisions which are often not subject to review. The incumbent may have to handle unique problems, know how to ask key questions even on subject matters with which he or she is not intimately familiar, engage in freewheeling, or unstructured thinking to deal with problems which are themselves abstract or unstructured.

VIII. FINANCIAL COMMITMENT APPROVAL

A high score on this factor in a management position indicates that the incumbent has the authority to approve large financial commitments and obligate the company. The incumbent may make final and for the most part irreversible decisions, negotiate with representatives from other organizations, and make many important decisions on almost a daily basis.

IX. STAFF SERVICE

A high score on this factor in a management position indicates that the incumbent renders various staff services to supervisors. Such activities can include fact gathering, data acquisition and compilation, and record keeping.

X. SUPERVISION

A high score on this factor of a management position indicates that the incumbent plans, organizes, and controls the work of others. The activities are such that they require face-to-face contact with subordinates on almost a daily basis. The concerns covered by this factor revolve around getting work done efficiently through the effective utilization of people.

XI. COMPLEXITY

A high score on this factor of a management position indicates that the incumbent has to operate under pressure. This may include activities of handling information under time pressure to meet deadlines, frequently involving his or her personal and/or family life.

XII. FINANCIAL MANAGEMENT

A high score on this factor of a management position indicates activities and responsibilities concerned with the preservation of assets, making investment decisions and other large-scale financial decisions which affect the company performance.

XIII. HUMAN RESOURCE MANAGEMENT

A high score on this factor of a management position indicates that the incumbent has reponsibility for the management of human resources and the policies affecting it.

B. MANAGERIAL PERFORMANCE DIMENSIONS

1. KNOW-HOW

Demonstrating a thorough knowledge of the technical speciality, keeping informed of the latest developments in the technical speciality, seeking ways to improve managerial and/or consultant proficiency, keeping in touch with events happening outside the organization which impact the functional area.

EXHIBIT 4-8 (Continued)

2. PLAN AND ALLOCATE

Taking into account all available information to make timely decisions, formulating goals, policies, and plans; monitoring the progress toward objectives and adjusting plans and actions as necessary to meet them; anticipating obstacles and contingencies; and allocating and scheduling resources to assure their availability when needed.

3. DOCUMENT

Processing paperwork promptly, properly, accurately, and with attention to details, maintaining accurate and current records about projects, personnel, costs, schedules, and equipment, documenting important aspects of decisions and actions.

4. EFFORT/PERSISTENCE

Working extra hours when necessary to complete assignments, performing "beyond the call of duty," seeking and willingly accepting challenging assignments and added responsibilities, persisting and overcoming difficult obstacles, sacrificing personal convenience in the pursuit of company objectives.

5. INNOVATE

Developing and applying innovative procedures to accomplish assignments; developing new ideas and unique solutions in planning and problem solving; anticipating and coping effectively with change in circumstances which impact the functional area.

6. CRISIS ACTION

Recognizing critical problems and acting promptly and decisively to alleviate them; taking charge quickly in crisis situations; behaving deliberately and rationally under stress; deciding promptly on an alternative course of action when necessitated by unforeseen emergencies.

7. RESPONSIBILITY/ACCOMPLISHMENT

Meeting objectives (i.e., budget, profit, headcounts), accepting accountability for the unit's performance, performing duties conscientiously without requiring close supervision, meeting deadlines, being punctual for meetings.

8. INTEGRITY

Behaving according to high standards of business, professional, and social ethics; unimpeachably correct ethical conduct.

9. ORGANIZATIONAL COMMITMENT

Accepting company goals and complying with orders and directives from above, endorsing the policies and actions of superiors, offering constructive criticism about policies and decisions formulated by higher management.

10. COMMUNICATE

Providing complete, concise, accurate, and prompt information to superiors, disseminating full information to subordinates about company policies and objectives, sharing information with other units as necessary, reporting truthfully job activities and progress toward objectives.

EXHIBIT 4-8 (Continued)

11. COORDINATE

Coordinating and cooperating with other organizational units to achieve company goals with maximum efficiency, volunteering his or her experience and expertise to assist other units reach their objectives, negotiating with other units for organizational resources, showing broad knowledge about the operations of other units and the company as a whole.

12. REPRESENT

Promoting a positive company image to the public, participating actively in community affairs as a company representative, showing genuine concern for the community and society at large, exercising tact and sensitivity while conducting economically advantageous transactions with consumers and suppliers.

13. CONSIDERATION

Maintaining smooth working relationships among and with subordinates, showing consideration for subordinates' feelings, showing interest in their personal problems, expressing genuine concern for subordinates' morale and general welfare.

14. TRAIN

Determining subordinates' training needs, instituting standardized training programs to meet those needs, monitoring the training and development of subordinates on technical matters.

15. DELEGATE

Delegating, giving orders, and assigning tasks; ensuring that assignments are clearly understood; scheduling and allocating work among subordinates equitably and for maximum efficiency; monitoring and evaluating subordinates performance.

16. MOTIVATE

Setting high performance standards for subordinates, establishing challenging goals for subordinates, giving them increased responsibility and stimulating assignments, setting an example of dedication and conscientiousness for subordinates by working diligently, putting in long hours when necessary.

17. COACH

Conducting regular performance appraisals, correcting subordinates whose job performance is not acceptable; using appropriate disciplinary techniques when necessary; rewarding subordinates suitably for superior job performance.

SOURCE: Reproduced with permission from "An Integrated R&D Program for Enhancing Managerial Effectiveness at Control Data." prepared by Walter W. Tornow and Timothy C. Gartland, Personnel Research Report#100-77 (February 1977).

EXHIBIT 4-9
Job-Person Matrix Showing which Performance Dimensions are Thought to be Most Important in Successfully Accomplishing Particular Position Factors

Performance Dimensions

Position Factors	1. Know-how	2. Plan and Allocate	3. Document	4. Effort/Persistence	5. Innovate	6. Crisis Action	7. Accomplishment/ Responsibility	8. Integrity	9. Commitment	10. Communicate	11. Coordinate	12. Represent	13. Consideration	14. Train	15. Delegate	16. Motivate	17. Coach
I. Strategy Planning	●	●			●										●	●	
II. Organizational Coordination			●			●				●	●						
III. Internal Business Coordination		●				●				●			●		●	●	
IV. Products and Services Responsibility		●					●						●		●		
V. Public Relations								●		●		●	●				
VI. Internal Consulting	●				●									●			
VII. Autonomy								●	●								
VIII. Financial Commitment Approval							●										
IX. Staff Service	●		●														
X. Supervision										●			●	●	●	●	●
XI. Complexity						●						●					
XII. Financial Management			●									●					
XIII. Human Resource Management		●				●				●						●	

Source: Based on analyses by Walter W. Tornow and associates, Control Data Corporation.

Source: Based on analyses by Walter W. Tornow and associates, Control Data Corporation.

5

Strategic Succession Planning and Management Development
Concepts and Applications

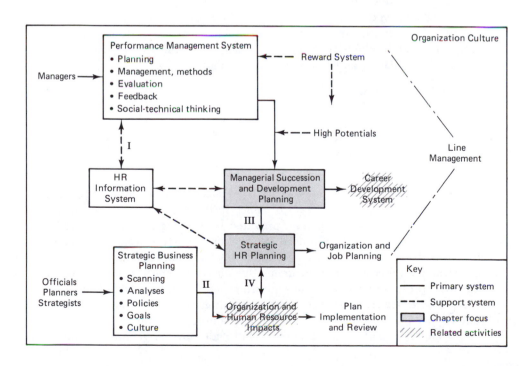

PART I: GENERAL CONCEPTS AND EXPERIENCE

Succession planning and management development remain as central activities of human resource planning, and this preeminence has been extended into the realm of strategic planning approaches. Although, traditionally, senior positions have been involved in succession analysis, the importance of these analyses has by necessity forced a broadening of focus. It is now frequently necessary to encompass middle- and even lower-level managerial ranks. Succession planning, which involves position planning, continuity, or replacement analyses, and development strategies among other activities, serves as the "centerpiece" for strategic management development.

This section is the first of a two-part discussion. In Part I, succession planning approaches are described generally and in a strategic context. In Part II, succession planning is viewed pragmatically. Stress is placed on the experiences of many different firms in starting programs, improving existing systems, and refocusing directions and thinking to achieve a greater strategic thrust. These discussions provide a foundation and framework for emphasizing systems development in the next chapter.

Strategic Succession Planning and Management Development Systems

Two mainstreams of activities feed strategic succession planning and management development approaches. The *performance system* includes performance planning, evaluation, and the underpinning provided by the organization's reward system. The second major source of crucial information is derived from the *strategic planning system,* which includes longer-range business and human resource planning and strategic processes (face diagram, this chapter). These planning and strategic activities proscribe management's future planning and decision-making environment; future organization structures; configurations; and numbers of senior (and junior) positions, staffing requirements, and timing for change.

Chapter 1 (particularly Exhibit 1-1) provides further general orientation information regarding this referenced diagram. Also, additional details regarding the systemic aspects of these two mainstreams of activity relative to management development are presented in the next chapter. This chapter emphasizes succession planning and management development to the extent that it supports succession approaches.

The essential difference brought about by "succession" analyses relative to general position planning and individual development emerges as a matter of degree or emphasis. In succession or continuity planning, senior positions are most frequently involved. The success of business planning strategies will rest on how well these positions are staffed, although the importance of sound performance planning continues undiminished. Now, however, still greater demands are made on management development planning. This is needed to fulfill successfully human resource strategic plans, the main thrust of which is succession. Due to the fact that senior (people and) positions, highly rated succession candidates, and high-potential people are involved, the sources of information and utilization of these for succession purposes are more complex than for lower-level positions. The area is also highly sensitive to political matters.

It is perhaps interesting to note in passing that, in recent years, interest in succession planning processes has been (re)awakened. But the more general supporting activities related to management development planning, including those for succession purposes, are often handled too casually. To the extent that this happens in an organization, a relatively *insecure* base exists for succession purposes.

There are some other essential features of succession planning in the strategic perspective which need to be brought out (face diagram, this chapter). Succession planning occupies a central position because much of what takes place in human resources ultimately affects succession activities. The processes and information generated in the "performance system" have to be artfully blended and integrated with various analyses in the strategic planning system. In succession work, the most complex and highest order of analyses usually involve attempting to systematize and draw inferences from the results of performance measurement and management. The higher the level of positions involved, the more numerous the needed information sources. Correspondingly, since more senior people (in length of service) also tend to occupy higher-level positions, the sheer amount of information is roughly correlated with the position involved.

The succession planning system also frequently includes capabilities for the identification and nurturing of high-potential people which is also shown in the face diagram. "High potentials" are those seen as promotable for (at least) two levels, forming a dynamic component in succession processes. They include individuals whose creative ability and leadership contribute heavily to organizational continuity, growth, and renewal.

Career development too is firmly embedded in succession processes. Succession planning and development of managerial resources seeks to stimulate, guide, and integrate individual career needs. From the individual's viewpoint, promotion and development moves will need to be seen as fulfilling important and valued career objectives and motivational requirements to maintain the person's interest, drive, and even affiliation. Succession moves typically lead to the expansion of individual responsibilities involving a substantial commitment of individual time, energies, and psyche. Personnel involved in succession planning processes play, potentially, a central role in the success of the organization's career management activities. For both the organization and person, the significance of succession discussions is great.

Benefits of Formalizing Succession Planning and Development Approaches

At this point, many readers will say that the reasons are obvious for formalizing succession approaches "so why belabor the point?" Perhaps an equal number, many in senior positions, feel that the complex and often secretive nature of succession sets it outside of useful description. Still others feel that attempts to describe the process implies procedurizing things—and thereby flexibility is lost or confidentiality is possibly jeopardized. As with most other important and complex activities of this nature, there is some truth in these assertions. But many strong and persuasive factors do command attention for rationalizing these approaches. The agenda of items in Exhibit 5-1 provides some of the essentials for more deeply probing succession approaches. These are discussed briefly in the paragraphs that follow.

The benefits itemized in Exhibit 5-1 can be organized into several broad categories. Perhaps the single most important set deals with the enlargement of the numbers of qualified candidates. Greater flexibility and choice is thus provided in succession planning and development decisions. Second, a more systematic approach reduces reactive responses to crises or emergency situations which characterize informal succession processes. More time is provided to anticipate some of these develoments and to take steps in advance for dealing with them. To the extent that top management is seen as doing its "homework," high-potential and talented people in the organization are more inclined to remain. They have the confidence that their career possibilities and desires for the future have been input into corporate needs, succession analyses, and development programming.

Another point favoring more systematic approaches is that a foundation is provided for better understanding of the corporate culture. Understanding is also required of the philosophy of management and ways of doing things, and how "culture" impacts particular succession analyses and decisions. Not to be ignored, too, is the fact that "fleshing out" succession approaches and the strategic aspects of these helps to move development strategies away from thinking that it is largely an art form or exercise in futility. It is moved into a realm where it can be treated in a more organized way—and with improved results.

EXHIBIT 5-1
Why the Interest in Succession Planning(?)

√ Provides a logical and specific connection to organization business and strategic planning.

√ Provides more systematic bases to judge the risks of making particular succession and development moves.

√ Assists developing systematized succession plans which fit with the distinct trend to codify, wherever possible, more general and comprehensive corporate planning actions.

√ Reduces randomness of managerial development movements.

√ Helps to anticipate problems before they get started—and thereby avoids awkward or dysfunctional situations.

√ Awareness is increased of state-of-the-art advances.

√ Increases managerial depth which can be called upon as needed.

√ Provides a logical approach for locking succession planning into the processs of human resource planning—connecting formats (data, timing) with process (judgments, discussions, analyses).

√ Facilitates integration of the many components of human resource planning after having done many of these separately in the past.

√ Improves the identification of high potentials and/or future leaders.

√ Exploits the use of computer power or capabilities to improve succession planning formats and processes further.

√ Broadens the use of "cross-functional development" techniques to improve competencies and quality of decision making.

√ Stimulates inquiry into the fit of succession planning with the philosophy of the organization.

√ Improves internal promotion opportunities.

√ Overcomes the limitations of "reactive management" approaches and goes to planned management of managerial positions.

√ Establishes a logical basis for widening choice among qualified candidates.

√ Improves fulfillment of "equal employment opportunity" objectives.

√ Makes informal but critical criteria such as "fit" of the person more explicit.

Succession Options: Inheritance of Traditions

Succession planning and development approaches have not lacked for a "rich" heritage of options. Not surprisingly, many of these have been anchored in past traditions, managerial philosophy, formal organization structure, or the peculiarities of an organization's legal form. Perhaps the most influential factor for the succession tradition was the valuing by top management of particular functional experiences, which, in turn, came to form an established line of succession. These included functional promotion sequences as in marketing, operations, engineering, and finance. Also, traditions in particular industries favored certain routes and the development experiences attendant to these. Examples included finance in utilities, engineering in heavy industries, marketing in mass-market consumer products, and buying and store management in retail merchandising. Small(er) types of businesses arrived at strategies which reflected largely their legal (often entrepreneurial) form or family orientation—thus development usually meant a rounding out of background which was often reserved exclusively for family members.

A common assumption in the succession tradition was that experience (time) correlated highly with performance. Thus, organizational members needed considerable seasoning before being actively considered as a succession candidate. Implicit within this philosophy was that extended length of service would also provide ample opportunity to observe acts of loyalty, dependability, political astuteness, and competency. People were often expected to play a passive role, with senior management making the overtures (or invitation) to join the inner, senior management circle.

Under these circumstances, the strategic aspects of succession and management development were often reduced largely to dependence on experience (albeit a guided experience) through particular functional or job sequences. Competitive trends; growth in organizational size and complexity; economic, social, and technological trends; the growing scope of legal regulations; and substantial improvement in developmental methods changed all this. Succession planning and improved means of carrying it out assumed new strategic importance beyond the power of traditional approaches.

Systems also had to be developed which helped to retain young, career-seeking, capable people for the period of time required to nurture their abilities, making them suitable candidates for succession purposes. These systems had to do a superior job of recognizing the growing complexities of contemporary organizations and how this affected career mobility. At the same time, individuals had to better understand the effects of individual business trends on their expectancies and the conduct of their affairs.

Actualizing Continuity or Succession Planning

Succession planning analyses assume a time orientation which dovetails into long-range business and strategic planning. The process is usually "bottoms up." In this approach, recommendations and reviews are made at successively higher organization levels. The events triggering continuity analysis stem from both long(er)-range business planning and strategic analyses and internal movement cycles keyed to promotion, retirement, and turnover. At times trigger events result from relatively unique situations. Examples include corporate reorganization, change of competitive mission, merger, or internalization of a business.

Business and strategic planning analyses have a marked influence on the thrust of succession planning and thereby the form and composition of development programming. The following listing of relationships is typical of these connections:

Strategic business issues	Human resource implications, thrust of development
• Business expansion	• Development of newer/expanded managerial cadre, often with significantly different competencies
• Improved profit performance	• Improvement in cost-benefit and profit analyses, exploitation of computer technology, introduction of cost containment strategies
• New product introductions	• Grafting on new product development skills and capabilities in marketing
• Introduction of new technology	• Technical training
• Revamping competitive philosophy	• Reorientation of key managers and executives—involving knowledge, skills, abilities, and concepts
• Merger	• Assessing areas of strengths and incompatibilities: people, talent, cultures, salaries, and joining of different value systems; obsolescence potential related to positional needs
• Internalization	• Use of foreign nationals as managers, culture issues, compatability, and costs of incorporating foreign nationals in continuity planning programs

Management Succession Planning Information

Succession or continuity planning involves many different information sources and reports. The extent to which these are formalized depends on organizational circumstances. The scope of these is suggested in Exhibit 5-2. Documents such as a "management inventory" are often basic in succession planning systems and include assessments of promotability, long(er)-term potential, and competencies. The same holds for "performance evaluations," but some firms feel that assessment center results, for example, are not needed because they have too few people involved or assessments are still (unjustifiably!) questionable as to validity. "Analysis of fit" with corporate value structure (or culture) is a newer and potentially rich source of information in the cultivation of succession candidates. There is the possibility of "discovering" seriously conflicting values among top people.

Reports that provide "functional summaries" or profiles of the type of data described here are helpful in planning internal or external development programming and even applying these more precisely to authority levels or areas of the organization which may pose special problems.

"Position information" serves to concentrate particularly on work analyses and the status of current staffing. A new and growing source of important information is the identification of lines of progression that reflect a conscious effort to systematize the analyses and determine succession positions and lines.

"Succession analysis reports" include basic documents such as a summary of direct reports (people supervised) and individual readiness to move, as well as

EXHIBIT 5-2

The Scope of Succession Planning Information and Reports

Information Sources, General

- Management inventory and assessments
  Assessment of potential (involving individual or multiple judgments)
  Assessment of promotability
  Inventory of knowledge, skills and abilities, experience, and past training
  Adaptability and capacity to learn new concepts or approaches
  Adaptability to changed circumstances—coping with change
- Performance evaluations
  Performance appraisals
  Evaluations related to performance (behavioral) dimensions
  Single and multiple evaluations
- Psychological evaluations
  Assessment of potential and various traits (job related)
  Analyses of developmental needs
- Management assessment center results
- Analyses of "fit" with corporate value structure (or culture)
- Individual career planning—objectives
- Self-nominations
- Personnel files

Position Information

- General organization staffing patterns, retention rates, and forecasted needs
- Position audits including estimates of positional vacancies
- Position qualifications—performance/behavioral dimensions (current ones and new ones).
- Lines of progression
- Succession summary, individual readiness, and disposition of direct reports (subordinates)
- Forecasts of individual potential
- High-potential lists
- Reserve and replacement candidates (variable composition)
- Individual development plans and summaries by type of strategy
- Development tracking (objectives/designs and results)
- Individual career pathing (planned)
- Attrition analyses (incumbents)
- Position blockages: individual readiness and positional move information
- Vacancy analyses (current positions)
- Performance summaries of key and critical human resources and change patterns
- Functional summaries: knowledge/experience (basic requirements, learning needs and qualities, functional, expertise)

(Continues)

EXHIBIT 5-2 (Continued)

- Contingency or "what if" types of analyses
- Action research components
  Effectiveness of developmental actions, strategies, candidate responses to developmental actions, programming-researchable questions for analysis.

Corporate Policy Determinations

- Equal employment (affirmative-action) objectives
- Recruitment policies and strategies (e.g., external/internal mix)

"development tracking" that summarizes incumbent moves and comparison of planned versus actual outcomes. "Vacancy analyses" and "position blockages" are examples of reports that "zero in" on particularly difficult or pressing problems or areas of future concern.

A type of report warranting comment (Exhibit 5-2) is that of the "action research components." The interest has grown considerably in establishing data base lines for comparative purposes. In other words, attitudinal surveys and other organizational studies provide the results by which the effectiveness of succession planning activities can be judged in the future. Contingency or "what if" types of analyses result from the consideration of alternate planning assumptions. For example, a common analysis involves alternate ratios of outside hires to inside promotions and considers the consequences of this type of decision on future staffing distributions and career expectancies of incumbents, including the time to reach particular salary/position levels.

It is important to state that few corporate succession programs incorporate all these information inputs and reports. They should be viewed, in consequence, as good possibilities that can yield a strong succession planning effort. As a matter of information, these reports and information comprise the inputs and outputs within the range of some currently available ("off-the-shelf") computer software packages described in detail in Chapter 11. In short, the state of the art regarding these information needs and capabilities has been established and is being exploited by an increasing number of organizations.

Succession Analyses as a Key Line Management Responsibility

It has often been said with much truth that if continuity planning becomes largely a staff activity, the overall quality of planning and results are likely to be poor. Human Resource staffs can plan systems, monitor the progress of succession candidates, design new system components, and help to improve the functioning of various methods and systems activities. However, if Human Resources or others take on too much of the planning, procedural, and decision-making aspects of succession functions, executives and senior line managers are likely to disclaim association, let alone responsibility for their fulfillment. Since the results of long-range and strategic business planning often take years to unfold, the results of staff assuming too much of the burden of "doing" may not be detected for a long time. In the meantime, serious cost or financial matters may crop up for which line management may well disclaim responsibility.

No formula approaches exist as to precisely what the level of staff involvement should be. But it is clear that line management holds the keys to the identification and cultivation of succession candidates. Thus, staff needs to be able to play an important supportive and guidance role. The discussions in Chapter 1, I hope, help to reinforce the "desired" role of Human Resource support. Because of the technical nature of some continuity analyses, procedures are vulnerable to shifting of responsibilities from line to staff. Continuing vigilance is required to avoid this unfortunate result.

Succession Development Data: Hard and Soft

Although many of the areas of information previously enumerated are a matter of record, they represent a combination of both hard and soft data. That is, information which is both factual as well as judgmental. Both are equally valuable in succession analyses and development but pose quite different problems in usage. This occurs because of the relative number of and importance assigned to judgmental inputs. Some selected categories of problems and issues will clarify these points. Further discussions of development data are provided in the next chapter on management development systems.

Knowledge, Experience, Obsolescence

Seemingly hard data such as past experience or participation in workshops or skills acquired in the past need to be interpreted in terms of current and future relevance. Examples of interpretive problems include programming skills in now obsolete computer software languages, business experience which is outdated because of greatly changed competitive tactics, and management motivation methods (training) based largely on various "hygiene" or "motivator" factors. These examples illustrate situations in which dynamic changes have greatly altered the form or relevance of information.

Performance and Assessment Ratings

Many of those highly experienced in succession planning and development processes view the subject ratings (judgments) as being among the most difficult factors with which to contend. The problem is made doubly difficult because of the impreciseness of performance standards related to senior managerial roles and highly subjective bases for rendering judgments. Academics, researchers, and corporate staff units have become acutely aware of those problems and, through intensive study, have made some notable improvements in the reliability and validity of these judgments. "What's been accomplished?" Both performance standards and the bases for rendering judgments have profited from job-analytic schemes that have led to an emphasis on end performance/behavioral dimensions for success (as discussed in Chapters 2 and 7). These are based on "critical incident" studies of actual managerial jobs and performance. Developing uniform sets of general dimensions, backed up with the detailed particulars of specifically assigned positions and behaviorally anchored rating scales, has greatly aided making performance and training judgments. These advancements also have aided comparisons of positions or candidates. Formal training in the use of "behaviorally anchored rating scales" has improved the use of these job-descriptive tools and has helped to assure greater uniformity in their application.

Another part of the difficulty in the succession tradition has been the great reliance placed on firsthand knowledge or direct contacts as a basis for rendering judgments. Improvements in the bases for developing information and performance standards have reduced somewhat the need for this type of personal or firsthand knowledge, though it continues to be of much importance. Growing attention has been directed toward multimethod approaches (i.e., multiple sources of information), and these have proven valuable in succession analyses and prescribing development programs. Greater reliance on information has also come from improvements in assessment center results based on work-related managerial situations, problems and roles, and the use of the types of behavioral dimensions referenced above. Further confidence in succession information has also resulted from psychological assessments by trained psychologists, especially where senior-level managerial or officer positions are involved.

"Chemistry" and Fit of the Person

Regardless of the amount and type of data, an absolute condition in most organizations is "fit" which lies mostly in the emotional realm. It is a fact of organization life. The importance of succession decisions to the organization *and* person warrants more explicit attention to this aspect of succession.

Needs Analysis for Development Planning

The core of development analyses for continuity planning rests squarely on needs analyses. Needs analysis simultaneously uses three different perspectives for specifying developmental actions. The three perspectives are those for the individual, position/job, and organization. No one of these is more important than the other—all are required in arriving at a clear specification of development requirements and timing. For the person, information on demographics, knowledge, skills and abilities, performance, and career interests are among the basic set of data considerations. From the viewpoint of the position, characteristic items include responsibilities, essential communications relationships, behavioral performance dimensions for success, and potential changes in these due to business and strategic planning considerations. Organizational aspects of needs analyses increasingly stress longer-range organization requirements. This is to help assure that business and long-range planning needs, staffing patterns, and potential changes in structure, philosophy/culture, or requisite competencies have been considered.

Successfully Marketing Continuity Planning

Anecdotal information gathered from literally dozens of organizational experiences provides a useful group of prescriptions which can help to improve the success of continuity planning and development programs. A primary reason for poor results is the lack of appreciation of apprising key people, or others, of succession objectives, problems, or the reason(s) for a particular action. Failures also result from the lack of involvement and commitment from line management. Additionally, there is a tradition, very strong in the United States and other Western cultures, that encourages quick moves, readily demonstrable results, and "fast" evaluation. Severe disappointments are likely for those pursuing this approach. These points and others are summarized in the following general guidelines. They hardly exhaust the subject, but they do provide a point of departure for analysis. (See Exhibit 5-3.)

Exhibit 5-3 indicates that the point of departure for formalizing succession/management development programs is the conscious and thoughtful consideration of top management's major urgencies and priorities. Knowing that the succession program, for example, is a direct response to improving the likelihood of succession for a new and major program, or for meeting continuity requirements in a key division, will immediately give it identification as responding to a critical and active organization need. Support by the president and various powerful officials legitimizes the undertaking and clarifies from the beginning the high priority assigned to the undertaking (point 2) and helps to enlist the essential involvement of line management (point 3). Support and communications are further ensured by an advisory group or sounding board committee (point 4).

In the experience of many working with these processes, it has been repeatedly demonstrated that successful undertakings hinge more on common sense, workable plans, and support of key people rather than sophisticated methods or technology. Slowly building a pattern of successful steps or results provides encouragement to the organization reflecting thoughtful, deliberate steps (Exhibit 5-3). Trying to bring in significant and widespread changes involving traditions and the customary ways of doing things in the past further underscores the need for building a success pattern and consciously dealing with change per se. Finally, Exhibit 5-3 suggests that regular monitoring approaches and adaptation to emergent problems or new situations are very much part of successfully marketing continuity planning. Human Resource's involvement in monitoring and adaptation will have to

EXHIBIT 5-3
Successfully Marketing Continuity Planning

- Identify top management's urgencies, priorities.
- Gain the direct endorsement and involvement of the president (and chair).
- From the beginning, build in line management involvement and commitment.
- Utilize an advisory group of senior and powerful people to confirm continuity needs and lend valued insights and power to program directions.
- Where important changes are being considered, be prepared to deal with senior people having major reservations or misgivings regarding the "new" approach. One-on-one explanations and attentive, active listening regarding specific problems, while seeking to resolve these where possible, further enlists support.
- Take a small step at a time and one that has a high likelihood of success.
- Recognize that the workability of planned approaches turns more often on the process (or approach) and having a sensible plan rather than one which is technically sophisticated.
- Link with business and strategic planning activities and more conventional personnel processes.
- Recognize that formalizing continuity planning is typically a challenge in change involving corporate culture (i.e., traditions and customary ways of doing things).
- Consciously acknowledge and be prepared to deal with long-term change. Because of the basic organizational values, and processes involved, it will likely take months or even years to take place fully in most organizations.
- Provide for mediation of disputes and differing viewpoints—but also indicate how and when a final decision is to be made where agreement (e.g., on moves or candidate selection) can't be reached.
- Establish a succession committee drawn from the original advisory group to facilitate a more permanent arrangement and to signal the move from the stages of marketing and installation to a more permanent arrangement.
- Monitor regularly to make needed changes.

be organized and staffed in such a way that follow-up is facilitated over an extended time period.

Interim Summary

There has been a conscious attempt here to avoid emphasizing one portion of succession planning and development approaches relative to the others. They are all equally important such that there is no point in a strong marketing effort if the program is poor procedurally. Conversely, there is no point in developing a thoughtful succession philosophy and planning strategy if the program hasn't been "marketed" to the organization. The keys to success are flexibility, a well-balanced effort, "fit" of the person, and understanding of existing issues and how to deal with these. The focus is on the longer-term and taking incremental steps which build success one step at a time.

Part II provides some tangible examples of how the philosophy, perspective, and general approaches described here have been translated into functional programs. In contrast to the chapter formats used elsewhere in this book, "applications" are incorporated as an integral part of developing this subject. These corporate experiences are central to actualizing the general guidelines and anecdotal information contained in Part I.

PART II: CORPORATE SUCCESSION PLANNING
APPLICATIONS AND EXPERIENCE
IN THE STRATEGIC FRAMEWORK

The central importance of succession processes to strategic planning approaches, and the need to customize systems to many different situations, is the primary rationale for Part II. Thus the thrust of Part II is quite different from that of Part I. It is pragmatic and concerned with applications and actual corporate experiences. Its purpose is to present a representative cross-section of experiences and applications related to succession processes. Also, two rather lengthy examples are provided of corporate succession/management approaches including, selectively, some of the documents used. These are entitled "An Insurance Company" and "Mayfair Corporation," a consumer products company.

Corporate Experiences with Succession Planning and Development Systems

There is probably no area of human resource planning and development so molded to the characteristics, culture, and processes of organizations as succession planning and development. For example, some of the corporations with which we are acquainted are old line and relatively conservative organizations. Over time, as they grew larger, and even international in scope, a cadre of powerful senior executives emerged who "reigned" over major divisions or sectors of the business. The diversity of competitive conditions and geographic decentralization of facilities and offices placed much responsibility for executive succession and development in the hands of these senior and powerful people. This focusing of succession responsibilities was further reinforced by a profit center orientation which effectively said, "We will judge you on the basis of the profitability of your unit and use of corporate assets. How you accomplish it is up to you—*so long as* you are meeting targeted (mostly) financial measures." For the company(ies) represented by this profile, managers demonstrating these competencies to the powerful leaders of these business sectors exhibited the potential for upward mobility into senior management ranks. More generally, these organizations were often described as traditional enterprises. For the firms profiled, top management's involvement in succession processes was limited to succession candidates for the top sector or divisional posts plus, of course, key positions at corporate headquarters. Human resource planning and development responsibilities related to succession were mostly lodged within divisions for reasons already mentioned. For this and similar situations, the role of Human Resources was often played out behind the scenes as counselor to top management, occasional consultant, and often as change agent.

In successful organizations where corporate size was not an overriding consideration, as in medium or small firms with domestic markets or limited international markets, quite different models of succession planning and development often emerged. General corporate culture characteristics for these firms frequently included such descriptors as creative, adaptive to needed change, and well-shared values. Other characteristics included heavy emphasis on human resources, strong resourceful leaders, reward climates geared to performance, and cross-fertilization of manager skill development to build competency. In these organizations, Human Resource officials often occupied high-level positions that gave them visibility and power enough to deal with entrenched line executives. Human Resource officials were usually politically astute and knew how to get things done. Thus, HR served various roles at the corporate level including coordinator of executive and management development planning, liaison with a corporate-level executive succession and development group or committee, broker of key personnel among group heads, consultant, and systems planner. In these organizations the active endorsement by top management of comprehensive and thoughtful human resource development planning was never in doubt—nor was the emphasis on performance, practical outcomes of individual needs analysis, and considerations of individual career planning as well.

Just described were two characteristic groups of companies whose succession systems were still evolving and taking on quite different features. However, another type of corporate experience was also encountered. The "middle-group" companies have varied mixtures of the characteristics just described. A tabular summary of six organizations (Exhibit 5-4) included in a corporate study (Burack, 1985, 1986) helps to bring out some of the features of these organizational approaches. Further, two of these firms are described in somewhat greater detail with emphasis on "why" and "how" their approaches worked in their organizations. These corporate profiles and company discussions complete the introductory material for Part II. This introductory section is then followed by two pragmatic cases, the purpose of which is to provide concrete examples of succession/development procedures and documents supporting these.

Example 1: A Bank

This large bank had worldwide operations, though its activities in the United States were still a major part of the picture. In general, competitors viewed them as tough competition, creative, seeking to accelerate growth, and managing their organization as a business ("not as an old-line bank"). Yet the organization had strong subcultures bound together by overriding core values. The organization was highly decentralized and divisional management was strengthened by both mainframe and personal computers positioned within divisions. The increasing growth enjoyed by the bank led to an organization in which mobility was the keynote and where horizontal transfers were frequent—at times several moves in one year.

Top management evolved a strategy for maintaining a dynamic growth quality in the organization through increases in business volume and a deliberate policy of regularly moving people. Although they were decentralized and well entrenched in foreign operations, all senior managers had to conduct annual needs analyses in their responsibility areas. These emphasized succession planning and development analyses which took into account general corporate requirements and individual career planning. With the decentralized character of the bank, management development programming was carried out within divisions. Yet divisional programs, including overseas operations, benefited from an extensive group of both outside and internal courses. These were cataloged in corporate materials. Although having said that, their primary emphasis for development was (still) job-related experiences reinforced by rotational assignments and coaching.

Succession thinking at the corporate level made it clear that high priority was assigned to those identified as high potentials. However, "officer candidate" designations were never formally communicated to the individuals involved, although it was obvious that some became aware of this classification. "Candidates" had to be both job and geographically mobile. High-potential people became "fast trackers." They were deliberately moved at least once every three years and frequently, much more often, sometimes once or twice in the same year.

Dual-career couples were an accepted part of organization life and the bank went to much trouble to help arrange job situations for the spouse. Women had always been an important part of the banking scene though upward mobility had been restricted to senior levels in the past. But a rapid turnaround took place in this industry. The result was that in this bank as in others, "the spouse" as frequently turned out to be male as female. To an important extent this bank viewed the college recruiting process as the primary inputting source for the "fast trackers" or high-potential people.

Much development programming time and thought were devoted to nurturing individial potential and moving these people along rapidly. MBA recruiting was selective and aggressive. New training cohorts of trainees were intermingled with more traditional banking types; this approach proved especially beneficial for many of the women since (at that point in time) they often lacked extensive work/job experiences. Individual development was accelerated through a very well-developed (internal) "effective management of people" program; it provided feedback from instructors, supervisors, co-workers, cohort members, and video-taped role simulations.

The Succession Planning Cycle.   All senior managers and officers (based on salary grade) were reviewed twice per year by the president and chair. All these executives reported in detail on their own development plans and those whom they had nominated as backup(s). These semiannual meetings served as a clearinghouse for candidate information, planning for crossmovement of candidates, conflict resolution in jurisdictional disputes, and confirmation of nominees. Extensive files were developed on succession nominees and vigorous cases had to be presented on behalf of candidates—subject to close questioning by the president and chair.

An "executive development committee" handled the next level of senior managers. Its membership included the president, vice presidents for human resources and finance, and two rotating positions (considered an excellent development experience) occupied by senior vice presidents. The executive in charge of the management candidate's area or division was expected to organize presentations on behalf of their people. Human Resources provided helpful *informal* feedback to the area or division head prior to formal submission of their candidates. On behalf of the "executive development committee," Human Resources also coordinated the cross flow of candidates for developmental purposes and reviewed developmental proposals relative to strategic business plans.

Succession planning became a serious and highly intensive process in this bank. Attention was directed to officers and senior managers and the next managerial levels that comprised "tomorrow's" possible candidates. Senior management recognized its need to become intensively involved in succession processes; it required at least several weeks per year. This "interest" was reinforced by the chair, the president, and the bank's reward system. Also, these senior officers provided much feedback to senior managers on how well they were performing on behalf of succession. The system was successful because it tied in with long-range planning and strategic thinking and the most senior people assured the connections with development planning. Also, it was flexible and blended in with the needs and level of detail seen as important in a particular area—as determined by the key people involved. The system grew through past successes, word of mouth, and willingness to change as needed. Systems in particular areas grew in depth or scope as need dictated and the people learned how to operate and improve on the system.

The continuing interest and attention of the president and chair assured long-term stability of their succession approaches. The "long run" was taken as a point of departure for reviewing short(er)-term proposals. As the system matured, Human Resources found it possible to shift its role from systems planning toward consultation and being a facilitator of change (including dealing with organizational politics).

Example 2: An Engineering-Consulting Organization

This firm provided a wide range of engineering and consultive services on a worldwide basis. Well known and highly regarded in its field, the company's staffing included a high proportion of technical and professional personnel who worked frequently in teams and often as a part of a "matrix" structure. Within the framework of the "matrix" structure, considerable flexibility and interpersonal skills were

EXHIBIT 5-4

Summary of Organization Features: Strategic Planning Examples
Types of Organizations

	Example 1	Example 2	Example 3	Example 4	Example 5	Example 6
	Bank	Consumer Products Company	Life Insurance Company	Pharmaceuticals and Chemicals Company	Manufacturing Company	Engineering Consulting Organization
Scope of activity*	• Large • United States and foreign	• Medium-large • United States and foreign	• Large • United States	• Medium-large • United States and some foreign	• Medium • United States and Canada	• Medium • International
Features of corporate culture	• Aggressive • Innovative • Decentralized • Rewards geared to performance	• Stability • Conservative • Decentralized • Heavy emphasis on "company way" • In process of change—conflict with traditional values	• Conservative in past • Many long tenure personnel • Current change: infusing new people at key levels • Cross-fertilization not encouraged	• Conservative • Slow-paced change • Decentralized power structure	• Changing to more aggressive, innovative form • Growing emphasis on systematic management • Business has become volatile—sense of uncertainty	• Formal • Systematic • Impersonal • Close control • Rewards geared to performance
Positioning of HR planning	• Centralized	• Centralized group • Decentralized function to groups	• Centralized group	• Centralized as function • Decentralized as activity in divisions	• Centralized as function • Decentralized as activity in divisions	• Centralized

Role of HR planning	• Consultants • Change agents • HR strategic planning • EEO orientation	• Advisory to chief executives • Incorporated in Personnel at group level	• Monitor and coordinate • Planning focused on executives • Transitioning to strategic emphasis on high potentials • Development of executives • Career planning advisory	• Coordinators • Consultants • Facilitators • Internal "marketers" • Division oriented • Career planning advisory	• Consultants to top management • Systems design • Coordinators • Decentralized • Division oriented • Career planning advisory	• Active administrative role • Consultants, systems planner • HR strategic planning
S.P. systems approach	• Integrated—top officers; otherwise decentralized to major sectors/or divisions • Integrate career planning	• Development of executive and middle management	• Development of executives at all managerial levels • Comprehensive • Integrate with career planning	• Development of executives and middle-level managers	• Executive development	• Comprehensive • Integrated • Integrate career planning

*Based on employment or assets and relative to its industry. In banking for example, large would be in excess of 8,000 employees.

required. Group members and activities cut across many different functional lines and authority levels. Computers were used extensively in the organization and were one of the main factors in its achieving a comprehensive strategic business and human resource planning system. The computer-based system greatly facilitated information flow and communications based on authoritative information.

The Strategic and Operational Planning System.   Strategic business planning was geared to its far-reaching project activities; environmental scans were regularly translated into business opportunities (and threats), demand and supply forecasts, and aggregate staffing planning. Operational planning, which was shorter range, helped to establish professional staffing parameters and the areas of shortages or surpluses in human resources. The operational planning analyses also served as the main basis for management development planning and defining the related requirements for their work systems. Individual interests were recognized too and became a part of broad-scale career development planning and widely available counseling. Cognizance of career development was tied into discussions of business directions and strategies.

This concludes the introductory note for Part II. The next two case applications are quite pragmatic, including selected documents used to support succession planning approaches. Both bear the stamp of longer-range business and strategic planning.

CASE APPLICATIONS

ENTON INSURANCE COMPANY

This insurance company was a diversified organization handling many different forms of life and casualty insurance. This traditionally organized company employed over 6,000 people. The life and casualty companies operated as essentially separate organizations under different presidents. Structurally, each company was organized as "areas," and within these "departments," and within these "divisions."

Fast-growing competition in the insurance industry, growing complexity of its own organization, and a forecasted gap between needed and available managers for succession forced the company to study means of meeting short-run needs and establishing longer-term managerial career development. Much more attention was required for succession analyses and candidate tracking. In addition, it had to look closely at how to cultivate personnel and identify people with potential for senior managerial and officer positions. This painstaking examination, covering a period of several years, resulted in a strategy of "grounds-up" revamping of corporate development practices. In the *initial program phase* lasting about three years, the basic personnel system was reorganized and greatly updated. Job planning, job analysis, performance appraisal, and assessment capabilities were all affected.

In *phase 2,* attention was focused on the design of a succession planning system. Critical to its success was the integration of long-range and strategic business plans (*both* life and casualty) with succession planning. The initial bridge between business and strategic planning was established through a "corporate succession planning committee" which included the chair and CEO, presidents of the life and casualty companies, senior vice president of administration, vice president of human resources, and two rotating positions. Many of the committee members also "sat" in the corporation's planning committee. Thus the initial succession design "locked together" business planning and planning for senior human resources. The initial design provided for these informal connections along with more formal procedures, plus analyses slated for future incorporation. Because of the company's newness to these procedures and its historical roots and culture anchored in traditional approaches, the first steps in the succession effort were concerned with meeting the "obvious" corporate shortage of senior talent. The line of authority included areas (top), departments, divisions, and then small(er) administrative units. The initial succession systems design strategy was unique in that it incorporated a department-level pilot program that ran in "parallel" with a program for all senior-level officials that was corporatewide and only involved senior and officer positions. This approach provided much flexibility for the pilot divisions (within the department) to take account of many different organizational situations and to maintain the important decentralized character and involvement of middle-level managers. It also provided the opportunity to test out a feeder ("farm")-system approach within a given department. The corporatewide plan and the department pilot program dovetailed at the senior officer level. That is, the succession plans for senior heads of divisions within the pilot area had to be merged successfully with the corporatewide succession program. All heads of areas were senior managers (vice president or senior vice president) and many heads of departments (vice president titles) were too.

The corporation's approach proved highly effective in getting the active cooperation of many different managerial levels and also provided for a department by department, or area by area phasing in of units in the future.

Next, a basis was to be established for introducing more systematic means of carrying out succession planning and development processes attendant to these. New development procedures were to involve cross-functional moves, agreement on a set of key corporate values for desired behaviors, points of decision making, and candidate identification. Many of the newer procedures were contrary to past practices. Thus top officials preferred to err on the side of slow change. Stage 2 emphasized obvious corporate needs as a rationale to gain support and a pilot-type implementation with several friendly and cooperative corporate groups. The intention was to learn from this implementation experience and to gain support for further formalization and corporatewide implementation in subsequent years.

A pragmatic corporate succession planning manual was developed which provided executive guidelines. This "manual" included two main parts and details on all the main phases of the succession planning system. Representative sections from this manual are reproduced in these case notes because the manual is a comprehensive description for a workable system, readily modified to suit many different application situations. The manual was forwarded to all senior managers and was accompanied by a letter signed by the chair and the presidents of the life and casualty companies. The two main parts of the manual were orientation and approaches and procedures. Details follow.

ENTON INSURANCE COMPANY SUCCESSION PLANNING MANUAL
PART 1: ORIENTATION AND APPROACHES

I. Statement of Purpose

    A. Our corporate philosophy is based importantly on the belief that the talent exists within the companies to meet the challenges we face. It is a management responsibility to develop employees to their fullest potential to fulfill corporate needs. The systematic planning of management succession at all levels of the companies is fundamental to the attainment of this objective. This program is designed to achieve the following goals:
        1. Assure that a group of qualified managers is available to meet future business needs.
        2. Provide career advancement opportunities for minorities, females, and other "designated" groups.
        3. Provide a mechanism for the review of corporate talent for succession and development training.
        4. Encourage inter- and intradivisional/functional development to broaden experience.
    B. Succession planning is a flexible process that changes as our strategic business plans and corporate structures change. Therefore, the plan presented here will require alterations as we grow and change. These alterations will be tailored to our changing future needs and also reflect the growing body of our experience with these approaches.
    C. This plan represents the first stage of the introduction of a comprehensive succession planning program. It will be treated as a pilot program in several departments or divisions but will be corporatewide at the area level. As we learn from this "pilot" experience, the cooperative participation of other divisions will be sought until a fully comprehensive program has been achieved.

II. Benefits

The succession planning process will enable us to

A. Have the right people in the right place at the right time to accomplish corporate goals and objectives.
B. Identify blocked positions and areas which lack good managerial replacements.
C. Identify the most promising managerial candidates, their readiness for promotion, and their developmental needs.
D. Emphasize the importance of planning for future personnel requirements to meet business plans.

III. Overview of Succession Planning Process

A. The succession planning process involves two separate groups with somewhat different guidelines for each. (See Section V, Part I, and Exhibit D in Part II.)
 1. Group 1, the senior officers, includes all individuals above grade 20.
 2. Group 2 includes grades 13–20.
B. The process for group 1 is well defined and specific because of the numerous and different corporate functions involved.
 1. Area heads develop a succession plan for their individual areas.
 2. They review their plans as a group with the Succession Planning Committee.
 3. The committee evaluates and approves the plans.
 4. Area heads implement the plans.
C. The process for group 2 is much more flexible than is that for group 1. Flexibility is essential because each area or department possesses its own organization structure and technical knowledge requirements, as well as other differences. Because of this diversity, a flexible plan is necessary to provide latitude of decisions. Therefore, the points outlined here represent guidelines and suggested approaches to achieve a workable system. Various areas may wish to modify it to suit the needs and requirements of their particular area.
 1. Department manager level
  a. Department managers develop succession plans for their areas.
  b. The area head conducts a meeting of all department managers to review their plans together, followed by approval and implementation.
 2. Division manager level
  a. Division managers develop succession plans for their areas.
  b. Division managers review their plans with their individual department managers for input and approval, followed by implementation.
D. Interrelationship of Groups 1 and 2
 Group 2 represents the succession planning process of each area of the company. Once each area has completed its own internal plan, that plan is merged into and related to the plans of the other areas. These merged and integrated plans become the succession plan for the top executives of the company. The plan for senior managers is the group 1 plan.

IV. Staffing Planning and Its Relationship to Succession Approaches

Activity	Characteristic level	Succession approaches
Succession planning (Group 1)	Presidents Senior vice presidents Vice presidents	Designated successors (talent pool)
Succession planning (Group 2)	Department managers Division managers High potentials Hard-to-replace positions	Designated positions—note position emphasis (talent pool) Functional promotions, Transfer strategies (cross-functional)
Staffing planning	All of the above Supervisory personnel Promotables from the nonexempt ranks	Functional movement patterns Transfer strategies (cross-functional)

V. Specific Steps and Supporting Materials

A. Group 1 Level

   1. Vice-presidential level

      a. The vice presidents review the most current performance evaluation and management inventory and other relevant information (See Exhibit F, Part II) to complete the *individual development plan* for each "direct report" (Exhibit A).

      b. Using data from the management inventory, performance evaluation, other appropriate sources, and Individual Development Plans, the vice presidents complete the Replacement Planning Chart (Exhibit B). Whenever feasible, this should include individuals other than "direct reports" about whom there is sufficient knowledge or experience to evaluate their potential. Several new systems and sources of personnel data are being developed to enlarge the pool of promotable talent.

B. Group 2 Level

   2. Division manager level

      a. Managers review the most current performance evaluation and management inventory as well as other pertinent materials to complete the Individual Development Plan for each report (Exhibit A).

      b. Using data from the management inventory, performance evaluation, other pertinent sources, and the Individual Development Plan, managers complete the Replacement Planning Chart (Exhibit B). Managers should try to include individuals other than "direct reports" about whom they have sufficient knowledge or experience to evaluate their potential.

EXHIBIT A
Individual Development Plan. PART I

1. Use label-type form for employee name, number, office/department, job title, manual code, sex, job code, month/year as assigned to present position.

2. Employee strengths: use card sort items for checklist.

3. Employee development needs: include development for both present job and preparation for future jobs.

Needs	Plan	Date Planned	Date Completed

Approved by _____ Date _____
(individual's supervisor)

4. Assessment of potential: employee possesses potential for the following positions or moves.

Cross-functional _____
Two levels higher _____
More than two levels higher _____

5. Possible future assignments within next 4 years

Job Title   Date When Ready

Approved by _____ Date _____
(preferably
supervisor
two levels
above individual)

6. Employee's preference for future jobs (include interest in other functions)

Job Title   Location

EXHIBIT B

Replacement Planning Chart 19_____

This form should be completed in keeping with the company's objectives to promote equal employment opportunities.

Area	Job Title	Job Code	Month, Year Assigned to Current Position	Promotability rating, Section of Management Inventory	Assessment of Potential, Section 4 of Individual Development Plan	Current Performance Evaluation Rating from P.E.* Form	Prior P.E. Rating, If Available
Incumbent's name and employee number							
Replacements—include job title location							

Prepared by _____ Date _____

Approved by _____ Date _____

*P.E. = performance evaluation.

    c. The managers then discuss the Individual Development Plan for each direct report and the Replacement Planning Chart with their department managers and obtain input and approval. Finally, managers implement the Individual Development Plans to help individuals develop to their fullest potential.

3. Department manager level

    a. Managers review the most current performance evaluation and management inventory as well as other pertinent materials (Exhibit F) to complete the Individual Development Plan for each "direct report."

    b. Using data from the management inventory, performance evaluation, other pertinent sources, and Individual Development Plans, managers complete the Replacement Planning Chart (Exhibit B). Managers should attempt to include individuals other than "direct reports" about whom they have sufficient knowledge or experience to evaluate their potential. Note new(er) sources of personnel information to help in widening the pool of promotable talent.

    c. Managers then discuss the Individual Development Plans for all "direct reports" and the Replacement Planning Chart in a meeting with area peers and the office head. In this meeting they should also obtain approval for their chart and plans.

    d. Finally, managers implement the individual development plans to help individuals fulfill their potential.

VI. Information Sources for Succession Planning

Level	Performance appraisal*	Management inventory†	Assessment center	Psychological evaluation	Corporate values
Vice president	✓	✓		✓	✓
Department manager	✓	✓		✓	✓
Division manager	✓	✓	✓		✓
Supervisor	✓	✓	✓		✓

Also, see Exhibit F for an analysis of the status of current information sources.
Data Management: accurate, up-to-date, and complete information is required to assure and to establish confidence in these data.

*Performance appraisal: performance evaluation; employee development; review, action plan, and results.

†Management inventory: assessment of potential, assessment of promotability, knowledge and skills inventory, ability to learn new material.

VII. Corporate Summary

After the meeting among area heads and the Succession Planning Committee, a corporate summary of the succession plan will be developed for presentation to the board of directors by the chief executive officer.

VIII. Succession Planning Committee

The committee consists of seven members. The permanent committee members include the chairman of the board and chief executive officer, the two presidents, the senior vice president of administration, and the vice president of human resources. The two rotating committee members are area heads who hold the position for two years each.*

THE CORPORATION'S SUCCESSION PLANNING PROGRAM:
PART 2: PROCEDURES

> THE COMPANY'S CORPORATE PHILOSOPHY STRESSES THE NEED TO IDENTIFY AND DEVELOP LEADERS WHO CAN MAINTAIN ORGANIZATION GROWTH WHILE MEETING FUTURE CHALLENGES.
>
> FUNDAMENTAL TO THE ATTAINMENT OF THIS GOAL IS SYSTEMATIC PLANNING OF MANAGEMENT SUCCESSION.

The Succession Planning Program is designed to

- Ensure that a group of talented and qualified managers is available to meet future business needs.
- Provide a system for the identification and development of corporate talent.
- Encourage cross-functional opportunities.
- Enrich our equal employment opportunities in a practical way.

Since succession planning is an adaptive process, it will need to be changed as our long-range and strategic business plans and corporate structure change.

Since systematic succession planning involves new corporate procedures and approaches, and because of the urgency of the program, key parts have been developed for *current planning activities*. Additional planning features will be added next year and as circumstances dictate in the future. Currently, succession planning will be introduced in three of our key divisions; learning gained here will be made available to other divisions as our program is expanded in subsequent years. We expect to make changes in procedures next year based on what we learn in the first succession cycle. This is normal and to be expected.

---

*In the initial implementation phase this will be staggered so that the rotating membership includes both old and new members.

I. Highlights: Succession Planning Activities and Responsibilities

  A. Group 1 (all corporate officers)
- Area heads–vice presidents develop succession plans for their areas. Succession plans include Succession Planning—Management Development Forms (Exhibit G) and Replacement Planning Charts (Exhibit H). See Forms section.
- Area heads–vice presidents review their succession plans with their senior vice president or president if no senior vice president.
- Senior vice presidents and vice presidents who report directly to the presidents or chairman separately present their succession plans to the Succession Planning Committee.
- The Succession Planning Committee* evaluates and approves the succession plans.
- Presidents review their individual succession plans with the chair.
- The succession plans are implemented.

  B. Group 2 (pilot group)
- Division managers develop succession plans for their areas and review them with their respective department managers.
- Department managers develop succession plans for their areas and review them with their respective vice presidents.
- Each area head–vice president conducts a meeting of all department managers in his or her area to finalize succession plans.

Group 1 succession plans are considered by the Succession Planning Committee. The Group 2 succession plans support the Succession Planning process of Group 1 and provide the primary candidates for cross-functional transfers.

The human resources administrator (vice president of human resources) will monitor the process and the progress of candidates and periodically provide the chair of the succession planning committee with a progress report.

II. Succession Planning: The Bottom-Up Approach (see Exhibit C)

Division Manager Level

1. Managers review the most current performance evaluation, management inventory (see Exhibit I) and other appropriate information (see Succession Planning Information Sources Chart, Exhibit F) for their direct reports. Then they complete the Succession Planning—Management Development Form (SP-MDF), Section III and Exhibit G, only for high-potential individuals (i.e.,

---

*The Succession Planning Committee includes the chair, presidents of the life and casualty companies, senior vice president of administration, vice president of human resources, and two rotating positions, one each representing (other) senior vice presidents and vice presidents.

EXHIBIT C
Overview: Succession Planning Process

The Succession Planning Process for the current year includes:
- **Group 1 — All employees at the V.P. level and above**
- **Group 2 — Grade 13 and above employees in (an) area(s)**
  (specific areas to be determined)

Succession Planning Groups

General Chairperson	* * * *	# # # #
Presidents		Group 1
	* * * *	# # # #
Senior Vice Presidents		
	* * * *	(Corporatewide)
Vice Presidents		

Grades:		
20	x ● ● ● ●	
19	x ● ● ● ●	
18	x ● ● ● ●	
17	x ● ● ● ●	
	Group 2	
16	x ● ● ● ●	
15	x ● ● ● ●	
14	x ● ● ● ●	
13	x ● ● ● ●	

Pilot Group

Key:

● ● ● ● ● ●	Participate in first-year pilot succession program.
* * * * * *	Will require integration.
# # # # # #	Corporatewide officer participants. In all cases, cross-functional moves will have to be coordinated.
x x x x x x	High potentials.

EXHIBIT D
Annual Timetable for Key Succession Events

Time	*Level*
January–February	Division managers complete succession plans and meet with their department managers.
March–April	Department managers complete succession plans.
By end of April	Department managers hold joint meetings with their vice presidents.
May–June	Vice Presidents complete their succession plans and meet with senior vice president or company president if no senior vice president.
By end of June	Senior vice presidents and vice presidents who report directly to presidents or chair meet with Succession Planning Committee.
July	Presidents complete succession plans and meet with the chair.
August	Corporate summary succession plan is completed.
	Chair presents corporate summary of succession plan to the board of directors.

EXHIBIT E
The Succession Planning Process Is Bottom Up

General Chair and CEO

↑

Succession Planning Committee/Presidents

↑

Senior Vice Presidents *

↑

Vice Presidents *

↑

Department Managers

↑

Division Managers

↑

Exempt Employees

* Area head may be a vice president or senior vice president. Also includes headquarters' officers.

EXHIBIT F

Succession Planning Information Sources and Status Estimates (as of _____)*

Source \ Management Level	General Chairman	Presidents	Senior Vice Presidents	Vice Presidents	Department Managers	Division Managers	High Potential Individuals	Supervisor	Notes
Management assessment center						X	X	X	
Management inventories Assessment of potentials				x	X	X	X	X	Computerized
Knowledge and training	x	x	x	x	X	X	X	X	Computerized
Performance evaluations	x	x	x	x	x	X	X	X	For grades 7–15†
Psychological studies	X	X	X	X	X	X	X	X	
Job descriptions	X	X	X	X	X	X	X	X	‡
Personnel/department files	X	X	X	X	X	X	X	X	§
Supervisory identification process								X	

X = Appropriate information sources for succession planning which are currently available.

x = Appropriate information sources for succession planning which are *not* currently available.

* By corporate human resources department.

† Grades 7–15 cover all but the highest division manager grade (i.e., division manager grade, 16).

‡ Not computerized and no plans exist to do so.

§ Some *personal file* information is computerized.

EXHIBIT G
Succession Planning—Management Development Form (MDF)

Employee name _____   Disbursement code _____
Employee number _____   Job code _____
Work location _____   Job title _____
Prepared by _____   Date _____
Reviewed by _____   Date _____

Section 1, Strengths: Dimensions valued by top management—evaluate the employee's strengths on each of the following corporate values using the attached definitions and rating scale.

_____ Leading and influencing   _____ Sensitivity to others
_____ Problem solving   _____ Productivity
_____ Decision making   _____ Personal development
_____ Communicating   _____ Planning
_____ Managing company resources   _____ Organizational sensitivity
_____ Energy level   _____ Performance in current position
_____ Integrity   _____ Skills for future position

Section 2, Future Assignments: List any positions for which this employee has long-term potential—four or more years. Special consideration should be given to cross-functional positions.

Job title _____   Office _____
Job title _____   Office _____
Job title _____   Office _____

Section 3, Employee Career Preferences and Goals: Indicate office(s) employee prefers and organizational level this employee has expressed a desire to achieve three or more years from now. Include any cross-functional preferences.

Office 1. _____   2. _____
Organizational level 1. _____   2. _____

Optional (provide when employee has expressed specific preference):

Job title _____   Office _____   Location _____
Job title _____   Office _____   Location _____

Section 4, Developmental Activities: Specify the employee's developmental activities for future positions.

Developmental Needs	Planned Activities	Date to Be Completed	Actual Result
1. _____	_____	_____	_____
2. _____	_____	_____	_____
3. _____	_____	_____	_____

DIMENSIONS VALUED BY TOP MANAGEMENT: RATING SCALE AND DEFINITIONS

Use the following rating scale to evaluate the strength of the employee in question on each of the dimensions valued by top management. Enter 1–5 next to each dimension in Section 1 of the Succession Planning—Management Development Form.

The definitions on this and the following sheets provide detailed descriptions of the dimensions valued by top management. Please refer to these definitions when making your ratings.

Rate the extent to which the employee meets proficiency in each of the dimensions:

Well Below	Below	Meets	Above	Well Above
1	2	3	4	5

Communicating—Ability to clearly convey ideas and listen actively in a variety of both oral and written communication situations; to persuade and negotiate; and to speak and write clearly, logically, and concisely with a smooth flow of ideas.

Managing Company Resources—Ability to recognize where and when to utilize company resources (e.g., personnel, material, equipment, and to create an accurate budget which most effectively utilizes these resources).

Leading and Influencing—Ability to establish the trust and confidence of others; to select, evaluate, develop, and motivate employees toward performance objectives and useful goals; to serve as a model of desired behavior, and to help in establishing challenging performance objectives.

Problem Solving—Ability to reason, analyze, and evaluate; ability to draw appropriate conclusions considering relevant data; and ability to integrate seemingly unrelated information and develop alternatives.

Decision Making—Ability to reach appropriate and timely conclusions, to select solutions for short- and long-term problems, to generate alternative solutions, and to consider and develop contingency plans.

Energy Level—Ability to do hard work for sustained time periods; sense of urgency, and commitment to achieve company and personal goals.

Trustworthiness—Commitment to honesty and integrity in all work undertakings; ability to interact with others in an open, nondeceptive manner.

Sensitivity to Others—Ability to interact appropriately with subordinates, peers, superiors, and the public; to consider others' feelings and opinions; to understand and respond to others' needs; and to recognize situational demands.

Performance in Current Position—Ability to perform one's current tasks, responsibilities, with required skills (see performance appraisal information).

Competency for Future Position—Possession of the abilities and knowledge necessary to perform effectively at higher levels in the organization. (This should relate to Sections 2 and 3 of the Personal Development Plan.)

Personal Development—Ability to recognize opportunity areas and engage in appropriate self-development activities (e.g., seminars, professional courses, on-the-job behavioral changes).

Productivity—Skills to produce satisfactory work in a timely way.

Planning—Ability to establish objectives and a course of action for self and/or others to provide for effective task performance; ability to develop strategies and schedules for meeting goals, anticipate obstacles to goal attainment, and anticipate future organizational requirements.

Organizational Sensitivity—Evidencing an awareness of the implications of one's actions and decisions on other units and people in the organizaton; demonstration of an understanding of the corporate culture.

---

individuals they consider to possess potential for management positions at least two levels above current positions).

2. Using data from performance evaluations, management inventories, and SP-MDFs for the high-potential employees, managers complete their Replacement Planning Charts (RPCs). Managers should consider individual preferences as expressed through the SP-MDF and the management inventory. They should also include high-potential individuals other than "direct reports" about whom they have sufficient knowledge or experience to evaluate their potential.

3. Managers discuss the SP-MDF for each high-potential candidate and the RPC with department managers. Managers obtain input and approval from their respective department managers, then implement SP-MDFs.

SUCCESSION PLANNING FLOW

Review key information sources, including Performance evaluations and management inventories for direct reports (see Exhibit I)	→	Complete SP-MDFs for high potentials	→	Complete RPC	→	Discuss plans and chart with department manager as part of over-all planning approach.	→	Implement succession plan

The three steps are repeated at successive management levels ending with an executive review by the succession planning committee and chair/CEO.

III. Instruction for Completing Forms

A. Succession Planning—Management Development Form (SP-MDF)—Exhibit G

1. This form was designed to identify an employee's strengths on the dimensions valued by top management (Section 1), potential for specific future assignments (Section 2), career goals (Section 3), and developmental needs (Section 4). Division managers complete this form for high-potential individuals only (individuals they consider to possess potential for management positions two levels above current position). Managers at and above the department level complete this form for each "direct report."

EXHIBIT H

Replacement Planning Chart (RPC)

Confidential

Employee name _____   Work location _____

Job title _____   Employee number _____

Reviewed by _____   Job code _____

Date _____   Disbursement code _____

Indicate qualified replacement candidates for your position. Consider both "direct reports" and other high-potential candidates in different functions. In keeping with the company's affirmative-action objectives, consideration should be given to qualified women and minority candidates and other designated groups.

READINESS (Check One)			Year/Month Assigned to Current Position	Promotability Rating (Section 2 of Management Inventory)	Performance Evaluation Rating
IMMEDIATE 0–1 Years	SHORT TERM Up to 3 Years	LONG TERM Over 3 Years			

Name _____
Job title _____
Location _____

Name _____
Job title _____
Location _____

Name _____
Job title _____
Location _____

Name of Emergency Replacement _____

EXHIBIT I
The Management Inventory Process

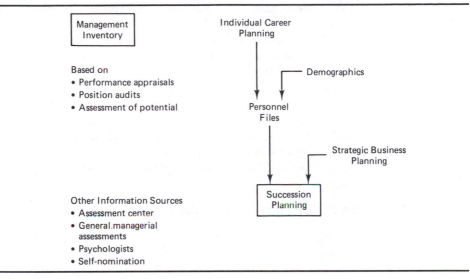

2. Managers should use supporting documentation from the management inventory, performance evaluations, and other pertinent sources (e.g., Management Assessment Center, Supervisor Identification Program and other sources indicated on the Succession Planning Information Sources Chart, Exhibit F) to aid completion.

3. Section 1 (Strengths) consists of a list of 14 corporate value dimensions. These values are considered by top management to be important qualities or characteristics for company employees to possess. Carefully read the attached definitions of each of the values prior to completing Section 1. Use the rating scale provided to indicate the extent to which you agree that the employee in question exhibits each of the corporate values.

4. Section 2 should be completed with long-term potential in mind.

5. Section 3 (employee career preferences and goals) should be completed only after these issues are discussed with the employee. While this discussion may take place at any time, for grades 7–15 the employee development review meeting is a logical time to discuss career goals. Organizational levels are division manager, department manager, vice president, senior vice president, etc. Locations are regions and headquarters.

6. The completed form(s) must be reviewed and signed by your immediate manager.

B. Replacement Planning Chart (RPC)—Exhibit H
   1. This confidential form is completed by managers to identify qualified replacements for their own positions.

2. Managers should use data from performance evaluations, management inventories, and personal development plans to aid completions.
3. List no more than four individuals (including job title and location, if known) who you think would make appropriate replacements for your job. Include individuals other than "direct reports" about whom you have sufficient knowledge or experience to evaluate their potential.
4. The promotability rating requested on the form should reflect what you feel the individual can attain within the next 12 months. If a management inventory was completed, use the rating in Section 2 as the promotability rating.
5. Managers may not have the year/month assigned to current position, promotability rating, and performance evaluation rating available. In such cases, these sections should be left blank.
6. The completed form(s) must be reviewed and signed by your immediate manager.

IV. Glossary of Key Terms Used in Succession Planning

(Thirty-three key terms used commonly in succession planning discussions, ranging from "affirmative action," to "environmental scanning," to "succession planning.")

Glossary of Key Terms Used in Succession Planning

Action Research involves studies to establish positional requirements, changes in position requirements due to longer-range plans, responses of individuals to succesion procedures, and related matters.

Affirmative Action is an organized effort by the company to recruit, promote, train, and develop minority group members, females, handicapped individuals, and Vietnam era veterans to ensure their representation in the organization and to overcome the effects of past discrimination.

Career Counseling involves discussions of current job activities and performance, individual job and career development objectives, and action plans. This component of *career planning* may involve people both within and outside of the company. However, the individual's immediate manager is the most common counselor.

Career Focus is the company's comprehensive program aimed at coordinating personnel services. The two main goals of this program are to help organization members develop their careers and to help meet our human resource needs.

Career Paths are paths by which people move between jobs, positions, departments, divisions, etc. Career paths are increasingly being formally defined within organizations.

Career Planning is the process whereby employees receive assistance in planning and developing their individual careers.

Career Vistas is the program the company will provide to employees in planning their careers. Examples include career workshops and a learning center.

Career Development is a process by which career-related activities are established simultaneously to meet the future needs of both the individual (*career vistas*) and the organization (*career management*).

The Corporate Mission of the company is to provide financial and security services to individuals, families, and organizations by offering products and services which meet and respond to changes in consumer needs. The corporate mission is accomplished through combining the processes of *strategic business planning* and *human resources management*.

Employee Development Review is a part of the company's performance appraisal system. It is a confidential document discussed between employees and their managers. The purpose of the EDR is to identify the employee's strengths and developmental needs so that the employee's performance can be improved. It is not a part of the employee's personnel file.

Environmental Scanning is a process in which the organization attempts to identify trends and changes (e.g., new competitors, tax law changes, availability of skilled individuals) and analyze factors that may affect corporate strategic objectives.

Equal Employment Opportunity is a policy that the company adheres to in hiring and promoting on the basis of ability, regardless of race, color, religion, creed, sex, age, handicap, or national origin.

Executive Development is the long-term process by which the company provides individuals at or above the director level with the opportunity to secure the special knowledge, skills, and experiences necessary to provide leadership within the organization.

High-Potential management employees are individuals who possess the long-term potential to hold management positions two levels above their current position.

Human Resources Management encompasses both corporate goals to have individuals prepare to meet future labor needs (*workforce forecasting* and *succession planning*) as well as the needs and goals of the individuals who will comprise the work force of the future (*career planning*). A key focus of HRM is the coordination, integration, and administration of these two efforts.

Human Resources Planning is a process through which the company projects the future personnel needs of the organization (*workforce forecasting*) while simultaneously monitoring the availability and development of individuals to meet these needs (*succession planning*).

Job Description is a summary of the most important features of a job: the objective or general reason the job was created, the nature of the work, important behaviors for successful performance, and the key accountabilities stated as tasks to be performed. Company job descriptions also include placement criteria which describe employee characteristics—knowledges, skills, abilities, and experience—which are commonly needed to perform the job successfully.

Job Opportunity List is a process by which the company posts job openings to give priority to company employees. Internal candidates fill out a job interest form through the Employment and Placement Office. Consideration is based on qualifications.

Management Assessment Center is a process used to assess the potential of organization members for division management positions. A variety of dimensions or characteristics of successful division managers are measured through activities such as an interview and group problem-solving exercises.

Management Inventory is a process of identifying an employee's promotability, knowledge, and training. It is composed of two parts: assessment of potential and the knowledge and training inventory, both of which are used for human resources planning purposes.

Manpower Planning (synonym: *Workforce forecasting*).

Performance Appraisal is a process of evaluating an employee's performance on the job.

Performance Evaluation is a part of the performance appraisal system. It is completed by the manager on an annual basis to summarize an employee's performance during the past evaluation period. It is used to support merit pay and other employment decisions. Completed performance evaluations are maintained in the employee's personnel file.

Psychological Studies are assessments of managerial and other high-potential employees prepared by consulting psychologists. A narrative description of the individual's personality is produced based upon psychological testing and an interview. Psychological studies are appropriate information sources for succession planning.

Replacement Planning Chart, a part of the succession planning process, is a confidential form completed by managers to identify qualified replacement candidates for their own positions. Using data from performance evaluations, management inventories, and succession planning—management development forms, the replacement readiness of appropriate individuals is assessed.

Staffing Planning (synonym: *workforce forecasting*).

Strategic Business Planning is the process by which the company sets organizational or business objectives and decides upon comprehensive programs of action which will achieve these objectives. The goal of this long-range planning is to help fulfill the corporate mission.

Succession Planning is a process that will enable us to know who is ready for upper management assignments and what developmental activities are essential to prepare individuals for such assignments.

The Succession Planning Committee consists of seven members who review and approve the succession plan of office heads. The permanent committee members include the chair and chief executive officer, the two presidents, the senior vice president of administration, and the vice-president of human resources. The rotating members (2) are office heads who hold the position for two years.

Succession Planning Dimensions are characteristics and abilities which top management consider to be important for management employees to possess. Employee strengths on these dimensions are assessed in Section 1 of the Succession Planning—Management Development Form.

Succession Planning—Management Development Form, a part of the succession planning process, is designed to identify an employee's strengths on succession planning dimensions, potential for specific future assignments, career goals, and developmental needs. Managers at and above the departmental level complete this form for each "direct report." Division managers only complete the form for high-potential individuals.

Succession Planning Information Sources Chart is a matrix which shows the appropriate information sources (e.g., performance valuations, personnel/department files) to be used when making succession plans for each of the company's management levels (i.e., division managers up through the general chairman).

Supervisory Identification Process is a program used to identify employees with the potential to become effective supervisors.

Work Force Forecasting is a process that will enable us to tie human resources with strategic business planning, integrating labor market forecasts, turnover and retirement data, organizational changes, economic and demographic projections, and staffing projections.

MAYFAIR CORPORATION: CORPORATE SUCCESSION PLANNING PROGRAM (A Consumer Products Company)

Management Continuity Planning

Mayfair Corporation is an old-line firm marketing consumer-related products on an international basis. The firm was highly profitable for many years, but severe competition in both its domestic and international markets cut severely into its dominant market share. No small part of the problem was its loss of young talented managers with considerable growth potential but who felt frustrated with the lack of systematic internal planning for their development and growth. The chairman of the board who also served as CEO took an active role in changing the situation. A new and systematic continuity (succession) planning program was introduced. His personal endorsement and support were reflected in a letter (Exhibit 5-A) which headed up a new continuity planning document distributed to all top managers. Excerpts from this letter and other internal documents follow.

I. Succession (Continuity) Planning Defined

Succession, or continuity, planning as it is often called, is a strategy to ensure uninterrupted progress toward the organization's goals and objectives. Both these terms are used in the discussions that follow. They capture the essence of our needs: the identification and development of talented people for key organizational positions and the fact that the success of this development will help to assure continuity in managerial and corporate processes. This planning is particularly concerned with human resources and the following main activities:

EXHIBIT 5-A

MAYFAIR CORPORATION
Executive Offices
Office of the President

Dear Colleagues and Organization Members,

A major goal for our Company in the next five to ten years is found in the corporation's Strategic Planning Statement. It says that "organization welfare and healthfulness continue to rest on both corporate continuity and renewal. Basic to this strategy is that we create and continue to enrich an environment in which all employees have equal opportunities to grow, develop, and advance in our firm." No statement could set out more convincingly our responsibility to make sure that the most effective and qualified of these managers move to the top of MAYFAIR.

Management succession (continuity) planning and development that is carried out in systematic fashion is basic to this process. More particularly, all senior managers have the responsibility to identify succession candidates *and* to assist their subordinates' development and fulfillment of their potential. This is beneficial to MAYFAIR CORPORATION and the individual as well.

Several documents have been developed as tools that can assist each senior manager in identifying succession candidates and highly qualified people, preparing development plans, and following their progress. These important documents include Executive Performance Appraisals and Management Inventory information including functional knowledge, and experience.

Your active cooperation and support is needed and appreciated.

Paul White
President and Chairman

- *Management Succession (Continuity) Planning*—To assure that individual potential is reviewed regularly and that backups have been designated for critical positions.
- *Management Development*—A system for assuring that managers/groups have the necessary knowledge and skills to perform effectively and to prepare themselves for future organization responsibilities and challenges.
- *Identification of High Potential*—A system for assuring that employees are identified, developed, and retained who can make significant contributions to the organization.
- *Career Development*—A system for supporting career planning needs of each employee and assuring, wherever possible, that these plans are meshed thoughtfully with those of the organization.

II. Organization Benefits and Top Management Committment

In general, the major benefits of continuity planning for the company will be that of having the right people in the right place at the right time and with the right skills to accomplish its goals and objectives. This means developing managerial capabilities to meet changing business conditions in an effective way. At the same time, we expect that the return on investment in the company's human resources will be more than justified. Continuity planning will also help to identify and correct areas needing strengthening with respect to candidates for key and critical positions. Also, to the extent possible, succession or continuity planning will also figure prominently in achieving equal opportunity for our human resources displaying the competencies and desires to advance themselves. Finally, continuity planning will help to assure that the most qualified and effective managers rise to the top of the organization. At a more specific level, these additional benefits should result:

1. Corporate headquarters will serve as a clearinghouse for matching placement and development needs (e.g., cross-functional moves) to take advantage of opportunities wherever these may exist.
2. Business planning information will provide important data to management planning and organization development as to what programs are needed within/across areas or divisions.
3. Management and organization development planning will be able to provide support in meeting line management needs to promote, develop, and implement divisional management continuity programs.

Management Commitment   Top management is fully committed to the support of this program which is part of our worldwide system for succession planning. Coverage will involve the first three levels of every division, regardless of where it is located or its marketing or operational area. Our objective for this year is that Paul White, president and chairman, review the top people identified as candidates for senior company positions. Also, he will review 125 additional people from all divisions who are considered to have long range, high potential.

III. Overview of the Succession Planning Process

A. Process Is Bottom Up

1. For each subordinate considered, managers determine the promotion readiness and the development needs. This is the management succession plan for their unit.

2. Managers then review the management succession plan with their superior for approval, which is then followed by implementation.

3. The first two steps are repeated at successive management levels ending with an executive review by Paul White and the Succession Committee.

4. Managers will also identify high-potential individuals who may or may not be in the top three levels within their respective organizations.

Responsibility and Control of Succession

The responsibility for planning and execution rests with each division and location. The system is designed to maximize managerial involvement in meaningful planning and to reduce paperwork to a minimum. The emphasis is on materials and analyses really needed for planning purposes.

B. Levels of Management Involved

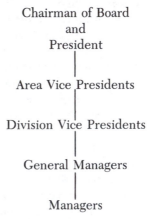

Chairman of Board
and
President

|

Area Vice Presidents

|

Division Vice Presidents

|

General Managers

|

Managers

C. Specific Steps and Supporting Materials

1. Managers complete a Forecast of Potential for each direct report and any others in whose development they and the organization have an interest (e.g., high potentials).

2. The *Forcast of Potential(s)* is forwarded to the corporate organization and Management Development Department (or local analysis units) who will have them scored, summarized into Individual Forecast of Potential Profiles, and quickly returned to you.

3. Individual Forecasts of Potential Profiles are then used as an information base for managers who complete their unit's Management Continuity Plan for review with their superior.

4. Once approved by senior division management, managers implement the individual development plans.

5 After approval by the senior management of each division, copies of the Management Continuity Plan are forwarded to the corporate organization and Management Development Department for integration with other divisions and for a presentation to Paul White and the succession planning committee at the fall conference.

6. Steps must be taken to assure all information used is complete, timely, and accurate.

D. Timetable

1. The Forecasts of Potential—at headquarters or local analysis sections by June 1st.

2. Individual Potential Profiles—scored and returned within seven days.

3. Review meetings on contents of the Management Continuity Plan should begin in June.

4. All Management Continuity Plans are to be completed, approved, and returned by the first of August.

E. Major Continuity Succession Groups

	Number
Senior manager and officer positions, succession/continuity candidates, Group 1	50
Sucession/continuity candidates, Group 2 (reserve and replacements)	125

IV. Continuity Planning Process—Key Features and Details

Assessment procedures and forecasts of individual potential	→ Promotion readiness and development needs high-potential list	→ Succession summary and management continuity plan (unit)	→ Development plans	→ Repeat at successively high levels	→ Review meetings • Input of business planners	→ Implement development plans • Schedule activities • Monitor progress
1.	2.	3.	4.	5.	6.	7.

V. Forecast of Potential

A. Approach

The "forecast of potential" provides an opportunity to assess subordinate managers *and* others who have been observed as having high potential. This form provides a systematic way to organize first hand experience, views, and observations. These data are analyzed in the form of "managerial assessment profiles" and then returned. Representative information is provided for the rating form. A regular form will be sent under separate cover.

"Managerial assessment profiles" help to

1. Identify qualified candidates for succession.
2. Identify people with high potential.
3. Identify individual development needs.

Although these analyses and ratings are considered confidential, the ratings may be shared with the individual being rated if the rater so chooses. In any case, the scoring of the "forecasts of potential" are only for use of the rating managers and will be returned to the rater.

B. Procedure

Emphasis is placed on performances and actions you have observed. Information is developed in the following three areas:

1. Individual skills and experience as these relate to *potential*
2. Rating of individual *functional knowledge* and experience
3. *Readiness* of individuals for promotion

Stress is placed on *job-related behaviors* required for successful performance of assigned responsibilities. Individual *personality traits* are often questionable predictors of behaviors and thus they are not used.

Scales, Ratings, Interpretations

Each scale has seven possible ratings—from a very "low" level to a very "high" level. A rating in the middle would be considered as satisfactory or average, thus the following interpretations as applied to Question 2.

Questions	Possible responses and interpretations:
2. For situations where the person has leadership authority, rate their ability to influence, persuade, or guide the actions of others	____ ____ ____ X ____ ____ ____ effective ineffective *Interpretation:* satisfactory performance. X ____ ____ ____ ____ ____ ____ *Interpretation:* person has demonstrated a high level of leadership effectiveness. ____ ____ ____ ____ ____ ____ X *Interpretation:* person is performing in an ineffective way—they accomplish little in so far as this leadership skill is concerned.

C. Summary of Behavioral Features for Rating Potential

Relations with People (4)
   Task supervision
   Influencing others
   Communications, oral
   Communications, written
   Examples:

Subordinate Development (3)
   Work delegation
   Coaching
   Use of feedback techniques
   Examples:

Management and Direction (3)
   Exercise of leadership
   Listening to subordinates
   Dealing with other managers
   Examples:

Administrative Performance (8)
   Factoring in the business context
   Making decisions under complex
      conditions
   Making decisions under uncertain
      conditions
   Problem analysis
   Short-run planning
   Longer-range planning
   Strategic thinking
   Innovative/creative approaches
   Examples:

General Management (4)
   Initiative in decision situations
   "Smart" risk taking
   Fit of leadership style to situation
   Managing change
   Examples:

Self-management (9)
   Stress management
   Willingness to learn new or novel
      approaches
   Self-development priorities
   Setting personal priorities
   Adaptation to changing conditions
   Energy level to see things through
   Relative objectivity/own performance
   Expressing personal integrity
   Expressing professional integrity
   Examples:

Corporate Culture (2)
   Reflected in decision making
   Incorporation in subordinate
      development
   Examples:

Total categories: 7
Total factors: 33

D. Functional Knowledge and Experience

general familiarity			working knowledge (most general (applications)		expert (could consult/mastery)	
1	2	3	4	5	6	7
	basic knowledge (limited application)			experienced (work without supervision)		

Knowledge/Ability Scale

Functional areas:	1	2	3	4	5	6	7
Marketing	___	___	___	___	___	___	___
Operations	___	___	___	___	___	___	___
Engineering	___	___	___	___	___	___	___
Research and development	___	___	___	___	___	___	___
Human resources administration	___	___	___	___	___	___	___
Finance	___	___	___	___	___	___	___
Accounting	___	___	___	___	___	___	___
Management information systems	___	___	___	___	___	___	___
Quality control	___	___	___	___	___	___	___
International operations	___	___	___	___	___	___	___
Legal	___	___	___	___	___	___	___
Public affairs	___	___	___	___	___	___	___

E. Individual Promotion Readiness—Overall Evaluations

1. Own functional area

    ___   ___   ___   ___   ___   ___

    now   up to one year   up two years   over two years   at potential   too early

2. Two levels beyond current assignment (see special note under Section VI)

    ___   ___   ___   ___   ___   ___

    now   up to one year   up to two years   over two years   at potential   too early

3. General management

    ___   ___   ___   ___   ___   ___

    now   up to one year   up to two years   over two years   at potential   too early

4. Working with candidate as a peer

    ___   ___   ___   ___   ___   ___

    un-attractive   very pleased

5. Working with candidate as a project team member

    ___   ___   ___   ___   ___   ___

    un-attractive   very pleased

F. Bar Chart Summary

Each of the behavioral/performance factors, readiness areas, and functional areas will be summarized in bar chart form. The behavioral/performance factors are summarized as weighted averages of the individual factors; for example, "Relations with People" (page 8) has four subfactors. A bar summary might be as follows for subfactors rated as 1, 4, 6, 3 (average = 3.5).

Relations with people   XXXXXXXXXXXXXX   Avg.
                                                            3.5

                        1   2   3   4   5   6   7

VI. Development Planning

Development Plan

A. Approach

For each candidate, please provide the following:

Overall performance (1 = excellent, 7 = poor)	Promotion readiness (when?)	Potential (no. of levels—stay in current position)	Next position to consider for succession	Job code	Development needed
(a)	(b)	(c)	(d)	(e)	(f)

Development strategies (suggestive)

1. Coaching
2. On-the-job (current)
3. Cross-functional (specify)
4. Geographic move (same function)
5. Skill training (seminar/workshop)
6. Rotation (other jobs, same lead

7. Task force assignment
8. Classroom/institute (one to two weeks)
9. Classroom/formal courses
10. Classroom/executive program

Comments on Development Plan

B. High Potentials—A Special Note

In general, the designation "high potential" will reflect

1. Outstanding performance ratings.
2. Advancement potential at least two levels beyond current.
3. Readiness to absorb significant additional responsibility—next two years.
4. High ratings in multiple assessments.

The determination of development for "high potentials" should be worked out in connection with the senior division officer.

Chapter Summary

Companies that have developed a solid foundation of Personnel Management activities have found that they can increasingly direct their attention to strengthening their "life blood" processes. Successful succession planning and development systems are artfully linked to their long-range and strategic business planning components. They seek to maximize involvement of their line management groups, and they expect senior officers to assume active leadership and supportive roles. Active involvement and support of the enterprise head is crucial to both activating and improving systems. The "fit" or "chemistry" of the person with key people also is a critical consideration but often not discussed specifically.

The examples of succession planning approaches provided in this chapter illustrate that each organization's approach is unique to its circumstances. Situational factors frequently encountered that shaped program development included corporate leadership and its conviction of the importance of these undertakings; nature of the enterprise and its dominant work system; corporate culture; size and physical dispersion of facilities; and the opportunities, threats, and urgencies identified in strategic planning discussions.

A common thread visible in virtually all the company experiences referenced in this chapter is the need to systematize succession or renewal approaches. Establishing more comprehensive (but flexible!) approaches requires that activities be monitored and coordinated on behalf of top management. It is also required that expert help be available at all levels to assist managerial personnel work out the application problems and issues that follow in wake of these undertakings. Formats such as those presented in the two case applications meet some of these needs. They provide more uniform approaches to identify responsibilities, anticipate problems, and clarify corporate policies. They seek creatively to develop information sources and usage. Valid information that is available in adequate amounts and in a timely fashion is indispensible to the successful fulfillment of these succession undertakings.

REFERENCES

Burack, Elmer H. "Corporate Business and Human Resource Planning Practices: Strategic Issues and Concerns." *Organization Dynamics*, Vol. 9, no. 2 (Summer 1986): 82–94.

Burack, Elmer H. "Linking Corporate Business and Human Resource Planning: Strategic Issues and Concerns." *Human Resource Planning*, Vol. 8, no. 3 (1985): 133–145.

Carnazza, Joseph, Jr. *Human Resource Planning (1985): Succession/Replacement Planning Programs and Practices*. New York: Center for Research in Career Development, Columbia Business School, 1982.

Halberstam, David. *The Reckoning* New York: Morrow 1986.

Hall, Douglas T. *Careers in Organizations*. Belmont CA: Goodyear, 1976.

London, Manuel. *Developing Managers*. San Francisco: Jossey-Bass, 1985.

Lorsch, Jay and Louis Barnes. *Managers and Their Careers: Cases and Readings*. Homewood, IL: Richard D. Irwin, Dorsey Press, 1972.

Mahler, Walter R. and Frank Gaines. *Succession Planning in Leading Companies*. Midland Park, NJ: Mahler, 1984.

Mahler, Walter R. and W. F. Wrightnour. *Executive Continuity*. Homewood, IL: Dow Jones-Irwin, 1973.

Odiorne, George S. *Human Resources Strategy: A Portfolio Approach*. San Francisco: Jossey-Bass, 1984.

Ritti, R. R. and G. R. Funkhauser. *The Ropes to Skip and the Ropes to Know*. Columbus, OH: Grid, 1977.

Rhodes, David and James W. Walker. "Management Succession and Development Planning." *Human Resources Planning*, Vol. 7, no. 4 (1984): 157–173.

Schein, Edgar H. "The Individual, the Organization, and the Career: A Conceptual Scheme." *Journal of Applied Behavioral Science*, Vol. 7 (1981): 401–426.

Schein, Edgar H. *Organization Culture and Leadership*. San Francisco: Jossey Bass, 1985.

Walker, James W. *Human Resource Planning*. New York: McGraw-Hill, 1980.

Walker, James W. and R. Armes. "Implementing Succession Planning in Diversified Companies." *Human Resource Planning*, Vol. 2, no. 3 (1979): 123–133.

6

Strategic Management Development Systems

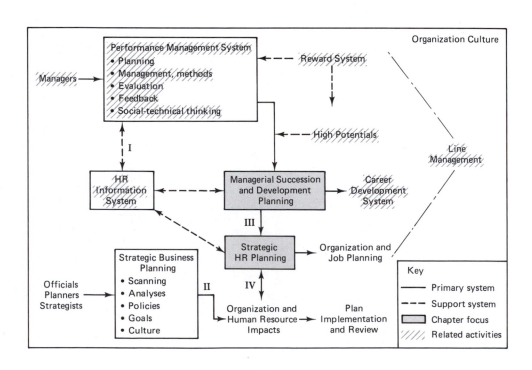

Among the greatest advances in human resource development (HRD) thinking and programming in the last decade was the achievement of comprehensive planning and action-oriented systems. This accomplishment, experienced by a growing number of firms, was underway for better than *two* decades (Burack and Walker 1972; Burack 1972). Comprehensive human resource development systems today combine in their approaches the business and human resource planning components with Personnel Administration and the active involvement of line management. Unfortunately, only a modest number of these results have been reported in the literature, although at last this reporting is starting to improve. The following notes provide some selected references for the convenience of interested readers.

Although a "comprehensive" HRD system is described, specific details differ markedly. For example, at EBASCO Services, Inc., an international engineering and consulting firm, intensive use of the computer was emphasized as an integrating device. It facilitated the translation of strategic business planning into operational plans, controls, and programs. Further, selective elements from these plans and programs were combined to provide an excellent basis for individual career planning and human resource development programs (Manzini and Gridley, 1985). As described in Chapter 4, Control Data Corporation developed an effective and comprehensive computer-based system for analyzing job and performance characteristics of this work. The information derived from this system was blended with staffing planning. This helped to establish a well-balanced corporatewide management development effort (Tornow and Gartland, 1980).

> The comprehensive system at Corning Glass Works (Beer and Ruh, 1975) was designed to solve the multiple needs of performance management and the dysfunctions or limitations of "management by objectives" and traditional types of salary programs. Their answer represented a workable system that combined MBO (management by objective), individual "performance development and review," and "performance results evaluation." The results from the MBO program and performance evaluation was an important basis for salary and promotion decisions. Their multiyear design effort resulted in a system covering some 4,000 managerial and professional people. It included a well-thought-out system with provision for describing key features of performance and relating these to individual development. It also served to facilitate developing strategies and tactics tailored to their competitive environment, management philosophy, and organizational climate.

For additional descriptions and details of comprehensive HRD systems, the reader may wish to review the discussions in DeVanna et al. (1982) and Tichy (1982), which emphasize the organizational culture/milieu and strategic aspects, or Burack and Mathys (1987) for a variety of systems geared to different corporate needs. Also, strategic management development (SMD) planning approaches and applications often can benefit from practical materials that provide useful guidelines and help to focus on issues or areas for analysis. Thus this chapter has a distinct pragmatic flavor.

The specifics of comprehensive HRD systems are *contingent* upon the particulars of organizational situations. Aside from corporate philosophy and climate, other common factors include

- Organization size and the number of people included in staffing plans.
- Technological base and the relative level of sophistication.
- Environmental change and the degree of "turbulence" it creates.
- Competitive environmental features and the degree of uncertainty and complexity associated with these.
- Geographic dispersion of facilities including the added complexities of multinational sites.
- Degree of decentralization of decision making.

Yet despite the number of factors that account for the unique characteristics of particular strategic systems, all rest on a common foundation of structural, system, and organizational elements.

Common Elements of Comprehensive HRD Systems

The term "systems," as used in connection with HRD, has had numerous understandings attached to it, some *erroneous!* Thus, we have found it useful in managerial briefing sessions to clarify the general meaning of this key term before getting too involved in specifics.

System: The Concept.   The basic concept of a system is "a purposeful group of interrelated activities designed to achieve particular goals or objectives." This definition sounds academic and is. But it is well to realize that "system" can and should communicate particulars for any organization or situation. To the extent that HRD can qualify as a *system* in an organization, it means that

- Goals or objectives it seeks to achieve are clear (few are single purpose in reality).
- Necessary or critical functions or activities have been identified.
- Functions have been brought together in appropriate relationships, structures, and *sequences* to carry out its work mission.
- Bases exist for measuring its performance.
- Monitoring and feedback provisions are made for appropriate adjustments over time.

- Audit capabilities exist that permit periodic reexamination of its performance in the light of efficiency and effectiveness criteria and changing needs.

In creating a system, a self-test of its completeness will invariably involve five questions:

1. *Why* was (is) it (to be) established? What are the problems, issues, and needs which suggest these approaches? How compelling are they?
2. *What* is it to accomplish? What are its main features?
3. *How* is the system to work so that it achieves what it is supposed to achieve?
4. *Who* will the system service and have we adequately accounted for individual needs? Also, who are the people to design and administer the system? Do they have the needed skills? Are sufficient numbers available? What are their responsibilities?
5. *When* is the system supposed to be completed procedurally? When will people have adapted themselves to the system? Systems can be installed in months. Developing needed information for strategic planning systems can well take a year or two and individual adaptation and change can take years! As a result, time estimates tend to consistently underplay the actual time needed for a system to be fully functional.

Aside from these general self-test points, organizations require a lot of specific and detailed information to audit existing systems and/or to start the necessary planning for designing a system to meet their needs. The applications section for this chapter includes a "Self-audit Readiness Questionnaire" (Exhibit 6-6), its purpose being to generate some detailed information in many of the main areas supportive of a comprehensive human resource planning and development system.

In Exhibit 6-1, a format is presented for examining 12 basic organizational features often found necessary in establishing a human resource development system with a strategic focus (SMD). It is included in the discussion portion of this chapter for convenience in referencing and to illustrate the importance of this type of information in systems planning. Thus the planner/strategist or policy official has these three representative bodies of data and information which can be drawn upon in planning analyses, namely, the five basic questions, the 12-item checklist described in Exhibit 6-1, and the general systems audit included in Exhibit 6-6. The discussions among planners, officials, and managers triggered by these types of formats are perhaps the most useful results of these approaches.

System Elements

Some of the complications and problems of these systems in the past were due to the fact that individuals or organizational units operated in (semi)independent fashion. As the need grew to coordinate related activities better, organizations were

EXHIBIT 6-1

Strategic Management Development Systems: Basic Elements

Item Number	Element	Doesn't Exist	Low Degree	Well Along	Oper-ative
		Degree of Development			
1.	Strategic and long-range planning and programming capability	____	____	____	____
2.	Provision for orderly succession and staffing of key and critical personnel	____	____	____	____
3.	Corporate "culture" which is clear to officials and managers and matched with organizational goals	____	____	____	____
4.	Top management commitment and support	____	____	____	____
5.	Line management support with reinforcement through the performance management/reward system	____	____	____	____
6.	Human resource planning and development policy which is known and communicated	____	____	____	____
7.	Coordinated human resource planning and development system with both planning and career management components	____	____	____	____
8.	Management development programming reflective of the contingencies or characteristics of major business units or segments	____	____	____	____
9.	Structures, activities, processes, and defined relationships to coordinate and control the above elements	____	____	____	____
10.	Information base and management adequate to capture and disseminate business, performance, job, and individual information	____	____	____	____
11.	Basis to describe jobs or work and performance in a work-related, consistent and valid manner and to relate these to each other	____	____	____	____
12.	Facilitation of individual career planning	____	____	____	____

forced to identify clearly the basic functions, the sum total of which could help assure a strategic management development capability. Our experiences in this regard indicate that some 12 different elements must be in place. These are summarized in Exhibit 6-1. The number 12 is debatable because some people who work in this area combine features while others prefer to err on the side of more detail. The point is that there is a particular group of elements present that serves as the foundation for a SMD. They may not be sufficient, however, for a particular company's needs, but they do provide a point of departure for analysis. Officials and planners are in a position to start to judge the relative degree of maturity or usefulness of their organization's systems based on this type of approach. The presence or absence of a factor is a start in ultimately rendering a judgment as to system maturity and future needs.

The basic list covers 12 items included in the three main functions of business: planning and strategic processes; human resource planning, strategies, and development activities; and performance and development elements at the individual level. Note, for example, that at the strategic business planning level, a basic capability needs to exist and be operational (item 1). All these systems thrive on a wide variety of information inputs, from business planning information to individual performance data. However, it is vital that the information be capable of being disseminated (items 10 and 11). The complexity of these systems requires coordination at several different levels to assure that the parts operate in reasonable harmony with each other and that overall performance is seen as efficient and effective (items 7 and 9). Systems design for SMD also requires that general approaches accommodate basically different leadership and administrative needs which (often) exist in different businesses in which the organization is engaged (item 8).

The endorsement or support of these systems represents a substantial commitment of the energies and financial resources of the firm (items 4, 5)—indispensable to these, and basic as well, is top management's support. Top management is also instrumental in clarifying the internal environment, including the organization's culture. This is needed because the leadership's philosophy of business organization and operation, historically important promotion paths, seats of power, and valued decision-making patterns, for example, directly affect the characteristics of SMD (item 3).

Individuals are what this effort is all about! This is especially the case for those upon whose shoulders rest organizational continuity and renewal (item 2), plus those charged with the main responsibilities for carrying out its programs and activities. Individuals need to know what the organization stands for (item 6) and what's in it for them relative to their own career (item 12).

This discussion of basics for strategic management development systems has included its major elements. What is not clear yet is how all these parts are drawn together. This is suggested in Exhibit 6-2, Part I.

The SMD portrayed in Exhibit 6-2 has three main functions to be accomplished. The overall SMD program needs to

EXHIBIT 6-2

Strategic Management Development: Major System Features, Part I

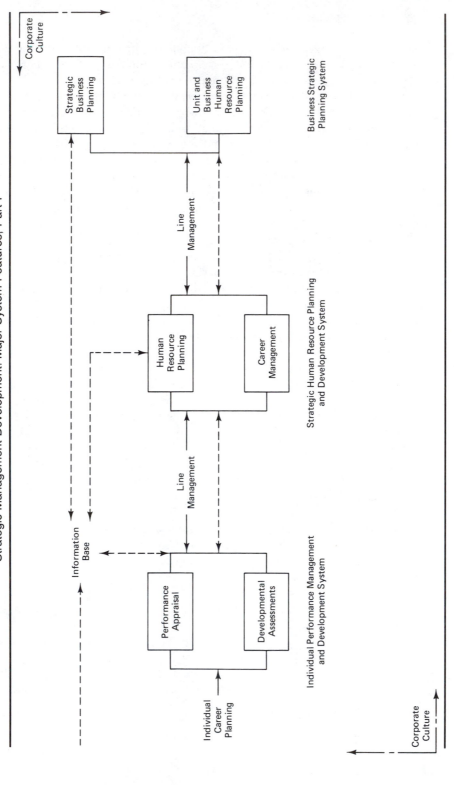

1. Encourage and channel individual performance while assuring the continuing knowledge, skill, and ability development to make this possible.
2. Organize numerous human resource/personnel activities in a way as to blend in smoothly with and support individual performance and development efforts as well as career programs.
3. Reflect business and strategic planning activities that establish direction or thrust for the enterprise.

Each of these three main functions has various and specific missions and responsibilities. Representative outcomes of each major subsystem, are detailed in Exhibit 6-3. Note that in Exhibit 6-3, the form of Exhibit 6-2 is reproduced but without the connecting lines showing system relationships. This is to facilitate exposition. When the results or performances of each of these "subsystems" is reviewed, the enormity of SMD starts to become apparent. A point to emphasize in Exhibits 6-2 and 6-3 is the critical role played by line management in the success of these strategic management development activities.

The activities and expected results from each of the major subsystems are discussed only briefly at this point since they receive much attention in subsequent chapters.

1. *Individual performance management and development system outcomes*—the results suggested in the leftmost panel of Exhibit 6-3 are tied into common performance-related programs such as "management by objectives" as well as those which primarily emphasize individual growth and development. In this "subsystem," there is a deliberate attempt to offset (the shortcomings of) overstressing performance results by a complementary development effort that helps people to strengthen needed knowledge and competencies for their current job responsibilities *and* also to further their career possibilities. In the development part, which usually takes place at a different point in time in order to stress its importance, needs analyses, including career development, are translated into specific knowledge-skill-ability requirements. This approach facilitates the identification of needs and targeted approaches for individual growth purposes. In the development mode, the supervisor's role is that of sounding board, coach, and behavioral model.
2. *Strategic human resource planning and development system outcomes*—activities include those shown in the central panel of Exhibit 6-3. Activities long associated with human resource planning and career management, the two basic elements of this system, are fused with strategic actions as well as those emphasizing coordination or linkage to the other main (sub)systems. Thus human resource strategies, system planning, data management, and environmental scanning receive added emphasis in strategic approaches and linking activities.
3. *Business and strategic planning system outcomes*—in this (sub)system, a distinction is made between long-range planning and strategic approaches. Our corporate studies indicate that these are distinct activities; the presence of a

EXHIBIT 6-3

Strategic Management Development: Major System Features, Part II

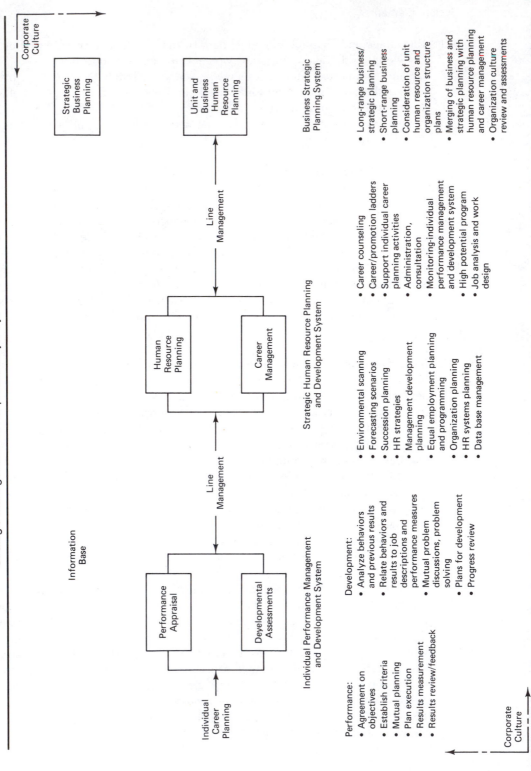

Corporate Culture

Strategic Business Planning

Unit and Business Human Resource Planning

Line Management

Business Strategic Planning System

- Long-range business/strategic planning
- Short-range business planning
- Consideration of unit human resource and organization structure plans
- Merging of business and strategic planning with human resource planning and career management
- Organization culture review and assessments

Information Base

Human Resource Planning

Career Management

Line Management

Strategic Human Resource Planning and Development System

- Environmental scanning
- Forecasting scenarios
- Succession planning
- HR strategies
- Management development planning
- Equal employment planning and programming
- Organization planning
- HR systems planning
- Data base management

- Career counseling
- Career/promotion ladders
- Support individual career planning activities
- Administration, consultation
- Monitoring-individual performance management and development system
- High potential program
- Job analysis and work design

Performance Appraisal

Developmental Assessments

Line Management

Individual Career Planning

Individual Performance Management and Development System

Performance:
- Agreement on objectives
- Establish criteria
- Mutual planning
- Plan execution
- Results measurement
- Results review/feedback

Development:
- Analyze behaviors and previous results
- Relate behaviors and results to job descriptions and performance measures
- Mutual problem discussions, problem solving
- Plans for development
- Progress review

Corporate Culture

long-range planning capability doesn't always signal that a strategic capability exists. Strategic approaches move beyond long-range planning in the sense that they involve an expanded base of participating staff units, officials, and key line managers; an expanded base of information; and an intensive study of existing resources, priorities, and alternatives. Also, as already noted, strategic approaches increase the importance assigned to organizational "culture" considerations as these affect the means, form and likelihood of success in specific strategic undertakings.

Strategic Planning Framework and Fit of Strategic Management Development

Corporate strategic planning is highly complex in the real world of multiproduct and/or multinational firms. There is a need to interpret competitive strategies and diverse environmental changes and generally to deal with the uncertainty inherent in the future. Some companies deal with the types of complexity described here by the use of profit centers or strategic business (planning) units (SBUs). These centers or units are then treated largely as independent planning units. Corporate-level strategies for the "decentralized model" provide for the integration of unit plans, a portion of which includes adjusting unit plans in comformity with general financial constraints and performance objectives. Some consultants and corporate officials argue, however, that these approaches are inherently suboptimizing since what is best or true for the parts (divisions, SBUs) is often *not* true for the whole.

One strategic planning framework that attempts to counter the inherent limitations of the approach described is to view the corporation as a whole. Comprehensive strategic planning is undertaken initially at the corporate level (the "centralized" approach). Corporate planning groups, strategists, and policymakers attempt to (best) match potential opportunity and/or threat with its resources— economic, technological, and human. In the "centralized model," it is quite common that the proposals or programs of various SBUs or divisions will be subordinated to those of others in an attempt to optimize overall corporate performance. We do not propose to enter into this debate since many arguments can be entered into both sides of the ledger. The key point to recognize from the perspective of strategic management development is that the role of human resource planning officials, line managers, and corporate policy and planning officials generally will differ greatly depending on the mode of approaches by headquarter's strategic and long-range business planning.

> For example, in one highly decentralized corporation, divisions comprise the basic planning units. Strategic planning takes place at the divisional level. Staffing analyses, succession planning, managerial inventories, developmental plans, and even specific aspects of human resource information and environmental data are geared to divisional needs. The control of staffing and development are divisional matters so long as decisions are made within the prescribed budgets or general constraints. However, when

managers in the divisions reach a predetermined salary level ("15" of 20 salary grades), headquarters reserves the right of review, though it is exercised infrequently.

In a highly centralized corporation, SBUs initially make proposals which were then reviewed at the corporate level. In this centralized approach, an overall strategic human resource plan emerges which was a resolution of business opportunities and corporate resource capabilities and limitations. The proposals were then "adjusted" to the corporation's overall strategic thrust. These corporate "adjustments" to SBU plans frequently created much concern, even conflict, because of the arbitrary way these changes were made. It was necessary to create a mediating role for Human Resources, to reduce conflict and come up with better strategic alternatives or solutions. Thus, corporate Human Resources assumed a highly interactive role in connection with corporate business and strategic officials, planners, and specialists. Eventually Human Resources' role was formalized as a "third-party" representative, sitting in on planning and strategic sessions involving corporate and SBU planners or heads.

Human resource scenarios were developed at the corporate level that matched the long-range planning and strategic business scenarios. Environmental business/economic scans were translated into strategic human resource planning analyses which were then reviewed and commented on by *both* SBU and corporate human resource people. The effectiveness of this centralized model and these working relationships required a long period of confidence building on the part of corporate Human Resources. It had to demonstrate its ability to understand fully, unit personnel interests while at the same time seeking to blend these with corporate needs and constraints artfully. Ultimately, the success of this approach depended on the expertise and personality of one or two key individuals and the full support of top management.

Design and Growth of Strategic Management Development Systems

The sophistication level of the organization and other organizational circumstances affect the characteristics of SMD systems. Companies differ widely with regard to their general state of systems maturity and the degree of refinement of particular processes (see Exhibit 6-4). Thus it is unlikely that a given organization would be wholly at stage I *or* II (Exhibit 6-4). For example, the current situation might be stage III on "top management commitment" (item 5), stage II on succession planning (item 3), and stage I on HRPD policy (item 7). The "stages" then represent characteristic points of advancement for any particular activity but not necessarily concurrent developments.

There are, however, important and underlying interrelationships among these SMD activities which need to be brought out. The first point to be recognized (Exhibit 6-4) is that some internal capability must exist before various advances can take place. For instance,

- Strategic thinking (item 2) and approaches assume that some degree of long-range organizational planning capability (item 1) already exists.

- Management development programming (item 9) is critically dependent on reliable position description and performance information (item 12) and is also reflective of individual's taking charge of their own career (item 13) in relation to corporate opportunities and requirements.
- The success with which corporate culture (item 4) is understood and serves as a unifying factor among top managers at all levels affects many elements in the strategic picture. The successful extension of strategic thinking (item 2) and its linking up with the human resource planning and development system (item 8) and bringing into reality management development plans (item 9) are some of the possible consequences of this understanding.
- Activities such as long-range planning (item 1), strategic planning (item 2), and succession planning (item 3) are critically dependent on solid external and internal information (items 11 and 12).
- The scope and usefulness of succession planning (item 3) is vitally dependent on long-range and strategic planning (items 1 and 2) for direction, timing, and specific needs, plus good information (items 11 and 12). Well-grounded succession plans help to assure adequate reserves of key and critical people resulting from a well-programmed management development activity (item 9).

Thus SMD systems don't just happen. Various stepping stones must be fashioned and set in place before system progress or advancements can be made. Exhibit 6-4 can be viewed in essentially two different ways: What is a fair representation of the current (systems) picture and what system *should* exist? Systems planning includes the identification of priorities, stepping stones, and links between activities which assure good communications and coordination.

A firm is regularly confronted with numerous problems and issues. However, only a relatively small number (say, five or six) at a given time are of the highest importance to organizational continuity, business success, and renewal for future growth. This critical set establishes the priorities and agenda for SMD system planning. For example,

> A large insurance firm, in the course of its long-range planning and strategic approaches, focused increasingly on territorial expansion. The geographic area identified was one in which very little business had been written in past years yet its "current" and projected growth indicated excellent future possibilities. Expansion into this area, however, was complicated greatly by an incompletely developed succession system. The situation was further complicated by poor job analysis information and performance data. There was a failure to identify and bring along an adequate flow of highly qualified backup people relative to impending retirements. Senior line managers were still uncertain of their role relative to SMD. The degree of system maturity, as it existed initially, is shown with the solid lines in Exhibit 6-5. System planning to strengthen this group of interrelated activities and to launch the (strategic) territorial expansion is shown with the dashed lines. The type of analysis highlighted here helped them to pull together the human resource side of their ambitious program. But it

EXHIBIT 6-4

Typical Growth Patterns of Strategic Management Development Systems

System Features	Stage of System Development			
	I Formative	II Emergent	III Contemporary	IV Advanced
1. Long-range planning	Informal speculation concerning possibilities—CEO and a few key officers form group; most actions geared to tangible issues.	Periodic attempts to develop some long-range plans; many senior managers view as temporary situation; emerges largely as offshoot of existing and main functions; often a financial orientation; attempt to use some planning models.	Regularized planning cycle and clear definition of "long range"; incorporate planning models; more flexible approach to planning horizons; link to budget and planning cycles; start to develop some scenarios based on environmental scans; planning functions still viewed somewhat apart from Human Resources—the latter seen as (still) providing the staffing numbers.	System orientation linking business planning and strategic elements to line management and functional units; regular use of planning models and simulations; variable time horizon based on changing external environment, internal environment, and business characteristics.
2. Strategic planning	Informal, speculative, irregular; often mixed up with "long-range" planning with no clear separation of the two.	Start to think in terms of alternative or fallback approaches, almost entirely in financial and business realm; HR considerations mostly deal with top leader; start to analyze organization as to what constitutes "logical" bases for planning.	Define strategic business units as bases for approaches; evoke strategy sessions as formal part of planning process; expand concept of "strategy" and thus identify new information needs; start to connect long-range planning scenarios	Most of strategic business unit problems of activities and linkages worked out; regularize environmental scans and develop scenarios for establishing contingency approaches; active expansion of information base and development of a user

			with strategic thinking; start to lose heavy financial orientation; start to identify critical qualities of leadership in this area.	friendly environment for personal computers to facilitate strategic thinking throughout organization.
3. Sucession planning	Informal; selected officer positions as needed.	Largely informal; extend officer leverage; add other critical positions.	Formalized; cover key and critical people, backups.	Formal; development strategy; talent pools; system for communications; review candidate tracking; dispute resolution.
4. Corporate "culture"	Identified primarily with corporate, owner or senior management philosophy and the historical roots of the organization.	Largely nonexistent as a functionally useful concept; people start consciously to identify "who we are," "what we stand for as an organization."	Corporate surveys start to identify key elements—top management starts to speculate as to the possible impact of these on behavior and/or performance.	Culture critically analyzed to determine impact on organization; considered somewhat variable thus questions of how defined it should be, the potential impact on performance, and should redefinition be sought; clarify features for incumbents and potential employees.
5. Top management commitment	No obvious signs or "signals"—rests mostly on generally understood philosophy of management—only vaguest connections to individual positions or effort; particular sponsors or mentors may be most reliable sign.	Some mentoring and/or sponsorship relationships firmed up and more in evidence; a key officer, at times the CEO, will evidence physical presence as show of support; key officers starts to participate regularly—often tends to be con-	Top management formally endorses strategic thinking and approaches by requesting their regularization; CEO and senior officers assume functional roles in strategic processes involving individual and committee assignments; en-	System defined, including structure, activities, responsibilities, and roles for all officers and senior managers; general and continuing reliance on system outputs; budgetary and reward systems further evidence of support;

(Continues)

EXHIBIT 6-4 (Continued)

Typical Growth Patterns of Strategic Management Development Systems

Stage of System Development

System Features	I Formative	II Emergent	III Contemporary	IV Advanced
		versational with informal written communications relied on; budgetary funding limited; use regularly scheduled meetings and informal formats to "voice" support.	dorse incorporation of supports via reward system and performance appraisals for lower management levels; confidence and reliance on system outputs growing.	mechanisms established for conflict resolution.
6. Line management support	Entirely on an individual interest basis—no "payoffs" for efforts; developmental results largely unpredictable and the quality of (limited) effort extended is highly variable; various managers enjoy reputation as "good teacher"; home and receiving managers link informally.	Cross-fertilization assignments more frequent—"home" and "receiving" managers link more formal and frequent; bosses ask about progress of people identified previously; sponsorship and mentoring somewhat more formal-based on interest and supervisory competency; supervisors will actively follow up on individual questions or problems; greater involvement "encouraged" by use on appraisal forms.	Supervisory competency developed to widen participation in program; appears regularly as a part of subordinate reviews in the agenda of human resource development meetings; highly competent managers assume regular posts as trainers and training units; greater career counseling and job-analytic skills in evidence.	Formalize mentoring sponsorship relationships as part of system; supervisory roles become more complex as they involve performances development, individual careers and planning components; performance appraisal and reward system actively "signal" desirability of system support.

228

7. HRPD policy	Nonexistent—general attitude and relationships taken as an extension of corporate philosophy and style of management.	Mostly informal; some policies evoked as particular problem situations occur or as defensive measures (e.g., succession matters or EEO); some attempts to frame a general policy statement signaling business interest in the individual and to support recruiting policies.	Formal policy statement evolves with varying degrees of specifics regarding individual and corporate roles and responsibilities; senior management briefing to facilitate familiarity and dissemination.	Formal studies to establish actively a policy reflective of the organization's current and future situation—various managerial levels contribute—Personnel/HR assumes leadership in design; most frequently in writing and widely disseminated; policy establishes foundation for structure, processes, activities and administrative practices.
8. HRPD system coordination	Primarily a topic of occasional discussion with important system elements missing; informal at best.	Largely informal but starting to assume definition as the system itself takes shape; informal links within involving Personnel Management and selected HR functions and line management and individuals.	Formalize and develop system linking main Personnel and Human Resource elements; elevation in importance of key official who serves to link planning and administrative functions; start to link to business planning system.	Develop comprehensive system linking Personnel and Human Resource elements and business planning and strategic functions; formalize position(s) for coordination; develop information baseline for measurement, periodic reviews, and audits.
9. Management development programming	Informal, largely in individual's hands.	Attempt to formalize—largely on an individual bases; primary reliance on external programming or extension of annual reviews; informal link-	Link to business and human resource planning; reliance on internal processes including immediate supervisor and external sources for general	Link development, performance management to planning and strategic system; situational/contingency approach reflective of company needs, indi-

(Continues)

EXHIBIT 6-4 (Continued)

Typical Growth Patterns of Strategic Management Development Systems

System Features	Stage of System Development			
	I Formative	II Emergent	III Contemporary	IV Advanced
		age of general staffing planning with business planning.	support; start to visualize in systems context; some degree of "action research" on effectiveness of approaches; heavily centered on annual performance reviews.	vidual, job and business planning/strategic units; HR policy clarifying issues and corporate commitments; action research component for performance and job improvement.
10. Coordination and control—general planning system	Informal; components not fully identified; rely on routine contacts and existing meetings and structures.	Emphasis on each functional unit coordinating its part of total; reliance on traditional form of control (e.g., financial officer/comptroller); various units consulted on an as-needed basis; build around previously scheduled meetings and events; start to develop feedback information system.	Identify major system components and formalize structures, responsibilities, activities and processes to carryout; seat coordination and control (C&C) with existing units and personnel; develop audit and feedback system; need growing for C&C position(s) per se; schedule mostly around existing meetings and groups.	Develop as a system with performance criteria reflective of career and general needs; develop comprehensive information base to form groups and establish time schedules reflective of C&C needs; formalize positions for C&C—by officers; regularly audit and review.
11. Information base and management inventory	Informally constructed, incomplete, reliance on verbal communications; internal orientation.	Formalizing much of records base; establishing performance standards and information;	Files mostly computerized and largely complete on standard information (e.g., per-	Computerized (mainframe and microcomputers) with multilevel retrieval, data reduc-

	internal information plus some external.	formance, performance standards, job availability data, demographics, some business and individual career data).	tion, and simulation possibilities. Data management of growing importance.
12. Job analysis and performance appraisal information	Oriented to traditional type job descriptions; various jobs not covered, incomplete or out of date; appraisals often use informal criteria.	Updating of job description base; incorporation of EEO language; development of job specifications; some job redesign; developing performance standards but often in terms unrelated (largely) to behavioral data.	Attempts to coordinate job and performance data base; growing attention to job descriptive and performance dimensions; growing interest in work design; planning for possible work-systems type changes; general checks for EEO conformity.	Job analysis incorporates job-descriptive and performance dimensions; careful re-analysis of job specifications; action research studies of jobs, job design, and system designs; regular review relative to EEO strategies; periodic audits.
13. Individual career planning	Informal, little career-related information available, quite incomplete; supervision main source of information and counseling; person does mostly on his or her own.	Routine job descriptive information and job availability information; traditional promotion-career progressions emphasized; some recourse to formal career counseling; career information—company rather than individually oriented.	Expand internal information base; increasing system orientation to individual and company needs; formal counseling available as back up to supervisor; vertical career ladders plus some growing of cross-fertilization or job change possibilities; some linking of personal development to career opportunity.	Balanced orientation to company and personal needs; job-posting system fully accessible; counseling system; individual filing and update on career-related information; link individual and corporate needs; review career interest and intentions relative to job/work design.

resulted in a necessary delay of over one year in getting their business expansion and marketing program underway. Failure to consider the human resource side of this program would have been costly due to lack of critical senior staffing and without adequate backup among supervisory and middle-management personnel in the marketing units.

The analyses of the human resource planning staff were furthered by a form of "impact analysis." This was carried out using the same system features as those shown in Exhibit 6-5. They were analyzed with respect to business-marketing components identified by the business planning staff. The format for this type of analysis is shown in Exhibit 6-7 of the application section.

Use of the Basic SMD Model in Focusing Strategic Systems Thinking and Planning

The preceding discussions have concerned various uses of the basic SMD model in system planning and analyses. Our experiences indicate that the type of format shown in Exhibit 6-5 can prove useful in strategic planning discussions. It permits key managers to reflect their impressions concretely on where matters stand regarding these important SMD elements. Not surprisingly, much erroneous information or unsupported attitudes or views come out in these discussions. This is precisely the type of benefit to be derived from these approaches. Top management thinking and planning is on much sounder ground with *common* understanding of "where" things are today as a basis for targeting future strategic thinking. This model or format lends itself readily to group discussions that can prove highly beneficial to understanding the essence of these systems and their fit into strategic planning.

Summary

Comprehensive strategic human resource planning systems represent a natural progression beyond existing human resource planning and career development activities. On the one hand, they are coupled to business and strategic planning, and internally to Personnel activities at the corporate and unit level. Of much importance in moving toward comprehensive systems is the fact that these activities include eventually three major functions or subsystems. These are tied to individual performance and development, human resource planning and systems management, and business and strategic planning.

The planning and achievement of comprehensive systems is a multiyear effort, the direction and composition of which needs to benefit from adequate and timely information. This chapter suggests several different sources of information and data, any or all of which may prove useful in preliminary or advanced systems planning. The three basic information sources described include "the five ques-

EXHIBIT 6-5

Strategic Management Development Systems Planning: A Large
Insurance Company

System Features	Stage of System Development			
	I Formative	II Emergent	III Contemporary	IV Advanced
1. Long-range planning			x	
2. Strategic planning		x		
3. Succession planning	x		o	
4. Corporate "culture" definition		x		
5. Top management commitment		x		
6. Line management support	x		o	
7. HRPD policy—definition		x		
8. HRPD system coordination		x		
9. Management development programming	x		o	
10. Coordination and control—general planning system		x		
11. Information base and management inventory		x		
12. Job analysis and performance appraisal information	x	o		
13. Individual career planning		x		

Key:
———————x = current state
— — ——o = projected system development

tions," assessing the presence of "basic strategic system elements," and the general state of (maturity) existing Personnel-Human Resources (Exhibit 6-6).

Strategic management development systems evolve in quite different and specific patterns. The bases for analysis includes viewing them in terms of basic points to establish a system (the 12 points, Exhibit 6-1) and as a stagelike growth process over time (Exhibit 6-4).

No particular pattern of system development "must" exist for a specific firm to achieve its possibilities. But key planning and line officials do need to reach consensus on "where" things are currently and possess commonly understood benchmarks for future systems designs. Thus, the comprehensive exhibit provided in this chapter (Exhibit 6-4) can serve as a recording and discussion vehicle for concretizing the outlooks of key people. Correspondingly, it can help to reduce the numerous communications problems which encompass this planning work.

Line management has come to play a central and key role in strategic management development systems. Their contributions and willingness to participate actively in strategic processes in a cooperative way is indispensable to planning and programming progress. Their role and contributory effort needs to be thought through more thoroughly than is characteristic of "today's" systems. In this regard, the role of line management is interleafed throughout discussions in this book.

REFERENCES

Allen, Gerald B. "A Note on the Boston Consulting Group Concept of Competitive Analysis and Corporate Strategy," HBS Case Services, No. 9-175-179. Boston, MA: Harvard Business School, 1975.

Beer, Michael and Robert A. Ruh. "Employee Growth Through Performance Management" *Harvard Business Review,* Vol. 53, no. 4 (July–August 1975): 40–52.

Burack, Elmer H. and Nicholas J. Mathys. *Human Resource Planning: A Pragmatic Approach to Manpower Planning and Development,* 2nd ed., rev. Lake Forest, IL: Brace Park Press, 1987.

Burack, Elmer H. and Nicholas J. Mathys. *Career Management in Organizations: A Practical Human Resource Development Approach.* Lake Forest, IL: Brace Park Press, 1980.

Burack, Elmer H. *Strategies for Manpower Planning and Programming.* Morristown, NJ: General Learning, 1972.

Burack, Elmer H. and James W. Walker. *Manpower Planning and Programming.* Boston, MA: Allyn & Bacon, 1972.

Buzzell, Robert D., Bradley T. Gale, and Ralph G. M. Sultan. "Market Share—A Key to Profitability." *Harvard Business Review,* Vol. 53, no. 1 (January–February 1975): 97–106.

Devanna, Maryanne, Charles Fombrun, Noel Tichy, and Lynn Warren. "Strategic Planning and Human Resource Management." *Human Resource Management,* Vol. 21, no. 1 (Spring 1982): 22–36.

Manzini, Andrew and John Gridley. *Strategic Human Resource Planning Systems.* New York, AMACOM, 1987.

Schoeffler, Sidney, Robert D. Buzzell, and Donald F. Heany. "Impact of Strategic Planning on Profit Performance." *Harvard Business Review,* Vol. 52, no. 2 (March–April 1974): 137–149.

Tichy, Noel. "Managing Change Strategically: The Technical, Political and Cultural Keys." *Organizational Dynamics,* Vol. 11, no. 2 (1982): 81–93.

Tichy, Noel. *Strategic Planning Systems and Approaches.* New York: John Wiley, 1984.

Tornow, Walter W. and Timothy C. Gartland. "Enhancing Managerial Effectiveness." In Edwin L. Miller, Elmer H. Burack, and Maryann Albrecht, eds., *Management of Human Resources*. Englewood Cliffs, NJ: Prentice-Hall, 1980.

Wilson, Ian H. "Environmental Scanning and Strategic Planning." *Business Environment/Public Policy: 1979 Conference Paper*. St. Louis: American Collegiate Schools of Business, 1980: 159–163.

APPLICATIONS SECTION

Exhibit 6-6 is a detailed instrument that has the purpose of providing preliminary information. Human Resource planners and strategists frequently find it necessary to examine the main systems, activities, and policies, the sum total of which can provide a "snapshot" of where the organization's Personnel–Human Resource activities are currently. Any major deficiencies disclosed by this type of activities are critical to the design of comprehensive strategic systems. Shortcomings or deficient processes and data usually need to be corrected *before* significant progress is possible in systems design. Each organization should draw on these data and render interpretations relative to its own particular circumstances.

Exhibit 6-7 was used as a basis for a form of impact analysis using the systems features and stage of maturity shown in Exhibit 6-4. Column heads, only a portion of which are shown, were focused particularly on the marketing effort. The purpose of the impact analysis illustrated was to establish more precisely which aspects of the strategic marketing program would be affected by particular strategic planning and staffing activities. This had implications for staffing (planning) needs, types of skills needed, orientation or training programs, and development and/or transfer of current personnel to meet the needs of the strategic marketing effort.

A. Organization Commitment

1. Has a policy statement been drafted and circulated to organization members indicating the company's commitment to human resource planning and supportive activities?

    Yes ☐   No ☐   Uncertain ☐

2. Is top management willing to commit organizational resources (e.g., time, money, staff) that are necessary to develop human resource planning and development systems?

    Yes ☐   No ☐   Uncertain ☐

3. Is staff available to assist in managing the human resource (HR) planning efforts?

    Yes ☐   No ☐   Uncertain ☐

4. Will the organization be able to integrate the human resource planning system with the strategic business planning system?

    Yes ☐   No ☐   Uncertain ☐

5. Is management receptive to evaluating its personnel every year (or more often) in terms of performance and potential?

    Yes ☐   No ☐   Uncertain ☐

6. Are employees informed about their opportunities within the organization, based on projected moves and competition among other employees for similar positions?

    Yes ☐   No ☐   Uncertain ☐

7. Is the organization willing to accept the transfer of talented people from one department to another as a way of life?

    Yes ☐   No ☐   Uncertain ☐

8. Is the organization willing to devote months or perhaps even one, two, or three years to research and develop the human resource planning system?

    Yes ☐   No ☐   Uncertain ☐

9. Is the organization's culture "known" to its members?

    Yes ☐   No ☐   Uncertain ☐

10. Is the organization's culture strong and supporting of human resource focused processes and activities?

    Yes ☐   No ☐   Uncertain ☐

B. Human Resource Planning—Forecasting

1. Are business and strategic planning analyses made regularly?

    Yes ☐   No ☐   Uncertain ☐

2. Are overall staffing requirements being established for future periods and regularly updated?

    Yes ☐   No ☐   Uncertain ☐

EXHIBIT 6-6 (Continued)

3. Are forecasts made for managerial and professional segments and regularly updated?

      Yes ☐   No ☐   Uncertain ☐

4. Are forecasts made and updated for key and critical managerial and officer slots to facilitate succession planning?

      Yes ☐   No ☐   Uncertain ☐

5. Do forecasts incorporate enterprise objectives for equal employment and utilization of all work force segments?

      Yes ☐   No ☐   Uncertain ☐

6. Are HR planning/forecasting analyses integrated with business planning and strategic analyses?

      Yes ☐   No ☐   Uncertain ☐

7. Are HR planning and forecasting analyses integrated with career management activities and the Personnel functions and system?

      Yes ☐   No ☐   Uncertain ☐

8. Is the overall systems and functions of human resources *and* the enterprise coordinated as an integrated whole?

      Yes ☐   No ☐   Uncertain ☐

9. Is there a willingness to reconcile differences between HR staffing forecasts and budgeting decisions?

      Yes ☐   No ☐   Uncertain ☐

C. Training and Development

1. Are appropriate promotion and mobility opportunities worked out for high potentials (i.e., are programs geared to HR planning)?

      Yes ☐   No ☐   Uncertain ☐

2. Are there sufficient (re: morale, turnover) training and development opportunities and coaching for people who are not identified as high potentials?

      Yes ☐   No ☐   Uncertain ☐

3. Is there regular monitoring and a special budget allocated for the development of high potentials?

      Yes ☐   No ☐   Uncertain ☐

4. Are unit heads and key line people adequately oriented and prepared to cross-train and work with and support the development experiences of high potentials?

      Yes ☐   No ☐   Uncertain ☐

5. Are adequate performance standards and criteria available to judge developmental efforts?

      Yes ☐   No ☐   Uncertain ☐

6. Are the development needs of top management identified/tracked?

      Yes ☐   No ☐   Uncertain ☐

7. Is (Will) there (be) staff and time available to orient managerial participants to the human resource planning system (when it is established)?

      Yes ☐   No ☐   Uncertain ☐

EXHIBIT 6-6 (Continued)

8. Is management receptive to a development program for new professionals who are hired into the organization from college?

    Yes ☐   No ☐   Uncertain ☐

9. Is management receptive to tracking new professionals over the initial career stages of their development (e.g., three to four years)?

    Yes ☐   No ☐   Uncertain ☐

10. Is there support for conducting organizationwide career planning discussions on a regularly scheduled basis with employees (nonsupervisory)?

    Yes ☐   No ☐   Uncertain ☐

11. Is there support for conducting organizationwide career planning discussions on a regularly scheduled basis with professionals, supervisors, staff, and managers?

    Yes ☐   No ☐   Uncertain ☐

12. Is management willing and able to identify both short- and long-range development needs for its professional and managerial personnel?

    Yes ☐   No   Uncertain ☐

13. Is management supportive in aiding the Human Resource planning staff to conduct training and development needs analysis?

    Yes ☐   No ☐   Uncertain ☐

14. Are career ladders identified that represent validated bases for individual development?

    Yes ☐   No ☐   Uncertain ☐

D. Employee Recruitment, Selection, and Placement

1. Is there a close relationship between the Human Resource planning and development administrator and the administrator of recruitment, selection, and placement?

    Yes ☐   No ☐   Uncertain ☐

2. Are employee recruitment objectives linked to human resource planning recommendations?

    Yes ☐   No ☐   Uncertain ☐

3. Do employees have realistic expectations regarding their development and career possibilities?

    Yes ☐   No ☐   Uncertain ☐

4. Are employment systems monitored for their conformance with equal employment plans?

    Yes ☐   No ☐   Uncertain ☐

5. Do accurate and useful descriptions of jobs exist to facilitate orientation and initial assignments?

    Yes ☐   No ☐   Uncertain ☐

6. Do bases exist as to future needs for establishing career plans?

    Yes ☐   No ☐   Uncertain ☐

7. Does the employment manager and the Human Resource planning manager report to the same supervisor or, this aside, are efforts made to assure coordination?

    Yes ☐   No ☐   Uncertain ☐

EXHIBIT 6-6 (Continued)

E. Career Management

1. Have managers and organization members accepted the basic proposition that people take charge of their own careers?

    Yes ☐   No ☐   Uncertain ☐

2. Have vertical and lateral mobility opportunities been identified for organizational personnel in the next three to five years?

    Yes ☐   No ☐   Uncertain ☐

3. Is management prepared to identify backups, potential successors, and/or to develop and maintain a talent pool?

    Yes ☐   No ☐   Uncertain ☐

4. Is management willing to identify (other) career opportunities for incumbents who have not been identified as backups?

    Yes ☐   No ☐   Uncertain ☐

5. Is there a career counseling and planning program for employees?

    Yes ☐   No ☐   Uncertain ☐

6. Is training provided for management in career counseling techniques?

    Yes ☐   No ☐   Uncertain ☐

7. Is management receptive to identifying and developing career paths for "targeted" job groups or those disadvantaged through prior treatment?

    Yes ☐   No ☐   Uncertain ☐

8. Is management willing to accept without prejudice the idea that some people may not wish to move up and prefer to do a good job but stay where they are?

    Yes ☐   No ☐   Uncertain ☐

F. Performance Appraisal

1. Are the organization's current performance appraisal systems and procedures effective?

    Yes ☐   No ☐   Uncertain ☐

2. Is management receptive to using standardized performance evaluation procedures—and control at the same time, nonstandard usage?

    Yes ☐   No ☐   Uncertain ☐

3. Do managers/supervisors receive training to assure uniform application of the system?

    Yes ☐   No ☐   Uncertain ☐

4. Are performance standards established for professional positions?

    Yes ☐   No ☐   Uncertain ☐

5. Are performance standards established for nonsupervisory positions?

    Yes ☐   No ☐   Uncertain ☐

6. Are performance standards established for supervisory/managerial positions?

    Yes ☐   No ☐   Uncertain ☐

7. Are managers at all levels willing to provide (sensitive) performance data and ratings of employees' potential to a central Human Resource planning group or information pool?

    Yes ☐   No ☐   Uncertain ☐

EXHIBIT 6-6 (Continued)

8. Is there a willingness among management to establish a performance objective setting and performance appraisal system that could be used with all professional and managerial levels concerned?

Yes ☐   No ☐   Uncertain ☐

G. Development and Use of Information

External Information

1. Are geographic job variances and area unemployment taken into account in HR analyses?

Yes ☐   No ☐   Uncertain ☐

2. Are occupational employment figures taken into account?

Yes ☐   No ☐   Uncertain ☐

3. Are technological trends considered as these impact work systems, skills, and internal training and development?

Yes ☐   No ☐   Uncertain ☐

4. Are general economic forecasts made, or take account of enterprise planning?

Yes ☐   No ☐   Uncertain ☐

5. Are general social, political, and ideological trends taken into account in deriving human resource forecasts?

Yes ☐   No ☐   Uncertain ☐

Internal Information

6. Is the information from business, functional area, and facilities planning available to HR planners?

Yes ☐   No ☐   Uncertain ☐

7. Are overall and detailed staffing plans available from the information system?

Yes ☐   No ☐   Uncertain ☐

8. Is internal job vacancies information available?

Yes ☐   No ☐   Uncertain ☐

9. Is an information base established and/or kept up to date as to demographic and performance data?

Yes ☐   No ☐   Uncertain ☐

10. Is behavioral-type data developed for incorporation in the information base?

Yes ☐   No ☐   Uncertain ☐

11. Is individual performance data validated against standards and made available in the information base?

Yes ☐   No ☐   Uncertain ☐

12. Is individual career planning data captured for the information system?

Yes ☐   No ☐   Uncertain ☐

13. Is job information developed that is oriented to the end behaviors needed for successful performance?

Yes ☐   No ☐   Uncertain ☐

14. Are right-of-privacy guidelines observed in information generation and access?

Yes ☐   No ☐   Uncertain ☐

EXHIBIT 6-6 (Continued)

Data Management

15. Is there support to monitor and control the quality of human resource data inputs?

    Yes ☐   No ☐   Uncertain ☐

16. Is there sufficient human resource staffing to monitor and process human resource data?

    Yes ☐   No ☐   Uncertain ☐

17. Are managers willing to treat employee data as a corporate resource rather than as a department resource?

    Yes ☐   No ☐   Uncertain ☐

18. Will the organization reach a clear policy as to sharing of human resource planning data with incumbents?

    Yes ☐   No ☐   Uncertain ☐

H. Needs Analysis: Human Resource Staff

1. Have all administrative and professional members had the opportunity to establish the "up-to-dateness" of their background relative to current organizational needs?

    Yes ☐   No ☐   Uncertain ☐

2. Have business and strategic planning activities been translated into their implications for Human Resource staffing *and* knowledge-skill-ability credentials?

    Yes ☐   No ☐   Uncertain ☐

3. Have all administrative and professional members had the opportunity to establish the "up-to-dateness" of their background relative to planned future directions?

    Yes ☐   No ☐   Uncertain ☐

4. Do means exist permitting Human Resource staff periodically to check out the relevance of their background relative to the state of the art in the field?

    Yes ☐   No ☐   Uncertain ☐

5. Has the organization structure of Human Resources been planned so as to make it fully responsive to future organization requirements?

    Yes ☐   No ☐   Uncertain ☐

6. Have new specialization needs been investigated, and if needs exist, have appropriate steps been taken?

    Yes ☐   No ☐   Uncertain ☐

7. Has Personnel, as a function, been integrated with Human Resource personnel and activities?

    Yes ☐   No ☐   Uncertain ☐

8. To the extent that constraints exist in staffing, have priorities been established and have adjustments been made in time or program commitments?

    Yes ☐   No ☐   Uncertain ☐

Source: Based in part on Robert L. Minter, College of Business Administration, University of Denver and as presented in *Training of Development Journal,* October 1980, pp. 54–55.

EXHIBIT 6-7

Impact Analysis: Strategic Management Development Planning and Marketing Planning

System features	Establish field sales offices	Public relations program	Advertising/ media program	Extend computer system capability and support	Hiring, training, field sales	Priority	Timing	Action program
1. Long-range planning								
2. Strategic planning								
3. Succession planning								
4. Corporate "culture"								
5. Top management commitment								
6. Line management support								
7. HRPD* policy								
8. HRPD system coordi- nation								
9. Management develop- ment programming								
10. Coordination and control—general planning system								
11. Information base and management inventory								
12. Job analysis and performance appraisal information								
13. Individual career planning								

*HRPD = human resource planning and development

7

Performance Planning, Management, and the Strategic Picture

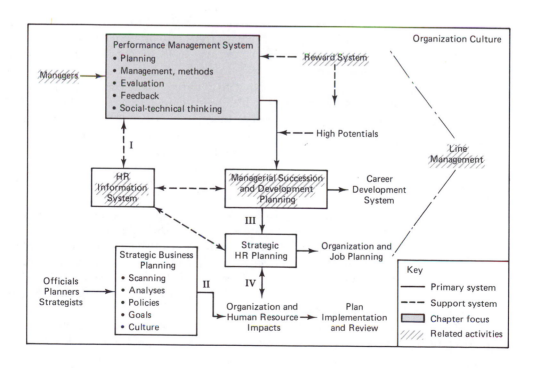

Performance Management System
- Planning
- Management, methods
- Evaluation
- Feedback
- Social-technical thinking

Managers

Reward System

High Potentials

HR Information System

I

Managerial Succession and Development Planning

III

Career Development System

Strategic HR Planning

Organization and Job Planning

Strategic Business Planning
- Scanning
- Analyses
- Policies
- Goals
- Culture

Officials Planners Strategists

II

IV

Organization and Human Resource Impacts

Plan Implementation and Review

Organization Culture

Line Management

Key
— Primary system
- - - Support system
▨ Chapter focus
▨ Related activities

The discussions in this chapter are of two forms. The initial focus is on performance planning issues and problems related to longer-range planning and strategic discussions, and how these affect general HR planning. Next, managerial performance and achieving "competence" are discussed in the context of strategic approaches. The shortcomings of traditional approaches form an effective point from which to discuss newer applications.

The final chapter discussion deals with newer performance planning and management issues brought about by some representative types of major corporate changes, including merger.

Strategic Business Planning for Performance Improvement

Strategic business analyses set the tone for performance planning and improvement and thereby related human resource planning approaches. An underlying consideration in many strategic discussions is a conscious and thoughtful approach by enterprise officials and strategists to minimize or avoid serious errors, although truly fortuitous or difficult-to-perceive circumstances will occur. The firm must be prepared to make necessary and feasible changes in its strategic plans or programs as these types of events occur.

Planners and strategists, in seeking to reduce serious errors, try to enlarge their understanding of their industry life cycle, demand characteristics, market/product substitution features, and their industry's basis for sales/cost competition. For example, understanding the cost structure of competition suggests corporate areas needing cost improvement or reanalysis of profit margins related to specific activities or even points of opportunity. Regarding the latter point, this information may, for example, indicate approaches to capitalizing on a firm's own (superior) competitive cost position (Mead and Stamm, 1985).

Even at a very general level of planning and strategic assessments, Human Resource planning officials need to understand the economic, marketing, technological, and competitive aspects of these analyses. This is necessary to be able to extrapolate their possible impacts on organization policies, structures, rewards, positional requirements, staffing, and managerial behaviors. The needed wisdom and competency to engage in these analyses is as great as the understanding required to develop HR planning scenarios.

Error avoidance at the strategic business planning level also involves studies to identify "trigger incidents" and "turning points" and then to decipher the organizational impact of these. The full effect of these change events often takes years to unfold, yet therein lies an opportunity for Human Resource planners. The successful fulfillment of long-term succession planning and management development processes can be materially assisted by HR strategists, who are able to draw out at an early point, the human resource aspects of turning points and trigger incidents.

> Japan's penetration of the U.S. automotive industry is an example of error avoidance factors at an international level. First, there was the continued production in the United States of full-sized, rear-drive vehicles, often lacking in durability and valued quality features. Also, there was the trickle of Japanese cars into California in the early 1970s, and the severe loss of market share of U.S. cars in international markets such Australia in the mid- to late 1970s. Both contributing to and reinforcing the speed and scope of the changes taking place was the shift in consumer tastes (turning points) toward reliability, quality, and economy of operation. These events eventually led to a major fallout and reorganization of U.S. automotive manufacturers and suppliers. The human resource impacts were dramatic. A few examples included rollback of managerial and technical work groups; reorganization and realignment of plant managerial and support staffs; reorganization of plants based on sociotechnical precepts (Chapter 2); creation of new participative roles for employees; refocusing of styling and engineering technology departments; and the need to foster a newer, more creative, managerial leadership. Penetrating human resource analyses of the effectiveness and efficiency aspects of these trigger incidents and turning points could in part have facilitated necessary corporate streamlining and other changes. These changes were needed to help prepare automotive companies for the competitive era of the 1980s and 1990s. It is also likely that loss of market share of U.S. companies could have been reduced if adaptability of personnel and organizational change had been accelerated (see Halberstam 1986).

Strategic Thinking and Operational Efficiency

Regardless of whether enterprises or their main work systems are oriented to information, transactions, or products, they usually assign high priority to improving operating efficiency. The appropriate and efficient application of technology is a common starting point in thinking about operating efficiency. The updating of mainframe computers from third to fourth (or fifth) generation, or the expansion of mini- and microcomputer usage (see Chapter 11), or new equipment processes and products are common in these approaches. Also, planners and strategists have been learning that *new* is not necessarily better and that dedication to getting more out of existing systems and being an efficient follower rather than leader may also represent viable corporate strategies.

There is a "point-counterpoint" for these planning discussions. Most major issues have significant human resource dimensions. Changes in Human Resource's role in strategy discussions, from follower to coequal, become more understandable in the light of growing HR challenges which are a part of these discussions. Establishing technology leadership, or playing an efficient "follower" role in innovation, equates to staffing planning and developing corresponding individual abilities.

Viewing Human Resources in a proactive and interactive role as a part of strategic processes imposes important and newer demands on their role. What new HR information systems or types of analyses should be considered to improve operational planning and decision making? How should operations be reorganized from a personnel and managerial standpoint to gain effectiveness? What positive results and problems can be expected from a "quality of work life" or "quality circle program?"

The Underlying Economics of Operations

Measurement systems need to reflect the underlying economics of operating efficiently. At times, the "logic" of beneficial approaches is counterproductive to past experience or depends on the point in the system at which costs are aggregated. Traditional-cost systems, for example, may distribute costs in proportion to sales for raw materials derived from the same source. Other traditional-cost approaches aggregate labor or managerial costs or services supporting these but lack the orientation or fine tuning needed to guide planning actions. Thus, these approaches often fail to provide information on decisionable costs and more generally what is needed for improving ("optimizing") results. Consider the following situation:

> A large manufacturer of consumer and industrial drug products was organized on a divisional and highly decentralized basis. Old-line product divisions continued to show above-average profits. Company officials felt that this (profit) resulted from long-established product markets and was not due to recent innovative marketing or product strategies. Recently introduced products had shown highly mixed results, in all divisions, in general, poorer than in previous years. Standard costs for these divisions were compiled in numerous ways and in depth. General financial measures (e.g., return on investment) were extensively developed and used at both the corporate and divisional level.

> However, most of the cost approaches shared a major deficiency; namely, they were financially oriented and lacked detailed cost information. That is, decisions to increase expenditures for technology or managerial resources, increasing performance bonuses, expanding marketing personnel, or tighter quality control, for example, were made *without benefit* of the returns to these expenditures. Only such general information as average cost per labor hour or thousands of items produced (or sold), was available.

> An extensive multiyear study was undertaken, the purpose of which was to identify the key cost structures underlying various divisional operations. Also of interest were the types of cost information which would be needed to improve division general management's planning and strategic decisions. In consequence of this study, a completely new set of cost figures resulted. It permitted the establishment of cost baselines and tracking of trends over time. The system also allowed for the isolation of managerial or

technical personnel expenditures, training costs, and workable accuracy concerning the calculation of returns to various personnel expenditures. Cost-benefit analyses, planning, and discussions were facilitated.

Human Resources played a major role in the indicated analyses because it provided counsel on the human resource aspects of these costs. It also was instrumental in (eventually) developing cost-decision models useful to division management and the training of divisional personnel to make effective use of these tools.

In summary, planning for performance improvement is a central concern in strategic discussions. Longer-range planning and fitting strategies to these sets the tone for involvement of Human Resources. Strategic discussions which initially enter into questions of performance efficiency and the improved use of technology rather quickly turn toward productivity issues involving human resources. Considerable knowledge and understanding of industry marketing, products, competitive profits, and cost structures help in minimizing errors in planning and strategic actions. The thoughtful identification of human resource options and expenditures requires cost-benefit information which is of workable accuracy and adequate detail.

Human resource issues may range from succession matters to developing a new managerial cadre, to staffing rollbacks or considering quality of work life programs. Planning scenarios built with HR represent the critical bridge from general business planning and strategic discussions to human resource assessments. A coequal and proactive role for Human Resources requires knowledgeable entry into these types of discussions and planning analyses.

Performance Planning and Surfacing Strategic Human Resource Issues: A Policy Perspective

A useful model for identifying strategic HR issues considers four main policy-related tasks with which officials and managers are generally confronted (Spector and Beer, 1985). Policies and strategic actions must be considered in regard to human resource flows, employee influence, reward systems, and work systems.

Human Resource Flows. These involve the movements of personnel into, through, and out of the organization. Aside from conventional personnel considerations such as recruiting, strategic analyses require planning and decisions concerning basic human resource planning questions ("the right number at the right place," etc.). Also, managerial and general employee needs related to job security, career progress, and equitable treatment are bound to be affected by various selection and stafffing approaches. "Flow planning and decisions" need to be consistent with organizational strategies, societal values at large, and individual competencies and expectancies.

Employee Influence. This deals with the extent to which authority, power, and responsibility (amount and level) is delegated in the organization. The appropriate degree of influence reflects a complex resolution of organization culture, individual member needs, societal values, work force maturity and competency, and task complexity and demands.

Rewards System.   This includes the amounts and types of rewards to use to achieve targeted performance and effectiveness levels and the desired degree of personnel participation. At an individual level, it is necessary to be aware of the current situation (motivation, morale, cooperation), the types of behaviors and attitudes likely to impact on organizational effectiveness, performance, and what is to be accomplished. For example, shall managerial (or individual) involvement be based primarily on monetary rewards and promotion, or is a deeper loyalty or commitment sought? If a deeper effect is desired, will the identified strategy conform with the organization's culture? Will there be improvements in long(er)-term effectiveness and efficiency?

Performance planning of necessity considers both extrinsic (e.g., salary) and intrinsic (e.g., the "job itself") rewards and the relative importance and role to be played by each. Compensation options, such as managerial bonuses, must also be factored into the strategic picture and their relative effectiveness established.

Reward systems planning also turns to general policy-level decisions related to the competitiveness of wages, merit-based rewards and promotions, and the possible gains from profit sharing. "Equal pay" legislation and regulations require that current and planned reward systems and compensation practices be carefully reviewed.

Job and Work Systems.   These strategic and policy-level issues relate in part to sociotechnical approaches described in Chapter 2. Arrangement of people, tasks, technology, and information access all form parts of the planning/policy matrix. On the one hand, decisions regarding work systems must take into account current human resource competencies and the desirability and feasibility of developing new ones. There must also be recognition given to the need for new levels of coordination or types of planning. Correspondingly, new managerial roles relative to the work force and requisite knowledge and skills to enact these are also very much a part of the picture.

Dynamics of Policy, Strategic-Planning Issues

In actuality, the four factors just described form a dynamic, interactive set of factors. A decision in any one of the four policy areas must also take account of the current status of other areas and the degree to which these will be affected. For example, strategies involving the expansion of employee influence for greater performance will involve job/work design options and have reward consequences. Also, greater managerial (employee) involvement may be achieved through new recruiting policies which bring in (personnel "flows") quite different types of personnel in the future.

> For example, a large manufacturer's strategic analyses led to the relocation of a major division to another area of the country. It was felt that it would be possible to gain greater employee involvement in this new area. Work systems in the new facility were radically different from conventional work systems and highly participative group processes were necessary to make the facility successful. Action research experiments in *existing* facilities and with the new work designs, had shown these to have highly mixed results. Analyses indicated that deeply entrenched and traditional ways of thinking about and approaching work were major problems in these attempted changes.
>
> When the new facility and work force were established, rewards relative to other units were changed greatly. These were built around group performance and included profit/performance sharing. Needless to say, the role of first-level supervisors and line management were greatly changed in their approach. In planning for the new facility, all four components of the policy-strategy model had to be considered. Results from the action research pilot study, and top management's longer-range planning objectives which stressed performance improvement, were an important part of their approach.

In summary, the four-phase policy–strategy planning model described in this section is helpful in surfacing key HR issues. The HR planning matters are a part of general business and strategic planning. Using the model in a dynamic way assists in drawing attention to the interrelated nature of many of these issues and thus the necessity of broad-based HR approaches.

Strategic Views on Managerial Performance—What Is It?

Previous chapter discussions, especially Chapter 2, indicated that no single number or measure will tell us with any degree of accuracy, how well a manager is doing. Multiple criteria are necessary to appraise managerial performance. One large "high-tech" company used 17 general dimensions plus many position–specific ones. A hotel chain used 20 in considering senior managerial positions.

Performance measurement is made more difficult when time effects are considered. The following questions indicate some of the problems:

- Are we considering short-term or long-term results? What happened subsequent to the measurement period(s)?
- What was the spoilage rate when we achieved *that* store volume? How many old accounts were lost while gaining the new ones?
- Although the average quality was acceptable, how bad did it really get and for how long?
- The number of units *produced* was good, but how many completed units were actually *shipped?*

Strategic thinking concerning managerial performance requires an enlarged perspective.

Efficiency and Effectiveness Measures of Performance

In the past, emphasis was often placed on efficiency measures that had heavy economic, financial, or production overtones. Examples of these included profits, quantity produced, and sales volume; others involved return on investment, number of patentable products developed, and relative cost increases or decreases. A performance measurement scheme such as management by objectives (MBO) fit well with these efficiency conceptions since it reinforced the identification of specific and measurable performance objectives. Also, MBO was said to foster a participative style. These accomplishments are important and are not being depreciated. But the positive aspects of goal clarity, participation, and (apparent) preciseness of the MBO model were often counterbalanced by negative "side effects." MBO encouraged focusing on short(er)-run results and preoccupation with the tangible aspects of managerial work. The "objectivity" of MBO approaches was often achieved at the expense of equally important qualitative results, or objective results which took a long time (say, two or three years) to play out. For example,

> The marketing department of a consumer products company introduced a redesigned line of garden tools. It was faced with overcoming a poor response by homeowners to its original line—the products didn't perform well and weren't durable. The first year's marketing plan for the redesigned line was based on sales programs negotiated with each of the field sales managers. The company stressed regaining its market share quickly and pushed heavily for first-year sales. Significant sales incentives (e.g., "a trip to Hawaii for you and your family") were established to support the sales program. The first-year marketing program was very successful in getting the line (back) into dealers, but dealer sales didn't follow. Virtually nowhere had enough time been spent to reorient dealers to the features of the new line. Nor had time been taken to overcome the negative feelings lingering in the minds of many consumers as a result of poor experiences with the original line. What in all likelihood should have been a two- or three-year program of confidence (and satisfaction) building, was compressed into a strong first-year effort, with poor longer-term results.

What are the strategic concerns in these aspects of performance? In the example presented, time phasing, company priorities, and performance measurement were all part of the picture. More broadly, many businesses in the United States and elsewhere in the Western world have a dominant, short-run orientation, although survival may preclude longer-term considerations. The glaring differences between U.S. and Japanese firms in performance horizons is perhaps overworked but nevertheless a reality commanding attention. The differences in results are *not* easily washed away even when cultural distinctions are taken into account.

The need for a longer time perspective for planning, decision making, and evaluation of results has impacted a growing number of firms. Concomitant with this need has been one of consistency in "thinking," "discussions," *and* "execution." It is pointless to plan with longer time horizons if most managerial actions are transacted based on a short-run outlook.

Performance Time Horizon and Responsibility Level. It is intuitively logical and generally verified by experience that the relevant time spans for managerial decisions are related to the scope and type of individual authority and responsibility. Thus another aspect of establishing relevant time frames for managerial performance management is the recognition of inherently different time perspectives for various levels of managerial positions. The general model, confirmed through years of study by Elliot Jaques, is that a time span gradient exists from lower to higher managerial levels. The time spans are related to planning horizons and decision commitments, managerial responsibilities, and authority. The following tabulation, based on the Jaques's study, suggests the relationships between time span and authority level.

Time span for goals and related decisions	Managerial position
10 to 20 years	CEO, group president
5 years	Division head
2 years	Unit manager
1 year	Department or section head
3 to 6 months	Supervisor
Hours to weeks	Line supervisor

This general model needs to be adjusted to the specific situations facing an organization and its managers—at all organization levels. It also requires reconciling time spans that are currently used and those that *ought* to be. The former may involve custom or the nuances of one's business ("corporate culture"). Even if Jaques's model is only approximately descriptive of particular situations, quite different managerial competencies and bases for judging performance are implied by these great time span differences (discussed further in Chapter 8).

A More Comprehensive Approach

The complexities of managerial work need to be recognized in an expanded framework that goes beyond immediate profits and figures. There is a need to incorporate general goal attainment (effectiveness measures) more explicitly into strategic thinking. Especially of interest here are the effects of managerial actions on employees (subordinates), customers, stockholders, suppliers, and community. It is also important to get our priorities and understandings straight among these groups. "Which one is our 'customer,' the one who purchases our product or our investor?" This

EXHIBIT 7-1
A Managerial Performance Model: Strategic Perspective

Time Frames	Performance Factors	
	Efficiency*	Effectiveness†
Short run		
Long run		

Notes: *Efficiency measures (examples) are economic measures, quantity, quality, profits, sales, costs, cost containment, return on investment, returns on research; often used in ratio form, for example, output to input.

†Effectiveness components are goal-related factors with human and social impacts. Included are employees (human experience, job-related satisfaction), executives, managers, supervisors, worker groups, customers, stockholders, suppliers, and community groups; also involved frequently is organization/corporate image.

conception of managerial performance incorporates time dimensions, organization goals, clientele, and aspects of individual behavior.

Model and Approach.   The model (Exhibit 7-1) is in reality a simple 2 × 2 table containing time and performance features. In brief, important short-run actions which are intended to improve *efficiency*, often impact both short- and long-run *effectiveness* factors, particularly goals (objectives). Correspondingly, actions which are thought to be largely long run in nature, affect short-run performance (behaviors) as well.

Effectiveness actions, which are (general) goal-related approaches affecting employees, suppliers, stockholders, or customers, also affect various aspects of efficiency (profits, costs, and/or returns). Corporate officials and strategy and policy planners, as well as managers, have a need to know the short- *and* longer-term implications of particular actions. However, the time needed to judge fully the impacts of major organizational actions varies widely, from as little as a few months, in some cases, to years in others.

Diffusion of Change.   Aside from organizational differences, part of the evaluation difficulty arises because there are several time-related phases of change involved. (Some designate these as primary, secondary, and tertiary effects.) Our studies in a highly diverse group of companies of many different sizes, services offered, product lines, and types of change (e.g., process automation, computer automation, and merger actions) indicate great differences in the time span for the full effects of changes to take place (Burack and Torda, 1979; Burack and McNichols, 1973). A short example of change follows, illustrating some efficiency and effectiveness issues.

> A large metropolitan bank identified what it believed to be an excellent and profitable new business service. A new department was to be established with a cadre of supervisors and managers drawn from other departments. The MBO for the newly appointed officer in charge was to establish the department as a functional unit within a calendar year. Also, it was to achieve profitable performance in the following year. The vice president did her job well, and the unit was up and functioning in 10 months. Her managerial incentive bonus reflected the excellent performance. Unfortunately, the heavy drain of supervisory resources transferred from other units created severe, general, operational problems. The profitable operation of the new department in the second year was almost completely offset by the dysfunctional results of other units. The "ripple effect" of the supervisory drain was felt organizationwide. The achievement of profitable operations for *all* the related units took better than *three years*.

Managing managerial performance from a strategic perspective necessitates a comprehensive approach to performance. It takes into account short and long(er) time considerations and considers both efficiency and effectiveness measures.

Policy Issues and Practical Problems with Longer Time Frames

Longer time frames can reveal some policy issues to which little thought had been given in the past. For example, management development approaches frequently exploit transfer or rotational assignments to strengthen individuals or develop new people. This approach can disrupt continuity or the strengthening of personal relationships within a particular unit, although the scope of individual acquaintances is improved. Also, in fast-growth or expanding organizational situations, such managerial movement may take place to cover jobs or to launch new activities. Both these situations, though quite different in specifics, pose substantial and quite similar problems. They both involve relationships which tend to be short term. Subordinates, reporting to people involved in these types of assignments or situations, will be wary of programs or approaches for which long-term evaluations are to be used. If a person is regularly confronted with a new boss, long(er)-term plans are more difficult to launch. Much time is lost due to (re)building trust and relationships. Also, these types of situations are accompanied by a degree of instability, the scope of which must be factored into program undertakings and evaluative processes. The greater the rotation of supervising managers, the more frequent the need to reestablish relations with subordinates, and the greater their sense of insecurity.

Senior officials need to think through the balancing of strategic management development plans with the implications of these designs for continuity in units or/and influencing subordinate actions.

Comprehensive Performance Planning

In discussing the strategic side of performance planning, it is easy to lose sight of the numerous challenges confronting less "lofty" levels of performance planning and its eventual translation into functional activities such as performance appraisal. This section has the purpose of drawing together various themes discussed in this and earlier chapters related to performance planning.

Performance Planning and Appraisal

In many organizations, the expressed dissatisfaction with performance appraisal systems may be a part of broader performance planning matters. Some of the problems may even be assigned to poor performance standards and supervisory ineptness. Yet even "good" performance standards and supervisory training may not solve the underlying problems that exist in these situations.

At a general level, supervisory and subordinate awareness is needed of performance objectives in terms of efficiency and effectiveness. Also, questions regarding relevant time spans for results must be surfaced and honestly resolved. Characteristics of the primary work system must be considered as these affect arrangements of jobs, responsibilities, and behaviors for managerial success. These affect supervisory and managerial roles in achieving the prescribed performance.

On the other hand, if organizational culture and planning dictate that work arrangements are to be a "variable" relative to the joint needs of the organization *and* person, different efficiency and effectiveness measures need to be identified. Also, the consequences of those revised approaches to the sociotechnical system will have major implications for defining performance roles and behaviors.

Time span is of such importance in interpreting appraisal results that some additional points need to be stressed. The planning and decision time horizons which (top) management finds to be functional at any particular organization level establish the time parameters for appraisal approaches. If, for example, the relevant time span for a particular managerial position is three years, it is likely that a whole new data base and approach will have to be developed relative to that used in the past. This change will be necessary because so many performance appraisal systems are attached to annual cycles. Performance appraisal criteria will have to take into account a three-year time horizon for achieving results, the characteristics of which may be counterintuitive to established corporate "wisdom."

Corporate Priorities, Planning, and Performance Appraisal.   Performance appraisal approaches, their capabilities, and their limitations need to be checked against the organization's planning directions, strategies, and priorities. If, for example, the expansion of an internal managerial talent pool is slated, then additional means such as self-nomination systems may have to be explored. Quite a different type of issue is involved if corporate strategies signal a longer-term shift in technology, business directions, or products. Performance appraisal criteria, organized around established work-product-service configurations, may have to be changed radically.

Succession Planning and Performance Planning: Too Little or Too Late?

In too many cases, serious planning discussions regarding succession candidates may be the "trigger incident" that reveals serious individual performance problems. Performance appraisal records are often "sterile" because of conflict in supervisor-subordinate relationships, lack of rater expertise, lengthy appraisal cycles, or record-keeping demands. "Raters" require expert coaching in establishing objectivity and consistent patterns of appraising subordinate performances. Yet this guidance often isn't forthcoming, and the behavioral dynamic of the rater "playing God" or personal relationships with the ratee are too much for many supervisors. They just provide the perfunctory information for the annual review and get on with other things. Supplementary notes are *not* added to the individual's personnel file, or sometimes a "desk file" is kept and then thrown out when the person is no longer their responsibility. Needless to say, development was not provided when it could prove beneficial, and so that the person gained insight into performance assessments or patterns. Many ratees are unaware that anything is wrong. So the sterile record grows and can easily represent a cumulative file spanning many years of employment—without revealing the real state of things. The "day of reckoning" comes when top management strategists and planners move into the picture and critical questions are asked regarding "so and so" and "what actions or evidence do you have to support your recommendations or turndown?" Individuals who could have been redirected down career-fulfilling paths and with valued performances for the organization fail to achieve their potential. Viable performance planning at both the strategic and operational level, and its thoughtful implementation into daily relationships, contain the makings of a comprehensive approach to this key area.

Performance Planning and the Individual: What's Expected of Me?

Appraisal is after the fact of performance. Critical self-examination may reveal that in truth, the first obligation of performance planning for the person has not been done or perhaps done poorly. The person needs to know what's expected of him or her. Many "wash out" concern for this general issue by substituting an MBO program. The objectives are clear and specific: they are discussed with the individual and, according to theory, are mutually agreed on. But is this the way the system really works? Do people fully understand in advance *all* the key or essential performances upon which they will be judged, although they may be perfectly clear on the MBO criteria? Can a person perform acceptably on his or her MBO priorities and still not progress? Is it possible for a person to be considered as plateaued or "making little real progress," although his or her performance has been recorded as acceptable?

Appraisal Results and Retrenchment

The shortcomings of performance planning and appraisal (PA) approaches are at times magnified as they enter into strategic HR applications. This occurs because the inherent uncertainties of dealing with the future may be confounded with serious PA data deficiencies. Important shortcomings of PA data and approaches not covered previously include

1. Failure to employ behaviorally relevant bases for judging levels of performance. Rating scales still continue to be a part of organizational procedures which lack behavioral relevance (anchorage) or which are inadequately defined. An example of a behavioral anchored rating scale is provided in the application section of this chapter (Exhibit 7-5).
2. Variability in the instrumentation used for deriving performance measures. This is particularly a problem in divisionalized organizations or those which in the past operated in highly decentralized or autonomous fashion. Where these differences have existed in data sources, comparability and interpretation of results is a large problem.

Despite this additional listing of (possible) shortcomings in PA data, it has a vital role to play in strategic human resource processes. Thus, large-scale corrective programs have been organized to overcome these deficiencies, and much progress has been made. Among the major improvements have been the use of uniform systems of behavioral dimensions for describing jobs and for appraising performance. These systems permit improved judgments regarding past performance and their possible relation to future work or positional needs. Important aspects of these were described in Chapter 4 and in a section that follows.

Retrenchment Decisions, Performance Appraisal, and Outplacement

The sharp bite of competition, price inflation, the shift of consumer markets and preferences, and foreign competition have been major contributing factors to the reorganization of many companies and even industries. Numerous examples of these results exist, including the U.S. (and elsewhere!) steel, automotive, and electronics industries. In these circumstances, performance appraisal has been delegated a relatively unique role of great strategic importance. In companies with up-to-date systems and modern practices, PA data has backed up and often helped to guide major staff reduction and outplacement efforts involving executives, managers, and technical personnel, let alone general employees. Other aspects of performance appraisal are dealt with shortly. In organizations lacking solid or up-to-date appraisal information, staff reductions have often been ill-advised, fraught with claims of bias or inequity, and destructive of the long-run welfare and survival of the organization. Two situations will clarify this point.

A large bank, in rather precarious financial shape, brought in a new president to help in its reorganization and to establish a sound basis for future growth. It was clear to the president that a major reduction, perhaps 10 to 15 percent of *both* exempt and nonexempt, would have to be accomplished for survival. But the president delayed any immediate decision in a force reduction strategy as it became clear that no solid performance (let alone potential) data existed for sound staffing decisions. The strategy elected was a reconstituting of the performance appraisal system—bringing it up to date quickly with relevant performance standards, behaviorally oriented rating scales, and training of appraisers and appraisees, among other approaches. Also, important areas of the system were computerized to facilitate analysis and comparisons. A series of interim moves were decided upon as a way to buy time. These involved expenditure and account controls and conservation of cash resources. Also, a major internal communications program was launched to apprise people fully of the company's financial picture, new performance system, and the use of performance results for future development moves *and* as a factor in staffing decisions (reductions). Two years of time were "bought" which allowed for a new and improved base of data to be generated. The time period also permitted dealing with most of the "glitches" that go along with launching a new system, especially under these tense circumstances. During the second year and into the third year, staffing reductions and development decisions were made. Where people were to be released, a strong outplacement and counseling activity was made available to ease personal trauma. Nobody enjoyed these difficult times but (even) many of those separated conceded the humanity and common sense with which the moves were handled.

A manufacturer of textile products achieved substantial and profitable sales, through acquisition and a substantial expansion in various consumer products related to residential and commercial construction. When a major construction downturn occurred and it appeared that it would last for a long period, the firm found management poorly equipped to handle the human resource aspects of the situation. In the past, half-hearted attempts had been made to launch a "performance management system," but in fact, data were available for less than 50 percent of the supervisory and managerial group. Much less data were available regarding nonexempt employee performance. The gathering of personnel development and potential data, another program that had been launched but not fully developed, showed the same poor results as the performance system. The whole situation was greatly complicated by the fact that longer-range planning and strategic analysis were done only informally. Consequently, only a partial picture was available of the rapidly changing situation. In short, a crisis stage was reached, and staffing reductions had to be made on a short-term, largely unplanned basis. To facilitate the cutback decisions, various managerial groups were brought together to gain the benefit of their collective experience. Reduction decisions were made and acted upon. Understandably, many employees felt that personnel decisions were arbitrary, unfair, and lacking sound data or were contrary to corporate traditions (culture). In many communities, the company's image was tarnished and, in a few, destroyed. Years passed before any important improvement took place in employee relationships. Correspondingly, performance suffered a great deal.

Having said all this, the importance of performance appraisal results to human resource planning/development processes continues. It forms a necessary part of strategic planning deliberations concerning individuals, but it must be critically viewed.

The Individual Perspective in Performance Planning

Many organizations such as Citicorp. feel that people management is a high priority and a long-term proposition. Further, they, as do many others, feel that the individual unit manager is the single most important determinant of an employee's performance (Berman and Mase, 1983). However, support planning for managing people means that the necessary conditions for successful performance be anticipated (planned for) and then established. Organization plans for the future need to incorporate adequate flexibility at the management level. One aspect of flexibility is that the supervising manager is able to adjust or control work conditions to a degree compatible with circumstances and performance targets. Another aspect of flexibility is that the individual manager has sufficient degrees of freedom in his or her job to meet performance commitments.

Information from Results Measurement

Comprehensive performance planning leans heavily on both macro and micro information resources of which several have already been discussed. (The discussion of managerial performance dimensions which follows echoes themes described earlier in Chapter 4.)

Two information sources are of such importance as to warrant separate treatment in this and the following section. The first deals with the motivation-behavioral aspects of individual performance, some aspects of which were developed in previous chapters. The second, performance appraisal, is discussed in terms of measuring managerial performance and a person's potential to take on higher levels of responsibility and perform well. Data for performance measurement usually start with basic information sources such as job descriptions, performance appraisals, and assessments of potential. It is desirable that position descriptions be comprehensive and have a data base facilitating understanding and comparison. As already established, most modern job descriptive systems involve general statements of responsibilities and reporting relationships *plus* information on competencies or end-job behaviors for success. Aside from the managerial characteristics described in Chapter 4, William C. Byham and his associates have also dealt with similar dimensions, but have related this information to successful managerial performance. This type of data materially assists performance planning as it affects selection and particular development designs.

This perspective takes on added importance in the light of the renewed interest assigned to the coaching role of trainer-managers (developed in the next chapter). If people are to be managed for results, then job-related performance has to be managed well, and the supervising manager must be skilled at dealing with and developing individuals.

Byham and the "Dimensions of Managerial Competence"

William C. Byham and his associates from Development Dimensions International (1982) identified 14 general managerial competency or performance dimensions. These dimensions are similar to those described in Chapter 4 except for those which are company specific (e.g., the work of Tornow at Control Data). Byham's dimensions included three different forms of communications (general oral, presentations, and written), four functional forms of management (planning/organizing, delegation, control, and subordinate development), and three interpersonal dimensions (general sensitivity to others, leadership with individuals, and leadership in groups). Their work is among the most extensive in this area and reflects numerous client assignments. Of particular interest here is the fact that their analyses helped to tie together behavioral characteristics of work and successful managerial performance.

What were some of the distinguishing features of successful and unsuccessful managers? Byham's work indicated, for example, that for middle-level managers in one organization, competencies which distinguished managers *prior* to development were oral communications; written communications; individual leadership; individual and group sensitivity; functional management areas, including planning and organizing, delegation, and control; and analysis, judgment, and initiative. However, thorough needs analyses and a well-organized development program proved helpful in correcting or strengthening performance competencies in all these areas. Assessment center technology served as a valuable diagnostic tool in needs determination and establishing competency benchmarks. Assessment center results helped in establishing baselines which were needed to judge knowledge and skill improvement through management development.

In another company program designed to strengthen interaction competencies of managers, substantially improved managerial behaviors included were individual leadership, individual flexibility, and listening and analytical abilities. *Good* improvement was evidenced in individual sensitivity and judgment. Greatly facilitating this effort was a reasonably concise scheme for defining performance competencies and the assessment center technology to facilitate measurement. Specifics aside, the results of Byham indicated that as a part of performance planning, major performance or competency deficiencies often can be remedied through carefully designed development efforts. These results, reinforced at various points in subsequent chapters, can have an important bearing on a variety of strategic matters. These include the expansion of the pool of qualified candidates for succession and/or venture projects.

Another type of analysis undertaken by Byham and his associates (1982) was the identification of performance competencies as these varied with responsibility or authority level. These results relate to the type of findings associated with the work of Baehr in Chapter 4. An example of performance competencies distinguishing lower- and senior-level managers is provided in Exhibit 7-2. More details of Byham's work goes beyond the scope of this discussion but are available from the referenced organization.

In summary, the work of Byham and his associates provides a helpful planning framework for viewing managerial competency needs and making more informed promotion decisions. This schema and comparative information provides a concrete basis for improving the understanding of factors contributing to the development of high-potential candidates. For example, lower-level managers who evidence particular competencies or characteristics of higher or senior managerial levels (Exhibit 7-2) are identified more easily and systematically through these approaches.

These behavioral-type factors are also related to individual mobility and, in some cases, the demonstration of high potential. These factors have facilitated identification and development of individual mobility within the organization; this is due to the identification of common position features within various job families. Mobility factors often associated with "high potentials" include flexibility, ready

EXHIBIT 7-2
Selected Performance Competencies Distinguishing Lower-Level and
Senior Managers after Byham

General Dimensions	Lower-Level Managers	Senior Managers
Interpersonal	Leadership as a staff person	Group leadership Negotiation
Management	Self organization, direction	Strategic planning, management of the job
	Follow up	Delegation, control, development of subordinates
Knowledge/skill	Technical/professional proficiency, knowledge	—

Source: Based on results reported by William C. Byham, *Dimensions of Managerial Competence*, Monograph II (Pittsburgh, PA: Development Dimensions International, 1982).

EXHIBIT 7-3
General Skill and Performance Factors Associated with "High
Potentials"

People Related

Oral communications skill	Effectiveness of expression, getting ideas across, in individual or group situations.
Written communications skill	Ability to express ideas clearly in writing in good grammatical form.
Leadership	Ability to get ideas accepted and in guiding a group or an individual to accomplish a task.
Interpersonal insight	Skill in perceiving and reacting sensitively to the needs of others; objectivity in perceiving impact of self on others and others on you.

Organizational

Planning and organization	Ability to establish efficiently an appropriate course of action for self and/or others to accomplish a specific goal and to appropriately use human and fiscal resources.
Problem analysis	Skill in identifying problems, securing relevant information, identifying possible cause of problems, and proposing alternative courses of action.
Stress tolerance	Ability to generate, recognize, and/or accept imaginative solutions and innovations in management situations.
Decisiveness	Ability to make decisions, render judgments, and take action or commit oneself.
Decision making	Ability to arrive at relevant and timely decisions through the appropriate use of logic or reason.

People Related and Organizational

Flexibility/adaptability	Ability to modify behavioral style and management approach to reach a goal, or to adapt to changing organizational needs and situations.

Source: Based on Elmer H. Burack and Nicholas J. Mathys, *Human Resource Planning: A Pragmatic Approach to Manpower Planning and Development* (2nd. ed.: Lake Forest, IL: Brace Park Press, 1987).

adaptation to change, and potential to absorb new(er) learnings. The applications section contains an expanded list of mobility factors (Exhibit 7-3).

Performance Appraisal

The subject of performance appraisal (PA) has been referenced a number of times in this chapter. It has been linked to planning approaches involving effectiveness and efficiency, organization culture, time span for evaluating performance or decisions, information support for succession planning, structural and job change, behavioral dynamics and the omission of important decision information, replacement or out-placement planning, and technical deficiencies (e.g., performance standards). This is indeed an imposing list! These discussions are justified because PA is the most impor-tant and widely used basis for managing managerial performance. PA results also are of major concern in assessment of potential, succession planning, and development plan-ning. The purpose of this section is to round out the discussion of PA, emphasizing several matters which have received little attention in the preceding material.

Recognition of the limitations of PA information, especially for analyses and decisions involving higher managerial levels, has encouraged the search for data needed for strategic purposes. Succession planning is a case in point. In general, the higher the position, the broader the scope of information (sources) needed for succession or replacement decisions. Even when PA results are timely and worka-bly accurate, it can serve only a portion of succession needs, albeit an important one. The point is that PA covers only past or current performance. At question is how well the person is likely to perform in the future in significantly (or wholly) different roles. This involves experience and competencies which may not as yet have been tested. Also, changes in managerial role resulting from strategic long-range plans still on the "drawing board" require information (much) beyond tradi-tional appraisal results.

Assessment center results have been used to supplement the meager informa-tion which often exists on individual potential, and it is also used to establish the fit of the person in higher-level positions with greater work demands and enlarged responsibilities. The increasing validation of assessment center results have made this an information source richly supplementing conventional PA data.

Appraising the Performance of Managerial Trainees.   Strategic human re-source planning approaches have helped to clarify the important linkage among recruiting, development, staffing availability, and replacement planning. Systematic approaches to performance appraisal have played a significant role in "quality assur-ance" (i.e., focusing trainee development and concretizing recruit expectations). An example of a form used in this regard is provided in the applications section (Ex-hibit 7-4). One feature of this company's appraisal approach, illustrated by the form, is the attempt to judge the trainee's enculturation and development of good co-worker relationships. These represent examples of a much expanded and useful approach to PA which take account of more comprehensive strategic needs.

Performance Planning, Management, and Individual Change

Performance management is often concerned with three pragmatic and primary conditions as they relate to the positionholder. The first condition is to assure that their people are "able to" meet performance requirements. This involves selecting the right people in the first place and providing early, appropriate training. Under-standably, as described previously, the systems capability must exist to describe the job in meaningful descriptive and behavioral terms. Yet, even where the person has the mental and physical potential, this is not enough. The person's potential must

EXHIBIT 7-4
Management Trainee Review Report

_____   _____
Name   (Date employed or transferred)

_____   _____   _____
Current Assignment   Home Department   Receiving Department

Rate the above management trainee as accurately as possible. Your *overall evaluation should be in comparison with other employees with the same length of service on this job.* Your analysis affects the employee's desirability and worth. Your thorough appraisal now may well prevent a critical problem later. No trainee will be retained beyond a probationary period if he or she fails to fulfill your specific requirements for the position. Termination form should accompany the review if the employee is unsatisfactory.

	Not Applicable	Unsatisfactory	Below Average	Average	Above Average
Accuracy, neatness	_____	0	1	2 3 4	5
Quality of work (Specify _____)	_____	0	1	2 3 4	5
Quantity of work	_____	0	1	2 3 4	5
Ability to follow directions	_____	0	1	2 3 4	5
Conscientiousness	_____	0	1	2 3 4	5
Use of judgment and imagination	_____	0	1	2 3 4	5
Initiative and responsibility as required	_____	0	1	2 3 4	5
Observance of departmental rules	_____	0	1	2 3 4	5
Understanding of organization's culture	_____	0	1	2 3 4	5
Attendance	_____	0	1	2 3 4	5
Promptness	_____	0	1	2 3 4	5
Response to supervision and instruction	_____	0	1	2 3 4	5
Courtesy and cooperation	_____	0	1	2 3 4	5
Attitude toward work	_____	0	1	2 3 4	5
Ability to relate to co-workers	_____	0	1	2 3 4	5
Ability to relate to clients, customers	_____	0	1	2 3 4	5
Appearance	_____	0	1	2 3 4	5

EXHIBIT 7-4 (Continued)

Comments: _____

_____

_____

_____

_____

6 month's recommendation: Retain ___   Dismiss ___

Orig: Human Resources   This will acknowledge that the review has
cc: Department Head (Home Dep't)   been discussed with me.

    Date reviewed _____   _____
                                               (Employee Signature)

                                       _____
                                               (Rater Signature)

Source: Based in part on Elmer H. Burack and Robert D. Smith, *Personal Management: A Human Resource Systems Approach* (New York: John Wiley, 1982). Competencies need to be drawn out through knowledgeable development actions that are accurately adjusted to performance needs. Building abilities involves knowledgeable coaching and effective goal setting and performance planning. Developmental *performance appraisals emphasize these constructive approaches. Successful cultivation of individual abilities builds confidence and often results in the person being more likely to be motivated to perform (discussed in the next section). They feel themselves more capable of achieving tough or high-level task requirements.*

be drawn out through knowledgeable development actions that are accurately adjusted to performance needs. Building abilities involves knowledgeable coaching and effective goal setting and performance planning. *Developmental* performance appraisals emphasize these constructive approaches. Successful cultivation of individual abilities builds confidence and often results in the person being more likely to be motivated to perform (discussed in the next section). They feel themselves more capable of achieving tough or high-level task requirements.

The second condition is that people *want to* perform, and the third condition is that they are *allowed to perform*. The second condition involves individual motivation, which is more fully described in the next section. The person's desire and encouragement to perform is importantly tied in with the work context including the "organization's culture." Top management values which are supportive of a performance management approach need to be clearly and widely communicated throughout the organization. From a strategic planning viewpoint, officials and planners need to know (or establish) what values are (should be) operational in the organization, their appropriateness for plans, and the linkage (if any) between values and performance management. Strategic planning provides the coordinating and planning mechanism to pull these elements together. It establishes a basic

EXHIBIT 7-5
Behaviorally Anchored Rating Scale for the Verbal Communications
Portion of a Car Fleet Supervisor

Scale	Anchor
1. Excellent performance	Always checks to make sure that others are heard correctly. Briefs replacement quickly and accurately, giving only relevant information. Checks verbal instructions against written procedures.
2. Very good performance	Informs supervising manager immediately if problems arise. Listens to others carefully and asks questions if she or he does not understand. Gives instructions and information in calm, clear voice.
3. Good performance	Apprises others of problems to look for. Avoids discussing nonwork-related subjects during conversation (communications).
4. Fair performance	Gives others detailed account of what should be done, but does not establish priorities. Occasionally mumbles when speaking to others. May not face the person during conversation and sometimes acts disinterested.
5. Poor performance	Fails to relate necessary details to replacements. Does not seek information and only offers it when asked. Does not check to make sure that others are heard correctly. Leaves out information about own mistakes when talking to others.
6. Unacceptable performance	Often does not answer when called. Does not brief replacements. Gives inaccurate information.

Source: See Exhibit 7-3

foundation from which performance actions take place. Top management needs to evidence its commitment and support of these approaches; communications, visible actions, and the organization's reward system are tangible bases to evidence supports. Senior officials need to make it known that important organizational values underlie their actions for which even their own performance will be appraised and rewarded (or otherwise).

Part of the challenge for strategic performance planning will be to identify strategies for communicating a positive program to the managerial group (Exhibit 7-5). Characteristically, these programs include reinforcement of performance standards, rewards including promotion, and the linkage of these to business planning objectives and results (Berman and Maze, 1983). More discussions on "wanting to," the role of motivation, follow in the next section.

The third condition ("being allowed to perform") involves the general supportiveness of the environment or work context. The confidence and trust of supervising managers will play an important role here. They need to demonstrate their confidence in their subordinate's competency to proceed in a knowledgeable, independent way. Also, conditions (may) have to be spawned to nurture creativity. It follows then that the supervising manager's power would have to be shared and that subordinate managers and perhaps others would be brought more fully into planning and decision processes. Also they would be provided with the resources and requisite authority to make things happen (Berman and Maze, 1983). At the same time, supervising managers must be able to plan, and bring into fruition, facilitative work decisions. These designs should help to achieve such widely desired personnel results as improved work identification, a sense of independence or being in control of one's situation, a sense of accomplishment, and sufficient and valid feedback for the person to gauge progress and judge future needs.

Facilitative work designs are particularly important for managers aggressively seeking to achieve a sense of personal growth. However, many individual actions take place in a group format, thus, supervising managers must improve or devise group structures which support communications and improve relationships within and between groups. This type of ability has become a valued and desired competency for performance planning and management.

To recap, strategic planning approaches need to anticipate the pragmatic aspects of individual performance management which center on three general conditions: "being able to," "wanting to," and "being allowed to" perform. The fulfillment of these through careful performance planning can help to establish the groundwork for a sound performance management program.

The Motivation-Behavioral Side of Planning for Performance Management: A Review and Analysis

Individual motivation ("wanting to") plays a key and instrumental role in performance management and is a highly relevant strategic planning consideration. The current status of motivational models useful for HR approaches is briefly reviewed and is then followed with a more general state-of-the-art discussion.

Motivators and Performance

For a large and dedicated following, motivating (managerial) performance meant exploiting the work of Abraham Maslow and Frederick Herzberg. Although their work was popularized years ago, it is likely that they are still the best known among practitioners today. Also, Maslow's work, upon which Herzberg's is based, has been acknowledged as one of the three major statements in motivational thinking (Pinder, 1984).

Maslow's "hierarchy of needs" underpins Herzberg's two-factor theory of "hygiene" and "motivator" factors. Hygiene factors include security, safety, policy, benefits, work hours and work conditions, supervision, and compensation. According to Herzberg's work, "hygiene factors" are all of continuing importance to people and need consistent replenishment—but they are believed to have little effect on performance. "Motivators," including achievement, recognition, independence, the job itself, and a sense of personal growth and fulfillment, are said to spark individual performance. The "motivators" vary in their duration and degree of impact from person to person. It is recognized that they also need periodic refurbishing or renewal. However, if an individual is concerned about "hygiene" factors such as business policy, money, and actions of the supervisor, use of the "motivators" as a strategy will not work well. *If hygiene conditions are met reasonably, then motivators can prove beneficial to the manager and to the organization.* Thus, "motivators" become the focus of strategic thinking regarding the individual, job, and work context. However, before contextual factors (related to "hygiene") are set aside too quickly, it's well to note that such factors as philosophy of management, security, and supervisory relations may also be important parts of an organization's culture. To this degree, they bear watching relative to their long-term impact on individual performance and effectiveness. Also, Herzberg's theory notwithstanding, security or good relationships, for example, may be very important and serve as "motivators."

Reinforcement Strategies and Job Design

The extension of B. F. Skinner's laboratory work to individuals and the work world represented a notable accomplishment in behavioral science. This approach rested on "operant conditioning" and "behavioral modification." Central to it was the recognition that a given behavior is only meaningful when viewed in the context of its antecedent conditions and consequences. That is, human activity (performance) was meaningful when seen in a sequence of ("cause-effect") time frames and acts that are interrelated. Thus for example, if a desired type of performance is *reinforced* within the context of work circumstances and under particular conditions, it is likely to be repeated in the future under the same set of conditions. In a corresponding way, undesired work performances which are responded to in "unpleasant ways," for example, negative feedback in an annual performance review, or reducing privileges or delaying a promotion are less likely to be repeated in the future.

Further experience with this reinforcement ("learning") approach suggested that the degree to which behavior is influenced is affected by (1) the schedule of reinforcement and (2) the type of learning required. For example, continuous reinforcement is best for *inducing new behaviors*. But *extinction* of the newly learned behavior is rapid if the reinforcement continues! Therefore, individuals need to be closely observed, say, through executive coaching, so that it can be determined when the initial learning experience has been (substantially) completed. Skinner's work also suggested that, after a basic behavior has been learned, more advanced or complex forms of that behavior can be gained through *variable reinforcement*. Pinder (1984) provides a good summary of Skinner's work. From a strategic planning and development viewpoint, Skinner's model(s) and application experiences have an important bearing on establishing conditions facilitating cultural change, management development planning, and the choice of managers to oversee development, among others.

Learning, Work-Life Experiences, and Reinforcement.   Organizational researchers have noted, that an individual doesn't suddenly perform in an achievement-oriented way. There is a relatively long period of gestation, say, starting in high school and stretching through college and the initial work years. It is during this period that the person starts to draw together in his or her mind, particular personal actions and the consequences associated with these. The links or relationships are initially quite vague, and the person usually isn't aware of the connections. Gradually, however, with general support (reinforcement) from friends, superiors, and business associates, the basic behavior pattern starts to take on shape and substance—it is "learned." As a consequence, the person may start actively to seek out (other) situations where personal or work-related actions result in positive feelings for the person. Thus, in a *practical reinforcement approach to assure long-term retention, managers who have met functional performance requirements are likely to prove increasingly responsive (vulnerable) to variable reinforcement schedules.*

The results related to variable reinforcement schedules indicate that a once-a-year performance review is not likely to be adequate for the achievement-oriented (high-potential) person! Informal and variable time contacts are needed with coach, mentor, and human resource officials. These contacts throughout the year need to be accompanied by *feedback* related to work accomplishment. Strategic planners need to establish a management development framework which includes these critical points in individual development cycles. Many of these types of ideas formed the planning framework for the Honeywell, Inc., management development program described elsewhere in this book (Chapters 5 and 8).

Putting Management Motivation into Perspective

Various approaches to motivating managerial behavior have in common the notion of *perception*—"what one sees is what really counts." It molds the reservoir of information that forms beliefs and attitudes, and thereby, the factors that affect individual desire and intentions to engage in a particular behavior. To the extent that managerial performance behaviors are volitional and felt to be feasible, the key to individual change is often one of altering perceptions. From the strategic planning aspect, there is a need to understand how perception enters into the picture as it is likely to affect managerial performance. What are the assumptions or beliefs held by various or particular managers? What is their risk-taking posture? What is their view of the culture? How are these views likely to affect their behaviors generally and their performance particularly?

Situational Uncertainty and Complexity as Viewed by the Manager.
Managers vary widely in the degree to which they possess accurate or valid knowledge regarding the possible results of their actions. *Situational uncertainty* refers to the quality and quantity of information possessed regarding their circumstances. At one level, uncertainty may involve business-related decision factors such as relevant environmental trends affecting their unit and the future results of

present or planned programs. However, uncertainty also involves how accurately the person interprets work circumstances affecting their career progress and mobility. What information is possessed by the person and its accuracy and relevancy? What steps need to be taken to assure, to the extent possible, that (the) manager(s) possess the requisite information for making informed business and personal career decisions.

Complexity too plays a role in individual perception, the results of which may be similar to that of uncertainty. Here the matter of relationships is involved as, for example, the linkage among their work behaviors, work results, and (more general) performance outcomes or rewards. The fact that managerial work environments have grown increasingly complex indicates that planning processes need to be more finely tuned. They must deal with these altered circumstances as well as those that are expected as these affect managerial roles and performance.

Attitudes, Beliefs, Intentions

Organizational attitude surveys have become so commonplace that it is perhaps prudent to reference these briefly as a part of general motivational approaches. Numerous studies indicate thaty there is *not* a simple or obvious connection between an individual's attitude regarding his or her job and a specific behavior. Predicting particular behaviors or reactions based on given attitudes is a poor bet. However, understanding more about the person's beliefs can prove helpful. Management strategists need to know much more about the *beliefs* (assumptions) of the individual regarding the "organization's culture," job or work situation, plus individual preferences and priorities. We know that personal beliefs are shaped by a variety of considerations and that three major sources are consistently operative:

1. *People observe things around them* and form beliefs based on these. A person may observe that most key managers belong to a certain club and this becomes part of the route upward.
2. *People "reason things out"* in a cognitive way. This may involve sequences of causal relationships which in turn provide a set of beliefs that can be drawn upon for a given situation (though perhaps leading to invalid conclusions!). For the example just stated in (1), a person may draw on multiple beliefs regarding club memberships, methods of promotion, and the weighting of criteria used in promotion.
3. *People draw on numerous sources of information* including friends, business associates, company documents, and the general (business) literature. Beliefs regarding the rationale for important organizational actions or policies may be widely shared in the organization, *even if incorrect*. The strategic implications of this point are so rich in the communications realm, that a chapter could be easily built around this subject. Space limitations don't permit this discussion, but the reader who is interested in pursuing this subject is likely to find it quite rewarding.

At this junction we can state that beliefs affect attitudes and further that the beliefs may create various *behavioral intentions* for the person. We would like to think that the more specific the intentions, the more likely the particular behaviors. We'll end this discussion with a slight digression. Organizations such as Weight Watchers have many members with very specific goals (e.g., "lose 40 pounds"), and many members reach their goals. Organizational affiliation, with Weight Watchers, for example, indicates a specific intention to lose weight as well as a given amount, and often in a particular time period. The pessimists tell us, however, that all kinds of people have intentions to lose weight but don't. Many members of these types of groups are initially successful, but fail to keep the (lost) weight off. In considering beliefs, attitudes, and intentions, one must consider the person's personality and the context of particular situations, the presence of behavior models for long(er) term support, and the potency and durability of particular actions ("behaviors").

Goal-Directed Behavior

Behavior is goal directed whether one is conscious of it or not, and typically more than one goal is involved. Also, goals are connected by various paths, and *alternatives* are a part of the consideration. Alternatives need to be evaluated in light of the value of work outcomes and a person's sense of the connection between work-related outcomes and valued goals. Also, consideration must be given to their belief(s) as to how well they are able to perform at a given level of output. In other words, people may "see" a (potential) connection among work performances, work outcomes, and valued goals. But they still need to judge their capability of accomplishing the task and the alternative which is most effective and capable of being pursued—at least as they see it.

Consider the following situation as an application of these points. Suppose that achieving a particular sales quota is seen by a sales manager as an overly ambitious objective and not realistic in the light of territorial potential. Thus, even if an attractive managerial bonus or generally valued incentive is attached to the accomplishment of this situation, the scheme probably won't work. The manager doesn't feel that he can accomplish it. Clearly, perceptions and the "reality" of these are important. However, executives and others *modeling* behaviors, initially seen as "impossible" by the person, may present sufficient (additional) evidence to alter that person's (perceptions of) intentions to engage in the activity.

Exchange and Equity

The heart of human relationships is the exchange of feelings, sentiments, and information. In social relationships, the motivation to participate in exchanges with others is due to the mutual values derived from the relationships or the value placed by a person on becoming part of the relationship. Equity exists where people derive benefits mutually valued, though these are frequently different for each person. This exchange and valuing of the relationship becomes the basis for establishing equity, fairness, and give and take.

The sense of equity also spills over into more formal organizational relationships. Of particular interest here are those connected to strategic management development considerations. For example, in compensation strategies for rewarding or evoking performance, individuals perceive a relationship among their effort, work outcomes, and rewards. Equity concerns the fairness of the possible bonus payoffs or promotion and even the likelihood that they will occur. Equity also concerns the fairness of rewards received by others relative to their effort and circumstances, both within and outside the organization. The result of people's feelings of *inequity* may result in (only) "adequate" performance, withdrawal, or chronic absenteeism and turnover. Thus, equity is a comparative built on one's subjective standards of fairness and involving all kinds of comparisons. From a strategic viewpoint, equity plays an important role in reward structures, making it an important part of planning approaches.

Contingency Approaches in Motivational Applications

Interest in *contingency approaches* to performance management has grown in recognition of the flexible ways in which motivational strategies need to be shaped to particular situations.

Modern strategic approaches to management development planning often exploit a contingency perspective that is related to situational requirements. This concept is of major importance today in performance planning and management thinking. In essence, different organizational and individual situations require the selective use of various motivational schemes. The application section for this chapter provides a summary of some of the more important bodies of motivational precepts commonly used in contingency approaches. These approaches can be incorporated in various managerial performance situations such as work relationships and work design, systems involving appraisal of performance and assessment of potential, reward schemes, policy statements, business and human resource plans, and career management.

Some Experiences of Researchers and Consultants with Behavioral Approaches. *No single conceptual framework or motivational approach will suffice for building management performance strategies.* Situational particulars included in contingency approaches are the person (e.g., skills, personality, experience), job features and work particulars, organization culture, and general organization features. The person dimension involving motivation is easily the most complex. Management performance strategies require an artful synthesis of the situation particulars noted and thoughtful reference to multiple motivational schemes. *First and foremost, performance management strategies focus on achieving the desired behaviors.* Initially, this may be sought irrespective of the person's attitude. It is recognized that attitudinal changes occur often after a behavior is engaged in. This results when the behavior is seen (eventually) by the person as a (valuable) means of avoiding negative consequences or a way of gaining positive ones. Conformity, in the sense of end results, can be achieved *without* attitudinal changes through strictly enforced policies, supervisory monitoring, manipulation of the reward system, and/or appropriate use of performance appraisal approaches. On a related point, the supposition that attitudinal change leads to behavioral change in an "expected" direction is questionable.

Some Experiences in the Use of Behavioral Approaches.   The sharing of some personal experiences may prove beneficial here. They are not especially profound but the fact that some are counterintuitive may prove useful.

In influencing behavior, the actions of the supervising manager as a "behavioral model" are basic. Extended discussions of this approach have been largely absent from management literature until the last few years. Much training experience has indicated the importance of supervisory "modeling" for bringing about particular subordinate behaviors. However, the reality of desired performances or behaviors may be that the person is unable to engage in a particular behavior even if they desire to do so, because they simply don't know how. Complex behavioral changes involve much more than book reading or learning. People need to know what's to be done and how to do it. They need to be given the opportunity to role play or practice it under controlled conditions or helpful observation, and then to have the benefit of general support when they are on their own.

There are some general points regarding factors which are operative in many different situations:

1. *Organization culture.* To the extent that values and ways of doing things are strongly embedded, this aspect of the internal environment will have much bearing on behavior and performance.
2. *Managerial technology.* Existing methods, information bases, and work systems directly affect management roles. If individual actions *have* to be taken which are in conflict with work guidelines to meet performance requirements, it may be with significant risk to the company and the person. This lack of fit between work requirements and needed actions may serve as a highly frustrating situation for the person.
3. *Work technology.* Computer and process technologies have an obvious and direct bearing on individual actions. Factors such as work pace, point or location to achieve control, and work space impose varying degrees of constraints on individual action.
4. *Individual factors.* Temperament, level of physical and mental energy, experience and skills, and knowledge and ability influence how a person reacts to a given situation.
5. *Structural features.* These include hierarchical authority and the centraliza-

tion/decentralization of responsibilities. The type and extent of rules and regulations (e.g., "bureaucratic conformity") may chill individual initiative.

6. *Communications.* Both the informal and formal systems greatly affect individual outlooks. Oral and written communications are also an important part of this picture. The function of feedback, the amount, accuracy, and accessibility to information are all part of the information picture.

7. *Outcomes and relationships known.* The manager having a good knowledge of the situation and results is likely to pursue a particular course of action. If a person believes that high performance leads to personally *valued* career, promotional, and/or salary opportunities, then motivational strategies based on this rationalization would probably be a good initial approach. In other words, applications of this concept indicate that the manager (person) will achieve high performance levels when he or she believes that this effort will lead to desired goals. Considering alternative approaches and corresponding outcomes, the person will go for the approach seen as most rewarding. Quite naturally, results will have to support the person's initial beliefs and analysis if they stick with the strategy.

8. *Outcomes and relationships not known.* This combination poses a difficult and perplexing situation and one understandably that is very confusing to the manager involved. To the extent that the situation is assessed accurately, people tend to proceed initially from their experiences and knowledge. Personal needs and values also guide their actions. There might be little else to do initially. When more information is developed, or events start to unfold, then the individual may be able to proceed in a more sensible way. Until then, the person's (motivational) "need" structure would be a workable starting point.

Trust and Motivation-Behavioral Approaches

As a strategic matter, no amount of knowledge of motivational models, or related experience, is likely to overcome a subordinate's mistrust of supervisory or organizational actions. Individual trust in one's manager and/or organization is basic to creating fertile conditions for high-level managerial performance. Unfortunately, the nuances of personality and human behavior may lead to individual perceptions of *mistrust*. It must be acknowledged that in establishing a climate of trust, individuals are vulnerable to personal attacks because these relationships must be open with colleagues, supervisors, and subordinates. But many people are willing to accept the risk if interactions are seen as motivated by the desire to do the right thing, and to be consistent and understanding. Needless to say, trusting relationships and a general organizational climate of trust are difficult to establish and are very fragile. But the rewards can be substantial in terms of creativity, cooperation, and people who can be counted on for performance. Characteristic barriers to establishing trusting relationships are as follows:

1. *Individual assumptions of "either/or."* This involves the visualization of only two outcomes such as reward or punishment, or high quality and high cost, or low quality and low cost. Thus, subsequent choices tend to be categorized as *either* good or bad. Middle ground is difficult to establish under these conditions. People won't accept counterintuitive thinking, for example, high quality is possible at an acceptable cost and under appropriate and achievable motivational and technological conditions.

2. *Mind set.* Once ideas have solidified into beliefs, then individual actions tend to be less compromising or adaptive. Individuals are less likely to consider alternative possibilities and approaches.

3. *Confirmed skepticism.* The basic assumption that people are naturally combative or *un*trustworthy is the point of departure for (too) many relationships in organizations. "The world is tough, and survival demands a tough shell, even aggressive behavior to survive." It follows that sound bases for communications may never be started. People will seem uncaring or unconcerned.

The *coaching relationship* involving supervisor and subordinate *builds importantly on trust*. If supervisory behaviors are to serve as a model of desired behaviors and if supervisory counsel and guides are to be accepted as valid, trust needs to be an important ingredient in these interactions.

Most readers are likely to be familiar with many situations where trust plays a key role. In strategic approaches, they span the range from the accepting of an individual's planning assumptions, to believability in committee discussions, to accepting counsel or advise in Human Resource–line manager interactions.

Behavioral Approaches and the Performance Planning Model

Before moving on to the discussion of other performance considerations and job/work design, it would be useful to tie in the behavioral approaches discussed here with the performance model discussed initially in the chapter. The approach described emphasized a lengthened time frame for planning and performance results. Thus, the success of any motivational scheme or work design to affect motivation positively, must generally involve a longer time period for judging results than that commonly exercised today.

Second, when alternate motivational strategies are being considered, it is necessary to consider that managerial (performance) behaviors will (eventually) affect *both* efficiency *and* effectiveness dimensions. Assessments of performance can no more be confined solely to employee or customers considerations than they can be assigned exclusively to operational or financial measures (e.g., profits). Thus the motivational picture based on the contingency approach will include numerous elements easily missed in more traditional approaches. The following example illustrates the complex human chemistry involved in these approaches.

Helen S. was a marketing manager for a manufacturer of personal computers (PCs). She was responsible for (market) development of their EXEC I line. Prior to the company's introduction of EXEC II, a highly improved version of their original model, Helen's boss, the marketing vice president, reviewed the marketing and sales situation with the vice president of Human Resources. Helen was being groomed for major responsibilities as head of a new international division. The vice president of marketing was perplexed because he had only been partially successful in getting Helen to broaden her outlook as department head. She still had a narrow problem-solving, task-oriented perspective that surfaced periodically in her current assignments. The strategy session was aimed at using the EXEC II situation as both a developmental and evaluation experience relative to the vice president of international position. Breadth of outlook and adaptability to a variety of cultures and competitive conditions were critical in the international job; they were also important to the introduction of EXEC II. Their management development strategy was conceived of along the following lines.

1. *Assessment of the current situation*. Both felt that Helen was ambitious and had strong growth needs. These included a need for independence in action and accomplishment. Although Helen was well qualified and had been in the company for five years, she had little chance to interact informally with others ("network") so that she didn't have a good understanding of how the company really operated. Her behavior in her current assignment and the circumstances of her rapid rise indicated that she probably was in a poor area for movement into executive ranks. It provided too little opportunity to gain a knowledge of effective organizational relationships. High uncertainty was the likely market situation in the EXEC II assignment. It would be further compounded by the international aspects.

   Helen had never had the responsibility of a new product introduction and probably didn't have a good sense of how she would react to these circumstances. Further, the opportunity had never arisen to apprise her formally ("to be more certain") of how the company's culture really operated, including the inner working of the performance appraisal/assessment of potential procedures. Based on their analysis of the situation, their strategy was to convert a situation potentially classified as "highly uncertain and low in understanding of relationships" to one with different situational features. Performance itself was thought of as involving a manageable level of uncertainty. The part likely to be troublesome was the need for the manager to be understanding of the complexities in the organization system and how to work things out with various key people. It would be important to be open with her regarding the demands of her current assignment as well as what she was likely to encounter subsequently. This approach, it was hoped, would help to build trust in the information and counseling being provided.

2. *Situational review with Helen*. The marketing vice president was a highly competent individual with solid professional qualifications and good interpersonal skills. The vice president of Human Resources was to assume responsibilities for needs analyses in connection with Helen's current and (possible) international assignments. The vice president of marketing was to deal with work performances related to her current responsibilities, the EXEC II introduction, and a "forecast" of what might be involved in the international

assignment. Both would jointly undertake discussions related to the corporate culture and the intricacies of how the performance and assessment systems operated. These discussions were scheduled to take place over a period of two months. This was to allow adequate time for the orientations to take hold and for Helen to raise questions and to experience some of the relationships or getting things done in a somewhat changed approach. The timing was partially governed by the EXEC II marketing program. They wanted to establish a sound base of understandings much in advance of the need to start her new promotion and development program. It turned out that four informal get togethers were needed (two with the new boss, one with the vice president of Human Resources, and one jointly with both vice presidents) to get the information across. Calendarwise, these four meetings were spread over a four-month period (instead of two) because Helen was tied up with some agency problems and had to be out of town several times. At first, when Helen's boss had the initial discussion, she felt threatened and was uncertain as to what the "real" purpose was. The second session was scheduled with the vice president of Human Resources who confirmed the content of the discussions and relieved her concerns. In the last discussion where both vice presidents were present, it was possible to get down to the specifics of how the system operated, what criteria would be used in her appraisals/assessments, and the relevant time frames for considerations.

By the end of the series of discussions, Helen's optimism and eagerness to move ahead were evident, and she entered into the discussion enthusiastically. It should be noted, however, that *no* promises were made regarding promotion, bonuses, and so on. These were to be reviewed in the light of results, *and* the company reserved the right of shifting its strategy should the situation warrant it. But Helen was to receive regular feedback on these so that they would not be "unknowns."

3. *Performance criteria, time frames, and longer-range motivational strategies.* The Marketing Department's strategic plans called for an intensive development program that lasted almost a year. Further, the performance criteria by which Helen would be judged would be tailored to the assignment. They would include a number of new dealerships opened, penetrations of competitive territories and market shares, product penetration, total cost expenditures, EXEC II's image among potential buyers, employee identification with the new line, and stockholder awareness of product capabilities and superiorities relative to competition. The base period for analysis was set as two years. At the end of the first year, results would be reviewed for progress and (possible) modification. Additional informal discussions would take place throughout this period to assure everybody was in touch with emerging events.

4. *Needs analysis.* Management development programming had to blend in with the considerable demands of Helen's current responsibilities—and expected knowledge/competency gains required for subsequent work needs. Her development program included the following:
   1. Helen was scheduled for two workshops dealing with
      a. "Strategies for new product introductions."
      b. "Planning for marketing organization and strategy development."

2. The vice president of Human Resources worked with Helen's boss in developing a market simulation with circumstances similar to the EXEC II introduction. Then Helen spent considerable time working through the simulation with appropriate coaching from her boss. The simulation provided an opportunity to put her learnings from the workshop to work. The expert coaching provided good guidelines, understanding and practical feedback.

3. About 15 months after the EXEC II introduction, the positive feedback she had received was further backed up with the second phase of developmental discussions regarding the international assignment.

Helen was promoted to vice president of international marketing about two and one-half years after the initial discussions with the vice presidents from marketing and Human Resources.

The complexity of modern organizations is such as to "reject" the use of simple models or guidelines when it comes to complex matters such as managerial performance and productivity. Technological systems are intertwined with social systems, and these are set in a context of "organizational culture" and the external environment. The nature of the organization, whether it is for-profit, nonprofit, or governmental, imposes its own demands as to managerial approaches. Managerial performance is linked to many factors, only one of which is motivation.

Many impediments stand in the way of a literal application of motivational strategies, not the least of which is the general receptivity of the organization, and particularly the cooperation of powerful senior managers. Motivational strategies cannot be used with precision because we still don't know that much about individual behavior. Yet our understanding today far exceeds that of past years.

The concluding topic in this section on motivation-behavioral approaches relates to individuals caught in the turbulent conditions of major organizational change. Merger or retrenchment situations, for example, pose major problems in individual adaptation and managing change. Behavioral approaches have an important role to play in this context.

Merger, Retrenchment, and Individual Change

The turbulence and highly unsettled conditions experienced by numerous companies is frequently part of a general economic restructuring of industries and organizations. Merger and retrenchment activities are a common part of this scene and thus reasonably incorporated as a part of comprehensive performance planning approaches. Other aspects of this subject are covered in the last chapter.

Turbulence in the general environment is likely to continue for many years. Automobiles, hospitals, steel, construction, "fast foods," hotels and motels, computers, airlines, chemicals, banks, insurance, and scientific instruments are examples of products and industries caught up in these widespread and unsettling changes. Foreign competition, creation of "free market" conditions in domestic industries, changes in state and federal tax and legal requirements, and the desire to establish more diverse and stable financial structures are among the main reasons for much merger and retrenchment activity. Internal reorganizations are a common outgrowth of these activities. Bank managers who were at one time specialists in "savings" operations may now be moved into "commercial." Insurance managers with much "life" background may now find themselves dealing with "casualty" problems. Managers from a merged-in, formerly "small" tool company may suddenly find that they need a "big picture" or corporate perspective in their approaches to new customers.

Age as a Policy Issue

Although tinged with legal controversy or even illegality, conventional wisdom underlying some corporate actions has been that "older" managers are higher risks relative to younger managers. The "reasoning" is that most older managers are prone to plateauing and/or obsolescence, that they are poor in adapting to new learning, and that they lack mobility. The foregoing notwithstanding, many senior managers have participated in education and (re)development programs. Even responding to this point in this way may give encouragement to some that they have a point. It is unintended! As the familiarity of education and training (E&T) officials has grown with respect to both successful and unsuccessful changes in management competencies, it is clear that some, perhaps many, notions regarding educability need renovation. The matter of age is an outstanding instance of where traditional assumptions need to be reexamined.

Carefully cataloged corporate experiences and research by health people indicate that age, per se, is often not the central point in predicting individual success.

> For example, in a corporate development program which had the purpose of retraining mostly older managers for new assignments, it turned out that the intentions or outlooks of the participant *prior to the program* had a major bearing on how well managers do! Age was not an issue unless it affected the ability of the person to participate in the program.

In this context, intentions or outlook mean the following:

- What do they expect to get out of the program?
- Will the program be seen as beneficial, is this something they really need and want?
- Will the organization prove supportive of the effort?
- Will they be able to use the learnings in a receptive environment or will people be hostile to the new learnings?
- To what extent do program participants feel that major personal sacrifices will have to be made in pursuing "this" development program, and will it be a stepping stone to changed (positive or negative) work circumstances?

These "questions" relate primarily to organizational and individual change and performance planning and management issues. Although age may be of some importance in energy level, there are too many mitigating circumstances to use the broad rubric of "age" as a key or qualifying factor.

Participants in management development programs of this nature find that they are very demanding. In the extreme where participants can't or choose not to change, a career shift or/and outplacement may be indicated. If program participants don't do well, it is often because they didn't expect to do well initially or weren't convinced of the relevance or validity of the program. Too, the person may have been unaccepting of the broader change circumstances. The outlooks or intentions of program participants involve motivational issues of the type already described. Individual perception may be the key to dealing with the situation, especially if distorted or in error. The challenge to the organization is one of motivating active participation and subsequently successful performance.

A Change Model to Facilitate Analysis

Viewing merger/retrenchment types of situations in the context of change permits the use of a strategic planning perspective which might not be initially apparent. A simple paradigm (AIMS) for checking out change circumstances and the individual's situation is as follows:

> A—*awareness* by the individual that important change is (has) taken place. At times these are not so obvious or have been misperceived. In a family-owned bank, for example, after several years of low profits due to poor investments, bringing in a new president from the outside was interpreted by organization members as a "house cleaning" move prior to sale. Managers who subsequently participated in management development programs felt that these were really an attempt to assess their competencies relative to outplacement. Many participants rated the program poorly at the time, though in retrospect many changed their mind when additional events unfolded. It turned out that the new president was brought in for lack of family successors and the desire of the family to establish a sound, professionally run business for the future.

> I—*impact* of work patterns or technology of reporting relationships and "why" and "how" these affect the particular person involved. People need to know, for example, that the requisite job-related behaviors for success will be altered and that new working relationships are indicated and the form these are likely to take. In this instance, change must be made job and individual specific to the extent that they are directly impacted. It also means that new performance appraisal objectives and criteria will have to be communicated.

> M—*motivation*, say, to participate in (the) management development programming. The need is to refocus knowledge, skills, and experience of the person toward different work objectives and to perform satisfactorily in these changed circumstances. The use of motivation-behavioral ideas presented in this chapter would, for example, suggest honest and frank discussions of new performance needs. These include: involving the

individual in their own needs assessment, achieving mutual agreement on the educational program dealing with the implications of the program for their career, providing a positive and supportive work environment, and *assuring* appropriate and supportive coaching is made available. Also, the reward system plays an important role in this picture through performance appraisals. This system should make it clear which behaviors are being rewarded (e.g., personal development and performance).

S—*skills* needed for change. If individuals feel (more) competent regarding their work circumstances, they are also likely to be positively motivated. There is an important synergy involving motivation and skills. People who feel that they are able to achieve the needed skills are "motivated" program participants. Consequently, the educational program has to be viewed as necessary and valid and one that will be supported. Important time commitments must be made by the supervising manager if the full benefits of development programming are to be realized, as for example, through coaching and guidance. "S" involves the methodology and processes of learning and development, but it is equally clear that they are part of a complex picture which includes the learning context and the supervisor's role.

Summary

The growing complexity of contemporary organizations requires a view of performance that includes efficiency and effectiveness and a much enlarged time frame. There is a dynamic interaction among these dimensions and multiple performance measures are integral to strategic analyses. Also, when planning analyses are undertaken in this framework, more powerful means are needed to describe work-related performance and the person's potential to undertake these in the future.

Performance planning, whether for general productivity improvement, introduction of new technologies, or doing business under greatly altered enterprise circumstances, assumes a key, often central, role in strategic descisions. Extrapolating HR problems and issues from these plans and strategies is an initial task for Human Resource officials and planners. Correspondingly, the greater acceptance and use of HR inputs offers an opportunity for it to play a much more proactive role. A second feature of performance planning is that of scaling it down or being able to visualize and anticipate the fit of operational planning with these more broadly focused discussions.

A growing number of behaviorally based, work-descriptive schemes have been developed to facilitate planning analyses and performance management. They improve performance appraisals, help to anticipate future work-related needs, improve the identification of high potentials, and strengthen the bases for individual needs analysis and development. Byham's work, cited in this chapter, is a good example of these newer behavioral schemes. It facilitates the design of jobs, judging performance, doing development planning, and dealing with the learnability of management competencies. Other specifics of behaviorally derived performance dimensions are provided in the applications section.

Performance appraisal has occupied a main "seat" in planning for performance. However, even this venerable model is undergoing vast and significant changes to outfit it for work in the strategic picture and to improve its operational role as well.

The importance assigned to performance appraisal information in human resource planning and management decisions has necessitated a reexamination of this data source. Important strategic planning decisions cited in this chapter using PA results included retrenchment decisions and work force reduction, development planning, management trainee progress appraisals, the identification of high potentials, and succession planning. Means for improving the use of PA-related information include better managerial training, behaviorly oriented work dimensions (as in Byham's work), behaviorally anchored rating scales, and standardizing the instrumentation used in the organization. Further important improvements in PA results have been achieved by using a uniform system of work dimensions for jobs and in appraising performance.

Strategic planning, overly concerned with the "how" or "what," may fail to recognize adequately the individual motivation in plan fulfillment or needed individual change. Three different motivational schemes were reviewed briefly which included needs-oriented approaches, rationality, and learning and individual adaptation. (Additional information on these approaches is provided in the applications section.) It was concluded that no single approach was adequate for the complex and diverse situations facing policy officials, planners, and strategists. Increasingly in a "situational-contingency" mode, an approach is called for with the components or approaches tailored to the circumstances.

One part of assessing the situation relates to judging the relative extent of uncertainty or complexity facing individual managers or officials. In the appraisal of uncertainty and complexity, it becomes important to identify the contributing factors or circumstances and to judge the behavioral/motivational consequences for the person. A knowledge of individual perception is important to understanding this picture.

Another aspect of the situation described had to do with organizational culture that effectively sets the tone for individual performance actions and often the supervising manager's role in this picture. The fast-growing file of corporate experience and research indicates the deserved attention to this factor in the future. Chapter 3 provides an extensive discussion of this factor.

Perceptions were linked to individual beliefs and, potentially, behavioral or performance "intentions." Perceptions affect the individual's evaluation of their decision context, expectations for career opportunities, and sense of environmental supportiveness. It also affects their reaction to development programs. Thus the individual's view (perception) of his or her situation may be instrumental in the success of strategically planned moves. The validity and adequacy of individual perceptions may well require examination as a part of planning assumptions.

The level of trust existing in particular relationships or exhibited in given settings is another factor to be contended within situational approaches. Trust is an essential basis for deriving the fullest benefits of coaching relationships and the type of progress expected of the developing manager. Put another way, lack of trust can seriously undermine the assumptions or rate of progress in fulfilling strategic plans.

The final discussion in this chapter dealt with change and possible applications of the AIMS model to render preliminary assessments of individual change situations. The fact that some and perhaps much of the growing uncertainty and complexity of organizations is attributable to strategically planned changes, improved bases can be established to approach performance management planning and issues.

REFERENCES

Agnew, Neil McKinnon and John L. Brown. "From Skyhooks to Walking Sticks: On the Road to Non-rational Decision Making." *Organizational Dynamics,* Vol. 11, no. 2 (Autumn 1982): 40–58.

Baird, Lloyd, Richard W. Beatty, and Craig Eric Schneier. "The Performance Appraisal Sourcebook." Reading, MA: Addison—Wesley, 1982.

Belcher, David W. "Pay Equity or Pay Fairness?" *Compensation Review,* Vol. 2 (Second Quarter 1979): 31–37.

Berman, David L. and Howard Mase. "The Key to the Productivity Dilemma: The Performance Manager." *Human Resource Management,* Vol. 22, no. 3 (Fall 1983): 275–286.

Bernardin, H. J. and Richard W. Beatty, eds. *Performance Appraisal: Assessing Human Behavior at Work.* Boston: Kent, 1984.

Bernardin, H. J. and P. C. Smith. "A Clarification of Some Issues Regarding the Development and Use of Behaviorally Anchored Rating Scales." *Journal of Applied Psychology,* Vol. 66 (1981): 458–463.

Borman, Walter C. "The Rating of Individuals in Organizations: An Alternate Approach." *Organizational Behavior and Human Performance,* Vol. 12 (1974): 105–124.

Burack, Elmer H. and M. Zia Hassan. "U-C Analysis; Management's New Tool." *Planning Review,* Vol. 10, no. 3 (May 1982): 2–6.

Burack, Elmer H. and Florence Torda. *The Manager's Guide to Change.* Belmont, CA: General Learning, 1979.

Burack, Elmer H. and Thomas J. McNichols. *Human Resource Planning: Technology, Policy and Change.* Kent, OH: Kent State University Press, 1973.

Burack, Elmer H. and Anant Neghandi. *Organizational Design.* Kent, OH: Kent State University Press, 1973.

Burnaska, R. J. "The Effects of Behavior Modeling Training upon Managers' Behaviors and Employees' Perceptions." *Personnel Psychology,* Vol. 26 (1976): 329–335.

Byham, William C. "Dimensions of Managerial Competence: What They Are, How They Differ Between Levels, How They Are Changing." Monograph VI. Pittsburgh: Development Dimensions International, 1982.

Campbell, John P., Marvin D. Dunnette, and Edward E. Lawler, III. *Managerial Behavior, Performance and Effectiveness.* New York: McGraw-Hill, 1970.

Carlyle, J. J. and T. F. Ellison. "Developing Performance Standards." Appendix B in H. J. Bernardin and Richard W. Beatty, eds., *Performance Appraisal: Assessing Human Behavior at Work.* Boston: Kent, 1984.

Cascio, Wayne F. *Human Resource Planning and Management,* New York: The Free Press, 1986.

Cascio, Wayne F. "Scientific, Legal, and Operational Imperatives of Workable Performance Appraisal Systems." *Public Personnel Management*, Vol. 11 (1982): 367–375.

Cherrington, D. J. *The Work Ethic: Working Values and Values That Work*. New York: AMACOM, 1980.

Cherrington, D. J. and B. J. Wixom, Jr. "Recognition Is Still a Top Motivator." *Personnel Administrator*, Vol. 28, no. 5 (1983): 87–91.

Cummings, Lawrence L. and Donald P. Schwab. *Performance in Organizations: Determinants and Appraisal*. Glenview, IL: Scott, Foresman, 1973.

Davis, Louis E. and J. C. Taylor, eds. *Design of Jobs*. Santa Monica, CA: Goodyear, 1979.

Dunnette, Marvin D., ed. *Handbook of Industrial and Organizational Psychology*. Chicago, IL: Rand McNally, 1976.

Equal Employment Opportunity Commission. "Uniform Guidelines on Employee Selection." *Federal Register*, Vol. 43, no. 166 (1978), pp. 38290–38309.

Field, H. S. and William H. Holley. "The Relationship of Performance Appraisal System Characteristics to Verdicts in Selected Employment Discrimination Cases." *Academy of Management Journal*, Vol. 25 (1982): 392–406.

Ford, Robert N. "Job Enrichment Lessons from AT&T." *Harvard Business Review*, Vol. 51, no. 1 (1973): 96–106.

Hackman, J. Richard and Greg Oldham. *Work Redesign*. Reading, MA: Addison-Wesley, 1980.

Henderson, Richard. *Performance Appraisal*. Reston, VA: Reston, 1980.

Herzberg, Frederick. "One More Time: How Do You Motivate Your Employees." *Harvard Business Review*, Vol. 46, no. 1 (1968): 53–62.

Kahalas, Harvey. "The Environmental Context of Performance Evaluation and Its Effect on Current Practices." *Human Resource Management*, Vol. 19, no. 3 (Fall 1980): 2–40.

Kirkpatrick, Donald L. *How to Manage Change Effectively*. San Francisco: Jossey-Bass, 1985.

Kopelman, R. E. and L. Reinharth. "Research Results: The Effect of Merit-Pay Practices on White Collar Performance." *Compensation Review*, Vol. 5 (Fourth Quarter 1982): 30–40.

Levine, E. L., R. A. Ash, and N. Bennett. "Exploratory Comparative Study of Four Job Analysis Methods." *Journal of Applied Psychology*, Vol. 65 (1980): 524–535.

London, Manuel. *Developing Managers*. San Francisco: Jossey-Bass, 1985.

Mahler, Walter. *How Effective Executives Interview*. Homewood, IL: Dow Jones-Irwin, 1976, pp. 111–125.

Mayes, B. T. "Some Boundary Conditions in the Application of Motivational Models." *Academy of Management Review*, Vol. 3 (1978): 51–58.

McCall, Morgan W., Jr. and Michael M. Lombardo. "What Makes a Top Executive?" *Psychology Today* (January 1983), 82–88.

Mead, Dana G. and Thoburn Milar Stamm, Jr. "Manufacturing Strategic Planning in Capital-Intensive Industries." In James R. Gardner, Robert Rachlin, and H. W. Allen Sweeny, eds., *Handbook of Strategic Planning*. New York: John Wiley, 1985.

Meyer, P. "Executive Compensation Must Promote Long-Term Commitment." *Personnel Administrator*, Vol. 28, no. 5 (1983): 37–42.

Pinder, Craig C. *Work Motivation*. Glenview, IL: Scott, Foresman, 1984.

Prue, D. M. and J. A. Fairbanks. "Performance Feedback in Organizational Behavior Management: A Review." *Journal of Organization Behavior Management*, Vol. 3 (1980): 1–16.

Schneier, Craig Eric and Richard W. Beatty. "Developing Behaviorally Anchored Rating Scales." *Personnel Administrator* (August 1979): 35–43.

Skinner, B. F. *About Behaviorism*. New York: Alfred A. Knopf, 1974.

Smith, Patricia, L. M. Kendall, and Charles L. Hulin. *The Measurement of Satisfaction in Work and Retirement*. Chicago: Rand McNally, 1969.

Spector, Bert and Michael Beer. *Human Resource Management*. New York: The Free Press, 1985.

Walther, F. and S. Taylor. "An Active Feedback Program Can Spark Performance." *Personnel Administrator*, Vol. 28, no. 6 (1983): 107–111, 147–149.

APPLICATIONS SECTION

Highlights from Three Motivational Models

The three motivational approaches summarized here include (1) needs-oriented approaches, (2) rationality, and (3) learning and individual adaptation. Highlights are presented, respectively, in Exhibits 7-6, 7-7, and 7-8. The rationale for includ-

EXHIBIT 7-6
Needs-oriented Motivation and Performance Approaches

1. A variety of needs may influence behavior at any particular time.
2. Needs may operate individually or in combination.
3. Individual needs strength varies both as to situation and over time as a concommitant of the person's career (human development).
4. Needs previously met lose their arousal ability and/or potency.
5. Intrinsic motivation has to do with "higher-order" needs, including achievement, recognition, self-esteem, independence, competence, and self-actualization.
6. Professional people (those with substantial education, 16 years or more, and those from higher economic status backgrounds typically view "intrinsic" factors as being of significant importance.
7. There are many who (also) see various "extrinsic factors" such as corporate policy, reward system, quality of supervision, and co-worker relationships of much more importance and who may assign as much value to these as various instrinsic factors.
8. Needs are operative to the extent that people see (perceive)
   a. A reasonable chance to succeed.
   b. A workable connection exists between their effort, results, and the value of their performance to their longer-range objectives or goals.

Source: Related points and an excellent discussion of motivation considerations can be found in Craig C. Pinder, *Work Motivation: Theory, Issues and Applications* (Glenview, IL: Scott, Foresman, 1984).

EXHIBIT 7-7
Rationality in Motivation and Performance Approaches

A. People process information based on what they see (perceive) or experience.
   1. Processed information shapes attitudes.
   2. Attitudes and experience shape beliefs and ultimately values.
B. Of immediate concern is recognizing that
   1. Attitudes shape intentions to engage in particular behaviors.
   2. Attitudes, even beliefs, often emerge out of behaviors, even if involuntary.
C. The most effective means to change
   1. Volitional behavior
      Change perceptions . . . and thereby attitudes, beliefs, and/or intentions.
   2. Nonvolitional behavior
      If a person engages in this type of behavior on a sustained basis and the results come to be seen as positive, nonthreatening, supportive, etc., positive attitudes and beliefs will often emerge.
D. Perception is the initial point of departure in shaping *rational* behavior(s). Considerations include
   • Task difficulty, likelihood of being able to cope with it, sense of "optimum" or desirable stress level . . . and thus (dis)inclination to engage in it.
   • *expected* satisfaction from outcome(s).
   • strength of connection between positively (or negatively) valued outcomes and work performance (or disinclination for work performance).
E. Perceptions of (in)equity underlie many forms of rational behavior:
   • These are based on exchange relationships between person and organization or with other individuals.
   • A sense of (in)equity is also shaped by one's perception of exchange relationships between the organization and other individuals or among other individuals.
F. Goal-directed behavior is purposeful and thereby is more readily initiated (energized) than vaguely described directions. It provides focus:
   1. Vague goals or objectives which can lead to ambiguous results negatively affect work motivation.
   2. Degree of goal specification needs to take account of the likelihood of ambiguous results *and* individual's need for structuring (e.g., methods, approaches, alternatives).
G. Intentions to undertake a given set of behavior or strive for a particular performance level is a central accomplishment in managing managerial performance. It reflects
   1. Perception(s) of the value (to them) of work-related *outcomes*.
   2. Personal beliefs regarding the *strength* of the *connection* between the *outcomes* and the likelihood of their being able to perform at a certain level (of energy expenditure) or to do what they feel has to be done.

Source: Related points and an excellent discussion of motivational considerations can be found in Craig C. Pinder, *Work Motivation: Theory, Issues and Applications* (Glenview, IL: Scott, Foresman, 1984).

EXHIBIT 7-8
Learning and Adaptation

A. Behavior most frequently occurs in sequences of actions.

B. Individuals learn from both the antecedents (or context) and consequences of given behaviors.

C. Managing managerial (behaviors) performance requires understanding of antecedent conditions, consequences, and the behavior itself.

D. Behaviors must be learned before any reinforcement strategy can be applied.

    1. (Re)establishing a given or similar set of antecedent conditions *and* reinforcing (or punishing) behavior in this context is more (or less) likely to establish a basis for similar occurrences in the future.

    2. Continuous reinforcement is most effective for initiating new behaviors.

    3. Extinction starts to take place rapidly where behaviors have been reinforced continuously (after being learned).

    4. Strategies of reinforcing behaviors that are variable ("variable ratio schedules") achieve the best results in higher levels of types of behavior.

Source: Related points and an excellent discussion of motivational considerations can be found in Craig C. Pinder, *Work Motivation: Theory, Issues and Applications* (Glenview, IL: Scott, Foresman, 1984).

ing these three approaches here is that no single approach is adequate for the complex and diverse situations facing management development strategists. It often appears that a "bit of this theory and some of that theory" is what is really needed. They often must be used in a complementary way, and somehow these must be drawn together to provide the stepping stone to a more comprehensive approach to dealing with managerial performance.

For example, Exhibit 7-6 highlights the needs-oriented approach. It is necessary to establish "where" a given manager is "today" in terms of personal needs and priorities. "Is the manager concerned about 'security' problems, such as stability of employment, or does he or she actively seek to meet 'recognition' needs for personal accomplishment, or perhaps more job autonomy or independence in decision making?"

As to Exhibit 7-7, rationality, getting to better understand a person's beliefs and attitudes, provides some insights into their intentions regarding performance, career pursuits, retirement, or perhaps even quitting. Perceptions, and "how" the person "looks" at his or her job's complex problems, especially if wrong, provides valuable insights into individual behavior and potentially *positive* and useful means of dealing with these. Also, although goal-directed behavior is purposeful, vagueness regarding goals or failure to involve the person in goal establishment may greatly reduce the positive results of formulating these.

In learning and adaptation (Exhibit 7-8), managing performance often depends on the manager's ability to learn from antecedent conditions and work results to grapple with these. Too, behaviors must be learned fully and in a way that they can be shaped to situational needs before any reinforcement schemes can be applied.

8

Management Development Methods
Individual Learning
and Effectiveness

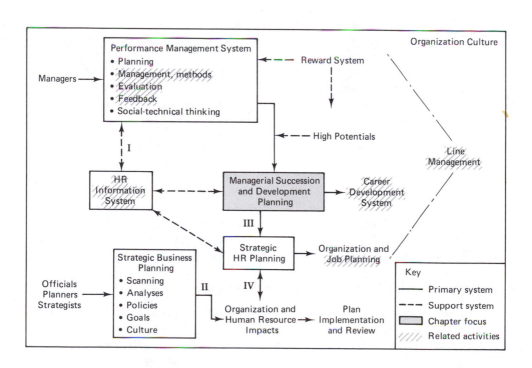

Much has been learned about the development of managerial personnel, and although these insights fall short of being a general theory, they do comprise a highly useful body of models, methods, and workable experiences. This is a complex area for which approaches are best undertaken by combining enlightened experience and insights with systematically derived results. Human Resource officials and line managers can use this information in a critical and selective way—and concentrate on those approaches that best fit their particular circumstances.

In strategic approaches, senior Human Resource officials are concerned with what managers "really need to know"; then they plan the processes and systems for "producing" these results. It is also important to detect shifts in these foci as business needs change and to judge the speed or pace of change. Supportive information for this planning includes how people learn and differences due to individual makeup, the relative effectiveness of alternate management development methods, characteristic requirements of adult learners, and the genére of successful managers, if this can be identified. Approaches are further complicated, for example, by the needed adjustments due to the position and function being considered. All these aspects are challenging, and the combination is rather humbling. Thus it is not likely that any single person or company has all or perhaps even most of the required knowledge or answers.

The purpose of this chapter is to identify and develop some of the major themes, questions, and approaches related to management development methods. Particular emphasis is on the planning or strategic aspects. Major chapter themes include

1. General approaches for making management development and learning more strategic.
2. Importance and involvement of line management.
3. Impact of organization culture.
4. Work characteristics and descriptions useful for development purposes.
5. Newer planning approaches reflecting how and why people learn.
6. Relative effectiveness of management development methods and processes, including newer approaches such as behavioral modeling.

Making Management Development More Strategic

Strategic approaches to management development increasingly enlist the active support of top corporate officials to reinforce the importance and high priority assigned to these programs. These programs are frequently seen as highly facilitative of corporate long-range business and strategic objectives and opportunities for individual career development. For example, a descriptive brochure for corporate management development programs was headed up by a letter "signed" by its CEO. In part, it read as follows:

> . . . These programs have proven to be helpful in assisting organization members to achieve personal and organizational potential more fully . . . the task before us involves self-development as well as developing our future leaders. The period ahead, though difficult, will be successfully accomplished if in addition to our considerable business expertise, we are able to utilize fully these management development programs and achieve our potential for excellence in individual performance, teamwork, and leadership.

It is of interest to note that this quotation reflects the relationship of management development to business welfare in terms of individual performance, teamwork, and leadership. The company involved was in the process of a major reorganization to contain costs and to meet competition more aggressively. The CEO and key staff members "saw" development as the key to creating more talent in depth, better teamwork due to improved abilities, strengthening leadership qualities, and facilitating individual career progress as well.

At times, too many problems are attributed to deficiencies in work methods or processes yet the basic issue may be one of failure by top management to support development programs. Even the best development procedures are destined for failure in situations where reward systems are not meshed with these approaches and/or top management appears to be disinterested. What's the use if a person undertakes an after-hour program to strengthen skills understood to be job related and important, but for which no recognition is provided? A similarly difficult situation is one in which top managers provide little or no recognition of efforts through *performance* planning, *appraisals*, or promotion considerations for supervisors or managers who take deliberate steps to develop their subordinates.

The overall orientation for the management development strategies discussed in this chapter is situationally focused. It considers (1) context or organizational features, including culture, structure, and work systems planning; (2) features of work and jobs; and (3) individual characteristics. The discussions which follow draw heavily on the experiences of seasoned Human Resource and development officials. Aside from our own corporate experiences and studies of management development methods, several executive conferences and special issues of major journals also proved helpful in providing resource material for this chapter.

Integrating Executive Perspectives on Management Development Approaches

The company's internal environment and work and administrative processes establish the basic direction and thrust of developmental methods and approaches. The organization's "cultural" context—including top management's philosophy regarding (and the importance assigned to) individual development, the degree of recognition of these in the reward system, and tangible acts of support—form the context for emerging methods and processes. They dictate the care and degree of attention given to these by line managers as well as the relative responsibility for development assumed by managers up and down the organization structure.

The nature of the business, structure, work processes, and products/services focus top management's strategic planning. Human resource analyses emerge from these and include organization structure planning, longer-range staffing requirements, and the specifics of the position responsibilities and behaviors needed for success. The number and types of these positions establish in a fundamental way, what behaviors are to be considered high priority or critical in the future and the planning time parameters for these accomplishments. If new corporate directions are taken in the future, these may result in a major refocusing of highly valued abilities and thus the need for developmental approaches.

Executives often won't agree exactly as to how to develop managers or methods that have proven most effective in their experience. But the substantive differences are often much less among seasoned senior managers than might be imagined. Rather than differing on fundamentals, the selection of approaches often reflects an emphasis on particular methods or priority needs in their organization. Taken collectively, they represent a group of approaches that straddle a range of highly useful and workable programs. In turn, most of these developmental orientations can be related to the models and approaches described in this chapter. Condon (1985) provides a good perspective of management development strategies, particularly in relation to the following important points.

Blending Work Experience and More Formal Instruction.   Companies tend to separate experience and instruction in episodic fashion and often over an extended time interval. The reinforcement potential of either one for the other is greatly reduced in this approach. *In general, the greater the time lapse between instructional experience and opportunity for work application (or vice versa), the less the reinforcement benefits.* In actuality, the staging of many development programs results in these being strung out over an extended time period—months in most cases and a year or more would not be unusual. This may pose severe learning problems unless more artful blending is undertaken of learning and application. A well-known example to many is the fast-growing popularity of cooperative educational programs where students work and learn. The considerable benefits from this mode of individual schooling, learning, and development have encouraged both corporate and educational officials to enter into or expand these programs. Another related experience is that of the part-time graduate student attending an evening program at a university. There is no doubt that this is a tough way to learn—occurring at the end of the workday and often on top of family, professional, or community responsibilities. Yet as many and difficult as these obstacles may be for the "learner," both students and corporate officials have reacted favorably to the excellent opportunity to "prove out management theory" or to "challenge the effectiveness of various corporate practices." Thus a learning strategy that seeks to coordinate and combine on-the-job or coaching experiences with more structured learning experiences (e.g., seminars, school, or self-study) *and* the application of these to one's work can prove beneficial to company and person alike.

Line Management Involvement and the Gestalt of Managing

A new appreciation has grown (or been reborn) for the importance of work-related experience as opposed to the reliance of many institutions on "classroom"-type instruction. The transfer of knowledge or information from off-site ("classroom") to on-site is only part of the issue in work-related development. "The job is where it happens" is an old cliché but is still quite applicable to many different circumstances. Newer approaches to work-related experiences, however, are quite different from those exercised many years ago. The awareness has grown that the job and attendant behaviors can serve as a rich source of learning. However, the full wealth of this learning resource can't be tapped if individual development responsibilities rest (too heavily) in the hands of Personnel/Human Resources, development people, or other staff groups. Line managers are in the best position to fully utilize positional resources and provide the requisite coaching so critical to management development progress. Deep involvement of line managers also helps to legitimize the "trainees" application of learning experiences to work-related situations. Although the line manager's role is central, "staff" has a very important role, too, in identifying educational strategies or alternatives, systems and methods planning, program designs, and coordination. Staff's support together with the line manager's expertise can help to assure a meaningful development experience.

The increased and purposeful involvement of line management also means that more of the subtleties of the managerial role can be communicated to the person ("trainee") in realistic fashion. There is a certain "Gestalt" about managerial actions in which many different factors are taken account of as information and experience are processed, a decision is made, and action is taken. Candidates need to get the "feel" for this complex process, experience it themselves, and know when to make a decision or perhaps to back off and get more information. It also means knowing what information is needed for managerial actions, where to get it, and how to use it.

Another part of line management's involvement and the role of work experience is the importance to the "trainee" of becoming more fully acquainted with the nature of the business. There is need to know what the organization is all about and how it functions as an economic enterprise. Some of these insights come alive through the eyes and experiences of those who are charged with making it happen and their sharing of these. It also means that people can enjoy the fruits of their insights and other learning experiences as well as the benefits of failure—while under the watchful eye of a coach who is often the person's supervisor. The (re)activated role of the line manager in development also means that feedback can be provided more frequently and when needed. It is quite apparent that line managers are increasingly cast into major roles that quite literally affect the welfare of the organization. The involvement in development provides considerable and needed stature for their efforts.

"Trainee" Performance and the Expectations of the Supervising Manager.
A body of both research and practical experience is growing that the expectations of the manager-coach or "trainee" (it is recognized that many trainees may be quite senior people) can have a substantial impact on the performance level of the trainee. Individual expectations are built on the basis of nonverbal communications cues, and explicit actions by the manager/trainer, with unmistakable messages for the trainee. People are sensitive to facial expressions signaling hope, support, disdain, or disgust. Obviously they are also conscious of the sincerity or emptiness in words of praise or acts, the obvious intent of which is to support or to write off a person as a poor risk. Managerial/trainer expectations thus are often translated into body language, attitudes, and overt actions that can become self-confirming for the person who they are coaching or training (see, for example, Baird and Wieting, 1985).

Receiving managers may size up a newly assigned person on the basis of sex, race, clothing, or mannerisms and attribute capabilities, potential, or limitations largely on the basis of these. Or these initial impressions (or attributions) may make just enough difference in a performance appraisal to "shift" a good performer to an average performer or even frustrate the person's display of managerial potential. Controlled lab experiments, numerous practical experiences, and research in educational settings suggest that manager-trainers (coaches) be briefed on these issues. Further, it is indicated that steps be taken through their own training, as for example, through role plays, to help gain assurance in the manner in which developmental situations are approached.

Key Steps in Making Learning More Strategic

When unanchored by corporate purpose or direction, development methods inevitably have been short run oriented and often given over to job pragmatics. Line managers who supervise "trainees," and thus serve as trainers, are for the most part held responsible for the budget/cost performance of their unit. Work-related problems, costs, complaints, and schedules are very real to them. If left to their own devices, these quite naturally will receive priority. Consequently even under the best of circumstances, a strong and well-organized effort must be made by the organization to break out of this circle of day-to-day issues and concerns and to cast candidate development in a broader perspective and with appropriate priorities. Part of this task includes individual development approaches which take into account changing organization circumstances, or alternate and superior learning opportunities that may exist elsewhere in the organization or outside. In consequence, a corporate presence must be well established at the grass-roots supervisory/managerial level to assure that a useful balance of short- and longer-run considerations is maintained.

Start with Comprehensive Needs Analysis.   Individual development needs to be approached in a systematic way that takes into account current and future work assignments and the broader context of the organization's strategic requirements. As already established, the tendency to do what is nearest at hand or most convenient is a strong impulse. Yet a full needs determination may indicate areas of individual strength with which people in the organization are unacquainted. An in-depth approach to individual needs determination for development involves joint analysis of the individual, job circumstances, and organizational requirements. Needs related to the individual depend on the level of responsibility and organization plans for the person but could include a profile of competencies, interests, learning abilities, aptitudes, experience, progress, potential, career interests, and at times, aspects of personality. Work needs include behaviors or actions of the job-holder for success, plus future changes in these. Organizational aspects include future plans for the person and major changes which may affect work characteristics. Comprehensive needs analyses also helps to assure that a more holistic approach is taken so that important points (needs) are not missed and so that better organization of the total effort becomes feasible.

Enlarging the Line Manager's Perspective.   Many supervisors who function as trainer-coaches draw from a narrow background or perspective of developmental approaches and limited information as to their effectiveness. Also, not surprisingly, the tendency is to use one's own background as a normative or developmental model against which comparisons are drawn for the person being "trained" (used in the development sense in this chapter). As a consequence it will often be necessary to train the trainer. This is needed to assure that full benefit is taken of the many corporate opportunities for development and that the most effective approaches are applied to the individual's situation.

Building Managerial Strength Progressively.   Successive assignments which gradually enlarge the demands imposed on the individual have been a longstanding approach to competency development. This process of knowledge, skill, and ability development is carried out within particular positions and through promotion to positions of greater responsibility and more demanding behaviors for job success. Being able to carry out assignments successfully and meeting particular emergencies as they arise fortifies individual capabilities and confidence. Many are then able to move into more demanding work. Organizations such as Johnson & Johnson pursue the practice of rotating individual line-staff assignments to broaden competencies and to enlarge the perspective of the individual. Interdivisional transfers are another common strategy. However, top management must often "pave the way" for these approaches, and the culture must be supportive of these developmental activities. The strategic perspective indicates that this area be approached in a way that adequately visualizes the "building block" possibilities inherent in any particular position and the connection to successively more demanding and comprehensive arrangements of "building blocks" in future assignments. Increasing management strength progressively and in a strategic way will thus reflect organizational human resource planning needs, positional demands, and the career desires and capabilities/limitations of the person.

Dual Career Paths with Equitable Rewards Systems.   Many organizations need to acknowledge the reward and promotion potential found in a variety of managerial tasks. It is important to recognize that some jobs may be inherently technical, while others lean heavily on general managerial or administrative skills or some combination of these. Technical work is the essence of some businesses. Typical activities include designing engineered products, computer systems planning, engineering services, architecture, actuarial-type analyses, and market research.

In the past, many technical types of jobs were deadends for careers because no viable career ladders existed to other organizational areas. The tardy recognition given to these types of technical assignments has resulted in career networks and dual-career mobility with rewards comparable to those found elsewhere in the organization. Similar statements can be made regarding general managerial or administrative positions in what otherwise are quite technical organizations. The point is that this duality of approaches requires *explicit recognition* in systems design and individual awareness and development.

Strengthening Selection Processes at Entry and Promotion

Many "problems" in developing managers could in part have been anticipated or perhaps avoided through improved selection procedures. At the point of entry into employment, whether in a special trainee classification or as a regular employee, too little attention has been given to developmental needs. Of course, priority must be assigned initially to those approaches which help to assure needed skills and performance in the first regular position assignment. Right from the beginning, a blueprint with timing is needed by the "trainee" to guide their achievement of the indicated knowledge-skills-abilities, to be appraised as a competent performer. Several characteristic types of problems commonly occur at this career/work stage: (1) systematic needs analysis procedures are ignored or carried out informally, (2) undue reliance is placed on the approaches of a particular supervising manager as a "trainer" without adequate thought given to "training the trainer" and/or ensuring reasonable uniformity between the approaches of various managers receiving new employees, and (3) there is a failure to use instrumentation or approaches that are oriented to successful performance. The last point concerns the end behaviors on the job that are needed for successful performance and then designing development actions accordingly.

Organizations also encounter numerous selection problems at the time of assessing potential for promotion. A continuing holdover from the past has been the heavy weight assigned to experience or past and current performance (discussed at length in Chapter 7). The problem is that too little recognition is given to the substantially different performance behaviors that are often required in the future. Another part of this selection problem is the reliance on informal judgments or a single criterion measure of potential. The complexity of these decisions has led to much heavier stress on multimethod assessments. A well-constructed assessment center organizes multimethod approaches in a systematic way; this model has been applied from supervisory to rather senior managerial levels. An interesting and newer addition to these approaches involves self-assessments by the individual and comparisons with their supervisor's assessments—often carried out in a workshop format.

Closely related to these issues has been the recognition of the need to build in more powerful approaches to assessing potential. The assessment center, previously referred to by incorporating multimethods and stressing end-job behavior, has substantially improved results in this area. Broadening the base of qualified candidates for selection purposes has also affected the features of development strategies. *Self-nomination options* as found in company posting systems, have typically resulted in a significant widening of qualified candidates to consider for development purposes.

Management Development: Scope and Focus

Although management development is being increasingly formalized and seen as integral to human resource management, significant numbers of organizations have "resisted" these trends. Also, as already brought out, the creation of comprehensive systems, including the integration of planning and development activities, is just starting to receive deserved attention.

According to one readership survey ("Who, What, and Where," *Training,* 1984), the average (annual) number of formal training hours for staff and managers ranged from 22 to 32. However, in some areas such as the business service group, policy-level managers received some 43 hours of training on the average. Interestingly, up to 30 percent of the surveyed organizations had no formal programs. The thrust of the training was heavily focused on managerial skills and technical and communications skills. Better than 80 percent reported concentration on these skills. Some 70 percent indicated the provision of some form of formal executive development, and a similar percentage focused on new methods and procedures. Sixty percent in the *Training* survey claimed to provide some focus on personal growth including career planning, but this percentage has varied a great deal based on other survey estimates with which we are familiar.

The bulk of the formal programs just described ("Who, What, and Where," 1984) were delivered "in house." However, executive development received relatively more outside programming time with many organizations using a combination of inside and outside strategies.

Types of Training and Development Approaches. The following selected results from the *Training* study are suggestive of topics related to problems and issues referenced at various points in these discussions.

Type of training and development provided	Percentage of total survey companies providing
Performance appraisal	77%
Time management	74
Leadership	73
Train the trainer	64
Interpersonal skills	64
Problem solving	61
Stress management	58
Decision making	57
Team building	57
Planning	55
Management information systems	52
Conducting meetings	51
Strategic planning	40

Source: Based on a survey by "Who, What, and Where," *Training* 21 (November 1984) p. 44. All numbers rounded.

Size of Organization and Provision of Development. Not surprisingly, size of organization had a pronounced effect on the scope of programs offered. Firms with under 1,000 employees concentrated primarily on management skills, supervisory skills, and communications and behavioral skills. Firms with over 1,000 employees had expanded programs that included executive development, newer management methods, and computer literacy.

Features of Work and Jobs

Development methods reflect the knowledge, skills, and abilities applied by jobholders to produce specified end results (Exhibit 6-3). Strategic approaches require timely and complete descriptions of positional responsibilities *and* required end behaviors to specify a position adequately for purposes of current assignment or future performance and development planning.

The *relational features* of a job, and its communications and working relationships, is an area of job-related competencies receiving increasing attention in developmental methods and specific attention in position descriptions. Position planners need to know what main work-related relationships are involved in any key posi-

tions and thus the competencies needed by the incumbent to make them successful. Communications acumen and interpersonal abilities are incorporated in relational analysis that need to be specified and for which people are "trained." Modern
job descriptions often have sections devoted to "main cooperative/work relationships." Various organizational changes modify these relationships in terms of types
of information flow, membership of the constellation of people interacting with the
incumbent, and the requisite communications and interpersonal requirements.

Refocusing Development to the "Adult Learner" Model

Another essential aspect of development is understanding how various learning
approaches will change as the individual develops competencies in the organization
and matures as an individual (see Exhibit 8-1). This area of learning is an enor-
mously complex one, so that the discussion in this section is focused particularly on
the strategic aspects. Additional information may be found in writings by R. M.
Gagne, Malcolm Knowles, J. D. Bransford, R. Glaser, and more recently by Jack
Martin.

The educational tasks confronting organizational members change based on
the individual's tenure within the organization, career progress, and personal
growth. The "adult learning" process comes into play here. In "adult learning"
often associated with the work of Malcolm Knowles (1970), and identified as "androgogy," individual learning is heavily self-directed, and the clear determination of
work and career-related needs is of great importance. The thrust is quite different
from "pedagogy," related to formal education during the individual's youth. Self-
assessment plays an important role for mature learners—especially those seeking
actively to improve their performance and further their careers. This trend represents an important enlargement of learning and methods diagnostics! Because of
their relative newness in the learning scene, development strategists and manager/
coaches may have to become acquainted with these. This trend also means that the
methods and technology to facilitate self-assessment need to be considered in the
broader context of formal, organizational development procedures.

The full thrust of "androgogy," the term increasingly used for adult education
and learning, is perhaps more fully appreciated by examining some of its major
assumptions and features (Knowles, 1970). A key and initial condition is that the
learner is both capable of learning *and* feels the need to learn (Knowles, 1970).
Individual learning is specific and problem centered and concerned with the imme-
diacy of application. Learning is usually improved where the learning environment
is seen as supportive; this often means that there is mutual trust and respect
existing between one's supervisor and the "learner," that there is reasonable freedom of expression, and that differences of opinion can be accepted and talked out.
As the person's body of experience expands, this helps to support the learning
process. Learners need to sense progress and consequently timely and accurate
feedback can help validate individual accomplishments. Individual commitment to

EXHIBIT 8-1
The Individual's Side of Development, "Adult Learners," and Careers

Features	Characteristic Elements
Adult learner	Self-determination of needs; increasing desire to learn by experience, self-paced learning.
Career stage(s)	Point in career/life cycle, goal orientation, human development, shifting psychological needs, career reentry.
Developmental tasks	Command of critical skills in preparation for movement between career stages.
Dual careers	Administrative management and/or technical career ladders.
Physical aspects and psychological makeup	Individual learning style, self-awareness, right-brain/left-brain thought and processes, and motivation to learn; mental dexterity, intelligence, adaptability to change, temperament, capability to manage stress; risk taking, assertiveness, and confidence; and energy level.

"adult learning" will mean that the person accepts substantial responsibilities for their learning experience as a lifelong process—but also with the needed and cooperative support of the company. Organization members need to be helped to develop attitudes and skills related to the adult as a "self-directed learner."

Emergence of the "Adult Learner" Model

In early schooling and systems of higher education, educators have been the main architects. The contributions of these educators are obviously valuable, but in various stages of work life, managerial learning has been increasingly tempered by individual situation and career needs. "*What* does a person need to know?" "*When* does a person have to know it?" "*What* learning options are available and what seem to be sensible choices, given one's learning style, time availability, proximity to learning resources, and so forth?" These are some of the questions relevant to newer managerial learning approaches dependent increasingly on advances in "adult learning" concepts.

The adult learner model proposes a substantially different development role for organization members and a much changed orientation for development planners and line managers. Managers and trainers need to

1. Assist learners in diagnosing their learning needs within particular organizational situations.
2. Plan with learners the types of methods or experiences likely to fill individual needs and produce the desired results.
3. Establish motivational conditions for the learner which will be seen as supportive of their efforts. Specific actions include thorough needs analysis, sound counseling, developmental performance appraisals, providing models of desired approaches and encouragement by one's supervisor, and the design features of the organization's reward system.
4. Arrange and allocate resources to support individual efforts.
5. Identify the most effective methods and techniques for desired learnings.
6. Assist learners to measure the results of their learning experiences.

Self-learning: A Major Challenge in Strategic Management Development

Self-learning in the adult learning framework is viewed here as an essential part of individual development and growth. This importance is reinforced where coaching by senior managers and learning through experiencing come to play major developmental roles for high potentials, subordinate managers, and trainees. This is fully compatible with the models of adult learning, which emphasizes people managing their own learning processes. The higher one moves in the organization, in general, the greater the value placed on individual flexibility and adaptability—this also places a premium on self-learning. In consequence, those who play dominant roles in strategizing learning for managerial personnel or literally carrying out these actions as in coaching, need to help individuals learn how to learn. This involves skill building and processes largely absent from the formal educational milieu. An additional and complicating circumstance is that the process of self-learning is often unplanned or dealt with informally by the individual's supervisor or development specialists. Attempts to systematize the process of self-learning has led to the types of step-by-step approaches outlined in Exhibit 8-2. Lists of this type can help to provide guides to senior managers serving as coaches for more junior managerial personnel. On balance, one of the major objectives for the development strategist or coach in this context, is to help the trainee-manager approach self-learning as a conscious personal strategy. Self-learning will be drawn on increasingly for various managerial situations confronted by the developing managers and will be indispensable for individual career planning purposes.

Management Development and the "Learning Function"

Managerial learning is a *highly individualized* matter that covers an extended time period and is beset with numerous behavioral problems and issues. The requirement of planning strategists for systematic ways to approach this complex and

EXHIBIT 8-2
Critical Steps in Self-Learning Strategies

1. Establishing learning need(s) or goal(s).
2. Preliminary assessment of information requirements.
3. Establishing information objectives and the processes for achieving these.
4. Information gathering through self-learning, whether by formal or informal means.
5. Reference to the problem or situation.
6. Evaluation of results, both short and long term.

Source: For related work and discussions, see Jack Martin and B. A. Hiebert, *Instructional Counseling: A Method for Counselors* (Pittsburgh: The University of Pittsburgh Press, 1985).

time-extended process has been facilitated by the "learning function" concept. Its roots were well established, with anchorage in research and practical usage going back to World War II and even earlier. Although often applied in the past to skill-oriented tasks rather than managerial work, it nevertheless offers many useful ideas for approaching managerial development strategically. The Honeywell, Inc., management development program reflects many of the concepts included in the "learning function." For a parallel discussion of the career development process related to management development, see Dalton and Thompson (1986).

Learning Function Highlights and Management Development

There are four rather distinct phases of the learning function which are of particular interest to management development strategists (Exhibit 8-3).

1. *Initial orientation and indoctrination period.* This corresponds to the time interval when the management ("trainee") person is first assigned to a particular position. This phase features becoming familiar with position responsibilities and the activities comprising successful performance, starting to build new or modified skills, becoming acquainted with different or more complex areas of knowledge, starting to establish working relationships, and starting to learn the "do's" and "don'ts" of job activity. This is a highly demanding and often anxious period for the newly assigned person or the individual whose job has been substantially changed. Modeling correct approaches, detailed review of job requirements, helpful coaching and frequent feedback, and talking out of problems are helpful means of starting to deal with performance requirements. The length of this time period varies considerably, reflecting both individual and job considerations. "Person A," for example, is an individual who is making faster progress than is "person B." That is, by the end of time period 1, "A" has been able to demonstrate greater competency than "B."
   Curves "A" and "B" can also be thought of as representing two different managerial development situations. For example, the "A" curve could show the "typical" time experience for a person in a given area to gain competency for a lower-level managerial position relative to the "average" experience at a

EXHIBIT 8-3
Management Development Learning Model

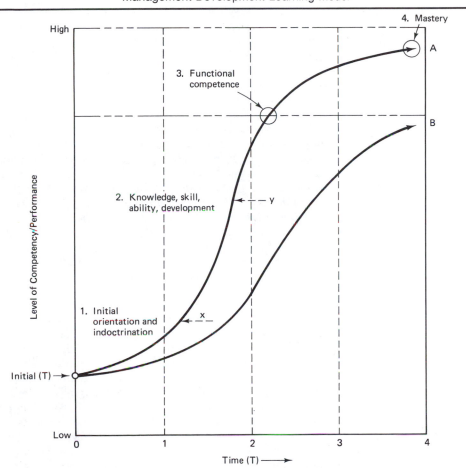

more advanced level (curve "B"). "Level of Competency" is established through performance appraisal ratings, comparisons with the initial learning requirements or experiences of previous jobholders and job analysis. "Average time" to achieve the initial competency level can be established in a similar manner and also provide an important development benchmark for the "trainee."

2. *Knowledge, skill, and ability (K-S-A) development.* The start of this phase is a critical transitional period. The awkwardness and mistakes of getting started are replaced by a growing concentration on learning combinations of knowledge, skill, and abilities that produce particular results. If basic K-S-As have been learned well in the initial phase, performance/competency improvement in this phase should be relatively more rapid suggested by an "inflection point," *x*, in the learning function. If this is the case, the anxiety

and concerns of early phases should be replaced gradually by more positive motivational feelings—individual job-related satisfaction should be improving. Positive gains in job proficiency are thus often linked to more positive feelings regarding ones work progress and attitude toward the job. It is well to note that even at the conclusion of this period, the work performance of the person will still be significantly less than "functional competence" or level of adequate performance. This may have "practical significance" for the unit, especially if the person in training is a unit manager or one with substantial or broad responsibilities.

3. *Functional competence.* This should correspond to that level of performance considered fully acceptable or satisfactory in performance appraisals. The approximation of this performance level is usually signaled by another inflection point (y) which for practical purposes means that rapid performance gains from new or additional learning have started to level off and most of the individual's concerns are with improvement or refinement. The overall elapsed time to achieve "functional competency" may be substantial, almost two years for person "A." If "B" were another manager being developed for a similar position, progress would probably be judged "unacceptable." On the other hand, if the "B" experience was typical, then "A" 's performance might provide a concrete basis to judge a individual as "high potential," at least on the key criteria of learning speed and adaptability to job conditions or requirements.

4. *Mastery.* This phase is often much longer than the total time involved in the first three. Competency here is equated to that at a consultive level or being able to lead or carry out research or product development, for example. If general managerial or administrative tasks were involved, this person would be seen as a sophisticated or seasoned manager, capable of rendering good, thoughtful decisions and providing sound advice to colleagues or those working under him or her. The length of the "mastery phase," individual differences aside, varies with authority level/salary grade and field of specialization. Specific situations vary so widely that generalizations regarding the length of this period are of little help. In technically oriented or general management positions, the "mastery phase" could easily be six or seven years if the first three entailed, say, one and one-half to two years.

Although specific situations vary greatly, what is of importance is that knowledge, skills, and ability levels at critical points be recorded. These can serve as benchmarks potentially for strategic planning analyses, self-assessment and development, individual career planning, performance appraisals, and assessment of potential.

The Learning Function, Individual Learning Style, and Individual Potential.   Acquaintance with learning function concepts and the fit of it to an individual's learning style and performance and career objectives is a key focus of individual development planning. It can help to strengthen individual self-assessment skills and thus the opportunity of the person to act in a more informed and independent way regarding their professional and career needs. To the extent that an individual's learning makeup and needs suggest a particular calculated time to achieve "functional competence," another "window" may be created for viewing individual potential. That is, by significantly bettering the time estimates for achieving requisite K-S-As, individuals may provide a concrete demonstration of learning competencies.

The Learning Function and Job Analyses.   The practicality of using learning functions as a guide for planning analyses depends greatly on the degree to which managerial positions are thoroughly analyzed relative to conventional position descriptions factors, required activities (behaviors) for successful performance, and the related time requirements. The required activities serve as a concrete basis for which needs analyses can be performed, required knowledge-skills-abilities identified, and time estimates developed to approximate each of the four learning phases.

The Planning Perspective in Development Approaches

The nature of management education and learning with its numerous options and complicating considerations requires a flexible planning framework. Contingency approaches that are oriented to the particulars of situation and permit the handling of these in an organized framework often prove helpful. A general framework for approaching managerial education and development in a reasonably disciplined way is as follows. *Establishing learning objectives*, which are central to strategizing development options, reflects the joint resolution, through general needs analysis, of person, job, and organization situation. Most immediately affecting the accomplishment of learning objectives is the instructor's or *supervising manager's competency and style*, the *framework* for organizing the learning experience, the *individual's learning style*, and the *development methods*. The work context of support (or otherwise) and the more general internal environment or organizational "culture" for support further affect how well learning objectives are achieved. These general factors and some related details affecting the meeting of learning objectives are summarized in Exhibit 8-4.

Some of the key points are further developed elsewhere in this or other chapters as they relate to strategic issues. Notes referring to specific corporate experiences as in the case of Honeywell, Inc., and Control Data are described more fully in other chapters. However, many details of this subject matter go far beyond the scope of this book.

Applying the Strategic Contingency Framework

What follows are some characteristic situations encountered in management development and how these might be viewed strategically using the framework presented in Exhibit 8-4.

EXHIBIT 8-4
Characteristics of the Management Development Learning Model

Learning objectives	• Education and development needs assessment • Needs analysis including person, job, and organization • Developmental tasks vs. job centered (current job) • Criteria of successful performance (e.g., successful end-job behaviors, specific competencies, or targeted knowledge improvement)
Supervisor's style and competency	• Supervisor's approach to "trainee" learning and interpersonal skills • Supervisor's own background, flexibility, and competency (e.g., use of feedback) • Quality of supervisor-trainee relationship • Supervisor's orientation (e.g., person centered vs. subject centered) • "Learning function" • Career stages and "developmental tasks"
Framework for knowledge—skill organization	• Inductive vs. deductive learning • Cognitive vs. experience based • Behavioral science, systemic problem solving, functional management, management processes, and/or historical (e.g., organization culture) • Requisite time spans inherent in position behaviors • Matrix of jobs and requisite knowledge or skills (e.g., as applied at Honeywell, Inc., or Control Data) • "Job grid" relating knowledge need and career stage (e.g., Honeywell, Inc.) • Requisite flexibility and adaptability
Individual learning	• Learning style (e.g., reflective, abstract conceptualization); hands-on/concrete experience, active experimentation, active discussion/information interchange • Combining methods (e.g., hear it, see it, experience it) for further reinforcement of learning gains • Moderating influences including maturity, experience, career/life-cycle position/ stage, and present social/cultural situation

(Continues)

EXHIBIT 8-4 (Continued)

	• Motivation to learn, clarity of objectives to person, and felt need or desire to learn
Development methods or technology	• On-the-job coaching, classroom format (e.g., lecture, film, cases)
	• Learning labs, simulation; programmed/ self-instruction
	• Active engagement/passive response
	• Behavioral modeling (e.g., by supervisor)
	• Use of feedback
	• Action learning, problem or theory centered
	• Learnee control (adult education mode) vs. instructor control

Source: Based in part on David A. Gray, James C. Quick, and Ann Laird, "A Contingency Model of the Management Learning Environment." *Academy of Management Proceedings* (Atlanta, GA), 1979; pp. 39–43.

Example 1: Management Trainee, Young Inexperienced. For this type of situation, and as brought out previously in the career/learning discussions, needs analyses usually initially emphasize knowledge acquisition. If trainees are assigned or rotated into a particular unit for initial development, they are expected to become familiar with a body of knowledge, including principles, concepts, and details of their functional area. A secondary but important theme of this assignment (and career stage) is to gain an initial acquaintance with how the organization works (i.e., the nature of the organization's culture). Another part of this initial learning or familiarization stage is to start developing relational competencies. The latter involves the ability of the person to work well with others, including those outside of his unit and also to learn how to learn from these people. Finally as the "trainee" moves toward the completion of this stage of learning, opportunities should be provided for the person to acquire or demonstrate the potential for competency in "developmental tasks." This is likely to be a good indicator of the person's future potential since they involve competencies associated with the next or generally higher-level positions.

Strategists will often have to present guidelines or some scenarios (alternate approaches) as to how the learning (or career) models can be actualized. The following is a representative scenario. To achieve the first learning objective of knowledge acquisition a supervisor could initially describe a (the) learning model and how the learning is going to be approached. Most "trainees," hearing this coming from a line manager, are likely to sense a greater ring of truth than if it were to come from staff person (e.g., a Human Resource/personnel department member). Further, as far as he or she is concerned, what the "boss" says does command attention. A specific approach then would be to organize department documents and processes in a structured way and to discuss these in a directive and subject-oriented style to assure specific content coverage and efficient use of time. These materials, in turn, could be further assigned to the "trainee" for reading along with some specific collateral readings. This initial strategy emphasizes cognitive or rational approaches. It provides the big picture and how things go together and/or are handled. The trainee would have to call into play reflective abilities and be able to move through these mentally in logical fashion, which should establish a basis for (actual) individual actions.

As the person starts to acquire important areas of knowledge, the learning strategy shifts toward more of an adult-oriented, person-centered approach. Quite naturally, the emphasis also shifts toward doing rather than merely understanding. Facilitation by the supervisor and the opportunity of the trainee to put the knowledge to work in a specific way "concretizes" the learning as the realities of application must be confronted. These ideas emphasize "hands-on" experience, and the "trainee" is (largely) in charge of putting the approaches to work. Additionally, as confidence is gained, the "trainee" will be more willing to experiment with modified approaches and this (it is hoped) will be supported by the supervising manager and others to assure generalization of the learning experiences. Supervisors also may role play difficult situations (in a protected environment) with the request that the "trainee" utilize a special programmed tape or perhaps a subject-specific workshop to gain further understanding and hands-on experience in application.

Also, keep in mind that the supervising managers and other authority figures constantly serve as models (good or bad!) for the trainee's actions.

The best learning situations are characteristically those in which multiple methods or processes can be combined and thus gain the reinforcement or synergy of these combined inputs. This avoids undue reliance on a particular approach. If the "trainee," for example, reads and participates in discussion and then experiences a situation, learning and retention are often affected favorably.

Example 2: Managerial Development.   Education and development for mature, experienced organization members are generally more complicated than in the trainee situation just described. Learning strategies are complicated, for example, by positional and environmental considerations. Also, these positions involve more complex sets of behaviors needed for success, the realities and politics of the organization, and organization culture and the encouragement or resistance to development methods such as cross-transfers. To deal with a realistic situation but one that is manageable in this context, for a moment assume that a major learning objective is to strengthen decision-making skills related to employee-centered problems. This learning objective involves communications skills (speaking, body language, style, mannerism), people sensitivities, and active leadership skills. This formidable array assuredly won't be "learned" in a short time period or in one "sitting." Building this competency is a long-involved task of successive approximation. The process is considered active and part of conscious strategy so long as progress is being made or new(er) learnings are in evidence; also, baselines and criteria must exist to judge progress. The learning requirement may go beyond the time available in a particular assignment or by a supervising manager. Thus the planning or individual development record will need the capability to track skill gains over an extended time period.

Unfortunately, many needs analyses turn almost immediately to "how to" types of questions related to education technology or method. We have experienced the best results for person-oriented learning objectives that center first on the learner! People who are seen as authentic to others in people-related decisions usually have a good sense of self. Therefore, initial learning approaches will often seek to encourage the person to "get more in touch with him- or herself." Areas of inquiry for the individual would include, for example, how they learn from or react to stress. What happens when they are physically or mentally tired? How do they respond when judged on the basis of subjective factors? How do they deal with conflict? The fulfillment of the potential in individual self-direction will depend on the person starting to get answers to these questions.

Following this phase of personal examination and encouragement of self-growth, greater attention is directed to such topics as

- Guidelines for dealing with situations characteristic of the position function or office.
- Decisions instituted in the past and why these did or didn't work.
- Sharing experience as to personal style found particularly effective for the situations previously outlined and why these (apparently) worked.
- Tips in dealing realistically with organizational/time pressures—which events can be delayed and which command immediate attention.

"Sessions," to the extent that they assume a formal flavor, are often didactic (one on one), are built around actual situations, and emphasize active discussion and feedback. To make the most of learning experiences, the trainee's manager would, it is hoped, be able to demonstrate adaptive approaches ("accommodation"), model desired behaviors, encourage active experimentation, and seek to strengthen individual ability to exploit concrete experience (see Gray et al., 1979, for an adaptive approach, modeling of desired behaviors, and excellent summary discussion on contingency approaches to learning). Also helpful support is gained from lab-type training, workshops, or classroom-type instruction; these usefully supplement coaching approaches, especially where concept or knowledge need to be studied and mentally "sifted through." Examples of these "challenging" applications include job redesign or restructuring, collective bargaining approaches or dispute resolution, marketing strategies, or the reorganization of units. Interlaced throughout these informal and formal learning situations should be various case studies and group discussions. This is especially helpful among peers where problem-solving exercises, use of behavioral instruments (e.g., attitude survey approaches and interpretation), and design of action research and its interpretation would also be integrated in these experiences.

Practical experience has been gained with various learning methods and their relative effectiveness. This information often proves useful in rounding out the planning perspective presented in this section. Selected points are summarized briefly in the next section.

Learning Processes and Methods

It is almost paradoxical that a discussion of learning methods and processes appears at this point relative to the length and scope of the preceding discussions. The rationale is that strategic planning approaches to management development have the purpose of sifting through the complex area of environmental, work, and individual considerations, as these will affect the selection of methods and processes. Development is often specific to a position and focused on strengthening individual performance to achieve a functional competency level as quickly as possible. Modern strategic approaches require that position or work context be dealt with adequately, both as it exists *and* for the form it is expected to assume in the future. Strategic analyses also seek to establish viable learning options relative to contextual considerations, job, person, and the availability and potency of learning processes and methods variables. A number of the options were summarized in Exhibit 8-4.

In this section, learning processes and methods are addressed in the following order: methods, ease of learning, and retention. Because of its considerable importance, many features of "coaching" are dealt with in a separate section that follows.

Management Development Methods

Although particular learning approaches such as coaching are strongly favored by most organizations, development strategies need to take account of the relative effectiveness of various methods for specific needs. Several corporate studies of management methods (e.g., Control Data, Honeywell) plus research studies conducted by ourselves and colleagues provide the basis for the generalizations that follow. For example, *coaching* relationships are excellent generally for communicating a sense of timing, gaining an understanding of organization politics, clarifying complex planning and decision issues, anticipating various managerial type of problems, and dealing with motivational issues. *On-the-job experiences* are particularly well suited for managers (trainees) gaining product knowledge, firsthand experience in dealing with conflicts, and familiarization with operational processes and work systems. *Formal learning* (defined as over two but less than six instructional days) *approaches* are typically favored in communicating structured knowledge such as mathematical modeling, interpretation or design of business systems, and planning methods. The *classroom-type* formal program (defined as six or more instructional days) is favored where much depth must be built in an area that is technically oriented, complex conceptually, or both. *Workshops* (defined as two or less instructional days) provide the advantage of facilitating hands-on experience and prove helpful where subject matter is technically "flavored" but not highly complex and/or where participants can draw on their experiences or general preparation.

In general, each of the learning strategies presents the following strong features.

Coaching/mentoring.   Featured here are understanding the nuances of organization politics, how the "culture" or system works, and how to deal with it effectively. Coaching approaches are excellent for sharing experience as to how to size-up problems or communicating approaches that work. Complex personnel, competitive, or policy situations frequently require interpretation of a seasoned person to make sense out of these. Even in techniques such as planning that frequently exploit "classroom learning," coaching provides the reality of interpretation and the problems that need to be grappled with, which are so necessary for successful planning. More on coaching appears in the next main section.

Education Courses and Seminars.   This involves efficient communication of much structured knowledge, where in-depth instruction is required or relatively complex or technical subject matter is to be covered. Platform skills, labor law, time management techniques, computer systems operation, job-(re)design principles, and planning models naturally lend themselves to these approaches.

On the Job.   Some situations simply must be experienced to gain familiarity. Work on the job builds familiarity with what is involved, helps to develop one's own feelings in response to the situation, and to gain an opportunity to build understanding, experiment with approaches, and build competence. "Discovering" good sources of information and use of lateral communications, and gaining confidence in the delegation of responsibilities, the believability of various employee commitments, and who has what talent—all are part of a critical reasoning process possible through on-the-job experiences.

Relative Effectiveness of Methods

A survey of a group of 160 senior management development people provided another basis for judging the relative effectiveness of various management development methods for particular skill or behavior areas.

These results confirm the confidence in coaching as a major factor in management development programming. Exhibit 8-5 makes it clear that coaching is seen as the most effective and widely used approach for a representative selection of 17 different management development knowledge, skill, and trait areas. It was named as among the most effective for 15 of the 17 subject areas. On the other hand, skill applications such as forecasting, planning, and written communications reflected high ratings for more formal learning activities.* Also, particular types of formal learning, as in "gaming," were seen as beneficial for problem-solving situations. For situations involving interpersonal relationships and dealing with behavioral issues, the high ratings to role-playing techniques are understandable. The foregoing not-withstanding, the strength ascribed to coaching is evident.

Another aspect of learning relative to particular skills or behaviors is that these methods vary in terms of ease of learning. Thus, time to learn or whether the person is likely to learn some of these skills or knowledge areas, as a practical matter, is an important strategic consideration.

Ease of Learning and Most Effective Methods

The ease of learning various skills or approaches "popular" in management development programming varies widely. The results from the survey previously referenced suggest that particular skills or behaviors, especially where personality features are involved, are the "most difficult" to (change) improve. The panel of senior managers felt, for example, that innovation, integrity, and even motivation were among the most difficult and challenging from a development viewpoint (Exhibit 8-6). For some additional and interesting expert experiences with the learning aspects of leadership and motivation, see the section on expert experiences ("What Works?"). Viewed as being far easier to deliver are skill areas involving written communications, monitoring the environment, technical areas, and even social skills.

Individual Learning and Retention

As noted earlier, the best learning situation for the person is usually one where multiple methods are used. For example, incumbents need to see, read about, and actually experience a particular situation. When all three learning modes are combined, learning and retention can go up dramatically. For a given period of retention, say, perhaps one year, the following hypothetical percentages (because there are so many variables) suggest the power of combining these approaches:

Approach	Retention
1. Read about it	20%
2. Read about it and see or visualize it	45
3. Read, see, and experience (or process) it	65
4. Read, see, experience, and reinforce it	75

The numbers aren't meant to be exact, but they do convey the potential power of learning and retention through the use of multiple methods.

---

*"Formal learning" involves seminar-type instruction with the instructors organizing and actively guiding the learning experience (workshop was defined as more informal). "Formal program" is learning largely in a school (or similar environment).

EXHIBIT 8-5
Most Effective* Methods for Skill Achievement
(in rank order)

Motivation/Leadership	*Social*	*Technical/Functional*
Coaching	Coaching	On-the-job-training
Role playing	Role playing	Formal learning†
Gaming	TV-video	Coaching
Workshops	Gaming (simulation)	Formal programs‡
Written Communications	*Verbal Communication*	*Interviewing/Appraising*
Formal learning	Coaching	Role playing
Formal programs	Workshops	Workshops
Workshops	Role playing	Coaching
Coaching	Formal learning	Gaming
Training/Coaching	*Forecasting*	*Planning*
Coaching	Formal programs	Formal programs
Role playing	Formal learning	Formal learning
Workshops	On-the-job-training	Gaming
On-the-job-training	Gaming	On-the-job-training
Problem Solving/Decision Making	*Delegation/Monitoring*	*Integrity*
Gaming	On-the-job-training	Coaching
On-the-job-training	Coaching	On-the-job training
Workshops	Workshops	General reading
Coaching	Role playing	Workshops
Innovation	*Monitoring Environment*	*Change Management*
On-the-job training	Coaching	Coaching
Gaming	On-the-job-training	Workshops
Workshops	Workshops	Gaming
Coaching	Formal programs	On-the-job-training
Consideration for Employees	*Organizational Commitment*	
Role Playing	Coaching	
Coaching	Job rotation	
Workshops	On-the-job-training	
On-the-job-training	Workshops	

*"Most effective" are: first-quartile items, $N = 156$.

†"Formal learning" is defined in terms of a structured learning experience (company program or in college/university setting, greater than two session days but equal to or less than five program days). ‡"Formal program" was defined as exceeding five program days.

The learning method or process is also viewed as a having a dramatic effect on individual retention. The retention factors presented in Exhibit 8-7 were identified and rated by a group of 160 senior development managers who were surveyed for these purposes. Rated as of the highest importance were immediate applicability, hands-on processing, the supervisor's reinforcement, and the willingness (motivation) of the person to enter into development programming initially. Interestingly, age and even financial recognition (e.g., salary increase) were seen only as modestly important factors.

EXHIBIT 8-6
Ease of Learning Managerial Skills and Attitudes
($N = 156$)

Factors	Mean Values*	
Innovation	1.500	Most difficult
Integrity	1.708	
Motivation/leadership†	1.727	
Managing change	1.902	
Problem solving/decision making	2.088	
Training/coaching	2.167	
Delegation/monitoring	2.223	
Organizational commitment	2.230	Moderate difficulty
Verbal communication	2.289	
Forecasting	2.298	
Consideration for employees	2.318	
Interviewing/appraising	2.367	
Planning	2.426	
Written communications	2.460	
Monitoring environment	2.466	
Social skills	2.496	
Technical/functional skills	2.763	Least difficult

†1 = Very difficult to learn, 2 = difficult to learn, 3 = easy to learn, and 4 = very easy to learn.

*See the "What Works?" section of this chapter for some alternate, expert views.

Source: Elmer H. Burack, "Survey of the Relative Effectiveness of Management Development Methods," Biennial Meeting, Australian Institute for Development, Adelaide, 1978.

Deductive Versus Inductive Information Processing.   Other things being equal, inductive learning (ground up to a generalization) may take longer, but as the person builds relationships, the processing of information and trying to figure out how things connect up often improves retention. On the other hand, deductive learning, often favored in formal schooling as in lecture methods, can efficiently provide an overview or main ideas in a time-efficient manner—but may lead to poorer retention experiences because of failure to stimulate the listener and/or confusion in meaning. Also, the nature of information or knowledge to be retained may be an additional consideration. These observations notwithstanding, the panel of experts gave a slight edge to deductive over inductive approaches. Efficient overall learning strategies have often led to combining both inductive and deductive approaches.

Importantly, these are survey results, and the findings must be approached critically as additional research provides more solid bases for planning purposes. Regardless, strategists will need to be sensitive to these differences in planning approaches.

EXHIBIT 8-7
Retention Factors in Skill Development

Factors	Mean*	Quartiles
(c) Immediate applicability	3.800	
(i) Experimental or "hands-on" learning	3.762	1
(o) Supervisor's reinforcement	3.734	
(a) Employee willingness to use/do (initially)†	3.662	
(b) Supervisor's counseling (preprogram)	3.393	
(g) Deductive teaching format‡	3.362	2
(p) Performance appraisal (postprogram)	3.293	
(n) Feedback by instructor (postprogram)	3.229	
(f) Inductive teaching format‡	3.190	
(h) Length of training program	2.985	3
(d) Participant's educational background	2.912	
(l) Promotion recognition after training	2.894	
(m) Administration of training program	2.800	
(j) Lecture-discussion format in program	2.750	4
(k) Financial recognition (e.g. more pay) after training	2.536	
(e) Age	2.316	

Note *1 = No effect, 2 = little effect, 3 = some effect, and 4 = significant effect.

†Recent studies (e.g., Sonnenfeld et. al., 1985) suggest that trainee expectations—(preprogram)—are a major factor in program success (and retention).

‡Other studies suggest that these factors be reversed; that is, inductive learning is superior to deductive for retention purposes.

Source: Elmer H. Burack, "Survey of the Relative Effectiveness of Management Development Methods," Biennual Meeting, Australian Institute for Development, Adelaide, 1978. Also, see Elmer H. Burack, and Robert D. Smith, *Personnel Management: A Human Resource Systems Approach.* (New York: John Wiley, 1982), for added details.

Combining Developmental Strategies

Although each developmental approach has its own particular strong points, strategic thinking dictates that these be thought of in combinations best suited to the situational reality with which one is dealing. Thus, a "formal learning" approach initially may be best, then a shift to coaching for clarification of organizational matters, on-the-job experiencing, and then perhaps later to "workshop" learning for experience sharing or updating on new developments. For example, when human resource planning methods were first introduced, many Human Resource managers lacked formal preparation in mathematics, statistics, modeling, computer approaches, and longer-range planning methods. Formal classroom-type instruction and workshops proved helpful to many in establishing general familiarity with these models and approaches. Coaching by senior Human Resource/personnel officials and those in "planning" and functional units as well provided the needed rounding out of effective and workable approaches. The subsequent introduction of human resource planning programs and the experiences gained from these provided an excellent and practical hands-on learning situation. As advances were made in these organizational programs and more companies introduced these methods, learning and shared experiences in seminars and workshops were additionally beneficial.

Coaching

Coaching has become the centerpiece for management development planning and strategic approaches. One shouldn't ignore, however, the fact that coaching may be accomplished through *various* position relationships, although the relationship with one's supervising manager is a primary one. These relations express varying degrees of interdependencies, exposure to alternate viewpoints, and needed bases for communications. They also reflect the degree of liking, respect, and general cordiality of the relationships.

Coaching is a method preferred in many organizations and with good reason. It is consistently rated as being among *the* most effective for development purposes. Some questions need to be asked here. Can supervising managers enter into the learning process (enthusiastically) and what is their capacity for teaching? Can we teach the "teacher"? Does he or she know the appropriate "whys" and "whats" to ask to be effective in building insightful experiences for the subordinates? Does the manager recognize the requirements for being a good teacher of mature people? a good coach? Can he or she accurately recognize the needs of subordinates? Ideally, of course, the answer to these questions regarding the supervising manager is "yes." What new or different considerations are raised by the coach whose role is *not* that of being the trainee's supervisor?

Since the line supervisor/coach is likely to be the main "teacher" in the individual's learning process, the quality of his or her relationship will be a key one in learning. The core of a coaching training method is the manager-subordinate relationship. This one-on-one relationship offers the (potential) advantage of personalized instruction and attention and a quick feedback mechanism. As the individual progresses in the organization, he or she may rely less on job learning or technical skills and be more concerned with socialization and development tasks (for career pursuits). The supervisor who can help subordinates to develop successfully in this manner performs a highly valuable service. The "coach" may also be a mentor, who can offer the appropriate types of guidance needed by the individual in moving into the organization's "inner circle" of key people. Over time, the manager/coach can help the individual start to transform further experience gains into useful insights related to the organization's culture and the type of insights (wisdom) needed in senior decision making. The difference between experience and knowledgeable insights or wisdom is considerable. Obviously, it is essential to find the coaching approaches that will assist the individual in achieving meaningful work and career experiences. It is also critical to involve (motivate) the coach/manager in a meaningful way, one that is supported by the organization's reward system. The organization's culture must both support the "trainee's" efforts as well as those of the coach/manager.

A pragmatic example of coaching related to behavioral modeling for development is presented in the applications section of this chapter.

What Works? The Views of Some Experts*

Most everyone concerned with management development, including planners and strategists, have confronted the pragmatic question of "what works?"

There are many professionals who work in the training and development field because of the great and continuing demand for these capabilities. Some have achieved expert status because of a long-established "track record" of superior results. Three members of this select group, a portion of whose work is the basis for this section, are Fred D. Fiedler, John Miner, and Phillip J. Decker. What do they share in common and why their inclusion in this section, aside from their high professional reputations? Put simply, each has worked with success in an area of much importance to the management development field. Fiedler's work in leadership has achieved international stature; his more recent work, described as "Leader Match," is one of the approaches described in this section. Miner's work in "managerial motivation" has led to good results in a very difficult and challenging area. And Decker is an acknowledged expert in the area of behavioral modeling; his application, refinement, and knowledge of this derived work from the field of social learning theory is impressive. Behavioral modeling is described in this section, and an example is presented elsewhere in this chapter.

"Leader Match"

"Leader Match" is a well-developed program that improves self-awareness and understanding of participants of the fit of leadership style and situation.† The program can be delivered in a comparatively short time (perhaps six to eight hours). It uses a variety of approaches and results in frequent, significant improvements in performance ratings and positive trainee responses. Programmed instruction and lecture, among other teaching approaches, have been used with equal effectiveness. Women seemed to change as readily as men, and in some cases their performance was superior. Some 19 studies of "Leader Match" have been undertaken in various industrial and military settings, and 18 of these indicated substantial improvements. Organizations included were Sears, Inc., Texas-Gulf Sulfur, and the U.S. Military Academy.

In brief, "Match" involves understanding one's capabilities, assessing three key situational factors, inferring the degree of situational control, and then electing an appropriate strategy. The three situation variables are

---

*This section based on a seminar held at the annual meeting Academy of Management, San Diego, CA, August 1985.

†Interpretations are those of the writer.

Leader-member relations and the extent to which the manager can count on group support or concurrence with his or her style or approach; *task structure*, which includes work objectives, procedures, and aspects of technology that affect individual actions; and *position power* of the manager, that is, his or her authority to reward, punish, or "carry weight" with decision makers in the organization. Based on their assessment of control of the situation, the "leader" may opt for a strategy of adjusting his or her leadership style or modifying the situation.

Based on reported results, it appears that deep-seated behavioral changes are difficult to achieve, and thus modifying the situation may prove to be a more practical approach. Although there may be some modification of attitudes, interests, or habit patterns, these usually don't involve deeply rooted behavioral changes. The general emphasis consequently is on situational modification. For example, managers may choose to vary the amount of information they share (affects the amount of power shared), or they may choose to involve various subordinates in decisions (affects task structures), or they may be less directive in follow-up of assignments (affects employee-leader relations).

What generalizations come out of this work which affect management development planning and approaches?

1. Important aspects of leadership, a key dimension of managerial activity, can be defined clearly and taught.
2. Learning effectiveness for the understandings involved is quite high and cost effective.
3. Women changed as readily as men.
4. Individual change experiences indicate that these are relatively stable—some results were checked out over an extended time period, and a continuous positive response to the program persisted.
5. Learning/training approaches for the desired leadership features, whether using programmed instruction, lecture, or a combination of these, seemed to make little difference in results.
6. Although individual change was desired, situational modification was frequently stressed as a more feasible approach. Sufficient alternatives existed that modifying the job was often unnecessary.

"Managerial Role Motivation" *

This management development approach focuses on casting the participant in a managerial role. The data emerge from 10 different studies involving 15 course presentations. They dealt with the types of problems which they faced, many of which involved aspects of supervisor-subordinate relationships. Eleven topics were dealt with, including performance, job-value conflicts, and verbal abilities. Based

---

*Interpretations are those of the writer.

on these motivation-related factors, the results involving four different trainers indicated that overall increases in "motivation to manage" were indicated in 90 percent of the studies. Also, the participant promotion record and recommendations for rehire (if they left the company) were substantially better than was that of nonparticipants.

In one five-year company study of promotion, based on comparing "before and after results," some 85 percent of those "trained" were promoted, while only about 55 percent of the "untrained" received promotions. Rehire recommendations for trainees who subsequently separated from the organizations were twice as high as the unexposed group (69 percent versus 30 percent). Thus even though some self-selection may have affected promotion decisions (i.e., for those receiving training), the ability of people to respond positively to managerial motivation training was given added support by the rehire recommendations.

What overall observations are suggested by this work with "managerial role motivation" training? (Miner, 1985b)

1. Important aspects of managerial motivation can be learned that affect managerial activities and performance.
   a. Components showing the most consistent changes were the development of a more positive or favorable attitude to authority; greater assertiveness and a mature, "take charge" attitude; and increased desire to exercise power over others.
   b. Variations in course administration (frequency of presentations, group size, and delivery mode) appeared to make little difference in results.
2. A range of learning media may be equally useful in managerial development training, though some may be more cost effective or individually attractive than others.
3. Women changed as readily as men, and change was often evident up to one and one-half years after training.
4. Relatively stable individual changes may be feasible in this area of managerial motivation.
5. The proportion of those exposed to training who increased their "motivation to manage" was in the range of 60 to 75 percent.
6. Basic personality changes are likely *not* involved. It appears that what is changing is people's interests or attitudes, which is (further) reinforced in their work roles and work environment (culture).
7. Change tends to occur only among those who have a predisposition toward change, and where no serious personality issues (or blocks) exist.

Behavioral Modeling

Decker's experiences and observations regarding behavioral modeling provided a helpful perspective for this development approach. They are heavily anchored in social learning theory. Aside from the clear distinctions (and differences) drawn in comparison with behavioral modification was the stress placed on it as a process. It capitalizes on the role of cognitive processes as an integral part of behavioral change (Decker, 1985). A well-developed body of theory and research indicates the comparative effectiveness of "social learning processes"—but these require clear and detailed identification of the managerial (performance-related, cognitive) activities and behaviors which are to be learned. This approach acknowledges that most human behavior is "learned observationally through modeling."

Social learning processes have a highly defined structure that can be tailored to a wide variety of learning needs. In management development based on these approaches, individuals have (frequently) experienced improvements in six areas: (1) attitudes, (2) social skills, (3) verbal skills, (4) cognitive skills, (5) memory (factual, material), and (6) manual skills. Observation by the trainee of a person who serves as a "model" can be a powerful basis for individual learning. Decker pointed out, however, that the features of the person serving as "the model" may greatly affect results. For example, "How well does the model (supervising person) fit the trainees' self-image?" and "How good is the model/trainee in sharing or communicating the substantive information needed to make the process effective?" Answers to these questions have a direct bearing on the selection and likely success of managerial coaches relative to trainee/subordinate needs.

Planners, strategists and officials may also wish to pursue a highly useful area of inquiry related to "modeling." The point of this analysis would be to determine the relative proportion of particular managerial roles which involve structured or loosely defined areas. Should additional structure be established through job design? Are there major areas of managerial role performance that depend on "wisdom" and how are people to be prepared to handle these? Answers of these types of questions affect staffing planning, assessment or potential, and the "trainability" of individuals for particular assignments.

Generalizations suggested by the foregoing discussions include the following:

1. *Behavioral modeling* needs to be clearly separated from *behavioral modification* as an individual learning-change approach.
2. Behavioral modeling can be highly effective as a development strategy including its application to the key areas of coaching or even mentoring.
3. The development of information regarding managerial functions, to facilitate application of the process, is likely to enlarge understanding of a particular managerial role which is highly useful in its own right.

General Observations

If now all the observational discussions and summary notes are viewed collectively, what inferences are suggested? On balance, it appears that

- The general theme that the managerial function has a substantive base which can be defined and learned is additionally supported.
- Women fared as well as men in these development approaches, further sup-

porting the contention of general learnability with no justification for sex distinctions.

- Important aspects of motivation, long thought difficult to acquire, can be learned. Miner sums this up well (1985b). Probably it is a process of sensitizing the individual to the managerial role. The process is facilitative of basic personality features of participants interacting with aspects of the managerial process and thereby producing individual changes.
- Important bases upon which the managerial function depends, including qualities of leadership, can also be learned.
- Inquiry into the nature of a particular managerial assignment, and the attempt to define content more precisely for development purposes, may of itself be highly beneficial for planning and strategic purposes.
- Alternative development approaches may be equally successful in bringing about improvements in performance or behavior, although costs of delivery may differ much. (The predisposition for learning or change is a major, perhaps critical, factor in the success of development efforts.)
- More credibility is lent to achieving relatively durable behavioral changes, for the types of behaviors described here.
- Controversy still exists as to whether any basic individual changes take place in development approaches. Regardless, added weight is lent to the possibility for important modifications ("imprints") in behaviors, attitudes, approaches, and performance.

Summary

Although this chapter was concerned primarily with management development methods, the viewpoint taken was that these needed to be viewed in a broader strategic planning context. This has involved organizational considerations, work features, and quite naturally the individual. Organizational and human resource planning provide the crucial translation of organization to individual needs.

The work scene is being approached in much more flexible fashion since it often provides a main stage upon which a variety of development approaches can be orchestrated and blended. In most of these approaches, the work itself, the competencies and personality of the trainee, and the relationship between the "trainee" and supervising manager form basic building blocks from which programs are designed and carried out. Even more to the point is the recognition of the central role played by line management in development programming. Thus, coaching and on-the-job experiences are combined with varying degrees and levels of more formal instructional/educational approaches, both on site and off site.

At this stage, sufficient options exist in developmental approaches and work descriptions so that these can be tailored to individual needs and situation—but with adequate flexibility for changes in the parameters of the learning experience or work-related needs.

Since managerial development typically extends over a considerable time period—months and even years—other considerations beyond the methods per se need to be introduced to understand, guide, and evaluate management development efforts. A number of these were discussed in this chapter and included the adult education model, learning models, and individual career phases. Among other considerations, these perspectives indicate that the individual needs to play an expanded role in his or her own needs determinations and will often have to be outfitted with competencies that facilitate self-assessment, learning how to learn, and learning how to integrate more fully thinking regarding his or her career with strategic career development designs in the organization. Correspondingly strategists, planners, and line managers will need to expand their understanding of the relationships and fits between personal career needs and development approaches related to organizational needs (organization career management).

This chapter also provided descriptions of some means by which the various themes and perspectives could be brought together in a more unified framework. The viewpoint proposed was that learning processes (and careers) should be approached in a phase or stage manner. The chapter on management development systems (Chapter 7) provides added details of this approach.

The final theme addressed in this chapter concerned learning processes and methods. Potentially useful information is being made increasingly available regarding aspects of development likely to be of growing importance to the strategist-planner. These include methods selection relative to skill need, trainability and retention, and judgments of effectiveness for particular learning needs. Also, newer studies or disclosure of expert or corporate experience in development methods will likely represent important future bases for shaping strategies related to methods. At this stage, these findings must be approached critically, but they do represent one basis for approaching strategic matters in a more systematic fashion and with potentially improved results.

Continuing studies of development methods and their underlying assumptions and relative effectiveness can be profitably consulted as these affect existing biases or preconceived notions affecting development. A case in point is that of "expert views" on learning aspects of managerial motivation, the use of alternate methods for particular skills, the use of behavioral modeling, and the time needed to effectuate individual change. In future years, with the prominence given to coaching approaches, behavioral modeling, and trainer-trainee relationships, more attention will likely be directed to these.

A pragmatic example of coaching based on behavior modeling concepts is provided in the applications section for this chapter. The applications section also provides a newer management development method entitled the "organization development, personal growth work shop" (O.D.P.G.).

Other material appearing in the application section for this chapter includes review questions, which have been used in connection with managerial training. It includes review questions and situational applications.

REFERENCES

Baird, John C., Jr. and Gretchen K. Wieting. "Nonverbal Communication Can Be A Motivation Tool." *Training* 22 (February 1985).

Bandura, Albert. *Social Learning Theory*. Englewood Cliffs, NJ: Prentice-Hall, 1977.

Burack, Elmer H. and Nicholas J. Mathys. *Human Resource Planning: A Pragmatic Approach to Manpower Planning and Development,* 2nd ed. Lake Forest, IL: Brace Park Press, 1987.

Burack, Elmer H. and Robert D. Smith. *Personnel Management: A Human Resource Systems Approach*. New York: John Wiley, 1982.

Burns, Herbert W. *Sociological Background of Adult Education*. Chicago: Center for the Study of Liberal Education for Adults, 1964.

Cass, Angelica W. and Arthur P. Crabtree. *Adult Elementary Education*. New York: Noble and Noble, 1956.

Condon, Mary. "How Do You Teach Managers to Think?" *Training and Development Journal,* Vol. 39, no. 3 (March 1985): 16–22.

Daloisio, Tony and Marsha Firestone. "A Case Study in Applying Adult Learning Theory in Developing Managers." *Training and Development Journal,* Vol. 37 (February 1983): 73–78.

Dalton, Gene W., Paul H. Thompson, and R. L. Price. "The Four Stages of Professional Careers: A New Look at Performance by Profession." *Organizational Dynamics,* Vol. 6 (1978): 19–42.

Dalton, Gene W. and Paul H. Thompson. *Novations: Managing Managerial and Professional Careers*. Glenview, IL: Scott, Foresman, 1986.

Darkenwald, Gordon G. and Sharon B. Merriam. *Adult Education Foundations of Practice*. New York: Harper & Row, 1982.

Decker, Phillip J. "Social Learning Theory and Leadership." Annual Meeting, Academy of Management, San Diego, CA, 1985.

Decker, Phillip J. "The Enhancement of Behavior Modeling Training of Supervisory Skills by the Inclusion of Retention Processes." *Personnel Psychology,* Vol. 35 (Summer 1982): 323–332.

Dessler, Gary. *Organization Theory*. Englewood Cliffs, NJ: Prentice-Hall, 1980.

Ely, Mary L. *Adult Education in Action*. New York: American Association for Adult Education, 1936.

Fiedler, Fred. *Leader Match*-in process (1987).

Fiedler, Fred. *A Theory of Leadership Effectiveness*. New York: McGraw-Hill, 1967.

Gray, David A., James C. Quick, and Ann Laird. "A Contingency Model of the Management Learning Environment." *Academy of Management Proceedings* (Atlanta, GA), 1979, 39–43.

Hall, Douglas T. *Careers in Organizations*. Pacific Palisades, CA: Goodyear, 1976.

Jaap, Tom. "Trends in Management Development: Introducing Theory P." *Training and Development Journal,* Vol. 36 (October 1982): 57–62.

Knowles, Malcolm S. *The Modern Practice of Adult Education: Androgogy Versus Pedagogy*. New York: Association Press, 1970.

Kolb, David A. *Experiential Learning-Experience as the Source of Learning and Development*. Englewood Cliffs, NJ: Prentice-Hall, 1984.

Likert, Rensis. *The Human Organization: Its Management and Value*. New York: McGraw-Hill, 1967.

Luthans, Fred and Tim R. V. Davis. "Beyond Modeling: Managing Social Learning Processes in Human Resource Training and Development." *Human Resource Management*, Vol. 20 (Summer 1981): 19–27.

Miller, Edwin L., Elmer H. Burack, and Maryann Albrecht. *Management of Human Resources*. Englewood Cliffs, NJ: Prentice-Hall, 1980.

Martin, Jack and B. A. Hiebert. *Instructional Counseling: A Method for Counselors*. Pittsburgh, PA: The University of Pittsburgh Press, 1985.

Miner, John. *People Problems*. New York: Random House, 1985a.

Miner, John B. "Managerial Role Motivation Training." Annual Meeting, Academy of Management, San Diego, CA, 1985b.

Owens, James A. "A Reappraisal of Leadership Theory and Training." James L. Gibson, John N. Ivancevich, and James H. Donnelly, Jr. eds., *Organizations Close-Up*. Plano, TX: Business Publications, 1985, pp. 219–235.

Schein, Edgar H. *Career Dynamics*. Reading, MA: Addison-Wesley, 1978.

Sonnenfeld, Jeffrey et al. As reported in his paper on "Career Progress and Executive Development Methods," Careers Workshop, Annual Meeting, Academy of Management, San Diego, CA, 1985.

Weiss, Howard M., "Subordinate Imitation of Supervisor Behavior: The Role of Modeling in Organizational Socialization." *Organizational Behavior and Human Performance*, vol. 19 (June 1977): 89–105.

"Who, What, and Where." *Training* 22 (November 1984): 39–47.

Wilson, Robert A. "Management Development: Whose Job?" *Human Resource Planning*, vol. 1 (1983): 49–53.

APPLICATIONS SECTION

1. Coaching and Behavioral Modeling

The coaching situation represents one of the outstanding opportunities to apply behavioral modification and modeling techniques to an area of great importance in strategic management development. Although all coaching situations involve some degree of modeling or attempts to modify behavior, the approaches described here are systematic and specific so as to increase the likelihood of positive results.

The importance assigned to coaching in management development suggests that some of its potential benefits be more thoroughly examined. One dimension of coaching that has been receiving growing attention is that of behavioral modeling. That is, recognizing that the supervising manager's role* and literally how it is

---

*Role models may also be managers other than the supervisor.

enacted, provides an important basis for knowledge and skill transfer to the "trainee." Thus combining the knowledge of how to handle particular situations with observation, practice, and doing represents a highly potent approach. These approaches are additionally important because they also serve very important motivational functions—providing positive support and reinforcement for their successful enactment. Those managers, officials, and planners familiar with these techniques may wish to skip this applied example. However, the experience of many suggests that too few of these proven techniques have been applied to management development which qualifies easily as one of the most important applications. The following is a characteristic situation which has been "scripted" for these management development situations and thus is representative of some of their possibilities.

Sales Supervision

Fred Block was employed as a "sales representative" for a major pharmaceutical-drug company, Jackson-Marsh, for better than 10 years. Fred graduated from Penn State with a B.A. in Business Administration and with a marketing concentration. He was recruited by Jackson-Marsh before graduating from school and joined a year-long training program shortly after finishing school. During his training years he worked in four major consumer products divisions which involved field sales and manufacturing experience. In addition, he spent almost two months in the headquarters unit of Jackson-Marsh located in Connecticut. In the headquarters, his experiences involved customer service, technical service, credit, sales planning, order processing, inventory control, quality control, planning, and traffic. When Fred was nearing the completion of his training program and because of superior performance in training, he was given a choice of assignments—one of the four selling divisions or the headquarters unit. Fred chose Chain-Store Sales/Consumer Products, Domestic (CSS/CPD).

In the next five years, he had a variety of assignments in CSS/CPD and gradually worked his way up in the division—his experiences covered everything from restocking and detail work to customer service to quality complaints, opening up new accounts, shelf displays, and even a "loan-out" assignment with CSS/CP Foreign. In the latter, he was part of a project team that helped to set up a major sales office in Mexico. He was chosen because of his excellent progress ("high-potential" rating for some four years) and language competency in Spanish. This assignment, his last as a sales representative, served as a direct stepping stone to CSS/CPD sales management.

Part of Jackson-Marsh's strategic business planning included a major expansion of its Sunbelt field sales (i.e., Florida to California) to meet the fast-growing opportunities as a result of major demographic shifts. Also, to gain better coverage, three new sales districts were to be established spanning from Florida to Southern California. These new districts would require highly competent and aggressive managers and salespeople, all of whom had to be bilingual (English and Spanish). These new assignments would also be excellent proving grounds for individual competencies and thus mobility toward more senior managerial positions. The company's approach was the "blueprint" most likely to affect Fred's future, and thus Fred was very attentive. Fred reviewed future organizational needs with his manager and the possible impact of this on his own knowledge, skills, and abilities. It was agreed that Fred be granted temporary leave to attend an eight-week middle management program of a major university.

Upon completion of the program, Fred was assigned to Walter Hicks, Southeast field sales manager. Hicks was just a few years older than Fred. He had been identified as "high potential" at an early point in his career after joining Jackson-Marsh and had benefited from careful guidance of his career development by his line manager and with the considerable support of the HR development manager. After a series of assignments which involved only general guidance, Hicks was able to get a much better "handle" on Fred's needs relative to a sales supervisory position. In Hicks's semiannual human resources report to CSS headquarters (copy to CSS Human Resources), he reported on the progress of all high potentials and the promotability of all his personnel. The summary assessments included a highly detailed analysis of progress on *10 managerial performance dimensions* (e.g., "successful introduction of new product lines"). Also, he had to provide examples of "trainee" actions demonstrating understanding, finesse or expertise relative to corporate philosophy, major missions, and corporate values and bases for internal managerial planning, problem solving, and decision-making activities.

One of Hicks's challenges in coaching Fred was to be able clearly and precisely to define sales management issues of major significance to the division and corporation—and means of dealing with these. A case in point had to do with the growing problem area of customer complaints involving sales supervisors. The sales supervisors for the most part were old-line salespeople who had been promoted to supervision, primarily for the purpose of breaking in new supervisors and showing them how to handle special problems and major customer complaints. Difficulties arose and the customer situation was greatly exacerbated because

1. Most of the new "trainees" were college graduates and much younger than the sales (training) supervisors.
2. Rapid expansion in the Sunbelt areas had led to the promotion of various supervisors, who themselves lacked training in dealing with some of the new products. Sales supervisors who were poor trainers could readily multiply negative results because of their influence among many new people.
3. Many supervisors were insensitive to the rapid growth in competition and the delicate attachment or questionable loyalty of customers.
4. Customer complaints were going unanswered or lacked full resolution—thus hanging on for months and leading to account dissatisfaction.

Hicks made the sales supervisor/customer complaint issue a high-priority matter in his coaching relationship with Fred. The fact that Hicks also had another management trainee with whom he was working gave him a chance to use some behavioral modeling approaches likely to prove beneficial to both. He tackled the coaching job in the following way.

1. *Issue/problem identification.* Walter Hicks, Southeastern regional manager and acting as Fred Block's coach, identified the sales supervisor/customer complaint issue and drew out in clear fashion, why this has become a problem and the rationale for assigning it such high priority for solution.

2. *Conceptual presentation.* Hicks chose to diagram the problem initially because of its complexity and the fact that two quite different elements were involved: "old-line" sales supervisors as trainers of sales representatives who had a pronounced affect on the customer approaches of the sales representatives and chain store personnel who typically became involved in complaints. Hicks then discussed the types of results that would be seen as successful for each, the behavioral challenges these involved, the different types of skills each would require, and several characteristic scenarios as to how each would be accomplished for different situations.

3. *Demonstration of desired performance.* Hicks then had both "trainees" accompany him on some visits with sales personnel and customers to give them a firsthand opportunity to observe the desired approach in action. He then reviewed the situation and the immediate results were critiqued in a joint discussion. Next, Hicks role played typical situations with Fred and the other management trainee. The general script he had prepared based on actual problem situations made the demonstrations very realistic. Role reversals and capturing the action on videotape gave Hicks a chance to point out in graphic fashion, his strategy in sizing up the situation, approaches, and the rationale for each important action. Also, the fact that Hicks had already established a reputation as a highly competent manager, particularly skilled in dealing with these types of situations, added further to the credibility of the presentation and its acceptance as a desirable way of handling the situations.

4. *Behavioral rehearsal.* In this phase of the coaching, both of the management trainees were involved. The two management trainees followed the prepared script that Hicks had initially used in demonstration—actions again were captured on videotape and critiqued in positive fashion by the observer. The fact that both management trainees were in the same development situation lent further reality to the rehearsals. The rehearsals were used until Hicks felt that both trainees had perfected the skills they would need with the sales supervisors and customers. General role plays were avoided because prescribed types of behavior were being sought for a specific group of characteristic situations. General role plays were used at a different stage in trainee development where only general behavioral guides could be provided by Hicks—and where a manager would conceivably behave differently depending on the circumstances.

5. *Feedback.* The fact that feedback was provided by Hicks and from each management trainee to the other proved highly useful since the viewpoints dif-

fered enough to make these complementary. Also the fact that feedback was relevant, constructive, and nonthreatening added greatly to its value and acceptance. Emphasis was on success—what to do and how to do it to assure a successful outcome. Videotapes also gave the participants a chance to view their performance during the behavioral rehearsals—visually to see aspects of verbal communications, body language, or mannerisms that were habitual or with which they were unaware. Discussions for correcting particular points were seen as supportive and workable. The feedback from the behavioral rehearsals was also immediate and thus allowed for quick correction.

6. *Transfer of training*. The acid test of the coaching and behavioral modeling approach was to assure their transfer to the (actual) job. This was accomplished in several different ways.

   a. A visit from Hicks to Fred (and the other sectional sales manager) to follow up on the coaching-modeling and to reinforce the approaches for actual situations Fred encountered. Fred was asked to maintain a (temporary) log on these types of situations, how he approached them, and the results.

   b. A post coaching-modeling meeting involving Hicks, Fred, and the other sectional manager to discuss situations encountered, problems of application and to rehearse suggested solutions.

Observations on Coaching and the Modeling Approach

The managerial role of coaching provides an opportunity to use a variety of effective techniques for development of junior (or even senior) managers or trainees. The six steps detailed in the marketing/sales example are characteristic ones in a modeling approach. Other sequences are possible and desired depending on the situation. An individual familiar with these approaches can think through a strategy for putting across effectively, ideas which are otherwise difficult to grasp or enact. From the viewpoint of strategic management development, needs and alternative approaches can be better planned. Also, results become more predictable so that coaching becomes more effective and time efficient in getting across complex learnings to the manager/trainee.

2. A Newer Approach to Management Development: The Organization Development Focused, Personal Growth Workshop

The field of management development has long awaited programming approaches that would successfully merge many of the important features of contemporary systems and processes. This need has became greater in recent years because of the rapidly growing complexity of these systems and the increasing danger that disparate parts may remain as such—unfocused, detached, or fail to evidence a unity of purpose. The Organization Development, Personal Growth Workshop (O.D.P.G.)

promises to respond to many of these needs. The fact that a number of management development consulting firms have successfully introduced various versions of this workshop approach (e.g., the managing personal growth, MPG, of Blessing and White) attests to its potential usefulness.

In general, the workshop sessions, anywhere from three to six or more, are an artful design combining individual career planning, organization career management, and performance management. Many of the workshop activities are carried out in an OD mode which, among other benefits, often facilitates much improvement in superior-subordinate relationships. Although many of the commercial programs and corporate organizational adaptations will understandably differ on details or specifics, most contain the following elements:

- *Individual career planning*, which includes values and goal(s) clarification, self-assessment of knowledge, skills, abilities and aptitudes, career focusing, career altneratives, and career pathing to achieve these.
- *Organization career management*, viewing individual careers within the frameworks of unit needs and organization possibilities; needs analysis for individuals which converge on development needs, considering career path alternatives.
- *Performance management*, including clarification of performance objectives and criteria and the resolution of differences in perception between the supervisor and subordinate, identifying means of improving individual performance, improving supervisory-subordinate working relationships, and improving communications (and getting acquainted!) with related or supportive personnel and services.
- *Role analysis and clarification* for both supervisors and subordinates, including seeing the supervisory role in perspective, improving definition of individual jobs and bases for successful performance, and helping new managers (supervisory or subordinate) better define their new role and mutual expectancies.

The great advances made in organization development approaches are evident in the structure, processes, and many of the activities of the workshop. The OD influence is being intentionally called to the attention of the reader because much of the methodology is so well known and widely understood.

The total contact time for this workshop is something in the area of 16 hours or two full days and at times extended to as much as the eqivalent of three or four (program) days. Some organizations have attempted to introduce condensed versions of these workshops, unfortunately, too often with poor results.

An early precautionary note is to avoid premature consideration of the O.D.P.G. Many commercially available workshops offer varying numbers of these activities and processes, divorced from the specific state or the maturity or degree of refinement of a particular company's systems. Although these are likely to provide some benefits to the participants, as a whole these workers are quite different from the O.D.P.G. delivery described here. O.D.P.G. involves only participants from one organization. Second, the "workshop" brings together supervising managers and their subordinates. Third, it is assumed that a sufficient groundwork of processes and environmental support has been established since one of the major current challenges in the organization is to improve work relationships and processes which are a part of the strategic management development system. In short, O.D.P.G. assumes that a given organization has already made significant progress in blueprinting and starting to erect its strategic management development effort.

The O.D.P.G. Workshop—Its Fit in the Strategic Picture

It is difficult to launch into a discussion of the planning and strategic aspects of the O.D.P.G. workshop without having first described its general format, major themes, and functioning. The design is a complex one, but it is hoped that the previous summary has been helpful in providing some familiarity with the approach.

At this juncture, the field of management development has assumed a form with many different elements. There is a need to develop more powerful means for bringing together many of these elements and for artfully carrying out the general planning and strategic thinking underlying contemporary systems. The systems models related to strategic management development provide a basis for integrating the many and varied elements of this approach. But the systems model is largely conceptual and needs to be fleshed out in terms of organization particulars. The methods described elsewhere in this chapter are for the most part techniques, useful for particular situations but not reflective of comprehensive approaches. Development procedures are often diluted because they are separated in time or space (enacted in different areas of the organization). The success of many also depend on the finesse of the supervising manager as supervisor, coach, human resource planner, and career counselor. The O.D.P.G. workshop approach represents an attempt to bring together many elements of modern management development programming, under more controlled conditions, and where these may be carried out in a more efficient manner. Also, there is a need to identify vehicles for program implementation. This is a problem that has continued to plague planners and strategists. In short, much planning and strategizing takes place, but too little time is given over to how to implement these so that they will be successful—and withstand the test of time. The O.D.P.G. is one vehicle which attempts to meet this need.

The workshop format of the O.D.P.G. approach is intended to help both supervising managers and their subordinates "see" how many elements of the strategic management development picture relate and to provide a practical vehicle for getting some of this work done. Our experience with some of these workshops and the responses of participants to (post) questionnaires indicate the possibility for some attractive results. In Exhibit 8-8, participant responses (postworkshop) are highlighted. These results are from one large insurance company which involved over 100 managers and their subordinates in six workshops. The results are summarized under subject categories which form major parts of the strategic management development effort. Although the overall rating was a "7" on a 9-point scale, the results are perhaps more impressive when it is recognized that this was a highly traditional bureaucratic type of organization. These workshops followed almost four years of groundwork that involved, among other things, the creation of a modern Personnel system and the basis for a human resource planning program.

If any generalization is in order, it is perhaps that the benefits of O.D.P.G. are very broad and substantial. A good opportunity is provided to advance individual career thinking and planning by helping to "connect" persons to their innermost needs and values and to consider these along side of their capabilities and career possibilities in *their own* organization. Quite naturally the latter represents potentially a logical direction to channel these needs and strengths. Second, the management of performance is another main "menu" item" which is strengthened considerably through improving supervisor-subordinate work relationships and communications and generally instilling an element of greater mutual respect, trust, and understanding. In many instances, "this workshop" was the first time in which supervisors and their subordinates had had open discussions in a (more) relaxed environment. It respresented an opportunity to uncover differences in outlook affecting communications or performance and to enlarge areas of mutual benefit. Also, subordinates were offered an opportunity to participate in processes leading potentially to the redesign of their jobs for greater job-related satisfaction.

The needs of organization career management have also been advanced by the O.D.P.G. sessions because many of the discussions involved supervising managers who most frequently have the responsibility for unit human resource planning and actualizing programs in their units. At the same time, no small benefit was achieved as supervisory managers gained a better understanding of their role, how managerial role needs are viewed by a subordinate, and practical bases for enacting their newer areas of responsibilities.

Some Reasons Why O.D.P.G. Has Failed

The lack of adequate time, failure to require advance preparation by participants, and lack of good internal organization for the conduct of activities are among the three most important reasons for workshops failing to meet their potential. There are other related problems too, and at times as much can be learned from why an activity doesn't succeed as from the guidelines for success. Participant views on the limitations or shortcomings of these workshops are as follows:

1. Individual Career Planning
    —Need for advance thinking and preparation because of the newness of approaches or areas of thought.
    —Insufficient time within the workshops to develop ideas fully.
    —Being unable to prioritize or "talk out" need areas in the workshops for lack of preworkshop thinking and analysis.

EXHIBIT 8-8
Summary: Participant Benefits of a Personal Growth and Development
Workshop

Individual Career Planning

A. Basics—"Who Am I"

- Personal values clarification.
- Influence of values on what a person does.
- Determination of own priorities.
- Framework to self-access knowledge, skills, abilities, and personality factors.
- Job factors as they affect my personal satisfaction.

B. Career Directions

- Supplementary and valuable format to weigh job alternatives.
- Enriching career decisions based on value-oriented information.
- Structured format to review and clarify value choices.
- Identification of new strength areas.
- Assistance in establishing what is really wanted.

Organization Career Management

- Clarification of constraints and possibilities in career thinking.
- Familiarization with organizational values and their relevance to individual careers.
- Establishment of a firmer basis for individual development planning.
- Critical examination of knowledge, skills and abilities, along with strengths and areas needing strengthening—much of which can be relevant to future career progress.

Performance Management

A. Individual Effectiveness and Performance

- Learnable techniques for brainstorming.
- Provision of workable formats for "selling" ideas.
- Helping new bosses define their expectancies for subordinates, thereby relieving some of the individual's anxieties.
- Motivation to discuss with boss, what I need and want from my job.
- Provision of insights to the boss's priorities and their relation to trainees.
- Development of format to define what is "the" job.

B. Supervisor Subordinate Relationships

- Provision of a basis for approaching one's boss.
- An understanding of outlooks of both on subordinates' skills and bases for these judgments.
- Supplementary and valuable way to get supervisory feedback.
- Surface opinions of boss.
- Motivation for subordinate to seek out boss's performance expectations.
- Communications format to enlist boss's support.

EXHIBIT 8-8 (Continued)

• Basis to improve longer-term relationships.

• Development of format for individual inputs on job design (of one's job).

• Recognition that boss may see things differently, which in some cases indicates a need to seek agreement.

• Catalyzing of thinking in areas of the job and work processes needing change.

C. *Supervisor's (Boss's) Outlook*

• Seeing how it would help "my" subordinates approach me.

• Helping new supervisors define their management role.

D. *Supervisory Management and Performance*

• Helping supervisors define bases for a valuable development program.

• Provision of format to communicate a workable development program.

• Creation of a participative friendly environment facilitating the confrontation of sensitive issues, problems, and priorities.

• Demonstration of a workable format to initiate change.

• Demonstration of an excellent format for communications with colleagues and subordinates on sensitive or controversial issues.

—Insufficient time to put together a development plan.

—Failure to see how pieces fit together.

2. Performance Management

—Surprise and concern as to the number of job objectives viewed by the subordinate that didn't "track" with those of the supervisory manager.

—Where relatively new relationships existed as with a newly appointed manager, it was difficult to arrive at concrete approaches or solutions.

3. Organization Career Management

—Managers (boss or supervising manager) ill informed regarding career possibilities in the organization.

—Managers lacking preparation in needs analysis or skills of coaching or counseling which is a part of the role in some workshop activities (e.g., regarding the individual taking charge of their career).

—Managers not "buying into" the joint interactive approach—are unaccepting of the concepts (e.g., cross-functional moves for development or open communications).

—Jobs lacking good documentation that involves both job-descriptive information and behaviors required for success.

4. Workshop Format and Contents
   —Insufficient time to clarify fully some of the key concepts and terms.
   —Widely varying background of participants and thus highly uneven contribution to group processes (e.g., brainstorming) or general workshop activities.
   —Need to develop in advance, study materials.
   —Failure to understand workshop processes—lack of orientation to reduce anxieties.
   —Failure to relate or link to other organizational programs.

Although this listing of workshops problems is obviously a significant one, where the O.D.P.G. can fall short of meeting expectations, all these points can be adequately dealt with in advance. It is clear that a significant amount of groundwork and advance preparation is needed to make the time spent worthwhile. For example, a supervising manager will have multiple roles to play as coach or counselor in the workshops—*and* back at the job as well! The supervising manager requires skill training in some of the techniques or roles which they will enact or carry out in the workshop. Another correctable type of problem is the lack of good job documentation—clearly, this problem can be corrected, but a good bit of time may be required.

Preworkshop Activities and the Workshop Format

The nature of this writing precludes detail of "workshop" programming, but a characteristic two-day workshop format is helpful is viewing main activities and processes. At the same time, the point has been made in several places that an important group of activities must precede the staging of the O.D.P.G. workshop. These are covered in the previous listing of workshop problems. The question of whether organization context is adequately supportive, including culture, planning and strategic approaches, and the documentation of jobs, is quite another matter.

Workshop Format

Exhibit 8-9 provides an outline of format and important preprogram activities. The description of activities and processes pre- and postworkshop plus the workshop itself suggest the comprehensiveness of this design. The preworkshop activities are considered as important to the workshop as the activities which are a part of the workshop. Many supervising and organization managers simply have not been exposed to these processes and techniques and often need much time to think them through. Another point to note in Exhibit 8-9 is the fact that supervising managers go through everything the subordinate does, although theirs are condensed versions. In summary, the O.D.P.G. workshop is one of a whole new series of innovations in development methods which are considered better suited to the need of modern, complex organizations than fragmented approaches used in the past. Because of its newness, much fine tuning will likely be required—but this is to be expected.

EXHIBIT 8-9
Preprogram Activities and a Format for an O.D.P.G. Workshop

Part I. General Organization Preparation (Representative Activities)*
- Establish a supportive climate, including policies, procedures, and reward system.
- Create a strategic planning capability.
- Undertake organization (structure and jobs) planning.
- Establish a foundation of job documentation, information base, and personnel procedures.
- Clarify Personnel/Human Resource functions and the relationship of these.
- Establish a framework for organization career management.
- Carefully review current organization processes to assure that preworkshop and workshop activities and materials are complementary and not redundant.
- Undertake attitude surveys to determine views on career needs, job related satisfaction, and sense of competencies.

Part II. Preworkshop Activities for Orientation and Processing

A. Subordinate
- Distribute resource materials describing individual career planning, definitions of key terms and insights, benefits of goal planning and values clarification, and some examples of career planning and career pathing completed for representative people.
- Provide materials that describe key features of the organization/corporation. These include career ladder and bases for employee mobility movement, key positions and job families, and the main qualifying characteristics for the positions described and the functions carried out.
- Provide self-assessment materials for a preliminary analysis of goals, values, and career interests.
- Have participants self-assess knowledge, skills, ability levels, and expertise; they also appraise their state of knowledge/understanding regarding career related approaches— covered in their resource materials.

B. Supervising Managers
- Direct reports contacted by their senior manager and apprised of program purposes.
- Assemble managers in small focus groups for a preliminary orientation to workshop processes, clarification of relation to other organizations processes and then provided with a small group of resource materials for background review, and personal processing. They also receive a copy of the packet of materials processed by the subordinate.
- Have each workshop participant review existing human resources documents (unit human resource plans, subordinate job descriptions, performance appraisals, previous "employee development reviews") and make notes in the forms provided for these purposes to make "recall" more accurate.
- Each participating manager reviews his or her own positional documents (e.g., position descriptions) as these might affect their subordinates.
- Provide each manager with a shortened version of self-assessment career materials for familiarization and processing.
- Request newer managers to review their functions and responsibilities with their senior manager to assure clarity and concurrence.

(Continues)

EXHIBIT 8-9 (Continued)

Part III. Workshop Activities and Processes

- Provide informal period during which participants review own preworkshop materials and questions are clarified.
- Arrange introduction by senior organization/corporate officers.
- Offer general orientation by workshop processors, including coverage of preworkshop materials and the materials and processes to be used.
- Give everyone a chance to work through a comprehensive set of career planning materials.
- Have groups brainstorm job-redesign approaches; serve as sounding boards for earlier ideas and propose ways of improving relational activities.
- Initiate one-on-one meetings of supervising managers and their subordinates, covering performance criteria exercised, development, and organization human resource needs.
- Hold small-group problem-solving discussions (performance and careers).
- Hold general workshop discussions of issues and problems.

Part IV. Postworkshop

- Develop attitude survey to establish possible areas of personal change and degree of change.
- Arrange for postaudit workshop for effectiveness.
- Review and follow-up development activities based on individual needs and wants.

*Details of these provided in other chapters.

3. Review and Application

A. Review Questions

1. What is the relevance of the following to internal recruitment and selections procedures?

Assessment center	Relational skills
Assessment of potential	Formal learning versus coaching
Adult learning model	Self-learning

2. What are the features of "androgogy?" self-learning strategies?

3. How does androgogy differ from pedagogy?

4. What is the fit of the "learning function" in
   a. New hiring?
   b. Performance appraisal?
   c. Selection for promotion?
   d. Designating a "high potential"?

5. What is meant by
   a. Functional competence?
   b. Learning objectives?

6. What is involved in learning strategies for the "inexperienced" management trainee?

7. What is meant by "supervisors serving as behavioral models"?

8. Compare and contrast learning strategies for management trainees and managers being groomed for promotion.

9. Critically examine the O.D.P.G. workshop described in the application section in terms of its training/development benefits and shortcomings.

10. For the coaching and behavioral modeling case described in the applications section, what qualifies Walter Hicks for his "modeling" role? Comment on Fred Block's experience in the light of chapter comments.

B. Application Issues and Questions

1. The Learning Function (Exhibit 8-3)

   Situation: The Loop Bank has recruited Mary Benson ("B") for a position in their newly opened marketing department. There was to have been two months of training (multiple department assignments) before she took up her work in marketing.

   Her supervisor carried out a two-month performance review and was displeased with the results. She decided to look at Mary's personnel file and noted the following from her record and college transcript.

   Mary Benson's Background (Person "B"/Exhibit 8-3)

   > 22 years old
   > Marketing Major, GPA (3.7/5.0; 4.0 in major)
   > Grades: Math, statistics and finance, 4.3 average
   >   "Organization behavior," 3.1 average

   Make and state necessary assumptions.
   How would you interpret this situation?
   What would you do?

2. Learning Function (Exhibit 8-3, person "A")

   Len Franklin was in the Systems Engineering Department of Computer Applications Corp. for some five years. Most of his work had been technical, and he performed well. Now it was being proposed that he go for "mastery" in this area and that he take leadership in their planned entry into micro (personal) computers. It is desired that he achieve this know-how in several years. As a consultant you know the characteristic form of the learning function for this situation is likely to be in the form of "A" (refer to Exhibit 8-3). What advice do you provide to Computer Applications Corp.? Make and state necessary assumptions.

3. What are you to infer as a management trainee at the Loop Bank concerning the learning task and based on the following training strategies in which you participate?
   a. Coaching
   b. On the job
   c. Formal learning
   d. Classroom-type instruction

4. Based on the discussion of methods effectiveness and behavioral considerations in this chapter, propose a training development strategy for the following situations and roles and your rationale and assumptions. Consider the following three settings for your responses:

    a. New super Dominick's (food store) with salad bar and catering, in addition to regular retail operation

    b. Marshall Field's (North Michigan Ave—a prestige location.)

    c. Central Scientific, International Division (high-tech instruments for export sales)

    Roles:

    a. A management trainee

    b. A trainee slated to work in marketing/advertising

    c. A mature woman returning to employment and slated for supervision

    d. A salesperson

    e. A person seen as having a "motivation problem"

    f. A person with poor writing skills

5. Wendy's (fast foods) is about to establish a new management training program for which people will be recruited directly from community colleges, four-year colleges, and universities. Future staffing needs will be greatest for two-year grads and significant though much less for MBAs. Those successfully completing the program will be assigned to field and HQ positions, with Domestic and International, based on their training/development (T/D) performance, background, skills, abilities, and educational credentials. Positions will be both line and staff based on availability and individual background and preferences. Set out a preliminary T/D design based on learning concepts discussed in this chapter. Rationalize your approach and clarify your assumptions.

9

Managerial Career Development
Strategic Approaches

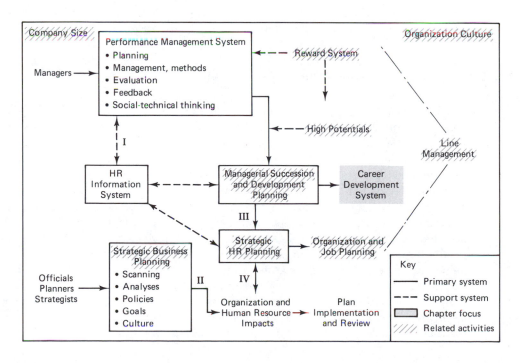

The strategic human resource orientation described in Chapter 1 is also highly applicable to career development. Managerial career development is concerned simultaneously with the thoughtful resolution of two relatively complex, at times, conflicting areas. In one, *organizational career management*, the major focus is on meeting the short- and longer-term staffing needs of the organization through individual development. Personnel-related activities such as recruitment and selection, training, performance appraisal, and assessment of potential serve as supportive processes for these purposes. The second area is that of *individual career planning*. Its primary concerns are focused directly on the individual and her or his career advancement. Involved in this approach are questions of job and occupational choice, work assignment, self-development for career mobility, and even organizational (or employer!) choice. A representative group of sources for *basic* career development systems are provided in the references for this chapter.

Career development seeks to establish a sufficiently broad base of common ground between career management and individual career planning so as to permit achievement of highly valued objectives in both areas. Adding the strategic dimension to managerial career development, however, increases the complexity of these analyses and by itself provides a rationale for this discussion.

The Strategic Perspective in Career Development

At an earlier point in the introduction of career development programs, it was often seen as a "quick fix" for equal opportunity or affirmative-action programming or simply what a public spirited corporation did for its employees. This rationale was not unimportant because it led to practical organizational actions with potentially valuable benefits for organization members. However, with more than 10 years of experience involving career development programs, corporate America has come to a more mature and sophisticated view of career development. Recognizing that some corporate programs have been in place for 10 years or better, pragmatically oriented officials have increasingly pressured Human Resource people for tangible results beyond the fact that programs were "satisfactory" or "liked" by organization members. In response, more specific results have started to be reported in various journals as well as newsletters of the human resource planning societies. These indicate that potential for significant benefits from well-organized career development programs. Cost-benefit calculations have included the added costs of counseling facilities, training expenditures, career materials, and supervisory time. Also included have been the monetary gains from reduced supervision, trainee turnover, lowering of other recruiting costs, improvement in various performance measures, and reduction in costs of training and development of personnel.

What is the order of magnitude of the benefits from these programs? In a bank with 8,000 employees, annual (net) benefits were estimated to be upwards of $100,000 per year. Regardless of what the calculations show in a particular situation, it is clear that the economic aspects ("benefits") of these programs are not to be discounted. Since the dollar benefits reported are usually based on short-term (annual) savings, the longer-term benefits could represent a substantial addition to these. For example, longer-term benefits include being able actively to pursue a business strategy because of the availability of motivated and appropriately developed people, improved cooperation and commitment among organization members, the willingness or active desire of people to contribute their creativity to corporate programs and activities, and the expansion of the pool of qualified internal candidates for various supervisory and managerial positions.

Strategic Managerial Career Development in Small(er) Companies

There is a widely held but erroneous belief that for the most part, career development programs are for large firms. If strategic thinking is also added into the picture, then "this for sure is for large companies." Small(er) company owners and senior managers often believe that the crucial elements of *strategic planning* and *managerial career* development create an expensive or sophisticated system, unworkable in the small(er) firm. This is probably a "logical" conclusion, given the fact that most books and magazine and newspaper articles describe applications in the Xeroxes, IBMs, Hewlett-Packards, or Honeywells. Workable systems and approaches at "Acme Tool," "Midstates Banks," or "Cantos Bros. Foods" go virtually unnoticed. What is important in all these applications, whether the company is *large or small,* is that *strategic approaches to succession planning and managerial development are a philosophy and way of thinking about your organization*. This was the "message" of Chapter 1. A central purpose of these processes is to spark thinking and discussions in human resource matters likely to affect the organization's long-term survival and renewal.

In reality, there are two initial challenges confronting small-firm applications of strategic thinking and career approaches. One of these is the lack of publicizing successful, small-company applications. The more basic problem may be a confusion in thinking. The philosophy and concepts of strategic and career approaches are blurred and perhaps lost sight of because of the formalization of application systems and products in many large firms. The structuring of systems, methods and procedures, use of staff specialists, and "hi-tech" computer applications are realistic means by which large firms cope with large work forces, decentralization of facilities, and diversity of products and services. "Formalization," "standardization," and "specialization" must be understood for what they are. They are tools of the "organizational management" trade to cope with size or diversity. In larger firms, they represent a tangible, fleshing out of the underlying strategic thinking of top management and other key people.

However, even under these circumstances, various systems and procedural options are exercised which are best suited to the circumstances of the organization. The diversity in the resultant career-related applications can be very great. For example, in one large corporation run essentially as a financial holding company, most planning and general management responsibilities were decentralized to divisions. Although the corporation coordinated advanced applications and interdivisional communications regarding these, the systems in place had little resemblance to each other. Great variations existed because divisional businesses ranged from military applications to industrial products to consumer products. Also, there were great differences in the numbers of employees in each and the philosophy and style of division general management. It is true that the growing importance assigned to succession planning for corporate continuity and growth forced some integration of divisional transfers, management development, and promotion plans. Yet, despite the overall size of the company, divisions continued to bear the "stamp" of their general management's philosophy and business circumstances.

"Is size per se, whether measured in employment or economic terms, the key factor separating strategically planned and directed firms from those more conventionally managed?" "Is size the primary determinant of the degree of formalization of approaches?" There is no question that larger firms tend toward greater formalization. Yet a "large" firm example was just provided in which a rich diversity of strategic planning and career approaches existed because of numerous situational considerations.

The number of employees as a measure of size also may be highly misleading. For example, an architectural-engineering firm with some 800 employees had a highly advanced strategic planning and career development system. With some 70 percent managerial, professional, and technical employers, long planning horizons, and fierce competition, it was forced to adapt internal management development methods fully equal to its technical capabilities. Underlying considerations were the need to plan future staffing needs; identify feasible human resource alternatives in the light of future business and economic conditions; attract new, capable people; reduce turnover; and generally improve working relationships and organizational effectiveness.

Two additional examples illustrate that many factors other than "size" affect an organization's use of strategic thinking and career development approaches.

Health Provider Example.   A company specializing in the provision of health care services had an employee force of less than 500. Yet it exploited a very advanced career development system to benefit both organization career management and individual career planning. Its most recent actions included greater formalization of its longer-range planning activities and strategic thinking and alternatives regarding future directions. At one point planning and strategic activities had been highly informal but the president found that there was too much diversity in planning approaches among senior managers. Also he felt that they often missed the benefit of the creative ideas or stimulation from various senior managers who were not a part of these processes. Further "encouragement" to pull things together came from the tough competition in this field, changes in the regulatory environment, and competition for high-talent people.

At one point the president knew almost everybody in the company on a firsthand basis. But by the time employment approached 400 people and 50 managers and supervisors, even the president and his two key officers started to realize that they were not tapping all the talent in the organization. Nor were they providing sufficient guides and support to cultivate senior managers in the future. But the concern of the senior officers was not just with succession matters. It seemed clear that they were in for a long period of change in which self-development would have to be encouraged and supported. Many organization members had to be encouraged to stay abreast of new developments or to update themselves in managerial, administrative, and technical aspects of their business.

The office manager who had a liberal studies degree with a minor in "behavioral sciences" became the key inside person for administering the career development program. Her attendance at several workshops and seminars and visits with a group of insurance companies and banks provided the needed theory exposure and practical experiences for internal career development applications. The exposure to these developments in the career field came as a surprise to her. Although burdened with many office management responsibilities, she initiated a slowly growing group of career activities, including a career library, career days, and individual career planning material. However, she found that these approaches, though satisfying some of the company's career requirements, still were far short of her original charge.

An updating of the company's job analysis system was a major accomplishment. It was based on successful applications in some similar types of organizations and work situations. It provided a more powerful basis for conventional personnel applications and a group of newer ones including developmental performance appraisals, assessment of potential, and needs analysis for development and career planning. Importantly, the personnel/human resource applications drew off of a common base of work characteristics and competencies.

The office manager was "invited" increasingly into planning and strategic discussions when it was realized that she could provide data of growing company value. Ratings of performance and potential were more uniformly drawn and thus provided a better basis for development and selection decisions. Another development also proved helpful to the changing directions of the organization, especially the planning and career picture. The office manager started to get more deeply into the career literature while meeting with professional acquaintances at other firms. She also informally "interviewed" various managers in the firm to see how their careers evolved. From these continuing contacts, a body of information evolved. Of great importance was a concept of career development within the organization that served as a model and framework for managerial career development. Subsequently it proved helpful in informal career planning discussions between managers and their subordinates. It also provided considerable insights to the president and his key officers as to the organization's development of managers and a basis for meeting their future succession needs.

Strategic Questions and Issues

Exhibit 9-1 provides a sampling of characteristic questions and areas of strategic inquiry focused on career development. It is noteworthy that the checkpoints concerning "the current situation" and future needs and plans are essentially *independent* of size or organization characteristics. They fit a large variety of situations.

The items in Exhibit 9-1 draw on the results of various organizational experiences and studies. It has been our experience that some companies have undertaken studies in the past which they have forgotten! It is understandable that some past studies were not strategically focused, yet their results may be useful. They may help crystallize viewpoints of key members or provide quantitative data useful for strategic analyses. For example, in a recent strategic planning study related to careers and human resources, the results from six different past studies were drawn upon in part in shaping strategic analyses. These included value analyses and surveys of preferences regarding career activities. These results were thoughtfully discussed and analyzed using the kinds of information, problems, and general matters suggested in Exhibit 9-1. Strategic discussions worked these down to a specific set of six comprising their high-priority items.

Other Dimensions of the Strategic Questions and Issues

The strategic related problems, issues, and questions shown in Exhibit 9-1 have been grouped into three categories for convenience in referencing. In the characteristic mode of strategic analyses described in Chapter 1, the first group of items relates to expanding the understanding of the organization's current (career development) situation. Note, for example, that these approaches seek to uncover how people are prepared for managerial promotions or senior-level positions. They also "ask" how careers are built "currently," the relatedness of various methods and systems in providing career-related information, the consciousness and urgency felt by employees in career matters, and the possible relation of major human resource problems and issues to career practices.

The second category of analyses shown in Exhibit 9-1 forms the basis for establishing future directions for career practices and activities to support these. The thrust of these analyses is directly linked to the organization of the future, its staffing and competency requirements, and career development likely to best support these.

The third group of questions and issues illustrated in Exhibit 9-1 is common

EXHIBIT 9-1

Issues and Questions in Establishing Strategic Priorities for Career
Development

The Current Situation

- What comprises our means and methods of building careers today? What is our "career management system" or its main functions? What functions have been formalized and how well are these working?
- What positions, job sequences, assignments, and types of experiences appear to have provided superior contributions to individual performance?
- Who are the people who have been instrumental in identifying (talented) "comers" or "high-potential people"? What types of supportive ("nurturing") relationships have emerged to further individual careers *within* the organization and in furtherance of corporate needs?
- What problems and/or priorities do employees assign to corporate support in furtherance of their career interests?
- Is it likely that the relatively high turnover among college recruits, if such is the case, reflects a failure to get a (comprehensive) career program underway?
- Have cross-functional moves in the past played a significant role in career advancement? What obstacles must be confronted in order to start a program of cross-functional moves?
- With regard to managerial and officer positions, to what extent are common performance or behavioral dimensions used to describe these and how are the related knowledge, skills, and abilities developed?
- Have job behaviors been defined which are critical to success and how are these developed?
- What is the relationship of performance management to career management activities? In turn, how do performance appraisals and assessments of potential relate to these?
- Have dual-career tracks (i.e., technical and more general managerial career ladders), been operative in the organization? If they have existed, how well have they functioned and why?

Future Needs, Possibilities, and Feasible Directions

- What is the character and direction of technological change likely to be in the future? What does it indicate for internal development strategies?
- What new organizational structures and work systems seem likely in the future and how are these likely to shape the direction of internal management development programs (i.e., requisite abilities and performance)?

Planning Feasible Career-Related Management Strategies and Surfacing Major Questions and Issues

- What are the nature of working relationships, roles, and responsibilities likely to be to improve career management processes in the future?
- Will a formalization of mentoring or sponsorship programs substantially improve the "growing" of top-level managers?
- Should "such and such" an activity be formalized as a part of our organization's career management system?

(Continues)

EXHIBIT 9-1 (Continued)

- How are we to expand the role and competency of senior managers as coaches to the extent that this approach is most important in gaining the subtleties of the managerial process and leadership?
- To what extent will our managers require more formal knowledge to deal with high technology or competition and how are we to motivate their involvement in development?
- Will we be able to encourage a sufficient number of organizational women and minority to undertake knowledge, or skill enhancement to meet targeted senior-level staffing? What approaches are likely to prove the most fruitful?
- How can we artfully gain more convergence in values (re: the organization's culture) shared by senior and powerful officers and managers, which are seen as instrumental to promotion?
- Given the expected future changes in the specifics of positional requirements and the organization's culture, what new rewards and reward systems will be indicated by these? How are we to facilitate major adaptive changes in the culture and positional requirements encompassed by our business and human resource planning?

in establishing career-related priorities. These relate to top-level strategic business/ planning priorities. Since the resolution of these questions and issues will focus development energies in the future, much must already have been learned about the organization as a business enterprise and "culture."

In summary, the questions and issues listed in Exhibit 9-1 form part of an essential process of analysis typical of strategic approaches. These approaches require highly informed judgments. Reducing this portion of an organization's study to checklists fails to capture the inherent subtleties, complexity, and uncertainties. Many of the difficulties with strategic approaches referred to in Chapter 1 emerged from unthinking, formulated approaches. There is a "Gestalt" involved in strategic processes which includes thoughtful discussions and the contemplation of complex issues combining objective information *and* judgments. This combination of factors cannot be ignored.

Career Development Systems Audit: An Action Research Approach

There are areas of strategic inquiry that lend themselves to (more) structured approaches, and a systematic type of audit can benefit these areas of anlysis (Exhibit 9-2). It provides an important source of information as to "where" the career development activities (system) are today and thereby indicates the possibilities for future systems development.

In the discussion that follows, some study results are provided which indicate the types of information which may come out of audit-based studies. It is recognized that all organizations don't have the need for comprehensive career development systems, now or perhaps even in the future. Recognition must be extended to

EXHIBIT 9-2
Strategic Analyses: An Audit of "Today's" Career Management System

	None Doesn't exist	(1) Informal	(2) Some structure	(3) Fairly well organized	(4) Functional
	None	1	2	3	4
1. Corporate policy (written or otherwise) reflecting corporate commitment—and recognition that individual career advancement necessitates corporate facilitation	___	___	___	___	___
2. Top management support	___	___	___	___	___
3. Business planning capabilities and its connection to human resource planning	___	___	___	___	___
4. An organizational culture that supports both organizational and individual career activities and in a consistent manner	___	___	___	___	___
5. Budgetary support	___	___	___	___	___
6. Active managerial involvement	___	___	___	___	___
7. Managerial support and counseling tied to performance appraisal/reward system	___	___	___	___	___
8. Up-to-date and complete position descriptions	___	___	___	___	___
9. Detailing of the work/performance actions needed for success, related to position descriptions	___	___	___	___	___
10. Open, equitable, internal communications systems (often includes valid posting system and opportunity for self-nomination)	___	___	___	___	___
11. Career counseling support: well-trained managers or personnel and counseling professionals	___	___	___	___	___
12. Career information support (e.g., organization career resource center and career materials)	___	___	___	___	___
13. Bases for individual auditing and update of personal experience, work, skill, knowledge, and interest record	___	___	___	___	___
14. Bases for individual auditing and update of personal experience, work skill, knowledge, and interest record	___	___	___	___	___

EXHIBIT 9-2 (Continued)

15. Bases for review of individual informa-
    tion inputs   _____   _____   _____   _____   _____

16. Availability of a management inventory,
    including position audits, promotion
    readiness, and performance information   _____   _____   _____   _____   _____

17. Cross-functional movement—policy and
    program   _____   _____   _____   _____   _____

18. Realization by individual personnel that
    individual career advancement is, first
    and foremost, their responsibility, al-
    though the organization needs to play a
    facilitative role   _____   _____   _____   _____   _____

the situational requirements and future directions of "your" organization. Exhibit 9-2 (to be discussed shortly) provides an audit-type checklist of 15 different features of a comprehensive career development system.

Not surprisingly, the relative number and combinations of career development elements or activities found in a particular organization or major units within it vary a great deal. Again, situational requirements and restraints are major considerations. For example, Gutteridge and Otte (1982, p. 16) reported the relative percentage usage of career-related activities as follows:

Seminars or workshops related to individual career planning.	78%
Career counseling	70
Posting of job availability	45
Workbooks for self-oriented analyses	40
Career pathing involving alternative career routes	23
Career discussions involving the individual's supervisor	18
Career resource center—stocking career-related material	18
Counseling, outplacement	10

Most of these types of activities are not difficult to launch, though some, such as career pathing, require some preparatory time. These results represent the relative frequency of usage in their sample of some 35 firms. As averages or summary results, they don't indicate the situational subtleties or needs previously referenced. There are several observations that can be made regarding organization progress in these career approaches which may provide some useful strategic planning insights.

Supervisory Career Counseling Capabilities. Career counseling by staff counselors (70 percent) was far more numerous than those involving the individual's supervisor (18 percent). To the extent that this counseling evolved in this way, it likely reflected a *serious deficiency in supervisory career counseling capabilities*. This is a good example of a career-related approach involving the path of least resistance. It is both feasible and desired that this supervisory capability be actualized, regardless of the firm's situation or size. Our experiences have indicated that the following underlying types of problems often exist: (1) supervisors' lack of confidence in their expertise to undertake these discussions, often due to lack of training; (2) failure to provide needed future staffing and job-related information; (3) supervisors' inability to establish open communications with their subordinate; and (4) failure to take a relatively even-handed or neutral approach that avoids criticism or self-interest. At times physical proximity is an issue to the extent that backup services or people are not convenient to the manager who is expected to do career counseling. Another point concerns the individual's supervisor and the need for a continuing working relationship that involves them in career-related discussions and assessments (e.g., performance planning, assessing potential). This point directs attention to the need to strengthen the supervisor's role.

Staff counseling by Personnel or other professionaly trained people (e.g., consulting, industrial/organizational (I/O) psychologists) may be important, especially for more mature or senior managerial people. Units that have this need for expert counseling but can't justify full-time people have used the services of outside firms or consultants.

Open, Equitable Communications, Job Posting.   Something less than one-half of these firms (45 percent) reported job-posting systems. If the survey had been administered to individual employees, including various supervisors and staff members, the percentage representing a *valid* and *functional* system would be much lower, perhaps 20 percent! The existence and perpetuation of an old boys' (or girls') network continues in many organizations. Promotables and succession candidates too often are identified on the basis of personal contacts or knowledge, and there is no opportunity to self-nominate. Further, if jobs are posted, they (may) have already been committed to particular individuals, and the organization is only going through the motions of running an "open" posting system. It is our experience that failure to establish some type of equitable and open system regarding job availability seriously undermines individual confidence in management's integrity or intentions. The fact that the pool of qualified candidates could be increased substantially, some 20 to 25 percent, based on various corporate experiences, indicates that these practices be questioned.

Availability of Individual Career Planning Materials.   Some 40 percent of the survey companies made available career workbooks or related materials. This was a rather large percentage, but as with posting, there is quite a different side to this practice. Making career materials of this type available is one of the easiest ways by which companies have been able conveniently to enter into a "career (related) program." Unfortunately for managers and general employees, it has represented the extent of their involvement. With these alternative interpretations in mind, how then are the results of a career development audit to be interpreted?

Career Development Audit: Administration and Interpretation

Many benefits can result from a strategic career audit in which a wide cross section of officials, line managers, and staff participate. The degree to which specific items are formalized depends on organizational circumstances and often is not the key issue. Audit results thus are used as a springboard to open up a number of issues, some extremely political or sensitive, in a relatively neutral discussion environment. To facilitate administration and subsequent discussion, nominal behavior anchors are fitted to the scale points to avoid absurd results and to assure workable reliability in (re)interpretation (see Exhibit 9-2). Also, the process of administering this type of instrument and getting officials and senior managers to focus on these matters is a major benefit as such.

The use of the "audit" is also readily undertaken in small(er) firms too, though some feel that this formality is unnecessary. This type of a check/rating list forces attention to a situation with which individuals may think themselves familiar. Yet the fact that different perspectives are drawn upon (from ours) is useful in identifying issues or problems overlooked in the past.

Getting Started Versus Program Refinement. Even though each firm will differ in specifics, it is clear that a company new to programming career development activities will be in quite a different position from those which have been at it for some years. In consequence, several characteristic modes of *start up* are reflected in Exhibit 9-3.

Models A and B (a typical, smaller-company pattern) illustrate strikingly different approaches to the planning for and programming of career development systems. Model A was strategically oriented from the beginning, and important information elements already existed. It was undertaken within the framework of the company's needs and resource limitations. It involved the use of a highly talented but very limited (in numbers) corporate Human Resources staff. The first two years of experience reflected a focus on the strategic objectives to the extent that the roster of qualified succession candidates was expanded by almost 50 percent. This need emerged because of a major wave of expected retirements in five years. Right from the beginning, priorities were assigned to establishing those career development components facilitative of succession planning. In turn, these helped to establish a solid base of information, orientation, and capabilities that permitted expansion in the third and fourth years to a much wider cross-section of talented managerial personnel, including a growing number of women and minority.

Model B represented a typical grass-roots approach and one characteristic of many smaller organizations. It started in response to requests from both profes-

EXHIBIT 9-3
Alternate Models of the Advancement of Career Development Systems

	Alternate Strategies in Systems Development	
	Model A: Conscious Systems Strategy—Information Base Partially Intact	Model B: Building the Information Base and a Basic System (grass- roots approach)
Year 1	Corporate policy (1)* Top management support (2) Counseling capability/line management (11) Career information support (13)	Update position descriptions (8) Career counseling support (12) Personnel information support (14)
Year 2 (add)	Business planning nominal (3) Reward system connection (7) Update position descriptions (8) Individual audit and inputs (14)	More updating of position de- scriptions (9) Identify job openings in most needed areas (10) Gain some managerial in- volvement (6) Emphasis on role of individual in career advancement (18)
Year 3 (add)	Business planning connec- tions increased (3) Budget support (5) Managerial involvement (6) Performance/behaviors (9) Internal communications (10) Career counseling support (12) Information review (15) Management inventory (16) Individual career direction (18)	Some top management in- volved (2) Detail of performance behav- iors for selected jobs (9) Expand internal job availability communications (10) Line management training in counseling (11)
Year 4 (add)	More integration of business strategic planning (3) Reexamining organizational culture (4) Advance performance behav- ioral dimensions (9) Employee self-nomination (10) Cross-functional movement program (17)	Top management support ex- panded (2) First attempt to tie in busi- ness/strategic planning (3) Nominal budget funds allo- cated (5) Managerial support introduced into performance appraisals (7) Start management inventory (16)

*Numbers in parentheses refer to those from systems audit, Exhibit 9-2.

sional and/or college-educated people for career counseling and information on promotion opportunities. This program was applied initially in the professional ranks, and then when positive results (reduction in turnover primarily) were seen by top management, it was decided to involve line management departments as well. Clearly, the means of establishing a strategic career development capability equal to Model B's would have involved much more time than Model A. On the other hand, the corporate Model A situation had high-priority human resource needs in an area directly affecting corporate continuity and renewal. Strategic thinking was appropriately assigned to the Model A situation at an early point. In B, the strategic implications became more obvious as time passed. It was "needed" (in B) as a part of strategic planning approaches—*but only* after the organizational groundwork (e.g., top management support) had been prepared.

Succession Planning and Career Development Linkage

The connections between succession and career development systems planning are varied and at times complex. The number and complexity of these tie-ins are directly dependent on

- Maturity of the succession and career planning systems and processes, including the strength and focus of the organization's culture.
- The number of authority levels included in the succession system and thus the number and the relative experience and sophistication of succession candidates.
- Size of the organization, which in connection with the number of authority levels, establishes the personnel included in this planning.

The maturity of succession and career planning activities and the organization's culture is a basic consideration in the degree of linkage between activities (if any). To the extent that succession planning assures timely staffing of key positions with appropriately developed people, career planning may play a key and facilitative role.

Assume, for example, that succession candidates are part of an *in*formal talent pool from which specific candidates are drawn. Career planning under these conditions is less tangible from the corporate viewpoint. Individual career plans are influenced in a general way by the validity and amount of information they receive related to corporate plans and future staffing plans and how well they understand the way the culture works in filling jobs. Career plans are further affected by the presence or absence of position posting and the individual's knowledge of his or her performance ratings and estimates of his or her potential. Individual career plans, to the extent that they affect succession, are further shaped by feedback from performance appraisals. Appraisal results may encourage (or discourage) individual determination for improvement and to be career mobile. From a behavioral viewpoint, much depends on the urgencies or needs experienced by the person. Do they feel a need to advance or achieve? What are their capabilities relative to the "criteria" for staffing of senior positions? And if gaps exist, What are the chances of strengthening deficiencies?

Individual career planning also ties into succession thinking to the extent of the validity of individual perceptions and the reality of their expectations. Supervisors and managers are often ignorant of or possess misinformation as to the qualifications for individual mobility. These need to be understood early in a person's career, or the company is placed in a position where it may lose capable people needlessly. Often, too, organizations may have (inadvertently) created such ingrained (negative) attitudes or mental sets that these are, at best, very difficult to change.

Another basic consideration in the link between succession and career planning is related to the organization's culture, power structure, and political system. The person's ability to work through the realities of the power or influence structure is a basic requirement in individual career advancement. Some companies take the view that if the person hasn't been able to piece things together for themselves (the "passive role"), he or she "wouldn't have made a good succession candidate anyway." This point is highly controversial; various officials would argue that failure of the company to take a more active role in this area is self-defeating.

A central concern related to career planning and succession is the extent to which the future supply of qualified candidates are affected by the culture and personnel policies. Neglect of succession-career connections "now" will simply delay dealing with this matter. It may also seriously jeopardize future succession plans because of the time lost in failing to think through these relationships and to organize appropriate approaches.

Where succession deals mostly with senior people, some of the previously mentioned points become less important, at least in the short run. The scenario is "you are dealing with a senior person who knows what the organization is all about." Thus main questions turn on corporate staffing needs, the capabilities of the individual, their fit with the corporate culture or milieu, and their knowledge and skill in working their way through the organization. However, this line of reasoning has its faults too. It may not be fully realized that the key need for establishing an efficient "feeder system" of candidates may have been postponed or covered up.

Career Systems Development: Pacing Growth and Support Capabilities

Strategic considerations dictate that individual interest in career-related matters be tempered with analyses of future staffing requirements and the scope and capacity of the organization to absorb and advance career-focused people. The characteristic problem that has existed in many organizations has been the lack of thinking or a philosophy (let alone system!) regarding organizational career development. However, an equally great problem is one in which a mature career development system exists and then creating levels of interest in career mobility for which the organization is incapable of satisfying. Thus the appropriate strategy is one that considers these extreme situations and paces the growth and thrust of career management systems accordingly. Two corporate experiences serve to bring out the strategic concerns in these types of situations.

Lack of a Career Development System.   After a considerable time in which basic information and procedural elements had been created, corporate HR staff felt that it was ready to launch its career development system. This system was to include career information, counseling, developmental performance appraisals, and cross-functional transfers. Corporate officials and Human Resources were greatly encouraged by the success of earlier efforts. They had moved to a critical juncture where developmental moves were being considered along divisional lines or throughout the corporation. However, further progress became possible only when it was realized that career development system advances depended on future staffing openings, reconstituting supervisory and managerial position information, the available time of line managers, and backup of the internal consultive staff. Put another way, enough survey information existed to indicate the widespread interest and concern of organization members in career matters. But a real danger existed that (far) too many people would be moved into a career thinking and behavior mode—with nowhere near the required capacity in the organization to deal with them in an effective way. Also, it became clear that a significant amount of work had to be done in creating up-to-date and behaviorally relevant position descriptions and supporting documents. Thus, the company elected a process of gradualism, with the installation of career development related elements that met its employee commitments, but paced the introduction and refinement of elements to its personnel, information, and job capacities.

Limited Growth Opportunities.   Over a long time period, a large retailer developed a comprehensive human resource planning and career development system. Strong managerial people and good candidates for senior succession positions were gradually developed. In addition, the average time required for candidate "ripening" continued to drop. In the past, it reached almost 18 years for senior managerial positions but was reduced to about 13 years on the average. The gradual reduction in the time "required" for achieving senior position status proved highly encouraging to younger organization members. It also became clear that further improvements could be made in this managerial growth process and thus individual progress accelerated. However, the strategic thinking that intervened in this analysis was the realization that overall sales and organization growth had slowed. Thus the *net* openings in middle management and senior positions (from retirements, quits, and expansion) would *not* support further reductions in this time period. Strategic discussions directed attention to creating more stimulating types of job situations where the creativity and energies of highly capable people could be absorbed. This approach led to a decrease in the (past) corporatewide emphasis (and support through its reward system) on upward movement (promotion) as the primary marker of success. In the past, promotion was the main way to achieve an interesting, responsible, and demanding job. The corporation finally devised a substantially revised internal climate, opportunity, and reward system. Job redesign and the entry of the corporation into newer business ventures met some of the requirements. They also reconstituted the elements of the reward system, for example, bonuses for good performance and recognition versus the emphasis on promotion. Workable elements were set in place which assisted in the refocusing of its career development system.

Strategic Approaches and Career Development: A Smaller Company's Experience

Many smaller firms are more recent entrants into this area or start with more modest resources; their growth patterns (Exhibit 9-3) are understandably different from relatively mature systems. The Pacific Tool case which follows traces the evolution of strategic and career capabilities in a small(er) firm.

Pacific Tool (PT) was the archetype of the small, family-owned business. Better than 70 years old, Henry Johnson, its president and a graduate of a state university, was the third generation in the business. His grandfather, a tool and die maker, had settled in an area which eventually was to become the outer reaches of "Silicone Valley" on the West Coast. The company's history bridged two world wars, a depression, recessions, and boom periods. As a small tool and die shop, it was taken for granted that boom and bust was characteristic of the business, and "you simply learned to live with it." When business was strong, the Johnsons built up their cash reserves (and credit) against the periodic business slides of the aircraft and automotive industries. When Harry formally came into the business in the late 1970s, he already had years (part-time and summers) of experience and indoctrination. But Harry was his own person and wanted to run the company in a "businesslike" way. He had the ingredients to do it: common sense, experience much beyond that normally found in a man of his age, years of expert coaching in the technical aspects of business, and an intense desire to succeed. Harry's father had been ill for years and shortly after Harry went into the business full time, his father retired. In the early 1970s, Pacific Tool employed some 175 people, including office help, tool and die makers, engineers, supervisors, superintendents, a general manager, and a vice president and business manager. Even by this time, it was evident that the character of PT was changing. Major technological changes had resulted in the use of computer-oriented shop equipment and engineering procedures. Also the character of the aircraft, electronics, and automotive industries they serviced was changing. Initially, these changes required more advanced knowledge of supplier firms. But it also became apparent that a more sophisticated understanding was needed of administrative and inventory management techniques as the planning, procurement, type of inventory, and internal management techniques of these industries changed.

One of the highest priorities for Pacific Tool after Harry came in the business was to create a more stable economic base. It was clear to the new president that he was going to need continuing expert counsel. He organized an advisory board consisting of the dean of the College of Business where he had attended school, an officer of the local bank, and the president of an electronics firm with whom the company had long done business. A professor of management, also from the College of Business, served as a consultant. The academic's areas of expertise were business and human resource planning. This cadre of talent served Harry well in the years to come. Longer-range business planning was increasingly the topic of advisory group meetings. Company resources were closely examined, and gradually, an imposing list of improved business approaches emerged. Strategic thinking led to the identification of two promising and new(er) areas of business that satisfied the "stability objective." Over the years the company had amassed much technical talent and know-how. Some of the industries it dealt with used die casting and plastic molding presses. Thus its general experience included all aspects of its basic tool and die activities, electronics, automotive and aircraft applications, and even knowledge of the presses and machines using this tooling. Out of its know-how emerged a strategy for modest diversification which both capitalized on and nurtured their core strengths.

Over the next 10 years, PT gradually took on a highly specialized repair business, design of custom fixtures, and the design and sale of a small line of high-quality plastic molding presses. Although PT expanded, only 25 employees or so were added. This was due to internal improvements in methods and shop automation. By 1980, it was clear that the "business and strategic planning" was starting to pay off. The company weathered the deep recessionary conditions of the late 1970s remarkably well. However, it was clear that continuing progress in stabilizing the business and achieving modest growth was going to require looking much more closely at its people and their competencies. Several different factors related to this shift in strategic focus and concerns. Part of the need reflected the fast-growing demand for technical *and* administrative management competencies to meet competition and the growing sophistication of their customers. Another point was that the early generation of tool and die makers had either retired or died. Promoting expert tool and die makers from the bench into supervisory or managerial ranks became less and less feasible with the changes in character of the business. Recruitment of engineers and technical personnel had changed too. Personal recommendations or firsthand knowledge of an individual had been the usual way in the past. This approach was no longer feasible because of a very tight labor market and the fact that engineers with these capabilities or potential had a dozen job offers. An additional consideration was the improved education and wider scope of interest of their new-era employers. They both talked about and expected their employers to respond knowledgeably and supportively regarding their career needs. In short, the traditional model for human resource planning, development, and promotion to meet work needs was no longer feasible.

The president had a general knowledge of corporate career development from his business publication readings. The company consultant was brought in and charged with developing the basis for a career development system. The design specifications were that

1. Current staff would be charged with maintaining the system; thus it had to be effective but quite straightforward.
2. The system should be state of the art in the sense of being timely and responsive to both company and individual needs, yet meeting the low-cost, simplicity of maintenance criteria.
3. The career development activities should effectively service managerial and professional development needs for fulfilling succession and promotion requirements. Especially important were those reflecting long(er)-range and strategic planning of the type increasingly in evidence in company planning discussions. In system planning discussions with the business consultant, the foundation of new strategic planning and career development was constantly reemphasized, namely, that the planned changes at Pacific Tool, were as much a way of thinking about their business's future (opportunities, threat and family goals) in relation to its resources, as any tangible method, career procedure, or activity.

The heart of the new approach had in part been created through the organization of a group whose periodic meetings were devoted to charting a sound future course for the business. These discussions also set the tone for subsequent succession planning discussions. What now had to be done was to organize internal activities that would strongly support the emerging strategic/planning guides and be seen clearly as supportive of individual career plans.

Steps in Establishing a Career Development System and Linkage to Company Planning.   The company consultant outlined a series of steps for meeting the design specifications. Timing of the moves called for approximately an 18-month period for phasing in the activities, since most of the work would have to be done by the office manager, department heads, and company officers. Key benchmarks reflecting the changes were as follows:

1. *Business and strategic planning and its human resource impacts*. Highlights of planning discussions were recorded to serve as a basic planning document for human resource planning, including succession analyses. Both the business school dean and consultant were helpful in identifying human resource developments and trends with which the company should be familiar. This information was usefully supplemented through several special labor market reports and trends prepared by a regional industrial association of which the firm was a member. The information concerned particularly human resources

and was further refined to the specifics of PT's current work force as well as its future profile of characteristics (competencies, knowledge, actions for success) and staffing.

2. *Organization planning.* The initial staffing estimates were further refined as a result of thinking through the changing structure of the business due to its new products and services. This action turned out to be a highly useful exercise despite the small size of the business. Since the products and services were changing, it was determined that some amount of internal reorganization would be called for. This affected staffing, particularly areas of responsibility, and thus related competencies.

3. *Job analysis.* All job descriptions were updated and expanded to incorporate competency information. The office's "word processing" system was used to facilitate current and future changes. This reflected a combination of job holder questionnaires and department head reviews (of questionnaires) for current duties and activities. This was no easy task since many job descriptions were out of date or "bare-bones" descriptions of major responsibilities. It was decided to stay with a conventional (but updated) job-description format to ease preparatory work, yet to create a document useful for individual career planning and company purposes. Job analyses were then looked at by the president and the consultant to see what additional changes would be indicated by business planning, organizational changes, and strategic discussions concerning new business directions. Selected department heads also were called in to help them think through the effects of the newer business directions and more general changes. The human resource discussions and analyses which accompanied the business discussions were quite helpful in making further adjustments to the revised job descriptions.

4. *Career development "model."* Company people, and particularly Harry Johnson, didn't want to glorify their career schema by designating it as a "model"; thus the use of the term here is descriptive. The approach combined information on professional and technical careers as studied for some 20 years by Dalton and Thompson (1986), human resource and career experiences of Walker (1980) and Burack and Mathys (1987), visits to several electronics and automotive units, and the collective experience of the advisory group. What was needed was a highly workable and simplified format that would serve company and individual needs. Features included the following:

   • *Career stages.* It was felt that most managers and technical personnel would develop in three broad phases. It was necessary to get specific as to numbers, concepts, and activities. This information was to be outlined in simplified form and distributed to all supervisory and managerial personnel, professional/managerial recruits, and other employees. The three phases identified were "indoctrination and competency development," "middle management preparation," and "senior management preparation including technical positions." These three phases seemed best to describe individual development from initial organization entry to highly valued senior organization positions—and to bridge their current situation with the one planned in the future.

- *Developmental career tasks.* Each career phase served multiple purposes. The first major job was to bring the person up to performance competency ("seasoned performance"). This represented the end point of the first stage's development. This career development was tied to a 12-level salary grade system which had been recently developed and installed: (1) covering their salary grade 1 (entry)–4 (end point represented competency); (2) middle-level managers (including professionals), covering salary grades 5–8; and (3) senior managerial competency, salary grades 9–12.

  Each career phase was looked at in two different ways. First, the competency developments to achieve "seasoned" performance and, second, the competencies identifying an individual with promotion potential. The former was covered by their newer job descriptions which also included competency statements. Inferences regarding the latter were documented by job descriptions (and competency statements) applying to the next higher career phase. Also, some judgments were made as to the overall elapsed time to achieve status as a "seasoned performer." Thus, in the future, each person had the benefit of knowledge regarding responsibility and performance criteria most affecting their immediate job, as well as guides to higher-level company job needs. The new job descriptions also served as the basis for individual needs analysis and development, for which determinations would be made by the individual's supervisor and the person himself or herself.

- *Line management involvement and participation.* As in the past, line managers or department heads had important roles to play in support of their subordinates. Now, however, much importance was assigned to "new era" skills such as coaching, counseling, and people planning.

- *Management development methods.* The "dean" serving with the advisory group as well as the company consultant identified various college and university courses likely to fit in with each of the career phases. A simple chart was then prepared, describing the three phases, job characteristics and competencies related to each stage/phase, typical job titles, applicable salary range data, formal courses and training programs thought to be useful for development, and estimated ranges of time spans for progress through the phase. Since department heads and officers would have important roles to play in the potential success of the program, an informal development program was arranged for them. The "program" consisted of meetings among the president, managers, and the consultant; one-on-one sessions with the consultant and manager, and tailored to individual need; and several university-based workshops (e.g., "calculating human resource costs and benefits" and "management development and planning").

- *Integrating business and human resource plans and programs.* Semiannual development and planning meetings were scheduled and attended by the officers and department heads. Ratings of people, future plans, and progress of each person were reviewed and future moves discussed and authorized. Where changes in business or strategy planning had occurred, these were noted and incorporated into future development plans. Cross-transfers between departments were also arranged at these sessions.

- *Individual career planning.* A bookcase in the office was dedicated to career materials are recommended by their consultant. Also, individual career counseling started to grow as department heads and floor managers became increasingly involved. At times the president too got into counseling sessions, especially where a department head, senior manager, or key person was involved. However, a conscious attempt was made by the president to avoid undercutting the position of the department heads' relationship with his or her subordinates.

Individual Career Planning in Respect to Talent Pools and Succession Planning

Individual career planning takes on new complications when it faces the realities of organizational systems for handling managerial promotion candidates. Common approaches include designated candidates and promotion pools. In the former, the danger of the heir apparent exists, and (other) qualified people, recognizing that a selection has been made, become discouraged. Performance often suffers, and at times people will elect to quit and go into other organizations. Sometimes those quitting have not shared their frustrations or engaged in exploring alternate possibilities. In the case of managerial talent pools, the determination of "membership" is characteristically a confidential matter. Information is shared by members of an executive development committee, senior officers, or some selected group. The lack of general knowledge regarding "membership" may instill a good deal of uncertainty in the minds and outlooks of many people in the organization—including those viewed as high potentials. As a consequence, a strategy is indicated in which positive encouragement is provided for self-development in reference to legitimate organizational opportunities in the future. Yet the encouragement needs to stop short of direct identification of pool candidates since its composition can and does change regularly. Customarily, "pool" members are reviewed every 6 or 12 months.

Much harm can be done by creating unrealistic expectations about individual promotion. The practical means of handling this situation is to create a positive environment for individual development where future opportunities are made known to organization members. This situation can be regularly updated and communicated to people. What is more important is that people have at their command adequate and reliable information so that they can make informed judgments regarding their future careers. Also, people need to be treated in an equitable way. If people are trusting of the sincerity and intentions of key officials whose actions affect their lives, much of the "battle" has been won.

Our experience indicates that people will accept the strategy of talent pooling if the management development system is seen as equitable, professional in outlook, and one from which they can gain reliable information for personal career planning. Even if the relative chances of upward mobility are modest, people prefer to have the benefit of a realistic assessment of their chances for upward mobility than fanciful stories that turn out to be false. It is also true that a significant number of people seen as highly talented and exhibiting senior management or high potential may choose *not* to move. Many personal considerations may motivate this type of decision and increasing numbers of organizations are "accepting" of it.

At times people go along with the promotion or transfer decision because they have been goaded into it—and with adverse longer-term results for themselves and the organization. Thus, from a strategic viewpoint, the organization needs to do the best job possible in judging future staffing requirements *as well as* qualifying competencies and the career interests and mobility intentions of its members. Nothing will destroy a situation faster than the uncertainties created by poor information or reliance on "old boy/girl" network candidates.

This series of discussions has had the purpose of highlighting major and general policy-level issues related to the launching and maturing of career development efforts. Subsequent discussions take up selected topics in successfully merging organizational requirements and valued behaviors with the needs of the person.

Careers and the Cognitive Development of Managers

The rather imposing term "cognitive development of managers" turns out to be one receiving increasing attention in career development discussions. Individual career progress in organizations depends on a variety of considerations not the least of which are various personal qualities of the "trainee." The existence of a (the) critical set of personal qualities and traits, let alone its composition, is hotly debated. Regardless of the outcome of the debates, cognitive skills and abilities that are needed for problem solving, reasoning, and abstract thinking rank high in many managerial jobs, whether in general administrative or technical areas. Additionally, the higher reaches of management and senior positions in many organizations stress strong abstractional skills for mental visualization, conceptualization of complex economic or competitive situations, or creative processes. These qualities are indispensable to strategic processes, although, they are necessary but not sufficient to assure strategic planning success. However, there are study results regarding management development, most notably those of Elliott Jaques (1976), which indicate definite limits to the growth of one's ability to think in abstractions.

Jaques felt that "abstractional ability," a main component in managerial "capacity to work," was innately determined, but variable in its degree of development. He defined this concept as the biologically established period of time across which an individual could formulate and implement a goal(s). The ability of the manager to visualize a task, to break down its components in detail mentally, and to plan its execution are managerial responsibilities and performances which clearly demanded abstractional ability.

Jacques argued that while there are innate limits to growth, abstractional ability increased during maturation in some predictable patterns—an idea supported by other research findings. Jaques notes that for those who have high potential for senior organizational positions, this improvement can continue throughout that person's life span. For others, the growth process may proceed until perhaps age 40.

Experience, the use of systematic approaches to learning, and biological maturation are all thought to influence the development of abstractional skills. From a strategic planning perspective, it is only with suitable opportunities and experiences that individuals can reach the upper boundaries of their potential abstractional ability. The most useful experiences, Jaques suggested, are to challenge but not overwhelm individual ability at a given stage of career development. This is consistent with the findings of Douglas Bray and his associates at AT&T (Chapter 3) that challenging and diverse early job experiences benefited most managers. However, they also noticed that these early job challenges especially benefited those well endowed with the managerial attributes fundamental to managerial success.

To fit the results of Jaques's comprehensive studies more into an organizational framework, it is necessary to consider the *span of time* for managerial actions to achieve major corporate objectives and how the type and complexity of issues vary with one's (authority) level of responsibilities. In general, the higher the level, the greater the abstractional abilities required. Also, as organizations grow and their activities become more complex, increasing demands are placed on abstractional qualities of the corporate leaders.

New levels of abstractional requirements, not just improved versions of the old ones, appear as one advances up the hierarchy. Generally, the crucial movement is from a form of thought which deals with practical situations and concrete approaches to situations requiring thoughtful analyses and the extensive use of concepts and ideas. Jaques hypothesized that seven levels of bureaucratic strata and abstractional abilities existed and that individual performance and work capacity was affected by the increasing cognitive demands in the hierarchy of management work assignments (Exhibit 9-4). In general, the results from studies of Melaney Baehr (Chapter 4) concerning job content changes with authority levels corroborate the general relationships described by Jaques. Also, an excellent discussion and interpretation of Jaques's work is provided in a publication by Manzini and Gridley (1987).

Although Jaques's work proposed a seven-level stratification of time spans and authority levels, these specifics are affected by the general societal and organization's culture, technological character of the business, and use of computer technology. Of importance to strategic management development are the ideas that the need for abstractional abilities varies with authority level and that substantially different forms are involved. A second point is that individual career advancement may be supported or inhibited by the individual's potential expressed in abstrac-

EXHIBIT 9-4
Characteristic Time Spans of Managerial Planning and
Work Orientation After Elliot Jaques

Characteristic Time span of goal or objective	Authority level	Typical managerial role
20 years	7	CEO, chair or president
10 years	6	Chief officer, acquired firm
5 years	5	Head, major group or area
2 years	4	Division- or departmental-level manager
1 year	3	Section-level manager†
3 months	2	Section-level manager
Days or weeks	1	First-line supervisor

†Larger or more complex responsibilities relative to level 2.
Source: Based on Andrew O. Manzini and John D. Gridley, *Integrating Strategic Business and Human Resource Planning* (New York: AMACOM, 1987).

tional skills. Closely related to this second point are the (strategic) means elected by a given organization to develop managers. This approach should reflect an understanding of the interplay among assignment, personal challenge, and level of abstractional ability which is a part of the trainees' assigned area of responsibilities (and authority level).

The variation of time spans of managerial planning, a third point, involves varying degrees of uncertainty faced by the decision maker. A rough correspondence exists between these different time spans and thus the type and scope of uncertainty involved and the requisite abstractional abilities of the manager.

Good managers cannot afford to get involved in the day-to-day details of their organizations. Increasingly high positions demand more perspective. These positions require of the incumbent greater competencies to guide their organizations based on the opportunities, threats, and barriers which they anticipate.

Corporate Innovations in Strategic Management Development

The new and growing emphasis on career development has affected organizations and their members alike. At this point, numerous studies, research, and experience exist that can be exploited. Various organizations have launched workable career development and human resource planning programs that help to meet the needs of individual career growth. They serve as valuable examples of means to assist organizations in meeting their long-range objectives. Considering the variety of managerial characteristics needed in different business environments, it is easy to see why this approach is becoming more popular.

Self-assessment of career interests, objective appraisals of skills, and counseling are career management tools. However, it is important to know how individual career behavior, motivation, and career-related problems change over time. John Leach (1980) has provided a useful framework to consider these issues. He sees a career as an "unfolding involvement or behavioral pattern." The seven different phases or stages of a typical career for an individual are summarized in Exhibit 9-5.

Career-related behaviors, motivation, and potential problems vary greatly across time (Exhibit 9-5). The significance for organizations is that various attitudinal and behavioral changes become more understandable when viewed in a career-stage context. Individual career planning is improved, and supervising managers can approach these situations in a more knowledgeable and helpful way. For example, during the organizational entry phase (3), it is important that interest be expressed for the individual's development and that this concern be backed up with useful information. As he or she becomes established, advancement tasks and protocols needed for advancement will have to be clarified (phase 4). Mentors and ("significant") others who can assist in relieving the person's anxiety and channel energies toward improving performance and skills for advancement (needed in the "getting ahead" stage) can help prevent the "burnout" problem which often happens in the advancement stage (phase 5). These significant (organizational) "others" can also serve as mirrors to individuals, helping them to probe the reality of their career plans and helping them to develop needed contingency plans.

Phase 6 also poses some issues of significance to strategic thinkers, especially that part related to "plateaued" performers. Options may need to be generated to help individuals deal with differences between their present career realities and career expectations. Individuals who experience midlife crises or skill obsolescence may exercise the option to return to the "career exploration" stage.

In career work, it is important for supervising managers to recognize that they are dealing with "adult learners" who need to be in charge of their learning experience. An important part of individual learning is motivated by personally defined career needs; most frequently, individuals deemphasize the importance of formal learning settings. Work, work experience, and coaching serve as important settings for adult learning.

Honeywell's educational and development approach consciously attempted to factor in their many years of experience with "adult learners" and seasoned managers. They also had the benefit of top-notch consultants. Some of their "precepts" included

- Individual abilities develop over time.
- Career development needs change across the organization life span of the individual. They are influenced by the outlook, expectations and reality of perceptions of the organization (adult learner) members.
- Job requisites differ across position and authority levels and change over time as the person gains experience and competency.

- The content of classroom teaching is inadequate as the exclusive means of developing managers. Of equal importance are "guided" on-the-job experiences, plus those which strengthen the person's ability to relate to others.

"Developmental Task Competencies" and High Potential: The Foundations

The conceptual basis for individual development in programs such as Honeywell's meshes well with many of the research findings in this study area (e.g., Dalton and Thompson, 1986). These concepts serve as a *general model* for many different programs. Central ideas follow.

Career Development Stages. Career development proceeds as a series of stages with each representing substantially different sets of job-related behaviors for success. Although particular types of knowledge, skills, and abilities might be required in successive stages, the emphasis or demands of work lead to quite a different set of behaviors (as compared to previous stages) for success. For example, in one stage, product knowledge could mean understanding of functional specifications. At another level, product knowledge might involve the ability to *visualize new* applications. This concept of "visualization" needed at a higher authority level is precisely the same one identified by Jacques and described earlier.

Developmental Tasks and High Potential. People with good promotion potential have to master certain "developmental tasks." People gain competency or know-how in a critical set of knowledge, skills, and abilities that are seen as critical to promotion. Promotion in terms of salary increases and sometimes in movement to a higher level of responsibility usually takes place on the basis of doing a good job for one's currently assigned responsibilities—as determined by performance appraisals. However, those who are seen as having good, even *high, potential for promotion* (i.e., at least two grades beyond the current position) start to display certain "developmental task competencies" often not connected to the current job but considered as important at higher managerial levels. For example, a young engineer at the time of employment had to learn the discipline of procedures and even be able to follow detailed directions. Yet at the same time, through ad hoc assignments, he or she may start to display leadership qualities and creative approaches beyond current job needs. Some of these might be highly valued in senior technical or management positions.

Hierarchy of Positional Demands. Numerous crossroads or decision points exist in the evolving managerial careers. In one sense, the connecting "roads" represent different stages of individual responsibility and demands; this point was made earlier. Another perspective is that management competencies and strengths are also tempered by successively more demanding and comprehensive work activities. For example, in administrative career tracks, successive problems may involve

EXHIBIT 9-5

Seven Phases of Career Development

Career Phase	Time	Career Behavior Focus	Motivational Issue	Potential Career Problems
1. Exploration	First appears during pre-adult or early adult years. However, may be elicited at numerous stages in later life.	Random or premeditated behaviors are focused upon the question: "What shall I do with my life?"	Career choice.	Making choices with only limited (at times incorrect) information.
2. Preparation	Overlaps with career exploration stage.	On educational experiences—one or more of which may vary in length, structure, or content.	In essence, this is a more concrete step in the career choice exploration.	Education is too limited, too extensive, or inappropriate for career choice.
3. Entry	Job placement. Stage may (also) overlap with next one.	Security and access to the chosen career role and situation. Initial integration into career setting.	Interfacing own conception of career role with realities of career situation.	Must separate career choice from the organizational setting. May often give up career choice because setting is unreceptive to individual.
4. Becoming Established		Trainee or apprentice-type behavior and "paying dues."	Assimilating the organization's norms and values for acceptance. Deciphering which behaviors are associated with career advancement.	Indiscriminately accepting all the organization's values and norms at the cost of ignoring one's own feelings and work- and career-related solutions.

5. Advancement	After achieving a career platform or more stable career situation.	"Pure advancement behavior", advancement vigilance, calculating (perhaps unconsciously) career potential risks/returns. Also contingency planning may emerge.	Highly motivated and, potentially, highly anxious for the advancement "race."	"Burnout" or exhausting all career energies.
6. Stabilization	When advancement opportunities are exhausted.	"Holding pattern" or plateau.	Comparing career goals or aspirations with external career realities.	Unless this plateau is viewed as a fulfilling option, uncertainty about the chosen career role may appear (i.e., return to phase 1). Also, the "midlife crisis" is associated with difficulties here.
7. Resolving the plateau situation	Follows career stabilization.	Behaviors will depend on which of the four solutions are chosen for the "plateau." Essentially the career cycle may be repeated entirely for a new career choice, and repeated partially for the same choice in another setting, or terminated to retire while on the job.	To resolve the potential conflict between career aspirations and goals and external career realities.	Depends on which behavioral routes are taken.

Source: Based on John J. Leach, "The Careers of Individuals in Organizations," in Edwin L. Miller, Elmer H. Burack, and Maryann Albrecht eds., *Management of Human Resources*. (Englewood Cliffs, NJ: Prentice-Hall, 1980).

individual specialization, group (project leadership), department management, plant or district management, area or division direction, product groups, and senior or executive responsibility. Each stage, though related, is featured by its own priorities and competency demands. Thus individual confidence grows as a result of facing increasingly challenging assignments.

Career Crossroads and Dual-Career Paths.   Numerous organizations in many different fields, service and high technology included, have come to appreciate the significantly different demands imposed on managerial personnel as a result of the general administrative versus technical "flavor" of assignments. This is particularly true in "hi-tech" or technically oriented organizations, but many service companies, including banks, have these technical career tracks too (e.g., as in data processing). The *network* of career stages and cross-over points between administrative and technical tracks have implicit within them alternate (viable) structures of career development. In technically related areas, these might, for example, represent career movement from engineer, to development engineer, to project leader, to development supervisor, to manager of applications engineering, and so forth. The point is that these sequences of technical stages co-exist with administrative management sequences as illustrated previously. Another feature of these complex networks is that technical or general administrative management sequences of jobs are accessible from various positional assignments—especially at earlier phases of career development. In consequence, dual-career paths exist but cross-over points or bridges are established so that (some) cross-functional career track movement is possible, especially before the "executive" designation is achieved in a particular area.

Positional "Competency" Versus "Expertise or Mastery."   The learning curve to achieve functional competency and consistently good performance in a given position varies greatly. The time range may be from several months to four, five, or more years for people who initially had (at least) entry-level qualifications. In the "learning phase," knowledge, skills, and abilities are gradually cultivated toward "functional competency." Ordinarily, because of the organization's economic considerations, people will remain in the position assignment for some while after achieving positional competency. This period is one in which future potential can be demonstrated. It is also a period in which, given the accomplishment of competency, the dual-career path option becomes operational. For example, election of a technical path puts the individual on a ladder moving toward "expertise or knowledge mastery." The achievement of this status means that the person has the background to consult in his or her area of specialization and lead original work or/and make key planning decisions affecting the future direction(s) of the area. It may also mean that the person represents the company to the government or key community groups and/or mentor's key talent.

Modern career development programs incorporate various of these development basics. The program at Honeywell, Inc., attempted to encompass substantially all these features.

Coaching and Counseling Impacts.   The progress of K-S-A gains for managerial candidates is dramatically affected by the manner and quality of relationships with the person's supervisor, staff, and various organization members. Individual development benefits greatly from coaching and counseling but the role of coach and counselor is enacted by many different people. Also, the role played by each varies with job assignment, individual maturity, the person's job-related needs, and the point in his or her career progression. Thus, at a given career point, the candidate's line manager might provide coaching and guidelines in handling difficult customer problems; a department head from a different organization area or a staff member might provide guides on technical aspects of using a planning model; and another line manager, pointers on resolving a tough corporate policy issue.

The Honeywell Development Model

In 1980, Corporate Human Resources at Honeywell created a task force "to learn how management development took place, what was important to this process, and what was not important." Survey information about careers and professional development was collected from 302 managers plus discussions and group meetings with over one-half of those surveyed. The managers represented all the company's functional areas and managerial levels. From this information, the task force established a plan to be implemented between the years 1981 and 1985. It was one of the most comprehensive management development programs initiated among corporate units. With many of the ideas just discussed as background for their approaches, a number of specific models and procedures were developed. Common to all their activities/approaches was the need to launch a program that would be compatible with their organization's culture: it had to be workable and linked reasonably to corporate processes and the information base. Also, it would have to improve substantially current managerial processes and provide a template for effectively incorporating strategic human resource planning designs in the future. The approach also had to take account of the highly decentralized approach to management in the past plus the diverse businesses characteristics of this company.

Obviously the specifics of the plan and formalization of activities also had to take account of the fact that Honeywell was a large, complex organization. Yet underlying the structuring of its systems were extensive discussions, studies, and a body of viable precepts. The last comprised a foundation with features to suit many different organizational situations.

One key model and framework (the "Grid") included managerial salary grades and an overlay of stages of individual career development and dual-career paths. Exhibit 9-6 is a sketch of this model. Features of this model (Exhibit 9-6) included the following; note the direct correspondence with their precepts, itemized earlier.

- Knowledge, skill, and ability (K-S-A) development took place over time through a combination of many different experiences and educational inputs

EXHIBIT 9-6
A Managerial Development Grid, after Honeywell

Authority Level Dimensions					
Vice Presidents and Senior Executives					
Area Division Directors					
Department Managers					
Supervisors					
Nonmanagers (e.g., specialists)					

Phases of individual skill building

job entry – – ➤ skill building – – ➤ performance – – ➤ mastery
"orientation"   "basics"   full scope work   expertise
                                          dimensions   (e.g., consultive
                                                               level)

Source: Based on Honeywell, *Management and Development System Study—Team Report on Developing Managers in the 80's,* Final Report (November 1980).

to the person. Some reflected formal or classroom experience, on-the-job and coaching experiences, and the benefits of numerous "relational" contacts with "boss," staff, and various line managers.

- For any particular position, job, or occupational family, individuals evidenced learning gains (initially) toward functional competency which required quite different times depending on the person and situation. On the other hand, fast trackers or *high-potential people* established records of progress that could be used as benchmarks of career program potential.
- Progress toward functional competency was marked by advancement in the salary-grade structure and achieving progressively higher-position skill designations.
- On-the-job coaching and counseling were necessary for improvements in KSAs and also aided integration of formal educational inputs.
- Achievement of "functional competency," though significant in itself as a mark of personal accomplishment and value to the corporation, set the stage for significant career development decisions. These reflected corporate needs and individual career preferences and K-S-A competencies.

- Promotion potential and often "high potential" could be signaled by an individual's display of competencies *beyond* current positional behavior requirements and which were valued much at more advanced levels.
- The decidedly technological focus of the organization dictated that substantial career development opportunities (challenge and rewards) be achievable in technical career paths, more general administrative management careers or some combinations of these—a dual-career ladder model. Individuals might elect either of these options depending on situation, corporate needs, and personal competency.
- A logical progression beyond positional competency, often requiring much time, was a demonstration of "mastery." The positionholder's grasp of knowledge and experience and their application were effectively woven into behaviors at an administrative level. Those in administrative tracks might undertake policy-level speeches or take the lead in forecasting human resource requirements at an area or division level, for example. It was possible to anticipate many of the specifics of needed formal knowledge gains, work-related experience, and crucial relational contacts for successful management development. Thus, an agenda of work and educational experiences could be prepared in advance to anticipate particular individual requirements at specific career points.

More details concerning Honeywell's "Grid" approach are in the applications section of this chapter.

Applications of the "Grid" Concept of Management Development. There are numerous ways in which a given organization can exploit the type of management development model used by Honeywell in their strategic processes. First, average or typical career paths can be charted for various functional areas of the organization. These might include for comparison, high-potential time-career moves and career paths with less rapid advancements. Another approach would be to chart specialized career paths as, for example, that for general administrative management. Also to be included would be characteristics of technical or staff careers which could serve as baselines for comparison against an individual's actual progress. These would help to promote remedial strategies if progress appeared to be too slow.

A third application approach, discussed subsequently in greater detail, is to integrate development programming (educational and on the job) with the type of career path information referenced here. In this approach, differences in approaches become clearer as these are affected by authority level or phase (e.g., "basics" or "full scope") of individual development (see Exhibit 9-6).

Another fruitful area of analysis is to develop actual comparative cases where conscious attempts have been made to accelerate or alter the timing or features of individual career progress. Closely related to this approach is charting, for analysis purposes, careers that crossed from technical to administrative functions or perhaps even some that went in the other direction. Other details of interest include timing of appraisals, performance objectives, and career plans attendant to these.

The time needed for an individual to progress to a particular combination or authority level and development phase varies greatly depending on the situation and individual involved. The charts and applications help to make sense out of what otherwise is a very murky or complex situation.

Summary

In this chapter, managerial role development has been considered in a career context and as part of a company's strategic approach to planning. Career development of managers and other organization members, long ignored in formal corporate systems and approaches, has started to receive deserved attention. It has become clearer to officials that the fulfillment of strategic plans increasingly will turn on *jointly* reconciling both organization and individual needs. The successful fulfillment of management development plans, often stretching over extended time periods, represents a significant part of an individual's career and thus a matter commanding attention. Cross-functional moves, improved performance management, and the nurturing of high potentials assume new significance and importance under the concept of "career development." Career "ladders," specific corporate policies, and the modification of organizational cultures are some of the "instruments" used in the furtherance of career development designs.

Strategic inquiry has been increasingly directed toward identifying career-related means of bettering major human resource planning activities. These include succession planning and the reduction of turnover among high potentials. Audits of career-related activities, for which a sample form was provided, have facilitated the focusing of these discussions and analyses. Clearly, companies already in an advanced application position will be dealing with quite different issues from those seeking to launch these types of programs. In both cases, however, approaches are tailored to the organization and situational requirements. There are many points which must be established before a program can be launched. Of much importance in this regard is an assessment of longer-term organizational needs and possibilities so as to assure that human resource flows, especially toward higher-level positions, have been coordinated with these. An equally important question but one decidely different is that relating to the state of internal information regarding managerial positions and their performance-related requirements. Both types of questions have often been ignored or only partially answered in the past by firms entering the career development picture. Poor long(er)-term results have been a frequent outcome of firms ignoring these kinds of matters.

In the strategic perspective as applied to career development, some analyses have moved toward establishing basic competency and learning questions related to managers and executives. One example of this approach dealt with "cognitive development," especially that work undertaken by Elliott Jaques. Results in this area may shed valuable, new(er) insights into the factors that "make" the manager or executive and thereby the approaches to be considered in strategic designs and approaches.

A "Fit" for Smaller Organizations

Managerial career development and strategic approaches can be combined effectively in small(er) organizations. The full use and benefits of these approaches rests on generating viewpoints and discussions regarding issues and problems vital to the long-term survival and growth of the organization. The mechanics of systems, procedures, and technology provide a framework for the conduct of the activities in various organizations, *but* these can be minimal and yet effective. It is also true, however, that some "small" firms may require quite elaborate systems based on their situation and needs. Size is an uncertain guide to these requirements. Formalization of systems and staff is a coping mechanism for complexity or uncertainty, some of which accompanies size. Feasibility of these approaches, however, does not rest on "size" per se.

Firms almost without regard to size have a need to undertake planning, entertain strategic thinking, and be concerned about careers simply as a survival tactic. People have to be developed who will assume important managerial roles; additional staffing requirements have to be considered relative to the firm's future leadership. Any company discussions involving people's future automatically projects the discussants into the realm of people's careers. The need is manifest in today's society for career thinking which is sensitive to individual concerns and priorities. The firm for its part needs to meet its needs and commitments. Thus career development, which bridges both of these requirements, needs to be linked effectively with broader organization planning and strategizing to form a unified structure for these approaches.

Leading edge firms such as Honeywell, Inc., have undertaken extensive studies in this area and all types and sizes of organizations can benefit from selective use of their findings and approaches. They have devised plans and programs which jointly take into account many of the crucial factors in this picture. One example discussed in this section concerned a "management development grid." It incorporated Honeywell's salary system, organization structure, individual career stages, and characteristic development needs relative to key career points. Additionally, educational approaches tied together the job and formal learning experiences, which are related to dual-career possibilities. This "Grid" provided a general structure integrating these elements and easing the task of relating strategic planning analyses. Some details of this approach are provided in the applications section. Yet despite the formal systems and procedures underlying this particular application, the discussions and studies generated by these types of approaches can prove rewarding in their own right.

REFERENCES

Burack, Elmer H. and Nicholas J. Mathys. *Career Management in Organizations: A Practical Human Resource Planning Approach*. 2nd ed, Lake Forest, IL: Brace-Park Press, 1987.

Burack, Elmer H. "Linking Corporate Business and Strategic Planning to Human Resource Planning," *Organization Dynamics* (Summer 1986): 82–94.

Dalton, Gene and Paul H. Thompson. *Novations: Strategies for Career Management*. Glenview, IL: Scott, Foresman, 1986.

Gutteridge, Thomas G. and Fred L. Otte. *Organizational Career Development: State of the Practice*. Washington, DC: American Society for Training and Development, 1982.

Honeywell. *Management and Development System Study–Team Report on Developing Managers*, November 1980.

Jaques, Elliott. *A General Theory of Bureaucracy*. London, Heinemann, 1976.

Leach, John J. "The Careers of Individuals in Organizations." In Edwin L. Miller, Elmer H. Burack, and Maryann Albrecht, eds., *Management of Human Resources*. Englewood Cliffs, NJ: Prentice-Hall, 1980.

Manzini, Andrew O. and John D. Gridley. *Integrating Strategic Business and Human Resource Planning*. New York: AMACOM, 1987.

Schein, Edgar A. *Career Dynamics: Matching Individual and Organizational Needs*. Reading, MA: Addison-Wesley, 1978.

Walker, James W. *Human Resource Planning*. New York: McGraw-Hill, 1980.

APPLICATIONS SECTION

Other Specifics of the Honeywell Approach

Program architects devised other specifics for their comprehensive management development approach. Various time values served as guides to individual career development. For example,

1. Entry, up to 2 months
2. Skill building, 2 months up to 2 years
3. Performance, 2 years up to 10 years
4. Mastery, 10 years and beyond

As already noted, the management study found that the development of managers occurred optimally with a combination of three experiences: on-the-job counseling, coaching, and classroom instruction. The Honeywell task force took this information one critical and difficult step farther. It integrated each mode of education into the managerial development grid, which was shown in Exhibit 9-6. The architects of the Honeywell system actually devised a job grid with five hierarchical salary levels and four competency stages for a total of 20 cells. Inside each cell, defined by one of the four time or competency stages and one of the five job levels, were listed the skills or knowledge which should be developed from the job experience. The job content set the stage for "teaching" these objectives. The designation of job content also established the parameters for job design discussed in Chapter 2.

Career progress and management development also depended on establishing good interpersonal relationships. This competency facilitated learning (from others) while recognizing that various people played quite different roles in this learning process, depending on where the person was in his or her career ("job matrix"). Each cell lists the person or persons from whom the individual should learn (see Exhibit 9-7). Honeywell saw these relevant relationships as a network of role models and sources of information—people who recommended actions and reinforced job improvement. It noted that subordinates also could be an important part of this learning network although they were not listed.

The last of the three grids, integrating an educational model into the management development model, was called the educational grid (see Exhibit 9-8). It served as an example of matching in-house training with different job and competency levels as well as providing an excellent range of development courses for managers as well as nonmanagers.

EXHIBIT 9-7
Honeywell's "Relationship Grid"

	Entry	Skill Building	Performance	Mastery
Role of coaching	Advice on how to perform the basic job	Advice on how to perform the basic job	Counseling on performance	Advice, interactions on state of art developments
Executive (VPs and up)	Immediate executive	Peers, inside and out Consultants	Outside executives Community leaders Assoc. memberships	National authorities Academic specialists Executives of other companies
Department directors	Immediate vice president Corporate employee relations managers	Corporate staff	Consultants Professors Manager's manager	Professional society members Colleagues, other companies
Managers of managers	Immediate director Employee relations directors	Division trainers Non-Honeywell trainers Division trainers	Interfunctional peers Honeywell functional groups Manager's manager	Learning by teaching, in and out Consultants
Supervisors	Immediate manager Employee relations managers	Intrafunctional peers Non-Honeywell trainers Division trainers	Interfunctional peers Professional society membership Supervisor's Manager	Outside experts
Nonmanagers	Immediate supervisor Employee relations representative	Lead person Buddy/coach Functional trainers Intrafunctional peers	Outside trainers Interfunctional peers	External technical specialists Professional society membership

Source: Reproduced with permission from Honeywell, *Management and Development System Study Team Report on Developing Managers in the 80's, Final Report* (November 1980).

EXHIBIT 9-8
Honeywell's "Educational Grid"

	Entry	Skill Building	Performance	Mastery
Focus	Introductory basics	Skill builders for new appointees	"Augmenting" content for seasoned managers	State of art content for specialists
Executive (VPs and up)		Outside functional workshops (Management 111, if missed) Selected standard university programs (Exeter,* if missed)	Honeywell executive seminars Selected senior university programs (Exeter,* if missed)	Outside executive seminars
Department directors		Management III Corporate functional programs Outside	Exeter* Electives Standard university programs	University programs
Managers of managers	Orientation to group	Management II Group functional programs Outside functional programs	PHM* Multicompany Electives Andover* Career workshops	Honeywell functional workshops Outside functional programs
Supervisors	Division purposes, policies, procedures orientation	Management I Division functional program Outside short courses	IMDP* Supervisor electives Outside short courses	Honeywell functional workshops Outside short courses
Nonmanagers	Honeywell orientation	On-hours vocational courses Off-hours specialty education Electives	On-hours, advanced vocational courses Electives Off-hours specialty Education Presupervisory skill courses Career workshops	On-hours, advanced vocational and supervisory courses Electives Continuing professional education

*Special corporate programs.

10

Wellness, Stress, and Aging
Strategic Aspects

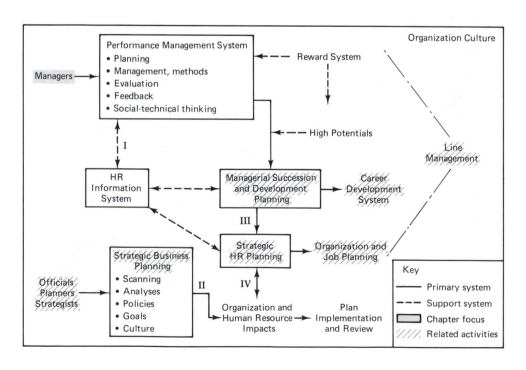

Employee wellness and issues in aging have started to come into their own as top-level planning and strategic matters. The reasons and circumstances are relatively straightforward. Employees, and particularly managers and senior executives, often make a major life commitment to the organization. This becomes the context for their satisfactions, accomplishments, social needs, and also a major, contributing source (potentially) of stress and major physical and mental illnesses. Second, changing work force demographics and age legislation have brought to the fore the need to deal more creatively with a fast-growing component of the work force, the older worker. Third, more people have realized that wellness relates to organization performance as well as providing obvious returns to the individual.

This chapter is developed in two major parts: one deals with wellness and stress, the second with aging.

PART I: WELLNESS AND STRESS

Background

Longstanding societal values, as for example, "machoism" or being stoic, are held firmly by many officials. People have been expected to battle their way out of stressful situations as a test of their mettle. To some extent, these attitudes or values have merit. But there are a growing number of situations in which excessive stress can't be easily dismissed because of its connection to various organizational processes and activities, let alone the new person's health. Many managers view dealing with stress as among their highest personal and professional priorities. This fact and its recognition have elevated stress-related issues and problems to strategic importance.

Studies of managers at all levels, within companies and across many industries, rate "coping with stress" as among the top problems and challenges with which they are confronted (Maddi and Kobasa, 1984; Friedman and Rosenman, 1974; Elliott and Eisdorfer, 1982). In one study conducted by mental health people, of some 27 different areas of potential managerial problems, dealing with stress was related among the top three challenges. From the organization's viewpoint, assessing sources and levels of stress can prove useful in improving organization/personel wellness, strengthening performance, and reducing conflict. Common high-stress situations are found in both anticipation and the wake of strategic business changes or in connection with "high-pressure" jobs. Research has determined that stress issues often represent a complex interplay of organizational matters *and* personal and life issues. Thus there is a need to (1) understand stress problems, (2) plan for and anticipate stress (trigger) incidents, (3) systematize stress-resolution approaches, and (4) establish corporate possibilities and limitations in these situations.

Increasingly, connections have been drawn between high stress and many phenomena of importance to organizational planners and strategists. These include absenteeism and productivity, job design and work-related satisfaction, mental health and potentially disabling results for managers and executives, turnover, "peaked-out performers" (burnout), and potentially, managerial obsolescence (De Frank and Cooper, 1985; Burack and McNichols, 1973). Recognizing stress sources connected with major enterprise plans can provide a basis for formulating major strategic planning objectives. These can comprise a basis for corporate stress management strategies and thus serve as a basic feature of its personnel policy and programs. From an individual viewpoint, the ability to self-manage stress is another consideration. It has moved into the set of critical appraisal factors which serve as a measure of professional potential and success.

Dealing effectively with stress is a pronounced challenge in both the personal *and* professional lives of managers since the two are closely linked. For some 10 years, we have periodically looked at factors which individuals feel contribute to their career development and the achievement of both personal and professional career success. These analyses generally support the point made earlier that coping with stress has been consistently among top-rated factors (among 14) scored by a wide cross section of people. Participants have included managers and supervisors, women and men, people in manufacturing and service industries, and graduate and undergraduate students as well! One of the important changes that has taken place among females we surveyed over this extended time period was the elevation of coping with stress to "high importance" as they became a growing factor in managerial ranks. The failure to cope adequately with high-stress events in the personal lives of managers spills over into their business functions, relationships, and performance. Needless to say, the effects go in the other direction as well; job stress greatly affects the family life of organization members.

Stress as it relates to the work and personal sides of individual lives is not especially new to business and human resource planning strategists. It's all part of work or living. What is new is recognition that stress is so pervasive, and that dealing with it effectively is seen as a problem or challenge by many. Also, high stress or the inability to cope with it can negatively affect managerial performance, personal relationships, and assessments of individual potential. Job and work environment features provide a complex and potentially beneficial or "lethal" stress mixture when combined with individual characteristics and work habits. Understanding the interplay of these factors, their connection to corporate plans, and what to do about them from a strategic viewpoint may provide beneficial results for both the organization and the manager. These points are dealt with in the following discussions.

Stress and Performance

In past years, many of the arguments mounted in support of dealing with stress were largely in the same category as job satisfaction. "It is very hard to quantify, but it makes sense intuitively to do something about it." "It will probably improve performance or the person's sense of well-being." However, in recent years, the area of stress has received more systematic attention. Results generally confirm that there is a desirable ("optimum") range of individually felt pressure or stress ("arousal") where people seem to perform best. Within the "optimum" stress band, stress is at a level where it can be controlled by the person yet it is high enough to serve as a strong motivating force—and negative side effects are minimized. If people become over-stressed, control may be lost, both real and perceived. Being overstressed brings with it a familiar litany of responses: highly emotional reactions leading to conflict escalation, loss of creativity, narrowing of alternatives to "this *or* that," and "blow-ups," or withdrawal or/and sullenness. Typically, these emotional states involve mistake rates which escalate, customers who are offended or turned off, people who can't "get it together" as deadlines approach, and loss of sensitivity to mistakes which otherwise would be noticed. People also frequently make poor decisions, lose focus or concentration, and may be inclined to precipitous actions.

The "low side" of the optimum stress range has negative performance consequences too, but for quite different reasons. Everyone needs some degree of (pressure) stress to function. With little pressure to accomplish or take care of "this or that," people become bored or have too much time on their hands. The individual may feel that there is no rush to develop the fallback plan or that "there is no hurry to start developing the succession candidate, the need is years off."

Stress analyses are still at a relatively early state of development, so that stress planning and management must be entered into carefully. Available information both anecdotal and empirical, emerges from a limited group of studies. However, the systematic studies are being carried out and are part of a new and growing body of more systematically derived study findings. These types of analyses are likely materially to assist more rigorous planning for and management of stress as well as provide a more solid basis for considering corporate policies and programs. Individuals too will be better able to undertake coping responses.

The following findings are from some of the stress studies referenced here. They suggest some possibilities for planning and strategic thinking. These types of findings are likely to be expanded greatly in the future and assume a much more substantive nature.

Some key findings from stress studies include the following:

1. High performance of complex (managerial) work assignments can be sustained over extended time periods, even under high-stress conditions. This becomes workable if the individual (manager) receives relief periodically from these types of challenging work assignment(s). Thus, alternative, low(er)-pressure,

and less complex assignments; temporary transfers; or recreating and/or time-off–all can break the high-stress–adverse (effects) pattern.

2. Parameters of managerial work vary greatly so that the positive results of stress management assume many forms aside from those seen as obviously performance related. For example, the degree of work consistency has been identified as a positive stress management outcome.

3. Some types of stress pattern–breaking activities, especially recreating, may have positive benefits for *both* overstressed people and for stimulating those whose stress levels are relatively low. Corporate wellness programs have the intention of promoting healthful living, exercise, and good diets. Studies suggest an interplay between healthful living, including recreating and performance—a relationship not fully appreciated in the past.

Stress Sources

To an important extent, successful stress management requires that the manager and his or her supervisor and associates recognize stress sources and their impact on themselves as well as on the "focus managers." Planners and strategists can help people gain a more *realistic* view of their situation and help to strengthen boss-subordinate relationships by using instrumentation, the purpose of which is to audit or identify major stress sources. Strategic studies of organizations are facilitated by the type of stress tolerance form in the applications section (1) of this chapter.

Before describing stress sources in some detail, it needs to be emphasized that the mental and physical makeup of the individual and, therefore, the "optimum" stress range for each person, differs. Individual tolerance for stress and individual healthfulness receive attention in the next section.

What are stress sources and what are some useful ways to think about them? A helpful classification of stress factors are *work role* versus *personal* sources. Also for either one, it is important to consider the degree of control which can be exercised. More on this point shortly. Work role stressors deal with technological change, business events, work, administrative processes, and even bombings as in some international assignments.

The magnitude of change correlates generally with the attendant stress level and degree of adaptation needed. A sense of uncertainty or loss of control over circumstances are psychological aspects. Finally, the conditions surrounding the need for individual adaptation may also be stress producing, including severe time constraints and/or supervisory pressures.

Managers too are constantly involved in work/career-cycle changes. These may involve quite common occurrences such as promotions or transfers that alter relationships with colleagues, bosses, and subordinates.

At the personal level, change is a natural product of life-cycle changes. Life-cycle events include aging, role changes (marital state), parenting, taking on community responsibilities, and home ownership and health (physical and mental). For the person, the extremes of the "stress range" may involve a range of feelings from between bordom and challenge. Many managers have a need for challenge and autonomy, or opportunity for achievement motivation. Many need a realistic sense of control over their work circumstance and ability to respond to uncertain situations in a way that seems reasonable or sensible under the circumstances. Put another way, individual needs for structure in their professional (and private) lives vary greatly. What is a challenge for one because of some uncertainties or risks may be threatening or even shattering to another person. Individual perceptions play an important role here to the extent that particular circumstances may appear (far) worse than they are or people are "locked in" to particular attributions that mask the real circumstances. If a person fells highly uncertain about things, they may well feel that their situation is out of (their) control. An individual sense of *control* turns out to be a complex one in stress analyses. Some sources of stress clearly cannot be affected by the individual and need to be viewed as fixed or "givens," at least in the short run. Other situations may be controllable by the person's supervisor or by still higher authority levels.

Another aspect of "control" is the level of control which the person believes he or she can exercise. "What is the reality of the situation versus what they believe to be true?" Individual managers react to circumstances as they "see" them. Supervising managers are often well advised to try and better understand the outlooks of their subordinates and to correct, where possible, misunderstandings.

Potency, Duration, and Frequency. Stress features and the patterns in which they occur are important to understanding what people are experiencing. This understanding can also help to open up possible channels for dealing with these. Some events, say, an accident, may cause high stress at the moment, but its effects rapidly subside. Other events, for example, an annoying but continuing office situation, may lead to a highly emotional showdown or some precipitous action.

Stress capacity among people varies widely, and there is a need for individuals to understand their capabilities as well as limitations. However, in our experience, more people seem to underestimate (rather than overestimate) their capacity to deal with change and/or stress situations. Environmental and person stressors and typical outcomes are summarized in Exhibit 10-1.

Stress—A More General Framework. Exhibit 10-1 summarizes many of the points from the preceding discussion. The two general classes of stressors referenced here, environmental and personal, are labeled as (1) in the sketch. The exhibit attempts to bring out the critical part played by the person's perceptions of events or the situation (2). Although wishing to avoid a detailed discussion on the perception factor, its central importance in understanding and dealing with stress warrants a slight digression.

The senses—sight, sound, and touch—come into play in the communications

EXHIBIT 10-1

Common Stress Sources—Their Impact on the Manager

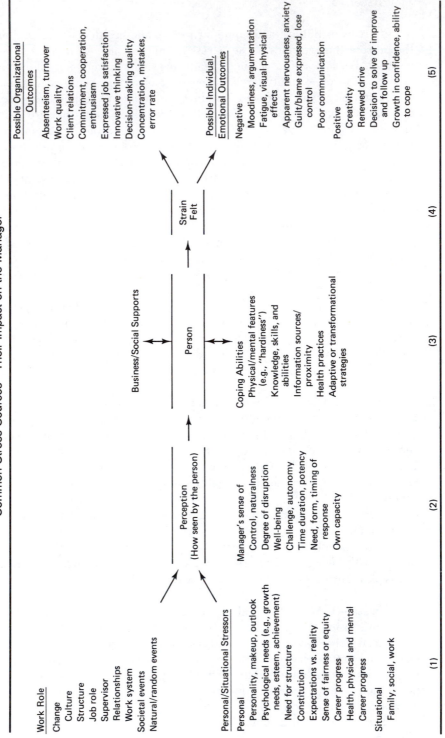

Work Role

Change
Culture
Structure
Job role
Supervisor
Relationships
Work system
Societal events
Natural/random events

Personal/Situational Stressors

Personal

Personality, makeup, outlook
Psychological needs (e.g., growth needs, esteem, achievement)
Need for structure
Constitution
Expectations vs. reality
Sense of fairness or equity
Career progress
Health, physical and mental
Career progress

Situational

Family, social, work

(1)

Perception
(How seen by the person)

Manager's sense of
Control, naturalness
Degree of disruption
Well-being
Challenge, autonomy
Time duration, potency
Need, form, timing of response
Own capacity

(2)

Business/Social Supports

Person

Coping Abilities

Physical/mental features (e.g., "hardiness")
Knowledge, skills, and abilities
Information sources/proximity
Health practices
Adaptive or transformational strategies

(3)

Strain Felt

(4)

Possible Organizational Outcomes

Absenteeism, turnover
Work quality
Client relations
Commitment, cooperation, enthusiasm
Expressed job satisfaction
Innovative thinking
Decision-making quality
Concentration, mistakes, error rate

Possible Individual, Emotional Outcomes

Negative

Moodiness, argumentation
Fatigue, visual physical effects
Apparent nervousness, anxiety
Guilt/blame expressed, lose control
Poor communication

Positive

Creativity
Renewed drive
Decision to solve or improve and follow up
Growth in confidence, ability to cope

(5)

of events or situations to a person. The initial interpretation and potential distortion
of this "communication" by the person sets into motion potentially stress-related
processes. The person's initial "view" of the event or situation may in part reflect a
connection with his or her sense of need, say, for challenge or autonomy: "How
good is the fit or match?"

People may also construct a view of a potentially stressful situation and its
consequences based on their sense of capacity to deal with these matters. Another
part of analyzing stress events is to establish their number, potency, and duration
and to checkout their similarity to past occurrences. Individual coping abilities
(physical and mental) and business/social supports (3) reflect both personal considerations as well as those of the work environment. The latter include sensitivity of a
supervising manager to stress-related events as well as attitudes arising from the
organization's culture.

Physical deterioration due to illness or some aspects of aging or the person's
(sense of) "hardiness" are other factors affecting the felt strains of the person (4) or
the performances outcomes of the person (5). Admittedly Exhibit 10-1 is simplified
since most stress circumstances are complex. Thus the exhibit is intended primarily
to highlight various aspects of the organization. These are a part of the milieu
within which the manager works. They affect daily work activities and routines as
well as potentially the environment with which the person is likely to work. The
person stressors have to do with personal makeup (e.g., temperament, personality)
and more general human development patterns as in life or career cycles. They
include also family and social events that affect the "personal role." Although at
times it appears that there are almost an infinite variety of these sources and
factors, the most important ones seem typically to involve:

1. Matters directly affecting the person's life, now or in the immediate future
   (e.g., family, marriage, health, children, moving; job-related problems and
   events), and longer-term events, such as careers for which decisions must be
   made "now."
2. How the person perceives these (e.g., as a threat with or without alternatives,
   solvable or disruptive) and their mental makeup, character, and state of psychological and mental health.

Change.   Change forces and circumstances underlie many stress situations.
It is a dynamic factor which is frequently incorporated in these studies. Characteristically, it challenges individual adaptation. Changes in the organization or work
environment involve customers, products, competition, and technology. It may
threaten (perceived) career opportunity or mobility, or it may affect organizational
performance expectations, or it may involve unfamiliar cultures in international
assignments. (In Chapter 1, even more major forms of organizational change were
discussed, including merger.) In drastic situations, professional relevance or job
security is threatened. In many of these situations, past work or habit patterns are
disrupted and a loss of control is common. At times physical considerations or

threats to bodily safety also enter into the picture, such as noise level or tempera-
ture, or kidnapping, or variables and relationships likely to be of interest to human
resource planners, strategists, and policy officials. However, this type of sketch has
also been useful in orientation discussions with managers.

Adaptive Strategies.   Individual coping responses for stress involve a range
of adaptive activities and processes. Exercise, an activity over which the person
exerts control, helps to work stress-related chemicals out of the body. Another
approach over which the person can exert some control is how the person thinks
about his or her situation or the stress-inducing event.

Quite a different set of adaptive responses involve actually seeking to "transform" (modify or change) the stress-causing event or circumstance. This is a more
permanent solution approach. Examples of transforming strategies include improving time scheduling for a chronically packed calendar, changing travel patterns to
avoid unreliable transportation or taking advantage of more favorable timing, or
choosing different times of the week to meet certain people when more scheduling
flexibility exists. Some of these "transformations" are not easily undertaken. Solution approaches like these are obviously appealing, but often involve changes in
habit patterns—behavioral modification at a basic level.

Personality, Constitution, and Coping.   The makeup of some people is to
some extent "changeable." These factors involve quite a different approach to coping. Some stress research (Maddi and Kobasa, 1984, pp. 30–32) indicates that
people who are active and self-reliant and work because they enjoy it appear to
have a greater likelihood of dealing with stressful events. Although confronted with
risk or uncertainties and strenuously engaged in business or social events, this
group of people enjoys a life-style that is relatively satisfying. However, if a member of this group is in a key managerial position, he or she may have little compas-
sion for any overstressed subordinates!

Change Characteristics.   Research, including our own studies of change in
many different types of organizations (Burack and Torda, 1979; Burack and McNichols, 1973), indicates that change takes on many different forms. Individual managerial coping may be facilitated when change forces are slow paced and people have
sufficient time to adjust to moderate changes. Much most dangerous, however,
have been large changes that take place suddenly or unexpectedly and/or that are
such as to force abrupt adaptive measures by the manager. If a manager feels that
he or she has been *plunged* into a change situation, that person often feels a high
level of uncertainty or lack of control. The circumstances may range from a sudden
change potentially in a competitive situation or a "suddenly" announced takeover
involving loss of prestige, power, responsibilities, or even one's job.

Stress Sources, an Industry Study.   It is not surprising that every industry
and business within it has its own characteristic stress sources that shape its form,
frequency, and potency. At the same time, quite general sets of factors also exist.
For example, Richard J. Mirabile has conducted studies in the banking industry,

identifying factors with which many managers, officials, or strategists can readily relate. The most common general factors identified by better than three-fourths of the managers in his study include:

- Customer demands, contacts
- Government legislation
- Customer demands, contacts
- Government legislation and regulations
- State-of-the-art change in one's professional field—and lack of adequate training or information to deal with these
- Problem solving for matters outside of a manager's control
- Unrealistic requests requiring responses
- Time constraints

It is worthwhile to examine this group of stress factors more closely since they arise for quite different reasons, and thus individual coping responses will vary much. For example, "customer demands" and "time constraints" may be due to particular types of customers or businesses over which little control exists, at least in the short term. The staffing of projects or assignment of people for dealing with these client groups or customers becomes important as persons must evidence stress tolerance for these types of circumstances. Another stress source, "unrealistic requests," is likely to be solvable if the affected parties can be brought together or the situation altered.

"State-of-the-art change" poses a difficult and complex problem. Other considerations may include the number of people involved and the scope, speed, and depth of change. But this is only the start of it. Quite a different side of this change form may have to do with the people involved, adequacy of information sources, lack of (adequate) individual training, access to relevant information, and awareness that changes are taking place and/or the need exists to update one's self. Changes in the state of the art are a central stress source and also a major contributing factor to individual obsolescence. More on individual obsolescence shortly.

Over 20 additional stress sources were identified in Mirabile's study, though some of these were not as significant as those listed or they were industry specific. Some of these other factors included (Mirabile, 1983)

- Subordinates who are aware of their supervisor's lack of confidence in them
- Lack of senior management direction
- Economic circumstances as in cost reduction demands
- Pressure to make or close sales.
- Power politics
- Slow response to customer needs
- Periodic meetings requiring some presentation on the part of the person
- Unduly close supervision

EXHIBIT 10-2
Common Business Sources of Managerial Stress

Very Frequently Mentioned
  Client-customer demands (for service information)
  Dealing with client/customer complaints
  Government regulation, compliance procedures
  Dealing with problems not wholly within the manager's control
  Time constraints
  "Unrealistic" requests for information or detail
  Lack of knowledge, skills, or abilities relative to field or profession changes
  Unexpected change
  Lack of information/feedback regarding work performance or results

Frequently Mentioned
  Lack of superior's confidence or support
  Salaries perceived as noncompetitive
  Multiple and conflicting assignments, responsibility
  Miscommunication, conflict between "headquarters" and divisions or branches
  Miscommunications or lack of cooperation between departments or units
  Lack of senior management guidelines or policy
  Income/job instability
  Pressure to make sales calls/close sales
  Delays by superior/senior management in making decisions—stalling action(s)
  Responsibility without authority
  Dealing with organizational policies and/or politics
  Sense of inequity
  Job responsibilities poorly defined

Common
  Lack of continuity in policies/programs due to turnover
  Close monitoring of one's activities
  Failure to provide workable independence in decision making
  Work at variance with job descriptions
  Trying to work through "bureaucratic" structures
  Career mobility blocks

Source: Based in part on Richard J. Mirabile, "Stress," *Training and Development Journal* (August 1983): 40–44.

General business-related stress factors are summarized in Exhibit 10-2. As already noted, a particular factor may be of small consequence in a given situation. Yet the collective impact of this and other factors may prove disruptive. At the same time, the same factor(s) may be seen by another person in quite a different way—they may take it (them) as "challenging."

   It is true that some of the general stress sources itemized in Exhibit 10-2 may be of little direct interest to planners or strategists. But some of these may be of high interest to line managers in ongoing relationships with their direct reports. Yet all the "very frequently" mentioned factors are often involved in strategy planning discussions. Their relative impact must be determined for particular organizational circumstances and the people (potentially) affected.

The remedies for some of the stressors just listed are fairly obvious, as for example, coaching or instruction to help managers cope better with new pieces of legislation or regulations. In other cases where the stress source is more ambiguous or affected by external circumstances (i.e., external to the organization), solution approaches may be much tougher!

Person Stress Sources

Before concluding this discussion of stress sources, it would be prudent to once more turn to personal circumstances, since these form a complex overlay with work and career matters. Thomas A. Holmes (1978), for example, studied in great detail, common life-cycle events affecting the individual. His studies indicated that individual success in coping depends much on stress potency (and thereby stress source) and frequency of occurrence. The cumulative result of various stress-producing events occurring in a given time interval can result in physical illness, emotional problems, or a person's sense of loss of (behavioral) control. For purposes of study, Holmes chose a one-year time period. He estimated the probability of occurrence of physical illness or emotional-behavioral problems based on the cumulative effects of stress-producing events which he scored for potency. The study did not deal with the effects of a supportive or nonsupportive environment. The following is illustrative of the events and scoring (Holmes, 1978):

Total Points in One Year

Over 300	80 percent probability of individual malfunction occurring
200–300	50 percent chance of the malfunction occurring
150–200	Increased chance of malfunction occurring

Life events	Points	Life events	Points
Death	100	Merger, reorganization	39
Divorce	73	Career (work) change	36
Major injury	53	Taking on a large	
Being fired	47	mortgage	30
Retirement	45	Major change of work	
		responsibility	29
		Change in residence	20

These results are obviously general ones and involve such things as averaging over large numbers of people and estimates of potency. Also, the study results did not include stress-time pattern. That is, the number of stress events occurring in a particular period of time. The experiences of particular individuals will vary from these results based on their physical and emotional makeup and particular circumstances. For example, reorganization was assigned 39 points. If a person perceived that there was a good chance of losing his or her job, this figure would likely be much higher. If the person also was a mature (older) executive with concerns regarding available employment, the stress points might be still higher. Our experiences with outplacement suggest exactly these kinds of results.

The study results indicate that various life-cycle and business events vary widely in their potency for individual stress. Planners and strategists have a need to understand and project the stress consequences of strategic planning actions as these impact managers and organization members generally. This is a new and valuable planning direction likely to get much attention in the future.

Managing Stress

Senior human resource officials and line managers, planners, and strategists, let alone individual managers, need to know that many organizational situations and events are major stress sources. These have widely different effects on organizational members.

The evidence at this point indicates that stress "turns up" the body's "fight or flight" chemical juices (Maddi and Kobasa, 1984, pp. 17–18). A complex series of biological and physiological responses ensue, affecting blood pressure, release of stress hormones, blood sugar, and brain enzymes. When people are overstressed, the consequences may be negative for performance, working relationships, client relations, and/or the individual's physical and/or mental health. As already noted, external events and forces often combine with individual makeup and circumstances to produce the damaging effects of overstress.

Stress sources help planners and strategists to establish a framework for coping. Work role factors are numerous and diverse. A representative group of these plus individual ("internal") factors and potential consequences of them are summarized in Exhibit 10-3.

Viewing the "work role" factors (Exhibit 10-3) suggests an agenda of approaches for strategists and managers to both anticipate and relieve stress events and situations. Stress needs to be approached as a two-pronged strategy which is directed toward organizational situations and persons. This has the obvious benefit of working on both sides of the problem/issue and dealing with both symptoms *and* causes. The applications section of this chapter includes an example of self-administered stress instrumentation and individual approaches to deal better with stress.

The "Hardy" Executive and Stress Resistance
(Maddi and Kobasa 1984)

The research on executive stress of Maddi and Kobasa (1984) is part of a newly emerging body of findings permitting much more systematic treatment by organizational strategists, planners, and policymakers. Their study is of interest because of the care with which it was undertaken, the size of the executive group (some 250 members of Illinois Bell Telephone Company), and the close involvement of the

EXHIBIT 10-3
A Stress Model for Strategic Analyses

Work Role or Work Features	Person's Role Factors	Potential Outcomes
• Excessive change reflecting the external and internal environment • Organization culture; contradictions, vagueness • Excessive work structuring beyond situational need • Thoroughness in the workings of the human resource planning system • Job roles, high conflict, or ambiguity • Jobs equated to red tape; characteristic stress overload • Poor communications • Quality and type of relationships (superior, subordinates, co-workers, public) • Equity in the exercise of the career system	• Perception, view of the situation or stress-related events • Progress toward personal goals • Personal temperament, tolerance for ambiguity (need for structuring), flexibility • Sense of equity, fairness • Expectations: what's denied or believed to be rightfully theirs; personal needs or aspirations; or colleague or associate expectancies • Value placed on independence • Desire/need for control • Sense of career progress, career mobility	• Burnout: moodiness, fatigue, anxiety, anger • Professional obsolescence • Deteriorating performance: decision making, creativity, mistakes, forgetfulness • Personnel impacts: absenteeism, client complaints, lessened cooperation, decreased commitment, turnover, job-related satisfaction • Personal: physical (e.g., illness), emotional • Conflict

company's well-known medical director (Dr. Robert R. J. Hilker, Jr.) and his associates with the study team. The study included most of their executive group and ran for some seven years (until 1982). One hundred and forty executives remained a part of the study at its conclusion. Their average age at the beginning of the study was 42 years. Perhaps the major limitation in the findings was that the participants were all male.

A combination of personal characteristics including commitment, control and challenge, termed "hardiness" by Maddi and Kobasa, helped executives to deal with stressful life and work events. On the positive side, the presence of these factors reduced the likelihood of physical or mental illness. Put another way, "high-stress/low-illness" executives scored high on "hardiness factors." Other executives proved vulnerable to physical and mental illness under comparable stress circumstances. Results from the study further confirmed the point that stressful situations are not always debilitating. Some factors, "if present, can have a buffering effect" for the person (Maddi and Kobasa, 1984, p. 24). Managers working under similarly stressful conditions may "process these" quite differently and thus some cope in good fashion while others prove to be quite vulnerable to stress dysfunctions. How are we to explain these results?

Exhibit 10-1, the stress model described earlier in this chapter, identified "hardiness" as a factor in several different ways. First, "hardiness" factors moderated the debilitating effects of various stressful situations so that the person could cope better or even respond positively to the situation. Second, some aspects of "hardiness" reflected an individual's constitution or personality makeup, so that their response to specific stress circumstances were quite different from their associates or colleagues to the same or similar circumstances. Third, some "hardiness" factors were linked possibly to health practices (e.g., biofeedback, diet, exercise) or were responses (positively) to development programs. Thus the strain experienced by people was either reduced or better managed from a personal standpoint. In general, the "hardy" person enjoys leading an active life and is hard working, displays a resilience in the face of adversity, and is self-reliant. More particularly, in terms of factors familiar to the business community, the "hardy" person tends toward being committed, in control (rather than powerless), and responsive to the challenge of change.

Exhibit 10-4 compares and contrasts the "hardy"/high-stress tolerance executive and those low in "hardiness" characteristics and stress tolerance. The exhibit highlights the distinct features of high-versus low-stress tolerant executives. Strategists, officials, and planners are likely to perceive that many features of the "hardy" or high-stress–tolerant executive are those often ascribed to high-potential people or those receiving high marks on performance appraisals. It is also apparent that those executives finding it difficult to deal with stress, or not knowing how, often engaged in actions that rationalize passive responses to stress conditions or simply maintain the status quo. Too, chronic pessimism regarding the problems or issues faced can readily "rub off" on associates and serve as a model of inaction. This would obstruct development of creative strategies, let alone gaining agreement to undertake positive actions. High-stress–tolerant people analyzed in this study, when viewed in profile, were well-rounded individuals possessing balanced (excellent) business-*and* social-related features. Consequently, this research provides an important and additional stress perspective, which enlarges the understanding of how individual differences may contribute to coping abilities.

"Type A Behavior" and Its Connections to Hardiness

The research undertaken by Friedman and Rosenman (1974) is widely known for its identification of behavioral features said to be associated with those prone to (severe) physical or mental disorders or heart attacks. Their behaviors were termed "Type A." Type A behavior assumes special significance in the corporate world because it represents a prototype of the aggressive, upwardly mobile person likely to be identified as excellent "managerial candidates," yet those who may also be quite vulnerable to serious health disorders including heart attacks. The general representation of the Type A person is one who is quite impatient, highly competitive and aggressive, experiences great time pressures, never seems content with themselves or their work, and generally seems to be highly active and on the move continuously. Relative to the profile of "hardy" and "low-stress–tolerant" persons drawn in Exhibit 10-4, there are similarities. However, according to the data from

EXHIBIT 10-4
Model of High- and Low-Stress–Tolerant Executives

	High stress tolerance	Low stress tolerance
1. General Characteristics	• Resilient in the face of adversity • Hard working, active, full lives, including social activities • Situational essentials can be varied or controlled • Committed • Oriented to challenge • Optimistic	• Compulsive, reactive • Situational essentials taken as given • Sense of boredom • Lack a leisure-time agenda • Respond to tasks as threat or become superficially involved • Pessimistic
2. Responses	• Maximum effort, cheerfully made • Reflect on how to look at things in a different way, seek out the "positive" side • Attempt to change their own feelings or reactions to more positive ones • Seek to transform situational constraints by varying time, place, event, or circumstance • Into health matters, exercise, and/or into sports at a conscious level and as a means of coping • Evidence commitment • Deal with change in an active and constructive manner • Seek out personal development and evidence lifelong commitment to learning • Relatively lesser signs of strain (e.g., anxiety, depression)	• Alienation, disinterest, or hanging back • Act powerless or passive—a victim of circumstances • Poor in identifying resources or alternatives • Avoid change, seek out stable situations, support the status quo • Personal development interpreted in terms of time involved or inconvenience • Seek out social relationships that support frequently a lack of action, or "playing it low profile" • Relatively high levels of strain when exposed to stressful situations (e.g., anxiety, depression, and suspicion) • Occurrence or increase of illness appears to parallel the path of stress events

Source: Based on research results from a study by Suzanne C. Kobasa and reported in Salvatore R. Maddi and Suzanne C. Kobasa, *The Hardy Executive* (Homewood, IL: Dow Jones-Irwin, 1984).

the Kobasa study (Maddi and Kobasa, 1984, pp. 40–41, 106–108), the two are unrelated insofar as vulnerability to stress was concerned. "Hardy" people evidenced interest and involvement in the things they were doing. Type A reflected impatience, felt great time pressures, and wanted to get on with things. Type As seemed to be driven, whereas the "hardy" persons appeared to be (somewhat) more congenial with their associates, situations, or circumstances.

Coping—One Approach.   Those who have dealt extensively with executive stress often reflect on broad characterizations such as "Type A" or "Type B" and point out that these are just that, general descriptions and not diagnoses. Experts such as Steven Zifferblatt of the La Costa Lifestyle and Longevity Center indicate that many managers and executives experience a variety of pressures—people need to learn to live with pressure but avoid (excessive) stress. Zifferblatt feels that (undue) executive stress is due to three conditions (Chicago *Tribune*, August 18, 1985): people promoted into a job that turns out to be too advanced for their talents, changes in major work characteristics (e.g., due to competition, technology, or market conditions), and a sudden or marked changed in their social or personal situation (e.g., diagnosis of a major illness, death of a spouse). In stress therapy, clients are "asked" to take a closer look at themselves and decide what if anything they would like to change. The effort is focused on helping them to *understand* their situation better, often many things they were already aware of. "Life doesn't have to be all or nothing; you can lead your life differently."

Hardiness: Social Background or What?

Are "hardy" executives really born that way (nature) or largely the product of their home environment or upbringing (nurture)? This is a tough question, but the results from the referenced study indicated that education, religion, ethnicity, and parents' education and age had *little or no relationship* to "hardiness." Thus, in general, socioeconomic background was largely irrelevant.

Certain aspects of background, however, can have a pronounced effect on "hardiness" characteristics. For example, an individual's sense that they can influence or control events may reflect early childhood training in independence. Also, a generous "climate" of affection during early years may facilitate general social development, individual adaptability, and involvement with one's work environment subsequently. This "climate" may help as well to build an individual's willingness to make commitments. Insightful counseling and coaching may be able to override the *lack* of these background features and contribute to the strengthening of individual "hardiness."

Developing "Hardiness" and Stress Adaptability: The Strategic View

The research results described are in the nature of associations; that is, "hardy" executives were found to possess such and such "features," but can these be learned? The answer is a qualified "yes" for many different individual situations. Some of these aproaches are suggested by the results in Exhibit 10-4. The "hardy" person uses basically two sets of mechanisms in stress coping: internal knowledge of self, which may serve as a basis to alter how they view their situation, and strategies that are based on varying time, place, or events transforming events or circumstances. Both adaptive mechanisms can be either established or strengthened through thoughtful counseling and coaching. They may benefit further from behavioral modeling by supervisors and lab-type sensitivity training. Some individual characteristics are more easily strengthened than others. For example, a commitment is difficult to strengthen. Yet is is feasible to build a person's belief (and, eventually, the reality) that he or she can successfully alter circumstances. This may strengthen confidence and the person's sense of the situation. People also can learn that "regressive coping" such as ignoring a situation or withdrawal usually doesn't solve anything. Old stereotypes often have to be unearthed as a part of individual sensitization so that these can be dealt with in realistic fashion. Also, this and other research indicates that a supportive environment involving supervisory relationships, organizational policy, availability of training, and the like can benefit "hardiness" development.

A number of strategic considerations are suggested from this discussion. One set of approaches includes reducing some of the dysfunctional aspects of managerial and executive work features. Also, improving the understanding of the existing situation through "audits" can help to establish the goodness of fit between work requirements and managerial strengths (and weaknesses). Similarly, surveys to establish the profile of "hardiness" characteristics among the existing managerial group and which benefit from the types of results cited here may provide a whole new assessment dimension for judging individual potential or identifying "high-potential" people. Feedback of these results to the people involved may also prove highly beneficial, and thus communication channels need to be identified for this purpose.

These newer types of HR programs seek to anticipate the individual impacts of change, strengthen managerial development planning, salvage executives who may plateau or become obsolete, and improve the quality of work life (work-related) satisfaction. To some extent positive results may come about from the company's communications *and* actions demonstrating a real effort to improve these situations. If change is impending, change briefings which are timely and thorough can ameliorate personnel transitions. Similarly changes in positional documents (job descriptions) or performance criteria require clear and timely explanation. Although organizational strategists and policymakers may at times *not* be able to alter circumstances significantly, viable options may (still) exist based on improving the coping abilities of the managerial group and providing strong internal support.

Work Stress—Sex Differences?

Examination of a group of 19 stress studies suggests that there may be some important differences between men and women in stress vulnerability and coping approaches and abilities (Jick and Mitz, 1985). The initial comparisons of study results indicated that women tended to report higher rates of (symptoms of) psychological and emotional stress such as tension, anxiety, perceived dissatisfaction, and depression. On the other hand, men appeared to be more vulnerable to severe physical and psychological problems, illnesses such as coronary heart disease, and withdrawal behavior such as problem drinking. In general, women seemed less likely to display Type A coronary-prone characteristics (as referenced in the "hardiness" discussion) than men (Jick and Mitz, 1985, p. 412).

Although various explanations were sought for why these apparent differences occurred including genetic, social/psychological, and situational/structural ones, the information was inconclusive. At this point the best explanation regarding the adverse results for women seem to be with the situational or structural factors. Women's role in the work situation is frequently such as to generate disproportionate strain or place them at a disadvantage relative to lack of influence or due to low-power/authority roles. Adverse comparisons relative to comparable worth, absence of a mentor, or inadequate networks of support groups are additional factors. Other causal factors may include disproportionate representation in high-stress jobs and with little individual discretion; lack of mobility; and role overload, or conflict due to joint work-home or family responsibilities. Clearly, more information is needed to understand these situations resulting in (potentially) different results for men and women.

Stress Agenda for the Organization

Organizational strategies for stress containment and management are situational. This recognizes differing situations including the stress tolerance of individuals. A set of basic assumptions underlie these approaches. One basic assumption is that some level of individual stress (tension or pressure) is needed and beneficial for many processes, activities, creative efforts, and good performance. It is also assumed that conditions can and do exist that can lead to overstressed people with potentially negative effects for the people and various aspects of performance. An additional assumption is that various degrees of freedom exist to alter the patterns, potency, and impacts of stress but that a significant group of these lie outside of individual control! In truth, some may be very difficult for the organization's control as well. Situational or people constraints vary a great deal and thus the scope or depth of remedial or preventative actions will differ.

Some useful guides can be set out, although not enough about this area is known to set forth precise actions or prescriptions. A basic plank in a strategic effort is the recognition of the range of events contributing to stress and the relative differences among these. A representative group of these were summarized in Exhibit 10-3. The type of action research in banks described by Mirabile can generate useful lists of stress events or sources as seen by the staff assigned to these work units. Also, participants can share their view of the relative potency of these occurrences. Admittedly, this type of study may lead to average results and general characterizations, but the results serve to profile stress forces as seen by organization members and thereby provide an initial point of departure for further study. A side benefit may be that the sharing of these feelings are therapeutic because they relieve much internal pressure.

A significant group of work role factors related to stress involves the organization's external environment. Thus forecasting or scanning efforts can take on new significance. Information for the types of stress analyses described here represent a logical extension of business and strategic planning studies. To the extent that the human resource function serves as an organizing point for stress analyses, a helpful first step would be the drawing up of an agenda of the type illustrated in Exhibit 10-5. It serves as a working document from which useful guides or types of analyses are initiated for planning and strategic actions as well as processes and programs.

Since the type, frequency, and duration of stress factors is likely to differ among various corporate units due to differences in their competitive and work environments and personnel staffing, both general and situation-specific lists will prove useful (point 3, Exhibit 10-5).

The fact that many organizations regularly survey their people on various performance, job satisfaction, and culture matters provides a natural vehicle for appraising stress developments (point 4) over time. Senior personnel will often get deeply involved in the business of their area and fail to recognize important shifts or changes taking place that may have highly negative stress effects. Staff reductions, cost containment programs, or bringing in "outside" senior staffing may be considered as "usual" situations. In brief, changes need to be monitored and evaluated for their stress effects.

The clarity with which policy officials and senior managers establish the ground rules of promotion or career mobility form another important link in the strategic approach (points 6 and 7 of Exhibit 10-5). Too often these ground rules are poorly understood, vague, or subject to different interpretation. The exercise of important *but different* promotion criteria among officials can and does create havoc with managers or fast trackers who aspire to be upwardly mobile.

Undeniably, the job itself, assigned responsibilities, and the necessary behaviors for success are very much part of the picture. These need not be seen as being "cut in stone." Commonsense rebalancing of responsibilities or shifts in event patterns can have a pronounced, remedial effect. The intent of these approaches is not to "coddle" managers but to capitalize on a new body of information likely to prove helpful to the organization and individual.

Agenda for the Individual Manager

Inspection of the factors included in Exhibit 10-5 indicates that an agenda of possible actions for the individual will require determined actions by the organization and person alike. Stress sources are often ingrained, linked to habits, values, beliefs, or experiences. Thus, rooting out causes and fostering individual change is challenging! The "personal role factors" referenced in Exhibit 10-5 are comprised

EXHIBIT 10-5
Managing Excessive Stress: An Organizational Agenda

1. Train line managers and human resources and selective staff as in planning, to monitor their respective environments for change forces which in potency, sequence, timing, or combination are likely to have adverse results for individual work activities and patterns.

2. Help senior managers and officials to gain the needed detachment to recognize the degree of change in their units likely to prove disruptive for their personnel. Use models such as "hardiness" or Type A as a basis for (adult) educational or remedial approaches—provide feedback.

3. Encourage senior officials and supervising managers to initiate activities whose purpose is to start to recognize the warning signs of high stress among their staffs and to identify people who are prone to being overstressed.

4. Periodically review in some systematic way, potential high-stress sources or situations as a basis for identifying means of dealing with these.

5. View job and situation design strategically. Generate options which serve to reduce high stress, improve work features for greater personal "rewards," or both.

6. Recognize that communications clarity regarding various organizational situations, processes, and policies can play a major role in a stress program. Examples of application areas include identifying career ladders and promotion criteria, job openings, clear performance criteria, and knowledge of required job behaviors for success.

7. Reappraise the organization's culture for circumstances, policies, decision making, and the like which encourage unduly high-stress individual actions. Also seek to identify areas of culture contributing to uncertainty regarding performance expectancies, valued bases for behavior, and/or exercise of the punishment/reward system.

8. Start to build useful stress indicators and measures into the human resource data base which can then serve as benchmarks for subsequent comparison and so that these can be increasingly used for strategic planning purposes.

9. Introduce wellness programs that help to put organization members in fuller control of their stress circumstances. Consider self-assessment instrumentation to assist individuals in profiling their own stress features and situations.

of how events are seen (perception), makeup of the person, personal goals and needs, commitments, and skills. General experience in many different training and development situations indicates that individuals change slowly. Results initially will be modest and not spectacular. Perhaps the most important "weapon" at the disposal of the individual manager is to encourage (help) them to understand themselves better. *Build self-awareness!* What situations appear to be stressful to the person and why? How are they viewed? What is assumed? "Are they seen in an accurate and/or realistic way?" How does the person respond to these physically (e.g., pacing) and behaviorally (e.g., anger)? Without these first-hand personal sensitivities and knowledge, the manager is in a poor position to know what's happening to him or her, let alone what to do about it. More details of a "personal agenda for managing excessive stress" are included in the applications section for this chapter (S1 and Exhibit 10-8). Also, a self-scoring Managerial Stress Tolerance Form is provided in the applications section of this chapter. This type of instrumentation is used widely in training sessions with many different managerial groups. Instructions are provided for self-scoring and general interpretations.

Many devices have been used to build self-awareness, including biofeedback, time/stress diaries or logs, and observations from associates. These form a part of the stress literature of the training field and are not detailed here.

Interim Summary—Stress Planning and Management

Stress management is assuming strategic importance in a growing number of organizations because of its connection to organization performance, wellness, and individual vitality. Both work and individual role factors are a part of the picture. It is well to realize, however, that the occurrence of changes in both simultaneously can result in mutually reinforcing effects with still greater negative outcomes. Practical bases exist to mount stress management efforts that affect the timing, pattern, and events of specific situations. Also, improved means are at hand to strengthen personal knowledge and responses to overstressful conditions.

PART II. AGING AND PERFORMANCE—A STRATEGIC PERSPECTIVE

Introduction: Age, Performance Issues

Executives and strategy planners have many good reasons to involve themselves in questions of age, aging, and performance. Not the least of these is that senior succession matters inherently involve age, aging, and retirement issues. The fast-growing numbers of more senior people and the extension of mandatory retirement to age 70 thus are very much a part of these strategic concerns. Also, work force projections of middle-aged people indicate that they will comprise a large part of the future work force.

There are increasing numbers of "young-old people" in their late 50s, 60s, and even the early 70s who are relatively healthy and vigorous. Many are organization members, and a significant portion of them hold senior managerial positions. Corporate policymakers are challenged to identify and exploit ways in which this human resource potential can be fully developed, used, and maintained.

Also there is quite a different side to these matters which hinges specifically on age stereotyping (see Exhibits 10-6 and 10-7). That is, generally held beliefs exist regarding individual characteristics in different age groupings. Many reflect over-generalizing or lack of understanding of the specifics of a situation.

Various studies indicate that beliefs regarding age consider the older person as having less potential for managerial positions, being less interested in change, and more reluctant to cope with future challenges. These views, often distorted ones, also propose that older or more senior people are less productive relative to job demands and often less enthusiastic or creative in their work situation (Rosen and Jerdee, 1977). The fact that these stereotypes exist and may be held by people in key positions is likely to affect key human resource decisions as, for example, promotion. The number of viable, promotable people could well be narrowed relative to older personnel if a new job or assignment were seen as requiring particular crisis management skills, flexibility, creativity, and/or mental dexterity.

The results of Rosen and Jerdee (1977) and other studies clearly confirm the existence of many of these stereotypes. Thus it behooves strategists and policy official to examine their organizations critically and to identify and examine these stereotypes for their functionality or validity. There is a real need to know the degree to which (understood) policy and/or practice leads to adverse results for older personnel in a self-confirming way, and what planning and strategic actions are indicated. We do know that lowered expectations for individual performance per se can be self-confirming.

Human resource planners and strategists need a more factual base of information to counter the possible stereotyping or biases that have grown up around age-related matters generally (see Exhibit 10-7). When it is recognized that the longstanding age 65 for retirement was, in reality, an arbitrary cutoff point engineered by New Deal politicans and planners, the linkage of age to function and performance requires serious examination. Longstanding assumptions and biases

---

EXHIBIT 10-6
Age Stereotyping and Succession Decisions: The Classic Model

Rigidity	Absence of enthusiasm
Change resistance and lack change adaptability	Presence of high absenteeism
Less mental flexibility	Poor memory
Uncooperativeness	Undependability
Preference for the status quo	Physical impairment
Lack of reliability	Proneness to mistakes
Uncertainty in decision making	Irritability

The Passing Scene:

John Bigelow, age 72, is a tennis coach for a community high school and plays competitively. He is also the track and swimming coach.

Frances Berg Sherman, age 91, retired as president of Wakem-McLaughlin, a public warehousing firm, at age 80.

EXHIBIT 10-7
Aging, Development, Performance: Myths and Reality

Intellectual Functioning

1. The large majority of older people do not decline markedly in intellectual and social competence until very advanced old age (mid-70s and beyond).

2. Intellectual functioning is relatively stable. If decrement does occur, it is probably more attributable to poor health, social isolation, limited education, or lowered motivation.

3. Isolation or/and shunting aside of older personnel into undemanding work frequently hastens the decline of individual contributions—and the (erroneous) assumed correlation of age and infirmities become self-fulfilling.

Change

1. To the extent that personal crises or major change events occur (e.g., death of loved one, stroke), the degree of effect is greatly moderated by earlier life-styles of coping, colleagial counseling, social support (e.g., friends), and timing of the events.

2. Those experiencing a series of psychologically stressful events are often more vulnerable to illness or disease that impair of performance; some of these can be ameliorated through counseling, education, and intervention programs.

Physiological Aspects, Learning, Decision Making

1. Sensory processes are generally age related and decline, especially vision and to some extent hearing.

2. Reaction time tends to decrease with aging—but becomes especially relevant where speed of response is important or (really) needed.

3. Most learning difficulties of older people result from the problems of acquiring and recalling information rather than retention. That is, "memory" problems are usually connected to the short term—when information *reaches* long-term memory, it is more readily retained.

4. Short-term memory blockages are connected to learning difficulties experienced in problem solving and decision making. Facilitating learning through better data organization, slower pacing, and good feedback can improve short-term memory processes. Training and development and unit procedures should be examined.

5. Age has surprisingly little effect on the physical strength of people whose work is very physical, at least until about age 50. Even at that point, and perhaps into the lower 60s, although physical strength decreases perhaps 10 to 15 percent, this may have little functional significance.

6. Older persons tend to take longer to reach decisions and appear to express somewhat greater hesitancy or lack of confidence in dealing with risk or uncertain situations. However, older managers appear to be able to assess more accurately the value of new(er) information.

Source: Based on National Advisory Council on Aging, *Our Future Selves,* National Institute of Health, No. 80-1446. (Washington D.C.: U.S. Government Printing Office; 1980). See the bibliography for other studies underlying this summary. Since some of these points are based on modest-scale research studies, they must be taken as advisory or suggestive at this point.

need to be challenged. A good example of these deep-seated attitude biases regarding age are assumptions that older managers (workers) are poor performers or that they have high rates of absenteeism. Yet studies of scholarly professional and artistic groups reveal multiple peaks at "midcareer ages and beyond" (age 40 and the late 50s). Also studies of older salespeople, for example, suggest that age may be a positive factor in performance and that the absenteeism record of older persons often matches or is better than that of younger people. Reliability, too, is generally greater (National Advisory Council, 1980). A representative group of these "myths and facts" is brought together in Exhibit 10-7.

For added convenience of the reader, the points in Exhibit 10-7 are grouped under several categories of study results. No attempt is made to delve into the details of these results from psychological and biomedical research. What is clear is that there is enough evidence to warrant a much more serious and studied approach of this area and its impacts on organizational policies, processes, and activities. Representative citations are provided at the end of this chapter. Since some of the studies were modest in scope, these summary points must be taken as suggestive. There are many gaps in this informtion, and much research is currently underway to fill in important omissions in this information. However, what can be said with much certainty is that there are many differences in each situation involving older or more senior persons. The generalizations regarding adverse work effects with aging are likely to be off the mark or completely wrong.

Functional Competence

Modern managerial job and needs analyses are concerned with end-job behaviors for success. This focus is especially relevant in considering age issues. "What is it that the person has to do in a particular job assignment to be rated as successful?" This view places development and staffing questions in a more realistic light. Programming for management development and vulnerability to charges of "age discrimination" in promotion or employment decisions can both be more effectively served by dealing with functional criteria of competence. Other corporate benefits are also likely to be realized when it is recognized that various job features or work conditions may be redesigned or reorganized to achieve functional competence. "Functional competence" was also an important concept used in the Honeywell approach described in the previous chapter. This approch, focusing on end results, helps to reduce the influence of prior beliefs (biases) related to aging and performance and places the emphasis on functional actions to meet performance (appraisal) criteria for success which are job related.

Older Managers, Change, and Strategic Considerations

The apparent lack of mobility on the part of some older managers reflects a combination of circumstances, some portion of which may be self-confirming based on past organization practices. It must be acknowledged that with aging, people often improve various connections and involvement with groups and situations outside of the organization. These include professional and community groups, family, and various recreational activities, all of which affect mobility to varying degrees. Also, where managers have worked largely under stable conditions with little change, the sudden introduction of change becomes threatening. Under these conditions, people feel threatened because, in the past, their niche in the workplace was defined by a stable work situation and activities. This niche included recognition and prestige, power, friendships, identification, and well-worked-out routines. Sudden change under these conditions is seen as "a crisis," "a disruption," or "an upheaval"—emotion-ladden terms used to express feelings of anxiety or uncertainty.

Planners and strategists, however, can't afford to ignore the fact that the change dilemma is often a self-confirming one. Job incumbents have been permitted, even encouraged, to cut deeper and deeper work grooves built around (then) existing work routines. At times, staying in a particular functional area or specialization was seen as being "for the convenience of the organization" or a demonstration of loyalty which was reinforced through salary increments or promotion. Thus tracking of managerial movement or change patterns and developing models with which comparisons can be made can prove highly useful in reducing the organization's complicity in creating the very conditions it often decries.

The Older Manager and Succession Decisions

Many policy officials prefer not to deal openly with issues related to promotion decisions where there is a "question" of "years of useful work life (remaining)." This matter is often not so much a problem of performance per se but rather the "useful" business life of the executive involved. This is a highly sensitive and difficult area because of the legal issues, practical concerns for the organization, and of course impact on the person. The amendments to the Age in Retirement Act in 1978 made it clear that age per se cannot be the primary reason for failure to promote. Yet the underlying issues are usually not as clear cut as this. It is well known that in some promotion situations, organizations will have to make a long-term commitment to developing the individual to meet promotion requirements fully. Some clarification is provided for all involved where positions have been studied carefully in terms of their work-related requirements. This is especially true where these needs have been brought out clearly through needs analyses relative to the (older) candidate being considered. Undoubtedly, some of the legal suits brought in this area reflect insufficient study of positions in detail, and in job-relevant terms.

Aging Matters in Perspective

The evidence seems to indicate that age stereotypes influence major human resource decisions in a variety of ways. The classic age prototype is rigid, change resistant, less mentally agile, uncooperative, less enthused over future challenge, less creative, steeped in the status quo, often unreliable, uncertain in decision making, and less adaptable to changing circumstances. These biases have become operational in particular organizations. Supervising managers shunt the older person aside as one who is too costly to retrain or a high-risk promotion candidate. Stereotyping leads easily to self-confirming actions which can reinforce the classic prototype of the older manager. Yet the term "older" is clearly a relative one, and the timing, circumstances, functional requirements, and such indicate that these terms could be put aside with beneficial results. "Older" is not a calendared event that automatically takes place at a particular point in a person's life. What is relevant in major planning and strategic decisions are such considerations as functional requirements of positions, meeting the continuity and renewal needs of the organization, and creating as broad a talent pool as possible to service these requirements. Age biases and stereotyping have no place in this picture.

Summary

The rapidly growing body of research and practical information concerning personnel wellness, stress, and aging provides a unique opportunity to business and human resource planners and strategists. Although much of this information is suggestive of possibilities and not complete, it is clear that strategic thinking can benefit from the information that is already available. Unbounded stress-producing conditions, often the product of both unplanned and planned business change, can adversely affect individual performance. Key efficiency dimensions such as absenteeism and work output can and do suffer. Managerial stress can lead to conflicts, undercut cooperation, diminish creativity and decision quality, and contribute to (serious) physiological and psychological disorders. Also it appears that stress may have somewhat different effects related to the sex of the individual. For females, there may be greater effects in the emotional realm; for males, results suggest higher incidences of serious physical diseases or extremes of regressive types of coping responses (e.g., problem drinking and perhaps addiction).

Corporate stress experiences suggest that strategists can improve the quality of longer-range planning through increased sensitization as to the adverse impact of change on the (managerial) work force. Also, a new agenda for strategists is emerging from recognition of the working of stress forces under existing organizational conditions. Also contributing to the agenda is an understanding of the stress profile of the managerial group, and what it implies by way of adaptive approaches for these. Work and structural redesign, revised tactics for the introduction of change, providing higher levels of internal support, and strengthening the stress-coping capabilities of the managerial group, form part of the new agenda of planners and strategists. These organizational actions have their counterpart in actions designed to strengthen individual coping responses.

In general, individuals need to be increasingly aware of their own stress features, situational stress sources, and various coping options. Guidelines are often established by models of successful stress coping. The scope and content of development programming too become a part of the strategist's planning agenda.

The individual has several workable approaches that can be drawn on to better deal with stress. Part of a personal strategy includes the person's ability to transform time, place, or situation circumstances to make these more congenial or less threatening. Another part of the individual's approach involves a personal reorientation as to the nature of stress forces plus personal coping responses which involves health fitness, exercise, and diet. These examples of individual coping strategies are highly flexible permitting their adpatation to many different individual circumstances.

Aging

Nobody had figured out how to stop or arrest (very much) the aging processes, but we do know enough now to introduce a "healthy level" of critical thinking when it comes to more senior personnel. This thinking should also facilitate strategic thinking and human resource planning processes. These will affect such areas as succession, management development, candidate selection, assessments of performance and potential, and promotion and retirement decisions. The listing of "myths and reality" in Exhibit 10-6 and 10-7 are symbolic of the growing pool of information needed to improve strategic thinking and planning. It also serves to encourage more realistic (often healthful) outlooks for the person. Longstanding biases connecting aging, individual function, and performance are being set aside in favor of a much more careful and selective view of the individual's work context and situation. Emerging challenges for planners and strategists include qualifying considerations such as "functional competence," strategies to introduce a "healthful level of change," and developing appropriate measurement criteria for individual stress.

REFERENCES

Part I

Aikman, Ann and Walter McQuade. *Stress, What It Is, What It Can Do to Your Health, How to Fight Back*. New York: Dutton, 1974.

Bartolome, Fernando. "Must Success Cost So Much?" *Harvard Business Review*, Vol. 58, no. 2 (March–April 1980): 137.

Beehr, Terry. "Relationship of Stress to Individually and Organizationally Valued States: Higher-Order Needs as a Moderator." *Journal of Applied Psychology*, Vol. 61 (1977): p. 41.

Benson, Herbert. "How Much Stress Is Too Much?" *Harvard Business Review*, Vol. 58, no. 5 (September–October 1980): p. 86.

Beuson, Herbert. "Your Innate Asset for Combating Stress." *Harvard Business Review*, vol. 58, no. 4 (July–August 1974): 49.

Blaker, Karen. "Easing Up—A Prescription for Learning How to Cope with Stress." *USA Today,* (May, 1984), p. 67.

Breo, Dennis, J. and Robert S. Eliot. *Is It Worth Dying for?* New York: Bantam Books, 1984.

Burack, Elmer H. and Thomas J. McNichols. *Technology, Policy and Change.* Kent, OH: Kent State University Press, 1973.

Burack, Elmer H. and Forence Torda. *The Manager's Guide to Change.* Belmont, CA: Reichold Publishing, 1979.

Cooper, Cary. *Understanding Executive Stress.* New York: PBI Books. 1977.

De Frank, Richard S. and Cary L. Cooper. "Worksite Stress Management Interventions: Their Effectiveness and Conceptualization." Paper presented at Annual Meeting, Academy of Management, San Diego, CA, August 1985. More information on worksite stress research is available from De Frank at the University of Texas Medical Branch, Galveston.

Elliott, G. R. and C. Eisdorfer, eds. *Stress and Human Health: Analysis and Implications of Research.* New York: Springer, 1982.

Ewing, David. "Tension Can Be an Asset." *Harvard Business Review,* Vol. 42, no. 5 (September–October 1964): 71.

Frew, David R. *Management of Stress: Using TM at Work.* Chicago: Nelson Hall, 1977.

Friend, Kenneth E. "Stress and Performance: Effects of Subjective Workload and Time Urgency." *Personnel Psychology,* Vol. 35 (Autumn 1982): 623–626.

Furst, M. Lawrence and Donald R. Morse. *Stress for Success.* Dallas: Van Nostrand Reinhold, 1979.

Friedman, M. and R. H. Rosenman. *Type A Behavior and Your Heart.* New York: Knopf, 1974.

Fulvey, Jack. "How Burnout Affects Corporate Managers and Their Performance." *The Wall Street Journal,* April 1979, p. 1.

Gupta, Nina. "Job Stress and Employee Behaviors." *Organizational Behavior and Human Performance,* Vol. 23 (1983): 373–387.

Holmes, Thomas H. *The Broken Taboo.* Seattle: University of Washington, School of Medicine, 1978.

Ivancevich, John. "Who's Liable for Stress on the Job?" *Harvard Business Review,* Vol. 63, no. 3 (March–April 1985): 60.

Ivancevich, John M. and Michael T. Matteson. "Stress Diagnostic Survey" (copyrighted, circa 1982). School of Business, University of Houston, 1982.

Ivancevich, John M., Michael T. Matteson, and Cynthia Preston. "Occupational Stress, Type A Behavior, and Psychological Well-Being." *Academy of Management Journal,* Vol. 25, no. 2 (1982): 373–391.

Ivancevich, John M., H. Albert Nafier, and James C. Wetherbe. "Occupational Stress, Attitudes, and Health Problems in the Information Systems Professional." *ACM Journal,* Vol. 26, no. 10 (October 1983): 800–806.

Jamal, Muhammad. "Job Stress and Job Performance Controversy: An Empirical Assessment." *Organizational Behavior and Human Performance,* Vol. 24 (1984): 1–9.

Jick, Todd D. and Linda F. Mitz. "Sex Differences in Work Stress." *The Academy of Management Review,* Vol. 10, no. 3 (July 1985): 408–420.

Johnson, Wista. "How to Tame the Stress in your Life." *Essence,* April 1983, pp. 82–83.

Kindler, Herberts. "Time Out for Stress Management Training." *Training and Development Journal* (June 1984): 64.

Kindler, Herbert S. and Richard J. Perle. "The Personal Stress Assessment Inventory: Its Use in a Study of Managerial and Professional Employees." Working Paper, Center for Management Effectiveness, Los Angeles, CA, College of Business Administration, Loyola University, 1985.

Kindler, Herbert S. and Richard J. Perle. "The Personal Stress Assessment Inventory," rev. Center for Management Effectiveness, Los Angeles, CA: College of Business Administration, Loyola Marymount University, 1981.

Mackay, Colin and Tom Cox. *Response to Stress.* London: IPC Business Press, 1979.

Maddi, Salvatore R. and Suzanne C. Kobasa. *The Hardy Executive: Health Under Stress.* Homewood, IL: Dow Jones-Irwin, 1984.

Matteson, Michael T. and John M. Ivancevich. *Managing Job Stress and Health.* New York: The Free Press, 1982.

Mirabile, Richard J. "Stress," *Training and Development Journal.* (August 1983): 40–44.

Moss, Leonard. *Management Stress.* Reading, MA: Addison-Wesley, 1981.

Murphy, Lawrence, "Occupational Stress Management: A Review and Appraisal." National Institute of Occupational Safety and Health (circa 1982).

National Advisory Council on Aging, No. 80-1446 Special Report, *"Our Future Selves: A Research Plan Toward Understanding Age.* Washington, D.C.: U.S. Government Printing Office, 1980.

Parasuramen, Saroj. "Sources and Outcomes of Stress in Organizational Settings: Toward the Development of a Structural Model." *Academy of Management Journal,* Vol. 27 (1984): 330–350.

Peters, Ruanne. "Time Out from Tension." *Harvard Business Review,* Vol. 56, no. 1 (January–February 1978): 120–124.

Seliger, Susan. "Making Stress Work for You." *McCalls,* June 1984, pp. 125–128.

Shaffer, Martin. *Life After Stress.* New York: Plenum, 1982.

Stoner, Charles. "Developing a Corporate Policy for Managing Stress." *Personnel* (May–June 1983): 66.

Theorell, T. "Selected Illnesses and Somatic Factors in Relation to Two Psychosocial Stress Indices." *Journal of Psychosocial Research,* Vol. 20 (1978): 7–20.

Wyler, A. R., M. Masuda, and T. H. Holmes. "Seriousness of Illness Rating Scale." *Journal of Psychosomatic Research,* Vol. 11 (1968): 363–375.

Part II

Aaronson, B. S. "Personality Stereotypes of Aging." *Journal of Gerontology,* Vol. 21, no. 3 (1966): 458–462.

"Age and Performance in Retail Trades," Ottawa, Canadian Department of Labor, 1959, as referenced in Carol H. Kelleher and Daniel A. Quirk, "Age Functional Capacity and Work: An Annotated Bibliography." *Industrial Gerontology,* Vol. 19 (1973): 80.

Bowers, W. H. "An Appraisal of Worker Characteristics as Related to Age." *Journal of Applied Psychology,* Vol. 36, no. 5 (1952): 296–300.

Burack, Elmer H. and Florence Torda. *The Manager's Guide to Change*. New York: Reichold, 1979.

Cunningham, Robert M. "What Old People Want: More Work, Less Talk." *Hospital*, (May 16, 1980), pp. 85–89.

Dennis, Wayne. "Creative Productivity Between the Ages of 20 and 80 Years." *Journal of Gerontology*, Vol. 21 (1966): 1.

Green, R. F. and G. Remanis. "The Age–Intelligence Relationship–Longitudinal Studies Can Mislead." In G. M. Shatto, ed., *Employment of the Middle-Aged*. Springfield, IL: Charles C Thomas, 1972.

Hall, Douglas T. "Socialization Processes in Later Years: Adult Development in Organizations." Paper presented at the 39th National Academy of Management meetings, Atlanta, GA, 1979.

Hill, Raymond E. and Edwin L. Miller. "Job Change and the Middle Seasons of a Man's Life." *Academy of Management Journal*, Vol. 24, no. 1 (1981): 114–127.

Hulin, Charles L. and Patricia C. Smith. "A Linear Model of Job Satisfaction." *Journal of Applied Psychology*, Vol. 49 (1965): 209–210.

Kelly, J. M. "Women, the Handicapped, and Older Workers." In J. Famularo, ed., *Handbook of Modern Personnel Administration*. New York: McGraw-Hill, 1972.

Levenson, Daniel J. *The Seasons of a Man's Life*, pp. 97–106. New York: Ballantine Books, 1978.

National Advisory Council on Aging. *Our Future Selves: A Research Plan Toward Undertaking Aging*, National Institute of Health Publication, No. 80-1446. Washington, DC: U.S. Government Printing Office, 1980.

Neugarten, Bernice L. A Developmental View of Adult Personality." In J. E. Birren, ed., *Relations of Development and Aging*, pp. 176–208. Springfield, IL: Charles C Thomas, 1964.

Pelz, Ronald C. "The Creative Years in Research Environments." Industrial and Electrical Engineering, Transaction of the Professional Technical Group on Engineering Management, 1964, EM-II, p. 23.

Riley, M. W. et al. *Aging and Society*. Volume 1. *An Inventory of Research Findings*. New York: Russell Sage, 1968.

Rosen, Benson and Thomas H. Jerdee. "Too Old or Not Too Old," *Harvard Business Review*, Vol. 55, no. 6 (November–December 1977): 97–106.

Rosen, Benson and Thomas Jerdee. "The Influence of Age Stereotypes on Managerial Decisions," *Journal of Applied Psychology*, Vol. 61, no. 2 (1976): 180–183.

Schein, Edgar H. *Career Dynamics: Matching Individual and Organization Needs*. Reading, MA: Addison-Wesley, 1978.

Sheppard, Harold L. *New Perspectives on Older Workers*. Kalamazoo, MI: W. E. Upjohn Institute for Employment Research, 1971.

Smith, N. W. "Older Worker Efficiency in Jobs of Various Types." *Personnel Journal*, Vol. 32, no. 1 (1953): 19–23.

Sonnenfeld, Jeffrey. "Dealing with the Aging Work Force." *Harvard Business Review*, Vol. 56, no.6 (November–December 1978): 81–92.

Taylor, Ronald N. "Age and Experience as Determinants of Managerial Information Processing and Decision Making Performance." *Academy of Management Journal,* Vol. 18 (1975),
p. 602.

Vaillant, George E. *Adaptation to Life.* Boston: Little, Brown, 1977.

Van Maanen, John, ed. *Organizational Careers: Some New Perspectives.* New York: John
Wiley, 1977.

Vroom, Victor H. and Bernd Pahl. "Age and Risk Taking Among Managers." *Journal of
Applied Psychology,* Vol. 13 (1971): 22–28.

Walker, James W. and Harriet Lazer. *The End of Mandatory Retirement.* New York: John
Wiley, 1978.

Welford, A. T. "Thirty Years of Psychological Research on Age and Work." *Journal of
Occupational Psychology,* Vol. 49 (1976): 129.

Work in America Institute. *Mid-Career Perspectives: The Middle-Aged and Older Popula-
tion.* Washington, DC: WAI, 1978.

APPLICATIONS SECTION

1. Managing Excess Stress: A Personal Agenda

The first items in Exhibit 10-8 emphasize building individual self-awareness including the idea that "if you are going to get worked up about something, make sure
you have seen it clearly and accurately." "Is your response to current situations
being triggered by past or similar circumstances?" "Have you seen the situation for
what it is?" And if the event has been interpreted correctly and it is a stressful one,
"Will you recognize it as such?"

The balance of the items in Exhibit 10-8 represent specific actions that individual managers can undertake to build stress management strengths. Here are
some additional background factors (Holmes, 1978, pp. 224–233):

- *Stressful language* (no. 3): Thought and self-talk related to stress events are
  natural. However, the person needs to realize that bodily responses and
  behavior can be triggered by these just as easily as by external circumstances.
  Many people need to adopt a new self-language that plays down the "awfuliz-
  ing" and attempts more accurately to represent what is really hapening—"has
  everything fallen through or in reality are most things going well and is it
  'such and such' that is the real problem?"
- *TSS* (timing, sequence, situation, no. 5). As in the organization or external
  circumstance, the individual must recognize that pattern, sequence, timing,
  and situation can be varied. "Schedule certain kinds or numbers of appoint-

EXHIBIT 10-8
Managing Excessive Stress: A Personal Agenda

---

1. Get to know yourself better, what situations are stressful, the signs and symptoms of stress, and your bodily and behavioral responses.
2. Determine that your situation as such is being seen in a reasonably accurate way.
3. Purge high-stress, body, demand/command language.
4. Use a more accurate, less emotional, self-dialogue language.
5. Examine critically the "TSS" (i.e., the timing, sequence of stress situations for alteration or elimination).
6. Improve your change coping abilities by regularly reviewing or monitoring your own situation or environment for change (events, frequency, potency); avoiding multiple (situational) changes—where possible and maintaining useful habits and areas of nonchange (stability).
7. Establish a small network of people with whom you can talk out stressful problems and issues—your "stress sounding board."
8. Develop a regular exercise pattern. Also use exercise as a selective personal strategy when faced with tough circumstances.
9. Develop a good knowledge of diet and nutrition to avoid overstressing the body.
10. Learn how to engage in relaxation exercise.

Source: Based in part on Thomas H. Holmes, *The Broken Taboo* (Seattle: University of Washington, School of Medicine, 1978), pp. 224–233.

ments at different times," or "change the time at which certain types of events are handled," or "use different people for problem solving" are example of positive individual steps.

The balance of the items in Exhibit 10-8 are likely clear and discussed in detail in the literature.

2. Managerial Stress Tolerance: Self-scoring Form*

EXHIBIT 10-9
Managerial Stress Tolerance: Self-scoring Form

Stress is a normal situation in everyday work and personal life. Our bodies help us to organize and deal with stress. Stress (tension) is often a positive force and brings out creative approaches or prepares us for special situations. The real problem is being overstressed whether due to *external* factors such as overload or working too long under high-pressure conditions or *internal* factors reflecting how we look at things or a combination of these. This form should help you start thinking about yourself, your particular situation, and what is good for you.

For the following situations check the item (NRSOUA) that seems to best describe your situation. If the situation is one you haven't experienced, indicate your likely response if faced with it. There are no right or wrong answers—it is how you feel. The "C" column is scored later as a part of the interpretation (see last section).

N	R	S	0	U	A	C
never	rarely	sometimes	often	usually	always	changeability

Situations	N	R	S	0	U	A	C
1. Often I feel under much stress without any warning.	——	——	——	——	——	——	——
2. It's upsetting to have my day laid out and then to have things disrupted by a last-minute meeting or "emergency" situation.	——	——	——	——	——	——	——
3. I never seem to get the salary or increase that I'm really worth.	——	——	——	——	——	——	——
4. I like the challenge of tough competition.	——	——	——	——	——	——	——
5. "Bad news" through public communications media such as TV or the newspaper can make me feel in the dumps for days.	——	——	——	——	——	——	——
6. My work style is such that I prefer to work alone—this way I don't depend on them nor they on me.	——	——	——	——	——	——	——

*Two excellent forms with a similar format are John M. Ivancevich and Michael T. Matteson. "Stress Diagnostic Survey," School of Business, University of Houston (circa 1982), copyrighted; and Herbert S. Kindler and Richard J. Perle, "The Personal Stress Assessment Inventory," Center for Management Effectiveness, College of Business Administration. Loyola Marymount University, Los Angeles, CA, rev. 1985, copyrighted.

Situations	N	R	S	O	U	A	C

7. Negative feedback or criticism makes me sullen or de-pressed—and I find it hard to snap out of it.

8. When taking a vacation. I feel guilty— as if I should be working.

9. If projects are not clear I get "uptight," frustrated.

10. The fact that I am (will be) fac-ing a new situation makes me tense.

11. I carry that extra work project or correspondence with me just in case I get a few extra free moments.

12. When I am receiving feedback I tense up—waiting for the negatives to come.

13. I am apt to think less of a per-son who has revealed a per-sonal problem to me—or asked for advise.

14. When I calendar an important event (e.g., a meeting or speech), I feel uncomfortable about it almost immediately.

15. When stalled in traffic, I get angry or uptight.

16. I feel quite anxious when faced with target dates or deadlines.

17. I constantly am figuring out ways to increase my work capacity.

18. I find changes in my work rou-tines upsetting.

19. I've never been able to discuss personal matters with associates.

20. My associates see me as a workaholic—always seems to be "at it."

21. I get "uptight" if I can't control all the factors in a situation.

22. I arrive right to the minute for appointments.

Situations	N	R	S	O	U	A	C
23. I usually leave at the last minute for meetings or appointments so that I can get some added things out of the way.	___	___	___	___	___	___	___
24. In making a presentation, I would be/am reluctant to involve group members for fear of losing control.	___	___	___	___	___	___	___
25. When I'm under pressure I can usually tell—I blow it (e.g., the diet or overdo the coffee or cigarettes).	___	___	___	___	___	___	___
26. Differences of opinions with associates almost always seem to end up in an argument or debate.	___	___	___	___	___	___	___
27. Groups or individuals over whom I have little or no control (e.g., clients, staff, and public administrator often get me up tight).	___	___	___	___	___	___	___
28. It really gets to me if my boss or somebody I know well says they can't make a decision "now."	___	___	___	___	___	___	___
29. If I had to please the changing power structure in my company due to replacements or promotions it would be both frustrating and irritating.	___	___	___	___	___	___	___
30. Faced with lack of cooperation or lack of direction, I would be frustrated or uptight.	___	___	___	___	___	___	___

Scoring and Interpretation of This Managerial Stress Tolerance Form

Scoring

This Managerial Stress Tolerance Form is scored in the following way:

1. Count up the number of checks in each column (N, R, S, O, U, A) and enter under "Frequency."
2. *Check* the "frequency" count to make sure you have accounted for all your responses—there are exactly *30* questions.
3. Multiply each frequency value by the indicated number and enter *Total*.
4. Add all the numbers in the *Total* column to get the grand total. Compare your total with the scores and interpretations below.

Interpretation—Overall Score

Response	Frequency* (total no. of checks)		Multiply each by		Total points
Never	_____	(x)	0	=	0
Rarely	_____	(x)	1	=	_____
Sometimes	_____	(x)	2	=	_____
Often	_____	(x)	3	=	_____
Usually	_____	(x)	4	=	_____
Always	_____	(x)	5	=	_____
Total (Check) 30*	_____		Overall Total		_____

*Total number in this column must equal 30.

The results as summarized are general guides. It is important to remember that everybody has a different tolerance for stress and thus reacts to stress differently.

Score Interpretation:

150	100	75	50	0
subject to high stress maximum score	relatively high stress	midpoint or average score	low stress	

Interpretation: Areas of High Stress and Stress Reduction

Now go back to your Stress Tolerance form and circle each response number that you have rated as "usually" or "always." Also for each of these, rate its changeability (your ability to affect a change in it) as low (= L), good (= G), or high (= H). Insert these in the "C" column.

If you are subject to high stress (overall score) or simply wish to improve your dealing with stress, examine your high-stress items critically. Consider reviewing some of these with a colleague or friend. Can you vary the (1) timing, (2) situation, or (3) pattern, or other contributing circumstances? Review your ratings of changeability—perhaps a friend or associate will see an approach that you have missed. Make a note below of the stress items you would like to work on and when.

Stress Item	Start	Initial Approach (?)
_____	_____	_____
_____	_____	_____
_____	_____	_____
_____	_____	_____

11

Viewing Information and Computers Strategically

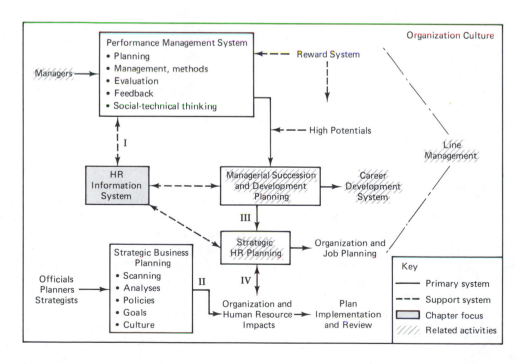

Introduction

In future years, progress in the advancement of strategic management development (SMD) systems will most likely rest on two considerations: people and information. The real story underlying the why, what, and how of SMD topics previously discussed was that of people. Of major interest to the successful advancement of strategic thinking and human resource programs are those individuals who have the vision, understanding of the organization, and flexibility needed to market successfully their vision to the organization. They must project their understandings of human resource development to the CEO, line management, and personnel as a whole. Yet the ability of this human resource leadership to achieve its vision for the organization will be either facilitated or, in the extreme, frustrated by the character of information available.

The issue, however, is much more than one of information technology (e.g., computers). Technology and systems as such never made a major human resource undertaking successful, though these are obviously necessary and important. Accessability to good information, in the appropriate quantities, and when needed, has made the critical difference in establishing a useful SMD system. The architects of a strategic planning program will have to think through "where" the organization is currently by way of information. This approach requires determining the likely needs at particular points in the future, and then how the needed information (quantity, quality, timing, access, and capabilities) will be achieved so as to facilitate and not constrain the actions of managers.

There are two approaches which together help to define information needs and the computer-based technology to achieve SMD systems development. The "status" of HR information is addressed to an important extent by auditing the existing information and system supporting human resource applications. A format for undertaking this type of analysis is provided in the applications section of this chapter. The second approach is one of judging the relative degree of maturity of the various activities comprising or in support of management development and in likely future needs. Correlating the present state of information and human resource planning systems development with the planned or targeted systems and applications is a form of "information needs analysis" for future planning. Then strategies need to be established from an information viewpoint, as to how to achieve this future systems.

The form provided in the applications section, *Auditing the Existing Information System and State of Information*, is similar to the one described in Burack and

Mathys (1987, Chap. 8). Since management development applications are very broad in scope, the scope of detail indicated by this form is appropriate. The form covers both external and internal information as well as some aspects of information systems development. Because of the numerous and varied types of information needed, the "internal information" category has been subdivided into 11 different sections. The audit form facilitates the determination of "where" the organization is today. No particular state of information/systems development is "correct." What is important is that planners, stategists, and human Resource people are in general agreement as to "current information needs and availability" and "future needs," and when and how the latter is to be achieved.

Information Systems Planning: Where We Are and Where We Are Going

The second approach to information systems planning involves profiling the current and desired future state of information systems development. The stage-type approach referenced frequently in preceding chapters works well here too. The diagrams are readily understood and permit each individual initially to "register" his or her judgment. Also, the form readily lends itself to group discussion and eventual consensing on plans and strategies.

The chart illustrated in Exhibit 11-1 features three main phases or stages of information/systems development. In addition, five areas of information applications relevant to strategic analyses are compared across these three stages. Since each organization's experiences are unique to its circumstances, profiles of current and planned activities are generated to develop an agenda for planning discussions.

Phase I. "The Personnel Systems Era"

The "personnel systems era" is perhaps best typified by the computer-based information system ("automation") of most conventional personnel applications. Understandably, the computerization of this record base has facilitated reporting procedures (1a in Exhibit 11-1) and basic planning activities such as employment planning. However, the latter was focused primarily on shorter-range staffing or recruiting needs. In this phase, succession planning applications (1b), because of data sensitivity and the need for confidentiality, were primarily informal and maintained by "hand." In this phase of information/systems development, the generation of data for development purposes typically involved numerous, separate records. These then had to be reconciled because of their substantially different basis for collection (1c, 1e). Career planning data (1d), to the extent it existed, was primarily oriented to organization purposes ("career management") and was mostly a derivation of conventional personnel demographic data (e.g., "location preference").

EXHIBIT 11-1

Phases of Information/systems Evolution: Implication for Strategic Management Development Systems Planning

Major Applications Areas	Phases of Information/Systems Evolution		
	I "The Personnel Systems Era"	II "The Human Resources Planning and Development Era—Macro"	III "The Human Resource Planning and Development Era—Comprehensive"
Human resource planning	Some employment planning and information for shorter-run staffing needs; applicant processing; govermental reporting; collection and dissemination of posting information. (1a)	Human resource forecasting data—relate to employment planning and staffing requirements; utilization of some external data; some applicant tracking data; incorporate EEO data regarding candidate selection; automate job posting system; access and privacy issues. (2a)	Emphasis on line management needs for planning; seek to establish data and system requirements for a comprehensive information system including data access; download main information base data for unit and department staffing planning; expand external data base; develop planning scenarios, emphases on user evaluation or user "friendly" access; informally link business planning and human resource planning data; microcomputer applications; informally generate data for organization structure planning. (3a)

Succession	Informal data collection and records maintenance methods. (1b)	Development of management reserve and replacement data; build and maintain separate data files representing assessments of (high) potential; regular data on succession candidates moves; anniversary dates, retirement, etc.; access and privacy issues. (2b)	Candidate tracking; development of data and indices for high-potential identification reflecting multiple data sources (e.g., assessment centers, psychological assessments); data from organizationwide scans to facilitate systems monitoring; microcomputer applications; access and privacy issues. (3b)
Management development	Attempt to enlarge and "fill in" performance appraisal and assessment of potential data; needs analysis data on a person-by-person basis; maintain files on development programs; informal connection to compensation system. (1c)	Skill banks; attempts to generate data for person-job matching; attempt to extend performance appraisal and assessment of potential data for needs analyses determinations; tuition reimbursement data generation; access and privacy issues. (2c)	Candidate tracking: attempt formally to link needs analysis components including organization, job, and person requirements; automate job-person matching applications; separate out performance management and career planning data; microcomputer applications; access and privacy issues; data for educational facilities utilization. (3c)

(Continues)

EXHIBIT 11-1 (Continued)

Major Applications Areas	Phases of Information/Systems Evolution		
	I "The Personnel Systems Era"	II "The Human Resources Planning and Development Era—Macro"	III "The Human Resource Planning and Development Era—Comprehensive"
Career management	Most individual career information a derivative of conventional personnel information with some indication of individual characteristics; skills and preferences. (1d)	Enlarge base of individual-career planning information and seek to link to future positional requirements; informal translation of human resource planning data into "career planning" requirements. (2d)	Enlarge and stabilize individual career planning data formats; provide for regular updating of individual file information; start to establish a basis for wellness analyses, including stress management; microcomputer applications; track individual "adult learning" progress and use of educational resources. (3d)
Job analysis	Most information "off-line" or simply automation of conventional job description information. (1e)	Basis established for end-job behaviors description of performance features of jobs; seek to unify data form and descriptors across various human resources/personnel applications (e.g., performance appraisal, job evaluation, and assessment of potential). (2e)	Data derived from job analyses to establish job families and data for job/work design; regularize job and performance action research to establish benchmark data for analysis; microcomputer applications. (3e)

Phase II. "The Human Resource Planning and Development Era—Macro"

Phase II represented a substantial updating in the character and thrust of the information system. The growing prominence of business planning led to the introduction or expansion of human resource planning capabilities. Data and systems in this phase reflected a better overall understanding of ("macro") systems design, development, and needs (2a). Human resource planning applications and appropriate data had to be developed to back up the business planning applications. Typical applications included data for general managerial staffing and EEO planning and automating posting systems. Expansion of the external information data base was also a part of this phase. Other notable developments in Phase II witnessed the rapid expansion of information and systems capabilities to back up the succession and management development activities (2b, 2c). These information developments permitted a better correlation of management development activities with succession planning and more general organization planning activities. Phase II was also featured by a sharpened focus on data for career planning purposes (2d) which at last gave much greater emphasis to individually derived data. This phase also witnessed rapid advancement in the consolidation of data coding and job-descriptive approaches permitting much more powerful analysis for job planning, work-design applications, and more powerful (but conventional) personnel applications (2e). For an excellent discussion of both Phase I and II types of applications, see Albert Walker's (1984) treatment of these based on his years of experience at AT&T.

Phase III. "The Human Resource Planning and Development Era—Comprehensive"

Phase III was as different from Phase II as Phase II was from Phase I. The general theme for this phase was creating a user-friendly (computer/information) environment facilitating planning and decision making for individual managers as well as more general analyses (3a). The rapid expansion of micro ("personal") computers permitted the introduction and use of numerous software programs geared much more to the needs of individuals, offices, departments, and units. It also facilitated line management's involvement and increasing commitment to these approaches (3b, 3c). In this phase, there was also a commensurate expansion of the career planning data base (3d) facilitating career-related analyses and decisions. Data available for work-design and organization planning were much improved, needs analyses became more comprehensive, and utilization of data from these was facilitated. The enlargement of human resource planning and development decisions necessitated an expansion in the conduct and recording of action research analyses (3c) facilitating multiyear comparisons against established baselines. The information/system developments in this phase have been of such importance that additional topics are addressed in the following section.

In brief, the sweep of changes covering Phases I–III witnessed a vast updating in human resource information and the systems supporting these. These accompanied a much-altered organizational approach relative to planning, management, administration, and decision making.

Human Resource Planning and Development: A Comprehensive Strategic Application at EBASCO, Inc. (Phase III)

Over a period of many years, Andrew O. Manzini and his associates at EBASCO, Inc., including John D. Gridley (Manzini, 1982; Manzini and Gridley, 1987), have fashioned a highly advanced and comprehensive application of computers for strategic, operational, and human resource purposes. EBASCO offered worldwide engineering and technical services. Many of its activities were project oriented and could easily last from one to three or more years. Its processes and activities, from planning to negotiations to operations, were highly dependent on timely and accurate information. The project format and technical nature of many of its services often permitted specific description and programming. The creativity with which these were approached and architected into a highly workable and useful information system made it part of the state of the art in this field. A detailed description of this system world be far too voluminous for the available space here. Thus, what is presented are some highlights of human resource applications; details are available in Manzini and Gridley (1987).

Selected Highlights—EBASCO's Strategic Human Resource Planning Approach*

EBASCO successfully integrated three distinct but related systems: (1) strategic planning, (2) operational planning, and (3) human resource planning (including career planning).

The *strategic planning system* established the direction for the total organization since financial, marketing, and corporate planning activities were fully correlated in this approach. Key information/data outputs from these strategic analyses included environmental and business scenarios that became the basis for more specific corporate strategies and business plans. One product of these analyses was the corporate data base of business-related information that drove the *operational planning system*. The operational planning system data, when fully developed, comprised the demand for EBASCO services. It included the numbers, type, and scope of human resources required in great detail. Thus, the operational system had to satisfy the required ("demand for") staffing for various (future) business

---

*The descriptions in this section regarding EBASCO reflect the writer's interpretations of lengthy discussions with Henry O. Manzini and review of various corporate documents. Nevertheless, the interpretations of system developments, capabilities, and the rationale for these developments are those of the writer and not to be taken as official corporate statements of position or approach.

processes and activities (projects). It also helped to crystallize thinking regarding the future leadership and management structure needed to meet the specifics of operational requirements ("demand forecast"). At the same time, thinking regarding leadership and structure was impregnated with the flavor of strategic planning directions. Put another way, human resource planning was charged with meeting ("supplying") forthcoming operational requirements. Although many of these were project oriented, they were at the same time helping to assure corporate continuity and renewal in the future.

Human resources planning (and development) was a comprehensive, integrated system combining all phases of the information/system features shown in Exhibit 11-1. For example the computerized personnel system (Phase I) provided for detailed data collection and distribution (personnel action form). In a particular, these related to personnel transactions/changes, basic personnel demographics (corporate, biographical, and historical), compensation administration and benefits, "resume retrieval," EEO reporting, and performance appraisals. Also included were individual potential data categorized on key dimensions such as experience, job categories, and education. Phase II types of applications included human resource planning and forecasting, skill inventories, career planning and development, managerial and professional development and development applications, applicant tracking, and position control.

The creative way in which Manzini and his associates (1982, 1987) approached computer applications and information development resulted in a solid basis for architecting a Phase III type system. For example, key Phase II information and system applications were refined by improving a basic "HRIS personnel model," incorporating service records and statistics for force planning and length of service data, strengthening EEO/AA administration, providing labor relations information, generating turnover analyses, and producing of employee profiles. Also, Phase II applications related to human resource planning were refined to include comprehensive forecasting models and career planning information which extended the usefulness of Phase II applications and informations.

Many benefits resulted from these advancements, including reduction of turnover, performance improvement, and better bases to staff projects and support individual career advancement. These benefits resulted because of the expansion of information system capabilities which helped to capture individual career goal information, enabled longer-range availability forecasting, facilitated interunit movement, resulted in better matching of individual and organization needs, and provided systematic bases for individual development and even retirement planning. A conscious attempt was made to meet personal career requirements while focusing on the work-related needs of the organization. Needless to say, the career program greatly improved the opportunity for internal promotions. The corporation backed up its computerized programs with substantial updating of basic documents to guide career planning, manuals describing career path options, and complete descriptions of positions and skill coding (Manzini, 1982).

The years required to develop the Phase I and II types of applications reflected a major investment of creativity, thoughtful analyses, and anticipation of future corporate requirements. This careful architecting of systems and information paid off in establishing a firm foundation for Phase III approaches. However, their task of information and system development was not complete. In dynamic organization, this process of refinement is never ending. Much remains to be done and the key people involved were carefully monitoring what had been accomplished relative to "current" needs and future corporate directions—and were prepared to adapt information systems to these requirements.

The following are suggestive of (other) Phase III types of accomplishments, particularly in the human resource area:

- *Succession planning*—managerial replacement analyses at all prescribed levels; identification of candidates, backups, and succession gaps; identification of promotion readiness and "high" potentials; and replacement status charting.
- *Position control*—status reports on jobs including the monitoring of (un)authorized positions, information on current and planned positions, and cost effectiveness of salaries and position utilization.
- *Management development*—individual records on succession planning, training, and development; managerial/employee tracking; comparison and evaluation of internal and external programs; and interfacing of succession planning, career development, and EEO/AA data.
- *Career planning*—identification of needed information for career counseling; bases for retirement planning, computerized career and guidance services, and job/skill matches and searches.
- *Action research*—survey analyses of job skills, individual career aspirations, and individual self-assessment data.
- *Equal employment opportunity and affirmative action*—bases to relate goals in this area against succession plans and individual career planning, salary information to provide support data as this might be required for litigation purposes, and improved bases to establish internal and external recruitment objectives and to track progress of these.

Based on EBASCO's information and system accomplishments, one could readily speculate that the further adaptation and use of microcomputers would have been readily accomplished.

On balance, EBASCO's information systems development played a central role in its strategic planning, operational, and human resources processes. These activities, though distinct, were interfaced in such a way as to assure smooth blending of all their major systems and organizational processes. Admittedly, some of the aspects of its business and internal processes facilitated design in more defined information and systems terms. This fact notwithstanding, it achieved notable advances in the information/systems area and thus stood as an important benchmark of Phase III information/systems possibilities.

Other Phase III Types of Applications

Strategic Planning Applications

Although established in the mid-1970s, the Industrial Relations Information System (IRIS) of Union Oil Company was notable for its integration with corporate planning processes (Bright, 1976). The use in this system of an extensive data base in connection with several simulation and forecasting models provided planning data for a five-year period which was reviewed and used in strategic planning by top management. The comprehensive nature of this application and extensive access to this information supported its usage by line management in shorter-range planning approaches. At the same time, IRIS provided the usual "recipe" of personnel housekeeping data. Another part of the information outputs available from this application facilitated projections and extensive analyses of personnel movements under various types of assumptions. As a matter of information, planning analyses of personnel movements were among the many human resource applications developed extensively at General Electric. General Electric's approaches provided an excellent basis for developing recruiting strategies, studying promotion patterns, identifying factors affecting managerial mobility, establishing bases for generating numerical information to identify high potentials or "fast trackers," and reviewing EEO/AA policies and objectives. See Hayes (1980) for an excellent discussion of these; added details are also available in Burack and Mathys (1987).

Aside from the indicated benefits at companies such as Union Oil and General Electric, availability of this type of information in a "user-friendly" environment alerted managers of the need for and potential to think through the long-term human resource requirements of their units as well as the goodness of fit with organization plans. In short, these information/system advancements provided a practical demonstration of the interrelatedness of decisions dealing with human resources. Managerial sensitivity to these issues was increased and perspectives enlarged. Participation in succession planning and management development processes was greatly improved where contributing managers had a tangible idea of the interaction of future needs and current plans under alternate sets of assumptions. These scenarios included assumptions regarding staffing, recruiting sources, skill mix, individual mobility, and career development policies.

Micro ("Personal") Computers and the Human Resource Information System

The microcomputer has been heralded as one of the most significant technological advancements in computer development during the 1980s. Its year-to-year sales growth alone is impressive; in a few short years from its introduction, annual unit sales of micros rose to over 4,000,000, and future prospects were very promising. Two companies, familiar to the writer, ordered, respectively, 100 and 400 each—to provide their line managements with hands-on experience in the use and application of the "personal" (micro) computer. (Technical questions, of obvious importance in the acquisition and development of these systems, are not dealt with here.)

No speculation is required at this point as to whether microcomputers will be successful in business applications. Rather, the more relevant questions are

- As an organization, are *we* prepared to capitalize on the potential these offer?
- Are support personnel available and prepared to develop the programs and information needed to gain the full benefit of computer capabilities?
- Are senior managers supportive of their usage so that needed training, budgets, and "active" encouragement is provided?
- For the many possible application areas, to which should the highest priorities be assigned for initial usage and will these actions reflect a longer-term application/planning strategy?

No mistaking, with the micros as with other managerial/technological innovations, there will be situations of mismatch or "going overboard" with attendant confusion and some poor results. But the micros have already established a trail of applications that have many implications for strategic planning and strategic processes. Additionally, they can be coupled together or operated in connection with a centralized mainframe system using information that is "downloaded to the micro," or in a decentralized (distributed) mode with information that can be "rolled up to central computer information facilities." Also, various combinations of these have emerged which give the micros power and flexibility commanding the attention of management development strategists. The range of applications cover all those already described in this chapter—with the added benefit of the indicated options and use of a variety of application packages.

Application Packages—Facilitating Strategic Usage

At this juncture, so many different application packages have appeared with acronyms or "creative" titles that the features common to many of these are hidden. Applications of particular interest to strategic human resource approaches reflect some of the types of applications associated with larger or mainframe systems in past years. But much recent emphasis has been placed on new(er) application approaches. Popular and representative applications include

1. Job- and work-related information for work design and analysis of performance and potential.
   Job content and behavioral information with a common structure of descriptive terms.
   Job structure and job relationship information including job families, reporting/authority relationships, and data related to job families.

2. Human resource and job planning data indicating the future status of positions, staffing information (e.g., when it is to be filled), and career ladder networks or typical developmental moves connecting one position to another.
3. Position audit data related to incumbents, position backup, and replacements.
4. Individual information to facilitate career planning and development including demographics, personal qualities, work histories, performance appraisals, assessments of potential, career preferences, and retirement planning information.

A general framework of information and application relationships with particular emphasis on strategic approaches is presented in Exhibit 11-2. The types of information described above form a basis for the "inputs" described in the exhibit. The time required for systems development and the demands for data completeness, uniformity, and up-to-dateness is considerable. It usually means that, initially,

EXHIBIT 11-2

Microcomputer Systems: Information and Strategic Planning
Applications

Information/data inputs	Standard document outputs	Outputs related to strategic planning and processes
Job content and structure	Job descriptions and job evaluations	Search, selection Needs analysis determinations
Human resource and job planning data	Performance appraisals	Development plans
Position audits	Organization (structure) charting	Performance profiles (individual, group, or unit) Position blockages
Individually focused descriptions	Turnaround documents*	Performance baselines and standards for comparisons
		Knowledge/skill/ability inventories
		Assessments of potential
		Succession planning, general managerial or executive analyses, equal employment planning, compensation planning
		Job design
		Systems/data research/ action research studies

*Demographics, career preferences, performance information, unique capabilities, and so on, for incumbents to check out.

companies will only be able to use a small part of (computer/program) application potential. "Rules of thumb" based on application experience with several micro systems indicate that

- Existing company information can be converted to limited microcomputer applications (e.g., basic succession planning approaches for senior managers and officials) in under six months.
- When microcomputer applications are installed initially, perhaps 20 to 30 percent of standard application possibilities will have been tapped. Customizing and special adaptations often increase the application possibilities greatly.
- Easily two to three years might be required in a medium-sized organization to develop the data base needed to take *full* advantage of application possibilities.

These are obviously "ballpark" figures and will vary greatly with corporate circumstances. They are provided here to express some of the application parameters, and the great potential existing in these approaches, as well as some of the realities of time requirements.

Standard types of applications referenced in Exhibit 11-2 include "automating" files to produce job-description and job-evaluation documents which are shown in the second column of Exhibit 11-2. Also, the capability to produce "turnaround documents" permitting people to check out these data inputs is useful. These standard applications should not be lightly dismissed. Of course, they have been available for a long time, at least in theory, using the capabilities of mainframe computers. For large organizations, the sheer volume of data has made mainframe applications a necessity. On the other hand, experienced Human Resource systems officials and specialists have realized that organization priorities are often such that getting desired information when needed has been difficult at best. In consequence, micros have provided a necessary expansion of capabilities which permits accessing large data bases ("downloading") and organizing this information in formats *best suited to human resource applications*. The growing complexity of managerial work has led to a cordial reception for this flexibility, even for conventional applications.

Some applications, as for example, succession analyses, often involve gathering data that are confidential. Decentralizing portions of these files so that they are secure makes sense in any organization. Moreover, it means that some data gathered in the course of these applications can be used in a convenient way, for example, to update "mainframe" files ("roll up" of information). In the last column of Exhibit 11-2, an important list of applications is provided which directly support or become a part of strategic planning/management development analyses. The listing is a long one and is likely to be familiar to many. Many of these are also described in detail in the application examples provided in a subsequent section. Many of the microcomputer applications deal with analyses of current staffing arrangements and organization members ("supply-type" analysis). However, some of the applications also incorporate planning data ("demand" related). For example, general succession analyses may incorporate data on the future staffing requirements (addition, deletion, change). Systems/data (action) research, listed in Exhibit 11-2, means that a capabilitiy can be provided to human resource planning officials or line managers to test out in advance, the consequence of particular decisions, changes in information formats, or modifications in available information.

In general, microcomputer systems should provide the following types of benefits:

- *Be user friendly* (encouraging usage)—they involve a level of technology in size and use that people can relate to ("can put their hands around") and gain a real sense of being in command of what is happening.
- *Offer ease of operation*—permitting inputting, updating, executive accessing, and executive report generation.
- *Have high operating flexibility*—can be operated in decentralized, independent fashion or "distributed" fashion with information inputs to mainframe equipment.
- *Have high application flexibility*—for currently popular applications and newer ones on the "drawing board."
- *Facilitate improved security*.
- *Achieve relative cost efficiencies* in terms of software acquisition and maintenance and data processing.

The large number of application packages that have become available for microcomputers suggests that these too become a point of planning considerations. These are considered briefly in the following discussion.

Microcomputer System Applications

Because of the relative ease of programming, the power of newer software languages, and a comparatively well-developed base of human resource methods, "off-the-shelf" software has become available (see the subsequent discussion for more on this) for numerous micro applications. Some companies customize these for special uses or needs. To the extent that specific programming packages are identified in subsequent discussions, these are meant to illustrate a particular application capability and area with relevance for strategic approaches. They do not represent the endorsement of a given vendor's product. A complicating aspect of off-the-shelf package capabilities is the fact that real differences exist in competitive products affecting both usage and output capabilities. Representative applications are the main focus of subsequent discussions—available off-the-shelf packages, however, may go significantly beyond the indicated applications.

Management Job Analysis Systems

Some Housekeeping Issues.   A comprehensive base of managerial position description information forms one of the basic building blocks for management development applications, but the content of this record differs greatly from traditional data files. Micro ("personal computer") application packages typically incorporate both conventional position description information *and* information regarding end-job behaviors or behavioral dimensions for successful performance. However, there are circumstances where some of these capabilities would likely be of little *current* interest:

- Applications planning was primarily concerned (only) with behavioral informa-tion—other applications are of little interest—and it is unavailable currently.
- A comparatively small managerial group is involved, say, under 50.
- Available budgets or systems staff are limited.
- Limited time to carry out studies of managerial positions and create a data base of behavioral or job descriptive information.

Other types of micro application for strategic processes could nevertheless be car-ried out. However, it is important to realize that much application potential would go untapped.

Job analysis applications gain their power through information gained from in-depth study of managerial positions. The heart of this application potential usu-ally rests with the determination of managerial (end) behaviorial dimensions, *after* up-to-date and detailed position descriptions have been established. For off-the-shelf packages, these behavioral dimensions have been organized on the basis of pilot studies involving representative management populations from various corpo-rate settings. This approach is workable since well-organized studies undertaken by different researchers in this field indicate a general type of convergence toward a similar set of dimensions. Standard job analysis packages can be applied to many different corporate situations—with the well-known limitations due to the use of general rather than customized information. (Chapter 4 provides results from some of these well-organized studies.)

This application potential for standardized packages, however, is not without its costs. Establishing a comprehensive position analysis record can take much time—several months for a group of perhaps 200 managers which would not be unusual. Also, once having committed to a particular format, subsequent corporate applications are not readily undertaken which go beyond this information structure, at least from an economic viewpoint. However, because of the rather stable record of these job-analytic structures put together by reputable experts in this area, the need for major changes are not likely to be great for periods of perhaps four to seven years. But the capability should exist to add new information readily (within the data structure) as required. What will change, however, and this is *basic* to file maintenance, are the behavioral acts or critical incidents, the set of which usefully describe a specific managerial position. Put another way, basic position analysis information which is gathered in depth, is usually guided by a well-designed job questionnaire. Behaviorally related incidents or actions are identified which are critical to success—these may comprise 100 or more critical elements or types of information which are organized into families (dimensions) of related elements. The latter may involve perhaps 10 to 20 different families (clusters) of related activities depending on the particular scheme used. These clusters or dimensions provide the basis for establishing profiles of position activities critical to success and also the basis for interposition, intergroup, or even unit-by-unit comparisons. In consequence, from a strategic standpoint, the critical concern is usually not with the job-analytic structure (as such) for clarifying job data (given the relevancy assumptions). Rather, the greater problem is to assure that the descriptive behavioral data are regularly updated to reflect long(er)-range business and human resource planning that affects organization and job structures and individual positions.

Dangers of Too Much Computer Power.   A growing problem in some companies has been one of exceeding information maintenance capabilities. The integrity of data and the system itself can be readily lost if applications or the number of people covered is allowed to go beyond the capacity of systems people to capture valued and useful data—and then use it.

Application—the FOCUS System.   FOCUS* was developed by Control Data Business Advisors as a management job analysis system. It exploits a long history (over 10 years) of job-analytic research at Control Data, much of it guided by Walter Tornow and carried out by associates (Timothy Gartland, Patrick Pinto, and Ronald C. Page) who successfully bridged theory and practice. The instrumentation for data gathering, the Management Position Description Questionnaire (MPDQ), was used for better than ten years. It was proven out in three pilot companies involving over 8,000 managers in both domestic and foreign assignments. Some 300 response categories provided the type of comprehensive job-related information needed for this approach. Major features of the MPDQ are summarized in Exhibit 11-3.

Eight different reports can be produced with the FOCUS package. At a basic level, narrative summaries of position descriptions can be produced which cover individual jobs as well as familes or groups of related positions. This type of information is very helpful for initial position orientation affecting new jobholders and individual career path planning. Individual development and performance management is greatly improved by the behavioral dimensions and performance appraisal data which can be incorporated in this software program. The FOCUS package also lends itself to profiling key areas of knowledge, skills, and abilities for position incumbents—some 30 elements can be detailed in this manner.

Executive TRACK†

Executive TRACK was developed especially for succession and career planning applications using a micro ("personal") computer. Because of its general utility and

---

*Based on Control Data Business Advisors' technical bulletin, 1984. Interpretations are those of the writer and not the supplier. Regular changes can be expected in these capabilities.

†Based on briefing seminars and technical information from Corporate Education Resources, Inc. Interpretations are those of the writer and not the supplier. Regular changes can be expected in these capabilities.

EXHIBIT 11-3

Features of the "Focus" Job Analysis System

General Organization: Management Position Description Questionnaire (MPDQ)

15 different parts for information gathering

5 major categories of data, including

- General information (background, human resource, and financial responsibilities and a narrative of primary responsibilities)
- Functional categories of position activities (10) plus an overall rating (e.g., "decision making," "representing").
- Proficiency ratings: knowledge, skills, and abilities.
- Organization charting information.
- Respondent comments on the utility of the approach.

General Application Areas

- Performance analysis.
- Job evaluation.
- Selection.
- Job design.
- Training.

Highlights of Application Specifics

Data base—contains questionnaire data for all people who fill out the MPDQ. Terminal capabilities greatly ease the inputting of this information.

Reports—a menu of eight different reports which can be run, including

- Management position description narratives for individual jobholders, a narrative summary for selected groups of jobholders, and over 100 possible areas of position activity and the degree of each.
- Behavioral/work dimensions for individual jobholders and an overall summary for selected groups of jobholder.
- Knowledge, skill, and ability summaries for individual and selected groups of jobholders. These include profiles on performance factors (e.g., managing work, business planning, and communication) and 31 detailed elements making up the knowledge, skill, and ability categories, for example, leadership, coaching, and developing; planning; group process skills; oral skills; judgment/decision making; professional (technical knowledge and knowlege of organizational practices).
- Group comparisons.
- Performance appraisal, formatted for general information, overall performance ratings, and nine factor dimensions (managing work, business planning, problem solving/decision making, communications, customer/public relations, human resource development, human resource management, and job knowledge). The nine performance categories are backed up with some 46 specific critical incidents associated with success on the job.

Source: Based on Control Data Business Advisors' technical bulletin, 1984. Interpretations are those of the writer and not the supplier. Regular changes can be expected in these capabilities.

fit with the indicated application, approaches were discussed at some length in the succession planning chapter. In this section only summary highlights are presented.

This software program was selected for description ("personal") as an example of a growing family of programs designed around microcomputer capabilities *and* with considerable strategic human resource application possibilities. The three main functions of this system are as follows:

- *Records storage* (personnel data) for a managerial, executive, or other designated populations, including important individual data. Data include conventional resume information and demographics plus performance and potential data, career path information, and developmental needs. Provision is made so that it is possible to capture data based on behavioral or special dimensions facilitating person job matching, person to person comparisons, and career planning.
- *Position data* concerning functional or conventional types of job descriptive information, including reporting requisite skills plus position audit information including replacement timing, candidate readiness, and position disposition in the future.
- *Search and report capabilities* permitting the identification of candidates relative to specified features and person-job matching approaches including consideration of desired education and training experience, skill competencies, and salary levels. *When*, and it is important to emphasize, *when* adequate data have been captured in the research base, an impressive group of analyses or reports can be outputted.

Perhaps the best picture of the Executive TRACK potential is presented by summarizing briefly the potpourri of outputs which can be run, *if* the data base is complete.

Strategic Planning Applications—General:

√ succession planning
√ staffing replacement needs
√ five-year plans (person/position)
√ candidate search
√ equal employment opportunity
√ duplicate candidates, position coverage
√ aspects of organization structure planning

Management Development Planning Analyses:

√ position blockages
√ development plans
√ outdated ratings

Maintenance and Special Usage:

√ special status tracking
√ outdated/obsolete rating
√ reconciliation
√ daily updates
√ executive/managerial records

A final note concerns the potential of this software/system capability relative to the existing state of data/information development. Most organizations have *not* reached Phase III maturity insofar as their HR data base is concerned. Thus possibly 25–40 percent of the potential of this system would be utilizable immediately. Yet this is a very substantial capability and provides a strong foundation for planning and data (system) development. Also, the relatively large number of users provides a valuable action-oriented network of contracts which the vendor has tapped to provide valuable application information to users.

Application Software—Planning Criteria for Selection

The large number and diversity of micro software packages which suddenly appeared with the introduction of micros attest to the widespread interest in these— but with the concomitant need to develop systematic bases for comparing them. Any set of criteria will be seen as arbitrary or reflecting personal biases of some sort or another. Thus the following points should be seen as advisory—each set of organization circumstances will require some number of special considerations. As a precautionary note, some times basic points as included in the following listing are missed as more technical or sophisticated answers are sought out. In this spirit, the first set of assessment questions seeks answers to basic questions, the next group refer to application specifics.

Answers to Basic Questions. The following are representative questions concerning basic matters in the (possible) acquisition of software packages:

1. Is the software compatible with the micro technology in use or to be acquired?
2. Does the vendor have expertise or good knowledge of our industry or types of applications?
3. Considering budgetary constraints, will the application software, training of personnel, and maintenance agreement be less than the specified amount or available budget?
4. Is the vendor prepared to provide a demonstration of their application software for our type of application(s) prior to acquisition?
5. Does the vendor have contact with a user network, especially where applications are new or developmental?

6. Is a "hot line" service available for problem solving and/or to answer questions regarding programming, applications, or malfunction?
7. Will system documentation be provided if the system is acquired? Is it clear and useful for training?
8. Will the vendor provide a reasonable amount of service time without charge during the initial use period for working out "bugs" and carrying out the first wave of training? If the cost of the application package does not include this backup, are the documents adequate for training?
9. Is internal staff available for training if this is not be purchased from the vendor?
10. Does the vendor have a good training staff; that is, how do the staff members stack up as trainers?

Specific Application Criteria.   Creating a user-friendly environment, often for people unfamiliar with computer usage or at best skeptical of its merits, requires attention to numerous application factors.

1. *User friendliness*

   Can the system be used by relatively unsophisticated people after a short period of training and follow-up assistance?

   Is the system "menu driven," providing easy access or bases for user selection? Are key strokes minimized? Is the designation of "operations keys" standard? logical?

   Are the screens laid out well for ready reading and interpretation? Do the screens anticipate user questions and handily provide for these? Correspondingly, do error messages communicate readily the nature of the error and simple means of correcting these?

2. *System capabilities*

   Is the capacity adequate for current applications and those already blueprinted or anticipated in the near-term future?

   Will the system be able to absorb "enhancements" or new types of information as these are introduced?

   Can work processing capabilities be linked to the system as these are often required for other managerial purposes?

   Does the range of available reports fully cover those needed now or those planned for the future?

   Will the system accommodate ad hoc reports or flexible formats relative to available information?

The type of basic and specific criteria outlined here can be assigned numerical values and weighted to compare comparative products including those which might be developed internally. In microcomputer applications it is important to recognize that these often involve the term "personal computers"—the term must be taken literally. It is important to note that many of the specific criteria listed deal with the *user-friendly, personal* aspects.

Summary

The viewpoint expressed in this chapter is that information and information systems represent one of the two main foundation stones for the erection of a comprehensive, strategic management development system. Acknowledging the central importance of individual planners and architects, the other foundation component, information, needs to be viewed broadly as an indispensable ingredient in creating a basic personnel system capability (Phase I). At the same time, it needs to provide a broad avenue to achieving more advanced Phase II and III possibilities.

The three-phase/stage perspective presented in this chapter provides an opportunity for planners and strategists to profile their existing information systems and the desired features of future systems. However, before alternate strategies can be studied, it is also important to know in detail, the current status of information data so that realistic planning, costs, and time frames can be considered. The information Audit Form in the application section of this chapter should be useful in this regard. Another component that needs to be fitted into this study is the planning for the management development system (described in earlier chapters). Thus the information/systems blueprint will reflect an "information needs analysis" with joint consideration of human resource planning, development, and information/system factors.

The advent of microcomputer technology and the need to once more vest line management with a major planning role have come together in time and space— they represent the possibilities for a workable marriage. This joining of information technology and line management's role is being played out against a backdrop of further information systems developments. More often than not, line managers will not be in a position to exploit this capability for their area of responsibilities.

These newer applications are more comprehensive in nature than those in the past. Whereas Phase II was largely "macro" oriented, Phase III thoughtfully incorporated individual users as well and additionally presented a still broader picture of applications. In Phase III, the comprehensive character of systems was exemplified by EBASCO's interfacing of strategic and operational systems, overlayed with the human resource system. In Phase III applications, a conscious attempt was made jointly to consider business planning strategies, operational plans, and the implications of both for human resources planning. Information systems tie these application components together while at the same time bridging individual planning (e.g., careers, management development), and succession, to aggregate planning including general staffing, organization, and work design.

REFERENCES

"A Structural Human Resource Management System for Data Processing Personnel." Manufacturers Hanover Trust Company, New York, circa 1980.

Bright, William E. "How One Company Manages Its Human Resources." *Harvard Business Review*, Vol. 54 (1976): 81–93.

Burack, Elmer H. and Nicholas J. Mathys. *Human Resource Planning: A Pragmatic Approach to Manpower Planning and Development*. Lake Forest, IL: Brace Park, 1980.

Control Data Business Advisors. *The Micro-Based Management Job Analysis Reporting System*. Minneapolis, January 1, 1985.

Control Data Business Advisors, Human Resource Service. *FOCUS*. Minneapolis, 1984.

Control Data Business Advisors. *Position Description Questionnaire*. Minneapolis, 1984.

Hawkins, Michael. "Micros and Mainframes: New Developments." *Human Resource Planning*, Vol. 11 (1988)—in process.

Hayes, Harold. *Realism in EEO*. New York: John Wiley, 1980.

Manzini, Andrew O. "Human Resource Planning and Development at EBASCO Services, Inc." A Presentation, Conference on Strategic Human Resource Planning and Development Systems, University of Chicago (1982).

Manzini, Andrew O. and John D. Gridley. *Strategic Human Resource Planning: A Business Perspective*. New York: AMACOM, 1987.

Walker, Albert. *Human Resource Information Systems: Design and Application*. New York: John Wiley, 1984.

APPLICATION SECTION*

EXHIBIT 11-4
Auditing the Human Resource Information Base: Needs, Usage

	Current Needs			Current Availability			Future Need		
	Lo	M	Hi	Lo	M	Hi	Lo	M	Hi
External Information									
1. Competition	—	—	—	—	—	—	—	—	—
2. Job vacancies/area unemployment	—	—	—	—	—	—	—	—	—
3. People movement patterns	—	—	—	—	—	—	—	—	—
4. National, area data on people	—	—	—	—	—	—	—	—	—
5. Technological trends	—	—	—	—	—	—	—	—	—
6. Wage levels, rates of change	—	—	—	—	—	—	—	—	—
7. Occupational employment and Unemployment	—	—	—	—	—	—	—	—	—

(Continued)

---

*The form contained in this section involves three assessments: (1) current (information and data) needs, (2) current availabilities, and (3) assessing future needs. Several different approaches have proven workable in using this rating form. First, it may be used as a basis to stimulate discussion among knowledgeable people in this area so that points or areas of disagreement can be highlighted and these differences resolved. Second, it can be used as a basis for validating strategic management development planning to assure that the information/system implications are considered. Third, this information/system assessment form can be used to dramatize to executive groups or others serious areas of deficiency relative to general business planning as these affect human resources. Naturally, these discussions will suggest features for incorporation in the data base.

EXHIBIT 11-4 (Continued)

	Current Needs			Current Availability			Future Need		
	Lo	M	Hi	Lo	M	Hi	Lo	M	Hi
8. General (economic social political) forecast									
a. (specify) _____	—	—	—	—	—	—	—	—	—
b. (specify) _____	—	—	—	—	—	—	—	—	—
9. Legislative trends	—	—	—	—	—	—	—	—	—

Internal Information: Part I

A. Overall

	Lo	M	Hi	Lo	M	Hi	Lo	M	Hi
1. Business (strategic) plans	—	—	—	—	—	—	—	—	—
2. Facility plans	—	—	—	—	—	—	—	—	—
3. New product, service plans	—	—	—	—	—	—	—	—	—
4. Market forecasts	—	—	—	—	—	—	—	—	—

Internal job vacancies

	Lo	M	Hi	Lo	M	Hi	Lo	M	Hi
5. Overall	—	—	—	—	—	—	—	—	—
6. Supervisory	—	—	—	—	—	—	—	—	—
7. Managerial	—	—	—	—	—	—	—	—	—
8. By division, international	—	—	—	—	—	—	—	—	—
9. Timing	—	—	—	—	—	—	—	—	—
10. Age, age distribution retirement possibilities/intentions	—	—	—	—	—	—	—	—	—
(specify) _____	—	—	—	—	—	—	—	—	—
B. Educational level, distribution, continuing education	—	—	—	—	—	—	—	—	—
11. Credentialing	—	—	—	—	—	—	—	—	—
12. "Decay" of time senitive knowledge, skills									
(specifiy) _____	—	—	—	—	—	—	—	—	—

C. Work experience, salary

	Lo	M	Hi	Lo	M	Hi	Lo	M	Hi
13. Prior to current employment	—	—	—	—	—	—	—	—	—
14. Since employment in firm	—	—	—	—	—	—	—	—	—
a. (specifiy) _____	—	—	—	—	—	—	—	—	—
b. (specify) _____	—	—	—	—	—	—	—	—	—
c. (specify) _____	—	—	—	—	—	—	—	—	—

Pay/salary

	Lo	M	Hi	Lo	M	Hi	Lo	M	Hi
15. Current	—	—	—	—	—	—	—	—	—
16. Expected									
(specify) _____	—	—	—	—	—	—	—	—	—

D. Work experience: general, other

	Lo	M	Hi	Lo	M	Hi	Lo	M	Hi
17. Knowledge	—	—	—	—	—	—	—	—	—
19. Training	—	—	—	—	—	—	—	—	—
20. Behavioral	—	—	—	—	—	—	—	—	—
21. (specify) _____	—	—	—	—	—	—	—	—	—
22. Relevant health considerations*	—	—	—	—	—	—	—	—	—

(Continued)

EXHIBIT 11-4 (Continued)

	Current Needs			Current Availability			Future Need		
	Lo	M	Hi	Lo	M	Hi	Lo	M	Hi

Internal Information: Part II

A. Manning/staffing requirements
   1. Different employed groupings — — —   — — —   — — —
   2. Within divisions — — —   — — —   — — —
   3. Impact of change: _____ — — —   — — —   — — —
   4. Likely range of activity — — —   — — —   — — —
   5. Officer succession — — —   — — —   — — —
   6. Managerial — — —   — — —   — — —
   7. Supervisory — — —   — — —   — — —
   8. Managerial talent pool — — —   — — —   — — —
       a. (specify) _____ — — —   — — —   — — —
       b. (specify) _____ — — —   — — —   — — —
       c. (specify) _____ — — —   — — —   — — —

B Individual career planning
   9. Location preference
  10. Job preferences

   Self-awareness of abilities, needs
  11. Managerial personnel — — —   — — —   — — —
  12. Supervisory personnel — — —   — — —   — — —
  13. Women and protected groups — — —   — — —   — — —
  14. Valued skills identified — — —   — — —   — — —
  15. (specify) _____ — — —   — — —   — — —
  16. Time decay code data use — — —   — — —   — — —
  17. Work style — — —   — — —   — — —
  18. Development, needs assessment — — —   — — —   — — —
  19. Development plans — — —   — — —   — — —
  20. Measures of productivity — — —   — — —   — — —

C. Job analysis
  21. Up-to-dateness of job analysis — — —   — — —   — — —
  22. Accuracy of job analysis — — —   — — —   — — —
  23. Completeness of job analysis — — —   — — —   — — —
  24. Job behaviors for success? — — —   — — —   — — —
  25. Transferability of key skills — — —   — — —   — — —
  26. Understanding of how to carry out — — —   — — —   — — —
  27. Identificiation of key skills
      in meaningful terms? — — —   — — —   — — —

D. Career ladders, job structures
  28. "Entry ports" to job structure — — —   — — —   — — —
  29. Knowledge of traditional
      promotion path? — — —   — — —   — — —
  30. Bases for lateral job moves — — —   — — —   — — —

(Continued)

EXHIBIT 11-4 (Continued)

	Current Needs			Current Availability			Future Need		
	Lo	M	Hi	Lo	M	Hi	Lo	M	Hi
E. Performance and potential data									
31. Appraisal of performance in operational/generalizable terms	—	—	—	—	—	—	—	—	—
32. Accuracy of appraisals, standards	—	—	—	—	—	—	—	—	—
33. Development/appraisal data	—	—	—	—	—	—	—	—	—
34. Assessment of performance in generally useful terms	—	—	—	—	—	—	—	—	—
35. Accuracy of assessments	—	—	—	—	—	—	—	—	—
Information Systems									
1. Computer capabilities	—	—	—	—	—	—	—	—	—
a. Main frame	—	—	—	—	—	—	—	—	—
b. Minis	—	—	—	—	—	—	—	—	—
c. Micros	—	—	—	—	—	—	—	—	—
2. Systems planning/design	—	—	—	—	—	—	—	—	—
a. Centralized/headquarters	—	—	—	—	—	—	—	—	—
b. Decentralized	—	—	—	—	—	—	—	—	—
3. Access to system	—	—	—	—	—	—	—	—	—
a. Business planners	—	—	—	—	—	—	—	—	—
b. Senior officials	—	—	—	—	—	—	—	—	—
c. Line officials	—	—	—	—	—	—	—	—	—
d. Line managers	—	—	—	—	—	—	—	—	—
e. Human Resources									
Centralized/headquarters	—	—	—	—	—	—	—	—	—
Decentralized	—	—	—	—	—	—	—	—	—
4. Coordination of applications	—	—	—	—	—	—	—	—	—
5. Systems "housekeeping" and updates	—	—	—	—	—	—	—	—	—

*Must conform to relevant EEO guidelines.

12

Implementation Strategies

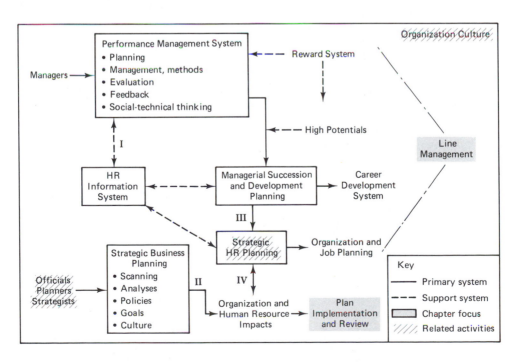

The Pilot Project—General Rationale

In large complex organizations, the sheer size and number of variables and unknowns involved in a systems installation present ample reasons in favor of a strategy with the highest possible chance for success. Pilot projects or installations confined to a particular division, business, or sector often answer this need since it is easier to provide necessary support controls *to help assure* a successful outcome. There are, however, no *guarantees* of success, and all concerned must realize this. A business area is selected where senior management and the nature of the business seem most supportive of strategic managerial development (SMD) and where important benefits are likely to result. The organization area proposed as a "candidate" needs to

- Have a high likelihood for success.
- Serve as a model for implementation strategies.
- Provide learnings and tangible results that will be useful for expanding the SMD program.
- Serve as a model of what is possible in an internal marketing sense—when the "word spreads," more senior officers will be inclined to participate in the undertaking.

Programming SMD requires a flexible, adaptive approach involving many choices and some important compromises.

A program as comprehensive as SMD is bound to run into roadblocks, events, and/or competing priorities, some of which cannot be avoided or anticipated. The pilot project carried out under the most favorable circumstances possible helps to meet some of the situational needs. But the choice of a pilot program is in itself in the nature of a compromise that needs to be explored more fully in terms of general installation planning and the usefulness of the results.

Some Necessary Compromises or Choices

For reasons already made clear, the installation of a companywide strategic managerial development system often is not practical. Thus choosing to move along divisional or sector lines decentralizes important processes and decisions to this area. This is the case even though the longer-range organizational design calls for positioning major coordinating or decision responsibilities at a more centralized or headquarters level. In other words, a comprehensive systems design for SMD may visualize headquarter's human resources with important coordinating and consultive responsibilities. Also, an "executive development committee" may be established with right of review and serving as a dispute resolution body. In a pilot program, some of this "apparatus" simply wouldn't be needed or would impede matters. A pilot SMD program, in a relatively large division or sector, involving perhaps 100 to 200 supervisors and managers, would be established initially on largely a self-contained basis.

As a consequence, important organization-structural changes can be expected as a more comprehensive SMD activity starts to emerge. Of course, this assumes that the early stages have been reasonably successful and that valuable experiences were derived.

Interpreting Pilot Program Experiences Relative to Subsequent Installation. "Organization culture" forms an important overlay with a strategic management development effort. Part of the "culture" analysis described in an earlier chapter was the recognition of powerholders and how they, in turn, influenced the way in which the system really operated. It was precisely this same recognition that provided some of the important criteria in determining (the) unit(s) that served as the pilot program. Desirably, a "typical" business unit with a powerful person favorable to SMD and human resource approaches would become a part of the pilot effort. For various practical and general considerations the "ideal" often is not to be found. Complicating considerations include pressing business problems, lack of adequately trained staff, and the diversity of functional activities found in a modern business. Whatever considerations dictate the final choice, there will be a wide spectrum of favorable/unfavorable situations. As a consequence, interpreting the results from a pilot program must take into account the favorability of the situation and the unit head's power. Explicit recognition of these matters influences the nature of strategic change strategies that will have to be mounted in other organization areas.

Managing Strategic Change Based on the Pilot Study

In proceeding forward from the pilot study results, two different types of actions must be carried out simultaneously. In one approach, there is the "systemic side" of the issues—the needed systems development as it involves procedures, information, communications, and organization. This was the central subject of the SMD systems chapter (Chapter 6). The fact that specific divisions or business sectors are at quite different points in terms of support system and trained personnel, and they possess diverse needs and priorities, will require that each installation respond to the unique conditions of that situation.

The other viewpoint to be factored in for strategy planning is the general cordiality and adaptability of the business unit to change. In units where change has been slow paced in the past or where key managers (have) actively resisted change, the difficulty (or ease) with which the pilot programs emerged or prominence (or lack) of particular types of problems may be highly misleading! For whatever comfort it provides, we have found no model or specific technique that is a "safe bet" (i.e., for a high probability of success). Much organization experience, diverse analyses, convenience, and sometimes plain gut feel or intuition are all involved. Pooling the results of various installation experiences indicates that there are workable approaches to managing strategic change based on pilot unit selection and capitalizing on data derived elsewhere in the company. Exhibit 12-1 represents a diagnostic-type approach for establishing the "favorableness" of a situation for change. It summarizes the points discussed in this section.

EXHIBIT 12-1
Managing Strategic Change: Selecting a Pilot Installation and
Generalizing Results

	Favorableness relative to other organizational unit		
Situational factors	high	moderate	low
A. Managerial group			
• Size in terms of the number of managers	____	____	____
• Dispersion of managers (domestic/international)	____	____	____
• Age range and age profile (e.g., relative to retirement)	____	____	____
• Background and training of manager	____	____	____
• Degree to which management training needs are expected to change	____	____	____
B. General			
• Power of key officials/senior managers	____	____	____
• Likelihood of support of key official(s) and senior managers	____	____	____
• Degree of change in past	____	____	____
• Degree of change current and anticipated	____	____	____

Facilitating Strategic Change

Discussions about changing attitudes or motivating (senior) managers and officials to undertake or adapt to change appear widely in the literature. But many of these writings are anchored in "theory" and not real-life circumstances. It is true that some people find change stimulating and welcome it, but there are large numbers, perhaps the majority, who find it uncomfortable and even threatening. These are natural feelings because the types of organization and systems changes described in this book often upset traditional routines or customary ways of handling things. These changes are destablizing, and the lack of familiar routines in the course of change build a sense of individual uncertainity due to the lack of structure. Furthermore, head-on confrontations to get people to change their attitudes or ways of doing things are sure to increase conflict and lead to questionable results. Also, it is true that what may be appropriate for one official may prove quite ineffective for another. For example, in one company situation, a senior and powerful manager made it perfectly clear that he "wasn't buying into the new system" and, in effect, to stay away from his area lest its good profit record be disrupted. Prudence dictated starting elsewhere in the organization and delaying SMD approaches for at least two years—which happened to coincide with the retirement of this senior official.

From these observations it should be clear that a diverse repertoire of change strategies must be drawn upon to match appropriately the numerous and diverse people and situations met in implementing SMD programs. We have compiled a list of bases for catalyzing change and a format for examining these relative to key people likely to be involved and/or those whose approval ("blessing") is needed to launch an SMD (change) program (Exhibit 12-2).

The basis for launching change, or "motivating" officials to move in particular directions, that are itemized in Exhibit 12-2 reflect some common features which may not be initially apparent. Bases for change which are (largely) in the hands of the officials involved frequently represent an ideal springboard to get things started. Officials who are the focus of change may at first "awfulize" the system or approach, but if the rationales or circumstances are compelling ones, people start to accept them and get moving. Such factors as legal requirements (e.g., court orders, affirmative action as with OFCC contractors), stockholder returns, commitments to key customers, financial limitations, and "corporate survival" are among the compelling but largely *impersonal factors in change*. In the Western world, these types of factors have a high level of acceptance since they are supported generally by societal norms. Undoubtedly many have experienced the situation where the explanation for a particular action is that it's "policy" or "the rules." People may not like it but they accept it—and these factors reflect the same type of approach.

A second group of factors is oriented much more to behavioral considerations. These include open discussions to gain consensus, strong executive leadership, and/or a strong "corporate culture." Implementation or change strategies indicate that these can be used individually or collectively. Where, for example, strong

EXHIBIT 12-2

Impact Analysis for Key Officials and Managers in Managing Strategic Change

Bases for undertaking strategic change	Key officials and managers								
	(Person) Impact			(Person) Impact			(Person) Impact		
	low	moderate	high	low	moderate	high	low	moderate	high
Budgetary controls	—	—	—	—	—	—	—	—	—
Financial considerations, controls	—	—	—	—	—	—	—	—	—
Incorporate in reward systems	—	—	—	—	—	—	—	—	—
Performance appraisals	—	—	—	—	—	—	—	—	—
Salary	—	—	—	—	—	—	—	—	—
Bonus	—	—	—	—	—	—	—	—	—
Legal requirements	—	—	—	—	—	—	—	—	—
Economic necessity (e.g., survival, continuity)	—	—	—	—	—	—	—	—	—
Timing (e.g., delay, accretion)	—	—	—	—	—	—	—	—	—
Transfer, promote retire	—	—	—	—	—	—	—	—	—
Open discussions	—	—	—	—	—	—	—	—	—
Strong executive leadership	—	—	—	—	—	—	—	—	—
Corporate culture	—	—	—	—	—	—	—	—	—
Return to stockholders, profitability	—	—	—	—	—	—	—	—	—
Top executive order	—	—	—	—	—	—	—	—	—

precedence exists for a particular line of innovative actions or change or commitment to human resources, this aspect of "corporate culture" can exert a powerful influence on the actions of individual officials.

We have found that open and freewheeling discussions often provide effective means of getting out "onto the table" serious reservations or negative attitudes (unvoiced) held by key people. A successful basis for establishing this format is to convene a meeting of key people whose participation and support is critical to the success of the SMD program. An agenda is circulated which lists the focus project (e.g., SMD system or pilot program) and some of the key and controversial issues attached to its implementation. Beforehand, people can even receive questionnaires (which are returned without signature) indicating their opinions or preferences. More viewpoints will surface as the discussion gets under way. The purpose of the "open" meeting format is to encourage an open discussion among peers that will help to reveal controversial issues and reservations regarding participation. This type of discussion is central to strategic processes. If spade work has been done carefully, at least a few of the key and powerful members will be able to mount (positive) persuasive reasons and considerations relative to the "negative" points thrown on the table. If the executive or consultant leading the discussion is skillful in these matters, results can be quite positive and greatly facilitative of the change program. Closely related to this approach is that of "strong executive leadership" that has been able to exert a major influence on executive actions—and with a "track record" of good results.

This discussion concludes the introductory remarks for this implementation/ application chapter. The balance of the chapter is given over to the cases illustrating some of the key circumstances surrounding strategic management development undertakings and the manner with which these have been handled. *Valley Stores, Inc., deals with strategic human resources planning approaches* with emphasis on *deriving strategies and gearing up human resources for its role.*

Hi-Tech Electronics deals with corporate culture and establishing strategies in SMD systems planning and approaches. A commentary is also provided. *The Acme-United Case deals with launching a corporatewide career development system.*

APPLICATIONS AND IMPLEMENTATIONS OF STRATEGIC HUMAN RESOURCE DEVELOPMENT CONCEPTS AND APPROACHES

VALLEY STORES, INC (Strategic Approaches)

"Chuck" Krammer founded Valley Stores in 1956, almost 10 years after his discharge from the U.S. Air Force. Chuck joined the Air Force in 1944 after receiving an engineering degree from Cal Tech and was trained as a flight engineer. After his discharge in 1946, he quite naturally turned to the airlines for employment. Unfortunately, many other discharged Air Force vets had the same idea. The few available jobs were filled quickly, and Chuck finally had to settle for employment at a firm making airplane components, including guidance and control systems. In a few years, Chuck was made director of engineering and production because he had exceptional abilities to think broadly and see the interrelationships between producing a product of uniformly high quality and good profits.

Chuck also developed a good reputation in the local community. The Chamber of Commerce was looking for a speaker at its monthly luncheon meeting, and Chuck's boss, a Chamber member, suggested him. Although Chuck was told that he could pick his own subject, the area of great interest to Chamber members was the likely course of area development and its possible impact on local business. The topic also interested Chuck, but he didn't know how to go about researching it. He visited one of his friends in the College of Business at a regional campus of the University of Texas. When Chuck was interviewed, he described his visit at U.T. as "an incredible, eye-opening experience." Chuck and his friend discussed business planning and reviewed general marketing trends; he also received a "laundry list" of references for business planning, marketing, and "futures"-type publications. The talk prepared by Chuck and delivered to the Chamber luncheon meeting was entitled "Business Opportunities—The Next Ten Years."

This experience completely changed Chuck's professional life. He went to his boss, the vice president of operations, and said that he wanted to go back to school and earn a master's degree in business. He was told in no uncertain terms that he was too valuable to be granted an extended leave of absence and further that "he was getting plenty of practical experience that would be more than enough for (their) business needs and his future in the company."

Chuck could not be dissuaded from pursuing a Business School program, so he enrolled in the night program at one of the regional campuses of the State University. It took Chuck almost five years of night school to complete his degree requirements, but in that time, he developed a career game plan for himself that involved a radical change in career direction, including a whole new occupation.

The work he did in preparing the talk for the Chamber of Commerce had convinced him that mass merchandising was just coming into its own, and he wanted to position himself to be a part of that growth. When he received his degree, he gave the company one month's notice and set out to establish a "new" business and concept. With savings accumulated from the war and line of credit from the local bank, he founded Valley Stores, Inc.

Valley's Marketing and Merchandising Concepts

From the very beginning Chuck was determined that Valley Stores would combine the best in merchandising, marketing approaches, and management to deliver to customers good-quality merchandise at reasonable prices. Further, Valley Stores merchandising approach was to be highly flexible. It was to anticipate important new regional (and national) consumer patterns and integrate these into their marketing program.

Chuck had been watching closely the merchandising patterns developed by the food chains. He decided that this would be the format for Valley's retail outlets. That is, mass merchandising of good-quality goods and services from a ground-level (one-story) type of structure. Furthermore, reasonable flexibility would also be incorporated into regional store units so that they could adjust operations to the demographic trends and economic needs of their areas. Relative to the then-existing Sears and Montgomery Ward stores, the merchandising approach appeared radical. It was an almost instant success. In the first store operation were featured women's and men's wearing apparel, hardwares, and white goods (appliances, large and small). By 1965, Valley Stores, Inc., had established a well-organized and fast-growing regional store chain. New store operating techniques and lines of merchandise continued to be introduced. Managerial structure and processes were also carefully developed and related to the primary store merchandising functions. The combination of merchandising and managerial approaches led to exceptional profits.

Organization and Business Planning and Strategic Developments

In 1967, Krammer in his capacity as CEO, asked the vice president of finance to establish a formal business planning capability and to get somebody trained (or hired) to take over this responsibility. Since the managerial organization was very lean, no staff people could be freed up for the planning assignment, so a recent MBA graduate, Bob Turner, was hired to take over these responsibilities. After an initial period of getting acquainted, Bob proved quite equal to the job, and by 1972, long-range business planning had been introduced at the executive level. In 1973, Bob Turner, manager of business planning, attended a three-day workshop on strategic business planning and a few months later presented a proposal to Valley's executive committee for establishing a strategic planning capability which was subsequently approved.

The original concept of the strategic business plan contained several essential features:

1. A five-year revolving planning period with an annual update.
2. Grass-roots, bottom-up planning, with consolidation and integration of these at the corporate level. For these purposes, stategic business units were to be organized based on regional marketing areas and the major corporate business functions.
3. Identification of central business issues that were likely to impact Valley Stores in the future and development of strategic alternatives by staff people working with senior officers.
4. Determination of the impact of various strategic alternatives in marketing/merchandising approaches on store operations and "manpower."
5. Decision making, that is, choice among the feasible strategic alternatives and launching of the appropriate programs or activities.

In the years subsequent to the launching of the strategic business planning program, two additional and important changes took place. For one, Bob Turner recognized that a considerable amount of managerial and executive time was being consumed by planning and strategic processes and was determined to improve this process. Through a contact at a professional meeting, he became aware of some computerized modeling approaches taken to long-range and strategic planning with what appeared to be good success. Although the underlying business planning model was both elaborate and complex, the inputs were relatively straightforward and involved various assumptions concerning costs, profits, volume, consumer preferences, and strategic options. With managerial and executive time at a premium, many managers and officers were happy to delegate the number crunching and manipulations to the (computerized) strategic modeling approach. True, some "hands-on" feel of the numbers might be best, but the speed of turnaround and reduction of time commitments were impressive.

Role of Human Resources

The second major planning-related development after launching of the strategic planning activity related to the Human Resources department. Fred Gerstien was director of human resources and reported to the vice president of administration. As he became aware of the long-range and strategic planning at corporate headquarters through his unit's strategic planning inputs, it seemed quite natural to him that Human Resources should be positioned to assume a more active role in the planning cycle. Although the founder, and CEO, Chuck Krammer, was a visionary when it came to the marketing or economic side of the business, Krammer had provided little impetus to strengthening Valley's Personnel capabilities other than in regard to succession planning analyses.

There were, however, several disquieting signs with which Krammer was becoming increasingly aware. One was the "recent" failure of the store operations function to have sufficiently well-developed store people to move up into all of the new store management slots. His intuition also told him that an insufficient number of second-level managers existed as backups or candidates for middle-level and senior managerial positions. Krammer asked both Turner and Gerstien to stop by his office and "review" planning coverage for human resources. He was told that human resources were a general part of all planning and strategic analyses but didn't enter into the process explicitly. Krammer indicated that "Next year, I would like to see Human Resources provide some interpretations of the business and strategic options *before* they are finalized and also to come up with a concept of structure that will assure we have top-flight managers in the future." The expansion of long-range and strategic planning to include Human Resources was seemingly a straightforward move, but it came at a time when various problems were being experienced with the business and strategic process itself. Thus two different levels of internal planning process problems started to emerge:

1. Several area general managers and some senior officers felt that they had lost touch with and control of some of the key numbers and parameters attached to strategic business planning. As one officer put it, "Although our time involvement is much less, we are getting buried in paper output that we can't possibly digest. We are losing touch here with what's happening, and if it continues, I won't be responsible for the results."

2. Human Resources got involved almost immediately in providing planning interpretations, but as Fred Gerstien said, "I'm getting the right kinds of questions but at the wrong time. There were some situations where our inability to staff certain key positions, for example, should call for a (temporary) halt to a particular business plan unless the people side of the question can be dealt with."

Revision of Business and Strategic Planning Processes and Organization of a Human Resource Planning Capability

By 1982 a major change was made in business and strategic planning process, the purpose of which was to reestablish management involvement and commitment to planning numbers and approaches. The computerized planning models were only to be used on an advisory basis to check out various options, but even then only if entered into and controlled by senior line managers. Otherwise, long-range planning and strategies were to be viewed as feasible *proposals* that were economic and which would receive careful executive review. Another major change concerned the role of Human Resources in the business planning and strategic process. The old and newer approaches are illustrated in Exhibit 12-3. The old approach affecting Human Resources (on the left side) placed it in a secondary and largely reactive role, providing information or interpretations but largely on request—and at later stages in the planning cycle. The flow on the right depicts the newer approach, with Human Resources having much greater inputs to the planning and strategic process. In this latter role, Human Resources started to interact informally with various line managers and officers regarding *tentative* staffing plans for key and critical positions. Also Human Resources assumed more formal responsibilities to the extent that it was expected to develop organization and job structure interpretations of various planning and strategic options. Human Resources also had a new role to the extent that it was to work closely with Turner in business planning and come up with human resource planning scenarios. This work involved interpretations of environmental and business trends in terms of their human resource implications as a basis for guiding various planning and strategic approaches. An example of these planning scenarios is provided in Exhibit 12-4.

On the left side are presented some important business and competitive developments that were anticipated in the early 1980s and, on the right side, some of the human resources interpretations fitted to these. For example, an important consumer trend that emerged was growing weight and health consciousness. It was

EXHIBIT 12-3

Valley Stores: Old and New Process Flows in Business and Strategic
Planning

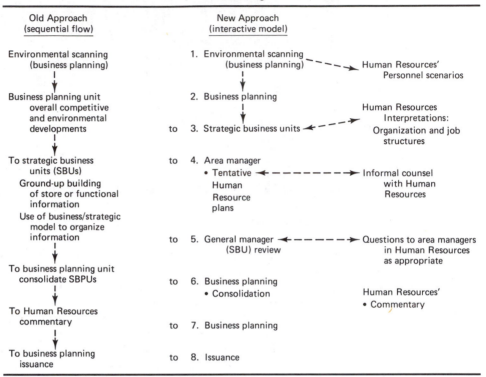

Old Approach (sequential flow)		New Approach (interactive model)
Environmental scanning (business planning)		1. Environmental scanning (business planning) — — → Human Resources' Personnel scenarios
Business planning unit overall competitive and environmental developments	to	2. Business planning
		Human Resources Interpretations:
	to	3. Strategic business units ← — — → Organization and job structures
To strategic business units (SBUs) Ground-up building of store or functional information Use of business/strategic model to organize information	to	4. Area manager • Tentative ← — — — — → Informal counsel Human with Human Resource Resources plans
	to	5. General manager ← — — — → Questions to area managers (SBU) review in Human Resources as appropriate
To business planning unit consolidate SBPUs	to	6. Business planning • Consolidation
		Human Resources'
To Human Resources commentary		• Commentary
	to	7. Business planning
To business planning issuance	to	8. Issuance

visualized that this trend translated into diet programs and health readings, exercise equipment programs, and still more outdoor sports. Some of this undoubtedly would be fadish, and others would likely grow in the long term. Also, the videotape acquisition and viewing habits of millions of people was about to explode. Similarly, "personal" computers were likely to grow at an incredible rate. Valley Stores was seen as playing potentially a major role in exploiting the thrust of these trends. However, this approach would drain large amounts of capital from its store growth programs. The business strategy adopted for this aspect of future planning was to shift to concession management for some of these new enterprises and in other instances to reorganize and consolidate some of the stores functions around these new concepts. To provide more opportunities for its own managerial work force, some of the concessions were to be organized as "entrepreneurial venture businesses." These were managed by former Valley Store employees, but with managerial development and external financing facilitated by Valley's excellent reputation and other internal capabilities.

EXHIBIT 12-4
Examples: Business and Strategic Planning and
Their Human Resource Implications

IA. *Representative Trends Identified*

Consumer health consciousness
Diets
Exercise equipment
Recreation equipment
Consumer/adult learning
Food supplements, vitamins, drugs
Health diagnosis

Information and computers
Use of personal computers
Business and personal applications
Adaptation to consumer/household
needs

Consumer entertainment
TV, VCRs
Home recording
Home movies
Videotapes

IIA. *Strategic Planning Possibilities (representative)*

Establish venture businesses, independently owned by former employees (logical personal growth opportunity for entrepreneurial-type people).

Reorganize portions of store operations built around new business/merchandising clusters (e.g., "home entertainment centers").

IB. *Key Strategic Objectives, Constraints*

Assure adequate supply of competent succession candidates.

Preserve store flexibility/marketing.

Conserve capital for store expansion.

Seek greater involvement and commitment of organization members.

Fully use computer resources.

Provide high level of product and service quality at reasonable prices—maintain merchandising leadership.

IIB. *Human Resource Outcomes*

Develop and install a comprehensive management plan and training program.

Reassess Corporate Human Resource Development capabilities in terms of programming and tracking people.

Develop and install a comprehensive management continuity plan and program.

Redevelop some operations and work with staff personnel evidencing the potential to move into new store business clusters as unit managers—providing appropriate consumer advice.

Review general management development and succession programs for staff capabilities and thrust of programs.

Reorient merchandising, advertising, and marketing personnel to new concepts.

(Continued)

EXHIBIT 12-4 (Continued)

IIB. Survey employee job satisfaction and
opportunity—to determine their perception of career development
opportunities.

Expand management development
programs—incorporate selective
and new entrepreneurial development components.

Human Resource Continuity (Reserve and Replacement) Planning System

Part of Fred Gerstien's "charge" was to come up with a continuity or succession planning system that would adequately back up the types of business strategies sketched out in Exhibit 12-4. It was also to inspire more confidence in finding successful replacements for succession. To develop a sound program and one that has the highest chance for success, Fred interviewed a number of managers in both middle-level and senior positions. His study indicated the great informality that accompanied the current replacement or filling of new managerial and executive positions and attendant development approaches.

The continuity planning program that Fred designed had several essential features, which he felt would meet the main deficiencies experienced in the past and furnish a sound foundation for future growth. Main parts of this program were as follows.

Designation of Two Types of Positions and Three Classes of Talent. These included

1. *Continuity positions* (40)—a group of officer, senior managerial positions, and positions identified as critical because of their relation to business process or supply/demand factors. Incumbents in continuity positions were not to be transferred or reassigned without review by the CEO.
2. *Key positions* (90)—positions which most commonly served as direct building blocks for succession or feeders to other critical jobs in the past plus newly designated positions which, through cross-transfer development, could also serve as building block positions. This part of the program proposal was greatly facilitated by a recently completed reanalyses of managerial positions based on a common set of behavior dimensions. This study permitted expansion of backup people for "key positions" by almost 25 percent over what they would have been otherwise.
3. *Key managerial pool* (110 people)—these comprised a flexible grouping of people who through performance assessments as "high potential" in any particular year were classified as "pool" members. However, "membership designation" shifted year to year to avoid an "heir-apparent" problem and unrealis-

tic expectations and disappointments among designees. Thus membership information was kept confidential, though supervisors were encouraged to discuss individual ratings and issues of promotability with the ratee.

Establishment of a New Candidate Review and Planning Cycle.   Design of a planning/strategic calendar with the following key dates and events.

January–February	• Store replacement planning cycle: business and strategic planning cycle starts.
March–April	• Strategic business unit (SBU) planning cycle based on interaction with store managers and other key personnel—proposal of individual development plans.
May	• Review and approval of SBU plans by general manager; review and acceptance of development plans at planning meeting.
June	• Executive committee —Review long-range and strategic plans and identify areas for revision or change. —Analyze "continuity" positions (every six months). —Analyze "key" positions. —Review "key managerial pool" designees and in conjunction with their general managers. —General review performance, assessments of potential, and development plans ("continuity" and "key" positions). —resolve jurisdictional and turf issues and approval of cross-functional moves of "key" people and also similar moves for "key managerial pool" designees that hadn't been otherwise resolved.
December	• Intersession meeting —Review program of business and strategic plans. —Review continuity plans. —Resolve new continuity problems.

Other features of the new review and planning program are described in the paragraphs that follow.

Managerial Development Program.   Management development planning was to be carried out with its incorporation into store and strategic business unit planning as well as at the semiannual executive committee reviews. Also cross-functional movements, managerial coaching, classroom-type learning, and self-learning were to be incorporated into all human resource planning discussions. Appropriate combinations of these were to be designated as individual career developmemt strategies. To support their program fully, a substantial management development budget was earmarked to support SBU activities. Also noted was the "support of permanent development," a note added to the managerial performance appraisal forms.

Career Development Program.   This program component was to be eventually introduced to help managers think through their own career plans and the meshing of these with Valley Stores. Additional budget was also earmarked for this program in support of individual career planning materials and services. These included the use of external psychological and career assessment services as these might be appropriate for middle-level and senior people.

Computerized Information Capability.   All its record-keeping and movement-tracking functions in connection with developing and managerial tracking were to be consolidated. Further, these were to be committed to a microcomputer system lodged in Human Resources.

Managerial and Executive.   Although larger computer system capabilities were still needed to back up the micro capability, needed information was "downloaded" to form a comprehensive information base to support the continuity system. Confidentiality was maintained through removable diskettes, limited access, and a typical lock/key arrangement.

Hi-Tech Electronics (Culture and a Corporatewide Strategic Management Development Approach)

Background

Hi-Tech Electronics employed some 7,000 people in five major establishments (divisions) located in both the metropolitan and suburban areas of a major Eastern city. The plants differed greatly in size, with one multiproduct suburban location employing some 3,000 people and a specialty products unit in the "inner city" employing about 800. Company products involved many computer-related products, and each establishment was self-contained in terms of systems, engineering, production, personnel, and marketing functions. Headquarters was at a separate location, where senior managers, directors, and officers took on supportive or coordinating roles.

To organize better and provide a companywide management development system, an audit of all managerial and supervisory positions was carried out. The audit's purpose was to establish a bank of up-to-date and complete information on organization people plus baselines or standards against which future progress would be measured. Soon after completion of the audit, the president called in the vice president of human resources (HR) and asked for "an explanation" of the numerous complaints he was receiving from all of the divisions regarding the recently completed management development audit (MDA).

The Management Development Audit

The audit was conducted by HQ staff and based on a carefully designed questionnairing approach (see attached) carried out in two parts (Exhibit 12-5). Prior to interviewing managers, each one received copies of the MDA forms for their immediate subordinates' as well as their own jobs. They were requested to complete these prior to discussing with the interviewer, job requirements, and information

EXHIBIT 12-5
Job Audit Job Performance Factors

(Part A)

Behavioral Skills | *Rating**

1. *Human relations*—works effectively with people at various organization levels; is empathetic; has ability to relate. _____

2. *Leadership*—is able to build team effort, rally support, and motivate; has consistent pattern of good decisions or reliable information; can be counted on; takes a stand. _____

3. *Oral communications*—can get across ideas clearly; can be persuasive; makes self understood; provides feedback. _____

4. *Self-appraisal*—is able to detach self from ideas—can self-analyze; has awareness of shortcomings, areas to improve. _____

5. *Conflict resolution*—is able to deal with tense situations and resolve these; can remain detached without emotional involvement; can see other viewpoints. _____

6. *Mentoring*—can serve as good sounding board for others' ideas; has skill in providing career assistance—counsel and guidance. _____

Managerial Functions | Rating

7. *Planning*—can identify with workable accuracy, relevant trends or future events; can develop contingency approaches. _____

8. *Control and coordination*—monitors relevant events; is able to work between people or units; deals with complex situations. _____

9. *Results orientation*—can prioritize activities and efforts so as to make the greatest impact on the final results. _____

10. *Time management*—self-organizes work and activities and delegation as needed to assure on-time performance. _____

11. *Problem solving*—recognizes and clearly defines key situational elements, identifies relevant assumptions—carries out relevant cost-benefit analyses. _____

12. *Decision making*—can identify alternatives, evaluate alternatives, and make choices. _____

13. *Job knowledge*—utilizes professional or technical knowledge, experience; uses appropriate tools needed to carry out responsibilities. _____

Personal Qualities

14. *Written communications*—organizes ideas in writing; recognizes impact of communications; accurate conveying of intended message. _____

15. *Oral communications*—can present ideas in a clear way, understands the impact of word choice, facial expression, etc., in getting points across convincingly; is a good listener. _____

16. *Creativity*—is able to conceptualize difficult situations; formulates unique ideas; is receptive to new(er) approaches. _____

17. *Persistence*—is able to resist pressure of others while maintaining progress in desired direction. _____

(Continues)

EXHIBIT 12-5 (Continued)

Individual-Management Inventory—Preliminary Form Summary

(Part B)

Date _____

Name _____   Position _____

Division _____   Department _____

Date of Hire _____ Year, Current Job _____ Age _____

Rating, Current Position:

	1 2	3 4	5 6	7 8	9 10	
	Mar- ginal	Accept- able	Compe- tent	Very Good	Out- stand- ing	Too Early (Less than One Year)

Potential:

_____	_____	_____	_____
Suited, Current	Promotable One Level	Promotable Two Levels	Too Early to Judge

Promotable
When (?):

_____	_____	_____
Under 6 Months	Under 1 Year	Type of Position

_____	_____
1 to 2 Years	Type of Position/Work

Performance Summary (Strengths, Development Needs)

_____

_____

_____

_____

Development Plan

_____

_____

_____

Supervisor's   Review and
Signature _____Date _____ Approval _____ Date _____

*1–2 (marginal): is variable in quality/quantity, can't be counted on, just meets requirements.

3–4 (acceptable): is fairly consistent in meeting performance standards, usually reliable, quality/quantity usually acceptable.

5–6 (competent): works with little supervision, has good command of necessary skills, reliable.

7–8 (very good): can often work independently, has most of necessary expertise, sometime assists others.

9–10 (outstanding): is highly reliable, operates independently, excellent command of skills, highly reliable and competent.

456

concerning personnel backgrounds as to knowledge, skills, abilities, interests, and career objectives. Also during the interview, the manager's supervisor joined the discussion to help validate the job information and to become more familiar with the background and goals of their subordinates. Interviews on the average lasted two to three hours and required the effort of three headquarters' people for almost three months to cover the 700 included in the MDA. Typically, managers distributed the MDA forms to their subordinates to get both the job and career information prior to their interviews with headquarters' staff. Where they felt the information was inaccurate or incomplete, it was corrected.

Details of the Audit

The systemwide human resource audit (HRA) dealt with both people and jobs. It was desired to determine for the company as a whole, individual strengths and developmental needs, managerial performances, and managerial potential in the future—this was the human resources side of the analysis. Jobs were analyzed additionally to determine needed job behaviors for success and the likely direction of future changes. The headquarters' development staff had the responsibility for conducting the HRA. Information was collected from all exempt employees after they were oriented as to the general purposes of the audit. Interviews were then conducted with department and administrative heads to sift through the performance, background, and job information secured from the employees. A particularly useful part of this program was to secure individual information that would be used for ultimately establishing a *management inventory*. Final reports were prepared for each division head (their data only), executive officers, vice president of Human Resources, and the president. Based on subsequent events, this approach to developing individual and job information proved inadequate for employees and a source of much confusion and even threat. In past analyses, it became clear that the initial briefings were superficial as to the purpose and use of the data and that jobholders had no opportunity to review the completed information file. Thus the HRA as a *process* for collecting information was viewed negatively. Its merits in terms of the technical aspects of its format or contents were not recognized.

The HRA was carried out in two parts:

1. Jobholders filled out a questionnaire that provided knowledge, skill, and ability information, personal interests, and future career objectives. They also described their concept of current job demands based on a 17-item inventory provided by the development staff (the form in Exhibit 12-5A was the basis).
2. Supervisors were interviewed based on a structured format and then asked to review the job and demographic data regarding their subordinates (a copy of the interview format was provided prior to the interview).

Aftermath of MDA

All senior managers of Hi-Tech had been told of the purposes of MDA and for the most part were quite understanding and supportive of the important outcomes which could result. Thus, when various managers questioned the purposes of the study, bases for eliciting information, and the usefulness of information resulting from the questionnaire-interview format, it was assumed that this was only natural interviewee tension and that senior managers would smooth things out. The assumption proved to be wrong.

The vice president of Human Resources, after the meeting with the president, quickly checked out all the divisional Personnel units and several senior managers. The latter were friends of long standing. Although it was not possible to put together a complete picture, it took little imagination to fill in the missing parts. It was clear that communications had broken down between senior managers and their immediate subordinates as to the purposes of MDA. Perhaps more serious, however, was the fact that many supervisors and managers seemed to be questioning the basic assumptions underlying the study. For example, misgivings were expressed regarding the "company's willingness and desire to undertake a forward-looking, creative, management development design program." Also questioned was the adequacy of systems and policies to support the effort and "the inclusion of only a select few in the subsequent development effort." The vice president of Human Resources consulted with the headquarters' director of management development and some of the divisional personnel managers. A plan resulted which was to salvage the MDA results and ultimately strengthen the organizationwide management development program (IMPACT) subsequently launched.

A Participation Plan and Program for Employee Involvement

The heart of the strategy set forth by the Human Resource group for opening up communications and gaining commitment was built around four employee task teams. The teams were staffed with (exempt) employees selected on a companywide basis. Each member reflected a range of company experiences, responsibilities, technical and more general managerial tasks, types of product orientation, age, and sex. Teams consisted of ten members and two alternates to fill in should somebody be unavailable for meeting attendance. Each team was assigned a central question directly related to the nature and specifics of the "feedback" from the audit experience. In the main, four central issues and areas of problems concerned employees. These dealt with the character of a management development program and some of the potentially useful results that could come from this effort. In particular,

1. *The supervisory/managerial role* and specifically what it should involve in an effective working relationship with employees.
2. *The culture of Hi-Tech Electronics* and how it affected employee mobility and sense of promotion opportunities seen by supervisors and managers.
3. *Organization career management and individual career planning*—relationships, systems, and approaches.
4. *Organizational support systems, capabilities, and facilitative efforts*—seen by employees as prerequisite to widespread member involvement and commit-

ment to the program. These covered a broad scope of activities ranging from longer-range and strategic planning ("to add more certainty into future planning to information position availability for career counseling").

Each task team was given 90 days to study its assigned area and to develop a summary report. All reports were then consolidated into a participant package for discussion at three half-day meetings. The meetings involved officers and senior managers, a representation of key department heads, and the employee committees. The purpose of the general meetings was to sort out matters common to various reports; clarify the assumptions or intent of particular recommendations; establish the company's position as to objectives of IMPACT, feasibility or fit of task team recommendations, and areas requiring further study; and to develop a time-activity game plan covering the next 24 months for moving forward with IMPACT.

Task Team Reports

The information provided by the task teams was notable for its crystallization of key management development issues and similarity to widespread matters found in many other companies. What follows is a brief summary of task team findings and recommendations in each of the four previously identified areas.

The Supervisory-Managerial Role. The supervisor-employee relationship was the essential building block for creating a job-supportive climate for management development and performance management and identifying individual potential and individual career development. The supervisor also served as an essential role model signaling both desired performances and those activities to be avoided; they were in a position to convey graphically organization culture and means of dealing with it in an effective way. At the same time, the supervisory role contained within it the necessary options and freedom of individual action to really make a difference to the employee. Thus the "literal" intent and reality of IMPACT, whatever these might be, emerged from the supervisor's role as it impacted his or her work group member.

The supervisor had various and different roles to play as *manager and career developer*. Some supervisory actions directly supported performance or the specific employee developmental needs resulting from the nature and needs of the business. Yet the latter was also seen by employees as possessing potentially, an important opportunity for personal growth and advancement. The supervisor, as a result, needed to do a good job in his or her additional roles as *mentor* or *sponsor*. *Mentors* were seen as those having desirable types of knowledge, skills, and abilities—and therefore served as behavioral models. Also, mentors served as trainers or teachers who could share know-how without personal threat and further served as sounding boards for employee ideas and concerns. Too, mentors assisted in providing guidance and direction impartially (as needed) but recognized that employees of necessity had to make career decisions for themselves. Mentors often served particular or specialized purposes so that a given employee could easily be interacting with several at different times and for different purposes.

The supervisory-managerial role also involved *sponsorship*. It was recognized that many managers played the role of sponsor even though it was informal. Sponsors could directly affect individual career development through a rather active role in counseling and guidance and as a power figure who directly affected employee progress. Whereas individuals often had several mentors, typically only *one* manager or supervisor (if any) served as a *sponsor*.

Task group recommendations included the following:

- Educate managers and supervisors as to the many roles they play, with clarification of mentoring and sponsorship activity.
- Help clarify the conflicts that were likely to arise from mentoring and sponsorship roles and bases for reaching these
- Strengthen coaching skills and techniques of informal interviewing.
- Consider formalizing a mentoring system and launch a pilot study to gain more information on its usefulness.
- Help the supervisor to understand that some issues will arise in the many roles they carry out that require referral to staff specialists or the assistance of others.
- Recognize individuals desiring to strengthen skills or/and advance learning so that they be given access to those who can be facilitative.

The Culture of Hi-Tech Electronics.   Many employees, even relatively new ones, came to realize that many company or *internal* environmental factors affected career mobility and opportunity. Few, however, really understood all these factors or how they influenced individual progress and career growth. In truth, ability was important but unless accompanied by insights into the inner workings of the organization could be diluted as a central factor in promotion. This was far more than a matter of "who you know," although this too could be a factor. The more experienced members of the task team used the term "company culture" to describe a set of informal but highly important "rules" which were felt to be indispensable to access long-term promotion opportunities, including succession to upper-level positions. The features of company (organization) *culture* thought to be most important included

1. Jobs or departments seen as "favored" by key managers that involved valued skills or the gaining of particularly important experiences at an early point in one's career.
2. Particular sets of knowledge, skills, and abilities or managerial qualities often sought out in high-potential or promotion candidates. For the most part these seemed to fall into two major categories:
   a. Generic managerial skills, including stress management, planning, decision making, communications, and dealing effectively with people.
   b. Company awareness skills, including the financial marketing and operational bases for corporate success, finesse in working with the company's "culture," and technical competencies in one's field of specialization.

3. A general sense of timing and understanding norms of behavior that led to a realistic basis to judge how long it took to gain certain abilities, or when to apply for promotion, or the implications of various company communications for individual career progress.
4. Organizational communications and its timing that informed people of promotional opportunity.
5. Knowledge of company trends and intermediate-range objectives and the further impact of these at the divisional level—and how rate of growth and types of future jobs available were affected.
6. Acceptable bases for employee competition and conflict.

In addition to identifying this list of organization culture (related) features, the task team was able to identify what appeared to be some of the specific behaviors of members that were valued by the organization. (See Exhibit 12-6.)

Career Management and Individual Career Planning.   The task teams that studied this area identified many sources of confusion that existed in the organization, namely, the intermixing of events and objectives of individual career planning with those of management planning. It was obvious that management development

EXHIBIT 12-6
Valued Company Behaviors

- Being in command of key job–related problems.
- Being assertive with work-related problems, making clear one's interests in career advancement.
- Making organization commitment and *demonstrating* loyalty to the company.
- Being stoic, that is, getting on with things and avoiding being known as a complainer.
- Being seen as one who meets one's management-by-objective targets consistently.
- Having flexibility and being adaptable to changing situations.
- Reserving judgment until the "facts" are all in.
- Exhibiting good survival qualities involving a high energy level, hanging in when the going is tough, and being able to absorb conflict.
- Having the ability to convert a problem or an apparent lack of resources to an opportunity—making the best of things and then some.
- Receiving consistently good performance ratings and a significant number of excellent ratings.
- Having command of valued information needed for making good decisions or getting things done in a practical way.
- Being willing to commit one's self and make a decision, but not to be seen as foolhardy.
- Being willing to commit personal time or energies considered as voluntary or "extra effort" by key organization managers.
- Having educational preparation in the "right" areas.

(MD) usually served as a vehicle for strengthening individual competence—but to meet particular company needs in the future. What wasn't clear, however, was the relationship of the MD activities to individual career planning and development. Discussion and analysis by this task team indicated the need to establish clearly a linkage between the two but also to be able to distinguish between the somewhat different purposes served by both. Individual career planning represented the hopes of the person for his or her future.

The Person of Necessity Takes Charge of His or Her Own Career.   It was quite possible that the satisfaction of individual career goals might be through participation in IMPACT. But it was also true that the person might wish to stabilize the job situation—do a good job—and remain in the same position. Another alternative to pursue in an individual career design is to leave the company, which might be mutually beneficial to the person and the company.

The expected results for management development were (somewhat) different from those from an individual viewpoint. To begin with, the company's future staffing of managerial positions and officer succession was directly dependent on the success of the management development program. Another rather obvious consideration, yet one at times overlooked, was the exclusive focus of MD on the fulfillment of organizational *company* options, alternatives, and needs. The corporation's strategic planning was the engine that powered this activity and focused directions. To the extent that individual career objectives could be (largely) met through the company's MD program, mutual reinforcement was provided. Yet in reality, objectives of the two could *diverge* and thus pose significant problems of individual frustration or even turnover. For the company, failure to converge to a workable degree could mean lack of fulfillment of company staffing objectives.

This task team also brought out what its members felt to be an inequitable system of company communications and competition for available positions or program participation. Even more to the point was the task team's statement that "employment and promotion decisions should be part of an open system. The system should have competitive recruitment and selection of the most qualified and able candidates—for any position outside of senior officership. Job posting, to the extent that it was carried out, was a failure because of inadequate job data, preselected candidates, and poor feedback of evaluation or decision information. Thus, any information or activities that could be seen as improving one's career possibilities as, for example, awareness of a position opening, clarifying job criteria for open positions or skill building, was seen as a necessary part of an authentic MD program. In the view of the task team, Hi-Tech employees generally lacked adequate information to make decisions regarding self-development that could realistically complement the career management objectives of the organization. Closely related to this point was the notion expressed by the team that far too much emphasis was placed by the management on vertical mobility. More thought had to be given to what constituted career opportunity, especially for specialists who worked to pursue technical careers.

Members of this task team also felt that many promotions in the past had been poorly made. Good work performance in one job was no sure indicator that the individual possessed the technical qualifications or professional education to stay relevant in some other job.

The final point made by this task team concerned the apparent lack of company and managerial awareness of the need for and potency of self-assessment. Employees wanting to take charge of their career needed periodically to inventory knowledge, skills, abilities, interests, and personal features. It was also important that this information be validated (reasonably) so that *sound* planning could take place.

Organizational Support Systems and Facilitative Efforts.   Company support of a management development program needed to be clearly signaled to the person's supervisors. In the view of this task team, the signals at best were mixed and inconsistent. Long-range business planning information seemed to be unavailable, even at a general level, making career planning and development difficult at best. The annual review, customarily the main time to reinforce MD priorities in terms of performance and reward, often failed in this mission. Another dimension of company support was its willingness to train supervisor/managers in mentoring or sponsorship roles as previously noted. This task team felt that at best these roles were incompletely understood and that supervisors lacked the needed information, even if well motivated and skilled.

This task team also criticized what it felt to be the overdependence on past performance information and lack of emphasis on competencies related to future position requirements including those at higher authority levels. Further, appraisal date was often incomplete or lacked comparability for lack of good performance standards.

The next deficiency area noted by this team was the need for a formal system. The system should be formalized on behalf of all organization members and assure proper coordination and control. In particular, it was felt that functions needed to be established to

- Formalize a human resource planning unit and forecast future staffing needs and the appropriate knowledge, skills, and abilities for these.
- Assume responsibility for human resource development, coordinator, and control—that focused on a system which was clearly defined as to paths of movement, job-descriptive material, equitable dissemination of information, and the like.
- Clearly identify and coordinate corporate and divisional activities related to MD and individual development and to make these known to the employee.

Exhibit 12-7 recaps, *from an employee viewpoint,* the primary problem areas related to Hi-Tech's management development program, identified by the committees.

EXHIBIT 12-7
Major Problem Areas Related to the Hi-tech Management
Development Program: Employee Viewpoints

The Supervisory/Managerial Role
- Understanding and training required in roles as mentor and sponsor.
- Using staff or company resources needed (e.g., the career counselor).
- Strengthening skills for management development planning.

Career Management and Individual Career Planning
- Needing clearly to distinguish meaning and implications of these two approaches to development and careers.
- Clarifying company policy or position as to "fit" of these.
- Understanding nature of existing jobs, let alone future needs.
- Needing to formalize career management and development system at headquarters and divisional level and to link these to personnel and line managers.
- Defining individual success only as upward moves—not taking into account limitations of specialist roles or definitions of career development that need not include job changing or promotion to higher level positions.
- For managers and employees, lacking knowledge of the potency and use of self-assessment instruments and approaches.
- Needing mechanisms for conflict resolution involving divisional interests or those of individual and division.

Company Culture
- Not understanding informal ground rules or valued skills often crucial to advancement.
- Establishing relative importance of ability ("doing") to "knowledge or understanding"
- People not controlling their own career decisions.

Organizational Support
- Poor base of long-range business planning information.
- Poor communication of available planning information.
- Human resource information questioned as to adequacy, type, frequency, and timing.
- Overdependence on performance appraisals for promotion.
- Inadequate job posting system: coverage, timing, and access.
- Need to define career ladder.
- Need for reward system for supervision that supports MD objectives.
- Promotions emphasize performance on current job rather than demands of future jobs.
- Need for monitoring and review of MD decisions.
- Need for complete and detailed employee orientation *prior* to position audits.
- Positionholders not given opportunity to review information collected in audit.
- Organization charts and job description incomplete or out of date.
- Company policy and priorities unclear regarding management development.
- Lack of disclosure of company plans or medium-range objectives.
- Need to open up to candidates cross-divisional mobility without prejudice.

Commentary: Hi-Tech Electronics

This case illustrated the organizational situation which eventually gave rise to strategic analyses for constructing an organizational foundation to support a management development and succession system. Symptoms of deep-seated human resource problems reflected major neglect in both the business planning and human resource areas. Major progress was not possible until top management fully recognized what needed to be done to assure better corporate continuity and growth in the future. Part of the solution turned on establishing an internal intelligence. What was needed was to get a better grasp on major problems and from the viewpoint of superiors and managers, whose help or opinions had not been solicited in the past.

The task force teams provided a vehicle for gaining involvement of many key employees and served as a demonstrable act of top management's intentions to improve things. It also provided an internal communications hub to many other persons in the organization through the grapevine. This permitted top management's objectives to become widely known outside of formal communications.

The recommendations of the task force teams made it clear that widespread problems existed and that no appreciable progress would be made until an infrastructure of information and basic systems was created. The audit instruments and task force recommendations provided concrete means of focusing strategic analyses, identifying options and priorities, and establishing an actionable base for future activities.

Acme United Case (Corporate Career Development System)

These case notes describe the strategic considerations and the critical incidents and activities that established a comprehensive career development program. Readers interested in the details of basic human resource planning and development systems forming the underpinning for their strategic approaches are referred to sources referenced elsewhere in this book. Since this case also provides an example of an organizationwide change strategy, the literature of organization development and change may also prove helpful. Selected references are provided at the end of this chapter.

The author would like to acknowledge with thanks the research study developed by Nancy A. Tiffany (University of San Francisco, September 1984) and with the guidance of her project advisor Sandra L. Gill, principal, Organization Development Associates (Santa Clara, CA), which was shared with me. This study and discussion provide a fine example of a corporation's introduction of a career development program and an excellent discussion of general change and organization development concepts widely applicable to this and many different situations. Nancy Tiffany's results provide further confirmation of the types of approaches described in the Acme United Corporation Case.

Background

Acme United Corporation was very much a product of contemporary societal change and corporate directions—it was "created" through fast growth and acquisition. The 12,000 employee firm specialized in banking and financial services and operated both domestically and internationally. As competition in their fields grew, it was increasingly confronted with the reality of reducing its growth rate and providing significantly fewer promotion opportunities. Its aggressive and highly active chair and president wanted to exploit opportunities in what otherwise might have been a period of consolidation and perhaps even reduction of operations. Thus the approach was aggressive and planning oriented, with strategic thinking slated to play an increasingly important and major role. Thoughtful strategic approaches were to point toward promising opportunities in the future. Also, the means were to be developed for utilizing its resources in constructing the organization of the future (Exhibit 12-8). Corporate continuity and preserving the dynamic spark of renewal indicated that the initial targets of its efforts should be improving managerial and executive mobility and strengthening succession planning. It also needed to reduce the turnover of high-potential people. Discussions in the executive committee established the initial focus of its human resource–related activities. These were to be the identification of high potentials, especially for succession (senior management) positions, an expansion of capable women and minority in managerial and executive ranks, dealing with individual career-related issues, and dealing with the growing problems of dual careers. The last involved both men and women who

EXHIBIT 12-8
Corporate Planning Strategies: Major Human Resource Planning Issues

---

1. Likely reduction in overall managerial staffing.
2. Imminent retirement of various key executives.
3. A bimodal age distribution with a major gap between numbers of younger and older managers.
4. Changing employee skill mixes with the potential for much methods or technical obsolescence.
5. Growing business competition and slowing of general business growth—likely to affect general promotional opportunities.
6. Physical decentralization affecting the development of facilities and personnel on a regional, national, and worldwide basis.
7. Divestment of some corporate holdings likely to reduce somewhat, promotional and cross-functional career growth opportunities.
8. A growing number of dual-career problems involving male and female members of the corporation. In some cases, both were employed in the firm.
9. Continuing corporate commitment to improve the quality of work life of all its employees and to maintain a stable employment policy and program.

---

were pursuing professional careers. Key initial steps in establishing "where things were" and taking the first major step in organizing a strategic planning approach were to (1) authorize the conduct of an executive survey by the corporate vice president of Personnel and Human Resources ("Key personnel issues and personal concerns") and subsequently (2) authorize the hiring of a director of management development. The chronology of key events in mounting a strategic planning initiative involving management and career development is shown in Exhibit 12-9. The first steps shown in Exhibit 12-9 were the specific moves that got things started.

In the light of strategic considerations, their situations emphasize several features seen as widely applicable to a number of different organization circumstances. These features were

1. The major human resource planning issues and developments which brought about the needs for strategic approaches (Exhibit 12-8).
2. Executive communications which helped to establish the focus and direction of strategic thinking for career development planning and programming (Exhibit 12-9).
3. A chronology of critical incidents which highlight the considerable time required to launch a program of this nature (Exhibit 12-9).
4. Viewing the strategic planning and programming effort as a challenge in planning and managing change and thereby applying many organization development techniques to various phases.
5. Creating a career development network (CDN) which in connection with the management and career development system elements provided a durable foundation for a long-term sustaining change effort (see Exhibit 12-12).

The Chronology of Critical Events

This log of events and activities serves to bring out several different features of strategic thinking and approaches at Acme United. Perhaps the most apparent point is that the chronology spanned a time period from the summer 1980 to spring 1985, almost five years. Over a year was required after the executive survey before the first concrete steps were taken, namely a study of managerial positions/descriptions in fall 1981. However, this activity was directed more toward building information for underpinning the system rather than the career development system as such. Another point to be noted in Exhibit 12-9 was the authorization for hiring a new director of management development. This capability was *not* resident in the organization nor did it appear that people were available who could be groomed for this key role. Thus, several events had to take place before action could be initiated. First, the particulars of the career development system and formulating alternate strategic approaches related to this undertaking had to be established. Second, the needed know-how called for the hiring of a specialist in this area. Further, it would be necessary to position this job at corporate headquarters to make the person

EXHIBIT 12-9

Timing of Critical Events: Background and Programming of Career
Development Directions and Strategies

Timing	Events

Part I. Background

Summer 1980   Executive survey: "key personnel issues and personal concerns (I)." Provided baseline information for subsequent comparisons.

Spring 1981   Executive meeting: authorization to hire a director of management development.

Summer 1981   Formalize long-range business planning.

Fall 1981   Study of managerial positions—updating of position descriptions.

Spring 1982   Start assessment center for identifying high-potential personnel, feedback of developmental assessments to participants.

Summer 1982
1. General managerial survey: "key personnel issues and personal concerns (II)." Provided baseline information for subsequent comparisons.
2. General employee survey: "Job satisfaction and personal issues." Provided baseline information for subsequent comparisons (III).

Part II. Career Development Directions and Strategies

Fall 1982
1. External consultant identified to work with Human Resources in establishing a career development strategy and framework for programming.
2. Proposal to top management for establishment of a career development task force team. *Focus:* career needs analysis, corporate need for change, divisional career related needs.

Winter 1982–1983
1. Executive communications (letter) to all senior and key officials regarding corporate interest in career development.
2. Executive interviews by task force.
3. Start strategic business planning informally in connection with business planning.

Spring 1983
1. Feedback of executive survey results to participants and corporate president.
2. Recommendations and approval of executive training program: "managing managerial careers and performance."
3. Task force review: human resource system activities in place (Review I)." Highlights of their review indicated
   - Generally understood policy on top management support for managerial development.
   - Long-range business planning and increasing formalization of strategic planning.
   - Updated managerial position descriptions.

(Continues)

EXHIBIT 12-9 (Continued)

	• Managerial assessment center for identifying high potentials.
	• Performance appraisal system (conventional) established.
	• Computerized personnel system (basics, conventional reporting) functioning.
Fall 1983	Career development program design. Task force team review, critique.
Fall 1983	Executive presentation of corporate career development program including a proposal for a pilot career development activity and a career development network.
Winter 1983–1984	1. Launch pilot career development program (two major divisions).
	2. Launch line management career orientation program.
Spring 1983	Establish career information centers in pilot divisions.
Summer 1984	1. Career development network conference, including pilot program review.
	2. Formal postnetwork conference meeting of CD task force team—recommendations for managerial training and expansion of staff counseling.
	3. Establish executive development committee.
	4. Transfer and train former corporate employment manager as career development manager.
Winter 1984–1985	1. Task force review: total human resources *system* activities in place (Review II). Their audit identified
	• Business and strategic planning.
	• Computerization of job analysis and job descriptions.
	• Computerized job posting—selected positions.
	• Managerial personnel file inputting and review.
	• Developmental component, performance appraisal system.
	• Assessment center for managerial appraisal and development.
	• Executive assessment and counseling program.
	• Human resource forecasting.
	• Succession planning.
	• Formalization of "affirmative-action" program.
	• Establishment of cross-functional transfer policy for management development.
	• Executive development committee functioning.
	• Corporate policy statement circulated on corporate management of human resources and individual career development.
	• Career information center established.
	2. Authorization to expand career development pilot program to additional divisions; initiation of line management careers orientation program in additional divisions.

(Continues)

EXHIBIT 12-9 (Continued)

	3. General surveys of executives, managers, employees (forms similar to those used in 1980, 1982) to judge progress against baselines established earlier.
Spring 1985	1. Expand scope of career development program to include supervisory levels with attendant support (i.e., posting, career information, staff counseling, and managerial careers orientation program), and balance of corporate units.
	2. *Annual meeting,* Career Development Network Conference (institutionalized).
	3. Proposal to link business and strategic planning system more formally to human resource planning system.

physically proximate to key decision makers. The Personnel/Human Resource Staff who were to work with the new director were to remain as a highly specialized corporate planning staff. Their activities were to include planning, design, and monitoring progress of managerial and career development activities (systemswise and individually) and strategic planning. Most operational activities were to be carried out within divisions. An example of the headquarters' functioning of the management development unit was the reassignment and training of the employment manager as the career development manager in summer 1984. This person assumed responsibility for overseeing assessment center activities, coordinating the "career orientation program" and career information centers, and working with "career development network" members.

The career development system proposal was not made until fall 1983. This was *several years after the initiation of activities* and about one year after a consultant was brought into the picture to discuss additional organization strategies and systems design. However, the fact that the various elements of the strategic approach and management organizational change were taking hold is attested to by the summary of accomplishments in winter 1984–1985.

Strategic Management of Change

The crux of a successful strategic program was interpreted as the implementation of widespread and massive changes in organization planning procedures, decision patterns, and the human resource assumptions underlying these. A broad scope organization development design was elected at a very early point by the vice president of Personnel/Human Resources and the director of management development. Necessary internal changes were likely to involve the modification or change of longstanding values and modes of personnel development, succession, communications, and decision making. Beliefs were widely held that high-potential people moved ahead on their own power and that development was largely a matter of pursuing individual interests and taking aggressive action. Career development thinking, which brought along with it mutual responsibilities, career lad-

EXHIBIT 12-10
Bases for Success in Introducing Career Development Programs: The
Change Strategy

- Clear goals or objectives.
- Sound information gathering for planning—often involving key people to gain early commitment to the change program.
- Counseling and direction by an internal expert or external consultant for enhanced acceptance.
- Top management commitment.
- Involvement of key and powerful people.
- Identification and evaluation of alternatives, risks and options, and sound rationalization for chosen direction.
- Readily communicated plans.
- Harmonious with "organization culture."
- Active involvement of line managers.
- Agreed on criteria for measuring change effectiveness.
- Establishment of realistic time frames.
- Implementation by skilled and committed personnel. Early establishment of a success pattern.
- Gradual implementation with provision for information feedback and program adjustment once underway and after installation.

ders, and systematic bases for performance management and cultivating potential, was likely to run afoul of traditionalists in the corporation. Thus the strategy for change was to gather critically needed information for planning from officers and managers. It would also be necessary to involve key powerholders and err on the side of slow but positive steps in change. Other important steps included soldifying corporatewide communications, gaining involvement and commitment of key people, and securing the backup of top management leadership. Finally, for overall support of these newer directions, a newer reward system had to be created. Key elements of their approach are summarized in Exhibit 12-10 and form part of the discussion that follows.

Change Strategy

The key elements seen as comprising an agenda for organization change were as follows:

1. *Collection of information and data* that were reasonably representative of managerial experiences, attitudes, and important areas or points of deficiency that needed to be addressed. This information and data had in common the

idea that it related to some aspects of career development. These needs were met (Exhibit 12-9) by the executive survey (summer 1980) and the survey of managers and employees (summer 1982) which established data base lines to use in making subsequent comparisons for progress. The general surveys taken in winter 1984–1985 were used to judge progress against the baseline data established earlier.

2. *Enlisting the assistance,* and ultimately gaining commitment, of the *key powerholders* for guidance on approaches and the handling of difficult problems which would arise. Thus the establishment of the career development task force (fall 1982).

3. *Top management's strong commitment to the program* which was then made visible through meetings and the president's letter to senior and key executives (See Exhibit 12-11).

EXHIBIT 12-11
Acme United Corporation

From: The Office of the
         President and Chair

The future welfare of Acme United, literally its survival, future growth, and renewal, is dependent on its managerial leadership, expertise, and adequacy in staffing. Our view of future organizational directions visualizes a period of intense competition and environmental changes. Career development is seen as a major corporate strategy for strengthening our future situation since it represents a major cornerstone of employee relations and cultivation of managerial leadership. Career development is also seen as crucial in meeting our corporate goal of more fully utilizing our human resources, including an expanded managerial role for women and minority personnel. This is fully in keeping with our company's sense of fair and equitable treatment, rewards for superior performance, improved quality of work life, and encouraging self-growth and achievement.

An integral part of every manager's role is the development of people. In the future, increasingly our success as a corporation will depend on how effectively managers perform in the role of developing their subordinates. A career development program will further these purposes and thus better serve our succession planning programs. At a more general level, career development will prepare people for more ready adaptation to change and strengthen self-management of careers. Your creative support and thoughtful suggestions would be much appreciated in connection with the executive survey "key personnel issues and personal concerns." We believe that the findings from this study will enable us to organize a career development effort that will fully meet the corporation's needs for sound future growth.

Thanks for your cooperation and support,

President and Chair

4. *Securing the services of (a) person(s) with obvious professional qualifications* who would take the lead in organizing a workable program and practical strategies for implementation. Thus the hiring of the director of management development, reassessment and training of the manager of career development, and securing the services of the outside consultant (fall 1982).

5. *Clear and accurate internal communications,* including description of the plans, strategies, and programs to assure that officials and managers would understand the essence of the systems and the programs underway and those being considered.

6. *Anticipating the threat to senior managers of value changes.* Major departures from existing values or assumptions regarding "proper" managerial approaches would be seen as threatening and would be likely to create uncertain or destabilizing conditions. Thus many formal and informal communication channels were established to keep people informed and to gain involvement and commitment of key people.

7. *Making visible highly regarded senior people serving as models for change.* Thus, the president and chair, key officials, the pilot study in a major and well-regarded division, and the makeup of the project group provided critical and needed visibility for change efforts.

8. *Gradualism and establishing an early and winning track record* to help assure recognition and growing acceptance when the program was expanded. The establishment of the pilot program played a major role in this approach.

9. *Establishing a (more) permanent underpinning of offices, systems, procedures, and confidence to "institutionalize" long-term changes* described here, the establishment of an executive development committee and the career development network, and the newly created position of director of management development.

The Career Development Network and System

An integral part of the career development system strategy was the need to introduce means by which long-term change would be facilitated *and* sustained. Some two and one-half years were required (Exhibit 12-9) to arrive at a point in systems development where activities would be seen as "regular" or recurring (winter 1983–1984 to spring 1985). Sustaining these changes, however, as part of a broader management development strategy, required the building in of activities, processes, groups, and structures that would provide nurturing energies and guidance for the long term—much beyond the initial installation period. A career development network became a central mechanism in this strategic approach. In brief, the CDN represented an internal, corporatewide system with specified members, responsibilities, and activities. The CDN had several main purposes. One objective was to build in a corporatewide communications network assuring information dissemination and feedback regarding career resources, services, and system-related needs. A second important activity was to facilitate the training of Personnel staff

EXHIBIT 12-12

Responsibilities and Major Roles of the Career Development System

Career Development Task Force (temporary)→	Career Development Network Coordinators	Executive Development ←Committee (permanent)
	• Clearinghouse for information dissemination in respective unit or division • Managerial counsel on the effective use of career development resources • Regular participation in network meetings and proposal of means of improving system performance	
Personnel Human Resource (Divisional)	Personnel/Human Resource Corporate Staff	Line Management
• Divisional training of line managers or other active system members • Coordination of career activities in the divisions • Consultation • Serve as CDN member along with appointee	• Corporatewide resource for strategic Human Resource systems training and strategic management development approaches • Recommendations to corporate Executive Development Committee • Corporate systems feasibility analyses • Development systems planning and design • Monitoring systems development and progress of candidates • Coordinate human resource planning and career development with strategic business planning.	• Provide career information and counseling as needed or desired by their subordinates. • Carrying out developmental performance appraisals assuring good performance management and individual development. • Providing employee feedback to help assure realistic expectations and as a basis for individual performance and career planning. • Taking the lead in assuring the successful conduct of career management activities related to management development and succession. • Make assessments for high potentials.

The Individual Employee

• Takes active charge of his or her own career, but with the support of corporate personnel and Human Resources.

• Seeks out whatever information and services needed in support of his or her (own) career development.

• Demonstrates a willingness to listen to career counsel but recognizes that he or she must make career-related decisions independently.

and line management people who would assume responsibility for introducing career development concepts and approaches in their respective divisional organizations. A third objective was to assist corporate Human Resources staff in the improvement or development of career-related tools, services, and programs.

Establishing CDN Members

Members of the CDN were appointed in each division through consultation between the division general manager and the division personnel manager. The appointee and the personnel manager were to serve as CDN members. In most cases the appointee was from the Personnel area, but in two instances a line supervisor and a field sales supervisor were appointed. In general, people were appointed who had the appropriate background and who were interested in career matters. In all cases the activities of the CDN members had to be coordinated with the responsibilities of other career system roles. Exhibit 12-12 briefly summarizes these responsibilities; these positions collectively were the basis for carrying on the work of the CDN and many career-related activities as part of an ongoing system. The membership roles summarized in Exhibit 12-12 illustrate the scope of the "network" and the necessary support provided by key system members. The "network" included all divisions and also tied into corporate headquarters. It included staff *and* line management members. Network coordinators served as divisional communications hubs and also played an increasingly important role in detecting problems, and passing along problem solutions and suggestions for systems improvement. The corporate Personnel/Human Resource staff, though small, was able to "multiply" greatly its efforts through cooperating members of the network. Corporate staff did the forward strategic planning for management development, succession planning, and helping to bring together systems designs. Line management roles included that of counselor and information provider plus serving as part of the appraisal and assessment processes. Juxtaposed to the role of the "network" coordinator in Exhibit 12-12 is that of the individual—the focus of the entire effort. Emphasized here is the basic proposition of career development, namely, the fact that the individual takes charge of his or her career. Also acknowledged, however, was the critical and needed support of the organization.

13

An Emerging Agenda for Strategic Management Development

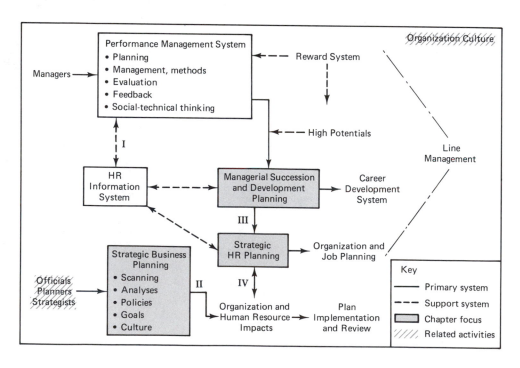

This concluding chapter presents several issues and concerns likely to be on the table in various strategic discussions in coming years. The challenging issues described here include

- *Growing organization size and complexity and the increasing difficulty of retaining* and harnessing the energies of *high potentials* and *good performers*.
- *Organizational and managerial adaptation to growth or rapidly changing environments*. These involve strategic planning and development postures for the confrontation of complex and major changes from economic, competitive, environmental, and technological sources.
- *Countercyclical versus procyclical hiring strategies* as these affect the availability and development of key and critical personnel.
- *Mergers and acquisitions* and some of the unique strategic issues and problems accompanying these.

Entrepreneurial ("Intrapreneurial") Units: A Corporate Response to Organization Complexity and Development of High Potentials

Many businesses in the United States are actively engaged in attempting to (re)infuse entrepreneurial-type enthusiasm, dedication, and creativity into various segments of their complex enterprises. The sheer size, complexity, and diversity of many corporate units limits the scope of conventional improvement strategies such as monetary incentives, job redesign, or even expanding computer applications. The potential frustration of these constrained situations for strategists instills an urgency to explore new directions. George Gendron of *Inc.* magazine claims that there is afoot, "a rediscovering of business as enterprise . . . limited only by the boundaries of each individual's intelligence, imagination, energy and daring." One of the newer approaches is entrepreneuring ("intrapreneuring") *within* established businesses. Another is a return to truly decentralized decision units which are largely autonomous. These approaches represent a confrontation of specific factors contributing to organization complexity, which include growing size; interchange of products, services, or staff among units; multiple and simultaneous events which make tracking these difficult; and strategic commitments to new products or service ventures constrained by established marketing or organizational process patterns.

In "intrapreneuring," the traditional model of the entrepreneur has been bent to the purposes and needs of modern corporations. Enterprises capitalizing on this approach include Control Data, Fuqua Industries, 3M, Baxter-Travenol, Hewlett-Packard, Emerson Electric, and Johnson & Johnson. The situational context is often one of high risk/high reward. These organizations have tapped varying combinations and degrees of individual need for achievement and autonomy, as well as single-mindedness, and the aggressive spirit. Harry Levinson of the Levinson Institute puts it well when he notes (Lee and Zemcke, 1985) the "unique constellation of psychological factors" often making up the entrepreneur. Many organizations would be unaccepting of these qualities if enacted in their own pure or extreme form. Taken together, these features could be disruptive economically or behaviorally if unleashed on conventional business forms and processes. Yet it must be acknowledged that the organizational milieu frequently stifles some of the very qualities needed for business survival, continuity, and renewal. At risk are the loss or dilution of such key activities as innovation and active experimentation. On the other hand, this innovation is not without problems, one of which may be incompatibility with existing cultures. Other concerns are brought out in subsequent discussions.

Entrepreneuring within established businesses takes several different forms. These approaches have substantial implications for strategic management development. The first point is the recognition that establishing a new structural form or reorganizing an existing structural arrangement, is often a strategic planning matter. A good example of this approach includes the creation by Control Data of Control Data Business Advisors as a self-standing business comprised of many key people from the parent corporation. It provided services such as managerial training, consulting, and computer systems packages to Control Data and other businesses. Also, the parent corporation, Control Data, created business centers in building complexes as a form of franchised activity, many owned or run by (former) Control Data people.

Entrepreneuring is often the spirit with which various companies approach complexity and leadership development, formal programs aside. Digital Equipment Corporation and Hewlett-Packard are both illustrations of this approach. The events of Hewlett-Packard (H-P) are used to illustrate this point.*

> H-P used product divisions as its major building block for developing leadership, sustaining creative product growth, and effectively dealing with complexity. By 1981, H-P had same 40 divisions organized within 10 product groups. The division concept created at H-P was that of a self-sustaining organization containing six basic functions involving marketing, manufacturing quality assurance, research and development, finance, and personnel. Division creation was part of a life-cycle process. Birth took place when it was clear that the unit could be self-sustaining from the profits it contributed. Also, divisional ground rules required that all six basic organization functions be a part of the "new baby."

---

*Viewpoints expressed are those of the writer and don't necessarily reflect the official position of the referenced company. See the excellent case developed by Richard O. Von Wessowetz, and Michael Beer (1982) for added details.

No formula-determined point existed for division creation. Commonsense guidelines such as sustainable profit and the decline of employee identification with a product were signals to which senior officials were tuned.

The divisional unit assisted in leadership development at H-P. It provided a relatively small and tightly defined area within which was exercised much freedom of action. The working environment encouraged creativity, planning, and problem solving close to the point where the needs, possibilities, and problems existed. The creation of "little companies" kept the decision making highly decentralized. It permitted the existing and future leaders to nurture each other and to gain direct familiarity with the people who made things happen. It also provided the hands-on feeling needed for practical problem solving and was very much in the spirit of preserving H-P's culture and traditions. The division permitted leadership role modeling, excellent communications, and reinforcement of desired behavioral patterns.

The foregoing examples suggest the range of variations of entrepreneuring within established businesses. One "boundary" was defined by the establishment of largely autonomous, self-standing units. In this approach, the redeployment of managerial and staff resources and other organizational capabilities was involved. A variation of this form has been acquired or merged in firms which have been allowed to remain largely intact.

An Alternate Strategic Model

A strongly decentralized organizational mode of planning, decision making, and control is an alternate strategic approach. This approach has often involved a conscious and sustained top management effort over an extended time period to realign assigned managerial responsibilities and performances needed for success. This was the approach taken at Fuqua Industries. Here decentralized decision making was strongly encouraged. Its president strongly endorsed decentralized operational controls and informal, open communications.

Since organizational situations differ so greatly, it is not surprising that many variations exist of the two forms described. Correspondingly, the degree of autonomy and requisite initiative or entrepreneurial acumen in each of the "boundary" situations differ.

Limits to Strategic Choice.   Strategic options and limits to choice in entrepreneuring are frequently dictated by business circumstances. Considerations include economies of scale in purchasing or mass advertising, as, for example, in food store chains or women's wear outlets. Economies in advertising in these situations often dictate centralization of this function. Another reality weighted heavily into the election of a strategic option is the "currently" existing situation. For example, the characteristics of the corporate culture or climate and the degrees of freedom or restraints on entrepreneurial thinking, inquiry, and pursuit of ideas affect strategic options. 3-M is another instance where strong encouragement of entrepreneurial thinking existed. The pursuit of ideas was supported, and individuals who were models of internal success were well known to company members.

Quite a different type of constraint on strategic options is presented by product lines which have grown increasingly interdependent on purchasing patterns or marketing approaches. Changes in customer needs posed difficult adaptive problems for the strong independent leadership spawned under Hewlett-Packard's "division" concept. Integrated systems applications contributed to growing problems of internal integration. Application systems and related hardware and electronic gear purchased independently by customers in the past, become more of a systems decision because of their relatedness in application. Delivery timing and components and systems design had to be increasingly coordinated and some divisional prerogatives subordinated to general organizational welfare. Understandably, these posed significant adjustment problems for divisional managers geared to independent thinking and action! Precisely this same type of problem has occurred in other organizations at varying points as they matured and the needs of their customer groups shifted.

The number of organizational members with the desire *and* capability to assure internal entrepreneurial roles is not likely to be great. But the potential benefit to the organizations goes much beyond the numbers involved. It is probably true that a great number of organization members desire a reasonably stable and perhaps structured environment. At the same time some of those who have experienced strong needs for growth and creativity have found ways to manipulate their environments. They have felt the need to do this to achieve increased personal satisfaction relative to use of their abilities. Others, however, may remain frustrated by restrictive circumstances. Additional people, possessing much self-confidence, eventually leave to try things on their own. Internal entrepreneuring taps to varying degrees. all three of these groups. This approach, thereby, may harness more of the existing managerial or creative energy potential as well as reduce the loss of highly talented people. Another corporate situation well illustrates this point.

> An old-line company had achieved a highly diverse and profitable line of products supplied to organizations in health care and allied fields. In recent years, though most products continued to enjoy growth and good profits, market sales penetration had stabilized. Highly talented managers including some senior personnel were increasingly dissatisfied with the lack of fast-paced change, growth, and personal challenge. Many had reasonably high incomes so that salary wasn't the primary issue, though obviously it was an important consideration. Too, corporate strategists were not pleased with the situation as it started to become clear that the emerging trends were going to affect long-term profitability and return on investment.
>
> One of the senior officers crystallized the situation by pointing out that both the corporation *and* various key people might benefit from a more creative approach to creating and managing new business. A series of discussions among top officials led to the rather surprising discovery that at various points in time, most had been approached with new(er) venture proposals by highly rated people in their units. In fact, many of these very same people were now the ones complaining about blunted growth

opportunities. Out of this ferment emerged the concept of internal entrepreneuring and the creation of a money pool for new business development (ventures).

Undertakings proposed in the recent past were to be sifted through and reviewed, and the go-ahead given for a detailed feasibility study. If the project looked promising relative to a number of corporate financial, business, and organizational criteria, then a pilot or limited-scope project was to be undertaken. If the project still appeared attractive, commercialization was to be considered.

The entrepreneurial heads of these new business ventures were in complete charge of the feasibility studies and the demonstration or pilot projects, should these be undertaken. Special monetary incentives were also attached to these new ventures with the payoffs tailored to individual situations.

Corporate management saw these projects as a positive step in the preservation of its financial situation, importantly assisted by these entrepreneurial undertakings. That is, projects were *not* undertaken just to keep talented people busy. Rather, it had a potentially important role to play in the corporation's strategic planning and financial picture and each activity (and its head!) would be carefully monitored and evaluated. Successful managers were likely to be candidates for major succession positions in the future.

In truth, it must be said that some highly talented people will leave because they want to try things out on their own. Another reality is that some of those with strong entrepreneurial feelings may not prove out when faced with the entrepreneurial circumstances. Regardless, for those situations where internal entrepreneuring may be considered, and there are many, a newer strategic option may exist in management development planning.

Management Development Approaches Under Entrepreneuring

Entrepreneuring brings with it much change in needed managerial knowledge, skills, and abilities for success relative to those in traditional structures. Even where it is thought that people desire and have the potential for these assignments, nurturing the related skills will often be indicated. Strategic planners will need to establish the possibilities and limitations of existing structural and managerial arrangements and organizational processes.

The following represent basic areas of strategies for internal entrepreneuring analyses and provide a foundation for management development planning.

1. *Skills and know-how for the running of a business.* Most candidates or appointees will be unfamiliar with the financial, accounting, and operational thinking and procedures needed for the survival of small business units. These are far different from the characteristic corporate environments where these responsibilities are widely distributed and discharged by specialists in many different areas.

2. *Group leadership and organizational skills.* Entrepreneurial teams or units are likely to be staffed with a generous assortment of people with diverse skills, personalities, and talents. The highly demanding business circumstances, and at times ambiguous nature of the entrepreneurial venture will likely dictate a substantial degree of know-how and competency of its members and head.

The group or unit leader also needs to be able to bridge effectively and deal with widely different situations. Part of the leader's role involves the necessary coordination and communications between the volatile entrepreneurial units and the more deliberate pace of the parent or corporate unit. The head's role also necessitates substantial group skills to be able to channel creative processes, carry out development, and yet come up with tangible economic results. Internal entrepreneurial managers must recognize that their units or team represent proving grounds and opportunities for career development and the realization of career possibilities for their members. Thus the head needs to nurture, coach, guide, or mentor group members.

Exhibit 13-1 highlights the key points related to entrepreneuring. Planners and strategists are well advised to examine closely existing organization structures, processes, and needs for entrepreneurial possibilities. To the extent that these possibilities exist, a strong commitment to this approach by powerful people, plus adequate resource support, are requirements that have to be addressed. An important group of points also noted in Exhibit 13-1 relates to monitoring carefully the internal environment and staying in close touch with managers of candidates at various levels.

The final group of points noted in Exhibit 13-1 relate to developing the person, the "management development aspects." Two points that should be noted are (3) and (5), namely, that failure, too can be instructive and developmentally desirable if severe damage to the organization and individual are avoided. Also indicated is the need to adjust the reward structure to the high-risk, often tense, climate of the entrepreneurial unit—high risk and high reward.

Rapid Growth and Organizational Adaptation

Rapid-growth companies place heavy demands on corporate resources. Examples of rapid growth companies in the past have included Wendy's, Pizza Hut, and McDonald's in the fast-food business, Marriott in the hotel and resort area, K-Mart department stores, and Hewlett-Packard and Apple in computers. Internal reorganization and attempts to adopt operational procedures and administrative controls to the expanded and more complex operations are potentially rewarding but taxing situations. Planning for management structure, succession, and development are among the keys to realizing successfully, business strategic and planning objectives although adaptation to rapid growth and change are challenging. Illustrative of strategic development issues in a period of rapid growth is that of Wendy's.

EXHIBIT 13-1
Guidelines for Strategically Approaching Internal Entrepreneuring

General Planning Approaches

1. Determine that a match exists and it is an appropriate one for the intended products and services. Also, establish that the organization's flexibility and adaptation in cultural, structural, and financial approaches will be adequate.

2. Undertake projects in scope or complexity that are manageable and have a good likelihood of success to help establish a successful pattern for future expansion.

3. Examine organization structures so that these facilitate fast adaptation, good communications, and a high level of interaction and involvement.

4. Approach this area with a results orientation, assuming realistic opportunities to achieve measurable results with commensurate rewards for achievement. Clarify thoroughly such matters as available resources and the details of results measurement.

5. Maintain sensitivity to people who aggressively express an interest in entrepreneurial types of activities.

6. Regularly monitor the organization for high-potential people who display strong needs and motivation in such areas as personal growth, achievement, change, and independence and/or who display creativity, good adaptive qualities, and the ability to organize and lead.

7. Provide thorough orientation to those key executives and powerful people whose co-operative assistance will be vital to the program's success.

8. Commit financial resources and support that are realistic for success but that require in themselves "stretching" and creative use to stay within budgets or established guidelines. That is, don't make it too easy but avoid austere approaches such that failure is likely to be self-fulfilling.

Management Development Aspects

1. Help the prospective head or high-potential person to develop further and refine the knowledge, skills, and abilities likely to be critical to a successful internal entrepreneurial effect. Recognize that the essential core of individual traits, skills, and abilities should already be in place.

2. Consider the (further) building of entrepreneurial strengths through activities or project assignments displaying many of the characteristics of a full-scale project.

3. Recognize that success and failure can both be instructive for the person and thus factored into top management's criteria for judging individual progress and (future) capabilities.

4. Use feedback which is clear and unambiguous and involves mutually agreed-on goals in terms of form, timing, and bottom-line results.

5. Arrange reward levels so that they materially affect overall compensation and are clearly linked to success of the activity, *both* short and long(er) term.

6. Strengthen interpersonal skills permitting a high level of effectiveness both within the entrepreneurial activity and between it and the organization. Consequently, entrepreneurial heads will need to be good coaches for their own units or teams and be capable integrators between their units and "parent" organizations and support groups.

Source: Draws in part on ideas developed by Chris Lee and Ron Zemke in "Intrapreneuring: New-Age Freedoms for Big Business?" *Training,* Vol. 22, no. 2 (February 1985): 26–42; Keith Atkinson, "Intrapreneurs: Fostering Innovation Inside the Corporation," *Personnel Administrator* (January 1986): 43–46; and Terrance Deal and Arthur Kennedy, *Corporate Cultures* (Reading, MA: Addison-Wesley, 1982).

Wendy's International, Inc: A Case of Rapid Growth and Strategic Challenge in Change*

The enormous changes that took place at Wendy's and the strategic challenges these provided to business, officials, and planners are reflected in many of Wendy's annual reports. For example, some highlights from the annual reports indicated that:

- The company was founded in 1969, yet by 1984 had already opened (approximately) 3,000 stores, of which 2,000 were franchised and 1,000 company owned. Additionally, it had strategically targeted another 1,000 store additions for 1990, of which perhaps 50 percent would be company owned.
- Volume and profits were substantially ahead of a five-year strategic plan established in 1982, in some cases by as much as two years.
- Strategic planning also indicated a significant expansion of its international operations. This included the conversion of numerous Canadian units to company-owned stores and the establishment of new units in England, Spain, West Germany, and elsewhere.
- Store profit and market segment objectives were achieved through a multi-pronged strategic program including extended store hours and new products such as breakfasts, salad bars, and an expanded menu. In the wake of the expansion of store products, menus, and services, item inventories, a pragmatic measure of growing complexity, increased *three* times.

Maintaining its established pattern of leadership in quality, variety, dining atmosphere, and nutrition (as described in *Consumer's Reports*), required new procedures, controls, and operating efficiency. It also indicated a need for stronger management with increased depth.

From the beginning, Wendy's corporate philosophy, bearing the strong stamp of its founder Dave Thomas, reinforced its concentration on its number one asset, people. Its culture and orientation also included the allied ideas of individual development, good morale, high productivity, and a good retention record. People were seen as the critical asset, and management expertise, organization, and processes were viewed as being critical to the company's successful achievement of strategic objectives. Wendy's tackled head on the adaptation of its managerial group to these new business challenges and "new dimensions of employee opportunities." The fact that profitability rose steadily in subsequent years bears witness to the soundness of its general managerial program. What were the major themes expressed in this program?

---

*Notes regarding Wendy's International, Inc., are presented for illustrative purposes and not to depict right or wrong ways of handling human resource situations. Opinions and interpretations are those of the author and do not necessarily reflect the opinion of Wendy's or its officials.

Change and Adaptation of Development Planning and Programming Strategies. The managerial prototype so successful in past years had to be altered greatly to cope with the fast-changing business situation. Managerial responsibilities had to be changed to incorporate job-related behaviors to help assure maintaince of high store standards in quality and service. The strategic objective of expanding the number of company-owned stores relative to franchises meant a major increase in managerial staff both in numbers and depth. In turn, a much stronger recruiting and development program had to be mounted. But the *qualitative changes* in the managerial work force were also great. Better qualified managers had to be identified and developed. Newer motivational strategies were evoked to help support managers operating under more difficult work conditions and in a more complex organization. Top management thinking incorporated management development strategies. They were fully committed to support a new corporatewide development initiative.

Wendy's strategies for management development planning and execution went beyond its company-owned store group. A group of some 2,000 domestic franchisees provided a dynamic element in the organization contributing both business "vitality and flexibility." New franchisees were supported by an intensive 14-week development program targeted to strengthen store management capability. Their professional staff who were a part of this program possessed much operating and business experience. Franchisees infused an entrepreneurial spirit and perspective into corporate thinking and programs. This helped to provide added synergy to corporate and operations management groups.

Strategic Management Development Perspective in Rapid Growth

The virtual explosion of managerial structure and processes exemplified by the Wendy's situation established the parameters for strategic approaches to management development. Rapid expansion both multiplied and compounded change effects throughout the organization. First, rapid staffing expansions created a structural "domino" effect. Managerial staffing "voids" were created and major internal and external recruiting effort had to be mounted. For example, consider a five-level managerial protypical structure.

The lateral transfer or promotion of a manager at the top level to serve as cadre for expansion or to head an entrepreneurial enterprise "ripples" through the existing management structure. This ripple effect creates five moves up the line including the recruiting of a person for an entry-level supervisory positic (see Burack and Mathys, 1987, esp. Chaps. 5 and 6). The challenges to carrying out basic indoctrination and development programs are enormous.

Second, most conventional management structures and organizational processes find quick adaptation under these circumstances difficult. They are locked into bureaucratic rituals and conventional communications and working relationships are anchored in paperwork. Occasional coordination meetings are attempted to meet situational needs. Strategic thinking needs to confront these traditional approaches. Useful prescriptions to facilitate adaptation include much heavier reliance on organic relationships, improved communications media, establishment of coordinator roles, launching pilot programs which serve as models for change, and establishing sounding boards of key and knowledgeable people to facilitate liaison and stay in touch with change developments. The "sociotechnical" committee referenced in a previous chapter is an example of a group formed for these types of special needs.

Third, another aspect of strategic approaches has to do with increasing managerial depth rapidly. In the Wendy's case, this coincided with the extension of store hours. The addition of the night or assistant manager role served the dual purpose of staffing units and providing another source from which trained managerial people could be drawn. Of course, the expansion of the night or assistant manager category could well prove disruptive in the short run, but once this new structure was stabilized, more internal resources could be drawn upon.

Fourth, adaptation to rapid change and growing operational/service complexity, as in the Wendy's case, often means a major change in the qualitative character and role of the managers. Credentials for managerial qualification were upgraded, which reflected a more complex and difficult resident manager job. It involved the expanded need for people demonstrating flexibility or adaptive qualities much beyond those which sufficed previously. Consequently, new and more complex patterns of managerial behavior must be identified that become the "directing" factors in managerial needs analyses and preparation.

Fifth, the need for different types of managerial competencies and behaviors dramatically alters strategic assumptions as to the means of achieving these. On-the-job approaches, often relied on previously, prove inadequate. Much greater attention is needed to formalizing coaching and more formal classroom-type instruction. Note how the changes at Wendy's affecting the operating or service delivery level placed new demands on supervisors and even more highly ranked managers. The new importance of coaching and the ability to conduct needs analyses with subordinates were part of these role changes.

The interactive chain of events suggested by the preceding is portrayed in part in Exhibit 13-2. It could be continued for several additional iterations. Suffice it to say that strategic management development thinking must encompass these compound and interrelated effects and lay the groundwork so that the organization can better cope with these.

Problems of Mergers or Acquisitions: A Side Note

Mergers and acquisitions are often the basis for rapid growth. At times, corporate mergers result in the absorption of units, including entrepreneurial talent which fits poorly into conventional structures. Another common situation is one where highly limited opportunity exists for this talent. In small, merged-in companies, entrepre-

EXHIBIT 13-2
An Example of Interactive Organization Effects in Rapid Change

1. Rapid business expansion. . . . leads to
2. Increases of needed services and scope of operational activities. . . . leads to
3. Increases of staffing requests. . . . results in
4. "Ripples" through the management structure. . . . creates
5. Short-term disruptive effects. . . . creates
6. Need for greater management depth. . . . leads to
7. Changes in the qualitative character of managerial roles. . . . results in
8. Shifts of the emphasis of managerial needs analysis. . . . requires
9. Expansion of the repertoire of needed management development strategies.

neurial talent often involves senior officials or the president. Unfortunately, many poor "marriages" result from these types of mergers insofar as the key creative people are concerned. Lack of identification with the acquiring organization and poor internal communications are common problems which arise frequently. An early confrontation of these types of issues and planning for their resolution *prior* to merger could provide a more rewarding result. In some situations, there should be greater reluctance to pursue these types of mergers if the difficulty of fit with key people were taken into account more fully. Unfortunately, financial and timing considerations usually dominate the scene to the exclusion of much else.

The strategic, human resource outputs of mergers or acquisitions are difficult to generalize because individual circumstances differ dramatically. The following situation is a good example of this:

> A large firm in the food industry represented an attractive target for numerous merger discussions with different companies. Analyses by the successful acquiring firm indicated substantial economies of operation and administration, product consolidation, and benefits from integration. Staffing analyses indicated that the entire top management and one-fourth of second-level management could be bought out with "golden parachute" packages. Also work force analyses indicated similar economies though it was clear that the reductions would be highly traumatic because of the number of people involved and the impact on the life and income of several communities. Eventually, almost 1,000 employees were affected. Planners and officials of the acquiring company anticipated most of the major problems accompanying the merger and planned accordingly. Early retirement packages, out-counseling, and job placement services, and discussions with community officials were among the many steps taken. Also one-on-one career counseling and development planning was a strategic approach discussed and eventually carried out with all second- and third-level managers. It was almost uniformly successful. Cross transfers into the acquiring organization were numerous, supported, and handled well generally. The greatest problems of culture integration were at the production plant level. The fewest problems were among managers for the reasons to be outlined in the sections that follow.

Clearly, nobody was pleased with the loss of jobs but most agreed that the consolidation and integration of plants, offices, and people was communicated, well organized, and handled with dispatch. The surprising part of employee reactions was the fact that relative to the former owners, most believed matters were handled in a superior way, that is, the former owners would never have been so generous, thoughtful, or communicative regarding employee separations. If it had to happen, thankfully it was done by the acquiring firm!

Pro- and Countercyclical Hiring and Development

Conventional strategic wisdom often favored procyclical hiring and layoffs, especially for nonmanagerial personnel. It seemed like the obvious, economic approach. This thinking pattern spilled over into managerial development planning—"expand in 'good' times and pull in your horns when the business outlook is bleak." High inflation and the severe business recession, starting in the 1970s and extending well into the 1980s, led to even more dramatic events in the managerial area. Companies with a longstanding reputation for durable management development programs and no managerial/professional layoffs, such as General Electric and IBM, experienced the need to rethink and often alter their policies. Leading banks, high-technology companies, service and product companies alike were also caught up in these disruptive events.

However, many of these occurrences need to be examined in an enlarged framework. Company strategists have the need to confront the "intuitive logic" of traditional procyclical policies affecting human resource planning, staffing, and development. The same need holds true for those organizations in which at some time, important business segments or groups, plateau, or experience rather serious business downturns. The strategic perspective mandates that some of the key and related issues be thought through in advance to launch soundly conceived planning and policies. This subject matter is the main thrust of this section.

Procyclical Approach

Procyclical approaches possess an intuitive logic born of traditional employment and management practices. Thus many managers could readily list the types of benefits itemized in Exhibit 13-3. Conventional wisdom would readily identify the likely reduction of "current" salary or staffing expenditures, elimination of "dead timber," and the difficulty of make-work activities. There are other compelling and positive results likely from this strategic approach of which some may not be quite as apparent as those previously named. Based on this approach, groups of recruits are often brought in at similar times so that cohorts are created. These have the potential for significant retention and socialization benefits. Cohorts will usually be ·
of similar age and possess like educational credentials. This type of hiring practice helps to create groups which can truly relate to each other while building strong

EXHIBIT 13-3
Procyclical Versus Countercyclical Human Resource Strategies: Costs and Benefits

Costs	Benefits
Countercyclical Approach	
May be seen as "counterintuitive" to seasoned managers, thus lessening their cooperation in recruitment, selection, and development processes.	Provides greater selectivity in recruiting talented people.
May be difficult to assign meaningful challenging work.	Provides greater individual certainty in career planning and thereby is likely to increase organizational identification and commitment.
May pose serious assignment and utilization problems if the time period becomes an extended one.	Permits greater reliance and certainty in human resource decisions based on the *internal* labor market. Tends to even out the age-experience distribution providing a broader span of competencies.
Mobility and promotional opportunities likely to be more competetive as the pool of candidates is enlarged.	
Need to develop more comprehensive and long-range planning approaches, and to scan carefully emerging events for their impact on these policies.	Builds corporate reputation relative to employment stability.
	Increases senior management confidence in internal selection and development decisions.
	Helps to preserve staffing gains achieved, using affirmative actions as a guide.
	Can serve as a contributing factor in creating a strong culture.
	Increases loyalty and thereby lowers voluntary turnover.
	Strengthens image among personnel as a proactive organization exercising strategic initiatives.
	Lowers recruiting costs due to "off-cycle" efforts.
	Extends time to affect development strategies.
	Permits frequently, extension or greater use of coaching approaches in subordinate development.
Procyclical Approaches	
Intensifies competition for highly capable people during the "hiring cycles."	Sharing of adversity builds sense of group feeling.
Creates sense of managerial instability, insecurity.	Facilitates acceptable human resource cost strategy.

(Continues)

EXHIBIT 13-3 (Continued)

Requires a long(er)-run staffing/planning capability.

Tends to distort age distribution of personnel in management development tracks; creates experience gaps.

Tends to exacerbate problems in working relationships due to age gaps.

Weakens and at times disrupts, mentoring relationships.

Tarnishes the company image and may impair attracting qualified people in future.

Forces recruiting of talented people in the "expensive years" and in competition with many others.

Reduces depth of managerial personnel for continuity planning purposes.

Tends to force the greater use of stopgap development programs to assure availability of needed position coverage.

Compounds greatly the meeting of affirmative action policy commitments; may undercut previous progress.

May strip out critical talents.

Undermines the creation of a strong comprehensive culture.

Reduces short-run cost or salary outlays.

Lessens need to "create" work in slack periods.

Increases mobility opportunities for "survivors" during good times.

Provides opportunity to eliminate "dead timber" where the decisions otherwise may have been difficult to make.

Contributes to building of cohorts and subgroup identification and involvement, while strengthening social support and potentially lessening voluntary turnover.

---

subgroup identification. This type of socialization may provide an important and needed alternative to the remoteness experienced by many relative to older or/and much more senior people. Too, the "survivors" who bridge business-hiring-layoff cycles will likely experience less commpetition for desired positions—an award to survival of the fittest.

Cost. Not surprisingly, significant costs attend procyclical strategies, and here again many of these are well known to seasoned strategists and planners (Exhibit 13-3). People sense employment instability, and a feeling of insecurity easily emerges. Key people experiencing these downturns, and periods of "bloodletting" (attempt to) develop hardened exterior postures permitting them to live with these policies. But these policies also lessen their willingness to become fully involved and committed to the organization. It is also rather widely experienced that finding and developing capable people is tougher during boom or hiring phases. Many others firms are engaged in precisely the same approach at the same time.

A point which is often a subtle one is that procyclical policies often create major age gaps in staffing distributions. For firms out of the hiring business for extended time periods, these age gaps can become serious and intensify differences in understanding, orientation, and shared values among organizational groups. These age gaps and lack of shared values seriously impede attempts to solidify or create a viable, organizationwide culture.

All too frequently, strategic discussion stops at the point of enumerating the pros and cons of a procyclical strategy. There is, however, another viewpoint to be introduced into these discussions, namely, the *countercyclical strategy*. True, a number of points would be deduced from extrapolating procyclical ideas. Yet at the same time, additional perspectives and considerations also need to be explored.

Countercyclical Approaches

Managements typically can exercise greater selectivity in recruiting talented people and committing them to career tracks in which they can be both guided and observed closely (Exhibit 13-3). Thus, the characteristics of the "managerial pipe-line" in subsequent years is measurably affected. The distribution of knowledge, skills, abilities, and experiences is more uniform, and strategists can tap into this reservoir of talent to generate opportunities, even in periods of great adversity. The philosophy of Matsushita's president and founder, one of the largest Japanese electronic firms, is that there is "opportunity in adversity." Severe external economic conditions, competition, or change, for example, can force a company to draw on its resources or exercise creativity in a manner not experienced or thought possible previously. But these possibilities in adversity only come alive when a cohesive organization has been established previously. Characteristics of this organization prototype include people who have learned to work together well in supportive ways, one possssing a tradition of workable approaches and good relationships and one for which company members are clear as to what's happening and what needs to be done. In this instance, countercylical policies can help to weld in place the diversity of talent and practical support of organizational culture required to diminish the severity of difficult times.

Another aspect of countercyclical policies is the contribution to individual career progress and development. These approaches instill a greater sense of employment stability or certainty into the picture for competent people. In consequence, managers and candidates tend to view career planning seriously, especially where there appears to be a realistic opportunity to fulfill career targets. Also, career development, which includes organizational and individual needs and plans, can be approached more realistically and with a sense of *mutual* requirements to be served. A related point is the idea that development programming achieves stature through continuity. Longer-term development processes characteristic of senior, technical, or specialized positions are entered into more readily with greater probability of accomplishment.

Costs.   At times, extra human resource capacity will exist, and supervising managers will need assistance in planning how to use this time well. Extended time periods of relatively low activity will compound these assignment and monitoring problems. A consideration countering this point is the fact that supervising managers may have more time to think through development strategies and to participate directly in coaching. In the SMD methods chapter (Chapter 6), the latter was identified as the most potent development approach.

A requirement to be contended with in the countercyclical approach is the demand for strong, long-range planning approaches. Forecasting, staffing analyses, and alternate scenarios under varying future conditions are part of these requirements. Also, emerging events require careful monitoring for new developments or shifts in circumstances affecting countercyclical policies.

A problem encountered in various organizations using countercyclical strategies is the idea that it flies in the face of conventional logic. Many seasoned managers have a background anchored in procyclical adjustments of their work force including at times their exempt classifications. The latter becomes a part of the picture when things are particularly tough. A countercyclical strategy works against this experience and logic, at times with explosive results. The following situation illustrates this point.

> In a large diversified manufacturing company, conventional handling of swings in its business cycle was a three-tier layoff policy. Initially, nonexempt personnel were laid off, then paraprofessional or assistant supervisory classifications, and finally supervisors, engineers, and even R&D people. Due to highly unstable domestic and worldwide conditions, the third level of layoffs was being reached more often than in earlier years. This cycling proved disruptive to the development of high-potential personnel. It was also starting to make serious inroads into the talent pool slated (eventually) for important succession positions. An internal staff study indicated that recruiting costs had gone up substantially because employment people and hiring managers were out recruiting at the same time as everybody else. A thinning supply of technical-managerial talent placed added upward pressure on these costs. Also, substantial progress made in advancing toward affirmative-action targets, was seriously impaired. The same staff study previously referenced recommended a conversion to a countercyclical policy for key and critical occupations and positions. These positions were identified on the basis of being highly important to business operations or long-term business continuity. Classification of positions in this manner was difficult but, in reality, no more so than the task faced regularly in position audits and succession analysis.

> Although field managers were generally briefed as to the purposes of the new policy, it met with great resistance. Many managers found it difficult to use staff members fully in slack periods and didn't take readily to the idea of further exacerbating their problems by following the new policy. Also, the company tradition in existence for years and years had been the "three-tier" layoff policy. It made "obvious" economic sense and seemed to square with individual experience in cost containment.

> The situation was one in which longer-term considerations and general corporate interests had to be factored into the picture at the divisional level. This consideration proved to be the critical recognition that was needed to resolve the apparent impasse or outright rejection of the policy by key divisional people.

A senior corporate officer accompanied by the vice president of Human Resources met with divisional officers to thoroughly explain the countercyclical policy. Their briefing meetings provided details of the five-year staffing plans, implications for launching individual development programs, illustrations of staffing and succession decisions, special budgetary coverage for managerial salary variances during the slack periods, cost projections, alternate scenarios for pro- and countercyclical periods, and useful suggestions for making productive use of people which tied in with general plans. The direct communications and the constructive way with which the situation was approached broke the deadlock.

The events described in this situation were not unlike those described by William E. Bright at Union Oil of California in past years. Clearly, these are important and at times challenging situations to be dealt with in launching a countercyclical policy and approach.

General Observations

As with many things in life, too little may not be any better than too much. Having more qualified candidates available under a countercyclical policy approch has its attendant costs. Procyclical approaches reduce some "costs" but pose difficult problems in staffing for continuity or succession purposes. *Pure* procyclical or countercyclical policies may prove unworkable for many organizations because of the numerous dysfunctional elements in each. Each company's circumstances will differ and thus their needs and priorities. For one company, given its needs, an approach more toward procyclical policies may be appropriate. For another, more of a countercyclical policy may be best. Regardless, these policies require explicit consideration, involvement of line managers, and conscious decisions by strategists and policymakers.

Summary

This concluding chapter has presented several important issues likely to be a part of strategic human resource discussions currently and in years to come. The growing complexity of many organization and the insatiable appetite of many for highly qualified people demand creative approaches to coping with these circumstances. Internal entrepreneuring provides one avenue to dealing with complexity. In this approach business venture units or self-contained enterprises are created. Highly talented people can be both cultivated and observed within these "intrapreneurial" units. The units themselves permit the loosening up of formal structural bonds and more flexible, adaptive behavior geared to situational need or circumstances. Also, there is the recognition that for some number of talented people, the conventional ways of hierarchical structure may prove stiffling. For entrepreneurial heads, a realistic opportunity is presented to exercise creativity in dealing with significant organizational needs and problems. These approaches also provide a workable means for their head and members to experience or sustain enthusiasm and dedication while engaged in meaningful work. The strategic human resource perspective requires constructive means of anticipating and dealing with organizational complexity. The "intrapreneurial" unit provides one of these options.

Another theme emerging from general business development and competition has been that of firms experiencing rapid growth. In what has become a highly mixed economy, the trajectory of companies experiencing rapid growth has often crossed the path of those simultaneously moving into a cost containment, shrinkage, or retrenchment mode. For the former, sustaining profitable growth has signaled internal human resource strategies that, at times, have led to a drastic alteration in the objectives and means of management development. On the one hand, rapid change often requires the emergence of new managerial prototypes with responsibilities and capabilities quite different from those valued in the past. The Wendy's case illustrated the various and diverse elements accompanying rapid change and some of the means elected to cope with these. Strategic approaches dictated that the domino effect of rapid change be anticipated. Coping or adaptative actions need to be launched sufficiently far in advance to avoid serious and long-term disruption of these organizations. For companies having to shrink their operations, strategic human resource approaches can help to establish a more dedicated, productive, managerial group and work force.

This concluding chapter discussion was also concerned with strategic choice in pro- and countercyclical human resource staffing situations. Traditional and conventional wisdom favored procyclical approaches due largely to their short-run cost economies. The "reasonableness" of this approach was reinforced through tradition and the support lent by budgetary methods and the approval of senior management. However, strategic human resource approaches brought both a longer-range and more comprehensive orientation into the picture. Included with these was the need to reexamine the assumptions and cost-benefit calculations of traditional approaches and to identify and critically examine alternate approaches. The alternative examined in this context was countercyclical staffing policies.

Neither approach is a panacea for the problems and issues which are a part of this picture. Significant dysfunctional results attend either approach. Thus strategic thinking requires a careful examination of these alternatives and the election of a strategy responsive to corporate circumstances.

The strategic management development field is just coming into its own. This book represents a consolidation of issues, perspectives, systems, and methods for strategically grounded human resource management with particular emphasis on succession and management development. It is a logical next step beyond an era of systems and methods development and consolidation of past writings. This era has witnessed the solidification of the field of human resource planning and development. The growing stature of human resource programs and its leaders and architects has brought it into senior executive discussions and long(er)-range planning processes, let alone higher education programs. Because of these new and higher-level actions, the audience interested in these matters has expanded correspondingly. Aside from Human Resource officials and planners, the audience now includes strategists, general executives, line managers, and students in human resources policy and planning.

REFERENCES

Atkinson, Keith. "Intrapreneurs: Fostering Innovation Inside Corporations." *Personnel Administrator* (January 1986): 43–46.

Bright, William E. "How One Company Manages Its Human Resources." *Harvard Business Review*, Vol. 54 (January 1976): 81–93.

Burack, Elmer H. and Nicholas J. Mathys. *Human Resource Planning: A Pragmatic Approach to Manpower Planning and Development*. 2nd ed.: Lake Forest, IL: Brace-Park Press 1987.

Deal, Terrance and Allan Kennedy. *Corporate Cultures*. Reading, MA.: Addison-Wesley, 1982.

Edwards, John and Mick Silver. "Introduction—The Art of Designing a Manpower Strategy." In John Edwards et al., eds., *Manpower Planning*. Chichester, England: John Wiley, 1983.

Greer, Charles R. "Countercyclical Hiring as a Staffing Strategy for Managerial and Professional Personnel: Some Considerations and Issues." *Academy of Management Reviews*, Vol. 9 (1985): 324–338.

Lawrence, J. R. "Manpower, and Personnel Models in Britain." In A. R. Smith, ed., *Corporate Manpower Planning*. Westmead, England: Gower Press, 1980.

Lee, Chris and Ron Zemke. "Intrapreneuring: New-Age Freedoms for Big Business?" *Training*, Vol. 22, no. 2 (February 1985): 27–41.

Peters, Thomas and J. Robert H. Waterman, Jr. *In Search of Excellence*. Cambridge, MA.: Harper & Row, 1982.

Pfeffer, Jeffrey. "Organizational Demography: Implications for Management," *California Management Review*, Vol. 28 (Fall 1985): 68–77.

Wendy's *Annual Reports*, Columbus, OH: 1980–1985.

Wessowetz, Richard O. Von and Michael Beer. *Human Resources at Hewlett-Packard*, Case 482-125. Cambridge, MA.: Harvard Business School Case Services, 1982.

Index